MW01251571

THE SHIPS OF CANADA'S NAVAL FORCES

THE SHIPS OF
CANADA'S
NAVAL FORCES
1910-2002

KEN MACPHERSON
RON BARRIE

Vanwell
PUBLISHING LIMITED

St. Catharines, Ontario

Copyright© 2002 by Ken Macpherson and Ron Barrie. All rights reserved. No part of this book may be reproduced or utilized in any form or by any means, electronic or mechanical, including photocopying and recording, or by any information storage and retrieval system, without permission in writing from the publisher.

Vanwell Publishing acknowledges the financial support of the Government of Canada through the Book Publishing Industry Development Program for our publishing activities.

Design: Linda Moroz-Irvine
Cover: HMCS *Ottawa* (4th)

Vanwell Publishing Limited
1 Northrup Crescent
P.O. Box 2131
St. Catharines, Ontario L2R 7S2
sales@vanwell.com
phone 905-937-3100
fax 905-937-1760

Printed in Canada

National Library of Canada Cataloguing in Publication

Macpherson, Ken
    The ships of Canada's naval forces 1910-2002 / Ken Macpherson, Ron Barrie. — 3rd ed.

Previous ed. published under title: The ships of Canada's naval forces 1910-1993 : complete pictorial history of Canadian warships / Ken Macpherson, John Burgess ; foreword, H.F. Pullen 1st pbk. ed.

Includes bibliographical references and index.
ISBN 1-55125-072-1

1. Canada. Royal Canadian Navy—Lists of vessels. 2. Warships—Canada—History—20th century. I. Barrie, Ron, 1949- II. Title.

VA400.M366 2002   359.8'35'0971   C2002-900934-0

CONTENTS

Preface & Acknowledgments vi
Foreword vii

PREFACE AND ACKNOWLEDGEMENTS

THIS IS THE THIRD REPRINTING AND UPDATE of our book since it was first published in 1981. Even since the appearance of its 1993 printing, the Navy has undergone a radical transformation. The trend-setting St. Laurent class destroyers and destroyer/helicopter carriers of the 1950s have grown old and vanished from the scene, to be replaced by the City class of twelve ultra-modern patrol frigates designed, unlike their predecessors, to counter threats from air, surface or underwater. They have already proven themselves in a variety of peacekeeping missions far from home. A new class of twelve maritime coastal defence vessels has replaced the Bay class minesweepers of the early 1950s, and the three Oberon class submarines have been retired. The second of four successors has arrived in Canadian waters, modern Upholder class submarines purchased from the Royal Navy.

We wish to offer particular thanks to Vice-Admiral Gary Garnett, who so kindly wrote our foreword, and Lieutenant-Commander Richard Gimblett, whose compilation for us of an updated Commanding Officers' list was a truly heroic undertaking, and who is the author of the introduction to Part Four. Commander Fraser McKee contributed an introduction on the subject of the Maritime Coastal Defence Vessels, and Lieutenant-Commander Dave Freeman has been an unfailing source of advice and support. Others whose assistance in a variety of ways has been greatly appreciated are Ken Levert, whose superb photographs illustrate many of the ships in Part Four, as well as the book jacket itself; Ian McCorquodale; Sandy McClearn; Bill Schell and Dave Shirlaw. We are especially grateful to Ben Kooter, our publisher, and Angela Dobler, his editor, for their gracious acceptance of scheduling upsets occasioned by Ken's illness throughout much of 2001. Last, though certainly not least, we wish to thank Faye Barrie and Jane McCluskey for their support and encouragement.

KRM and RJB

FOREWORD

I AM PLEASED AND HONOURED to provide the foreword for this Third Edition of *The Ships of Canada's Naval Forces 1910-2002*. Each edition constitutes a definitive chronicle of the ships that have comprised the Canadian Navy from its beginnings in 1910, and this edition brings their story up to the present.

Canada is a country that often has trouble understanding its maritime heritage and appreciating the importance of the maritime dimension in its future. This history addresses the problem, providing a baseline for the depth of Canada's maritime tradition. The Navy has always responded to any call by the people of Canada. Two world wars and the Korean conflict stand as sterling examples. Indeed, at the end of the Second World War the Royal Canadian Navy was the third largest in the world. In more recent times the Navy has invariably been "ready aye ready," whether it was in the Cold War, protecting our national fisheries from incursion, engaging in coalition operations in the Arabian Sea, enforcing UN sanctions in the Adriatic or off Haiti, or waging war on terrorists.

There have been occasions in the history of the Navy when our ships have been only marginally capable of taking up the task. This, however, has never been the case with the ships' companies. They have always numbered among the very best. When ships have been among the most capable, the Canadian Navy has excelled and in recent years has often been called upon to take a lead role in operations. The current Canadian Patrol Frigates (CPF) and their crews are of such a standard that they regularly serve as integral members of US Carrier Battle Groups—something no other navy has done.

This volume will bring back memories to many of the readers: whether it be the record of commanding officers, pendant numbers, or the particulars of ships by class. The Third Edition also features the three newest classes of Canadian warships, the Halifax class patrol frigates, the Kingston class maritime coastal defence vessels (MCDV) and the Victoria class submarines. Most of these ships have been named after Canadian cities and this has provided the Navy with a new opportunity to establish wider relations with Canadians across the country. This is being achieved by developing close ties with the namesake municipal councils, engaging in major community activities, working with local naval veterans' organizations, taking countless Canadians to sea, and helping local sea cadet corps. In addition, the prominent individuals who act as ships' sponsors are kept apprised of the accomplishments of their respective vessels. In the finest naval tradition many of the current warships pictured in this handsome volume have antecedents and, therefore, carry not only their Battle Honours but maintain connections with the previous ship's companies. The long-term health of the Navy may well depend on how well the Navy succeeds in cementing relations with Canadians from coast to coast.

I salute Ken Macpherson for his continuing dedication to the Canadian Navy and its history. His previous colleague John Burgess, who passed away in 1997, is also remembered. Ken and his present co-author, Ron Barrie, are to be congratulated for this Third Edition of *The Ships of Canada's Naval Forces 1910-2002*.

Vice-Admiral (ret'd) Gary L. Garnett
November 2001

Affectionately dedicated to John Burgess, one of the original
authors, whose sudden death on 16 September 1997 left
Canada's naval historical fraternity immeasurably poorer.

PART I **1910–1939**

INTRODUCTION

THE CANADIAN NAVY came into existence on May 4, 1910, when the Naval Service Act became law, and later that year its first ships were commissioned – two cruisers purchased from the Royal Navy (RN). Permission to add the prefix "Royal" was granted by King George V in 1911. Apart from two submarines acquired in 1914, *Niobe* and *Rainbow* were the only offensive warships to serve in the RCN during the First World War.

The Act provided, however, that the Department of Naval Service should incorporate the fisheries patrol, hydrographic, tidal survey, and wireless telegraphic services of the Department of Marine and Fisheries. The ships associated with these services were the backbone of the young navy during most of the war. When not needed as naval vessels they carried on their regular peacetime duties, sometimes performing both roles simultaneously. There were also five former yachts and a number of ships commandeered from customs, post office, and navigational aids maintenance duties, as well as a host of tugs and motor launches. Information regarding their naval careers is now very scarce.

This motley assortment did a creditable job as patrol craft, minesweepers, and examination vessels, particularly off the east coast, the German threat in the Pacific having faded after Admiral Graf von Spee's defeat in December 1914. In 1914 three classes of minesweeping trawlers and drifters began to make their appearance from a variety of yards on the Great Lakes and St. Lawrence River. Four of the trawlers were to be among the few ships the Navy could boast during the lean years between the wars.

Niobe and *Rainbow* went to the scrapyard in 1920, to be replaced by the modern cruiser *Aurora* and the destroyers *Patrician* and *Patriot*. Doomed by budget cuts, *Aurora* was retired in 1922 along with two submarines acquired in 1919. With the creation of the Department of National Defence in 1922 the miscellaneous government ships mentioned earlier ceased to be considered, even on paper, as naval vessels and were transferred back to the Department of Marine and Fisheries. *Patrician* and *Patriot* were replaced in 1928 by *Champlain* and *Vancouver*, so that from 1922 to 1931 the RCN consisted in its entirety of a destroyer and two trawlers on each coast.

In 1931 the destroyers *Saguenay* and *Skeena*, the first ships designed and built for the RCN, were commissioned; *Fraser* and *St. Laurent* were purchased from the RN in 1937 as replacements for *Champlain* and *Vancouver*, and a year later *Restigouche* and *Ottawa* joined them. These six destroyers will be found in Part Two: 1939-1945, owing to their close kinship with the eight others of the River class. A class of four modern minesweepers was added in 1938, and the training schooner *Venture*, training ship *Skidegate*, and trawler *Armentières* made up the rest of the thirteen ships that constituted the RCN on the eve of the Second World War.

Rainbow.

Rainbow

On 4 August 1910 at Portsmouth, England, *Rainbow* was commissioned the first unit of the infant RCN. One of a class of twenty "protected cruisers," she had served in the RN since 1893. *Rainbow* arrived at Esquimalt on 7 November 1910, and carried out training duties, ceremonial visits, and some fisheries patrols until the end of 1912. She then lay largely idle until the outbreak of the First World War, during which, apart from two submarines, she was the sole defender of Canada's western seaboard.

The German threat in the Pacific ended with the defeat of Admiral Graf von Spee's squadron at the Battle of the Falkland Islands in December 1914, and thereafter *Rainbow* patrolled the Pacific coast as far south as Panama. In 1916 and early 1917 she was used in the transporting of $140 million in Russian bullion between Esquimalt and Vancouver. By 1917 her crew was needed to man patrol vessels on the east coast and on 8 May she was paid off. *Rainbow* was recommissioned on 5 July to serve as a depot ship at Esquimalt. Paid off again on 1 June 1920, she was sold to a Seattle shipbreaker.

RAINBOW				
BUILDER:	Palmers, Hebburn-onTyne		SPEED:	12 kts
LAUNCHED:	25/3/91		CREW:	273
DISPLACEMENT:	3,600		ARMAMENT:	two 6-inch, six 4-inch, eight 6
DIMENSIONS:	314.5' x 43.5' x 16.5'			pdrs., four 14-inch TT

Commanding Officers

CDR J. D. D. Stewart, RN	4/8/10	23/6/11	CDR J. T. Shenton, RCN		22/8/17	12/5/18
CDR W. Hose, RN	24/6/11	30/4/17	LT Y. Birley, RCN		13/5/18	14/10/19
CDR H. E. Holme, RCN	1/5/17	8/5/17	CAPT E. H. Martin, CMG, RCN		15/10/19	1/6/20
LCDR J. H. Knight, RCN	1/7/17	21/8/17				

Niobe, 1907.

Niobe

A good deal more imposing than *Rainbow*, *Niobe* had served in the RN from 1898 to 1910, one of eight sisters of the Diadem class. She was commissioned in the RCN on 16 September 1910 at Devonport and arrived at Halifax on 21 October. *Niobe* was almost lost during the night of 30-31 July 1911 when she went aground off Cape Sable, necessitating repairs that were not completed until the end of 1912. In the fall of 1914, after the ravages of two years' disuse had been made good, she joined the RN's 4th Cruiser Squadron on contraband patrol off New York.

Worn out, she returned to Halifax on 17 July 1915, never to put to sea again. She was paid off on 6 September and became a depot ship. Her upperworks were wrecked in the Halifax explosion of 6 December 1917, but she continued to serve as a depot ship until 1920, when she was sold for scrap. *Niobe* was broken up at Philadelphia two years later.

NIOBE		SPEED:	15 kts
BUILDER:	Vickers, Barrow-in-Furness	CREW:	677
LAUNCHED:	20/2/97	ARMAMENT:	sixteen 6-inch, twelve 12 pdrs, five 3 pdrs., two 18-inch TT
DISPLACEMENT:	11,000		
DIMENSIONS:	466' x 69' x 26'		

Commanding Officers		
CDR W. B. MacDonald, RN	16/9/10	-
LCDR C. E. Aglionby, RN	20/6/13	-
CAPT R. G. Corbett, RN	15/8/14	1/9/15
A/CDR P. F. Newcombe, RN	16/10/16	-
CDR H. E. Holme, RCN	22/12/17	1/6/20

Aurora with *Patrician* and *Patriot* at Esquimalt, 1921.

Aurora

One of the eight-ship Arethusa class, *Aurora* had served with the Grand Fleet from 1914 to 1916, and was the first British ship in action at the Battle of the Dogger Bank in 1915. She was on hand at the surrender of the German High Seas Fleet in November 1918.

Aurora was presented to the RCN in 1920, along with two destroyers, and commissioned on 1 November. After the three ships arrived in Halifax on 21 December they set out on a training cruise via the Caribbean to Esquimalt, returning to Halifax on 30

July 1921. A year later, drastic cuts in the naval budget made it necessary to pay off *Aurora*. Disarmed in 1922, she lay at Halifax in an increasingly embarrassing state of deterioration until 1927, when she was sold for breaking up.

AURORA					
BUILDER:	H.M. Dockyard, Devonport	DIMENSIONS:	436' x 39' x 14'	ARMAMENT:	two 6-inch, six 4-inch, two 3-inch, eight 21-inch TT (4 x II)
LAUNCHED:	30/9/13	SPEED:	25 kts		
DISPLACEMENT: 3,512		CREW:	318		
Commanding Officer					
CAPT H. G. H. Adams, CBE, RN		1/11/20	1/7/22		

Patrician and Patriot

These sister ships, commissioned in 1916, served in the RN for the duration of the First World War. In 1920, *Patrician, Patriot* and the cruiser *Aurora* were offered to Canada as replacements for the decrepit *Niobe* and *Rainbow*. The three were commissioned at Devonport on 1 November 1920, and left for Canada a month later.

When the naval budget was cut by a million dollars in 1922, the two destroyers became the only seagoing ships in the RCN. *Patrician* was ordered that autumn to the west coast, where she was to spend the next five years training officers and men of the naval reserve. *Patriot* performed the same function on the east coast. In September 1921, she assisted Dr. Alexander Graham Bell, towing his experimental hydrofoil craft *HD-4* at high speed on Bras d'Or Lake near Baddeck, Nova Scotia. As perhaps the strangest assignment of her career, *Patrician* was detailed in November 1924, to intercept a band of Nanaimo bank-robbers trying to reach the United States by motor launch. *Patriot* was paid off in December 1927 and *Patrician* on 1 January 1928. Both were sold for scrap in 1929, *Patriot* to be broken up at Briton Ferry, Wales and *Patrician* at Seattle.

Patriot at Halifax, 1923.

Patrician at Esquimalt, 1924.

PATRICIAN			
BUILDER:	Thorneycroft, Southampton	SPEED:	30 kts
		CREW:	82
LAUNCHED:	5/6/16	ARMAMENT:	three 4-inch, one 2 pdr., four 21-inch TT (2 x II)
DISPLACEMENT: 1,004			
DIMENSIONS:	274' x 27.5' x 10.5'		
Commanding Officers			
Lt G. C. Jones, RCN		1/11/20	2/9/22
LT C. T. Beard, RCN		3/9/22	31/10/22
LT J. E. W. Oland, RCN		1/11/22	30/9/24
LT W. J. R. Beech, RCN		1/10/24	14/8/26
LCDR R. L. Agnew, RCN		15/8/26	1/1/28

PATRIOT						
BUILDER:	Thorneycroft, Southampton			SPEED:	30 kts	
LAUNCHED:	20/4/16			CREW:	82	
DISPLACEMENT: 1,004				ARMAMENT:	three 4-inch, one 2 pdr., four 21-inch TT (2 x I"I)	
DIMENSIONS:	274' x 27.5' x 10.5'					
Commanding Officers						
LT C. T. Beard, RCN		1/11/20	2/9/22	LT C. R. H. Taylor, RCN	7/10/25	4/4/26
LT G. C. Jones, RCN		3/9/22	23/8/23	LT C. R. H. Taylor, RCN	5/4/26	23/10/27
LT H. E. Reid, RCN		24/8/23	6/10/25			

Champlain and Vancouver

Initially named *Torbay* and *Toreador*, respectively, these sister ships were originally commissioned in the RN in 1919. They were lent to the RCN while replacements for *Patrician* and *Patriot* were being built in Britain, and the transfer took place at Portsmouth on 1 March 1928. (As there was already a *Vancouver* serving in the RN, she was renamed *Vimy* to free the name for the new Canadian ship.)

In May 1928, *Champlain* arrived at Halifax and *Vancouver* at Esquimalt to provide reserve training, as did *Patrician* and *Patriot*, at opposite coasts. They were paid off at their respective bases on 25 November 1936 and sold for scrap the following year.

Champlain, 3 July 1931.

Vancouver.

CHAMPLAIN			
BUILDER:	Thorneycroft, Southampton	SPEED:	30 kts
		CREW:	90
LAUNCHED:	6/3/19	ARMAMENT:	three 4-inch, one 2
DISPLACEMENT: 1,087			pdr., four 21-inch
DIMENSIONS:	276' x 27.5' x 10.5'		TT (2 x II)

Commanding Officers

CDR C. T. Beard, RCN	1/3/28	20/5/28
LCDR J. C. I. Edwards, RCN	21/5/28	26/12/29
CDR V. G. Brodeur, RCN	27/12/29	26/12/30
LCDR A. R. Pressey, RCN	27/12/30	27/8/31
LCDR G. B. Barnes, RCN	28/8/31	15/10/31
LCDR A. R. Pressey, RCN	16/10/31	22/5/32
LCDR V. S. Godfrey, RCN	23/5/32	23/5/34
LCDR W. B. Creery, RCN	24/5/34	10/12/35
LCDR R. E. S. Bidwell, RCN	11/12/35	25/11/36

VANCOUVER			
BUILDER:	Thorneycroft, Southampton	SPEED:	30 kts
		CREW:	90
LAUNCHED:	7/12/18	ARMAMENT:	three 4-inch, one 2
DISPLACEMENT: 1,087			pdr., four 21-inch
DIMENSIONS:	276' x 27.5' x 10.5'		TT (2 x II)

Commanding Officers

LCDR R. I. Agnew, RCN	1/3/28	14/8/28
LCDR R. W. Wood, RCN	15/8/28	4/5/30
LCDR G. M. Hibbard, RCN	5/5/30	19/1/31
LCDR F. G. Hart, RCN	20/1/31	14/12/32
LCDR L. J. M. Gauvreau, RCN	15/12/32	19/12/33
LCDR F. L. Houghton, RCN	20/12/33	30/11/34
LCDR C. D. Donald, RCN	1/12/34	14/5/36
LCDR E. R. Mainguy, RCN	15/5/36	25/11/36

CC 1 (foreground) and *CC 2* at Halifax, 1918.

CC 1 and CC 2

These submarines, originally named *Iquique* and *Antofagasta*, respectively, were built at Seattle for the Chilean government. However, the deal with the Chilean government fell through, and on the eve of the First World War they were purchased by the premier of British Columbia, Sir Richard McBride. The Dominion government ratified the purchase and on 6 August the two boats were commissioned as *CC1* and *CC 2* because of their resemblance to the British "C" class submarines. After three years of cruising and training on the west coast they were ordered to Europe, and on 21 June 1917, set out for Halifax with their mother ship *Shearwater*. They were the first warships ever to transit the Panama Canal under the White Ensign. Unfit for a transatlantic crossing, they remained at Halifax until sold for scrap five years later.

CC1			
BUILDER:	Seattle Construction & Drydock Co.		
LAUNCHED:	3/6/13		
DISPLACEMENT:	313/373		
DIMENSIONS:	144' x 15' x 11'		
SPEED:	13/10 kts		
CREW:	2/16		
ARMAMENT:	five 18-inch TT		
Commanding Officers			
LT A. St. V. Keyes, RCN		7/8/1914	1/10/1914
LT F.B. Hanson, RN		1/10/1914	1/11/1917
LT F.B. Hanson, RN (refit)		1/9/1917	26/9/1918
LT F.B. Hanson, RN		26/9/1918	4/12/1918

CC2			
BUILDER:	Seattle Construction & Drydock Co.		
LAUNCHED:	31/12/13		
DISPLACEMENT:	310/373		
DIMENSIONS:	152' x 15' x 11'		
SPEED:	13/10 kts		
CREW:	2/16		
ARMAMENT:	three 18-inch TT		
Commanding Officers			
LT B.E. Jones, RCN		3/8/1914	17/4/1916
LT G. Lake, RNCVR		17/4/1917	1/11/1917
Lt F.B. Hanson, RN (refit)		1/11/1917	6/9/1918
LT A.C.S. Pitts, RNCVR		26/9/1918	14/12/1918

CH 14 and CH 15

As their nomenclature implies, these were Canadian members of the British "H" class, two of ten built during the First World War at Quincy, Massachusetts. *H 14* and *H 15* were on their way to Britain when hostili- ties ended, and were rerouted to Bermuda. Presented to the RCN, they were commis- sioned at Halifax on 1 April, 1921 as *CH 14* and *CH 15*. Scarcely used, they were paid off on 30 June 1922 and sold for scrap five years later.

CH 14 and CH 15			
BUILDER:	Fore River Co., Quincy, Mass.	SPEED:	13/11 kts
COMMISSIONED:	April 1921	CREW:	4/18
DISPLACEMENT:	363/434	ARMAMENT:	four 18-inch TT
DIMENSIONS:	150' x 15' x 12'		

CH14 - Commanding Officer

LT R.C. Watson		1/4/1921	6/1922

CH15 - Commanding Officer

LT R.W. Wood		1/4/1921	6/1922

Acadia.

Acadia

Acadia, a Dominion government hydrographic survey ship, was commissioned as a patrol vessel from 16 January 1917 to March, 1919, and carried out A/S patrol in the Bay of Fundy, off the south shore of Nova Scotia and in the Gulf of St. Lawrence. She then resumed survey duty until the outbreak of the Second World War when she was commissioned on 2 October 1939, first serving as training ship for HMCS *Stadacona*, later patrolling the Halifax approaches from May 1940 to March 1941. She also occasionally acted as close escort for small convoys between Halifax and Halifax Ocean Meeting Point. After refit in 1941, she served as a training ship at Halifax for A/A and DEMS (Defensively Equipped Merchant Ship) gunners and, in June 1944, went to HMCS *Cornwallis* as gunnery training ship. Paid off on 3 November 1945, she was returned to the Dominion government. *Acadia* retired from service on 28 November 1969 to become a museum ship at the Bedford Institute of Oceanography in Dartmouth Nova Scotia. On 9 February 1980 she was handed over to the Maritime Museum of the Atlantic.

ACADIA						
BUILDER:	Swan, Hunter & Wigham, Richardson, Newcastle		DIMENSIONS:	170' x 33.5' x 19'		
LAUNCHED:	1913		SPEED:	8 kts		
DISPLACEMENT:	1,050		CREW:	59		
			ARMAMENT:	one 4-inch, one 12 pdr.		

Commanding Officers

LT J. O. Boothby, RCN	20/2/40	1/4/40	LCDR J. C. Littler, RCNR	16/12/43	30/3/44	
LCDR H. G. Chadforth, RCNR	12/4/40	-	LCDR R. A. S. MacNeil, RCNR	31/3/44	6/6/44	
LT S. Henderson, RCNR	29/4/41	11/11/41	SKPR/LT F. W. Durant, RCNR	7/6/44	4/3/45	
LCDR J. L. Driver, RCNR	12/11/41	19/9/43	SKPR/LT C. C. Clattenburg, RCNR	5/3/45	-	
LCDR R. V. Campbell, RCNR	20/9/43	15/12/43				

Algerine.

Algerine

Built at Devonport Dockyard in 1895, this RN sloop was based at Esquimalt before the First World War. Her crew was sent east in 1914 to man *Niobe*, and *Algerine* was lent to the RCN in 1917 to serve for the duration as a depot ship at Esquimalt. Sold in 1919 and converted for salvage work, *Algerine* was wrecked in Principe Channel, British Columbia, on 13 October 1923.

ALGERINE	
BUILDER:	H.M Dockyard, Devonport
LAUNCHED:	6/6/1895
DISPLACEMENT:	1,050
DIMENSIONS:	210.5' x 32.5' x 11.5'
SPEED:	12 kts
CREW:	
ARMAMENT:	four 3 pdrs.

Canada

A fisheries patrol vessel built in 1904 along warship lines, *Canada* provided training for an embryo corps of Canadian naval officers before the creation of the RCN, and was commissioned as a naval patrol vessel from 25 January 1915 to November 1919. Sold for commercial purposes in 1924, she was lost off Florida on 2 July 1926.

Canada, 1918.

CANADA	
BUILDER:	Vickers-Armstrong, Barrow
LAUNCHED:	1904
DISPLACEMENT:	557
DIMENSIONS:	206' x 25' x 13'
SPEED:	14 kts
CREW:	60
ARMAMENT:	two 12 pdrs., two 3 pdrs.

Cartier/Charny

A Dominion government hydrographic survey ship that served as an armed patrol vessel on the east coast during the First World War. *Cartier* reverted to government service between the wars, but was commissioned as a training ship at Halifax on 18 September 1939. She was named *Charny* on 9 December 1941. Paid off on 12 December 1945, she was reported derelict and sunk at Sydney, Nova Scotia a dozen years later.

Charny (ex-Cartier), 1940.

CARTIER/CHARNY		
BUILDER:	Swan, Hunter & Wigham Richardson, Newcastle	
LAUNCHED:	1910	
DISPLACEMENT:	556	
DIMENSIONS:	164' x 29' x 13'	
SPEED:	12 kts	
CREW:	60	
ARMAMENT:	three 12 pdrs.	

Commanding Officers

LCDR J. J. DesLauriers, RCNR	18/9/39	-	LT L. J. Wallace, RCNVR	4/3/44	29/744
LT A. B. Taylor, RCNR	21/8/40	21/10/41	LT C. C. Love, RCNVR	30/7/44	17/9/44
LT E. R. Shaw, RCNR	22/10/41	8/5/42	LT L. J. Wallace, RCNVR	18/9/44	31/10/44
LT F. E. Grubb, RCN	9/5/42	/11/42	LT R. D. Brown, RCNVR	1/11/44	6/4/45
LT C. L. Campbell, RCNVR	/11/42	4/4/43	LT L. J. Wallace, RCNVR	7/4/45	20/4/45
LCDR C. G. Williams, RCNR	5/4/43	3/3/44	LT R. D. Brown, RCNVR	21/4/45	16/11/45
			SKPR/LT P. Perrault, RCNR	17/11/45	12/12/45

Constance and Curlew

These oddly shaped little sisters were built at Owen Sound in 1891 and 1892, respectively, for the Canadian government – *Constance* to serve the Customs department, and *Curlew*, the Department of Marine and Fisheries. Both were fitted for minesweeping in 1912 and promptly taken into naval service upon the outbreak of war. When required, they functioned as east coast patrol craft throughout the war, otherwise performing their regular duties. *Curlew* was sold in 1921, *Constance* in 1924.

A third sister, *Petrel*, was built as a fisheries patrol vessel at Owen Sound in 1892, but did not see salt water until 1905. Between 1914 and 1918 she was employed frequently as a patrol or examination vessel on the east coast. After the war she reverted briefly to her fisheries patrol duties before being sold in 1923.

CONSTANCE			
BUILDER:	Polson Ironworks, Owen Sound	DIMENSIONS:	115' x 19.6' x 11.?'
		SPEED:	10 kts
LAUNCHED:	1891	CREW:	23
DISPLACEMENT:	185	ARMAMENT:	3 machine guns

CURLEW			
BUILDER:	Polson Ironworks, Owen Sound	SPEED:	10 kts
LAUNCHED:	1892	CREW:	23
DISPLACEMENT:	185	ARMAMENT:	3 machine guns
DIMENSIONS:	116.3' x 19.8' x 11.3'		

Florence

Originally named *Czarina*, then *Emeline*, this American-built yacht was bought and renamed by John Eaton, who brought her to Toronto in 1910. He presented *Florence* to the RCN, which commissioned her on 19 July 1915, and for most of the ensuing year she served as guard ship at Saint John, New Brunswick and patrol vessel in the Bay of Fundy. However, she proved to be unsuitable and was paid off on 21 September 1916. Later that year *Florence* was sold to buyers in Martinique and is said to have been lost in the Caribbean in January 1917.

FLORENCE			
BUILDER:	Crescent Shipyard, Elizabeth, N.J.	DIMENSIONS:	144' x 22.5' x 7.5'
		SPEED:	12 kts
LAUNCHED:	1903	CREW:	
DISPLACEMENT:	257	ARMAMENT:	one 3 pdr.

Constance.

Curlew.

Florence before she joined the Navy.

Galiano.

Galiano

Built in Dublin, Ireland, as a fisheries patrol craft for the Dominion government, *Galiano* was sister to *Malaspina*. Although *Galiano* apparently was not commissioned until 15 December 1917, she alternated civil duties with those of a naval patrol and examination vessel throughout the war. She foundered with all hands in Barkley Sound, British Columbia, on 30 October 1918.

GALIANO			
BUILDER:	Dublin Dockyard	SPEED:	11 kts
LAUNCHED:	1913	CREW:	33
DISPLACEMENT:	393	ARMAMENT:	
DIMENSIONS:	162.3' x 27' x 13'		
Commanding Officer			
LT R. M. Pope, RCNVR		15/12/17	30/10/18

Grilse

Formerly the yacht *Winchester*, she was purchased in the US in June 1915, fitted with a torpedo tube, and commissioned 15 July as a torpedo boat. Since she was unsuited for winter service in Canadian waters, *Grilse* left Halifax on 11 December 1916 for the Caribbean and was reported lost in a storm. She turned up at Shelburne, Nova Scotia three days later, however. After several months' refit *Grilse* resumed her patrol duties until she was paid off on 10 December 1918. An effort was made to sell her in 1920, but no adequate bid was received, and during 1921-22, she was attached to a youth training establishment in Halifax dockyard. In 1922 she was sold to Solomon Guggenheim, who renamed her *Trillora*, and was still in his possession when, on 21 September 1938, she foundered in a hurricane on Long Island.

Grilse.

GRILSE			
BUILDER:	Yarrow & Co., Glasgow, Scotland	SPEED:	30 kts
		CREW:	56
LAUNCHED:	1912	ARMAMENT:	two 12 pdrs, one 14-inch TT
DISPLACEMENT:	287		
DIMENSIONS:	202.3' x 18.3' x 9.2'		
Commanding Officers			
LT J. K. L. Ross, RCNVR		15/7/15	15/7/16
LT W. Wingate, RCNVR		16/7/16	10/1/17
CDR J. T. Shenton, RCN		10/5/17	25/5/17
LCDR W. T. Walker, RCN		26/5/17	16/12/17
LT H. H. D. Wood, RCNVR		17/12/17	16/1/18
Mate T. C. M. Cotton, RCNVR		17/1/18	11/2/18
LCDR W. T. Walker, RCN		12/2/18	5/5/18
LT A. F. Thomas, RCNVR		6/5/18	10/12/18

Gulnare

Gulnare was purchased by the Canadian government in 1902 for fisheries protection work. From 1918 to 1919 she served as a contraband control vessel on the east coast, returning after the war to government duties, which included hydrographic survey. She was sold to Marine Industries Ltd. about 1938, and broken up about ten years later.

Hochelaga

An armed yacht formerly named *Walrus*, *Hochelaga* was purchased in the US in 1914. She served as a patrol vessel from 13 August 1915 to 1920, and from then until 1923 took up coast-guard duties. She then spent many years as a Pictou-Charlottetown ferry and was sold in 1942, to reappear briefly four years later when she was seized by the RN as an illegal Israeli immigrant ship.

Lady Evelyn

Built on the Mersey for a Blackpool firm and originally named *Deerhound*, she was acquired and renamed by the Postmaster-General's department in 1907. *Lady Evelyn's* new function was to meet transatlantic mail steamers in the Gulf of St. Lawrence and take off the mail for transfer to trains. She was commissioned in the RCN as a patrol vessel from June 1917 to 1919, and survived in commercial service on the west coast until shortly before the Second World War.

GULNARE			
BUILDER:	C.Connel, Scotstoun	DIMENSIONS:	137' x 20.5' x 13.6'
		SPEED:	10 kts
LAUNCHED:	1893	CREW:	25
DISPLACEMENT:	262	ARMAMENT:	

HOCHELAGA			
BUILDER:	Hawthorn & Co., Leith	SPEED:	12 kts
		CREW:	
LAUNCHED:	1900	ARMAMENT:	one 12 pdr.
DISPLACEMENT:	628		
DIMENSIONS:	192.6' x 27.6' x 14.8'		

LADY EVELYN			
BUILDER:	Tranmere, UK	SPEED:	9 kts
LAUNCHED:	1901	CREW:	
DISPLACEMENT:	483	ARMAMENT:	
DIMENSIONS:	189' x 26.1' x 9.5'		

Gulnare.

Hochelaga.

Lady Evelyn.

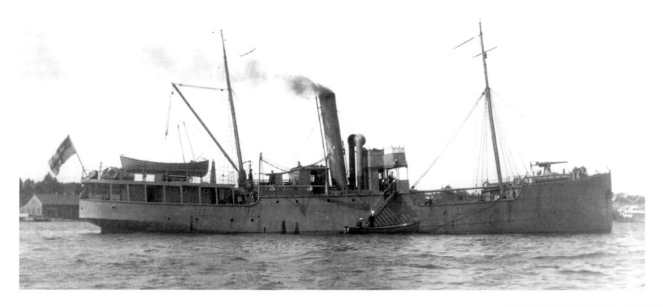

Laurentian

The Yorkshire-built *King Edward* was acquired in 1911 by Canada Steamship Lines and renamed *Laurentian*. She was sold to the RCN six years later and served as a patrol vessel from May 1917 to January 1919. Later transferred to the Department of Marine and Fisheries, she served as a lighthouse supply vessel and buoy tender until sold for scrap in 1947.

LAURENTIAN

BUILDER:	Cook, Welton & Gemmell, Beverly, UK	DIMENSIONS:	149' x 24' x 11'
		SPEED:	11 kts
		CREW:	
LAUNCHED:	1902	ARMAMENT:	one 12 pdr.
DISPLACEMENT:	355		

Malaspina.

MALASPINA

BUILDER:	Dublin Dockyard	SPEED:	11 kts
LAUNCHED:	1913	CREW:	33
DISPLACEMENT:	392	ARMAMENT:	one 6 pdr.
DIMENSIONS:	162.4' x 27.1' x 13.1'		

Commanding Officers

LT H. Newcombe, RCNVR	1/12/17	31/3/20
LCDR W. Redford, RCNR	6/9/39	-
LT G. S. Hall, RCNR	14/11/40	-
CH.SKPR W. R. Chaster, RCNR	17/4/41	-
CD/SKPR J. M. Richardson, RCNR	21/11/41	-
CH/SKPR A. W. Ogden, RCNR	28/1/42	-
LCDR J. S. Cunningham, RCNVR	8/3/43	-

Malaspina

Like her sister *Galiano*, she joined the Canadian government fleet as a west coast fisheries patrol vessel in 1913. With the outbreak of the war *Malaspina* took up a part-time career as a patrol vessel, but from 1 December 1917 to 31 March 1920 was commissioned solely for contraband control in the Strait of Juan de Fuca. Between the wars she served the Department of Transport, but on 6 September 1939 was again commissioned by the RCN for patrol and examination work. She was later taken over by HMCS *Royal Roads* as a training vessel. *Malaspina* was paid off on 31 March 1945, sold for scrap the following year, and broken up at Victoria.

Margaret

Margaret had scarcely been delivered to the Canadian Customs Department when, in August 1914, she was taken up by the RCN for patrol work, chiefly in the St. Lawrence River and Gulf of St. Lawrence. She was commissioned from 3 February 1915 to 3 April 1919, and soon afterward returned to the Dominion government. Acquired by the Brazilian Navy about 1935 and renamed *Rio Branco*, she was discarded in 1958.

MARGARET

BUILDER:	Woolston UK
LAUNCHED:	1914
DISPLACEMENT:	756
DIMENSIONS:	182.4' x 32.3' x 15'
SPEED:	15 kts
CREW:	
ARMAMENT:	two 6 pdrs.

Margaret.

Newington, May 2, 1944.

NEWINGTON

BUILDER:	Cook, Welton & Gremmell, Hull, UK
LAUNCHED:	1899
DISPLACEMENT:	193
DIMENSIONS:	115' x 21' x 11.5'

Newington

Originally a fishing trawler, *Newington* was purchased in 1908 by the Dominion government for use as a light-house tender. In 1914 she was crudely fitted as a minelayer to lay a defensive minefield in Johnstone Strait. She served the RCN on the west coast as a patrol vessel during the First World War, then reverted to government service until 1937, when she was sold. When she sank in Burrard Inlet, British Columbia, on 26 August 1959 she was sixty years old.

P.V. II.

P.V. I to P.V. VII

These seven New England-built menhaden trawlers made up a patrol and minesweeping flotilla based at Sydney, Nova Scotia. Purchased in the US, they served in the RCN between March 1917 and April 1919, subsequently reverting to their former names and occupation. Each was armed with a 12-pounder gun.

	FORMER NAME	WHERE BUILT	LAUNCH	DISPL.	DIMENSIONS	SPEED	ARMAMENT
P.V. I	William H. Murray	Rockland, Maine	1912	390	151.6' x 24.1' x 13'	8kts	one 12 pdr.
P.V. II	Amagansett	Rockland, Maine	1912	390	151.6' x 24.1' x 13'	8kts	one 12 pdr.
P.V. III	Herbert N. Edwards	Rockland, Maine	1911	323	151.6' x 24.1' x 12.9'	8kts	one 12 pdr.
P.V. IV	Martin J. Marran	Rockland, Maine	1911	323	151.6' x 24.1' x 12.9'	8kts	one 12 pdr.
P.V. V	Rollin E. Mason	Essex, Massachusetts	1911	323	151.6' x 24.1' x 12.9'	8kts	one 12 pdr.
P.V. VI	Leander Wilcox	Noank, Connecticut	1903	205	126' x 22.3' x 9.2'	8kts	one 12 pdr.
P.V. VII	Rowland H. Wilcox	Noank, Connecticut	1911	247	132' x 22.3' x 10.7'	8kts	one 12 pdr.

Restless

This innocuous-looking little ship was employed throughout the First World War as an examination vessel on the west coast. Built in 1906, she was purchased for fisheries patrol two years later. She served as a training ship at the Royal Naval College of Canada, Esquimalt, from 1918 to 1920, when she was donated to the Navy League of Canada for sea cadet training. She was sold in 1927, but remained in commercial service until about 1950, when she was destroyed by fire in Saanichton Bay, British Columbia.

Restless.

RESTLESS	
BUILDER:	New Westminster, BC
LAUNCHED:	1906
DISPLACEMENT:	76
DIMENSIONS:	71' x 17' x 7'

Shearwater

Stationed at Esquimalt, the sloops *Shearwater* and *Algerine* were, in 1914, the last remnants of the vanished RN Pacific Squadron. *Shearwater's* two 4-inch guns were put ashore to defend Seymour Narrows when the First World War broke out, and her crew was sent to Halifax to man HMCS *Niobe*. The Admiralty agreed to lend *Shearwater* to the RCN, and on 8 September 1914 she was commissioned as a tender to the newly acquired submarines *CC 1* and *CC 2*. In the summer of 1917 she sailed with her charges via the Panama Canal to Halifax. She was paid off 13 June 1919 and in 1924 sold into mercantile hands and renamed *Vedas*. Her register was closed in 1937.

SHEARWATER	
BUILDER:	H.M. Dockyard, Sheerness
LAUNCHED:	10/2/1900
DISPLACEMENT:	980
DIMENSIONS:	204' x 33' x 11.5'
SPEED:	12 kts
CREW:	
ARMAMENT:	four 4 pdrs., four 3 pdrs.

STADACONA	
BUILDER:	Crescent Shipyard, Elizabeth NJ
LAUNCHED:	1899
DISPLACEMENT:	682
DIMENSIONS:	196.4' x 33.5' x 11'
SPEED:	12 kts
CREW:	62
ARMAMENT:	one 4-inch gun

Stadacona

Originally named *Columbia*, this large yacht was purchased from her New York owner and commissioned on 13 August 1915 for patrol duty out of Halifax. She was also for a time the flagship of Vice-Admiral Sir Charles Kingsmill at Halifax. Early in 1919, *Stadacona* was sent around to the west coast and, after brief service as a dispatch vessel, was paid off 31 March 1920. After a few years' employment as a fisheries patrol and hydrographic survey vessel, she was sold in 1924. She then achieved a degree of notoriety as a rum-runner's depot ship under the name *Kuyakuzmt*. In 1929 she was rebuilt at Vancouver and once again became a yacht, successively named *Lady Stimson* and *Moonlight Maid*. In 1941 she became a towboat, and served in the US as such for a time in 1942. She was burned for salvage at Seattle in January 1948.

Tuna

This former yacht was built as *Tarantula* for W. K. Vanderbilt, Jr., and acquired by the RCN in 1914. Converted to a torpedo boat by the addition of two torpedo tubes, *Tuna* was commissioned on 5 December 1914. She was paid off on 10 May 1917, as a result of irreparable engine-mount fracture. Her hull, sold in June 1918 and stripped for salvage, still lay in Halifax's Northwest Arm in the 1930s.

Shearwater.

Stadacona.

Tuna.

TUNA			
BUILDER:	Yarrow & Co., UK	SPEED:	24 kts
LAUNCHED:	1902	CREW:	
DISPLACEMENT:	124	ARMAMENT:	one 3 pdr., two 14-inch TT
DIMENSIONS:	153' x 15' x 5'		

TR 9.

TR 1-6, 37-44	Port Arthur Shipbuilding Co. Ltd.		**TR 58-60**	Tidewater Shipbuilding Co., Trois Riviéres, Quebec
TR 7-12	Collingwood Shipbuilding Co. Ltd.		LAUNCHED:	1917-1919
TR 13-14	Thor Iron Works, Toronto, Ontario		DISPLACEMENT:	275
TR 15-18	Polson Iron Works, Toronto, Ontario		DIMENSIONS:	125' x 23.5' x 13.5'
TR 19-20, 54-57	Kingston Shipbuilding Co.		SPEED:	10 kts
TR 21-31	Canadian Vickers Ltd., Montreal Quebec		CREW:	
TR 32-34, 51-53	Government Shipyards, Sorel, Quebec		ARMAMENT:	one 12 pdr.
TR 35-36, 46-50	Davie Shipbuilding Co. Ltd., Lauzon, Quebec			

C.D. 27.

C.D. 1-50	Davie Shipbuilding Co. Ltd., Lauzon, Quebec		**C.D. 71-96**	Canadian Vickers Ltd., Montreal, Quebec	
C.D. 51-53	Government Shipyards, Sorel, Quebec		**C.D. 97-100**	Harbour Commissioners, Montreal, Quebec	
C.D. 54-59	Sorel Shipbuilding & Coal Co., Sorel, Quebec		LAUNCHED:	1917	SPEED: 9 kts
C.D. 60-61, 68-70	H. H. Sheppard & Sons, Sorel, Quebec		DISPLACEMENT:	99	CREW:
C.D. 62-67	LeClaire & Sons, Sorel, Quebec		DIMENSIONS:	84' x 19.3' x 10'	ARMAMENT: one 6 pdr.

TR 1 to TR 60

These large minesweeping trawlers were copies of the RN's Castle class. It seems impossible to determine how many were actually commissioned, but the number is likely about 45. *TR 37, 39, 51, 55, 56* and *58-60* were lent to the USN from November 1918 until sometime in 1919. Little used, the TRs found willing buyers as replacements for fishing tonnage lost during the war, and a good many were absorbed into the RN as auxiliary minesweepers during the Second World War. Two of them appear in the 1940s roster of the RCN as *Andrée Dupré* and *Macsin*.

C.D. 1 to C.D. 100

These wooden-hulled drifters were built along the same lines as those of the RN. All were launched during 1917, and thirty-seven are supposed to have been commissioned before the end of the war. They were intended for minesweeping and patrol duty, and fourteen served at Gibraltar, six at Bermuda and five in West Africa from 1918 to 1919. A further eighteen were lent to the USN during the same period. Like the TRs, they found ready employment after the war, and a few served in the RN from 1939 to 1945. Three of the drifters, unnumbered, were destroyed incomplete by fire at the Canada Steamship Lines plant at Sorel on 19 June 1917.

Arleux

Built at Montreal and commissioned 5 June 1918, *Arleux* saw only brief service before being handed over to the Department of Marine and Fisheries, though in common with several sisters she remained nominally a naval vessel until 30 June 1922. As a fisheries patrol vessel she frequently acted as mother ship to the winter haddock fishing fleet off the east coast. Taken up again by the RCN, she was commissioned 13 September 1939, and in 1940 designated *Gate Vessel 16* at Halifax. She was sold for commercial use on 15 February 1946, and foundered 19 August 1948 off White Head Bay, Nova Scotia.

ARLEUX	
BUILDER:	Canadian Vickers, Montreal
LAUNCHED:	9/8/17

Armentières

Commissioned from 5 June 1918 to 28 October 1919, *Armentières* re-entered naval service in 1923 only to be sunk in Pipestem Inlet, British Columbia, on 2 September 1925. Refloated on 26 October she was recommissioned the following year and continued in service, primarily as a training ship, but with occasional intervals on fisheries patrol. In the spring, *Armentières* would escort the fur seals en route to their breeding grounds in the Pribilof Islands to protect them from illegal hunting procedures. From 1934 until the outbreak of the Second World War she was the only one of her class still in naval service. She served as an examination vessel at Prince Rupert throughout most of the war, and after being paid off on 8 February 1946 was sold to become SS *A. G. Garrish*. Two changes of name later, she still existed in 1962 as *Laforce*. She was sold to an American buyer in 1972.

ARMENTIÈRES			
BUILDER:	Canadian Vickers, Montreal	LAUNCHED:	11/8/17
Commanding Officers			
LT T. MacDuff, RCNR	1/9/39	-	
LT A. H. G. Storrs, RCNR	31/3/41	-	
CH/SKPR G. Billard, RCNR	29/7/41	-	
CH/SKPR W. E. Eccles, RCNR	2/3/42	-	
CH/SKPR J. D. McPhee, RCNR	14/12/42	-	
SKPR/LT G. F. Cassidy, RCNR	20/9/43	-	
CH/SKPR J. G. A. Grandmaison, RCNR	-	-	
SKPR/LT H. R. H. Stratford, RCNR	24/6/44	-	
SKPR/LT W. E. Eccles, RCNR	9/12/44	-	
SKPR/LT H. R. H. Stratford, RCNR	-	-	
SKPR/LT J. Craig, RCNR	7/8/45	-	

Battle Class Trawlers

PARTICULARS OF CLASS:	
DISPLACEMENT:	357; if built at Polson Ironworks, Toronto: 320
DIMENSIONS:	130' x 25' x 13'; if built at Polson Ironworks: 130' x 23.5' x 13.5'
SPEED:	10 kts
ARMAMENT:	one 12 pdr.

Arleux as gate vessel, Halifax, 1940.

Armentières, December 9, 1940.

Arras, 1940.

Festubert, November 12, 1943.

Givenchy.

Arras

Built at Kingston, *Arras* was in commission from 8 July 1918 to 1919, when she became a fisheries protection vessel. As such, she frequently served as hospital ship to the Grand Banks fishing fleet. Taken up again by the RCN, she was in service from 11 September 1939 to 1 April 1946. Initially stationed at Halifax from mid-1941, she was employed at Sydney, Nova Scotia, as *Gate Vessel 15*, and was extensively damaged by fire in November 1943. She was broken up at Halifax in 1957.

Festubert

Built at Toronto, *Festubert* was commissioned on 13 November 1917, and after brief service was laid up until 1 May 1923. She was then recommissioned for training and other duties on the east coast until once more placed in reserve in 1934. From 1939 to 17 August 1945 she was again in service as *Gate Vessel 17* at Halifax. *Festubert* was sold in 1946 for commercial use and renamed *Inverleigh*. She was scuttled off Burgeo, Newfoundland on 30 June 1971.

ARRAS			
BUILDER:	Canadian Vickers, Montreal	LAUNCHED:	15/9/17

Commanding Officers		
LT R. R. Kennedy, RCNR	4/5/40	-
LT A. H. Cassivi, RCNR	28/1/41	-
LT J. Willis, RCNR	11/2/44	-
LT W. S. Arsenault, RCNR		
LT J. Willis, RCNR	17/4/43	-
SKPR/LT A. Currie, RCNR	26/4/45	-
LT W. S. Arsenault, RCNR	/45	-

FESTUBERT			
BUILDER:	Polson Ironworks, Toronto	LAUNCHED:	2/8/17

Givenchy

Built at Montreal, *Givenchy* was commissioned on 22 June 1918 and paid off on 12 August 1919 at Esquimalt. She then entered the service of the Department of Marine and Fisheries as a fisheries protection vessel, but was returned to the RCN on 15 April 1939. Though her principal function was that of accommodation ship (notably to the Fishermen's Reserve) she was actually in commission from 25 June 1940 to 18 April 1943. Sold on 19 September 1946, *Givenchy* is thought to have been broken up in the US in 1953.

GIVENCHY			
BUILDER:	Canadian Vickers, Montreal	LAUNCHED:	15/9/17

Loos

Launched at Kingston on September 27, 1917, *Loos* was in commission between 1 August 1918 and 1920. In 1922 she entered the service of the Department of Marine and Fisheries as a lighthouse supply ship. About 1937 she was sold out of government service, but was taken up again by the RCN on 12 December 1940. By June 1941, she had been converted to *Gate Vessel 14* and served as such for a time at Shelburne, Nova Scotia. In 1945 she was returned to her previous owner, Marine Industries Ltd., and broken up in 1949.

Loos

LOOS			
BUILDER:	Kingston Shipbuilding Co.	LAUNCHED:	27/9/17
Commanding Officers			
CH/SKPR N. H. Pentz, RCNR		3/12/40	-
SKPR E. T. Coggins, RCNR		15/5/41	-
SKPR J. A. D. Anthony, RCNR		1/5/42	-
SKPR J. Cossar, RCNR		22/6/42	-

Messines fitting out at Toronto, astern of *Ypres*, 1917.

Messines

Launched at Toronto on 16 June 1917 along with three sisters, *Messines* began a short commission on 13 November and in 1920 was handed over to the Department of Marine and Fisheries to become a lightship. Eventually designated *Lightship No. 3*, she was scrapped in 1962.

MESSINES	
BUILDER:	Polson Ironworks, Toronto
LAUNCHED:	16/6/17

St. Eloi.

St. Eloi

Built at Toronto, *St. Eloi* was commissioned on 13 November 1917. Like *Messines*, she was turned over to the Department of Marine and Fisheries in 1920 for conversion and ultimately designated *Lightship No. 20*. The RCN recovered her in 1940 and she became *Gate Vessel 12* for the duration of the war, spending at least part of that time at Shelburne. The Department of Transport, successor to the Department of Marine and Fisheries, took her back in June 1945 and she was not finally disposed of until 1962.

ST. ELOI			
BUILDER:	Polson Ironworks, Toronto	LAUNCHED:	2/8/17

Commanding Officers		
CH/SKPR N. H. Pentz, RCNR	15/5/41	-
CH/SKPR P. E. Blouin, RCNR	1/5/42	-
SKPR W. I. V. Power	31/5/42	-

St. Julien fitting out at Toronto, 1917.

St. Julien

Built at Toronto, and commissioned on 13 November 1917, *St. Julien* was transferred to the Department of Marine and Fisheries in 1920, and was known by 1934 as *Lightship No. 22*.

Sold out of government service in 1958, she was renamed *Centennial*, and still existed as recently as 1978.

ST. JULIEN			
BUILDER:	Polson Ironworks, Toronto	LAUNCHED:	16/6/17

Thiepval

Launched in 1917 at Kingston, *Thiepval* was in commission between 24 July 1918 and 19 March 1920, when she was turned over to the Department of Marine and Fisheries as a patrol vessel. Taken back into the RCN, she was commissioned 1 April 1923 for service on the west coast. In February 1924 she was detailed to proceed across the north Pacific to Hakodate, Japan, to deposit fuel and lube "dumps" for the round-the-world flight of Major Stuart MacLaren. Travelling over 11,000 miles in the process, *Thiepval* also salvaged what remained of the aircraft after it was wrecked at Nikolski, USSR, on 3 August. The trawler herself was wrecked on an uncharted rock in Barkley Sound, British Columbia, on 27 February 1930.

Vimy

The Toronto-built *Vimy* was in commission from 13 November 1917 to 30 November 1918, seeing even less service than the dates would indicate. In 1922 she was transferred to the Department of Marine and Fisheries for conversion, and eventually known as *Lightship No. 5*. She is thought to have been broken up about 1958.

Ypres

Built at Toronto and in commission from 13 November 1917 to 1920, *Ypres* was recommissioned as a training ship on 1 May 1923. She was placed in reserve in November 1932, but emerged from a 1938 refit as *Gate Vessel 1* of Halifax boom defence. On 12 May 1940 she was run down and sunk at Halifax by HMS *Revenge*, fortunately without loss of life.

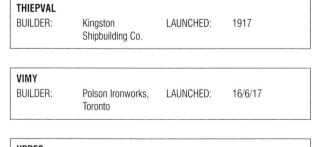

THIEPVAL			
BUILDER:	Kingston Shipbuilding Co.	LAUNCHED:	1917

VIMY			
BUILDER:	Polson Ironworks, Toronto	LAUNCHED:	16/6/17

YPRES			
BUILDER:	Polson Ironworks, Toronto	LAUNCHED:	16/6/17

Thiepval.

Vimy fitting out at Toronto, 1917.

Ypres, 1924.

Fundy Class Minesweepers

PARTICULARS OF CLASS:

DISPLACEMENT:	460	SPEED:	12 kts
DIMENSIONS:	163' x 27.5' x 14.5'	CREW:	3/35
		ARMAMENT:	one 12 pdr.

Comox, June, 1942.

COMOX

BUILDER:	Burrard Dry Dock Co., Vancouver	COMMISSIONED:	23/11/38
LAID DOWN:	5/2/38	PAID OFF:	27/7/45
LAUNCHED:	9/8/38		

Commanding Officers

LCDR H. W. S. Soulsby, RCNR	23/11/38	26/5/40	A/LT T. Gilmour, RCNR	23/6/41	2/8/41
A/LCDR D. C. Wallace, RCNR	27/5/40	27/7/40	Mate J. R. Biggs, RCNR	29/9/41	25/3/42
A/CDR S. H. Soulsby, RCN	28/7/40	9/10/40	LT F. G. Hutchings, RCNR	26/3/42	3/8/42
LT R. R. Kenny, RCNR	10/10/40	22/6/41	LT J. P. A. Duggan, RCNR	4/8/42	13/4/44
			LT J. E. N. Vezina, RCNR	14/4/44	27/7/45

Fundy, 1944.

Comox

Commissioned on 23 November 1938, *Comox* was stationed at Esquimalt at the outbreak of war, and carried out local patrol duties until March 1940, when, with *Nootka*, she was ordered to the east coast. Arriving at Halifax in April, she spent the entire war on local minesweeping duties with Halifax Local Defence Force. On 15 January 1945, with *Fundy*, she rescued survivors from the US Liberty ship *Martin van Buren*, torpedoed off Halifax. She was paid off 27 July 1945, sold for commercial purposes in 1946 and converted to a tug, the *Sung Ming*.

Fundy

Commissioned at Collingwood on 1 September 1938, she was at Halifax when the war began, and served almost continuously as a member of Halifax Local Defence Force on local minesweeping duties. In July 1942, her one change of occupation occurred when she escorted one convoy to Boston and another back to Halifax. On 15 January 1945, with *Comox*, she rescued survivors of the torpedoed *Martin van Buren*. *Fundy* was paid off at Halifax on 27 July 1945 and sold two years later to Marine Industries Ltd. Converted for mercantile purposes, she was finally broken up at La Malbaie, Quebec in 1987.

FUNDY

BUILDER:	Collingwood Shipyards Ltd.	LAUNCHED:	18/6/38
		COMMISSIONED:	1/9/38
LAID DOWN:	24/1/38	PAID OFF:	27/7/45

Commanding Officers

LCDR J. W. R. Roy, RCN	2/9/38	14/12/38
LCDR A. R. Pressey, RCN	15/12/38	26/12/39
LCDR O. C. S. Robertson, RCNR	27/12/39	22/2/40
A/LCDR A. G. Stanley, RCNR	23/2/40	7/3/41
LT A. Moorhouse, RCNVR	8/3/41	2/8/41
LT A. M. McLarnon, RCNR	3/8/41	17/8/41
LT A. Moorhouse, RCNVR	18/8/41	28/10/41
Mate J. B. Raine, RCNR	29/10/41	9/3/42
SKPR/LT F. A. Heckman, RCNR	10/3/42	27/7/45

Gaspé

Commissioned at Quebec on 21 October 1938, *Gaspé* was at Halifax when hostilities broke out. Throughout the war she served with Halifax Local Defence Force on local minesweeping duties. She was paid off at Halifax on 23 July 1945 and sold into mercantile service in 1946, becoming the Shanghai tug *Sung Li*.

Nootka/Nanoose

Commissioned on 6 December 1938 at Esquimalt, *Nootka* was based there when the war began. She performed local patrol duty until March 1940, when with *Comox*, she was transferred to Halifax. Arriving there in April, she was assigned to Halifax Local Defence Force where she remained throughout the war. On 1 April 1943 she was renamed *Nanoose* so that her original name could be allotted to a Tribal class destroyer. She was paid off at Halifax on 29 July 1945, and like two of her sisters, sold in 1946 to become a tug. Her Chinese owners renamed her *Sung Ling*.

Gaspé, 1940.

Nootka, September 23, 1942.

GASPÉ			
BUILDER:	Morton Engineering Co., Quebec City	LAUNCHED:	12/8/38
		COMMISSIONED:	21/10/38
		PAID OFF:	23/7/45
LAID DOWN:	24/1/38		

Commanding Officers

LCDR H. N. Lay, RCN	12/1/39	17/8/39
A/LCDR H. D. Mackay, RCNR	3/9/39	11/4/41
LT R. T. Ingram, RCNR	12/4/41	2/8/41
LT T. Gilmour, RCNR	3/8/41	17/8/41
LT R. T. Ingram, RCNR	18/8/41	26/10/41
CH/SKPR G. A. Myra, RCNR	27/10/41	2/8/42
LT W. S. Bryant, RCNR	3/8/42	24/6/43
SKPR/LT A. J. Burke, RCNR	25/6/43	7/1/45
SKPR/LT R. A. Doucette, RCNR	8/1/45	23/7/45

NOOTKA/NANOOSE			
BUILDER:	Yarrows Ltd., Victoria, BC	COMMISSIONED:	6/12/38
		PAID OFF:	29/7/45
LAID DOWN:	1/2/38	Renamed *Nanoose*	
LAUNCHED:	26/9/38		

Commanding Officers

LCDR H. Kingsley, RCN	6/12/38	14/5/39
LCDR K. F. Adams, RCN	15/5/39	21/8/39
LCDR M. A. Wood, RCN	22/8/39	13/9/39
LT A. T. Morrell, RCNR	14/9/39	27/9/40
LCDR W. J. Fricker, RCN	28/9/40	25/1/41
LT J. P. Fraser, RCNR	29/1/41	20/7/41
LT A. M. McLarnon, RCNR	21/7/41	2/8/41
LT J. P. Fraser, RCNR	3/8/41	14/9/41
Mate W. R. Nunn, RCNR	15/9/41	15/3/42
CH/SKPR G. F. Burgess, RCNR	16/3/42	13/9/43
SKPR/LT C. Burnham, RCNR	14/9/43	29/7/45

Skidegate, January, 1941.

Skidegate

Named *Ochecac* before her purchase, this diminutive vessel was commissioned on 25 July 1938 for training purposes in connection with the Fishermen's Reserve, formed that year on the west coast. Of declining use as the war progressed, *Skidegate* was paid off on February 18, 1942, finally sold into mercantile service in 1946 and renamed *Santa Rosa*.

SKIDEGATE	
BUILDER:	Vancouver BC
LAUNCHED:	1927
DISPLACEMENT:	15
DIMENSIONS:	47' x 13.5' x 5'
SPEED:	8 kts
CREW:	3/7

Venture.

Venture

The only sailing vessel among the thirteen ships serving in the RCN on the eve of the Second World War, this three-masted schooner was built at Meteghan, Nova Scotia, and commissioned on 25 October 1937 as a training ship. With war imminent, *Venture* was paid off on 1 September 1939 to become an accommodation vessel at Halifax for ratings on the staff of the Rear Admiral, 3rd Battleship Squadron, RN. In November 1941, she was commissioned as guard ship at Tuft's Cove, at the entrance to Bedford Basin. She gave up her name on 13 May 1943 to the former yacht *Seaborn* and thereafter was known as *Harbour Craft 190*. She was sold on 10 December 1945 to a Halifax firm and renamed *Alfred & Emily*. Engaged first in the sealing trade and then in carrying coal, she was lost by fire at sea in 1951.

VENTURE	
BUILDER:	Meteghan, NS
LAUNCHED:	6/37
DISPLACEMENT:	250
DIMENSIONS:	142' x 27' x 14.5'

PART II **1939–1945**

INTRODUCTION

DURING THE SECOND WORLD WAR the RCN grew from thirteen ships to some four hundred and fifty, excluding the smaller auxiliaries. The majority were engaged in the Battle of the Atlantic, which was fought for most of the war around several series of convoys running between North America and the United Kingdom. This battle was fundamental to Britain's survival, and the importance of the RCN's role in it can hardly be exaggerated.

This introduction presents the activities of the RCN against the background of the Atlantic struggle, which an anonymous Admiralty historian has divided into eight phases. More detail will be found in the histories of the ships themselves.

3 September 1939 to 9 June 1940

During this period the U-boats found most of their victims in the southwest approaches to the British Isles—about as far as they could handily operate from their home bases. Transatlantic convoys were initiated almost immediately on the outbreak of war. They were escorted by battleships, cruisers, or armed merchant cruisers, as the greatest threat at the time was the surface raider. Eastbound convoys were given a local escort of one or two Canadian destroyers, which would accompany the convoy to a point south of St. John's, Newfoundland. The first such convoy, HX.1, was escorted out of Halifax by *Saguenay* and *St. Laurent* on 16 September 1939, six days after Canada had declared war on Germany. Passive defences in the form of A/S nets were completed at Esquimalt in October and at Halifax in November.

The four destroyers based on the west coast had joined their sisters in Halifax by the end of the year, and the small force was augmented in November by the arrival of HMCS *Assiniboine*, transferred from the RN. The only other notable ships added to the RCN in this period were the three small Prince class liners, for conversion to armed merchant cruisers.

Orders for sixty-four corvettes and eighteen Bangor class minesweepers were placed with fifteen Canadian shipyards in 1940. In April the Germans overran Denmark and Norway, and four of Canada's destroyers were ordered to the UK.

10 June 1940 to 17 March 1941

Italy entered the war on 10 June and soon afterward France collapsed. The Canadian destroyers found themselves engaged in the melancholy business of evacuating troops from France, and in the process *Fraser* was rammed and sunk by HMS *Calcutta* on 25 June.

Able now to operate from bases from France and Norway, the U-boats could stay at sea longer and range farther out into the Atlantic. In the face of this threat, as well as that posed by E-boats and the Luftwaffe to Channel traffic, convoys ceased in July to use the southwestern approaches and were routed north of Ireland instead. The remaining three Canadian destroyers now served as local escorts in those waters. The newly acquired HMCS *Margaree* was lost in collision in convoy on 22 October with most of her ship's company, many of them survivors of *Fraser*.

From July to October the U-boats wreaked havoc with the weakly defended shipping and the German "aces" came into prominence. They favoured attacking on the surface and by night, and toward the end of the year introduced the "wolf pack" attack.

The destroyer shortage caused by losses and damage during the Norwegian campaign and the evacuation of France was to some extent made good through the agreement of 2 September 1940, whereby sites for military bases were leased by Britain in return for fifty over age US destroyers. Six of these were commissioned into the RCN that month and two more later. Corvette production was in full swing both in Britain and Canada, whose first eighteen were commissioned during this period. The period ended with the loss of U-boats commanded by three German "aces" in attacks on convoys between 7 and 17 March.

18 March 1941 to 11 January 1942

Faced with a growing number of convoy escorts in what had been so happy a hunting ground, the U-boats moved their patrols farther into the Atlantic. It was now imperative that continuous escort be provided across the ocean, and to this end Britain began basing escorts at Hvalfjord, Iceland, in April. In June 1941, an RCN base was established at St. John's, Newfoundland, and Canadian ships overseas were withdrawn to become part of what was called the Newfoundland Escort Force (NEF). Canada accepted responsibility for the ocean escort of convoys to the meeting point south of Iceland at the end of May.

In May the cast of the ongoing drama were upstaged by those engaged in the hunt for the German battleship *Bismarck,* finally sunk on 27 May. The victory was dearly bought, HMS *Hood* having been sunk by *Bismarck* three days earlier.

On 10 September the corvettes *Chambly* and *Moose Jaw* had barely arrived to reinforce the Canadian escort force of a beleaguered eastbound convoy when they attacked and sank *U 501*. HMCS *Lévis* was torpedoed and sunk nine days later with another convoy, not far away, and on 7 December *Windflower* was lost in a collision. She had been the first Canadian corvette launched.

A German long-range bomber, the FW 200 Kondor, became a serious menace to transatlantic shipping during this period, both as an attacker and as a spotter for U-boats. A countermeasure in the form of naval auxiliaries called fighter catapult ships was introduced in April, and in May the first of twenty-six mercantile counterparts called CAM (catapult aircraft merchant) ships went to sea. The types were alike in that they could not recover the Hurricane fighters, whose pilots had to "ditch" and hope for rescue. HMS *Audacity*, which entered service in June, remedied this defect. A German freighter captured by HMCS *Assiniboine* and HMS *Dunedin*, and later fitted with a flight deck, she was the precursor of the escort carriers—mostly US built—that would appear in growing numbers as the Battle of the Atlantic progressed.

Among decisions made at the meeting of Roosevelt and Churchill at Argentia, Newfoundland in August 1941, was one permitting US warships to escort convoys to and from the Mid-Ocean Meeting Point. This arrangement was initiated the following month, and was to cost the USN its first war casualty when, on 31 October, USS *Reuben James* was torpedoed and sunk in convoy HX.156.

Toward the end of the year an appreciable number of U-boats were withdrawn to serve in the Mediterranean and its western approaches, so that the Atlantic convoys had a comparatively quiet time until mid-January. During this period fifty new corvettes were commissioned, including the first four with extended fo'c's'les. The first nineteen Bangor class minesweepers and the first thirteen Fairmiles also entered service.

12 January to 13 July 1942

Four days after Pearl Harbor, Hitler declared war on the US, and in mid-January a large force of U-boats made their appearance off the eastern seaboard and in the Caribbean. In these waters they took a staggering toll of merchant shipping, especially tankers, as no convoy system had been established for coastal traffic. This was finally remedied in May, and by mid-July the system was effective enough that the U-boats returned to mid-ocean waters.

March 1942 saw the first use by the Germans of "milch cow" U-boats to refuel and replenish their smaller sisters at sea, nearly doubling the latters' endurance. Not to be outdone, the RN devised a method of refuelling escorts at sea from ordinary merchant tankers, which went into practice that summer. About the same time high-frequency direction finding (HF/DF or "Huff-Duff") was perfected for shipboard installation. It had been used since the beginning of the war by shore stations to obtain cross-bearings on U-boat wireless transmissions and fix their location at sea. Convoys could thus be warned of U-boats in their path or aircraft directed to attack them. In time all destroyers, frigates and convoy rescue ships were equipped with this device, which though largely unsung in histories of the sea war, played a very significant part in the defeat of the U-boats.

The RCN by now formed the backbone of the western Atlantic escort force, with thirteen destroyers and sixty-seven corvettes in commission, and by the autumn of 1942, bore almost half the burden of escorting North Atlantic convoys. Base facilities had been completed at Londonderry, Ireland, and in February 1942 Canadian mid-ocean escorts inaugurated the "Newfie-Derry run," seldom thereafter calling at Iceland. An escort of one of the earliest convoys on that run, HMCS *Spikenard* was torpedoed and sunk on 10 February on the way across.

In May two ships were sunk in the Gulf of St. Lawrence, leading to the formation of a St. Lawrence Escort Force based at Gaspé. This typically consisted of two corvettes, five Bangor minesweepers, and some of the Fairmile motor launches that had begun entering service the previous fall. In August and September U-boats were again active in the Gulf and the St. Lawrence River itself, and the armed yacht *Raccoon* and the corvette *Charlottetown* were torpedoed and sunk on 7 and 11 September respectively. On the other side of the ledger, the period ended with the sinking of *U 90* by *St. Croix* on 24 July, and of *U 588* by *Skeena* and *Wetaskiwin* on 31 July in mid-Atlantic.

1 August 1942 to 21 May 1943

This period began with a renewed effort by the U-boats against North Atlantic convoys, especially in what the Germans called "the black pit," a gap north of the Azores out of reach of land-based air cover. The wolfpacks were larger than ever before, and they were steadily refining their methods of intercepting convoys and calling in their comrades for the kill. Losses were appallingly heavy and U-boat sinkings disproportionately small. Canadian ships sank, or assisted in sinking, six U-boats in the Atlantic, three in the Mediterranean, and one in the Caribbean. HMCS *Ottawa* was torpedoed and sunk on 13 September, corvettes *Louisburg* and *Weyburn* on 6 and 22 February 1943. The latter two were lost in the Mediterranean due to their being among sixteen Canadian corvettes assigned to convoys supplying Allied forces in North Africa after Operation Torch, the invasion of November 1942.

An important development during this period was the formation in September 1942 of the first support groups—groups of ships that could be dispatched to bolster the escorts of threatened convoys, and which now could afford the luxury of hunting U-boats to death rather than merely "putting them down" and rejoining the convoy. Their effective use was, however, delayed by the needs of the North African campaign.

In February 1943, Dönitz, who had succeeded the less forceful Raeder as Grand Admiral of the Kriegsmarine, won Hitler's approval to mount an all-out onslaught on the North Atlantic sea-lanes. Allied fortunes there sank to an unsurpassed low, U-boats sinking one hundred and seventy-one ships in February and March. One of the deadliest attacks of the war was that delivered against the combined convoys HX.229/SC.122 in March by forty-four U-boats, which sank twenty-one ships for the loss of only one of their own.

At this inauspicious juncture, on 30 April, the RCN assumed control of the northwest Atlantic. Seven corvettes lent to the USN for Caribbean convoy duty were now returned, as were the fourteen from the Mediterranean. In addition six of the RN's veteran destroyers were to be transferred to the RCN. Commissioned between March 1943 and February 1944, they received the names of Canadian rivers. Canadian ocean escort groups were further reinforced at this time by the allocation of three RN frigates and six RN corvettes. In addition, six RN anti-submarine (A/S) trawlers were lent to bolster the escort force in the Gulf of St. Lawrence. Brief accounts of these fifteen ships will be found in Appendix One.

Through April the tide of battle began almost imperceptibly to turn in the Allies' favour, and May proved as disastrous for the U-boats as March had been to the convoys. The forty-two-ship convoy ONS.5 lost only thirteen ships despite having forty-one U-boats deployed against it, not to mention sinking seven of the attackers and damaging five, while SC.130 lost none despite the efforts of a wolfpack of thirty-two U-boats. In all, forty-one U-boats were sunk that month, and on 24 May Dönitz recalled most of the others. The Battle of the Atlantic had two years to run, but the Kriegsmarine lost the initiative in May 1943, and was never to regain it.

The U-boats were defeated by a combination of factors: improved intelligence, more and experienced convoy escorts, continuous air cover, and support groups. Each of five of the support groups contained one of the newly commissioned US-built escort aircraft carriers. These, together with shore-based Liberators, provided vital air cover across the "black pit," while elsewhere the U-boats were subjected to increasingly effective attacks by long-range aircraft from bases in Newfoundland, Greenland, Iceland, and Britain.

Two new weapons also made their appearance: the Hedgehog threw its twenty-four projectiles ahead of the ship, enabling the operator of the Asdic, a submarine-detecting device, to maintain contact with his quarry until the moment of firing. The second was the airborne rocket projectile, such as those used by a Swordfish from the aircraft carrier *Archer* to sink *U 752* on 23 May. The RCN's first two Tribal class destroyers, *Athabaskan* and *Iroquois*, were completed during this period.

22 May to 18 September 1943

At the end of May the first of nineteen MAC (merchant aircraft carrier) ships went into service. These differed from US-built escort carriers in that they carried regular cargoes—most of them oil, some of them wheat—as well as aircraft.

There were no attacks on North Atlantic convoys in June, but land-based bombers launched a devastating assault on U-boats transiting the Bay of Biscay en route to or from their bases in western France. Sixteen were sunk there in July alone, whereas merchant ship losses were negligible during the rest of the period. At the same time, US hunter/killer groups incorporating escort carriers were systematically eliminating the "milch cows" south and west of the Azores. During this period the RCN's second pair of Tribals, *Haida* and *Huron*, were commissioned, as were its first five frigates and the first Algerine class minesweeper.

19 September 1943 to 6 June 1944

The expected renewal of U-boat attacks on North Atlantic convoys began with a wolf pack attack on ON.202, 19-23 September. One of the first victims was HMCS *St. Croix*. The attack was notable as the first in which the U-boats were armed with acoustic torpedoes, which tracked their targets by the sound of the propellers. It was also one of the earliest occasions on which a homing torpedo was used against a U-boat by an aircraft, *U 238* being sunk by this means. HMCS *Chedabucto* was accidentally lost on 21 October in the St. Lawrence River.

Despite a determined effort throughout the autumn, the U-boats accomplished little in the North Atlantic and suffered heavy losses. During this period Captain F. J. Walker's group of RN sloops enjoyed its greatest success, sinking eleven U-boats. One of these, *U 264*, was the first operational boat fitted with a Schnorckel—a 26-foot tube that enabled the boat to run on diesels while submerged and to charge its batteries and refresh the air in the boat without surfacing. By autumn few boats went on patrol without it, and the device was to occasion a sharp decline in sinkings, especially by aircraft.

Another unsuccessful effort early in 1944 was abandoned in March, leaving only a couple of weather-reporting U-boats in the North Atlantic. All serviceable boats were now being held ready against the anticipated invasion of northern Europe. During this period RCN ships assisted in the destruction of eight U-boats. HMCS *Valleyfield* was lost south off Newfoundland on 7 May.

During the last quarter of 1943 the RCN Tribals were used extensively on convoys to Russia, then early in 1944 took part in a series of attacks on German shipping off the coast of Norway. Prior to D Day three of them participated in strikes against German shipping in the Channel; *Athabaskan* was lost in one of these strikes on 29 April.

While still committed to its duties in the North Atlantic, the RCN was deeply involved in preparations for the invasion. Early in 1944, sixteen Bangors and nineteen corvettes made the passage to the UK, the former to be equipped for minesweeping and the latter to help escort the ships massing for D Day. The nine remaining River class destroyers were withdrawn from the Atlantic for service in the Channel, and eleven frigates were formed into two escort groups for U-boat hunting, under operational control of Western Approaches Command. As well, the RCN now manned two flotillas of motor torpedo boats, which took part in a variety of operations in the Channel before, during, and after D Day.

During the night of 5-6 June, RCN Bangors swept a safe channel to Omaha Beach where American troops were to land, and on and after D Day itself (6 June) sixteen Canadian corvettes escorted shipping and artificial harbour components across the

Channel. Two new RCN destroyers, *Algonquin* and *Sioux*, provided inshore fire support during the landings, in which thirty RCN-manned infantry landing craft took part. *Prince David* and *Prince Henry* were also on hand in their new role as infantry landing ships.

7 June 1944 to 8 May 1945

With the Normandy beachhead secure, the British-based RCN ships shared with their RN sisters the task of defending the Channel approaches from Biscay-based U-boats, and of harassing German shipping both in the Channel and in the Bay of Biscay itself. The A/S sweeps were carried out principally by the frigates and River class destroyers, which sank four U-boats in August and September.

The Tribals specialized in dramatic night actions, *Haida* and *Huron* sinking a large German destroyer, *Z 32*, in one of these forays. The Bangors meanwhile busied themselves clearing German mines from the Channel and from liberated ports, a task that was to occupy them for some months.

The anticipated U-boat onslaught against post-invasion traffic failed to materialize; instead, attempts began almost immediately to resume operations in British coastal waters. These attempts increased toward the end of the year as the Biscay boats, driven from their bases, reorganized themselves in Norway for an effort that continued almost until the end of the war. They achieved little success while suffering heavy losses, but HMC ships *Regina*, *Alberni*, *Trentonian*, and *Guysborough* were among their victims. At the end of 1944, RCN ships made up fourteen of the thirty-seven escort groups based at Londonderry, whose primary duty was to counter the enemy's inshore campaign, and Canadian ships sank six U-boats.

No longer needed in the Channel, *Algonquin* and *Sioux* returned to Scapa Flow, and until early in 1945 escorted Russian convoys and assisted in strikes against German shipping off the Norwegian coast. On 22 August the Canadian-manned escort carrier *Nabob* was torpedoed while taking part in an air strike against the battleship *Tirpitz* in her Norwegian lair. *Algonquin*, one of the screening destroyers, took off two hundred and three of *Nabob's* crew as a precaution, but the carrier struggled back to Scapa Flow.

In mid-December, 1944, the North Atlantic convoys resumed the Western Approaches route south of Ireland, which they had been forced to abandon four years earlier. There were still a few U-boats on patrol in the northwest Atlantic, and toward the end of the year there were five or six off Halifax and in the Gulf of St. Lawrence. *Shawinigan* and *Clayoquot* fell prey to two of these, and *Esquimalt* to another in April 1945. That month the first operational Type XXI U-boat left her Norwegian base on patrol. She and her class represented the ultimate in submarine development; they had no need to surface while at sea, and had an underwater speed about equal to that of a frigate. Had they come into production a year earlier the course of the war would have been dramatically changed. As it was, they accomplished nothing.

On 4 May 1945, Dönitz ordered his U-boats to cease hostilities, and on 8 May, to surface and surrender. *U 190*, which had sunk HMCS *Esquimalt*, complied on 12 May and a day later *U 889* followed suit, the only two boats to surrender to the RCN.

The Pacific

The RCN's involvement in the war against the Japanese was negligible. A small force of seven corvettes and seven minesweepers, based at Esquimalt and Prince Rupert, was maintained for escort and A/S duties on the west coast. Apart from isolated Japanese submarine attacks off the California and Oregon coasts—in December 1941, June-July 1942 and October 1942—no threat to west-coast shipping materialized, and no ship was attacked in Canadian waters. Five of the seven corvettes were therefore transferred to the east coast in October 1942 to release a number of more experienced Halifax-based corvettes for Operation Torch.

The three Canadian armed merchant cruisers, together with the corvettes *Dawson* and *Vancouver*, left Esquimalt on 20 August 1942 to support the US Aleutians campaign, remaining in those waters for a little over two months. The corvettes later returned to Alaskan waters for escort duties from February to June 1943.

The only RCN ship to see active service against the Japanese was the cruiser *Uganda*, which served with the British Pacific Fleet between April and July 1945, in operations against Truk and the Japanese home islands.

When the Pacific war ended in August 1945, the newer war-built destroyers and a majority of the frigates were undergoing modifications for tropical waters and refit in Canadian yards for service in the Pacific, but were never required.

Cruisers

Uganda/Quebec

As HMS *Uganda,* the name ship of her class, she was completed 3 January 1943 at Vickers-Armstrong Ltd., Newcastle-on-Tyne. After working up with the Home Fleet she joined Plymouth Command in April for operations in the Bay of Biscay and the English Channel, and in July joined the 15th Cruiser Squadron, Mediterranean Fleet, as part of Force K. She was badly damaged by a German glider bomb on 13 September 1943, while supporting the Allied landings at Salerno, Italy, and arrived at Charleston, South Carolina in November for a year of repair work.

Presented to the RCN, the ship was commissioned HMCS *Uganda* on 21 October 1944 at Charleston, and in November returned to the UK for further modifications. She left in January 1945 for the Pacific via the Suez Canal, to join the 4th Cruiser Squadron, British Pacific Fleet. In April she joined Task Force 57 in the Okinawa area, and was thereafter principally employed in screening the Fleet's aircraft carriers operating against Japanese airfields in the Ryukyu Islands. On 14 June she participated in the bombardment of Truk, and in July supported carriers operating against Tokyo. She left the Fleet late in July

Quebec 1953.

and arrived at Esquimalt on 10 August for refit.

Uganda spent the rest of her career as a training ship, having been renamed *Quebec* on 14 January 1952. Paid off on 13 June 1956, she arrived at Osaka, Japan, on 6 February 1961 to be broken up.

UGANDA/QUEBEC				
BUILDER:	Vickers-Armstrong Ltd., Newcastle-on-Tyne		DISPLACEMENT:	8,800
LAID DOWN:	20/7/39		DIMENSIONS:	555' 6" x 63' x 16' 6"
LAUNCHED:	7/8/41		SPEED:	30 kts
COMMISSIONED			CREW:	730
IN RCN:	21/10/44		ARMAMENT:	nine 6-inch (3 x III), ten 4-inch
PAID OFF:	13/6/56			(5 x II), six 21-inch TT (2 x III)

Commanding Officers

CAPT E. R. Mainguy, OBE, RCN	21/10/44	4/7/46
CAPT K. F. Adams, RCN	5/7/46	1/8/47
CAPT P. D. Budge, DSC, RCN	14/1/52	10/9/53
CAPT E. W. Finch-Noyes, RCN	11/9/53	31/7/55
CAPT D. W. Piers, DSC, RCN	1/8/55	8/5/56
CAPT E. S. MacDermid, RCN	9/5/56	13/6/56

Ontario

Laid down by Harland and Wolff, Belfast, as HMS *Minotaur*, she was presented to the RCN and on 26 April 1945 commissioned at Belfast as HMCS *Ontario*. She was completed on 25 May, and after trials and workups, left the Clyde River on 2 July for the Pacific via the Mediterranean and the Suez Canal. *Ontario* joined the 4th Cruiser Squadron, British Pacific Fleet, too late to see war service, but was employed in a variety of duties that took her to Hong Kong, Manila, and Japan. She arrived at Esquimalt on 27 November for refit.

Ontario spent the remainder of her career as a training ship, and was paid off on 15 October 1958. She arrived in tow for breaking up at Osaka, Japan, on 19 November 1960.

Ontario, 1945.

ONTARIO					
BUILDER:	Harland & Wolff Ltd., Belfast, Ireland		DISPLACEMENT:	8,800	
LAID DOWN:	20/11/41		DIMENSIONS:	555' 6" x 63' x 16' 6"	
LAUNCHED:	29/7/43		SPEED:	30 kts	
COMMISSIONED			CREW:	730	
IN RCN:	26/4/45		ARMAMENT:	nine 6-inch (3 x III), ten 4-inch (5 x II), six 21-inch TT	
PAID OFF:	15/10/58			(2 x III)	

Commanding Officers

CAPT H. T. W. Grant, DSO, RCN	26/4/45	31/12/45	CAPT E. P. Tisdall, RCN	25/8/51	3/3/53
CDR E. P. Tisdall, RCN	1/1/46	4/3/46	CAPT D. L. Raymond, RCN	4/3/53	14/9/54
CAPT F. G. Hart, RCN	5/3/46	14/6/46	CAPT D. W. Groos, DSC, RCN	15/9/54	22/8/56
CDR J. V. Brock, DSC, RCN	15/6/46	29/6/47	CAPT R. P. Welland, DSC & Bar, RCN	23/8/56	21/8/57
CAPT J. C. Hibbard, DSC & Bar, RCN	30/6/47	13/7/49	CAPT J. C. Littler, RCN	22/8/57	31/8/58
CAPT H. F. Pullen, OBE, RCN	14/7/49	24/8/51	CDR D. G. Padmore, RCN	1/9/58	15/10/58

Armed Merchant Cruisers

Prince David at Taranto, Italy, as converted to infantry landing ship, 1944.

Prince David

Formerly a three-funnelled Canadian National Steamships liner, she was purchased on 19 December 1939, and after very extensive conversion commissioned at Halifax on 28 December 1940 as an armed merchant cruiser. After working up at Bermuda in January and February 1941, *Prince David* was assigned to the RN's America and West Indies Station for the rest of the year. That December she was transferred to Esquimalt and in May 1942, after refit at Esquimalt and Vancouver, joined Esquimalt Force. From August to November she served under USN con-

trol in the Aleutian campaign. She then resumed her former duties out of Esquimalt until the beginning of March 1943, when she was paid off for conversion to an infantry landing ship. The rebuilding, which took place at Esquimalt and Vancouver, was completed that December and shortly after recommissioning she left for the UK via Cristobal and New York.

Upon arrival in the Clyde in February 1944, *Prince David* joined Combined Operations Command and landed troops in Normandy on D Day. In July she left for the Mediterranean to take

part in Operation Dragoon, the invasion of southern France, on 15 August. She saw extensive service in the Mediterranean until damaged by a mine on 10 December 1944 off Aegina Island, Greece. Repaired at Ferryville, North Africa, she left in March 1945 to refit at Esquimalt, but saw no further service and was paid off in June. Sold in 1948 for mercantile purposes and renamed *Charlton Monarch*, she was broken up in 1951.

PRINCE DAVID			
BUILDER:	Cammell, Laird & Co., Birkenhead, UK	DIMENSIONS:	385' x 57' x 21'
		SPEED:	22 kts
LAUNCHED:	1930	CREW:	31/386
COMMISSIONED:	28/12/40	ARMAMENT:	four 4-inch (2x II), two
PAID OFF:	11/6/45		2 pdrs., eight 20-mm
DISPLACEMENT:	5,736		guns

Commanding Officers

CDR W. B. Armit, RCNR	28/12/40	24/3/41
CDR K. F. Adams, RCN	25/3/41	1/12/41
CAPT V. S. Godfrey, RCN	2/12/41	18/3/42
A/LCDR T. D. Kelly, RCNR	19/3/42	16/4/42
CAPT V. S. Godfrey, RCN	17/4/42	17/4/43
CDR T. D. Kelly, RCNR	18/4/43	1/5/43
CDR T. D. Kelly, RCNR	23/5/43	11/6/45

Note: particulars are for *Prince David* and *Prince Henry* as converted to LSI(M)s; for *Prince Robert* as A/A ship. Original armament as AMCs: four 6-inch, two 3-inch guns.

Prince Henry

Originally a Canadian National liner, later Clarke Steamship's *North Star*, she was bought on 11 March 1940 and given back her maiden name. Like her two sisters, *Prince Henry* was converted to an armed merchant cruiser, commissioning at Montreal on 4 December 1940. She arrived at Bermuda on 15 January 1941 to work up, afterward transiting the Panama Canal to take up patrol off Callao, Peru. On 1 April she intercepted the German freighters *München* and *Hermonthis*, which scuttled themselves. In May she arrived at Esquimalt and engaged in patrols off the west coast until 24 August when she left for Halifax via Bermuda. In January 1942, after brief employment at St. John's as depot ship for Newfoundland Escort Force, she was assigned to patrol duties in the West Indies but was soon again ordered to Esquimalt. Arriving 7 May, she served with Esquimalt Force until the following March, except for the months of September and October 1942, when she served under USN control in the Aleutians. On 6 March 1943 she commenced rebuilding into an infantry landing ship, was recommissioned on 6 January 1944, and left immediately for the UK. She was present on D Day as a member of Combined Operations Command and like *Prince David*, next took part in the

Prince Henry, 6 August 1941 as originally fitted as armed merchant cruiser.

invasion of southern France. She remained in the Mediterranean until March 1945, and then proceeded to London to refit in East India Dock. During the refit, on 15 April she was paid off, and used afterward by the RN as an accommodation ship first at Portsmouth and later at Falmouth. Sold to the Ministry of Wartime Transport in 1946, she was renamed *Empire Parkeston* and employed as a troopship between Harwich and the Hook of Holland. She was broken up in 1962 at La Spezia, Italy.

PRINCE HENRY

BUILDER:	Cammell, Laird & Co., Birkenhead, UK	DIMENSIONS:	385' x 57' x 21'
LAUNCHED:	1930	SPEED:	22 kts
COMMISSIONED:	4/12/40	CREW:	31/386
PAID OFF:	15/4/45	ARMAMENT:	four 4-inch (2x II), two 2 pdrs., eight 20-mm guns
DISPLACEMENT:	5,736		

Commanding Officers

CAPT R. I. Agnew, OBE, RCN	4/12/40	19/12/41
CAPT J. C. I. Edwards, RCN	20/12/41	31/12/42
CAPT F. L. Houghton, RCN	1/1/43	18/3/43
LCDR E. W. Finch-Noyes, RCN	19/3/43	22/3/43
LCDR T. K. Young, RCNR	23/3/43	23/5/43
CDR T. D. Kelly, RCNR	24/5/43	29/11/43
CDR K. F. Adams, RCN	30/11/43	11/12/43
CDR V. S. Godfrey, RCN	12/12/43	15/4/45

ARMED MERCHANT CRUISERS

Prince Robert

The third of the C.N. sisters, *Prince Robert* was purchased in December 1939, and fitted out as an AMC, commissioning at Vancouver 31 July 1940. She left in mid-September for patrol off Mexico and Peru, and on 25 September intercepted and captured the German freighter *Weser*. On 15 December she left Callao, Peru for Australia to act as escort to a Canadian-bound troop convoy, and in May 1942, returned to the South Pacific for three months of escort and patrol duties under RN control on the New Zealand Station. She left Auckland on 28 July 1941 for Easter Island to investigate reports of a Japanese supply ship in the area, and arrived at Esquimalt on 24 August for a short refit. In November she escorted a shipload of ill-fated Canadian troops to Hong Kong and on her return rejoined Esquimalt Force. In August 1942, *Prince Robert* was placed under USN control for duty in the Aleutians, arriving back at Esquimalt on 4 November. She was paid off on 2 January 1943 for conversion to an auxiliary A/A ship, and was recommissioned on 7 June at Vancouver, leaving Esquimalt twelve days later for the Clyde via Bermuda. In November she was assigned to Gibraltar Command, Mediterranean Fleet, and employed as A/A escort to UK–Sierra Leone and UK–Mediterranean convoys. Though reassigned to Plymouth Command in January 1944, she remained at the same duties, and from June to August escorted Mediterranean convoys. In September *Prince Robert* left Plymouth for Esquimalt, and upon arrival underwent a refit that lasted until June 1945. She left Esquimalt 4 July 1945 for service with the British Pacific Fleet, arriving at Sydney, Australia on 10 August. On 31 August *Prince Robert* entered Hong Kong, where her commanding officer had the honour to represent Canada at the surrender ceremonies, 16 September. On 20 October she arrived at Esquimalt with repatriated Canadian prisoners from Hong Kong, and on 10 December was paid off and laid up in Lynn Creek, British Columbia. Sold in 1948, she became the merchant vessel *Charlton Sovereign* and, in 1952, the Italian-flag *Lucania*.

Prince Robert at Gibraltar, fitted as A/A ship, 1943.

PRINCE ROBERT

BUILDER:	Cammell, Laird & Co., Birkenhead, UK	DIMENSIONS:	385' x 57' x 21'
LAUNCHED:	1930	SPEED:	22 kts
COMMISSIONED:	31/7/40	CREW:	33/405
PAID OFF:	10/12/45	ARMAMENT:	ten 4-inch (5x II), two 2 pdrs., six 20-mm guns
DISPLACEMENT:	5,675		

Commanding Officers

CDR C. T. Beard, RCN	31/7/40	7/10/40
CDR F. G. Hart, RCN	8/10/40	21/6/42
A/CAPT F. L. Houghton, RCN	22/6/42	31/12/42
CDR O. C. S. Robertson, RCN	1/1/43	23/3/43
LCDR E. W. Finch-Noyes, RCN	24/3/43	5/6/43
CAPT A. M. Hope, RCN	6/6/43	7/12/44
CAPT W. B. Creery, RCN	8/12/44	19/12/44
CAPT W. B. Creery, RCN	4/6/45	10/12/45

Aircraft Carriers

Nabob

Laid down as the merchant vessel *Edisto* but converted to an aircraft carrier while building, she was commissioned HMS *Nabob* at Tacoma Washington, on 7 September 1943. After working up, she entered Burrard Drydock at Vancouver on 1 November for modification to RN standards, completing 12 January 1944. About this time it was arranged that she and a near-sister, *Puncher*, should be manned largely by Canadians while remaining RN ships. In February she embarked 852 Squadron (FAA) of Avengers at San Francisco and sailed for the UK via New York, where she took aboard a flight-deck cargo of Mustangs for the RAF. She joined the British Home Fleet at Scapa Flow on 1 August, and that month took part in two operations off the Norwegian coast, the second being an attack on the *Tirpitz*. On 22 August *Nabob* was torpedoed by *U 354* in the Barents Sea, resulting in a hole some thirty-two feet square abaft the engine room and below the waterline. Amazingly, she made Scapa under her own power on 27 August, but was not considered worth repairing and was paid off at Rosyth on 10 October. She left there in 1947 to be broken up in Holland, but was resold and converted for merchant service, emerging in 1952 as the German MV *Nabob*. Sold Panamanian in 1967 and renamed *Glory*, she was broken up in Taiwan in 1978.

Puncher

Begun as MV *Willapa*, she was commissioned HMS *Puncher* at Tacoma Washington, on 5 February 1944, and arrived at Vancouver on 15 March for modification to RN standards. She left Esquimalt in June for Norfolk, Virginia, en route ferrying motor launches from New Orleans to New York. In July she left Norfolk for Casablanca with a cargo of forty USAAF aircraft, returning to Norfolk to load the Corsairs of 845 (RN) Squadron and a deck-load of US aircraft for the UK. On 1 February 1945, she joined the Home Fleet, and following VE Day was used for several months for deck-landing training. In September she was totally converted to serve as a troop carrier and employed the rest of the year repatriating Canadian troops from Britain. In 1946 she left Halifax for Norfolk and was paid off there 16 January for return to the USN. Converted for merchant service, she became the British *Muncaster Castle* in 1949, later to be renamed *Bardic* in 1954 and *Bennevis* in 1959. She was broken up in Taiwan in 1973.

Nabob, 25 January 1944.

NABOB

BUILDER:	Seattle-Tacoma Shipbuilding Corp., Tacoma, Wash.	DIMENSIONS:	495' 8" x 69' 6" x 25' 5"
		SPEED:	18 kts
LAID DOWN:	20/10/42	CREW:	1,000
LAUNCHED:	9/3/43	ARMAMENT:	two 5-inch, sixteen 40-mm (8 x II),
COMMISSIONED:	7/9/43		twenty 20-mm guns
PAID OFF:	10/10/44	About 20 aircraft carried. Canadian-manned, but commissioned as RN ship.	
DISPLACEMENT:	15,390		

Commanding Officer

CAPT H. N. Lay, OBE, RCN	15/10/43	30/9/44

Puncher, 1944.

PUNCHER

BUILDER:	Seattle-Tacoma Shipbuilding Corp., Tacoma, WA	DIMENSIONS:	492' x 69' 6" x 24' 8"
		SPEED:	18 kts
LAID DOWN:	21/5/43	CREW:	1,000
LAUNCHED:	8/11/43	ARMAMENT:	two 5-inch, sixteen 40-mm (8 x II),
COMMISSIONED:	5/2/44		twenty 20-mm
PAID OFF:	16/1/46	About 20 aircraft carried. Canadian-manned but commissioned as RN ship.	
DISPLACEMENT:	14,170		

Commanding Officer

CAPT R. E. S. Bidwell, RCN	10/4/44	16/1/46

Destroyers

The RCN entered the Second World War with an offensive force consisting solely of six destroyers. *Saguenay* and *Skeena*, essentially copies of the RN's 'A' class, had been the first ships built to Canadian order. In 1937 and 1938 they were joined by *Fraser, St. Laurent, Restigouche,* and *Ottawa,* 'C' class sisters purchased from the RN and given the names of Canadian rivers. A few weeks after the war broke

out the 'C' class flotilla leader was acquired and renamed *Assiniboine.*

Soon known as the River class, these were joined in 1940 by the ill-fated *Margaree* and, in 1943 and 1944, by *Chaudière, Gatineau, Kootenay, Qu'Appelle, Ottawa* (2nd), and *Saskatchewan,* representatives of four fairly homogeneous RN classes.

In September 1940 the RCN was given six of the

fifty over-age US destroyers transferred to Britain in return for the use of British bases. Those serving in the RN were called the Town class because of their names, and their RCN sisters received the same epithet despite being named for US-Canadian border rivers: *Columbia, Niagara, St. Clair, St. Croix,* and *St. Francis. Annapolis* was an exception to the rule. Two more of this class were

acquired later, *Hamilton* in 1941 and *Buxton* in 1943.

In 1942 and 1943 Canada's first four Tribal class destroyers were commissioned: *Athabaskan, Haida, Huron,* and *Iroquois.* Another four entered service shortly after the war: *Athabaskan* (2nd), *Cayuga, Micmac,* and *Nootka.* The last destroyers acquired before hostilities ended were two of the RN's 'V' class, renamed *Algonquin* and

Sioux. Had the Pacific war continued, Canada would also have received a flotilla of eight 'C' class destroyers to replace her aging Rivers, but only two were transferred, late in 1945, becoming HMCS *Crescent* and *Crusader.* The Tribals, 'C' and 'V' class units were the only Canadian destroyers whose careers extended more than a few months into the postwar period.

RIVER CLASS

Saguenay

Saguenay and her sister *Skeena* were the first ships built for the RCN. *Saguenay* was commissioned on 22 May 1931 at Portsmouth and made her maiden arrival at Halifax on 3 July. With the outbreak of the Second World War she escorted local convoys until late September, when she was assigned to the America and West Indies Station, and based at Kingston, Jamaica. On 23 October 1939, in the Yucatan Channel, she intercepted the German tanker *Emmy Friederich,* which scuttled herself. She returned to Halifax in mid-December to resume local escort duty until 16 October 1940, when she sailed for the UK to join EG.10, Greenock. On 1 December 1940, while escorting convoy HG.47, she was torpe-

doed by the Italian submarine *Argo* 300 miles west of Ireland. With her bows wrecked and twenty-one dead, *Saguenay* made Barrow-in-Furness largely under her own power, and was under repairs until 22 May 1941. She left Greenock on 23 May and arrived on 7 June at St. John's, where she joined the NEF, then forming. On 15 November 1942 she was rammed by the Panamanian freighter *Azra,* south of Cape Race, Newfoundland and lost her stern when her depth charges exploded. The ship was docked at Saint John, New Brunswick where her stern was sealed off. She was then taken to Cornwallis in October 1943 to serve as a training ship. Paid off 30 July 1945, she was broken up in 1946.

Saguenay.

SAGUENAY					
BUILDER:	John I. Thornycroft & Co. Ltd., Southampton, UK		DIMENSIONS:	320' x 32' 6" x 10'	
			SPEED:	31 kts	
LAID DOWN:	27/9/29		CREW:	10/171	
LAUNCHED:	11/7/30		ARMAMENT:	four 4.7-inch, eight 21-inch TT (2 x IV),	
COMMISSIONED				two 2 pdrs	
IN RCN:	22/5/31		Modified to: two 4.7-inch, one 3-inch, four 21-inch TT, six 20-		
PAID OFF:	30/7/45		mm, Hedgehog		
DISPLACEMENT:	1,337				

Commanding Officers

CDR P. W. Nelles, RCN	22/5/31	6/6/32	A/CDR D. C. Wallace, RCNR		8/4/42	14/1/43
CDR L. W. Murray, RCN	7/6/32	22/5/34	LT J. W. McDowall, RCN		15/1/43	11/3/43
CDR R. I. Agnew, RCN	23/5/34	5/5/36	LT J. H. Ewart, RCNVR		24/8/43	17/5/44
CDR W. J. R. Beach, RCN	6/5/36	29/6/38	LT W. C. Hawkins, RCNVR		18/5/44	6/10/44
LCDR F. L. Houghton, RCN	30/6/38	7/7/39	A/LT W. E. Hughson, RCNVR		7/10/44	15/4/45
LCDR G. R. Miles, RCN	8/7/39	21/4/41	LT K. P. Blanche, RCNVR		16/4/45	30/7/45
LT P. E. Haddon, RCN	22/4/41	7/4/42				

Skeena

Commissioned at Portsmouth on 10 June 1931, she arrived at Halifax with *Saguenay* on 3 July and proceeded to Esquimalt the following month. *Skeena* returned to Halifax in April 1937, and with the outbreak of war engaged in local escort duties until ordered to the UK. On her arrival at Plymouth on 31 May 1940 she was assigned to Western Approaches Command, taking part in the evacuation of France and escorting convoys in British waters. She returned to Halifax on 3 March 1941 for refit, and then joined Newfoundland Command, Mid-Ocean Escort Force (MOEF). In April 1943 she became a member of EG C-3. During this period she saw continuous convoy duty and on 31 July 1942 while escorting convoy ON.115, shared with *Wetaskiwin* in the sinking of *U 588*. In May 1944, she was assigned to EG 12 for invasion duties, and was present on D Day. That September she was transferred to EG 11 and on 25 October dragged her anchors in a storm and was wrecked on Videy Island, near Reykjavik, losing fifteen of her complement.

SKEENA				
BUILDER:	John I. Thornycroft & Co. Ltd., Southampton, UK		DIMENSIONS:	320' x 32' 6" x 10'
			SPEED:	31 kts
LAID DOWN:	14/10/29		CREW:	10/171
LAUNCHED:	10/10/30		ARMAMENT:	four 4.7-inch, eight 21-inch TT (2 x IV),
COMMISSIONED				two 2 pdrs
IN RCN:	10/6/31		Modified to: two 4.7-inch, one 3-inch, four 21-inch TT, six 20-	
PAID OFF:	25/10/44			mm, Hedgehog
DISPLACEMENT:	1,337			

Commanding Officers

CDR V. G. Brodeur, RCN	10/6/31	24/5/32	LT H. S. Rayner, RCN	10/3/40	1/4/40
CDR G. C. Jones, RCN	25/5/32	14/5/34	LCDR J. C. Hibbard, RCN	2/4/40	10/12/41
CDR J. E. W. Oland, DSC, RCN	15/5/34	7/1/36	CDR H. Kingsley, RCN	11/12/41	19/5/42
CDR H. E. Reid, RCN	8/1/36	24/3/37	A/LCDR K. L. Dyer, DSC, RCN	20/5/42	28/2/43
CAPT V. G. Brodeur, RCN	25/3/37	22/4/38	A/LCDR E. E. G. Boak, RCN	1/3/43	20/11/43
CDR H. T. W. Grant, RCN	23/4/38	30/11/39	LCDR P. F. X. Russell, RCN	21/11/43	25/10/44
LCDR E. P. Tisdall, RCN	1/12/39	9/3/40			

Sold in June 1945 to a local resident, she was refloated and later broken up.

Fraser, 1938.

Ottawa, September 1940.

Fraser

Built in 1932 as HMS *Crescent* and purchased for $978,527 by the RCN five years later, *Fraser* was commissioned on 17 February 1937 at Chatham, UK. She arrived at Esquimalt on 3 May and was stationed on the west coast until the outbreak of the war. Ordered to Halifax, she arrived on 15 September, and like her sisters was put to work as local escort to ocean convoys out of Halifax. In November, *Fraser* was transferred to operational control of the RN's America and West Indies Station, but continued to be based at Halifax until ordered in March 1940, to join Jamaica Force for Caribbean patrol service. On 26 May she left Bermuda for the UK, arriving at Plymouth on 3 June. A participant in the evacuation of France, she was returning to Plymouth from St. Jean de Luz when on 25 June she was sunk in collision with the British cruiser *Calcutta* in the Gironde River estuary, losing forty-seven of her complement.

FRASER			
BUILDER:	Vickers-Armstrong Ltd., Barrow-in-Furness, UK	SPEED:	31 kts
		CREW:	10/171
LAID DOWN:	1/2/30	ARMAMENT:	four 4.7-inch, eight 21-inch TT (2 x IV), two 2 pdrs
LAUNCHED:	29/9/31		
COMMISSIONED IN RCN:	17/2/37	Modified to:	two or three 4.7-inch, one 3-inch, four 21-inch TT, six 20-mm, Hedgehog
LOST:	25/6/40		
DISPLACEMENT:	1,375		
DIMENSIONS:	329' x 33' x 10' 2"	Ex-HMS *Crescent*	
Commanding Officers			
CAPT V. G. Brodeur, RCN		17/2/37	24/3/37
CDR H. E. Reid, RCN		25/3/37	31/8/38
CDR W. B. Creery, RCN		1/9/38	25/6/40

OTTAWA			
BUILDER:	Portsmouth Naval Dockyard, Portsmouth, UK	SPEED:	31 kts
		CREW:	10/171
LAID DOWN:	12/9/30	ARMAMENT:	four 4.7-inch, eight 21-inch TT (2 x IV), two 2 pdrs
LAUNCHED:	30/9/31		
COMMISSIONED IN RCN:	15/6/38	Modified to:	two or three 4.7-inch, one 3-inch, four 21-inch TT, six 20-mm, Hedgehog
LOST:	13/9/42		
DISPLACEMENT:	1,3/5		
DIMENSIONS:	329' x 33' x 10' 2"	Ex-HMS *Crusader*	
Commanding Officers			
CAPT V. G. Brodeur, RCN		15/6/38	1/10/38
CDR C. R. H. Taylor, RCN		2/10/38	20/11/38
CAPT G. C. Jones, RCN		21/11/38	1/4/40
CDR E. R. Mainguy, RCN		2/4/40	20/7/41
A/LCDR A. G. Boulton, RCNVR		21/7/41	18/8/41
A/CDR H. F. Pullen, RCN		19/8/41	13/11/41
A/CDR C. D. Donald, RCN		14/11/41	4/7/42
A/LCDR C. A. Rutherford, RCN		5/7/42	13/9/42

Ottawa

Completed in 1932 as HMS *Crusader,* she was purchased for $817,500 and commissioned as *Ottawa* on 15 June 1938 at Chatham, UK. She arrived at Esquimalt on 7 November and, the war intervening, left for Halifax almost exactly a year later. Though assigned to the RN's America and West Indies Station, she remained based at Halifax, as a local escort to eastbound convoys. She left Halifax for the Clyde, 27 August 1940, and on arrival was assigned to EG 10, Greenock, until the formation of Newfoundland Command in June 1941. *Ottawa* then shifted her base to St. John's and was employed as a mid-ocean escort from June 1941 onward, joining EG C-4 in May 1942. While escorting convoy ON.127, she was torpedoed and sunk by *U 91* in the North Atlantic on 13 September 1942, and one hundred and fourteen of her ship's company were lost.

Postwar reassessment of U-boat kills credits *Ottawa* with a share in the sinking of the Italian submarine *Faa di Bruno* in the North Atlantic on 6 November 1940.

Restigouche

Completed in 1932 as HMS *Comet*, she was purchased at the same time as *Ottawa* and was commissioned at Chatham, UK the same day. Like her sister, she arrived at Esquimalt 7 November 1938 and left for Halifax 15 November 1939. She performed local escort duties from that port until 24 May 1940, when she left for Plymouth. Upon arriving there on 31 May *Restigouche* was assigned to Western Approaches Command. While assisting in the evacuation of French ports she rescued survivors of *Fraser*. She left Liverpool at the end of August for a brief refit at Halifax, returning to the UK in January 1941. In June 1941, "Rustyguts" was allocated to Newfoundland Command, and in April 1943 became a member of EG C-4, in the interval toiling ceaselessly as a mid-ocean escort. On 31 December 1941 she suffered storm damage en route to join convoy ON.44, and extensive repairs were carried out at Greenock. She was allocated to EG 12 in May 1944 for invasion duties, including D Day, and afterward carried out Channel and Biscay patrols from her base at Plymouth. She retuned to Canada in September 1944 for a major refit at Saint John, New Brunswick and Halifax, and upon completion proceeded to Bermuda for working up. Returning to Halifax on 14 February 1945 she performed various local duties, and after VE Day was employed for three months bringing home military personnel from Newfoundland. Paid off on 6 October 1945, she was broken up the following year.

St. Laurent

Completed in 1932 as HMS *Cygnet*, she was purchased for $978,527 by the RCN and commissioned at Chatham on 17 February 1937 as *St. Laurent*. She arrived at Halifax on 8 April and soon afterward sailed for Esquimalt. Shortly after war was declared she returned to the east coast, arriving at Halifax on 15 September, and for several months escorted convoys on the first leg of the transatlantic journey. *St. Laurent* left Halifax for the UK on 24 May 1940, and on arrival at Plymouth on 31 May was assigned to Western Approaches Command, playing a brief role in the evacuation of France. On 2 July 1940 she rescued 860 survivors of the torpedoed liner *Arandora Star*. She returned to Halifax on 3 March 1941 for refit, on completion of which she joined Newfoundland Command as a mid-ocean escort, serving continuously for the following three years. In April 1943 she became a member of EG C-1. During this period "Sally" assisted in the destruction of two U-boats: *U 356* on 27 December 1942, while escorting convoy ONS.154; and *U 845* on 10 March 1944 while with convoy SC.154. In May 1944 she was transferred to EG 11 for invasion duties, remaining

Restigouche, 1941.

St. Laurent, off Larne, 1943.

with the group on patrol and support duties until the end of November, when she returned to Canada for major repairs at Shelburne, Nova Scotia. She afterward remained in Canadian waters as a member of Halifax Force and after VE Day was employed in transporting troops from Newfoundland to Canada. She was paid off on 10 October 1945 at Sydney and broken up in 1947.

RESTIGOUCHE						
BUILDER:	Portsmouth Naval Dockyard, Portsmouth, UK			DIMENSIONS:	329' x 33' x 10' 2"	
LAID:	DOWN 12/9/30			SPEED:	31 kts	
LAUNCHED:	30/9/31			CREW:	10/171	
COMMISSIONED IN RCN:	15/6/38			ARMAMENT:	four 4.7-inch, eight 21-inch TT (2 x IV), two 2 pdrs	
PAID OFF:	6/10/45			Modified to:	two or three 4.7-inch, one 3-inch, four 21-inch TT, six 20-mm, Hedgehog	
DISPLACEMENT:	1,375			Ex-HMS *Comet*		
Commanding Officers						
CDR W. B. L. Holmes, RCN		15/6/38	25/12/39	LCDR D. W. Groos, RCN	6/6/43	3/12/44
CDR H. N. Lay, RCN		26/12/39	23/6/41	LCDR P. E. Haddon, RCN	4/12/44	15/4/45
LCDR D. W. Piers, RCN		24/6/41	5/6/43	LCDR R. J. Herman, OBE, RCNR	16/4/45	6/10/45

ST. LAURENT						
BUILDER:	Vickers-Armstrongs Ltd., Barrow-in-Furness, UK			DIMENSIONS:	329' x 33' x 10' 2"	
				SPEED:	31 kts	
LAID DOWN:	1/12/30			CREW:	10/171	
LAUNCHED:	29/9/31			ARMAMENT:	four 4.7-inch, eight 21-inch TT (2 x IV), two 2 pdrs	
COMMISSIONED IN RCN:	17/2/37					
PAID OFF:	10/10/45			Modified to:	two or three 4.7-inch, one 3-inch, four 21-inch TT, six 20-mm, Hedgehog	
DISPLACEMENT:	1,375			Ex-HMS *Cygnet*		
Commanding Officers						
LCDR R. E. Bidwell, RCN		17/2/37	7/12/37	CDR H. F. Pullen, RCN	20/1/43	12/3/43
LCDR A. M. Hope, RCN		8/12/37	5/10/39	LCDR G. H. Stephen, DSC, RCNR	13/3/43	14/4/44
LCDR H. G. DeWolf, RCN		6/10/39	13/7/40	LCDR A. G. Boulton, RCNVR	15/4/44	7/11/44
LT H. S. Rayner, DSC, RCN		14/7/40	18/2/42	LT M. G. Stirling, RCN	8/11/44	7/4/45
LCDR E. L. Armstrong, RCN		19/2/42	13/11/42	A/CDR G. H. Stephen, DSC, OBE, RCNR	8/4/45	10/10/45
LCDR G. S. Windeyer, RCN		14/11/42	19/1/43			

Assiniboine

Completed in 1932 as HMS *Kempenfelt*, she was transferred to the RCN at Devonport on 19 October 1939, and arrived in Halifax on 17 November. Assigned to the America and West Indies Station, she left for Jamaica on 5 December to carry out Caribbean patrols. While so employed *Assiniboine* assisted in the capture of the German freighter *Hannover* in the Mona Passage and towed her into Kingston, Jamaica. She returned to Halifax on 31 March 1940 and was employed there as a local escort until 15 January 1941, when she sailed for the UK to join EG 10, Greenock. With the formation of Newfoundland Command in June 1941, "Bones" was allocated for mid-ocean escort service. While thus employed with convoy SC.94, on 6 August 1942 she rammed and sank *U 210*, necessitating repairs at Halifax from 29 August to 20 December. Not long after her return to service, while on passage to Londonderry on 2 March 1943 she attacked a U-boat with depth charges set too shallow, causing serious damage to her stern. Repairs were effected at Liverpool from 7 March to 13 July 1943, when she joined EG C-1 of MOEF. In April 1944 she returned to Canada for refit at Shelburne, Nova Scotia, and on 1 August arrived at Londonderry to become a member of EG 12 and, a few weeks later, EG 11. In December she was loaned to EG 14, Liverpool, and remained with it until VE Day. She returned to Canada in June 1945 and after brief employment as a troop transport, was paid off 8 August 1945. On 10 November 1945, en route for scrapping at Baltimore, *Assiniboine* broke her tow and was wrecked near East Point, Prince Edward Island. Her remains were broken up *in situ* in 1952.

Assiniboine.

ASSINIBOINE				
BUILDER:	J. Samuel White & Co. Ltd., Cowes, I.O.W., UK	SPEED:	31 kts	
		CREW:	10/171	
LAID DOWN:	18/10/30	ARMAMENT:	four 4.7-inch, eight 21-inch TT (2 x IV), two 2 pdrs	
LAUNCHED:	29/10/31			
COMMISSIONED IN RCN:	19/10/39	Modified to:	two or three 4.7-inch, one 3-inch, four 21-inch TT, six 20-mm, Hedgehog	
PAID OFF:	8/8/45			
DISPLACMENT:	1,375	Ex-HMS *Kempenfelt*		
DIMENSIONS:	329' x 33' x 10' 2"			

Commanding Officers

CDR E. R. Mainguy, RCN	19/10/39	2/4/40	CDR E. P. Tisdall, RCN	2/12/42	10/2/43
COM G. C. Jones, RCN	3/4/40	15/9/40	CDR K. F. Adams, RCN	11/2/43	8/6/43
CAPT C. R. Taylor, RCN	16/9/40	29/10/40	A/LCDR R. P. Welland, DSC, RCN	9/6/43	7/7/43
COM L. W. Murray, RCN	30/10/40	11/2/41	CDR K. F. Adams, RCN	8/7/43	30/9/43
A/LCDR J. H. Stubbs, RCN	12/2/41	1/10/42	A/LCDR R. P. Welland, DSC, RCN	1/10/43	13/10/44
LT R. Hennessy, DSC, RCN	2/10/42	1/12/42	A/LCDR R. Hennessy, DSC, RCN	14/10/44	21/2/45
			CDR E. L. Armstrong, RCN	22/2/45	8/8/45

Diana (later *Margaree*), 1933.

Margaree

Completed in 1932 as HMS *Diana*, she was serving on the China Station when the war broke out, and transferred to the Mediterranean for a short time before returning to Britain to join the Home Fleet. In May 1940 she took part briefly in the Norwegian campaign and in mid-July commenced refit at Albert Docks, London. There she was transferred to the RCN to replace the lost *Fraser*, commissioning as *Margaree* on 6 September 1940. On 20 October she left Londonderry for Canada with a five-ship convoy, OL.8, and two days later was lost in collision with the freighter *Port Fairy*. One hundred and forty-two of her ship's company were lost, many of them survivors from *Fraser*.

MARGAREE			
BUILDER:	Palmers Shipbuilding Co. Ltd., Hebburn-on-Tyne, UK	SPEED:	31 kts
		CREW:	10/171
		ARMAMENT:	four 4.7-inch, eight 21-inch TT (2 x IV), two 2 pdrs
LAID DOWN:	12/6/31		
LAUNCHED:	16/6/32		
COMMISSIONED IN RCN:	6/9/40	Modified to:	two or three 4.7-inch, one 3-inch, four 21-inch TT, six 20-mm, Hedgehog
LOST:	22/10/40		
DISPLACEMENT:	1,375		
DIMENSIONS:	329' x 33' x 10' 2"	Ex-HMS *Diana*	

Commanding Officer

CDR J. W. R. Roy, RCN	6/9/40	22/10/40

Chaudière

Completed in 1936 as HMS *Hero*, she saw extensive service in the Second World War, including the second Battle of Narvik, April 1940; the evacuation of Greece and Crete, April and May 1941; and the Syrian invasion, June 1941. As a unit of the Mediterranean Fleet, she also took part in the second Battle of Sirte in March 1942, and in May and October of the same year shared in the sinking of two U-boats. In April 1943 she returned to the UK for a major refit at Portsmouth, and there was transferred to the RCN on 15 November 1943, becoming HMCS *Chaudière*. In January 1944 she became a member of EG C-2, MOEF, and on 6 March shared in the destruction of *U 744*. In May she was assigned to EG 11, Western Approaches Command, for invasion support duty, and was present on D Day. On 20 and 28 August respectively she assisted in the sinking of *U 984*, west of Brest, and of *U 621* off La Rochelle. During the next three months she was employed in patrol and support duties in the North Atlantic, Bay of Biscay, and English Channel. She returned to Halifax at the end of November for repairs, and a major refit begun at Sydney two months later was still incomplete on VE Day. *Chaudière* was paid off 17 August 1945 to reserve at Sydney, and broken up there in 1950.

Chaudière, 25 August 1944.

CHAUDIÈRE

BUILDER:	Vickers-Armstrong Ltd., Newcastle-on-Tyne	DIMENSIONS:	323' x 33' x 9' 11"
		SPEED:	31 kts
LAID DOWN:	28/2/35	CREW:	10/171
LAUNCHED:	10/3/36	ARMAMENT:	two 4.7-inch, four 21-inch TT (1 x IV), two 6pdrs., six 20-mm, Hedgehog
COMMISSIONED IN RCN:	15/11/43		
PAID OFF:	17/8/45	Ex-HMS *Hero*	
DISPLACEMENT:	1,340		

Commanding Officers

A/LCDR C. P. Nixon, DSC, MiD, RCN	15/11/43	21/3/45	LCDR G. M. Kaizer, RCNR	2/8/45	12/8/45
A/LCDR W. Davenport, RCNR	22/3/45	20/6/45			

Gatineau, February 1945.

GATINEAU

BUILDER:	Swan Hunter & Wigham Richardson Ltd., Wallsend-on-Tyne, UK	DISPLACEMENT:	1,370
		DIMENSIONS:	329' x 33' 3" x 10' 10"
LAID DOWN:	23/3/33	SPEED:	31 kts
LAUNCHED:	29/5/34	CREW:	10/171
COMMISSIONED IN RCN:	3/6/43	ARMAMENT:	three 4.7-inch, four 21-inch TT (1 x IV) six 20-mm, Hedgehog
PAID OFF:	10/1/46	Ex-HMS *Express*	

Commanding Officers

CDR P. W. Burnett, RN	3/6/43	9/11/43	LCDR J. A. Bryant, RCNVR	30/9/44	9/11/44
LT E. M. Chadwick, RCN	10/11/43	22/11/43	LCDR G. H. Davidson, RCN	10/11/44	14/7/45
LCDR H. V. W. Groos, RCN	23/11/43	10/9/44	A/LCDR P. D. Budge, DSC, RCN	15/7/45	26/11/45
A/LCDR R. L. Hennessy, DSC, RCN	11/9/44	29/9/44			

Gatineau

Completed in 1934 as HMS *Express*, she saw strenuous war service with the RN. She was the second last ship to leave Dunkirk, having made six trips and evacuated 3,500 troops. On 31 August 1940, while laying a defensive minefield off the Dutch coast, she was herself extensively damaged by a German mine. Repairs carried out at Hull, UK, took more than a year, and included fitting a completely new fore end. She went to the Far East late in 1941, and on 10 December was on hand to rescue nearly 1,000 survivors of HMS *Prince of Wales*, sunk by Japanese bombs off Malaya. After long service with the Eastern Fleet she returned to Liverpool in February 1943 for refit, and in the process was transferred to the RCN. She was commissioned there as *Gatineau*, on 3 June 1943 and joined EG C-3 MOEF. On 6 March 1944 while escorting convoy HX.280, she assisted in the sinking of *U 744*. That May she transferred to EG 11, Londonderry, for invasion duties, and was present on D Day. She proceeded to Canada in July 1944 for major refit at Halifax, then sailed in March 1945 for workups at Tobermory. No longer needed after VE Day, she returned to Canada in June and two months later went to the west coast. She was paid off 10 January 1946 into reserve at Esquimalt, and is believed to have been scuttled at Royston, British Columbia in 1948 as part of a breakwater.

Kootenay, February 1944.

KOOTENAY

BUILDER:	John I. Thornycroft & Co. Ltd., Southampton, UK	DISPLACEMENT:	1,375
		DIMENSIONS:	329' x 33' x 10' 2"
LAID DOWN:	25/6/31	SPEED:	31 kts
LAUNCHED:	7/6/32	CREW:	10/171
COMMISSIONED		ARMAMENT:	three 4.7-inch, four 21-inch TT (1 x IV)
IN RCN:	12/4/43		seven 20-mm, Hedgehog
PAID OFF:	26/10/45		
		Ex-HMS *Decoy*	

Commanding Officers

A/LCDR K. L. Dyer, DSC, RCN	12/4/43	28/3/44	A/LCDR W. H. Wilson, DSC, RCN	29/3/44	26/10/45

Ottawa (2nd), May 1943.

OTTAWA (2nd)

BUILDER:	Vickers-Armstrong Ltd., Barrow-in-Furness, UK	DISPLACEMENT:	1,350
		DIMENSIONS:	323' x 33' x 10' 7"
LAID DOWN:	20/9/34	SPEED:	31 kts
LAUNCHED:	15/8/35	CREW:	10/171
COMMISSIONED		ARMAMENT:	two 4.7-inch, four 21-inch TT (1 x IV) six
IN RCN:	20/3/43		20-mm, Hedgehog
PAID OFF:	31/10/45		
		Ex-HMS *Griffin*	

Commanding Officers

CDR H. F. Pullen, RCN	20/3/43	8/6/43	LCDR R. J. Herman, OBE, RCNR	7/10/44	11/10/44
CDR K. F. Adams, RCN	9/6/43	6/7/43	LT N. Cogdon, RCN	12/10/44	4/2/45
CDR H. F. Pullen, RCN	7/7/43	18/5/44	A/LCDR P. D. Budge, DSC, RCN	5/2/45	14/7/45
CDR J. D. Prentice, DSO, RCN	19/5/44	9/9/44	A/LCDR G. H. Davidson, RCN	15/7/45	31/10/45
LT E. P. Earnshaw, RCN	10/9/44	6/10/44			

Kootenay

She was completed in 1933 as HMS *Decoy*, and at the outbreak of the war was with the 21st Destroyer Flotilla, East Indies Fleet. The flotilla was transferred later that month to the Mediterranean and in January 1940 to the South Atlantic. *Decoy* was reassigned in May 1940 to the Mediterranean Fleet, and on 13 November was damaged by bombs at Alexandria, requiring a ten-week repair at Malta. While in the Mediterranean she took part in the evacuation of Greece and Crete, and in the supply run to Tobruk. Then assigned to the Eastern Fleet in February 1942, she returned to Britain that September for a major refit at Jarrow-on-Tyne. There, on 12 April 1943 she was transferred to the RCN as *Kootenay*, and after working up at Tobermory was assigned to EG C-5, MOEF. In May 1944 she became a member of EG 11 and was present on D Day. In succeeding months she carried out patrols in the Channel and the Bay of Biscay, and while thus engaged took part in the sinking of *U 678*, 6 July, south of Brighton; *U 621*, 18 August, off La Rochelle; and *U 984*, 20 August, west of Brest. She sailed for Shelburne, Nova Scotia, in mid-September 1944 for a refit, returning to the UK in the spring of 1945. Following workups at Tobermory she operated out of Plymouth until the end of May, then returned to Canada, where she made six round trips as a troop transport between Newfoundland and Quebec City. She was paid off into reserve at Sydney on 26 October 1945 and in 1946 was sold for scrapping.

Ottawa (2nd)

Completed in 1936 as HMS *Griffin*, she took part in the evacuation of Namsos, Norway, in May 1940 before transferring in August to Force 'H' at Gibraltar and in November to the 14th Destroyer Flotilla in the Mediterranean. She subsequently took part in the evacuation of Greece and Crete, embarking 720 troops on one trip from Suda Bay. She also escorted a relief convoy to Malta. Transferred to the Eastern Fleet in February 1942, she returned to the UK that October for major refit at Portsmouth and Southampton, toward the end of which, on 20 March 1943 she was commissioned at Southampton as HMCS *Griffin*. On 10 April, despite the objections of her captain, she was renamed HMCS *Ottawa*. She joined EG C-5 based at St. John's as a mid-ocean escort, but was removed from this duty in May 1944 to take part in the invasion with EG 11. During post-invasion patrols in the Channel and the Bay of Biscay she took part with *Kootenay* in the destruction of three U-boats. *Ottawa* returned to Canada in October 1944 for refit at Saint John, New Brunswick, remaining in Canadian waters until paid off 1 November 1945 at Sydney. She was broken up in 1946.

Qu'Appelle

Completed in 1935 as HMS *Foxhound*, she was a member of the 8th Flotilla, Home Fleet, on the outbreak of war, and on 14 September shared in the sinking of *U 39* off the Hebrides—the first U-boat kill of the war. In April 1940 she took part in the second Battle of Narvik and that November was transferred to Force 'H' at Gibraltar. On 18 June 1941 she shared in the sinking of *U 138* west of Cadiz, and she took one convoy to Malta. From January 1942 to May 1943 she served with the Eastern Fleet, then transferred to West Africa Command, Freetown. In September 1943 she returned to the UK for an extensive refit on the Humber, and on 8 February 1944 was commissioned there as HMCS *Qu'Appelle*. She served on D Day with EG 12, and afterward took part in Biscay and Channel patrols, latterly with EG 11. She arrived at Halifax for the first time on 29 November 1944 and proceeded to Pictou, Nova Scotia, for refit. Completing this refit on 31 March 1945 she served as a troop transport between Greenock and Halifax from August to October. She was paid off on 11 October to serve as a stationary training ship attached to the Torpedo School at Halifax. Removed from service in January 1946, *Qu'Appelle* was sold in 1947 for scrapping at Sydney, Nova Scotia.

Saskatchewan

Completed in 1935 as HMS *Fortune*, she was serving with the 8th Flotilla, Home Fleet when the war broke out, and took part in the Norwegian campaign and the occupation of Iceland in May 1940. She also shared in the sinking of *U 27*, *U 44* and the Vichy French submarine *Ajax*. On 10 May 1941 while escorting a Malta convoy, she was badly damaged by bombs and spent six months under repairs at Chatham, UK. In February 1943 following two years' service with the Eastern Fleet, *Fortune* returned to the UK for major refit at London, and there on 31 May 1943 was transferred to the RCN as *Saskatchewan*. She was assigned to EG C-3, MOEF, until May 1944 then transferred to EG 12 for invasion duties. She proceeded to Canada in August 1944 to refit at Shelburne, Nova Scotia, returning to the UK in January 1945, first as a unit of EG 14 and then of EG 11. She returned to Canada the month after VE Day and, after employment as a troop transport, was paid off 28 January 1946 at Sydney and broken up.

Foxhound (later *Qu'Appelle*).

QU'APPELLE

BUILDER:	John Brown & Co. Ltd., Glasgow, Scotland	DISPLACEMENT:	1,405
		DIMENSIONS:	329' x 33' 3" x 10' 10"
LAID DOWN:	21/8/33	SPEED:	31 kts
LAUNCHED:	12/10/34	CREW:	10/171
COMMISSIONED IN RCN:	8/2/44	ARMAMENT:	two 4.7-inch, four 21-inch TT (1 x IV) six 20-mm, Hedgehog
PAID OFF:	27/5/46		Ex-HMS *Foxhound*

Commanding Officers

CDR D. C. Wallace, DSC, RCNR	8/2/44	19/4/44	LCDR I. Angus, RCNVR	3/4/45	21/6/45
CDR A. M. McKillop, RN	20/4/44	11/7/44	A/LCDR W. Davenport, RCNR	22/6/45	9/10/45
CDR J. D. Birch, RNR	12/7/44	9/9/44	LT J. H. C. Bovey, RCN	10/10/45	25/11/45
CDR J. D. Prentice, DSO, RCN	10/9/44	4/12/44	A/LCDR W. E. Harrison, DSC, RCNR	26/11/45	22/3/46
CDR E. L. Armstrong, RCN	5/12/44	6/1/45	A/LCDR J. C. Annesley, RCN	23/3/46	7/4/46
CDR E. G. Skinner, DSC, RCNR	7/1/45	2/4/45	LT D. Adamson, RCNR	8/4/46	27/5/46

Saskatchewan, 1 October 1945.

SASKATCHEWAN

BUILDER:	John Brown & Co. Ltd., Glasgow, Scotland	DISPLACEMENT:	1,405
		DIMENSIONS:	329' x 33' 3" x 10' 10"
LAID DOWN:	25/7/33	SPEED:	31 kts
LAUNCHED:	29/8/34	CREW:	10/171
COMMISSIONED IN RCN:	31/5/43	ARMAMENT:	three 4.7-inch, four 21-inch TT (1 x IV) six 20-mm, Hedgehog
PAID OFF:	28/1/46		Ex-HMS *Fortune*

Commanding Officers

LCDR G. H. Williams, RN	31/5/43	6/7/43	LCDR A. H. Easton, DSC, RCNR	7/4/44	8/8/44
CDR R. C. Medley, DSO, RN	7/7/43	22/3/44	A/LCDR T. C. Pullen, RCN	25/8/44	21/8/45
LCDR E. W. Finch-Noyes, RCN	23/3/44	6/4/44	A/LCDR F. C. Frewer, RCN	22/8/45	28/1/46

TOWN CLASS

Note: The armament for this group was typically modified to one 4-inch, one 12 pdr., three 21-inch TT, four 20-mm, Hedgehog

Annapolis

As USS *Mackenzie*, she served three years with the US Pacific Fleet before being laid up at Mare Island, California, in 1922. Briefly commissioned again during the first year of the Second World War, she arrived at Halifax on 20 September 1940, and four days later was transferred to the RCN. A month later she burned out her No. 4 boiler and as a result lost her aftermost funnel. Owing to reduced endurance, *Annapolis* never crossed the Atlantic, but spent her entire RCN career with Western Local Escort Force (WLEF). In June 1943 she became a member of EG W-8 and later, for a short time, W-10. In April 1944 she was relegated to training duties at HMCS *Cornwallis*, also functioning as escort to RN submarines between Halifax and Digby, Nova Scotia. Paid off at Halifax 4 June 1945 she left later that month in tow for Boston, where she was broken up.

Annapolis, 11 September 1944.

ANNAPOLIS

BUILDER:	Union Iron Works, San Francisco, Calif.	DISPLACEMENT:	1,069
LAID DOWN:	4/7/18	DIMENSIONS:	314' 3" x 30' 6" x 8' 6"
LAUNCHED:	19/9/18	SPEED:	28 kts
COMMISSIONED		CREW:	10/143
IN RCN:	24/9/40	ARMAMENT:	four 4-inch, twelve 21-inch TT (4 x III)
PAID OFF:	4/6/45	Ex-USS *Mackenzie*	

Commanding Officers

A/CDR H. Kingsley, RCN	24/9/40	10/10/40	A/LCDR G. H. Davidson, RCN	15/10/42	3/12/42
CDR C. D. Donald, RCN	11/10/40	28/3/41	LCDR A. G. Boulton, RCNVR	4/12/42	2/3/44
LCDR F. C. Smith, RCNR	29/3/41	1/7/42	LCDR H. C. Walmesley, RCNR	3/3/44	15/4/45
A/LCDR G. H. Davidson, RCN	2/7/42	4/10/42	SKPR/LT C. C. Clattenburg, RCNR	16/4/45	4/6/45
LCDR R. F. Harris, RCNR	5/10/42	14/10/42			

Buxton, 10 May 1944.

BUXTON

BUILDER:	Bethlehem Shipbuilding Corp. Ltd., Squantum, Mass.	DISPLACEMENT:	1,190
		DIMENSIONS:	314' 3" x 30' 9" x 9' 3"
LAID DOWN:	20/4/18	SPEED:	28 kts
LAUNCHED:	10/10/18	CREW:	10/143
COMMISSIONED		ARMAMENT:	four 4-inch, twelve 21-inch TT (4 x III)
IN RCN:	4/11/43	Ex-USS *Edwards*	
PAID OFF:	2/6/45		

Commanding Officer

LT J. F. Watson, RCNR	4/11/43	2/6/45

Buxton

Commissioned as USS *Edwards* in 1919, she saw brief service with the USN in Europe before being placed in reserve at San Diego in 1922. Recommissioned in December 1939, she was given an overhaul, and from April to September 1940 was on Neutrality Patrol in the Gulf of Mexico and off the east coast of the US. On 8 October she was commissioned HMS *Buxton* at Halifax and assigned to local duties, since serious defects prevented her crossing the Atlantic. Following a major refit at Boston from July to September 1941 she made her first transatlantic crossing in October, only to undergo further repairs at Chatham, UK, which kept her idle from December 1941 to April 1942. Returning to Canadian waters that August, she was assigned to WLEF, but her defects persisted and she was taken to Boston in December for further repairs. These repairs completed, she arrived at St. John's on 30 March 1943 to rejoin WLEF, three months later becoming part of its newly formed EG W-1. Her defects persisted, and *Buxton* was offered to the RCN for training purposes, arriving at Digby in December, having been commissioned on 4 November 1943 at Halifax. She continued as a stationary training ship until paid off 2 June 1945 at Sydney, and was broken up the same year at Boston.

Columbia

As USS *Haraden* she served in the Adriatic Sea during part of 1919 before returning to the US for training out of Norfolk, Virginia. Placed in reserve at Philadelphia in 1922, she emerged in December 1939 to take part in the Neutrality Patrol, and was transferred to the RCN as *Columbia* on 24 September 1940 at Halifax. At first employed on local escort duty, she left Halifax 15 January 1941 for the UK, where she was assigned to EG 4, Greenock. In June 1941 she joined the newly formed NEF, and in March 1942 following repairs at Halifax, transferred to WLEF. In January 1943 she went to the aid of her RN sister, HMS *Caldwell*, adrift without propellers southeast of Cape Breton, and successfully towed her 370 miles to Halifax. Following a major refit at Saint John from 1 February to 20 May 1943 she rejoined WLEF, becoming a member of EG W-4 at the end of June and of

Columbia.

W-10 in December. On 25 February 1944, owing to a combination of fog and faulty radar, she rammed a cliff in Motion Bay, Newfoundland without so much as touching bottom. Repairs only sufficient to make her watertight were carried out at Bay Bulls, though not until May. That September she was taken to Liverpool, Nova Scotia, to serve as an ammunition storage hulk for ships refitting there. Paid off on 12 June 1945 into reserve at Sydney, she was sold for scrap later that year.

COLUMBIA					
BUILDER:	Newport News Shipbuilding & Dry Dock Co. Ltd., Newport News, Va.		DISPLACEMENT:	1,069	
			DIMENSIONS:	314' 3" x 30' 6" x 8' 6"	
LAID DOWN:	30/3/18		SPEED:	28 kts	
LAUNCHED:	4/7/18		CREW:	10/143	
COMMISSIONED			ARMAMENT:	four 4-inch, twelve 21-inch TT (4 x III)	
IN RCN:	24/9/40		Ex-USS *Haraden*		
PAID OFF:	17/3/44				

Commanding Officers

LCDR S. W. Davis, DSC, RCN	24/9/40	13/5/42	LT M. L. Devaney, RCNVR	23/5/44	18/6/44
LCDR G. H. Stephen, RCNR	14/5/42	17/3/43	LCDR F. O. Gerity, RCNR	19/6/44	30/6/44
LCDR B. D. L. Johnson, RCNR	18/3/43	23/11/43	LT M. L. Devaney, RCNVR	1/7/44	22/7/44
LCDR R. A. S. MacNeil, OBE, RCNR	24/11/43	30/3/44	LT J. G. Hughes, RCNR	23/7/44	1/3/45
LT T. A. G. Staunton, RCNVR	31/3/44	22/5/44			

Hamilton.

HAMILTON

BUILDER:	Bethlehem Shipbuilding Corp. Ltd., Fore River Yard, Quincy, Mass.	DISPLACEMENT:	1,069
		DIMENSIONS:	314' 3" x 30' 6" x 8' 6"
LAID DOWN:	17/8/18	SPEED:	28 kts
LAUNCHED:	21/12/18	CREW:	10/143
COMMISSIONED		ARMAMENT:	four 4-inch, twelve 21-inch TT (4 x III)
IN RCN:	6/7/41	Ex-USS *Kalk*	
PAID OFF:	8/6/45		

Commanding Officers

LCDR N. V. Clark, RCNR	6/7/41	19/7/43	CDR F. Poole, RCNR	19/1/44	22/4/45
LCDR D. G. Jeffrey, RCNR	20/7/43	18/1/44	SKPR/LT J. D. Burnham, RCNR	23/4/45	8/6/45

Niagara.

NIAGARA

BUILDER:	Bethlehem Shipbuilding Corp. Ltd., Quincy, Mass.	DISPLACEMENT:	1,069
		DIMENSIONS:	314' 3" x 30' 6" x 8' 6"
LAID DOWN:	8/6/18	SPEED:	28 kts
LAUNCHED:	31/8/18	CREW:	10/143
COMMISSIONED		ARMAMENT:	four 4-inch, twelve 21-inch TT (4 x III)
IN RCN:	24/9/40	Ex-USS *Thatcher*	
PAID OFF:	15/9/45		

Commanding Officers

A/CDR E. L. Armstrong, RCN	24/9/40	2/7/41	A/LCDR W. H. Willson, RCN	10/9/43	5/3/44
LCDR T. P. Ryan, RCNVR	3/7/41	22/2/42	LT J. C. Smyth, RCNR	6/3/44	22/6/44
LCDR R. F. Harris, DSC, RCN	23/2/42	4/10/42	CDR R. B. Mitchell, RCNR	23/6/44	29/6/44
A/LCDR G. H. Davidson, RCN	5/10/42	14/10/42	LT R. N. Smillie, RCNVR	30/6/44	18/7/44
LCDR R. F. Harris, DSC, RCN	15/10/42	9/9/43	CDR R. B. Mitchell, RCNR	19/7/44	15/9/45

Hamilton

As USS *Kalk* she served the USN in European waters during 1919, returning to the US to perform training duties for a few months before being laid up at Philadelphia in 1922. Recommissioned in June 1940, she served briefly with the Neutrality Patrol in the Atlantic before being transferred to the RN at Halifax on 23 September 1940. Commissioned as HMS *Kalk*, she was renamed *Hamilton* (for Hamilton, Bermuda) at St. John's where, on her arrival on 1 October, she was damaged in collision with her sister HMS *Georgetown*. She was taken to Saint John, New Brunswick for repairs and while being undocked there on 26 October, ran aground and received damage sufficient to lay her up for half a year. She was therefore offered to the RCN, recommissioned at Saint John as an RCN ship on 6 July 1941 and assigned to WLEF. After escorting one convoy, she was in collision with the Netherlands submarine *O-15* at Halifax. After repairs she again took up local escort duties, and in June 1943 became a member of WLEF's EG W-4. She still had not made a transatlantic passage when in August 1943 she was allocated to HMCS *Cornwallis* as a training ship. She was paid off on 8 June 1945 at Sydney and broken up at Baltimore the same year.

Niagara

Completed in 1919 as USS *Thatcher*, she served with the Pacific Fleet until 1922, when she was placed in reserve at San Diego. Briefly recommissioned and overhauled in 1940, she was transferred to the RCN as HMCS *Niagara* at Halifax on 24 September 1940, and sailed for the UK on 30 November. There, in March 1941 she was assigned to EG 4, Greenock, but in June joined the newly formed NEF. On 28 August she was on hand to take aboard the crew of *U 570*, which had surrendered to a Coastal Command aircraft south of Iceland. In March 1942 she joined WLEF, that June becoming a member of its EG W-9, and in October of W-10. In common with the other "Towns," she required major refits on a number of occasions and on 2 March 1944 following one of these, she became a torpedo-firing ship for training Torpedo Branch personnel at Halifax. She was paid off at Sydney on 15 September 1945 and broken up in 1947.

St. Clair

Completed in 1918 as USS *Williams*, she served with the Pacific Fleet until 1922, when she was laid up at San Diego. Recommissioned in 1940, she served briefly with the Neutrality Patrol before being transferred to the RCN at Halifax on 24 September 1940 as HMCS *St. Clair*. Assigned to EG 4, Greenock, she arrived in the Clyde on 11 December to undertake escort duty for Western Approaches Command. On 27 May 1941 in company with three RN destroyers, she was attacked by five German bombers west of Galway, Ireland. HMS *Mashona* was capsized by bombs and *St. Clair* sank the hulk after picking up survivors. Assigned to NEF, she collided with the oiler *Clam* on 17 June 1941, shortly after her arrival at St. John's, and remained under repairs until 2 December. In March 1942 she joined WLEF and in June 1943 was assigned to its EG W-2. Except for two months' absence that summer, attached to HMCS *Cornwallis*, she remained with the group until December, when she was ordered to St. Margaret's Bay to serve as a depot ship for RN submarines used in A/S training. In May 1944 she was taken to Halifax for repairs, remaining there until paid off 23 August. She was then reduced to a firefighting and damage control training hulk in Bedford Basin, where her remains still lay as late as 1950.

St. Croix

Completed in 1919, she operated with the Atlantic Fleet as USS *McCook* until placed in reserve at Philadelphia in 1922. Recommissioned in December 1939, she again served with the Atlantic Fleet prior to being transferred to the RCN at Halifax as HMCS *St. Croix* on 24 September 1940. She sailed for the UK via St. John's on 30 November but ran into a hurricane and had to return. Arriving at Halifax on 18 December, she remained under repair until mid-March 1941, when she took up the role of local escort. In August 1941 she joined NEF, escorting convoys to Iceland. In May 1942, following six months' refit at Saint John, New Brunswick, she escorted her first convoy, SC.84, to the UK and was thereafter employed constantly on the "Newfie-Derry" run. In April 1943 she was assigned to EG C-1, and in June to C-5. During this period she sank *U 90* while escorting convoy ON.113 on 24 July 1942, and on 4 March 1943 while accompanying convoy KMS.10 from Britain to Algeria, she assisted HMCS *Shediac* in destroying *U 87*. In August 1943 *St. Croix* was allocated to support group EG 9 for an offensive against U-boats crossing the Bay of Biscay, but the group was diverted to assist a group of convoys beset by U-boats

St. Clair, 9 November 1942.

ST. CLAIR

BUILDER:	Union Iron Works, San Francisco, Calif.	DISPLACEMENT:	1,069
LAID DOWN:	25/3/18	DIMENSIONS:	314' 3" x 30' 6" x 8' 6"
LAUNCHED:	4/7/18	SPEED:	28 kts
COMMISSIONED		CREW:	10/143
IN RCN:	24/9/40	ARMAMENT:	four 4-inch, twelve 21-inch TT (4 x III)
PAID OFF:	23/8/44	Ex-USS *Williams*	

Commanding Officers

LCDR D. C. Wallace, RCNR	24/9/40	5/4/42	LT J. E. Burnett, RCNVR	8/3/44	23/8/44
LCDR G. O. Baugh, OBE, RCNR	6/4/42	11/1/44			

St. Croix, 28 June 1942.

ST. CROIX

BUILDER:	Bethlehem Shipbuilding Corp. Ltd., Quincy, Mass.	DISPLACEMENT:	1,190
		DIMENSIONS:	314' 3" x 30' 9" x 9' 3"
LAID DOWN:	11/9/18	SPEED:	28 kts
LAUNCHED:	31/1/19	CREW:	10/143
COMMISSIONED		ARMAMENT:	four 4-inch, twelve 21-inch TT (4 x III)
IN RCN:	24/9/40	Ex-USS *McCook*	
LOST:	20/9/43		

Commanding Officers

LT M. A. Medland, RCN	24/9/40	10/10/40	LCDR A. H. Dobson, DSC, RCNR	6/1/42	20/9/43
CDR H. Kingsley, RCN	11/10/40	10/12/41			

in the Atlantic. While thus engaged, with convoy ON.202, *St. Croix* was torpedoed and sunk by *U 305* on 20 September, south of Iceland. Five officers and seventy-six men were rescued by HMS *Itchen*, but only one of these survived the loss of *Itchen* two days later.

St. Francis

As USS *Bancroft*, her career almost exactly paralleled that of her sister, USS *McCook*, and she was turned over to the RCN at Halifax on the same day, becoming HMCS *St. Francis*. She spent the remainder of the year based at Halifax, and on 5 November searched for the *Admiral Scheer* following the latter's attack on convoy HX.84. She left Halifax 15 January 1941 for the Clyde, where she was assigned to EG 4 of Western Approaches Command, Greenock. On the formation of Newfoundland Command in June 1941 she was based at St. John's and continuously employed as a mid-ocean escort until early December 1942, when she began a major refit at Halifax. On completion of her refit in April 1943 she returned to the MOEF, but by November was again urgently in need of repairs, which were carried out at Shelburne, Nova Scotia. In February 1944 she was allocated to HMCS *Cornwallis* as a training ship. She was paid off at Sydney on 11 June 1945 and sold for scrap. In tow for Philadelphia, *St. Francis* sank off Rhode Island on 14 July 1945 after colliding with the American SS *Winding Gulf.*

ST. FRANCIS				
BUILDER:	Bethlehem Shipbuilding Corp. Ltd., Quincy, Mass.	DISPLACEMENT:	1,190	
		DIMENSIONS:	314' 3" x 30' 9" x 9' 3"	
LAID DOWN:	4/11/18	SPEED:	28 kts	
LAUNCHED:	21/3/19	CREW:	10/143	
COMMISSIONED IN RCN:	24/9/40	ARMAMENT:	four 4-inch, twelve 21-inch TT (4 x III)	
PAID OFF:	11/6/45	Ex-USS *Bancroft*		

Commanding Officers

A/CDR H. F. Pullen, RCN	24/9/40	25/8/41	LT G. L. MacKay, RCNR	16/11/43	27/12/43
LT C. A. Rutherford, RCN	26/8/41	3/7/42	A/LCDR J. F. Watson, RCNR	17/1/44	11/10/44
LCDR F. C. Smith, RCNR	4/7/42	17/2/43	SKPR/LT C. C. Clattenburg, RCNR	12/10/44	12/11/44
A/LCDR H. V. W. Groos, RCN	18/2/43	15/11/43	A/LCDR J. F. Watson, RCNR	13/11/44	11/6/45

Athabaskan, 1944.

TRIBAL CLASS

PARTICULARS OF CLASS:

DISPLACEMENT:	1,927
DIMENSIONS:	377' x 37' 6" x 11' 2"
SPEED:	36 kts
CREW:	14/245
ARMAMENT:	six 4.7-inch (3 x II), two 4-inch (1 x II), four 21-inch TT (1 x IV), four 2 pdrs., one 12 pdr., six 20-mm
AS REVISED:	four 4-inch (2 x II), two 3-inch (1 x II), four 40-mm, four 21-inch TT (I x IV), two Squid.

ATHABASKAN

BUILDER:	Vickers-Armstrong Ltd., Newcastle-on-Tyne	LAUNCHED:	18/11/41
		COMMISSIONED:	3/2/43
		LOST:	29/4/44
LAID DOWN:	31/10/40		

Commanding Officers

CAPT G. R. Miles, OBE, RCN	3/2/43	5/11/43
LCDR J. H. Stubbs, DSO, RCN	6/11/43	29/4/44

Athabaskan

Commissioned on 3 February 1943 at Newcastle-on-Tyne and assigned to the British Home Fleet, *Athabaskan* left on 29 March to patrol the Iceland-Faeroes Passage for blockade-runners. Stress of weather caused hull damage that required five weeks' repairs at South Shields, UK, following which, in June 1943 she took part in Operation Gearbox III, the relief of the garrison at Spitsbergen. On 18 June she collided with the boom defence vessel *Bargate* at Scapa Flow, occasioning a month's repairs at Devonport. In July and August she was based at Plymouth, carrying out A/S patrols in the Bay of Biscay, and on 27 August was hit by a glider bomb off the Spanish coast. She managed to reach Devonport, where she remained under repair until 10 November. Returning to Scapa Flow in December, she escorted convoy JW.55A to Russia, but in February 1944 rejoined Plymouth Command and was assigned to the newly formed 10th Destroyer Flotilla. On 26 April she assisted in the destruction of the German torpedo boat *T 29* in the Channel off Ushant, and three days later was sunk by a torpedo from *T 24* north of the Ile de Bas. Her captain and 128 men were lost, 83 taken prisoner, and 44 rescued by *Haida*.

Haida

Commissioned on 30 August 1943 at Newcastle-on-Tyne, *Haida* was assigned to the British Home Fleet and during the first three months of her career made two trips to North Russia as a convoy escort. In January 1944 she joined the 10th Flotilla at Plymouth, and for the next eight months was engaged in sweeps and patrols in the Channel and the Bay of Biscay. She was present on D Day. During this period she took part in the sinking of several enemy vessels, including torpedo boat *T 29* on 26 April off Ushant; *T 27* on 29 April off Ushant; destroyer *Z 32* on 9 June off Ile de Bas; *U 971* on 24 June off Land's End; and minesweeper *M 486* on 6 August off Ile d'Yeu. In September she sailed for Canada to refit at Halifax, returning to Plymouth in January 1945. In March she returned to Scapa Flow and escorted another convoy to Murmansk, as well as carrying out strikes against German shipping off the Norwegian coast. She returned to Halifax on 10 June to begin tropicalization refit, but with the surrender of Japan this was cancelled and she was paid off on 22 February 1946. She was recommissioned at Halifax in 1947 and for the next three years took part in training and NATO exercises, then in July 1950 began extensive modernization.

Haida was recommissioned on 11 March 1952, to prepare for service in Korean waters. Between 1952 and 1954 she did two tours of duty in that theatre, then resumed her training role until she was paid off for the last time on 11 October 1963, at Sydney. Purchased by a group of private citizens, she arrived at Toronto in tow on 25 August 1964 to become a floating memorial, and in 1970 was accorded a berth at Ontario Place. It was announced in 2001 that she is to be moved to Pier 9 in Hamilton, Ontario, adjacent to a site being developed by Parks Canada.

Haida, 4 July 1944.

HAIDA

BUILDER:	Vickers-Armstrong Ltd., Newcastle-on-Tyne		PAID OFF:	22/2/46
LAID DOWN:	29/9/41		RE-COMMISSIONED:	1/2/47
LAUNCHED:	25/8/42		FINALLY PAID OFF:	11/10/63
COMMISSIONED:	30/8/43			

Commanding Officers

CDR H. G. DeWolf, DSO, DSC, RCN	30/8/43	18/12/44	CDR V. Browne, RCN	16/12/54	10/7/56
LCDR R. P. Welland, DSC, RCN	19/12/44	2/9/45	CDR H. R. Beck, RCN	11/7/56	6/4/58
LCDR F. B. Caldwell, RCN	3/3/47	11/12/47	CDR J. Husher, RCN	7/4/58	2/9/60
LCDR A. F. Pickard, OBE, RCN	12/12/47	15/5/49	CDR G. S. Clark, RCN	3/9/60	2/8/61
LCDR E. T. G. Madgwick, RCN	16/5/49	12/1/50	CDR D. C. Rutherford, RCN	3/8/61	19/7/62
CDR R. A. Webber, DSC, RCN	13/1/50	31/12/51	CDR W. H. Atkinson, DSC, RCN	20/7/62	22/9/63
CDR D. Lantier, RCN	1/1/52	28/10/53	LCDR D. K. Gamblin, RCN	23/9/63	11/10/63
CAPT J. A. Charles, RCN	29/10/53	15/12/54			

Huron

Commissioned 19 July 1943 at Newcastle-on-Tyne, she was assigned, like *Haida*, to the 3rd Destroyer Flotilla of the British Home Fleet. She made a trip in October to Murmansk with technical personnel and special naval stores, and for the rest of the year escorted convoys to and from North Russia. In February 1944 after one more such trip, she joined the 10th Flotilla at Plymouth for invasion duties, spending the next seven months in the Channel and the Bay of Biscay. She was present on D Day. *Huron* assisted *Haida* in sinking torpedo boat *T 29* and destroyer *Z 32*, and in August made her first visit to Canada for refit at Halifax. In November she returned to the UK to carry out escort duties in the Western Approaches and to make one further trip to Russia. She returned to Halifax with *Haida* and *Iroquois* on 10 June 1945 and began tropicalization refit, but this was discontinued owing to VJ Day and she was paid off on 9 March 1946. She was recommissioned at Halifax for training purposes in 1950, but sailed on 22 January 1951 on the first of two tours of duty in Korean waters, the second being carried out 1953-54. She then reverted to her peacetime role until she was finally paid off on 30 April 1963 at Halifax. She was broken up at La Spezia, Italy in 1965.

Huron, 1944.

HURON

BUILDER:	Vickers-Armstrong Ltd., Newcastle-on-Tyne	COMMISSIONED:	19/7/43
		PAID OFF:	9/3/46
LAID DOWN:	15/7/41	RE-COMMISSIONED:	28/2/50
LAUNCHED:	25/6/42	FINALLY PAID OFF:	30/4/63

Commanding Officers

LCDR H. S. Rayner, DSC, RCN	19/7/43	22/9/44		CDR L. P. McCormack, RCN	25/6/54	9/8/54
LCDR H. V. W. Groos, RCN	23/9/44	24/10/45		LCDR E. D. Robbins, RCN	10/8/54	16/8/54
LT E. P. Earnshaw, RCN	24/10/45	21/2/46		CDR J. C. Pratt, RCN	17/8/54	7/8/55
LT J. C. L. Annesley, RCN	22/2/46	20/3/46		CDR R. A. Webber, DSC, RCN	8/8/55	27/1/57
LCDR E. T. G. Madgwick, RCN	28/2/50	23/3/50		CDR N. Cogdon, RCN	28/1/57	1/8/57
LCDR T. C. Pullen, RCN	24/3/50	6/4/50		CDR W. H. Howe, RCN	28/3/58	6/12/59
LCDR E. T. G. Madgwick, RCN	7/4/50	23/9/51		CDR H. H. Smith, RCN	7/12/59	3/11/61
CDR J. C. Littler, RCN	24/9/51	12/10/51		CDR W. C. Spicer, RCN	3/11/61	4/10/62
CDR R. C. Chenoweth, MBE, RCN	18/11/52	20/9/53		CDR D. S. Bethune, RCN	4/10/62	9/4/63
CDR T. C. Pullen, RCN	21/9/53	24/6/54				

Iroquois

The first of the Canadian Tribals to commission, she did so at Newcastle-on-Tyne on 30 November 1942. *Iroquois* was assigned to the 3rd Flotilla, Home Fleet, but proved to have structural flaws and was not fully operational until 30 January 1943. On a quick round trip to Canada in March, she incurred weather damage that kept her under repairs at Plymouth until early June, following which she was employed on Gibraltar convoys. In July three troopships she was escorting to Freetown were attacked by German aircraft 300 miles off Vigo, Spain, and two were sunk, *Iroquois* rescuing 628 survivors from the *Duchess of York*. *Iroquois* then spent several months escorting Russian convoys. In February 1944 she arrived at Halifax for a refit, returning

to Plymouth early in June to join the 10th Flotilla for invasion duties. After D Day she carried out patrols in the Channel and the Bay of Biscay, and for some months escorted capital ships and troopships in UK coastal waters. *Iroquois* rejoined the Home Fleet at Scapa Flow in March 1945, escorted one more convoy to Russia and, following D Day, sailed to Oslo as an escort to Crown Prince Olaf, who was returning to liberated Norway. Shortly afterward she visited Copenhagen, whence she escorted the German cruisers *Prinz Eugen* and *Nürnberg* to Kiel for their formal surrender. On 4 June she left Greenock with *Haida* and *Huron* for home. The end of the Pacific war brought a halt to her tropicalization refit, and *Iroquois* was paid off on 22 February 1946. The fol-

lowing year she began a long refit and on 24 June 1949 was recommissioned as a cadet training ship. In 1952 and 1953 she did two tours of duty in the Korean theatre, following which she returned to her training role until paid off at Halifax on 24 October 1962 and laid up at Sydney. She was broken up at Bilbao, Spain, in 1966.

IROQUOIS			
BUILDER:	Vickers-Armstrong Ltd., Newcastle-on-Tyne	COMMISSIONED:	30/11/42
		PAID OFF:	22/2/46
LAID DOWN:	19/9/40	RE-COMMISSIONED:	21/10/51
LAUNCHED:	23/9/41	FINALLY PAID OFF:	24/10/62

Commanding Officers

CDR W. B. L. Holmes, RCN	30/11/42	29/7/43		LCDR T. C. Pullen, RCN	24/6/49	30/9/49
CDR J. C. Hibbard, DSC, RCN	30/7/43	7/2/45		CDR W. M. Landymore, RCN	21/10/51	31/10/53
CDR K. F. Adams, RCN	8/2/45	2/7/45		LCDR S. G. Moore, RCN	1/11/53	22/3/54
CDR E. W. Finch-Noyes, RCN	3/7/45	10/11/45		CDR M. F. Oliver, RCN	23/3/54	7/8/55
LT C. G. Smith, RCN	11/11/45	30/1/46		CDR D. L. Hanington, DSC, RCN	8/8/55	23/5/57
LT A. H. McDonald, RCN	31/1/46	22/4/46		LCDR M. W. Mayo, RCN	24/5/57	19/11/57
LT D. Adamson, RCNR	27/5/46	23/12/46		CDR W. D. F. Johnston, RCN	17/10/58	7/9/60
LCDR J. Plomer, DSC, RCN	1/3/47	1/6/47		CDR H. W. Moxley, RCN	8/9/60	19/3/62
LCDR J. S. Davis, RCN	2/6/47	13/11/47		CAPT G. C. Edwards, RCN	20/3/62	30/9/62
LCDR B. P. Young, MBE, RCN	14/11/47	2/5/49		LCDR W. D. Munro, RCN	1/10/62	24/10/62

Algonquin, 6 June 1944.

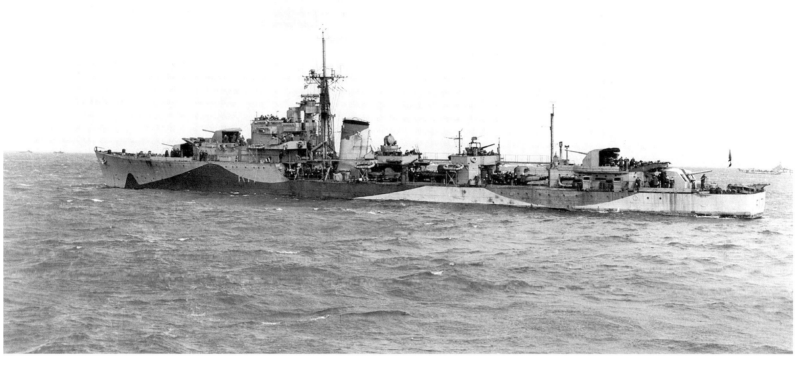

V CLASS

PARTICULARS OF CLASS:

DISPLACEMENT:	1,710
DIMENSIONS:	362' 9" x 35' 8" x 11' 6"
SPEED:	36 kts
CREW:	14/230
ARMAMENT:	four 4.7-inch, eight 21-inch TT (2 x IV) four 40-mm, four 20-mm
AS REVISED:	two 4-inch (1 x II), two 3-inch (I x II), two 40-mm, 2 Limbo, homing torpedoes

Algonquin

Not a Tribal despite her name, she was laid down as HMS *Valentine* but commissioned on 17 February 1944 at Glasgow as HMCS *Algonquin*. Assigned to the 26th Destroyer Flotilla of the British Home Fleet, she left Scapa Flow on 31 March to help escort a carrier attack on the *Tirpitz*. In April she escorted a similar attack on German shipping off the Lofoten Islands, Norway, and on 28 May left Scapa Flow for D Day operations. On 6 June she bombarded shore targets on the Normandy coast. At the end of June she returned to Scapa, from whence she carried out attacks on German convoys off Norway and, at year's end, escorted convoys JW.63 and RA.63 to and from Murmansk. On 22 August 1944 she took off 203 of *Nabob*'s ship's company when the latter was torpedoed in the Barents Sea. She returned to Halifax in February 1945 for refit, leaving on 12 August via Malta to join the British Pacific Fleet, but was recalled on VJ Day and left Alexandria for Esquimalt on 3 November. There she was paid off into reserve on 6 February 1946, but was recommissioned on 25 February 1953 after very extensive modernization, and sailed for the east coast that summer. After fourteen years' service with Atlantic Command, she returned to the west coast in March 1967, and was paid off for the last time on 1 April 1970, to be broken up in Taiwan in 1971.

ALGONQUIN

BUILDER:	John Brown & Co. Ltd., Glasgow, Scotland		PAID OFF:	6/2/46	
			RE-COMMISSIONED:	25/2/53	
LAID DOWN:	8/10/42		FINALLY PAID OFF:	1/4/70	
LAUNCHED:	2/9/43		Ex-HMS *Valentine*		
COMMISSIONED:	7/2/44				

Commanding Officers

LCDR D. W. Piers, DSC, RCN	17/2/44	19/4/45	CAPT D. G. King, DSC, RCN	29/11/57	23/9/58
LCDR P. E. Haddon, RCN	20/4/45	6/2/46	CAPT P. F. X. Russell, RCN	24/9/58	26/11/59
CDR P. F. X. Russell, RCN	25/2/53	27/8/54	CAPT A. F. Pickard, OBE, RCN	27/11/59	5/7/61
CAPT R. L. Hennessey, DSC, RCN	28/8/54	10/5/56	CAPT A. D. McPhee, RCN	6/7/61	2/7/62
CAPT D. W. Piers, DSC, RCN	11/5/56	6/7/56	LCDR D. C. Edwards, RCN	3/7/62	29/10/62
LCDR R. B. Hayward, RCN	7/7/56	28/7/57	CDR P. C. Berry, RCN	30/10/62	14/7/64
LCDR E. M. Jones, RCN	29/7/57	28/11/57	CDR J. W. Mason, RCN	15/7/64	-

Sioux

Laid down as HMS *Vixen*, she was commissioned as HMCS *Sioux* at Cowes, Isle of Wight, on 21 February 1944 and assigned to the 26th Flotilla of the British Home Fleet. She took part in escorting carrier attacks against the *Tirpitz* and against German shipping off Norway, and on 28 May left Scapa Flow for Portsmouth for D Day duties. Returning to Scapa Flow in July, she resumed her previous occupation and also escorted three convoys to and from Murmansk. She left the UK on 6 April 1945 for her first trip to Canada and, upon arrival, underwent major refit at Halifax. In November, *Sioux* was transferred to Esquimalt, where she was paid off into reserve on 27 February 1946. After some modernization she was recommissioned in 1950, and did three tours of duty in Korean waters, from 1951 to 1955. The last RCN ship to depart from Korean waters, upon her return to Canada *Sioux* resumed her training role until paid off at Halifax on 30 October 1963. She was broken up in 1965 at La Spezia, Italy.

Sioux, 1944.

SIOUX

BUILDER:	J. Samuel White & Co. Ltd., Cowes, I.O.W., UK	
LAID DOWN:	31/10/42	
LAUNCHED:	14/9/43	
COMMISSIONED:	21/2/44	

PAID OFF:	27/2/46
RE-COMMISSIONED:	18/1/50
FINALLY PAID OFF:	30/10/63
Ex-HMS *Vixen*	

Commanding Officers

LCDR E. E. G. Boak, DSC, RCN	21/2/44	29/6/45		CDR R. W. Murdoch, RCN	27/9/55	27/3/57
LCDR R. A. Webber, DSC, RCN	30/6/45	8/11/45		LCDR J. M. Calver, RCN	28/3/57	23/5/57
A/LCDR M. F. Oliver, RCNR	9/11/45	27/2/46		CDR P. G. Chance, RCN	24.5.57	1/7/58
CDR D. W. Groos, DSC, RCN	18/1/50	3/7/50		CDR A. B. C. German, RCN	2/7/58	1/2/59
CDR P. D. Taylor, DSC, RCN	4/7/50	9/3/52		LT H.D.N. Bridgman, RCN	2/2/59	4/3/59
LCDR P. C. Benson, RCN	10/3/52	6/5/52		LCDR J. D. Lowe, RCN	5/3/59	24/8/60
CDR P. E. Haddon, RCN	7/5/52	11/9/53		CDR L. J. Hutchings, DSC, RCN	24/8/60	20/9/61
LCDR D. R. Saxon, DSC, RCN	12/9/53	11/11/53		CDR C. A. Law, DSC, RCN	20/9/61	30/10/63
CDR A. H. Rankin, OBE, RCN	12/11/53	26/9/55				

Frigates

At first called twin-screw corvettes, this type was designed for the RN by the same William Reed who had designed the original corvette, and was intended to remedy the latter's shortcomings as an ocean escort. The name "frigate" was adopted by the Admiralty at the suggestion of Vice-Admiral Percy Nelles, Canada's Chief of Naval Staff. A far more habitable ship than the smaller corvette, it was also faster and had twice the endurance—7,200 sea miles at 12 knots. The RN frigates were named for rivers and hence known as the River class; the RCN units were named for towns and cities.

"The first of sixty frigates built in Canada for the RCN, HMCS *Waskesiu* was commissioned in June 1943. A further ten were built for Britain on a lease-lend arrangement with the US, which in the end kept two of them, and these are said to have been the basis from which the US destroyer escort was developed. In 1944 seven RN frigates, identifiable by their river names, were transferred to the RCN, along with three of the Loch class, a slightly larger model designed for prefabrication. Most of the RCN frigates were fitted with twin 4-inch guns, the only Canadian escort ships so armed except the Tribals

Many of the frigates were retained or recommissioned after the war to provide sea training for officer cadets and naval reservists. Between 1953 and 1958 the remaining twenty-one of the class underwent conversion to a flush-decked configuration, the once vast quarterdeck enclosed to house two Squid A/S mortars. The bridge was also greatly enlarged and the funnel heightened. Known as Prestonian class ocean escorts, all but *Victoriaville* had passed from the scene by 1968, and she had been renamed *Granby* two years earlier on assuming the duties of a diving tender.

PRESTONIAN CLASS CONVERSIONS

Twenty-one of the RCN's wartime frigates were radically modified between 1953 and 1958 to become a distinct class of ships. The first to undergo this conversion was HMCS *Prestonian*. As most of the frigates are illustrated in their wartime guise, and since many of our readers will have served in these ships, it is worthwhile presenting a sampling of photographs of them as Prestonians.

New Glasgow.

Sussexvale.

Victoriaville, 24 May 1960.

Antigonish, 11 November 1957.

Stettler.

RIVER CLASS, 1942-43 PROGRAM

PARTICULARS OF CLASS:

DISPLACEMENT:	1,445	FIRST 15 BUILT:	one 4-inch, one 12 pdr.
DIMENSIONS:	301' 6" x 36' 7" x 9'	PRESTONIAN	
SPEED:	19 kts	CLASS:	one twin
CREW:	8/133		4-inch gun, six 40-mm
ARMAMENT:	two 4-inch (1 x II), four		guns (one twin, four sin-
	20-mm, Hedgehog		gles), two Squid Mortars

Beacon Hill

Commissioned 16 May 1944 at Esquimalt, *Beacon Hill* arrived at Halifax on 11 July, having escorted *Puncher* from New Orleans to New York en route, and proceeded to Bermuda to work up. On her return to Halifax she left in September to join EG 26, an RCN support group based at Londonderry, but for varying periods was detached to Plymouth and Portsmouth. She remained in UK waters for the balance of the European war, leaving Greenock for home on 28 May 1945. Intended for Pacific service, she underwent tropicalization refit at Liverpool, Nova Scotia, from June to November, and sailed from Shelburne to Esquimalt on 22 December. She was paid off at Esquimalt on 6 February 1946, but recommissioned in the summer of 1949 for cadet training. She was again paid off in 1954 for conversion to a Prestonian class ocean escort, was commissioned as such on 21 December 1957, and served on the west coast until finally paid off on 15 September 1967. She was broken up in 1968 at Sakai, Japan.

Beacon Hill in characteristic west-coast camouflage, 5 June 1944.

BEACON HILL

BUILDER:	Yarrows Ltd., Esquimalt, BC	PAID OFF:	6/2/46
LAID DOWN:	16/7/43	RECOMMISSIONED	
LAUNCHED:	6/11/43	AS PRESTONIAN:	21/12/57
COMMISSIONED:	16/5/44	PAID OFF (FINAL):	15/9/67

Commanding Officers

A/CDR E. T. Simmons, DSO, DSC,RCNVR	14/10/44	12/8/45		LCDR A. G. Kilpatrick, RCN	19/8/59	24/8/61
LCDR H. L Quinn, DSC, RCNVR	13/9/45	5/2/46		LCDR J. L. Panabaker, RCN	25/8/61	17/5/62
LT J. E. Korning, RCN	16/5/49	15/9/49		LCDR A. C. McMillin, RCN	18/5/62	15/9/63
LCDR R. W. Murdoch, RCN	15/4/50	23/9/51		LCDR K. M. Young, RCN	16/9/63	27/10/64
LCDR J. W. McDowall, RCN	24/9/51	20/9/53		LCDR W. A. Hughes, RCN	28/10/64	-
CDR G. A. LaRue, RCN	21/9/53	4/1/54		LCDR G. V. Hartman, RCN	-	1/5/66
LCDR P. F. Wilson, RCN	21/12/57	14/11/58		LCDR P. E. Simard, RCN	2/5/66	11/9/66
LCDR F. G. Henshaw, RCN	15/11/58	1/12/58		LCDR S. C. Gould, RCN	12/9/66	15/9/67
LCDR W. S. Blandy, RCN	2/12/58	18/8/59				

Cap de la Madeleine

Commissioned 30 September 1944 at Quebec City, she arrived at Halifax 20 October, and soon afterward sailed for Bermuda to work up. Returning in December, she was allocated to EG C-7, MOEF based at St. John's. She left that port 28 December 1944 to accompany convoy HX.328 eastward, but was detached on 3 January to the westbound convoy ONS.39, as she had to return for repairs. These were carried out at St. John's, Halifax, and Quebec, and completed 7 May 1945. She then began tropicalization refit at Lauzon, but this was cancelled in August owing to termination of hostilities, and the ship was paid off 25 November at Shelburne. She was sold to Marine Industries Ltd., but later reacquired by the RCN and converted to a Prestonian class unit. Recommissioned on 7 December 1954, she served on the east coast until paid off on 15 May 1965. She was broken up the following year at La Spezia, Italy.

Cape Breton

Commissioned at Quebec City on 25 October 1943, *Cape Breton* arrived at Halifax on 28 November and worked up in St. Margaret's Bay in January 1944. Assigned to EG 6, a support group based at Londonderry, she left Halifax for the UK on 24 February. She operated at various times from Derry, Portsmouth and Plymouth, and in April 1944 sailed to North Russia, returning with convoy RA.59. She was also on hand at D Day. She returned to Canada late in 1944, arriving on 6 November at Shelburne for a major refit. This was completed in April and she was then sent to Bermuda to work up. Assigned to EG 9, she left St. John's on 9 May with convoy HX.354, and later that month sailed from Derry direct to Vancouver. A tropicalization refit begun on 26 June was cancelled before completion and the ship was paid off 26 January 1946, after several months in reserve at Esquimalt. She was sold in 1947 and expended as a breakwater in 1948, reportedly at Kelsey Bay, British Columbia.

Cap de la Madeleine off Quebec City, 1944.

CAP DE LA MADELEINE

BUILDER:	Morton Engineering and Dry Dock Co., Quebec City, QC	LAUNCHED:	13/5/44	RECOMMISSIONED	
		COMMISSIONED:	30/9/44	AS PRESTONIAN	7/12/54
LAID DOWN:	5/11/43	PAID OFF:	25/11/45	PAID OFF (FINAL)	15/5/65

Commanding Officers

LCDR R. A. Judges, RCNVR	30/9/44	18/10/45	LCDR D. R. White, RCN	9/1/61	6/2/61
LCDR W. O. O. Barbour, RCNR	19/10/45	25/11/45	CDR K. E. Grant, RCN	7/2/61	25/10/62
LCDR C. A. Gray, RCN	20/5/59	27/12/60	LT G. R. Ferguson, RCN	26/10/62	18/2/63
CDR K. E. Grant, RCN	28/12/60	8/1/61	CDR R. A. Beach, RCN	19/2/63	8/3/64
			LCDR F. J. French, RCN	27/11/64	15/5/65

Cape Breton off Quebec City, 1943.

CAPE BRETON

BUILDER:	Morton Engineering and Dry Dock Co., Quebec City, QC	LAUNCHED:	24/11/42
		COMMISSIONED:	25/10/43
LAID DOWN:	5/5/42	PAID OFF:	26/1/46

Commanding Officers

LCDR A. M. McLarnon, RCNR	25/10/43	3/12/44	A/LCDR J. C. L. Annesley, RCN	5/1/45	24/9/45

Charlottetown (2nd)

Commissioned at Quebec City on 28 April 1944, *Charlottetown* visited her namesake city en route to Halifax on 22 May. She arrived in Bermuda on 18 June for a month's working up, and on her return to Halifax was assigned to EG 16. She left Halifax on 7 March 1945 for Londonderry, the group having been transferred there, and was also briefly based at Portsmouth. In May she escorted two convoys to Gibraltar and two back, and in mid-June left Derry for Sydney, Nova Scotia. There she commenced a tropicalization refit that was completed at Halifax on 28 February 1946, and on 3 March left for Esquimalt. She spent the rest of the year training cadets and new entries, and on 25 March 1947 was paid off at Esquimalt. She was sold the same year and her hull expended as a breakwater at Oyster Bay, British Columbia.

Charlottetown (2nd), 1944.

CHARLOTTETOWN (2nd)

BUILDER:	Davie Shipbuilding and Repairing Co. Ltd., Lauzon, QC	LAUNCHED:	16/9/43
		COMMISSIONED:	28/4/44
LAID DOWN:	26/1/43	PAID OFF:	25/3/47

Commanding Officers

		A/CDR W. C. Halliday, RCNR	19/9/45	5/10/45
LCDR J. Harding, RCNR	28/4/44	23/4/45	LCDR S. W. Howell, RCNR	6/10/45	-
A/CDR W. C. Halliday, RCNR	24/4/45	9/7/45	LCDR J. E. Wolfenden, RCNR	13/4/46	

Chebogue, 17 March 1944.

CHEBOGUE

BUILDER:	Yarrows Ltd., Esquimalt, BC	COMMISSIONED:	22/2/44
LAID DOWN:	19/3/43	PAID OFF:	25/9/45
LAUNCHED:	17/8/43		

Commanding Officers

		A/LCDR M. F. Oliver, RCNR	24/7/44	21/1/45
LCDR T. MacDuff, RCNR	22/2/44	23/7/44	LT D. F. McElgunn, RCNVR	22/1/45	25/9/45

Chebogue

Chebogue was commissioned at Esquimalt on 22 February 1944 and sailed for Halifax on 15 March, arriving on 12 April. After working up in Bermuda in May she returned to Canada and was assigned to EG C-1. After visiting Yarmouth, Nova Scotia, from 12 to 14 June, she left St. John's on 23 June for Britain as part of the escort of convoy HXF.296. On her second return trip, this time as Senior Officer's ship of EG C-1 escorting convoy ONS.33, she was torpedoed by *U 1227* on 4 October, 800 miles west of the British Isles. She had made some 900 miles under tow, successively, of HMCS *Chambly*, HMS *Mounsey*, HMCS *Ribble*, and the ocean tug HMS *Earner*, when on 11 October the towline parted in a gale and *Chebogue* drove ashore in Swansea Bay, Wales. She was refloated the following day, taken to Port Talbot and placed in reserve. In December she was moved to Newport, Wales, to be made ready for a transatlantic crossing under tow, but instead was taken to Milford Haven and paid off on 25 September 1945. She was broken up locally in 1948.

Dunver

The name represents an odd effort to honour Verdun, Quebec, without duplicating the name of the destroyer HMS *Verdun*. The first frigate launched for the RCN, *Dunver* was commissioned at Quebec City on 11 September 1943 and arrived at Halifax on 3 October, having escorted a Sydney-Halifax convoy en route. After working up at Pictou she was allocated to EG C-5, and served continuously on North Atlantic convoys until October 1944. That July she had been Senior Officer's ship while escorting HXS.300, the largest convoy of the war, with 167 merchant ships. On 9 September she and HMCS *Hespeler* sank *U 484* near convoy ONF.202, south of the Hebrides. In October 1944 she commenced refitting at Pictou, completing on 27 December, and in April 1945 joined EG 27, based at Halifax, for the rest of the war. In June she went to the west coast for tropicalization, but this was discontinued in August and she was laid up at Esquimalt. Paid off 23 January 1946, *Dunver* was sold and her hull expended as part of a breakwater at Royston, British Columbia, in 1948.

Dunver, November 1943. Her unusually low pendant number, K03, was a bequest from *HMS Heliotrope*, transferred to the USN in 1942.

DUNVER

BUILDER:	Morton Engineering and Dry Dock Co., Quebec City, QC	LAUNCHED:	10/11/42
		COMMISSIONED:	11/9/43
LAID DOWN:	5/5/42	PAID OFF:	23/1/46

Commanding Officers

LCDR W. Woods, OBE, RCNR	11/9/43	6/5/44	A/LCDR W. Davenport, RCNR	25/8/44	26/3/45
LT W. Davenport, RCNR	7/5/44	9/8/44	A/CDR St. C. Balfour, RCNVR	27/3/45	26/5/45
A/CDR G. H. Stephen, RCNR	10/8/44	24/8/44	LCDR C. P. Balfry, DSC, RCNR	27/5/45	2/9/45

Eastview

Commissioned at Montreal on 3 June 1944, *Eastview* arrived at Halifax on 26 June and procceded to Bermuda to work up. On her return in August she was attached to EG C-6 as Senior Officer's ship, and on 18 September left St. John's with her first convoy, HXF.308. For the balance of the European war she was continuously on Atlantic convoy duty, and was one of the escorts of HX.358, the last HX convoy of the war, leaving St. John's 27 May 1945. That July she went to the west coast and had barely commenced tropicalization refit when work was stopped and the ship laid up in reserve at Esquimalt. She was paid off 17 January 1946 and sold in 1947, and her hull made part of a breakwater at Oyster Bay, British Columbia, the following year.

Eastview.

EASTVIEW

BUILDER:	Canadian Vickers Ltd., Montreal, QC	LAID DOWN:	26/8/43	COMMISSIONED:	3/6/44
		LAUNCHED:	17/11/43	PAID OFF:	17/1/46

Commanding Officers

			LT F. W. Bogardus, RCNVR	29/11/44	3/12/44
LCDR A. M. Kirkpatrick, RCNVR	3/6/44	16/9/44	LT R. E. Pare, RCNVR	4/12/44	7/12/44
LT W. D. H. Gardiner, RCNVR	17/9/44	26/10/44	A/LCDR R. C. G. Merriam, RCNVR	8/12/44	11/8/45
LT R. E. Pare, RCNVR	27/10/44	28/11/44	LCDR J. Morrison, RCNR	24/10/45	-

Grou

Grou was named for a French martyr of 1690, in lieu of the name Pointe-aux-Trembles, Quebec, the latter being considered overly long. Commissioned at Montreal on 4 December 1943 she arrived at Halifax later that month, worked up in St. Margaret's Bay and in March 1944 was assigned to EG 6, Londonderry. In April she went to Kola Inlet and returned as escort to convoy RA.59 from North Russia. Based at various times at Derry, Portsmouth, and Plymouth, she was present on D Day on A/S patrol. *Grou* left for home with convoy ON.285 on 17 February 1945 and on 4 March began a six-month tropicalization refit at Dartmouth, Nova Scotia. In October she left for the west coast, where she was paid off into reserve at Esquimalt on 25 February 1946. She was broken up at Victoria in 1948.

Grou, 1945.

Joliette, 1944.

Joliette

Commissioned at Quebec City on 14 June 1944, *Joliette* left for Halifax, then proceeded to Bermuda to work up. Returning to St. John's in August, she became a member of EG C-1 but on reaching Londonderry the following month was reassigned to EG 25. Returning to Derry on 22 November from her first round trip to Halifax, she ran aground in Lough Foyle, receiving extensive bottom damage. Repairs were effected at Belfast from 5 December 1944 to 5 April 1945, after which *Joliette* went to Tobermory to work up. She then returned to Londonderry, but sailed for Canada in June. On 19 November she was paid off at Sydney and laid up at Shelburne. In 1946 she was sold to the Chilean Navy, to serve as *Iquique* until disposed of in 1968.

GROU			
BUILDER:	Canadian Vickers Ltd., Montreal, QC	LAUNCHED:	7/8/43
		COMMISSIONED:	4/12/43
LAID DOWN:	1/5/43	PAID OFF:	25/2/46
Commanding Officers			
LCDR H. G. Dupont, RCNR		4/12/43	2/7/45
A/CDR B. D. L. Johnson, RCNR		9/8/45	14/11/45
LCDR R. D. Barrett, RCNR		15/11/45	25/2/46

JOLIETTE			
BUILDER:	Morton Engineering and Dry Dock Co., Quebec City, QC	LAUNCHED:	12/11/43
		COMMISSIONED:	14/6/44
		PAID OFF:	19/11/45
LAID DOWN:	19/7/43		
Commanding Officers			
A/LCDR G. N. Downey, RCNR		14/6/44	2/2/45
LCDR W. E. Harrison, RCNR		3/2/45	19/6/45
A/LCDR K. W. N. Hall, RCNR		20/6/45	19/11/45

Jonquière

Commissioned at Quebec City on 10 May 1944, she arrived at Halifax on 5 June and proceeded from there to Bermuda to work up. Returning in August, *Jonquière* was assigned to EG C-2 and after three Atlantic crossings was transferred to EG 26 at Londonderry. She was also based from time to time at Portsmouth and Plymouth, remaining in UK waters on A/S patrol until 27 May 1945 when she sailed with ON.305, the last westbound convoy. She was paid off 4 December at Shelburne and later taken to Lauzon for conversion to a Prestonian class ocean escort, recommissioning 20 September 1954. She was finally paid off on 12 September 1966, and broken up at Victoria in 1967.

Jonquière off Quebec City, 1944.

Kirkland Lake off Quebec City, 1944.

Kirkland Lake

Commissioned at Quebec City on 21 August 1944, she arrived at Halifax on 10 September and left on 20 November for Bermuda to work up. On her return to Halifax in December *Kirkland Lake* was assigned to EG 16, leaving on 8 March for Londonderry when the group was transferred there. She was based at various times at Derry and Portsmouth, and in May 1945 escorted two convoys to Gibraltar and two back. She returned to Canada in June for tropicalization refit at Quebec City, and when this was completed on 5 November, returned to Halifax. She was paid off 14 December 1945 to maintenance reserve in Bedford Basin and broken up at Sydney 1947-48.

JONQUIÈRE

BUILDER:	Davie Shipbuilding and Repairing Co. Ltd., Lauzon, QC	PAID OFF:	4/12/45
		RECOMMISSIONED	
LAID DOWN:	26/1/43	AS PRESTONIAN:	20/9/54
LAUNCHED:	28/10/43	PAID OFF (FINAL):	23/9/66
COMMISSIONED:	10/5/44		

Commanding Officers

LCDR J. R. Kidston, RCNVR	10/5/44	12/3/45	LCDR E. V. P. Sunderland, RCN	16/6/58	8/9/59
A/LCDR A. Marcil, RCNVR	13/3/45	16/6/45	LCDR H. V. Clark, RCN	9/9/59	28/11/61
LT J. H. Lincoln, RCNVR	17/6/45	4/8/45	LCDR R. L. Hughes, RCN	29/11/61	24/8/63
LCDR D. M. MacDonald, RCNVR	5/8/45	18/8/45	LCDR A. P. Campbell, RCN	7/9/63	14/9/65
LCDR H. R. Tilley, RCN	20/9/54	24/7/56	LCDR D. R. Donaldson, RCN	15/9/65	23/9/66
LCDR C. D. Gibson, RCN	25/7/56	15/6/58			

KIRKLAND LAKE

BUILDER:	Morton Engineering and Dry Dock Co., Quebec City, QC	LAUNCHED:	27/4/44
		COMMISSIONED:	21/8/44
LAID DOWN:	16/11/43	PAID OFF:	14/12/45

Commanding Officers

LT J. A. Tullis, RCNR	21/8/44	13/11/44	LCDR F. H. Pinfold, RCNVR	3/10/45	-
A/CDR N. V. Clark, OBE, RCNR	14/11/44	2/10/45			

La Hulloise berthing at Liverpool.

Kokanee, 23 June 1944.

La Hulloise

Commissioned at Montreal on 20 May 1944, *La Hulloise* arrived at Halifax in June. She proceeded to Bermuda in July to work up, and on returning was assigned to EG 16 at Halifax. In October she was reassigned to EG 25, and transferred with it to Londonderry in November 1944. She spent the remainder of the war in UK waters, based variously at Derry and Rosyth. On 7 March 1945 with *Strathadam* and *Thetford Mines*, she took part in sinking *U 1302* in St. George's Channel. Late in May she sailed for Canada to undergo tropicalization refit at Saint John. Work was completed 19 October, but the Pacific war had ended and she was paid off at Halifax on 6 December. Recommissioned for cadet and new entry training in 1949, *La Hulloise* was largely operational from then until 23 November 1953, when she was paid off for conversion to a Prestonian class ocean escort. She was commissioned as such on 9 October 1957, and remained in service until paid off 16 July 1965. She was broken up at La Spezia, Italy, in 1966.

LA HULLOISE			
BUILDER:	Canadian Vickers Ltd., Montreal, QC	COMMISSIONED:	20/5/44
		PAID OFF:	6/12/45
		RECOMMISSIONED AS	
LAID DOWN:	10/8/43	PRESTONIAN:	9/10/57
LAUNCHED:	29/10/43	PAID OFF (FINAL):	16/7/65

Commanding Officers		
LCDR J. Brock, RCNVR	10/4/44	16/8/45
LT J. C. Walker, RCNVR	17/8/45	2/10/45
LT J. A. Wyatt, RCNVR	3/10/45	6/12/45
LCDR M. J. A. T. Jette, RCN	24/6/49	31/12/49
CDR R. A. Webber, DSC, RCN	1/1/50	13/1/50
CDR T. C. Pullen, RCN	1/6/50	22/9/51
LT A. H. McDonald, RCN	23/9/51	27/11/52
LCDR H. A. Porter, RCN	28/11/52	6/11/53
LT E. J. Hyman, RCN	7/11/53	23/11/53
LCDR R. M. S. Greene, RCN	9/10/57	18/11/58
LCDR F. P. R. Saunders, RCN	19/11/58	9/9/60
LCDR W. J. H. Stuart, RCN	9/9/60	8/2/61
LCDR A. H. Grady, RCN	8/2/61	11/9/62
LCDR A. G. Lowe, RCN	11/9/62	11/8/64
LCDR E. A Makin, RCN	11/8/64	16/7/65

Kokanee

Commissioned at Esquimalt on 6 June 1944, *Kokanee* arrived at Halifax on 24 July and left for Bermuda in August to work up. On arrival at St. John's in September she was assigned to EG C-3 as Senior Officer's ship, and spent the rest of the European war on Atlantic convoy duty. She left Londonderry for the last time on 25 May 1945 with convoy ON.304, and soon after arriving left for the west coast. On 4 October she had completed tropicalization refit, but as VJ Day had intervened she was paid off into reserve on 21 December. She was sold to Canadian brokers in 1947, but resold in 1948 to the government of India for conversion to a pilot vessel for the Hooghly River and renamed *Bengal* in 1950.

KOKANEE			
BUILDER:	Yarrows Ltd., Esquimalt, BC	LAUNCHED:	27/11/43
		COMMISSIONED:	6/6/44
LAID DOWN:	25/8/43	PAID OFF:	21/12/45

Commanding Officers		
LCDR J. H. Marshall, RCNVR	6/6/44	14/12/44
LCDR F. W. T. Lucas, RCNVR	15/12/44	31/1/45
A/LCDR W. J. Kingsmill, RCNVR	1/2/45	14/3/45
LCDR F. W. T. Lucas, RCNVR	15/3/45	19/8/45
LT L. H. Reid, RCNVR	3/11/45	21/12/45

Longueuil

Commissioned on 18 May 1944 at Montreal, she arrived 30 June in Bermuda to work up. In July she became a member of EG C-2, and on 7 August left St. John's for Londonderry with convoy HXF.302. She spent her entire wartime career on convoy duty and for varying periods was Senior Officer's ship of her group. Returning to Canada in June 1945 she proceeded to Vancouver for tropicalization refit, but this was cancelled and the ship paid off 31 December at Esquimalt. She was sold in 1947 and reportedly expended as part of a breakwater at Kelsey Bay, British Columbia, in 1948.

Longueuil, 1945.

Magog, 1944.

Magog

After commissioning at Montreal on 7 May 1944, *Magog* arrived at Halifax on 28 May and worked up briefly in St. Margaret's Bay before sailing for Bermuda to complete the process in July. She then returned to Montreal for repairs, subsequently completing these at Halifax in August. There she joined EG 16, performing A/S duty in the Halifax, Gaspé, and Sydney areas. On 14 October 1944 while escorting convoy GONS.33 (the Gulf section of ONS.33), she was torpedoed and badly damaged by *U 1223* in the St. Lawrence River off Pointe des Monts. Lacking sixty feet of her stern, she was towed to Quebec and there declared a constructive total loss. Paid off 20 December to care and maintenance, she was sold in 1945 to Marine Industries Ltd., Sorel, who scrapped her in 1947.

LONGUEUIL

BUILDER:	Canadian Vickers Ltd., Montreal, QC	LAUNCHED:	30/10/43
		COMMISSIONED:	18/5/44
LAID DOWN:	17/7/43	PAID OFF:	31/12/45

Commanding Officer

LCDR M. J. Woods, RCNVR	18/5/44	18/7/45

MAGOG

BUILDER:	Canadian Vickers Ltd., Montreal, QC	LAUNCHED:	22/9/43
		COMMISSIONED:	7/5/44
LAID DOWN:	16/6/43	PAID OFF:	20/12/44

Commanding Officer

LT L. D. Quick, RCNR	7/5/44	20/12/44

Matane

Commissioned at Montreal on 22 October 1943, *Matane* arrived at Halifax 13 November and began working up in St. Margaret's Bay, completing the process at Pictou. In April 1944 she joined EG 9, Londonderry, as Senior Officer's ship, thereafter serving mainly on escort and patrol duty in UK waters. Postwar reassessment of U-boat kills credits *Matane* with a share in the sinking of *U 311* in the North Atlantic, 22 April 1944. She was present on D Day. On 20 July she was hit by a German glider bomb off Brest and towed, badly damaged, to Plymouth by HMCS *Meon*. In April 1945 she completed eight and a half months' repairs at Dunstaffnage, Scotland, worked up at Tobermory and on 13 May sailed from Greenock to escort convoy JW.67 to North Russia. She was detached on 16 May, however, to help escort fourteen surrendered U-boats from Trondheim to Loch Eriboll. In June after one round trip to Gibraltar as convoy escort, she left Londonderry for Esquimalt via Halifax. She arrived at Esquimalt in July and on 11 February 1946 was paid off into reserve there. She was sold in 1947 and her hull sunk in 1948 as part of a breakwater at Oyster Bay, British Columbia.

Matane, June 1944, typical of the first fifteen RCN frigates, with single 4-inch gun forward and no clinker screen to her funnel.

MATANE

BUILDER:	Canadian Vickers Ltd., Montreal, QC		LAUNCHED:	29/5/43	
			COMMISSIONED:	22/10/43	
LAID DOWN:	23/12/42		PAID OFF:	11/2/46	

Commanding Officers

LCDR A. H. Easton, DSC, RCNR	22/10/43	3/4/44	LCDR W. R. Stacey, RCNVR	4/2/45	28/3/45
A/CDR A. F. C. Layard, DSO, RN	4/4/44	26/7/44	A/LCDR F. J. Jones, RCNVR	29/3/45	19/7/45
A/LCDR F. W. T. Lucas, RCNVR	27/7/44	19/9/44	LCDR P. D. Taylor, RCNVR	20/7/45	27/11/45
LT J. M. Ruttan, RCNVR	20/9/44	3/2/45			

Montreal.

MONTREAL

BUILDER:	Canadian Vickers Ltd., Montreal, QC		LAUNCHED:	12/6/43	
			COMMISSIONED:	12/11/43	
LAID DOWN:	23/12/42		PAID OFF:	15/10/45	

Commanding Officers

LCDR R. J. Herman, OBE, RCNR	12/11/43	4/7/44	A/LCDR C. L. Campbell, RCNVR	27/11/44	26/7/45
LCDR S. W. Howell, RCNR	5/7/44	26/11/44			

Montreal

Commissioned on 12 November 1943 at Montreal, she arrived at Halifax on 29 November, worked up locally and on 25 February left St. John's for Londonderry to join EG C-4. She was employed continuously on convoy duty until late September 1944 when she joined EG 26, then forming at Derry. On 17 December 1944 she rescued survivors of *U 1209* wrecked on Wolf Rock southwest of Land's End. *Montreal* remained in UK waters and for short periods early in 1945 was based at Portsmouth and at Plymouth. She left Derry for the last time on 12 March 1945 as escort to convoy ON.290. Arriving at Shelburne, Nova Scotia, on 31 March she completed tropicalization refit there at the end of August, then performed odd jobs out of Halifax until paid off 15 October to reserve in Bedford Basin. Sold in 1947, she was broken up at Sydney.

New Glasgow

Commissioned on 23 December 1943 at Esquimalt, *New Glasgow* arrived at Halifax on 17 February 1944 and then proceeded to Bermuda to work up. On her return late in April she joined EG C-1. She left St. John's with her first convoy, HXS.291, on 15 May and for the next five months was steadily employed on convoy duty. Late in September she was allocated to EG 26, then forming at Londonderry, and for the remainder of the European war served in UK waters, based for short periods at Portsmouth and at Plymouth early in 1945. On 21 March 1945 she rammed and fatally damaged *U 1003* off Lough Foyle, and was herself laid up for repairs at Rosyth until 5 June. She then proceeded via Londonderry to Halifax and thence to Shelburne, where she was paid off to reserve on 5 November. Rebuilt in the long interval as a Prestonian class ocean escort, she was recommissioned on 30 January 1954 and served in a training capacity until 30 January 1967, when she was paid off at Esquimalt. She was broken up in Japan that year.

New Glasgow, 1944.

NEW GLASGOW

BUILDER:	Yarrows Ltd., Esquimalt, BC	PAID OFF:	5/11/45
LAID DOWN:	4/1/43	RECOMMISSIONED	
LAUNCHED:	5/5/43	AS PRESTONIAN:	30/1/54
COMMISSIONED:	23/12/43	PAID OFF (FINAL):	30/1/67

Commanding Officers

LCDR G. S. Hall, RCNR	23/12/43	23/7/44	LCDR J. G. Mills, RCN	14/8/61	3/3/63
LCDR T. MacDuff, RCNR	24/7/44	29/8/44	LCDR J. S. Hertzberg, RCN	4/3/63	21/4/64
LCDR R. M. Hanbury, RCNVR	30/8/44	28/3/45	LCDR O. J. A. Cavenagh, RCN	22/4/64	3/8/65
A/LCDR E. T. P. Wennberg, RCNVR	29/3/45	31/7/45	LCDR J. I. B. Donald, RCN	4/8/65	24/10/65
LT H. M. Palmer, RCNVR	1/8/45	1/11/45	LT S. W. Riddell, RCN	25/10/65	9/12/65
CDR G. A. LaRue, RCN	30/1/54	27/3/55	LCDR W. R. Vallevand, RCN	10/12/65	16/1/66
LCDR B. C. Hamilton, RCN	28/3/55	22/5/56	LCDR P. E. Simard, RCN	17/1/66	1/5/66
LCDR J. W. B. Buckingham, RCN	23/5/56	15/11/57	LCDR W. R. Vallevand, RCN	2/5/66	8/5/66
LCDR A. R. Pickels, RCN	5/5/58	6/1/60	LCDR T. A. Irvine, RCN	9/5/66	11/9/66
LCDR I. A. Macpherson, RCN	7/1/60	13/8/61	LCDR P. E. Simard, RCN	12/9/66	30/1/67

New Waterford, 1944.

NEW WATERFORD

BUILDER:	Yarrows Ltd., Esquimalt, BC	PAID OFF:	7/3/46
LAID DOWN:	17/2/43	RECOMMISSIONED AS	
LAUNCHED:	3/7/43	PRESTONIAN:	31/1/58
COMMISSIONED:	21/1/44	PAID OFF (FINAL):	22/12/66

Commanding Officers

A/LCDR E. R. Shaw, RCNR	21/1/44	23/3/44	LCDR F. Lubin, RCN	18/12/59	14/1/60
A/LCDR W. E. S. Briggs, DSC, RCNR	24/3/44	7/7/45	LCDR C. G. Pratt, RCN	15/1/60	22/6/61
A/LCDR W. E. S. Briggs, DSC, RCNR	13/8/45	11/11/45	LCDR J. H. Wilkes, RCN	23/6/61	9/10/62
LCDR J. M. Leeming, RCNVR	12/11/45	-	LCDR R. C. Brown, RCN	10/10/62	28/6/64
LT J. C. Payne, RCN	9/1/53	28/8/53	LCDR N. St. C. Norton, RCN	29/6/64	31/10/65
LCDR W. S. Blandy, RCN	31/1/58	26/10/58	LCDR N. D. Moncrieff, RCN	16/5/66	22/12/66
LCDR I. Butters, RCN	27/10/58	17/12/59			

New Waterford

Commissioned on 21 January 1944 at Victoria, she arrived at Halifax on 9 March and in Bermuda on 22 April to work up. Returning to Halifax, she was assigned to EG 6 as a replacement for the damaged HMCS *Teme*, and sailed for Londonderry on 19 June. She remained with the group until the end of the European war, detached for short periods to Portsmouth and Plymouth, and in April 1945 returned home for tropicalization refit at Liverpool, Nova Scotia. This was completed in November, and *New Waterford* left in January 1946 for the west coast, where she was paid off to reserve at Esquimalt on 7 March. Briefly commissioned in 1953, she later underwent conversion to a Prestonian class ocean escort, commissioning as such on 31 January 1958. She was paid off for the last time on 22 December 1966 and broken up the following year at Savona, Italy.

Orkney

Commissioned on 18 April 1944 at Victoria, *Orkney* arrived at Halifax on 8 June. After working up in Bermuda she returned to Halifax in August to join EG 16, but was transferred as Senior Officer's ship to EG 25 at Londonderry, sailing late in October with eastbound convoy HX.317. She remained on duty in UK waters until 13 February 1945 when she collided with SS *Blairnevis*, which sank, and was herself under repairs at Dunstaffnage, Scotland, until mid-April. Following a week's working up at Tobermory, *Orkney* briefly returned to Derry, then sailed late in May for home and tropicalization refit at Louisbourg. This was completed on 20 October, after which she served locally until paid off 22 January 1946 to reserve in Bedford Basin. Sold in 1947, she was renamed *Violetta* and served for a time as an Israeli immigrant ship before joining the Israeli Navy as *Mivtakh*. Sold in turn to the Singhalese (Sri Lanka) Navy in 1959 as *Mahasena*, she was broken up at Singapore in 1964.

ORKNEY			
BUILDER:	Yarrows Ltd., Esquimalt, BC	LAUNCHED:	18/9/43
		COMMISSIONED:	18/4/44
LAID DOWN:	19/5/43	PAID OFF:	22/1/46
Commanding Officers			
LT G. L. MacKay, RCNR		18/4/44	24/6/44
A/CDR V. Browne, RCNVR		25/6/44	28/3/45
CDR J. M. Rowland, DSO & Bar, RN		29/3/45	21/5/45
LT N. J. Cactonguay, RCNVR		22/5/45	2/9/45
IT H, R. Beck, RCN		19/10/45	22/1/46

Orkney, 1944.

Outremont

Commissioned at Quebec City on 27 November 1943 *Outremont* arrived at Halifax on 13 December and carried out working-up exercises in St. Margaret's Bay. She left St. John's on 17 February 1944 to join EG 6, Londonderry, and served mainly on escort and patrol duties in UK waters. She was present on D Day. She left the UK on 30 November for tropicalization refit at Sydney, which kept her idle until 20 August 1945, only to be paid off 5 November and sold to Marine Industries Ltd. Later reacquired by the RCN and converted to a Prestonian class ocean escort, she was recommissioned 2 September 1955 and served in a training role until finally paid off 7 June 1965 and broken up at La Spezia, Italy, the following year.

OUTREMONT			
BUILDER:	Morton Engineering and Dry Dock Co., Quebec City, QC	COMMISSIONED:	27/11/43
		PAID OFF:	5/11/45
		RECOMMISSIONED AS	
LAID DOWN:	18/11/42	PRESTONIAN:	2/9/55
LAUNCHED:	3/7/43	PAID OFF (FINAL):	7/6/65
Commanding Officers			
A/CDR H. Freeland, DSO, RCNR		27/11/43	11/8/44
LCDR F. O. Gerity, RCNR		12/8/44	5/11/45
LCDR J. M. Paul, RCN		2/9/55	7/5/56
LCDR P. G. Chance, RCN		8/5/56	25/4/57
LCDR M. O. Jones, RCN		26/4/57	8/10/58
LCDR C. J. Benoit, DSC, RCN		9/10/58	12/4/60
LCDR S. M. King, RCN		13/4/60	7/3/61
LCDR J. A. Fulton, RCN		8/3/61	2/9/62
LCDR J. R. H. Ley, RCN		3/9/62	20/6/64
LCDR R. L. Donaldson, RCN		21/6/64	7/6/65

Outremont, 1945, fitted with US-type SU radar.

Port Colborne

Commissioned at Victoria on 15 November 1943, *Port Colborne* arrived at Halifax 9 January 1944 and proceeded to Bermuda to work up in February. Late in April she sailed for Londonderry to join EG 9. She remained on patrol and escort duty in UK waters, including participation in D Day, except for a round trip to North Russia in December 1944 with convoys JW.62 and RA.62. She left Derry for Halifax 21 February 1945 and on 24 September completed tropicalization refit at Liverpool, Nova Scotia. On 7 November she was paid off at Halifax and laid up in reserve in Bedford Basin, and in 1947 was broken up at Sydney.

Port Colborne, 5 December 1943.

PORT COLBORNE					
BUILDER:	Yarrows Ltd., Esquimalt, BC	LAUNCHED:	21/4/43	PAID OFF:	7/11/45
LAID DOWN:	16/12/42	COMMISSIONED:	15/11/43		

Commanding Officers

LCDR C. J. Angus, RCNR	15/11/43	23/4/45	A/LCDR M. F. Oliver, RCNR	24/4/45	7/11/45

Prince Rupert

Commissioned at Esquimalt on 30 August 1943, she arrived at Halifax 21 October, worked up at Pictou, and in January 1944 joined EG C-3 as Senior Officer's ship. *Prince Rupert* left St. John's on 3 January to join her maiden convoy, SC.150, and was thereafter continuously employed as an ocean escort until late that year. On 13 March, with US naval units and US and British aircraft, she assisted in sinking *U 575* in the North Atlantic. In November 1944 she began a refit at Liverpool, Nova Scotia, and on its completion in March 1945 joined EG 27, Halifax. In June *Prince Rupert* sailed for Esquimalt, where she was paid off 15 January 1946. She was sold in 1947, and her hull expended as a breakwater at Royston, British Columbia, the following year. In 1985 seventy-four members of her ship's company held a reunion at the site.

Prince Rupert wearing the funnel emblem of EG C-3.

PRINCE RUPERT			
BUILDER:	Yarrows Ltd., Esquimalt, BC	COMMISSIONED:	30/8/43
LAID DOWN:	1/8/42	PAID OFF:	15/1/46
LAUNCHED:	3/2/43		

Commanding Officers

LCDR R. W. Draney, DSC, RCNR	30/8/43	31/7/44	LCDR R. W. Draney, DSC, RCNR	24/10/44	27/8/45
A/CDR C. A. King, DSO, DSC, RCNR	1/8/44	23/10/44	LCDR J. C. L. Annesley, RCN	24/9/45	15/1/46

St. Catharines

Commissioned on 31 July 1943 at Esquimalt, *St. Catharines* arrived at Halifax on 4 October and in November sailed for the UK as a member of EG C-2. She was continuously employed on convoy duty until October 1944 and from February to September that year was Senior Officer's ship. With six other escorts of convoy HX.280, she took part in the destruction of *U 744* on 6 March 1944. After refitting at Shelburne from October to December 1944 she went to Bermuda to work up, and on her return to Halifax commenced tropicalization refit there. By the time this was completed in August 1945 the war was over, and the ship was paid off on 18 November. In 1947 she was sold to Marine Industries Ltd. and laid up at Sorel, but was reacquired in 1950 and converted to a weather ship. Then owned by the Department of Transport, she was taken around to the west coast to be stationed in the North Pacific as of July 1952. Replaced in March 1967 by CGS *Vancouver*, she was broken up in Japan in 1968.

St. Catharines.

ST. CATHARINES

BUILDER:	Yarrows Ltd., Esquimalt, BC		COMMISSIONED:	31/7/43	
LAID DOWN:	2/5/42		PAID OFF:	18/11/45	
LAUNCHED:	5/12/42				

Commanding Officers

LCDR H. C. R. Davis, RCNR	31/7/43	14/3/44	LT A. B. Swain, RCNVR	25/5/45	3/8/45
LCDR A. F. Pickard, OBE, RCNR	15/3/44	13/12/44	LCDR L. C. Audette, RCNVR	4/8/45	18/11/45
LCDR J. P. Fraser, RCNR	14/12/44	24/5/45			

Saint John, May 1944.

SAINT JOHN

BUILDER:	Canadian Vickers Ltd., Montreal, QC		COMMISSIONED:	13/12/43	
LAID DOWN:	28/5/43		PAID OFF:	27/11/45	
LAUNCHED:	25/8/43				

Commanding Officers

A/LCDR R. M. Mosher, RCNR	13/12/43	20/2/44	LT C. G. McIntosh, RCNR	19/2/45	1/4/45
A/LCDR W. R. Stacey, RCNR	21/2/44	18/2/45	LCDR W. R. Stacey, RCNR	2/4/45	19/6/45

Saint John

Commissioned on 13 December 1943 at Montreal, she arrived at Halifax on 20 December and in January 1944 was sent to Bermuda to work up. On her return in February she was based for a short time at Halifax, but in April joined EG 9 in Londonderry. She was present on D Day. On 1 September 1944 she and *Swansea* sank *U 247* off Land's End, and on 16 February 1945 *Saint John* destroyed *U 309* in Moray Firth. In December 1944 she escorted convoys JW.62 and RA.62 on the North Russia run to and from Kola Inlet. She arrived at Cardiff for repairs on 27 February 1945, and when these were completed in April proceeded home for tropicalization refit at Saint John, from May to October. She was paid off 27 November 1945 at Halifax and placed in reserve in Bedford Basin until sold in 1947 for scrapping at Sydney.

Springhill, 17 April 1944.

SPRINGHILL

BUILDER:	Yarrows Ltd., Esquimalt, BC	LAUNCHED:	7/9/43	PAID OFF:	1/12/45	
LAID DOWN:	5/5/43	COMMISSIONED:	21/3/44			

Commanding Officers

A/CDR W. C. Halliday, RCNR	21/3/44	23/4/45	LCDR J. Harding, RCNVR	24/4/45	1/12/45

Stettler, May 1944.

STETTLER

BUILDER:	Canadian Vickers Ltd., Montreal, QC	COMMISSIONED:	7/5/44	RECOMMISSIONED	
LAID DOWN:	31/5/43	PAID OFF:	9/11/45	AS PRESTONIAN:	27/2/54
LAUNCHED:	10/9/43			PAID OFF (FINAL):	31/8/66

Commanding Officers

LCDR D. G. King, RCNVR	7/5/44	9/11/45	LCDR H. W. Vondette, RCN	9/3/61	18/10/62
CDR G. C. Edwards, RCN	27/2/54	2/9/55	LCDR R. F. Gladman, RCN	19/10/62	23/8/64
LCDR G. R. MacFarlane, RCN	3/9/55	9/9/57	LCDR T. A. Irvine, RCN	24/8/64	8/5/66
LCDR M. H. Cooke, RCN	10/9/57	11/8/59	LT S. C. Gould, RCN	9/5/66	31/8/66
LCDR R. A. Evans, RCN	12/8/59	8/3/61			

Springhill

Commissioned on 21 March 1944 at Victoria, she arrived at Halifax on 12 May and left in mid-June for three weeks of working up in Bermuda. In August *Springhill* joined EG 16, Halifax, as Senior Officer's ship. She left on 7 March 1945 for Londonderry, the group having been transferred there, but returned in April for tropicalization refit at Pictou. This occupied her from May to October, and on 1 December she was paid off at Halifax and laid up in reserve in Bedford Basin. She was broken up in 1947 at Sydney.

Stettler

Stettler was commissioned 7 May 1944 at Montreal, and arrived at Halifax on 28 May. She carried out work-ups in Bermuda in July. On her return to Halifax she was assigned to EG 16. On 7 March 1945 she left for Londonderry, EG 16's new base, and was thereafter employed in UK waters except for two round trips to Gibraltar in May and June 1945. She left Derry for home on 16 June, the last Canadian warship to do so, and began tropicalization refit at Shelburne. Work was suspended in August and the ship was paid off 9 November 1945. She was sold but later recovered and converted to a Prestonian class ocean escort, being recommissioned on 27 February 1954. She subsequently moved to the west coast, and was finally paid off there on 31 August 1966. She was broken up in 1967 at Victoria.

Stormont

Commissioned at Montreal on 27 November 1943, *Stormont* arrived at Halifax in December, worked up in St. Margaret's Bay and in mid-March 1944 sailed for Londonderry to join EG 9. She was present on D Day, and in July 1944 assisted the damaged HMCS *Matane* toward Plymouth. In October she escorted a convoy to Gibraltar and, in December, escorted convoy JW.62 to Kola Inlet and RA.62 back. She left Derry on 19 December 1944 for Halifax and tropicalization refit at Shelburne. The latter, begun in June, was discontinued on 20 August and the ship was paid off 9 November 1945. She was sold in 1947 to a Montevideo buyer for conversion to a merchant ship, but was resold in 1951. Converted at Kiel 1952-54 to a luxury yacht for Aristotle Onassis, she was renamed *Christina*. In 1978 she was turned over to the Greek Navy, and sold commercially in 1994.

Stormont.

STORMONT

BUILDER:	Canadian Vickers Ltd., Montreal, QC	COMMISSIONED:	27/11/43
LAID DOWN:	23/12/42	PAID OFF:	9/11/45
LAUNCHED:	14/7/43		

Commanding Officer

A/LCDR G. A. Myra, RCNR	27/11/43	9/11/45

Swansea at Godthaab, Greenland, 12 September 1949.

SWANSEA

BUILDER:	Yarrows Ltd., Esquimalt, BC	PAID OFF:	2/11/45
LAID DOWN:	15/7/42	RECOMMISSIONED	
LAUNCHED:	19/12/42	AS PRESTONIAN:	14/11/57
COMMISSIONED:	4/10/43	PAID OFF (FINAL):	14/10/66

Commanding Officers

A/CDR C. A. King, DSO, DSC, RCNR	4/10/43	29/7/44	LCDR J. R. Coulter, RCN	27/3/52	15/8/52
CDR A. F. C. Layard, RN	30/7/44	4/11/44	LCDR W. D. F. Johnston, RCN	14/4/53	6/11/53
LT J. T. Band, RCNVR	5/11/44	15/4/45	LCDR C. H. LaRose, RCN	7/11/53	10/11/53
LCDR G. A. LaRue, RCNVR	16/4/45	2/11/45	LCDR J. A. Farquhar, RCN	14/11/57	17/2/59
LT R. W. Timbrell, DSC, RCN	12/4/48	6/2/49	LCDR G. S. Clark, RCN	18/2/59	31/8/60
LT J. P. T. Dawson, RCN	7/2/49	11/8/50	LCDR W. E. Clayards, RCN	1/9/60	17/7/62
LCDR J. E. Korning, RCN	12/8/50	22/1/51	LCDR B. A. Cartwright, RCN	18/7/62	23/1/64
LT W. A. Manfield, RCN	23/1/51	28/2/51	LCDR D. K. Gamblin, RCN	24/1/64	-
LCDR J. E. Korning, RCN	1/3/51	26/3/52			

Swansea

Commissioned at Victoria on 4 October 1943, *Swansea* arrived at Halifax on 16 November and worked up off Pictou and in St. Margaret's Bay. Assigned to EG 9, Londonderry, she made her passage there with convoy SC.154, incidentally taking part in the sinking of *U 845* on 10 March 1944. On 14 April she repeated the process in company with HMS *Pelican*, the victim this time being *U 448*. Postwar re-assessment of U-boat kills credits *Swansea* with a share in the destruction of *U 311* in the North Atlantic, 22 April 1944. She was present on D Day, and for the next four months patrolled the Channel in support of the ships supplying the invasion forces. While thus employed, she and *Saint John* sank *U 247* off Land's End on 1 September. She left Londonderry on 5 November for a major refit at Liverpool, Nova Scotia, from December 1944 to July 1945. It was the first tropicalization of a frigate for Pacific service, and on VJ Day *Swansea* was assessing the results in the Caribbean. She was paid off 2 November 1945 to reserve in Bedford Basin, but was twice recommissioned for training cadets and new entries between April 1948 and November 1953. She was rebuilt, from 1956 to 1957, as a Prestonian class ocean escort, serving on the east coast until finally paid off 14 October 1966. She was broken up in 1967 at Savona, Italy.

Thetford Mines

Thetford Mines, 1944.

Commissioned on 24 May 1944 at Quebec City, *Thetford Mines* arrived in Bermuda on 12 July to work up, returning to Halifax on 16 August. Soon afterwards assigned to EG 25, she was transferred with the group to Londonderry in November, and served in UK waters from then until VE Day, working out of Derry and for a time out of Rosyth. On 7 March 1945 she helped sink *U 1302* in St. George's Channel, and on 11 May arrived in Lough Foyle as escort to eight surrendered U-boats. She returned home late in May and was paid off 18 November at Sydney and laid up at Shelburne. In 1947 she was sold to a Honduran buyer who proposed converting her into a refrigerated fruit carrier.

THETFORD MINES

BUILDER:	Morton Engineering and Dry Dock Co., Quebec City, QC	LAUNCHED:	30/10/43
		COMMISSIONED:	24/5/44
LAID DOWN:	7/7/43	PAID OFF:	18/11/45

Commanding Officers

LCDR J. A. R. Allan, DSC, RCNVR	24/5/44	12/6/45	LCDR J. A. R. Allan, DSC, RCNVR	1/7/45	20/7/45
LT J. M. S. Clark, RCNVR	13/6/45	30/6/45	A/CDR T. Gilmour, RCNR	21/7/45	18/11/45

Valleyfield

Valleyfield, 1943.

Commissioned 7 December 1943 at Quebec City, she arrived at Halifax on 20 December and commenced working up in St. Margaret's Bay, completing the process in Bermuda. She left Halifax at the end of February 1944 to join EG C-1 and sailed for the UK with convoy SC.154, but was detached to Horta en route, escorting the rescue ship *Dundee* with the corvette *Regina* in tow, which had fouled her screw while fuelling. Her next assignment was to escort a Royal Naval salvage tug with the disabled HMCS *Mulgrave* in tow from Horta for the Clyde. The three left the Azores on 14 March and joined convoy SL.151 (from Sierra Leone) three days later. *Valleyfield* made one return trip to Canada, and on her next trip left Londonderry on 27 April with convoy ONM.234. She parted company on 7 May for St. John's and shortly afterward was torpedoed and sunk by *U 548*, fifty miles southeast of Cape Race, with the loss of 125 lives. She was the only RCN ship of her class to be lost.

VALLEYFIELD

BUILDER:	Morton Engineering and Dry Dock Co., Quebec City, QC	LAUNCHED:	17/7/43
		COMMISSIONED:	7/12/43
LAID DOWN:	30/11/42	LOST:	7/5/44

Commanding Officer

LCDR D. T. English, RCNR	7/12/43	7/5/44

Waskesiu

The first frigate completed on the west coast, *Waskesiu* was commissioned at Victoria on 16 June 1943 and left for Halifax on 8 July. She worked up in Bermuda the following month, returning to Halifax on 11 September, and late in October left for Londonderry to join EG 5 (renumbered EG 6 on 21 November). *Waskesiu* served chiefly in UK waters, but early in 1944 supported Gibraltar and Sierra Leone convoys. On 24 February while escort to SC.153 she sank *U 257*, and in April made a trip to North Russia to bring back convoy RA.59. She was present on D Day. On 14 September she left Derry with ONF.253 for Canada, and soon after arriving began an extensive refit at Shelburne. On its completion in March 1945 she proceeded to Bermuda to work up, following which she sailed for Londonderry via Horta. She left Derry for Canada late in May, proceeding to Esquimalt in June to commence tropicalization refit, but work was suspended in August and she was paid off into reserve on 29 January 1946. She was sold to the Indian government in 1947 for conversion to a pilot vessel, and renamed *Hooghly* in 1950.

Wentworth

Wentworth was commissioned on 7 December 1943 at Victoria and arrived at Halifax 25 January 1944. She left for Bermuda to work up, but defects forced her to return and the working-up exercises were carried out in St. Margaret's Bay. In June she joined EG C-4, becoming Senior Officer's ship in August, and remained continuously on convoy duty until February 1945 when she commenced a major refit at Shelburne, from 7 March to 9 August. She was paid off on 10 October 1945 to reserve in Bedford Basin, and broken up in 1947 at Sydney.

Waskesiu.

WASKESIU						
BUILDER:	Yarrows Ltd., Esquimalt, BC			COMMISSIONED :	16/6/43	
LAID DOWN:	2/5/42			PAID OFF:	29/1/46	
LAUNCHED:	6/12/42					

Commanding Officers

LCDR J. H. S. MacDonald, RCNR	16/6/43	4/2/44	A/LCDR L. D. Quick, RCNR	14/12/44	22/10/45
LCDR J. P. Fraser, RCNR	5/2/44	13/12/44			

Wentworth.

WENTWORTH					
BUILDER:	Yarrows Ltd., Esquimalt, BC	LAUNCHED:	6/3/43	PAID OFF:	10/10/45
LAID DOWN:	11/11/42	COMMISSIONED:	7/12/43		

Commanding Officers

LCDR S. W. Howell, RCNR	7/12/43	4/7/44	A/LCDR J. B. Graham, RCNVR	16/1/45	10/4/45
LCDR R. J. C. Pringle, RCNVR	5/7/44	15/1/45	LT G. C. Campbell, RCNVR	25/8/45	10/10/45

RIVER CLASS 1943–1944 PROGRAM

Antigonish

Commissioned at Victoria on 4 July 1944, she arrived at Halifax on 22 August, and after undergoing minor repairs sailed for Bermuda in mid-October to work up. On her return to Halifax on 2 November she joined EG 16, transferring with the group to Londonderry in March 1945. During the next three months *Antigonish* was employed on patrol and support duty, including two round trips to Gibraltar. She left Londonderry in mid-June and on 3 July began tropicalization refit at Pictou, completing 17 November. On 22 December she left for Esquimalt and there, on 5 February 1946, she was paid off into reserve. She recommissioned for training on 26 April 1947 and was paid off 15 January 1954. The ship was converted 1956-57, to a Prestonian class ocean escort, and again took up her training role until finally paid off on 30 November 1966. She was broken up in Japan in 1968.

Antigonish, 27 July 1944.

ANTIGONISH

BUILDER:	Yarrows Ltd., Esquimalt, BC	PAID OFF:	5/2/46
LAID DOWN:	2/10/43	RECOMMISSIONED	
LAUNCHED:	10/2/44	AS PRESTONIAN:	12/10/57
COMMISSIONED:	4/7/44	PAID OFF (FINAL):	30/11/66

Commanding Officers

LCDR R. D. Barrett, RCNR	4/7/44	4/5/45	LCDR R. Phillips, RCN	28/9/50	3/8/52
A/LCDR J. A. Dunn, RCNVR	5/5/45	22/7/45	LCDR H. R. Beck, RCN	4/8/52	15/1/54
A/LCDR G. G. K. Holder, RCNVR	13/8/45	28/10/45	LCDR R. W. J. Cocks, RCN	12/10/57	16/8/60
A/CDR A. H. G. Storrs, DSC & Bar, RCN	29/10/45	5/2/46	LCDR G. M. DeRosenroll, RCN	17/8/60	8/8/61
A/LCDR J. E. Wolfenden, RCN	26/4/47	16/8/47	LCDR E. M. Jones, RCN	9/8/61	27/8/63
LCDR C. A. Law, DSC, RCN	17/8/47	3/12/48	LCDR H. J. Wade, RCN	28/8/63	26/4/64
LCDR W. S. T. McCully, RCN	4/12/48	27/9/50	LCDR P. L. McCulloch, RCN	27/4/64	2/9/65
			LCDR J. I. Donald, RCN	3/9/65	30/11/66

Buckingham, 29 October 1956, fitted with experimental landing pad.

BUCKINGHAM

BUILDER:	Davie Shipbuilding and Repairing Co. Ltd., Lauzon, QC	PAID OFF:	16/11/45
		RECOMMISSIONED	
LAID DOWN:	11/10/43	AS PRESTONIAN:	25/6/54
LAUNCHED:	28/4/44	PAID OFF (FINAL):	23/3/65
COMMISSIONED:	2/11/44		

Commanding Officers

A/LCDR M. H. Wallace, RCNR	2/11/44	7/11/45	LCDR T. L. Hebbert, RCN	14/12/59	–
LT R. M. Montague, RCNVR	8/11/45	16/11/45	LCDR R. F. Choat, RCN	15/9/62	7/6/63
LCDR J. W. Roberts, RCN	25/6/54	7/9/55	LCDR C. E. Leighton, RCN	8/6/63	31/3/64
LCDR T. E. Connors, RCN	8/9/55	30/9/57	LCDR N. S. Jackson, RCN	1/4/64	10/1/65
LCDR D. M. MacLennan, RCN	6/5/58	–	LT E. G. A. Bowkett, RCN	11/1/65	15/1/65
			LT J. T. Stuart, RCN	16/1/65	23/3/65

Buckingham

Commissioned on 2 November 1944 at Quebec City, she proceeded to the east coast and sailed from Halifax on 18 December for Bermuda to work up. She returned in mid-January 1945 and in February was assigned to EG 28 and carried out escort and patrol duty out of Halifax until VE Day. In May she arrived at Shelburne, escorting the surrendered *U 889*. In June she began a tropicalization refit at Liverpool, Nova Scotia, which continued at Shelburne until 20 August, when it was suspended. *Buckingham* was paid off on 16 November at Sydney and placed in reserve at Shelburne until 1946, when she was sold to Marine Industries Ltd. Reacquired by the RCN, she was converted to a Prestonian class ocean escort 1953-54, and recommissioned for training purposes. Further modified by the addition of a helicopter landing deck aft, she carried out trials October-December 1956, preliminary to the design of the destroyer helicopter carriers. She was paid off for the last time on 23 March 1965, and broken up the following year at La Spezia, Italy.

Capilano

Commissioned at Victoria on 25 August 1944, *Capilano* arrived at Halifax on 20 October. Following workups begun in St. Margaret's Bay and completed in Bermuda in November, she joined EG C-2 in St. John's, Newfoundland, and was continuously on North Atlantic convoy duty until VE Day. She left Londonderry for the last time on 30 May 1945 and on 10 June began tropicalization refit at Shelburne. The work was completed on 13 October, and on 24 November 1945 the ship was paid off at Halifax and placed in reserve in Bedford Basin. She was sold for mercantile use in 1947, and in 1948 appeared under Jamaican registry as *Irving Francis M*. She foundered in 1953 off the Cuban coast while en route from Jamaica to Miami in tow of *Bess Barry M.*, the former HMCS *St. Boniface*.

Carlplace

Carlplace was commissioned on 13 December 1944 at Quebec City, the last RCN frigate to enter service. En route to Halifax, she suffered serious ice damage to her hull, necessitating several weeks' repairs at Halifax and Philadelphia. She then proceeded to Bermuda to work up, returning to Halifax on 24 March 1945. In April she was allocated to EG 16, Londonderry, and sailed for the Clyde via the Azores, escorting an RN submarine homeward bound from refit in the US. She finally arrived at Londonderry on 23 April and left on 5 May to escort convoys to and from Gibraltar. Late that month she returned to Canada for tropicalization refit at Saint John, New Brunswick. Begun on 2 June and continued at Shelburne, Nova Scotia on 10 July, the work was called off on 20 August, and on 13 November 1945 the ship was paid off at Halifax and laid up at Shelburne. Sold to the Dominican Republic in 1946 for conversion to a presidential yacht, she was renamed *Presidente Trujillo* and, in 1962, *Mella*.

Capilano, 9 September 1944.

CAPILANO

BUILDER:	Yarrows Ltd., Esquimalt, BC	COMMISSIONED:	25/8/44
LAID DOWN:	18/11/43	PAID OFF:	24/11/45
LAUNCHED:	8/4/44		

Commanding Officers

LCDR H. E. McArthur, RCNVR	25/8/44	12/8/45	LT C. B. Hermann, RCNVR	13/8/45	26/8/45

Carlplace.

CARLPLACE

BUILDER:	Davie Shipbuilding and Repairing Co. Ltd., Lauzon, QC	LAUNCHED:	6/7/44
		COMMISSIONED:	13/12/44
LAID DOWN:	30/11/43	PAID OFF:	13/11/45

Commanding Officer

A/LCDR C. E. Wright, RCNVR	13/12/44	2/9/45

Coaticook

Commissioned on 25 July 1944 at Quebec City, *Coaticook* proceeded to Bermuda in mid-September for three weeks' working up. She was then assigned to EG 27 with which she served on A/S and support duties out of Halifax for the balance of the war. In June 1945 *Coaticook* sailed to Esquimalt, where she was paid off into reserve on 29 November. In 1949 her stripped hull was sold for a breakwater at Powell River, but was refloated in 1961. On 14 December 1961, while in tow for Victoria to be broken up, the hull was found to be structurally unsound. In February 1962, *Coaticook* was blown up *in situ* off Race Rock.

Coaticook, December, 1944.

COATICOOK	
BUILDER:	Davie Shipbuilding and Repairing Co. Ltd., Lauzon, QC
LAID DOWN:	14/6/43
LAUNCHED:	26/11/43
COMMISSIONED:	25/7/44
PAID OFF:	29/11/45

Commanding Officers

LCDR L. C. Audette, RCNVR	25/7/44	3/6/45
LCDR L. R. Hoar, RCNVR	4/6/45	22/7/45
A/LCDR J. W. Golby, RCNVR	6/8/45	19/8/45

Fort Erie, 1945.

FORT ERIE	
BUILDER:	George T. Davie & Sons Ltd., Lauzon, QC
LAID DOWN:	3/11/43
LAUNCHED:	27/5/44
COMMISSIONED:	27/10/44
PAID OFF:	22/11/45
RECOMMISSIONED AS PRESTONIAN:	17/4/56
PAID OFF (FINAL):	26/3/65

Commanding Officers

A/LCDR A. W. Ford, RCNR	27/10/44	20/2/45
A/LCDR E. F. Piper, RCNVR	21/2/45	5/8/45
A/LCDR R. C. Chenoweth, RCN	6/8/45	4/11/45
CDR W. W. MacColl, RCN	17/4/56	17/1/58
LCDR H. C. LaRose, RCN	3/7/58	17/9/59
CDR J. R. Coulter, RCN	18/9/59	10/8/60
CDR L. B. Jenson, RCN	11/8/60	30/9/62
CDR W. C. Spicer, RCN	4/10/62	12/8/63
CDR E. Petley-Jones, RCN	12/8/63	-

Fort Erie

Commissioned at Quebec City, on 27 October 1944 she did not arrive at Halifax until December. She worked up in Bermuda in mid-January and, on her return to Halifax, was assigned to EG 28, an RCN support group based on Halifax, for the duration of the European war. Tropicalization refit begun 2 June 1945 at Pictou was cancelled on 20 August and *Fort Erie* was paid off on 22 November, to be laid up at Shelburne. She was sold in 1946 to Marine Industries Ltd., but reacquired by the RCN and rebuilt in 1954 and 1955 as a Prestonian class ocean escort. Recommissioned 17 April 1956, she was generally in service as a training ship until paid off on 26 March 1965, at Halifax. She was broken up at La Spezia, Italy, in 1966.

Glace Bay

Commissioned on 2 September 1944 at Lévis, she arrived at Halifax 23 September. She carried out workups in Bermuda in mid-October and on her return was assigned to EG C-4, Londonderry. She left St. John's for that port on 17 November, escorting a number of US-built subchasers destined for the Russian Navy. *Glace Bay* was employed continuously on convoy duty until VE Day, and early in June 1945 left Derry for the last time to spend several months at a variety of tasks off the east coast of Canada. In October she made a round trip to Bermuda, and on her return was paid off on 17 November at Sydney. She lay in reserve at Shelburne until sold in 1946 to the Chilean Navy and renamed *Esmeralda* and then, in 1952, *Bacquedano*. She was broken up in 1968.

Glace Bay, 1944.

GLACE BAY

BUILDER:	George T. Davie & Sons Ltd., Lauzon, QC	LAUNCHED:	26/4/44
		COMMISSIONED:	2/9/44
LAID DOWN:	23/9/43	PAID OFF:	17/11/45

Commanding Officers

A/CDR J. H. S. MacDonald, RCNR	2/9/44	23/2/45	LT P. W. Lee, RCNVR	11/8/45	26/8/45
A/LCDR F. W. Bogardus, RCNVR	24/2/45	2/7/45	LT S. L. Slade, RCN	27/8/45	-
LT D. B. D. Ross, RCNVR	3/7/45	10/8/45			

Hallowell, October 1944.

HALLOWELL

BUILDER:	Canadian Vickers Ltd., Montreal, QC	LAUNCHED:	28/3/44
		COMMISSIONED:	8/8/44
LAID DOWN:	22/11/43	PAID OFF:	7/11/45

Commanding Officers

SKPR/LT E. S. N. Pleasance, RCNR	8/8/44	18/10/44	LT D. Davis, RCNVR	5/8/45	7/11/45
LCDR R. H. Angus, RCNVR	19/10/44	4/8/45			

Hallowell

Commissioned on 8 August 1944 at Montreal, *Hallowell* arrived at Halifax on 3 September and left a month later for Bermuda to work up. Returning early in November, she was allocated to EG C-1 and was Senior Officer's ship from December onward, remaining with the group until the end of the European war. She left St. John's 28 November to join convoy HX.322, and was thereafter continuously employed escorting North Atlantic convoys. Early in June 1945 she left Greenock for home, and in July and August was engaged in transporting troops from St. John's to Canada. She was paid off at Sydney on 7 November and placed in reserve at Shelburne. Sold to Uruguayan interests in 1946, she was resold to a Palestinian firm in 1949 for conversion to a short-service Mediterranean ferry and renamed *Sharon*. In 1952 she was acquired by the Israeli Navy, reconverted to a warship and renamed *Misnak*. In 1959 she was again sold, this time to the Singhalese (Sri Lanka) Navy and renamed *Gajabahu*. She was discarded in 1978.

Inch Arran

Commissioned on 8 November 1944 at Quebec City, *Inch Arran* left for Halifax on 3 December, visiting Dalhousie en route. In January she proceeded to Bermuda to work up, and on her return to Halifax on 4 February she was assigned to EG 28. She served for the rest of the war on A/S and support duties out of Halifax, and on 13 May escorted the surrendered *U 889* into Shelburne. Tropicalization refit, commenced on 6 June at Sydney, was suspended on 20 August, and the ship was paid off 28 November 1945. Placed in reserve at Shelburne, she was sold in 1946 to Marine Industries Ltd., but reacquired in 1951 by the RCN for conversion to a Prestonian class escort at Saint John. She was commissioned on 23 August 1954, serving on the east coast as a training ship until finally paid off on 23 June 1965. She was then acquired by the Kingston Mariner's Association for conversion to a nautical museum and youth club, but was eventually scrapped in 1970.

Inch Arran, November 1944.

INCH ARRAN

BUILDER:	Davie Shipbuilding and Repairing Co. Ltd., Lauzon, QC	PAID OFF:	28/11/45	
LAID DOWN:	25/10/43	RECOMMISSIONED AS PRESTONIAN:	23/8/54	
LAUNCHED:	6/6/44	PAID OFF (FINAL):	23/6/65	
COMMISSIONED:	18/11/44			

Commanding Officers

A/LCDR J. W. E. Hastings, RCNR	18/11/44	15/3/45	LCDR L. P. Denny, RCNR		8/8/45	28/11/45
LCDR F. A. Beck, RCNVR	16/3/45	23/3/45	LCDR P. C. H. Cooke, RCN		25/11/59	11/9/61
A/LCDR J. W. E. Hastings, RCNR	24/3/45	20/6/45	LCDR B. A. Mitchell, RCN		19/9/61	24/7/63
LT T. S. Dobson, RCNVR	21/6/45	7/8/45	LCDR C. R. Manifold, RCN		24/7/63	23/6/65

Lanark, 1944-45.

LANARK

BUILDER:	Canadian Vickers Ltd., Montreal, QC	LAUNCHED:	10/12/43	RECOMMISSIONED AS PRESTONIAN:	26/4/56
LAID DOWN:	25/9/43	COMMISSIONED:	6/7/44	PAID OFF (FINAL):	19/3/65
		PAID OFF:	24/10/45		

Commanding Officers

			LCDR R. W. Leslie, RCN	12/7/58	15/9/60
LCDR J. F. Stairs, RCNVR	6/7/44	5/4/45	LCDR C. H. P. Shaw, RCN	16/9/60	28/8/62
A/CDR B. D. L. Johnson, OBE, RCNR	6/4/45	9/5/45	LCDR J. M. Reid, RCN	29/8/62	22/4/64
LCDR J. F. Stairs, RCNVR	10/5/45	20/10/45	LCDR F. J. P. French, RCN	23/4/64	26/11/64
CDR W. M. Kidd, RCN	26/4/56	9/11/56	LT R. L. Clarke, RCN	27/11/64	15/12/64
LCDR P. H. Cayley, RCN	10/11/56	11/6/58	LT D. M. Swim, RCN	16/12/64	15/1/65
LCDR W. L. D. Farrell, RCN	12/6/58	11/7/58	LT J. T. Stuart, RCN	16/1/65	19/3/65

Lanark

Commissioned on 6 July 1944 at Montreal, *Lanark* arrived at Halifax on 28 July. She carried out workups in Bermuda in September and, returning to Halifax in October, was assigned to the newly formed EG C-7, Londonderry. She spent the balance of the European war on convoy duty, most of that time as Senior Officer's ship, and early in June 1945 sailed for home. In mid-July, she began tropicalization refit at Liverpool, Nova Scotia, but this was called off on 31 August and the ship was paid off at Sydney on 24 October. She was then placed in reserve at Shelburne, but was sold to Marine Industries Ltd. in 1946. Later repurchased by the RCN, she was converted to a Prestonian class ocean escort 1954-55, and on 26 April 1956 commissioned for training purposes on the east coast. She was paid off for the last time on 19 March 1965, and broken up at La Spezia, Italy the following year.

Lasalle

Commissioned on 29 June 1944 at Quebec City, she arrived in Bermuda on 31 August to carry out working up exercises. She left on 1 October for Halifax, there to become a member of the newly formed EG 27, and spent the remainder of the war in that area on A/S patrol and support duty. In June 1945 *Lasalle* sailed for the west coast and was paid off 17 December at Esquimalt. She was dismantled in 1947 and her hull expended as a breakwater in 1948 at Kelsey Bay, British Columbia.

Lasalle, 20 February 1945.

LASALLE

BUILDER:	Davie Shipbuilding and Repairing Co. Ltd., Lauzon, QC
LAID DOWN:	4/6/43
LAUNCHED:	12/11/43
COMMISSIONED:	29/6/44
PAID OFF:	17/12/45

Commanding Officers

LCDR F. A. Beck, RCNVR	29/6/44	2/7/45
LCDR R. D. Barrett, RCNR	3/7/45	14/11/45

LAUZON

BUILDER:	George T. Davie & Sons Ltd., Lauzon, QC	PAID OFF:	7/11/45
LAID DOWN:	2/7/43	RECOMMISSIONED	
LAUNCHED:	10/6/44	AS PRESTONIAN:	12/12/53
COMMISSIONED:	30/8/44	PAID OFF (FINAL):	24/5/63

Commanding Officers

LCDR W. Woods, OBE, RCNR	30/8/44	29/3/45	LCDR H. A. Porter, RCN	12/12/53	4/1/54
LCDR D. G. Jeffrey, DSO, RCNR	30/3/45	10/4/45	CDR M. J. A. T. Jette, RCN	5/1/54	17/7/55
A/LCDR J. B. Graham, RCNVR	11/4/45	29/6/45	LCDR J. C. Carter, RCN	18/7/55	12/4/57
SKPR/LT F. W. M. Drew, RCNR	30/6/45	3/11/45	LCDR D. O. Campfield, RCN	13/4/57	3/10/58
LT N. M. Stewart, RCNVR	4/11/45	7/11/45	LCDR W. G. Kinsman, DSC, RCN	5/6/59	-

Lauzon

Commissioned on 30 August 1944 at Quebec City, *Lauzon* arrived at Halifax in mid-October and in November spent three weeks working up in Bermuda. She arrived at St. John's 30 November to join EG C-6, and was continuously employed as a mid-ocean escort until VE Day. She left Londonderry 13 June for the last time, and that summer was employed as a troop carrier between St. John's and Quebec City. Paid off on 7 November 1945 she was laid up in reserve at Shelburne, Nova Scotia until purchased in 1946 by Marine Industries Ltd. The RCN reacquired her in 1951 for conversion to a Prestonian class ocean escort. She was recommissioned on 12 December 1953, and assumed a training role on the east coast until finally paid off on 24 May 1963. She was sold the following year to a Toronto buyer, presumably for scrap.

Lauzon, 1944-45.

Lévis (2nd)

Commissioned at Quebec City on 21 July 1944 she arrived in Bermuda at the end of August to work up, and a month later left for Halifax to join the newly formed EG 27. She spent the balance of the war with the group, on patrol and escort duty out of Halifax, and on 4 June commenced tropicalization at Lunenburg, Nova Scotia. The work was completed on 26 November and she sailed a month later for Esquimalt, arriving 30 January 1946. Paid off on 15 February to reserve there, she was sold in 1947 and her hull expended the following year as part of a breakwater at Oyster Bay, British Columbia.

Lévis (2nd), 5 July 1944.

LÉVIS (2nd)

BUILDER:	George T. Davie & Sons Ltd., Lauzon, QC			LAID DOWN:	25/2/43		COMMISSIONED:	21/7/44
				LAUNCHED:	26/11/43		PAID OFF:	15/2/46

Commanding Officers

LCDR P. C. Evans, RCNR	21/7/44	6/9/44	LCDR P. C. Evans, RCNR	18/9/44	19/9/45
LT P. T. Molson, RCNVR	7/9/44	17/9/44	LCDR P. C. Evans, RCNR	23/10/45	

Penetang

Commissioned on 19 October 1944 at Quebec City, she left on 6 November for Halifax and in December proceeded to Bermuda to work up. Returning northward in January 1945, *Penetang* joined convoy HX.331 at New York as local escort. She was allocated in February to EG C-9, and made the crossing to the group's Londonderry base as an escort to SC.168. She spent the rest of the war as a mid-ocean escort, returning to Canada in June 1945 to be employed as a troop carrier between St. John's and Quebec City. One of the new frigates not taken in hand for tropical-

ization, she was paid off on 10 November and laid up at Shelburne. She was sold in December to Marine Industries Ltd., but later reacquired and converted to a Prestonian class ocean escort, recommissioning on 1 June 1954. Again paid off on 2 September 1955, she was loaned to the Norwegian Navy on 10 March 1956 and renamed *Draug*. Transferred outright three years later, she served until 1966 and was then broken up.

Penetang.

PENETANG

BUILDER:	Davie Shipbuilding and Repairing Co. Ltd., Lauzon, QC		PAID OFF:	10/11/45
			RECOMMISSIONED	
LAID DOWN:	22/9/43		AS PRESTONIAN:	1/6/54
LAUNCHED:	6/7/44		PAID OFF (FINAL):	25/1/56
COMMISSIONED :	19/10/44			

Commanding Officers

A/LCDR A. R. Hicks, RCNVR	19/10/44	22/8/45	CDR V. Browne, RCN	5/11/54	13/12/54
LT E. M. Lutes, RCNVR	23/8/45	10/11/45	LCDR J. M. Paul, RCN	14/12/54	2/9/55
CDR B. P. Young, MBE, RCN	1/6/54	4/11/54	LCDR A. H. McDonald, RCN	5/1/56	25/1/56

Poundmaker

Poundmaker was commissioned on 17 September 1944 at Montreal, arrived at Halifax in October and worked up in Bermuda in November. In mid-December she arrived at St. John's to join EG C-8, serving as a mid-ocean escort for the rest of the war. She left Londonderry for the last time on 11 May 1945 to escort convoy ONS.50 westward, and on 31 May began tropicalization refit at Lunenburg. Work was completed on 20 August, and on 25 November she was paid off at Sydney and taken to Shelburne for disposal. She was sold to the Peruvian Navy in 1947 and renamed *Teniente Ferre* and in 1963, *Ferre*. Stricken from the Peruvian Navy list on 18 December 1965 and sold, she was towed to Chimbote for breaking up on 29 March 1968.

Poundmaker.

POUNDMAKER

BUILDER:	Canadian Vickers Ltd., Montreal, QC		LAUNCHED:	21/4/44	
			COMMISSIONED:	17/9/44	
LAID DOWN:	29/1/44		PAID OFF:	25/11/45	

Commanding Officers

LCDR H. S. Maxwell, RCNVR	17/9/44	14/4/45	A/LCDR A. E. Gough, RCNR	31/5/45	24/8/45
LCDR J. T. Band, RCNVR	15/4/45	19/4/45	LCDR W. P. Moffat, RCNVR	25/8/45	25/11/45
LCDR W. P. Moffat, RCNVR	20/4/45	30/5/45			

Prestonian 1944.

Prestonian

Commissioned 13 September 1944 at Quebec City, *Prestonian* arrived at Halifax the following month in need of repairs, and it was early January 1945 before she could go to Bermuda to work up. On her return to Canada she was assigned to EG 28, based at Halifax, and employed locally until VE Day. She then underwent tropicalization at Halifax, completing 20 August, and on 9 November was paid off and sold to Marine Industries Ltd. Later reacquired by the RCN, she was rebuilt to become the name-ship of the Prestonian ocean escort class. She was recommissioned on 22 August 1953, and finally paid off on 24 April 1956, having been lent to the Norwegian Navy. Renamed *Troll*, she was transferred outright in 1959, and in 1965 reclassified as a submarine depot ship and renamed *Horten*. She was discarded in 1972.

PRESTONIAN

BUILDER:	Davie Shipbuilding and Repairing Co. Ltd., Lauzon, QC		COMMISSIONED:	13/9/44
			PAID OFF:	9/11/45
LAID DOWN:	20/7/43		RECOMMISSIONED AS PRESTONIAN:	22/8/53
LAUNCHED:	22/6/44		PAID OFF (FINAL):	24/4/56

Commanding Officers

LCDR I. Angus, RCNVR	13/9/44	1/4/45	LCDR W. C. Spicer, RCN	22/8/53	9/6/55
LCDR G. N. Downey, RCNR	2/4/45	18/7/45	LCDR W. M. Kidd, RCN	10/6/55	24/4/56
LT E. M. More, RCNR	19/7/45	9/11/45			

Royalmount

Royalmount was commissioned at Montreal on 25 August 1944, arrived at Halifax on September 8 and carried out working up exercises in Bermuda later that month. She arrived at St. John's on 15 November to join EG C-1, and spent the remainder of the war with the group as a mid-ocean escort. She left Liverpool 21 April 1945 and escorted convoy ONS.48 on her homeward passage to refit at Sydney from 26 May to 5 October. She was paid off at Halifax on 17 November 1945 and placed in reserve in Bedford Basin until 1947, when a New York buyer purchased her for scrap.

Royalmount.

ROYALMOUNT			
BUILDER:	Canadian Vickers Ltd.,	LAUNCHED:	15/4/44
	Montreal, QC	COMMISSIONED:	25/8/44
LAID DOWN:	7/1/44	PAID OFF:	17/11/45

Commanding Officers

LCDR J. S. Davis, RCNVR	25/8/44	10/5/45
LT J. H. Dunne, RCNVR	11/5/45	8/8/45
LCDR J. S. Davis, RCNVR	9/8/45	17/11/45

Runnymede, December 1944.

Runnymede

Runnymede was commissioned on 14 June 1944 at Montreal and arrived in Bermuda for workups toward the end of July. On 21 August she returned to Halifax to become Senior Officer's ship of EG C-5, and was to wear its barber pole stripes the rest of her career. She left Londonderry toward the end of May 1945 and made her passage home as escort to convoy ON.305. She left Halifax on 20 June for Esquimalt, arriving 18 July, and early in August commenced tropicalization refit at North Vancouver. Work was soon suspended and she sailed for Esquimalt to be placed in reserve, though she was not paid off until 19 January 1946. Sold in 1947, she is reported to have been expended as part of a breakwater at Kelsey Bay, British Columbia, in 1948.

RUNNYMEDE			
BUILDER:	Canadian Vickers	LAUNCHED:	27/11/43
	Ltd., Montreal, QC	COMMISSIONED:	14/6/44
LAID DOWN:	11/9/43	PAID OFF:	19/1/46

Commanding Officers

A/LCDR R. C. Chenoweth, RCNVR	14/6/44	22/1/45
LT P. S. Milsom, MBE, RCNVR	23/1/45	22/3/45
LCDR R. C. Chenoweth, RCNVR	23/3/45	8/6/45
CDR C. A. King, DSO, DSC & Bar, RCNR	9/6/45	9/8/45

St. Pierre

Commissioned on 22 August 1944 at Quebec City, she arrived at Halifax in October and spent more than four months under repair. She carried out workups in Bermuda in March 1945 and on 5 April left for Londonderry via the Azores, having been assigned to EG 9. From Horta she picked up convoy SC.172, arriving at Derry on 21 April. On 13 May she left Greenock to escort convoy JW.67 to North Russia, but was detached three days later to accompany a number of surrendered U-boats bound from Trondheim to Loch Eriboll. She left the UK late that month for Canada, and on 4 June commenced tropicalization refit at Lauzon. The job was called off on 20 August and the ship paid off 22 November at Sydney, to be placed in reserve at Shelburne. In 1947 she was sold to the Peruvian Navy and renamed *Teniente Palacios*, shortened to *Palacios* in 1953. Stricken from the Peruvian Navy list on 18 December 1965 and sold, she was towed to Chimbote for breaking up on 29 March 1968.

St. Pierre, 1944.

ST. PIERRE

BUILDER:	Davie Shipbuilding and Repairing Co. Ltd., Lauzon, QC	LAUNCHED:	1/12/43
		COMMISSIONED:	22/8/44
LAID DOWN:	30/6/43	PAID OFF:	22/11/45

Commanding Officers

LCDR N. V. Clark, OBE, RCNR	22/8/44	13/11/44	A/LCDR A. E. Giffin, RCNVR	25/7/45	6/11/45
LCDR J. A. Tullis, RCNR	14/11/44	24/7/45	SKPR/LT E. L. Ritchie, RCNR	7/11/45	22/11/45

St. Stephen, 14 August 1944.

ST. STEPHEN

BUILDER:	Yarrows Ltd., Esquimalt, BC	COMMISSIONED:	28/7/44
LAID DOWN:	5/10/43	PAID OFF:	30/1/46
LAUNCHED:	6/2/44		

Commanding Officers

LCDR C. Peterson, RCNR	28/7/44	22/1/45	LCDR A. F. Pickard, OBE, RCNR	17/9/45	4/12/45
A/LCDR R. C. Chenoweth, RCNVR	23/1/45	22/3/45	LT W. G. Findlay, RCNR	5/12/45	30/1/46
LCDR N. S. C. Dickinson, RCNVR	23/3/45	8/8/45	LT E. M. Chadwick, RCN	27/9/47	25/8/49
LT G. F. Crosby, RCNVR	9/8/45	5/9/45	LCDR G. H. Hayes, DSC, RCN	26/8/49	31/8/50

St. Stephen

Commissioned on 28 July 1944 at Esquimalt, *St. Stephen* arrived at Halifax on 28 September and in October proceeded to Bermuda to work up. Returning in mid-November, she joined EG C-5 and spent the balance of the war as a mid-ocean escort. She left Barry, Wales, on 27 May 1945 to take passage home with convoy ON.305, and early in June began tropicalization refit at Dartmouth, Nova Scotia. This was cancelled in August and on 30 January 1946 the ship was paid off at Halifax and laid up in Bedford Basin. On 27 September 1947 she was recommissioned, having undergone alterations to fit her as a weather ship. She was stationed between Labrador and Greenland until August 1950, when she sailed to Esquimalt to be paid off on 31 August and lent to the Department of Transport. Retained primarily as a "spare" in the event of a mishap to *St. Catharines* or *Stone Town*, she was purchased by the Department in 1958. Ten years later she was sold to a Vancouver buyer, purportedly for conversion to a fish factory ship.

Ste. Thérèse, August 1945.

STE. THÉRÈSE

BUILDER:	Davie Shipbuilding and Repairing Co. Ltd., Lauzon, QC		
LAID DOWN:	18/5/43		
LAUNCHED:	16/10/43		
COMMISSIONED:	28/5/44		
PAID OFF:	22/11/45		
RECOMMISSIONED AS PRESTONIAN:	22/1/55		
PAID OFF (FINAL):	30/1/67		

Commanding Officers

A/CDR J. E. Mitchell, RCNVR	28/5/44	5/7/45
A/LCDR A. C. Campbell, RCNVR	6/7/45	4/9/45
LT J. Jackson, RCNVR	5/9/45	26/9/45
LT G. A. MacPherson, RCNVR	27/9/45	22/11/45
LCDR W. F. Potter, RCN	22/1/55	3/6/56
LCDR P. J. Pratley, RCN	4/6/56	12/1/58
LCDR A. R. Pickels, RCN	13/1/58	25/4/58
LCDR J. B. C. Carling, RCN	24/1/59	17/8/60
LCDR A. G. Murray, RCN	18/8/60	16/8/62
LCDR M. A. Martin, RCN	17/8/62	2/5/63
LCDR P. G. May, RCN	3/5/63	
LCDR K. M. Young, RCN	30/10/64	14/9/65
LCDR P. E. Simard, RCN	15/9/65	30/1/67

Ste. Thérèse

Commissioned on 28 May 1944 at Lévis, she arrived at Halifax early in July and, after preliminary workups in St. Margaret's Bay, proceeded to Bermuda to complete the process. Returning in mid-August, *Ste. Thérèse* left Halifax in late October to join convoy HX.317 for passage to Londonderry. There she joined EG 25 and served with it in UK waters until February 1945, when she was reassigned to EG 28, Halifax. She served locally with EG 28 until the end of the war, and on 22 November was paid off at Sydney and placed in reserve at Shelburne. She recommissioned on 22 January 1955, after conversion to a Prestonian class ocean escort, finally being paid off at Esquimalt on 30 January 1967. She was broken up in Japan that year.

Sea Cliff, 1944.

Sea Cliff

Sea Cliff was commissioned on 26 September 1944 at Quebec, and arrived at Halifax 20 October, proceeding to Bermuda in November to work up. On completion she sailed to St. John's to become a member of EG C-3, and left 23 December to join her first convoy, HX.237. She spent the remainder of the war on North Atlantic convoy duty, and on 21 May 1945 left Londonderry for the last time, to join ON.304 on her passage to Canada. She began tropicalization refit at Liverpool, Nova Scotia, on 10 June, but work was halted 28 August and the ship was paid off on 28 November. She was placed in reserve at Shelburne until 1946, when she was sold to the Chilean Navy and renamed *Covadonga*. She was broken up in 1968.

SEA CLIFF

BUILDER:	Davie Shipbuilding and Repairing Co. Ltd., Lauzon, QC		
LAID DOWN:	20/7/43		
LAUNCHED:	8/7/44		
COMMISSIONED:	26/9/44		
PAID OFF:	28/11/45		

Commanding Officer

LCDR J. E. Harrington, RCNVR	26/9/44	14/6/45

Stone Town

Commissioned at Montreal on 21 July 1944, *Stone Town* arrived at Halifax on 13 August, and on 3 September commenced a month's workups in Bermuda. On her return to Canada she was assigned to newly formed EG C-8 as Senior Officer's ship, and spent the balance of the war as a mid-ocean escort. She sailed from Londonderry on 12 May 1945 as escort to convoy ONS.50 on her way home, and on 22 July commenced tropicalization refit at Lunenburg. Work was stopped on 24 August and the ship was paid off on 13 November at Lunenburg, to be laid up in reserve at Shelburne. Sold to the Department of Transport for a weather ship, she was modified for the purpose at Halifax in 1950, and sailed that October for Esquimalt. In October 1967 she was replaced by CGS *Quadra* and sold in 1968 to a Vancouver buyer, purportedly for conversion to a fish factory ship.

Stone Town, June 1945.

STONE TOWN

BUILDER:	Canadian Vickers Ltd., Montreal, QC	LAUNCHED:	28/3/44
LAID DOWN:	17/11/43	COMMISSIONED:	21/7/44
		PAID OFF:	13/11/45

Commanding Officers

LCDR W. P. Moffatt, RCNVR	21/7/44	20/4/45	LCDR G. M. Kaizer, RCNR	20/8/45	13/11/45
A/LCDR J. T. Band, RCNVR	21/4/45	19/8/45			

Strathadam, 1944.

STRATHADAM

BUILDER:	Yarrows Ltd., Esquimalt, BC	COMMISSIONED:	29/9/44
LAID DOWN:	6/12/43	PAID OFF:	7/11/45
LAUNCHED:	20/3/44		

Commanding Officers

LCDR H. L. Quinn, DSC, RCNVR	29/9/44	6/7/45	LCDR H. L. Quinn, DSC, RCNVR	30/7/45	7/11/45
LCDR S. W. Howell, RCNR	7/7/45	29/7/45			

Strathadam

Commissioned on 29 September 1944 at Victoria, she arrived at Halifax on 21 November and left a month later for Bermuda to work up. Returning to Halifax, she was assigned to EG 25, Londonderry, and sailed from St. John's on 2 February 1945. Except for one trip later that month to Gibraltar, *Strathadam* was employed in UK waters until VE Day. On 7 March, with *La Hulloise* and *Thetford Mines*, she took part in the sinking of *U 1302* in St. George's Channel, and on 11 April she was carrying out another attack when a Hedgehog projectile exploded prematurely, killing six of her crew. She returned to Canada at the end of May, and in July commenced tropicalization refit. This was cancelled 20 August and the ship was paid off at Halifax on 7 November, to be laid up at Shelburne. She was sold to Uruguayan interests in 1947 but acquired by the Israeli Navy in 1950 and renamed *Misgav*. She was broken up in 1959.

Sussexvale

The last frigate launched for the RCN, *Sussexvale* was commissioned on 29 November 1944 at Quebec City, and arrived at Halifax on 16 December. She left on 8 January 1945 for a month's workups in Bermuda, on completion of which she was assigned to EG 26. She arrived in Londonderry to join the group on 6 March and spent the remainder of the war in UK waters, based primarily at Portsmouth. She returned home in May to begin tropicalization refit at Shelburne, but this was called off and the ship was paid off at Sydney on 16 November. Placed in reserve at Shelburne, she was subsequently sold to Marine Industries Ltd., but reacquired by the RCN and converted to a Prestonian class ocean escort. Recommissioned 18 January 1955, she served as a training ship until paid off on 6 December 1966. She was scrapped in Japan in 1967.

Sussexvale in the Channel, 1945.

SUSSEXVALE

BUILDER:	Davie Shipbuilding and Repairing Co. Ltd., Lauzon, QC	LAUNCHED:	12/7/44	RECOMMISSIONED	
		COMMISSIONED:	29/11/44	AS PRESTONIAN:	18/1/55
		PAID OFF:	16/11/45	PAID OFF (FINAL):	6/12/66
LAID DOWN:	15/11/43				

Commanding Officers

LCDR L. R. Pavillard, DSC, RCNR	29/11/44	16/11/45	CDR V. J. Murphy, RCN	28/11/58	26/4/60
CDR R. H. Leir, RCN	18/1/55	25/8/55	LCDR H. D. Joy, RCN	27/4/60	17/5/62
LCDR J. B. Young, RCN	26/8/55	20/11/56	LCDR A. N. Turner, RCN	18/5/62	26/7/64
LCDR E. P. Shaw, RCN	21/11/56	23/6/58	LCDR T. C. Shuckburgh, RCN	27/7/64	20/6/65
			LCDR F. W. Crickard, RCN	21/6/65	6/12/66

Toronto, 31 May 1945.

TORONTO

BUILDER:	Davie Shipbuilding and Repairing Co. Ltd., Lauzon, QC	LAUNCHED:	18/9/43	RECOMMISSIONED	
		COMMISSIONED:	6/5/44	AS PRESTONIAN:	25/11/53
		PAID OFF:	27/11/45	PAID OFF (FINAL):	14/4/56
LAID DOWN:	10/5/43				

Commanding Officers

LCDR H. K. Hill, RCNVR	6/5/44	17/3/45	LCDR W. D. F. Johnston, RCN	25/11/53	31/8/54
LCDR A. G. S. Griffin, RCNVR	18/3/45	17/6/45	LCDR A. H. MacDonald, RCN	1/9/54	3/1/56
A/LCDR E. B. Pearce, RCNVR	18/6/45	27/11/45	LCDR G. S. Clark, RCN	4/1/56	5/4/56
			LCDR W. W. MacColl, RCN	6/4/56	14/4/56

Toronto

Commissioned on 6 May 1944 at Lévis, she arrived at Halifax on 28 May, leaving on 18 June for a month's working up in Bermuda. In August *Toronto* was allocated to EG 16, Halifax, but for the next few weeks operated principally from Sydney. Following repairs in November she joined Halifax Force and was employed locally until May 1945, when she began five months' training duty at HMCS *Cornwallis*. Paid off on 27 November, she was placed in reserve at Shelburne, but was recommissioned on 25 November 1953, after conversion to a Prestonian class ocean escort. She was paid off for the last time on 14 April 1956, having been lent to the Norwegian Navy, which renamed her *Garm*. She was permanently transferred in 1959 and reclassed in 1964 as a torpedo boat depot ship. Simultaneously renamed *Valkyrien*, she served a further thirteen years before being disposed of.

Victoriaville

Commissioned on 11 November 1944 at Quebec City, *Victoriaville* arrived at Halifax on 3 December and late that month proceeded to Bermuda to work up. In February 1945 she was assigned to EG C-9, leaving Halifax on 27 February to join convoy SC.168 for her passage to Londonderry, where the group was based. *Victoriaville* spent the balance of the war on North Atlantic convoy duty. She left Barry, Wales, on 2 May to pick up convoy ON.300 on her way home to Canada, and on 12 May escorted the surrendered *U 190* into Bay Bulls, Newfoundland. She began tropicalization refit at Saint John, New Brunswick,

on 24 May but work was stopped on 20 August, and on 17 November the ship was paid off at Sydney and laid up at Shelburne. Subsequently sold to Marine Industries Ltd., she was reacquired by the RCN and recommissioned on 25 September 1959, following conversion to a Prestonian class ocean escort. On 21 December 1966 she assumed the name and duties of the retiring diving tender *Granby*, but was paid off 31 December 1973 and sold for scrap the following year.

Victoriaville, 1945.

VICTORIAVILLE

BUILDER:	George T. Davie & Sons Ltd., Lauzon, QC	PAID OFF:	17/11/45
LAID DOWN:	2/12/43	RECOMMISSIONED	
LAUNCHED:	23/6/44	AS PRESTONIAN:	25/9/59
COMMISSIONED:	11/11/44	PAID OFF (FINAL):	31/12/73

Commanding Officers

A/LCDR L. A. Hickey, MBE, RCNR	11/11/44	17/11/45	LCDR A. J. Norman, RCN	12/12/64	0/1/65
LCDR G. B. Wither, RCN	25/9/59	4/5/61	LCDR E. A. Makin, RCN	21/12/66	-
LCDR W. P. Rikely, RCN	5/5/61	10/3/63			

RIVER CLASS, ex-ROYAL NAVY

Annan

Named after a river in Scotland, *Annan* was transferred newly built from the RN to the RCN at Aberdeen on 13 January 1944. On completion of workups at Tobermory, she joined EG 6, Londonderry, for patrol and escort duties in UK waters. On 16 October 1944 while on A/S patrol south of the Faeroes, she sank *U 1006*, rescuing forty-six survivors. In April 1945 EG 6 was transferred to Halifax, but *Annan* sailed for the UK on 29 May and was handed back to the RN at

Annan, 25 September 1944. The gooseneck whaler davits were characteristic of the ex-RN frigates.

Sheerness on 20 June. That November she was sold to the Danish Navy and renamed *Niels Ebbesen*. She was broken up at Odense, Denmark, in 1963.

ANNAN

BUILDER:	Hall, Russell & Co. Ltd., Aberdeen, Scotland	LAUNCHED:	29/12/43
		COMMISSIONED:	13/1/44
LAID DOWN:	10/6/43	PAID OFF:	20/6/45

Commanding Officer

A/LCDR C. P. Balfry, RCNR	13/1/44	26/5/45

Ettrick

Named after a river in Scotland, *Ettrick* was completed in July 1943 as an RN ship and assigned to EG C-1, a Canadian escort group. On 29 January 1944 while undergoing a refit in Halifax, she was transferred to the RCN, and on completion of the refit on 6 May she was assigned to EG C-3. She arrived in Bermuda on 30 September for a month's working up, and on her return made two round trips to Londonderry with EG C-3 before being transferred in October to EG 27, Halifax. She was employed locally until VE Day, and on 30 May 1945 returned to the RN at Southampton. She was then converted to a combined operations HQ ship, though never employed as such, and in April 1946 was laid up at Harwich. In 1953 she was broken up at Grays, Essex.

Ettrick, December 1944.

ETTRICK

BUILDER:	John Crown & Sons Ltd., Sunderland, UK	LAUNCHED:	5/2/43
		COMMISSIONED:	29/1/44
LAID DOWN:	31/12/41	PAID OFF:	30/5/45

Commanding Officers

A/LCDR W. R. Stacey, RCNR	29/1/44	20/2/44	LCDR E. M. Moore, RCNR	16/3/44	28/4/45

Meon, May 1944.

MEON

BUILDER:	A. & J. Inglis Ltd., Glasgow, Scotland	LAUNCHED:	4/8/43
		COMMISSIONED:	7/2/44
LAID DOWN:	31/12/42	PAID OFF:	23/4/45

Commanding Officers

A/CDR St. C. Balfour, RCNVR	7/2/44	26/3/45	LT N. W. Adams, RCNVR	27/3/45	23/4/45

Meon

Named after an English river, *Meon* was completed in December 1943 at Glasgow and sailed on 16 January 1944 with convoy ON.220 for Canada. She was commissioned in the RCN at Halifax on 7 February, and in April worked up in St. Margaret's Bay. In May she was assigned to EG 9 and sailed with convoy HXM.289 to join EG 9 in Londonderry. For the next five months she was employed in UK coastal waters, and was present on D Day. She was then transferred to EG 27, Halifax, as Senior Officer's ship, arriving there on 19 October. Employed locally until 31 March 1945 she then left Halifax to join convoy HX.347 on passage to Britain, and was returned to the RN at Southampton on 23 April. Like *Ettrick*, she was converted to a combined operations HQ ship but was never used as such, and lay idle at Harwich for twenty years before being broken up at Blyth in 1966.

Monnow

Named after an English river, *Monnow* was transferred newly built to the RCN at Bristol on 8 March 1944. Following workups at Tobermory in April she joined EG C-2 in May and served with that group until August, when she was reassigned to EG 9, Londonderry. She served throughout her career in UK waters except for a round trip to Gibraltar in October 1944 and to Kola Inlet with convoys JW.62 and RA.62 in November and December. On 13 May 1945 she left Greenock to pick up JW.67 but was detached three days later to escort surrendered U-boats en route from Trondheim to Loch Eriboll. She left Londonderry on 25 May for Sheerness, where on 11 January she was paid off and returned to the RN. That October she was sold to the Danish Navy and renamed *Holger Danske*. She was broken up at Odense, Denmark in 1959. *Monnow* was one of two among the larger RCN warships that never saw a Canadian port.

Monnow. The unusually thick stanchions just ahead of the bridge support a "split" Hedgehog.

MONNOW

BUILDER:	Charles Hill & Sons Ltd., Bristol, UK	LAUNCHED:	4/12/43
LAID DOWN:	28/9/43	COMMISSIONED:	8/3/44
		PAID OFF:	11/1/45

Commanding Officers

| A/LCDR L. L. Foxall, RCNR | 8/3/44 | 16/7/44 | CDR E. G. Skinner, DSC, RCNR | 17/7/44 | 11/6/45 |

Nene at St. John's.

NENE

BUILDER:	Smith's Dock Co., South Bank-on-Tees, UK	LAUNCHED:	9/12/42
LAID DOWN:	20/6/42	COMMISSIONED:	6/4/44
		PAID OFF:	11/6/45

Commanding Officer

| LCDR E. R. Shaw, RCNR | 6/4/44 | 11/6/45 |

Nene

Named for an English river, *Nene* was completed in April 1943 as an RN ship but assigned to Canadian EG 5 based at St. John's. The group was renumbered EG 6 in November 1943 to avoid confusion with EG C-5. On 20 November *Nene*, with *Calgary* and *Snowberry*, sank *U 536* north of the Azores while escorting the combined convoys MKS.30 and SL.139. From February 1944 onward *Nene* was Senior Officer's ship of EG 6. She was transferred to the RCN at Halifax on 6 April 1944 immediately prior to a refit at Dartmouth, Nova Scotia which was not completed until mid-July. She then proceeded to Bermuda for workups, and in August joined EG C-5. After escorting three transatlantic convoys she was transferred in October 1944 to EG 9, Londonderry. Except for a trip to North Russia with convoy JW.62, *Nene* served in UK waters until the end of the war, based at various times at Londonderry, Plymouth, Rosyth, and Portsmouth. She left Greenock 13 May 1945 to join JW.67 for North Russia but was detached on 16 May to escort fourteen surrendered U-boats bound from Trondheim to Loch Eriboll. She arrived at Sheerness on 27 May and was handed back to the RN on 11 June, which placed her in reserve at Southampton. She was broken up at Briton Ferry, Wales, in 1955.

Ribble, 1944.

Ribble

Named for an English river, *Ribble* was built for the RN but commissioned in the RCN as a new ship at Blyth, UK, on 24 July 1944. After working up at Tobermory she arrived at Londonderry on 4 September to join the newly formed EG 26 the following month. She spent her whole career with this group, based much of the time at Portsmouth and Plymouth, and from 7 to 9 October 1944 towed the damaged HMCS *Chebogue* toward Swansea, Wales. She was paid off at Sheerness on 11 June 1945 and returned to the RN, and after twelve years in reserve at Harwich was broken up in 1957 at Blyth.

RIBBLE			
BUILDER:	Blyth Shipbuilding & Dry Dock Co. Ltd., Blyth, UK	LAUNCHED:	10/11/43
		COMMISSIONED:	24/7/44
		PAID OFF:	11/6/45
LAID DOWN:	31/12/42		
Commanding Officers			
LCDR A. B. Taylor, RCNR		24/7/44	20/11/44
A/LCDR A. A. R. Dykes, RCNR		21/11/44	11/6/45

Teme

Named after a river on the English-Welsh border, she was commissioned in the RCN at Middlesbrough on 28 February 1944. After working up, *Teme* was assigned in May to EG 6, Londonderry, and spent her whole career with this group. She was present on D Day, and on 10 June was rammed in the Channel by the escort carrier HMS *Tracker*, and cut almost in half abaft the bridge. She was towed by *Outremont* 200 miles to Cardiff, where she remained under repair until Christmas. In January 1945 she went to Tobermory to work up, returning to Londonderry on 9 February to rejoin her group. On 29 March, while escorting a coastal convoy, BTC.111, in the Channel off Falmouth, she was torpedoed by *U 246*, losing sixty feet of her stern. Surveyed at Falmouth, she was declared a constructive total loss, paid off on 4 May and handed back to the RN. She was broken up at Llanelly, Wales, in 1946.

TEME						
BUILDER:	Smith's Dock Co., South Bank-on-Tees, UK			LAUNCHED:	11/11/43	
LAID DOWN:	25/5/43			COMMISSIONED:	28/2/44	
				PAID OFF:	4/5/45	
Commanding Officers						
LCDR D. G. Jeffrey, DSO, RCNR	28/2/44	20/2/45	LT D. P. Harvey, RCNVR		21/2/45	4/5/45

Teme, 8 March 1944.

LOCH CLASS

PARTICULARS OF CLASS:	
DISPLACEMENT:	1,435
DIMENSIONS:	307' x 38' 7" x 8' 9"
SPEED:	19 kts
CREW:	8/133
ARMAMENT:	one 4-inch, six 20-mm, Squid

Loch Achanalt

Commissioned on 31 July 1944 at Leith, Scotland, she worked up at Tobermory and joined EG 6 in September at Londonderry. *Loch Achanalt* served with the group until VE Day on A/S patrol and support duty in UK waters, based for brief periods at Portsmouth and Plymouth. When the group was transferred to Halifax in April 1945 she accompanied it, but left Halifax on 29 May for Sheerness and there was paid off 20 June and returned to the RN. She remained in reserve at Sheerness until 1948, when she was sold to the Royal New Zealand Navy and renamed *Pukaki*. She was broken up at Hong Kong in 1966.

Loch Alvie

Commissioned on 10 August 1944 at Dalmuir, Scotland, she carried out workups at Tobermory and joined EG 9, Londonderry, in September. Briefly based at Portsmouth and Plymouth, *Loch Alvie* served in UK waters for the duration of the war, except for a trip to Gibraltar in October and to Iceland in March 1945 to escort convoy JW.67 to North Russia. She was detached from this convoy three days later to escort fourteen surrendered U-boats bound from Trondheim to Loch Eriboll. Like *Monnow*, she never saw a Canadian port. She was paid off at Sheerness on 11 July and returned to the RN, which laid her up in reserve there. She was later recommissioned for service in Far Eastern waters, following which she was laid up at Singapore. After being cannibalized for parts, she was broken up in 1965.

Loch Achanalt, August 1944.

LOCH ACHANALT

BUILDER:	Henry Robb Ltd., Leith, Scotland		LAUNCHED:	23/3/44
			COMMISSIONED:	31/7/44
LAID DOWN:	13/9/43		PAID OFF:	20/6/45

Commanding Officers

A/LCDR R. W. Hart, RCNVR	31/7/44	26/5/45	LT D. M. Saunders, RCNVR	27/5/45	20/6/45

Loch Alvie.

LOCH ALVIE

BUILDER:	Barclay, Curle & Co. Ltd., Glasgow, Scotland		LAUNCHED:	14/4/44
			COMMISSIONED:	10/8/44
LAID DOWN:	31/8/43		PAID OFF:	11/7/45

Commanding Officer

LCDR E. G. Old, RCNR	10/8/44	11/7/45

Loch Morlich

Commissioned on 7 July 1944 at Wallsend-on-Tyne, she joined EG 6 at Londonderry in September after working up at Tobermory. *Loch Morlich* remained with the group in UK waters until the end of the war, based for short periods at Portsmouth and Plymouth. In April 1945 the group was transferred to Halifax, but *Loch Morlich* left them on 29 May for Sheerness where, with *Loch Achanalt*, she was paid off on 20 June for return to the RN. She lay in reserve at Sheerness until 1949, when she was sold to the Royal New Zealand Navy and renamed *Tutira*. She was broken up at Hong Kong in 1966.

LOCH MORLICH					
BUILDER:	Swan Hunter & Wigham Richardson Ltd., Wallsend-on-Tyne, UK		LAUNCHED:	25/1/44	
			COMMISSIONED:	17/7/44	
LAID DOWN:	15/7/43		PAID OFF:	20/6/45	

Commanding Officers

LCDR L. L. Foxall, RCNR	17/7/44	25/5/45	A/LCDR T. Gilmour, RCNR	26/5/45	20/6/45

Corvettes

The corvette was designed by William Reed of Smith's Dock Co. near Middlesbrough, Yorkshire and patterned after his firm's whale-catcher, *Southern Pride*, of 1936. The proposed class name, "patrol vessel, whaler type" was not to Winston Churchill's liking, and he dubbed it "corvette" instead.

Impressed with the design, the Canadian Naval Staff ordered sixty-four corvettes early in 1940. Owing to their short length they could negotiate the St. Lawrence canal system, and many were to be built in Great Lakes shipyards. Ten, originally intended for the RN, were loaned to Canada and manned by RCN crews. Like their RN sisters, they bore the names of flowers, whereas the Canadian units were named for towns and cities. The ten were commissioned incomplete in Canada as RN ships, and sailed to UK yards for completion. There, on 15 May 1941 they were all formally commissioned as RCN ships.

Sixteen more corvettes were ordered under the 1940-41 Program, the first six identical to those built earlier but the remainder somewhat larger and of an improved design. In the original version the break in the fo'c's'le was located just ahead of the bridge, making the ship's low waist very wet in rough weather. In the improved design, the fo'c's'le was extended halfway aft and the bows given greater sheer and flare. All but twelve of the earlier corvettes had their fo'c's'les lengthened as the war progressed.

The last twenty-seven corvettes built in Canada differed little externally from the older ones but had twice the endurance—7,400 sea miles at 10 knots owing to increased fuel capacity. An additional four of these were acquired from the RN in exchange for Canadian-built minesweepers.

The corvette was originally designed as a coastal escort, but the shortage of ocean escorts forced it into the latter role throughout the worst years of the war. It met the challenge admirably, and in the process became the quintessential ship of the wartime RCN.

In 1944 a dozen Castle class corvettes were acquired, again in exchange for minesweepers. Originally named for British castles, they received town names in accordance with RCN practice. They were much larger than the Flower class, hence far more comfortable. They and the Loch class frigates were the only British ships of the period to be armed with the Squid, a triple-barrelled mortar which threw its projectiles ahead of the ship.

Unlike the frigates, the corvettes were nearly all disposed of at the war's end—most of them for scrap, some to minor navies, others to various mercantile pursuits including that of whale-catching.

FLOWER CLASS 1939-40 PROGRAM

PARTICULARS OF CLASS:	
DISPLACEMENT:	950
DIMENSIONS:	205' 1" x 33' 1" x 11' 6"
SPEED:	16 kts
CREW:	6/79
ARMAMENT:	one 4-inch one 2 pdr., two 20-mm, Hedgehog in many

Agassiz

Commissioned at Vancouver on 23 January 1941, *Agassiz* arrived at Halifax on 13 April and left on 23 May for St. John's to join the newly formed NEF. She sailed early in June with a convoy for Iceland and was thereafter in continuous service as an ocean escort until the end of 1943. In September 1941 she took part in a major battle around convoy SC.44 rescuing survivors of her torpedoed sister, HMCS *Lévis*. She was also part of the escort of the hard-pressed convoy ON.115 in July 1942. On 5 January 1943 she commenced a major refit at Liverpool, Nova Scotia, completing in mid-March, and in April was assigned to newly designated EG C-1. She arrived at New York on 16 December for another major refit, including extension of her fo'c's'le, completing 4 March 1944. After working up in St. Margaret's Bay in April, she joined EG W-2 of WLEF, transferring in August to W-7. She spent the remainder of the war with W-7, being paid off on 14 June 1945 at Sydney, and was broken up at Moncton in 1946.

Agassiz, May 1944.

AGASSIZ

BUILDER:	Burrard Dry Dock Co. Ltd., Vancouver, BC	COMMISSIONED:	23/1/41	
		PAID OFF:	14/6/45	
LAID DOWN:	29/4/40	FO'C'S'LE EXTENSION COMPLETED		
LAUNCHED:	15/8/40	New York City, N.Y.:	4/3/44	

Commanding Officers

LCDR B. D. L. Johnson, RCNR	23/1/41	14/3/43	A/LCDR F. E. Burrows, RCNVR	14/3/44	8/1/45
A/LCDR E. M. More, RCNR	15/3/43	13/3/44	LT J. P. Jarvis, RCNVR	9/1/45	-

Alberni

Commissioned at Esquimalt on 4 February 1941, *Alberni* arrived at Halifax on 13 April with *Agassiz*, and the two left on 23 May for St. John's to join the recently formed NEF. *Alberni* left the following month with a convoy for Iceland, serving as a mid-ocean escort until May 1942, when she was taken out of service to have a new furnace installed. In September 1941 she had taken part in the defence of convoy SC.42, which lost eighteen ships to as many U-boats. Assigned to duties in connection with the invasion of North Africa, she sailed for the UK in October with convoy HX.212, and until February 1943 escorted convoys between the UK and the Mediterranean. She returned to Halifax in March 1943 and served briefly with the WLEF before transferring to Quebec Force in May. For the next five months she escorted Quebec-Labrador convoys, leaving Gaspé on 6 November to undergo repairs at Liverpool, Nova Scotia. With repairs completed early in February, she proceeded to Bermuda to work up, and on her return to Halifax joined EG W-4. On 24 April she sailed for the UK for duties connected with the coming invasion, and was still engaged in these when, on 21 August 1944 she was torpedoed and sunk by *U 480*, southeast of the Isle of Wight. Fifty-nine of her ship's company lost their lives.

ALBERNI			
BUILDER:	Yarrows Ltd., Esquimalt, BC	COMMISSIONED:	4/2/41
		LOST:	21/8/44
LAID DOWN:	19/4/40	FO'C'S'LE EXTENSION:	
LAUNCHED:	22/8/40	Never done; ship lost	

Commanding Officers

LCDR G. O. Baugh, OBE, RCNR	4/2/41	4/4/42
LT A. W. Ford, RCNR	5/4/42	11/10/42
A/LCDR I. H. Bell, RCNVR	12/10/42	21/8/44

Algoma, 1941.

Algoma

Commissioned at Montreal on 11 July 1941, *Algoma* arrived at Halifax 18 July. She escorted her first convoy to Iceland in September, and was thereafter employed as an ocean escort until the end of May 1942. During this period she was involved in two major convoy actions: ONS.67 (February 1942) and ONS.92 (May 1942). In July 1942 after six weeks of repairs at Liverpool, Nova Scotia, she joined WLEF. In October, allocated to duties in connection with the invasion of North Africa, she left for Britain with convoy SC.107, which

lost fifteen ships to U-boat attacks. *Algoma* served under RN orders the next few months, escorting convoys between Britain and the Mediterranean. In February 1943 she was based at Bône, Algeria, but returned in April to St. John's via the UK She served briefly with Western Support Force based at St. John's, which existed only during May 1943, and with WLEF before joining Quebec Force in June. *Algoma* escorted Quebec-Labrador convoys until mid-November, when she was loaned to EG C-4 for one round trip to

the UK. She arrived at Liverpool, Nova Scotia, late in December for a major refit which included extending her fo'c's'le and was not completed until mid-April 1944. In May she joined EG C-5 and arrived in Bermuda on 1 June to work up.

Returning to St. John's on 27 June, she made three round trips to the UK before joining EG 41 (RN), Plymouth Command, in September. She was employed on patrol and escort duties in the Channel until the end of May 1945 when she

returned to Canada and was paid off 6 July for disposal at Sydney. In 1945 she was sold to the Venezuelan Navy, renamed *Constitución*, and was not discarded until 1962.

ALGOMA					
BUILDER:	Port Arthur Shipbuilding Co. Ltd., Port Arthur, ON		COMMISSIONED:	11/7/41	
			PAID OFF:	6/7/45	
LAID DOWN:	18/6/40		FO'C'S'LE EXTENSION COMPLETED		
LAUNCHED:	17/12/40		Liverpool, NS:	15/4/44	

Commanding Officers

LT J. Harding, RCNR	11/7/41	30/8/43	LT S. B. Kelly, RCNVR	27/3/44	5/4/44
A/LCDR J. P. Fraser, RCNR	1/9/43	10/10/43	LT L. F. Moore, RCNR	6/4/44	9/8/44
A/LCDR J. Harding, RCNR	11/10/43	3/2/44	LT W. Davenport, RCNR	10/8/44	24/8/44
LT E. R. Hammond, RCNVR	17/3/44	26/3/44	LT J. N. Finlayson, RCNVR	25/8/44	6/7/45

Amherst

Commissioned on 5 August 1941 at Saint John, New Brunswick, she arrived at Halifax on 22 August and after working up, joined Newfoundland Command in October. She was steadily employed as an ocean escort for the succeeding three years, during which time she was involved in two particularly hard-fought convoy battles: ON.127 (August 1942) and SC.107 (October 1942). She had joined EG C-4 in August 1942. Her only real respite was between May and November 1943 when she underwent a major refit at Charlottetown, including the extension of her fo'c's'le. After workups at Pictou, Nova Scotia, she returned to the North Atlantic until September 1944 when she began another long refit, this time at Liverpool, Nova Scotia. Following workups in Bermuda in January 1945 she joined Halifax Force, but in March was loaned to EG C-7 for one round trip to the UK. She was paid off 11 July 1945 at Sydney, and placed in reserve at Sorel. Sold in 1945, she was wrecked in the Gulf of St. Lawrence en route to become the Venezuelan Navy's *Carabobo*.

Amherst, 17 July 1941. A classic example of an early corvette in the original configuration of short fo'c's'le, foremast ahead of bridge, mainmast still fitted, and minesweeping gear aft.

AMHERST

BUILDER:	Saint John Dry Dock and Shipbuilding Co. Ltd., Saint John, NB		COMMISSIONED:	5/8/41	
			PAID OFF:	11/7/45	
LAID DOWN:	23/5/40		FO'C'S'LE EXTENSION COMPLETED		
LAUNCHED:	4/12/40		Charlottetown PEI:	1/11/43	

Commanding Officers

LCDR A. K. Young, RCNR	5/8/41	20/11/41	LT D. M. Fraser, RCNVR	25/5/44	16/12/44
LT H. G. Denyer, RCNR	21/11/41	19/9/42	LT K. W. Winsby, RCNVR	17/12/44	11/7/45
A/LCDR L. C. Audette, RCNVR	20/9/42	24/5/44			

Arrowhead, June 1942.

Arrowhead

Commissioned in the RN at Sorel on 22 November 1940, *Arrowhead* arrived at Halifax on 3 December, carried out workups and sailed on 21 January 1941 with convoy HX.104 for Sunderland. There she was in dockyard hands for the two months' work required to complete her fully. After working up at Tobermory, *Arrowhead* joined EG 4, Iceland Command (RN), and in June transferred to the newly formed NEF. For the rest of 1941 she escorted convoys between St. John's and Iceland, proceeding early in December to Charleston, South Carolina for refit. Returning to Halifax in February 1942 she made one round trip to Londonderry before joining WLEF. In July she transferred to Gulf Escort Force, escorting Quebec/Gaspé-Sydney convoys, and in October joined Halifax Force and for two months escorted Quebec-Labrador convoys. On 30 November she joined WLEF at Halifax, to remain with it until August 1944. When this escort force was divided into escort groups in June 1943 *Arrowhead* became a member of EG W-7, transferring to W-1 that December. During this period she underwent two refits: at Charleston, South Carolina, in the spring of 1943 and at Baltimore, Maryland, a year later. In September 1944 she joined Quebec Force and was again employed escorting Quebec-Labrador convoys. In December she transferred to EG W-8, WLEF, and served on the "triangle run" (Halifax, St. John's, New York/Boston) for the balance of the war. On 27 May 1945 *Arrowhead* left St. John's to join convoy HX.358 for passage to Britain, where she was paid off and returned to the RN on 27 June at Milford Haven. Sold in 1947 for conversion to a whale-catcher and renamed *Southern Larkspur*, she was finally broken up at Odense, Denmark, in 1959.

ARROWHEAD

BUILDER:	Marine Industries Ltd., Sorel, QC		PAID OFF:	27/6/45
LAID DOWN:	11/4/40		FO'C'S'LE EXTENSION COMPLETED	
LAUNCHED:	8/8/40		Charleston, SC:	2/1942
COMMISSIONED:	15/5/41			

Commanding Officers

LT V.H. Torraville, RCNVR	22/11/40	17/1/41	LT R. H. Sylvester, RCNVR	5/3/44	15/4/44
CDR E. G. Skinner, RCNR	18/1/41	19/4/43	SKPR/LT L. A. Hickey, RCNR	16/4/44	21/10/44
SKPR/LT L. A. Hickey, RCNR	20/4/43	10/2/44	LT R. H. Sylvester, RCNVR	22/10/44	27/6/45
LT W. P. Wickett, RCNVR	11/2/44	4/3/44			

ARVIDA					
BUILDER:	Morton Engineering and Dry Dock Co., Quebec City, QC	COMMISSIONED:	22/5/41		
		PAID OFF:	14/6/45		
LAID DOWN:	28/2/40	FO'C'S'LE EXTENSION COMPLETED			
LAUNCHED:	21/9/40	Baltimore, Md:	8/4/44		

Commanding Officers

LT A. I. MacKay, RCNR	22/5/41	20/9/42	LT D. W. G. Storey, RCNVR	5/12/44	30/12/44
A/LCDR D. G. King, RCNVR	21/9/42	15/3/44	LT J. C. P. Desrochers, RCNVR	31/12/44	17/1/45
LT D. W. G. Storey, RCNVR	16/3/44	19/11/44	LT D. W. G. Storey, RCNVR	18/1/45	14/6/45
SKPR/LT E. S. N. Pleasance, RCNR	20/11/44	4/12/44			

Arvida

Commissioned at Quebec City on 22 May 1941, *Arvida* arrived at Halifax on 6 June. She joined Sydney Force in July, acting as escort to local sections of transatlantic convoys until September, when she joined Newfoundland Command. She left Sydney on 5 September to join her maiden ocean convoy, SC.43 and was thereafter in almost continuous service as an ocean escort until the end of 1943. In June 1942 she became a member of EG C-4 and, in May 1943 of C-5. While escorting convoy ON.188 in mid-June 1943 she was damaged by her own depth charges and arrived at Iceland on 16 June for a week of repairs. Three of *Arvida*'s convoys received particularly rough handling by U-boats: ONS.92 (May 1942), ON.127 (September 1942), and SC.107 (November 1942). While with ON.127 she rescued survivors of HMCS *Ottawa* on 13 September. She had major refits at Saint John (January to April 1942); Lunenburg/Saint John (December 1942 to March 1943); and Baltimore, Maryland (January to April 1944). While at Baltimore she was given her extended fo'c'sle, afterward joining EG W-7 of WLEF. In mid-May 1944 she was sent to Bermuda to work up, returned to Halifax on 9 June, and in August joined EG W-2. In December she transferred to W-8, remaining with that group until the end of the war. *Arvida* was paid off on 14 June 1945 at Sorel and later sold for commercial use, entering service in 1948 as the Spanish-flag *La Ceiba*.

Baddeck

Commissioned at Quebec City on 18 May 1941, *Baddeck* arrived at Halifax on 29 May. She again left Quebec City late in June for Halifax, escorting SS *Lady Rodney*, but had to return to her builders at Lauzon owing to an engine breakdown. In September the two ships set out from Halifax for Jamaica, but again *Baddeck*'s engine failed, and she reached her destination only with difficulty. When further repairs had been completed, she was assigned to Newfoundland Command, leaving Sydney on 5 October for Iceland as ocean escort to convoy SC.48, which lost nine ships to U-boats. Engine repairs kept her at Hvalfjord, Iceland, until mid-December but failed to cure the problem and she was in dock at Halifax for the first six months of 1942. She worked up at Pictou in July 1942, then joined WLEF until allocated to duties in connection with the invasion of North Africa, arriving at Londonderry on 1 November. For the next four months she escorted UK-Mediterranean convoys, returning to Halifax on 4 April 1943. Later that month *Baddeck* was assigned to EG C-4 for two round trips to Londonderry, then in mid-July went to EG W-2, WLEF. In August she commenced a major refit at Liverpool, Nova Scotia, including fo'c's'le extension, and after working up in St. Margaret's Bay in January 1944 sailed in March to join EG 9, Londonderry. In April she transferred to Western Approaches Command for invasion escort duties, based at Portsmouth, and on 13 June beat off an attack by motor torpedo boats while so employed. In September she was transferred to Nore Command, based at Sheerness, escorting local convoys until her departure for home on 24 May 1945. She was paid off at Sorel on 4 July and sold for mercantile purposes in 1946, renamed *Efthalia*. After a number of name changes, she was lost ashore near Jeddah as the Greek-flag *Evi* on 11 March 1966.

BADDECK

BUILDER:	Davie Shipbuilding and Repairing Co. Ltd., Lauzon, QC	COMMISSIONED:	18/5/41
		PAID OFF:	4/7/45
LAID DOWN:	14/8/40	FO'C'S'LE EXTENSION COMPLETED	
LAUNCHED:	20/11/40	Liverpool, NS:	15/11/43

Commanding Officers

LT A. H. Easton, RCNR	18/5/41	5/4/42
LT W. E. Nicholson, RCNR	6/4/42	20/4/42
LT L. G. Cumming, RCNVR	21/4/12	5/10/42
LT J. Brock, RCNVR	6/10/42	17/10/43
LT G. C. Brown, RCNVR	18/10/43	19/4/44
A/LCDR F. G. Hutchings, RCNR	20/4/44	23/7/44
LT C. L. Campbell, RCNVR	24/7/44	14/10/44
LT D. H. Tozer, RCNVR	15/10/44	4/7/45

Barrie, 1945.

Barrie

Commissioned at Montreal on 12 May 1941, *Barrie* arrived at Halifax on 24 May and was initially employed as a local escort out of Sydney. On 5 September she left Sydney to join convoy SC.43 for Iceland, but defects necessitated her sailing on to Belfast for two months' refit. She served as a mid-ocean escort until May 1942, when she was assigned to WLEF on her return from Londonderry with ON.91, and she remained with this force until the end of the war. When individual escort groups were formed by WLEF in June 1943 she became a member of EG W-1, and continued so except for brief service with EG W-8 in the fall of 1944. In mid-March 1944 she commenced a long refit including fo'c's'le extension at Liverpool, Nova Scotia, working up at Bermuda afterward in August. On 19 May 1945 she left New York with HX.357, her last convoy, and was paid off on 26 June at Sorel. Sold for merchant service in 1947, she became the Argentinean *Gasestado* but was taken over by the Argentinean Navy in 1957 as a survey vessel and renamed *Capitan Canepa*. She was broken up in 1972.

BARRIE

BUILDER:	Collingwood Shipyards Ltd., Collingwood, ON	COMMISSIONED:	12/5/41
LAID DOWN:	4/4/40	PAID OFF:	26/6/45
LAUNCHED:	23/11/40	FO'C'S'LE EXTENSION COMPLETED	
		Liverpool, NS:	17/7/44

Commanding Officers

LT R. M. Mosher, RCNR	12/5/41	9/1/42	LT D. R. Watson, RCNR	9/10/43	18/3/44
CH/SKPR G. N. Downey, RCNR	10/1/42	28/3/42	LT H. O. Magill, RCNVR	19/3/44	15/6/44
A/LCDR R. M. Mosher, RCNR	29/3/42	13/3/43	LT W. D. Stokvis, RCNVR	16/6/44	26/6/45
LT H. O. Magill, RCNVR	14/3/43	8/10/43			

Battleford

Commissioned at Montreal on 31 July 1941, she arrived at Halifax on 4 August, remaining there for six weeks while undergoing repairs, radar installation, and workups. Briefly a member of Sydney Force, *Battleford* transferred to NEF and left Sydney on 28 November to escort convoy SC.57 to Iceland. Returning to Halifax on 7 January 1942 she went to Liverpool, Nova Scotia for a refit that kept her idle until the end of March. Arriving in the UK with a convoy early in May, she completed further repairs at Cardiff in mid-June, and then carried out workups at Tobermory. From July 1942 to May 1943 she was a member of EG C-1, and in December was escort to convoy ONS.154, which was badly mauled, losing fourteen ships. She participated with other RCN escorts in the destruction of *U 356* on 27 December. Arriving at Halifax on 23 April 1943 with her last ocean convoy, ONS.2, she commenced a two-month refit at Liverpool, Nova Scotia, joining EG W-4 of WLEF in mid-June. Early in April 1944 she commenced a long refit at Sydney, including fo'c's'le extension, following which she proceeded to Bermuda to work up. Returning to Halifax, she was employed for the balance of the war as a local escort with EG W-3 and was paid off at Sorel 18 July 1945. Sold to the Venezuelan Navy in 1945 and renamed *Libertad*, she was wrecked 12 April 1949.

Battleford, 1943.

BATTLEFORD

BUILDER:	Collingwood Shipyards Ltd., Collingwood, ON	COMMISSIONED:	31/7/41	
		PAID OFF:	18/7/45	
LAID DOWN:	30/9/40	FO'C'S'LE EXTENSION COMPLETED		
LAUNCHED:	15/4/41	Sydney, NS:	31/7/44	

Commanding Officers

LT R. J. Roberts, RCNR	31/7/41	5/10/42	LT H. H. Turnbull, RCNVR	8/5/44	19/6/44
LT F. A. Beck, RCNVR	6/10/42	5/7/43	LT P. A. F. Langlois, RCNVR	20/6/44	23/5/45
LCDR A. H. Easton, RCNR	6/7/43	20/8/43	LT F. D. Wickett, RCNVR	24/5/45	18/7/45
LT F. A. Beck, RCNVR	21/8/43	7/5/44			

Bittersweet about to be taken in tow by *Skeena*, May 1943.

BITTERSWEET

BUILDER:	Marine Industries Ltd., Sorel, QC	PAID OFF:	22/6/45
LAID DOWN:	17/4/40	FO'C'S'LE EXTENSION COMPLETED	
LAUNCHED:	12/9/40	Charleston, SC:	3/1942
COMMISSIONED:	15/5/41		

Commanding Officers

A/LCDR J. A. Woods, RCNR	23/1/41	30/11/42	LT F. W. Bogardus, RCNVR	10/7/44	7/12/44
LCDR F. B. Brooks-Hill, RCNVR	1/12/42	9/7/44	SKPR/LT F. C. Smith, RCNR	17/12/44	22/6/45

Bittersweet

Built at Sorel, *Bittersweet* was towed to Liverpool, Nova Scotia for completion so as not to be icebound. She was commissioned in the RCN 23 January 1941 at Halifax, and on 5 March left with convoy HX.113 for the Tyne. There, from 1 April to 6 June, the finishing touches were carried out, and after working up at Tobermory she left for Iceland on 27 June, having been assigned to Newfoundland Command. She was continuously employed as an ocean escort until 31 December 1941 when she arrived at Charleston, South Carolina, for refit including fo'c's'le extension, resuming her duties in March. *Bittersweet* served with EG C-5 and C-3 until October 1943, one of her most perilous convoys being ONS.192, which lost seven ships. She underwent a refit at Baltimore, Maryland, from October to November 1943, then proceeded to Pictou to work up. She then resumed her convoy duties, leaving Londonderry late in October 1944 to join her last convoy, ON.262. Upon arriving in Canada she went to Pictou to commence a refit that was completed at Halifax 10 February 1945. She was then assigned briefly to Halifax Force before transferring in April to Sydney Force, with which she remained until the end of the war. She was returned to the RN at Aberdeen on 22 June 1945 and broken up at Charlestown, Fife in 1950.

Brandon

Commissioned at Quebec City on 22 July 1941, *Brandon* arrived at Halifax 1 August. She joined Newfoundland Command in September after working up and left St. John's 26 September for her first convoy, SC.46. She served as an ocean escort to and from Iceland until December, when she arrived in the UK for three months' repairs at South Shields. From mid-March 1942, after three weeks' workups at Tobermory, she served on the Newfie-Derry run almost continuously until September 1944. From December 1942 onward, she served with EG C-4, helping defend the hard-pressed convoy HX.224 in February 1943 and in the following month escorting convoys t o and from Gibraltar. In August 1943 she began a three-month refit at Grimsby, England, including fo'c's'le extension. She left Londonderry 2 September 1944 to join her last transatlantic convoy, ONS.251, and after two-months' refit at Liverpool, Nova Scotia, worked up in Bermuda. On 5 February 1945 she arrived at St. John's to join EG W-5, Western Escort Force, in which she served until the end of the war. Paid off at Sorel on 22 June 1945 she was broken up at Hamilton, Ontario in 1945.

Brandon, in U.K. waters, 1942-43.

BRANDON

BUILDER:	Davie Shipbuilding and Repairing Co. Ltd., Lauzon, QC	COMMISSIONED:	22/7/41	
LAID DOWN:	10/10/40	PAID OFF:	22/6/45	
LAUNCHED:	29/4/41	FO'C'S'LE EXTENSION COMPLETED		
		Grimsby, UK:	10/10/43	

Commanding Officers

A/LCDR J. C. Littler, RCNR	22/7/41	19/8/42	LT H. E. McArthur, RCNVR	25/11/42	25/5/44
LT R. J. G. Johnson, RCNVR	20/8/42	20/9/42	LT J. F. Evans, RCNVR	26/5/44	26/4/45
A/LCDR J. C. Littler, RCNR	21/9/42	24/11/42	LT P. J. Lawrence, RCNR	27/4/45	22/6/45

Buctouche, December 1944.

BUCTOUCHE

BUILDER:	Davie Shipbuilding and Repairing Co. Ltd., Lauzon, QC	COMMISSIONED:	5/6/41	
LAID DOWN:	14/8/40	PAID OFF:	15/6/45	
LAUNCHED:	20/11/40	FO'C'S'LE EXTENSION COMPLETED		
		Saint John, NB:	29/1/44	

Commanding Officers

LT W. W. Hackney, RCNR	5/6/41	6/5/42	SKPR/LT E. S. N. Pleasance, RCNR	5/12/44	1/1/45
SKPR/LT G. N. Downey, RCNR	7/5/42	28/4/44	SKPR/LT H. E. Young, RCNR	2/1/45	15/6/45
SKPR/LT H. E. Young, RCNR	29/4/44	4/12/44			

Buctouche

Commissioned at Quebec City on 5 June 1941, *Buctouche* arrived at Halifax on 12 June. After working up she joined Newfoundland Force at St. John's on 28 July. On 26 August she left St. John's for Iceland with convoy SC.41 and thereafter escorted convoys to and from Iceland until January 1942, when Londonderry became the Eastern terminus. In June 1942 she was transferred to WLEF, with which she was to remain until the end of the war except for two months in the summer of 1944 when she was attached to Quebec Force. On 28 June 1944 she was damaged by grounding in Hamilton Inlet, Labrador, but made Pictou on her own for two months' repairs. After the formation of escort groups by WLEF in June 1943 *Buctouche* served principally with EG W-1. In October 1943 she commenced a four-month refit at Saint John, in the process acquiring an extended fo'c's'le. She was paid off at Sorel on 15 June 1945 and broken up at Hamilton, Ontario in 1949.

Camrose

Camrose, November 1943.

Commissioned at Sorel on 30 June 1941, *Camrose* arrived at Halifax on 6 July. She was assigned to Halifax Force after working up, but in October joined Newfoundland Command, leaving St. John's on 8 October for Iceland with convoy SC.48. She was employed as ocean escort to and from Iceland until February 1942, when she commenced a major refit at Lunenburg. Upon completion in May she resumed her mid-ocean escort duties for one round trip to Londonderry, but was assigned in June to WLEF. In October *Camrose* was allocated to duties concerned with the invasion of North Africa. She left Halifax on 20 October for the UK, and for the next five months escorted convoys between Britain and the Mediterranean. In April 1943 she proceeded to Pictou, Nova Scotia for a refit lasting five and a half months, including fo'c's'le extension, after which she worked up and was assigned to EG 6. She left St. John's early in December for Londonderry, where she was based for the next four months in support of convoys, especially to and from Freetown and Gibraltar. While with combined convoys OS.64/KMS.38, she shared with HMS *Bayntun* the sinking of *U 757* in the North Atlantic on 8 January 1944. In May she joined Western Approaches Command, Greenock, for invasion duties, escorting convoys to staging ports, and to and from Normandy beaches. She left the UK on 2 September for another refit at Pictou, followed by workups in Bermuda, returning in January 1945 to become a member of EG 41, Plymouth. She served with this group until VE Day, afterward participating in the re-occupation of St. Helier in the Channel Islands. *Camrose* left Greenock for home early in June 1945 and was paid off at Sydney on 18 July. She was broken up at Hamilton, Ontario in 1947.

CAMROSE			
BUILDER:	Marine Industries Ltd., Sorel, QC	COMMISSIONED:	30/6/41
LAID DOWN:	17/9/40	PAID OFF:	18/7/45
LAUNCHED:	16/11/40	FO'C'S'LE EXTENSION COMPLETED	
		Pictou, NS:	15/10/43

Commanding Officers

A/LCDR L. R. Pavillard, RCNR	30/6/41	7/11/44	LT J. B. Lamb, RCNVR	8/11/44	18/7/45

Chambly

Chambly, January 1945.

Commissioned at Quebec City on 18 December 1940, *Chambly* arrived at Halifax on 24 December. After working up she joined Halifax Force, and on 23 May 1941 left Halifax as one of the original seven corvettes forming NEF. She served continuously as an ocean escort between St. John's and Iceland until 8 December, when she returned to Halifax for refit. During this period she took part in two major convoy battles: HX.133 (June 1941) which lost six ships; and SC.42 (September 1941) which lost eighteen. In the latter case she had left St. John's on 5 September with *Moose Jaw* for exercises, and when SC.42 came under attack, they received permission to join the convoy off Greenland in support. Just before joining on 10 September, they came upon *U 501* trailing the convoy, and sank her. *Chambly* served as a mid-ocean escort to Iceland for the balance of 1941 and then underwent repairs at Halifax from 8 December 1941 to 22 February 1942. She then made a round trip to Londonderry as an escort in March 1942 and on her return to St. John's on 28

March, was based there to reinforce ocean escorts in the western Atlantic, doubling as a training ship. In September she resumed regular mid-ocean escort duties, with time out for refit at Liverpool, Nova Scotia, from 26 November 1942 to 13 February 1943. From March to August 1943 she was a member of EG C-2, then briefly joined the newly formed EG 9 at St. John's and, in September, EG 5. In December she returned to Liverpool, Nova Scotia for three months' refit including fo'c's'le extension. After workups in St. Margaret's Bay she resumed mid-ocean duties, this time with C-1, until her final departure from Londonderry on 11 March 1945. She was refitting at Louisbourg when the war ended, and was paid off and laid up at Sorel on 20 June. Sold in 1946 for conversion to a whale-catcher, she entered service in 1952 under the Dutch flag as *Sonja Vinke*, and was broken up at Santander, Spain, in 1966.

CHAMBLY

BUILDER:	Canadian Vickers Ltd., Montreal, QC	COMMISSIONED:	18/12/40
		PAID OFF:	20/6/45
LAID DOWN:	20/2/40	FO'C'S'LE EXTENSION COMPLETED	
LAUNCHED:	29/7/40	Liverpool, NS:	11/3/44

Commanding Officers

A/LCDR F. C. Smith, RCNR	18/12/40	25/3/41
CDR J. D. Prentice, RCN	26/3/41	13/11/42
A/LCDR A. F. Pickard, RCNR	14/11/42	26/1/44
LT S. D. Taylor, RCNR	27/1/44	22/6/44
LT H. A. Ovenden, RCNR	23/6/44	20/7/44
A/LCDR S. D. Taylor, RCNR	21/7/44	13/5/45
LCDR J. B. B. Shaw, RCNVR	14/5/45	20/6/45

Chicoutimi

Commissioned at Montreal on 12 May 1941, *Chicoutimi* arrived at Halifax on 17 May. She carried out workups and then joined Sydney Force, escorting ocean convoys on the first leg of their eastward journey. In September she joined Newfoundland Command and left Sydney on 29 September to escort convoy SC.47 to Iceland. She was employed for the next five months as an ocean escort between St. John's and Iceland, and later Londonderry. Reassigned to WLEF, she left Derry on 27 February 1942 to meet convoy ON.71. She served with WLEF until August 1944 (from June 1943 on with EG W-1), when she was transferred to HMCS *Cornwallis* as a training ship. In April 1945 she went to Sydney Force and on 16 June was paid off at Sorel for disposal. She was broken up at Hamilton, Ontario in 1946. A credit to her builders, Canadian Vickers, *Chicoutimi* required only three short refits during her active career, and she was one of the few corvettes to survive the war with a short fo'c's'le.

Chicoutimi, 6 September 1944.

CHICOUTIMI

BUILDER:	Canadian Vickers Ltd., Montreal, QC	COMMISSIONED:	12/5/41
LAID DOWN:	5/7/40	PAID OFF:	16/6/45
LAUNCHED:	16/10/40	FO'C'S'LE EXTENSION:	
		Never done	

Commanding Officers

LT W. Black, RCNR	12/5/41	10/5/42	LT A. E. Giffin, RCNVR	4/9/44	16/11/44
A/LCDR H. G. Dupont, RCNR	11/5/42	15/2/43	SKPR/LT C. C. Clattenburg, RCNR	17/11/44	26/11/44
LCDR J. F. Stairs, RCNVR	16/2/43	7/5/44	LT A. E. Giffin, RCNVR	27/11/44	14/4/45
LT F. Cross, RCNR	8/5/44	3/9/44	LT R. A. Wyllie, RCNVR	15/4/45	16/6/45

Chilliwack

Commissioned at Vancouver on 8 April 1941, *Chilliwack* arrived at Halifax on 19 June, was assigned to Newfoundland Command in July, and for the rest of the year escorted convoys between St. John's and Iceland. Early in February she escorted SC.67, her first transatlantic convoy, and was thereafter employed almost continuously as an ocean escort until November 1944. From June 1942 onward she was a member of EG C-1, and during this period escorted three convoys around which epic battles were fought: SC.94 (August 1942); ONS.154 (December 1942); and ON.166 (February 1943). In addition, she assisted in sinking two U-boats: *U 356* (when escort to ONS.154, 27 December 1942); and *U 744* (when escort to HX.280, 6 March 1944). In the course of a major refit from April to October 1943 at Dartmouth, Nova Scotia, she acquired her long fo'c's'le. Assigned on 4 December to EG W-8, WEF, she left for a month's workups in Bermuda. Reassigned in April 1945 to Halifax Force, she was temporarily loaned to EG C-1 the following month for one final round trip to Londonderry. Paid off 14 July and laid up at Sorel, she was broken up at Hamilton, Ontario in 1946.

Chilliwack, June 1942.

CHILLIWACK

BUILDER:	Burrard Dry Dock Co. Ltd., Vancouver, BC		COMMISSIONED:	8/4/41
LAID DOWN:	3/7/40		PAID OFF:	14/7/45
LAUNCHED:	14/9/40		FO'C'S'LE EXTENSION COMPLETED	
			Dartmouth, NS:	10/10/43

Commanding Officers

A/LCDR L. L. Foxall, RCNR	8/4/41	25/5/43
LCDR C. R. Coughlin, RCNVR	26/5/43	11/4/44
A/LCDR D. R. Watson, MBE, RCNR	12/4/44	14/7/45

Cobalt, 1942-43.

COBALT

BUILDER:	Port Arthur Shipbuilding Co. Ltd., Port Arthur, ON		COMMISSIONED:	25/11/40
LAID DOWN:	1/4/40		PAID OFF:	17/6/45
LAUNCHED:	17/8/40		FO'C'S'LE EXTENSION COMPLETED	
			Liverpool, NS:	20/7/44

Commanding Officers

A/LCDR R. B. Campbell, RCNR	25/11/40	19/5/41	A/LCDR R. A. Judges, RCNVR	6/5/43	3/3/44
LT C. J. Angus, RCNR	20/5/41	3/1/43	LT A. A. R. Dykes, RCNR	4/3/44	17/3/44
LT M. F. Oliver, RCNR	4/1/43	6/2/43	A/LCDR R. M. Wallace, RCNVR	26/6/44	17/6/45
LT C. J. Angus, RCNR	7/2/43	5/5/43			

Cobalt

Built at Port Arthur and commissioned there on 25 November 1940, *Cobalt* was taken to Halifax in advance of completion to beat the St. Lawrence freeze-up, arriving 24 December. Completing early in January 1941 she worked up and joined Halifax Force, but left on 23 May with the other six corvettes that first formed NEF. For the next six months she operated as an ocean escort between St. John's and Iceland, proceeding in mid-November to Liverpool, Nova Scotia for three months' refit. Following completion she made two round trips to Londonderry before being assigned in May 1942 to WLEF, with which she was to spend the balance of the war. She served with EG W-6 from June 1943; with W-5 from April 1944; and with W-7 from February 1945. During the second of two other extensive refits at Liverpool, Nova Scotia from April to 20 July 1944 her fo'c's'le was lengthened. She was paid off at Sorel on 17 June 1945 and subsequently sold for conversion to a whale-catcher, entering service in 1953 as the Dutch *Johanna W. Vinke*. On 31 December 1961 she suffered a boiler explosion while whaling, and was declared a constructive total loss. She was broken up at Cape Town in 1963.

Collingwood

The first RCN corvette to enter service, *Collingwood*, was commissioned on 9 November 1940 at Collingwood, arrived at Halifax 4 December, and joined Halifax Force in January 1941. She sailed on 23 May as one of the seven corvettes that were charter members of Newfoundland Command, and in June commenced six months' employment as an escort between St. John's and Iceland. Early in December she began a two-month refit at Halifax, following which she resumed mid-ocean escort duties between St. John's and Londonderry. These duties continued, with time off for three minor refits, until the end of 1944. From December 1942 onward she was a member of EG C-4. *Collingwood* was involved in one major convoy battle, that of HX.133 in June 1941, when eight ships were torpedoed and six sunk. During her refit at New York City from October to December 1943 she received her extended fo'c's'le. She left Londonderry on 16 November 1944 for the last time, refitted briefly at Liverpool, Nova Scotia and then went to Digby to serve as a training ship from April to June 1945. Paid off on 23 July 1945 and laid up at Sorel, she was broken up at Hamilton, Ontario in 1950.

Collingwood, September 1942.

COLLINGWOOD

BUILDER:	Collingwood Shipyards Ltd., Collingwood, ON	COMMISSIONED:	9/11/40
		PAID OFF:	23/7/45
LAID DOWN:	2/3/40	FO'C'S'LE EXTENSION COMPLETED	
LAUNCHED:	27/7/40	New York City, NY:	14/12/43

Commanding Officers

LT N. G. W. Bennett, RCNR	9/11/40	16/4/41	LT H. R. Knight, RCNR	5/7/44	2/5/45
A/LCDR W. Woods, RCNR	17/4/41	9/12/42	LT E. B. Pearce, RCNVR	3/5/45	17/6/45
LT D. W. Groos, RCN	10/12/42	5/6/43	SKPR/LT J. D. Burnham, RCNR	18/6/45	23/7/45
A/LCDR R. J. C. Pringle, RCNVR	6/6/43	4/7/44			

Dauphin, 1941.

DAUPHIN

BUILDER:	Canadian Vickers Ltd., Montreal, QC	PAID OFF:	20/6/45
LAID DOWN:	6/7/40	FO'C'S'LE EXTENSION COMPLETED	
LAUNCHED:	24/10/40	Pictou, NS:	5/9/43
COMMISSIONED:	17/5/41		

Commanding Officers

LCDR R. A. S. McNeil, OBE, RCNR	17/5/41	17/1/43	LT E. R. O'Kelly, RCNVR	11/10/44	20/6/45
A/LCDR M. H. Wallace, RCNR	18/1/43	10/10/44			

Dauphin

Commissioned at Montreal on 17 May 1941, *Dauphin* arrived at Halifax on 24 May. She joined Sydney Force late in June and in September transferred to Newfoundland Command. She left Sydney on 5 September to join her maiden convoy, SC.43, continuing on to the UK for further workups at Tobermory and returning to mid-ocean service in mid-October. *Dauphin* was almost continuously employed as an ocean escort until August 1944, after December 1942 as a member of EG A-3, (redesignated C-5 in June 1943). She escorted three particularly strenuous convoys: SC.100 (September 1942); ON.166 (February 1943); and SC.121 (March 1943). In the course of a major refit at Pictou from April to September 1943 her fo'c's'le was lengthened. *Dauphin* left Londonderry for the last time on 11 August 1944, underwent refit at Liverpool, Nova Scotia, then proceeded to Bermuda to work up. Returning in January 1945 she was assigned to EG W-7, Western Escort Force, for the balance of the war. She was paid off at Sorel on 20 June 1945 and sold for conversion to a merchant ship, entering service in 1946 as the Honduran *Cortes*. She became the Ecuadorian *San Antonio* in 1955, and still appeared in Lloyd's Register for 1987-88.

Dawson

Built at Victoria, *Dawson* was commissioned on 6 October 1941 and after working up joined Esquimalt Force for local patrol duty. On 20 August 1942 she arrived at Kodiak, Alaska to take part in the Aleutian campaign under US operational control, returning to Esquimalt 4 November. She resumed her duties with Esquimalt Force until February 1943 when she again proceeded to Alaskan waters to work with US naval units until the end of May. In September she commenced a major refit, including fo'c's'le extension, at Vancouver, worked up fol-lowing its completion 29 January 1944 and on 14 February left for Halifax. Arriving there 25 March, she joined EG W-7, WEF. Early in January 1945 she began a refit at Dartmouth, on completion of which in April she went to Bermuda to work up. The European war had ended by the time she returned, and she was paid off 19 June at Sorel. Sold for scrap, she foundered at Hamilton on 22 March 1946, but was raised and broken up.

Drumheller

Commissioned at Montreal on 13 September 1941, *Drumheller* arrived at Halifax on 25 September. She joined Sydney Force in November after completing workups, but soon afterward transferred to Newfoundland Command and left St. John's on 11 December to join her first convoy, SC.59, for Iceland. *Drumheller* was employed for two months on that convoy run, but on 6 February 1942 arrived at Londonderry—one of the first Canadian ships to do so. She left for St. John's the following week, but developed mechanical defects en route and returned to the UK to refit at Southampton. On completion of the repairs she arrived at Tobermory on 22 March to work up, resuming ocean escort service at the end of April as a member of EG C-2. She served with the group until April 1944 with respite only from mid-November 1943 to mid-January 1944 while undergoing a refit, including fo'c's'le extension, at New York City. Her most hectic convoy was the combined ON.202/ONS.18 of September 1943 which lost six merchant vessels and three escorts. On 13 May 1943 while escorting HX.237 she, HMS *Lagan*, and a Sunderland aircraft collaborated in sinking *U 456*. In April 1944 *Drumheller* was allocated to Western Approaches Command, Greenock, for invasion duties, transferring in September to Portsmouth Command and in November to Nore Command. She served with the latter until the end of the war, escorting convoys in UK coastal waters, and returned to Canada in mid-May 1945. Paid off on 11 July 1945 at Sydney, she was broken up in 1949 at Hamilton, Ontario.

Dawson, 6 July, 1942.

Drumheller, 1942.

DAWSON

BUILDER:	Victoria Machinery Depot Co. Ltd., Victoria, BC
LAID DOWN:	7/9/40
LAUNCHED:	8/2/41
COMMISSIONED:	6/10/41
PAID OFF:	19/6/45
FO'C'S'LE EXTENSION COMPLETED Vancouver, BC:	29/1/44

Commanding Officers

A/LCDR A. H. G. Storrs, RCNR	6/10/41	7/6/43
A/LCDR T. P. Ryan, OBE, RCNR	8/6/43	30/3/44
SKPR/LT J.B. Cooper, RCNR	31/3/44	19/6/45

DRUMHELLER

BUILDER:	Collingwood Shipyards Ltd., Collingwood, ON
LAID DOWN:	4/12/40
LAUNCHED:	5/7/41
COMMISSIONED:	13/9/41
PAID OFF:	11/7/45
FO'C'S'LE EXTENSION COMPLETED New York City, NY:	15/1/44

Commanding Officers

A/CDR G. H. Griffiths, RCN	13/9/41	15/10/42
LT L. P. Denny, RCNR	16/10/42	20/8/43
LCDR A. H. G. Storrs, RCNR	21/8/43	26/9/43
LT L. P. Denny, RCNR	27/9/43	7/12/43
LT H. R. Beck, RCNR	28/12/43	11/7/45

Dunvegan

Named for a village in Nova Scotia, *Dunvegan* was commissioned at Sorel on 9 September 1941, and arrived at Halifax a week later. She joined Sydney Force after working up, but in mid-November was transferred to Newfoundland Command, leaving St. John's on 18 November as ocean escort to convoy SC.55 as far as Iceland. On her return she underwent repairs at Halifax, and on their completion in January 1942 was assigned briefly to WLEF. Resuming her duties as ocean escort with Newfoundland Command, she arrived at Londonderry on 10 March. In succeeding weeks she made two more round trips to Derry, leaving that port for the last time in mid-June 1942. On reaching Halifax, she was assigned to WLEF and in June 1943 to its EG W-8. In October 1943 she proceeded to Baltimore, Maryland, for a refit which included fo'c's'le extension and lasted until the end of the year. She then carried out workups at Norfolk, Virginia, completing the process in Bermuda after some repairs at Halifax. On her return she resumed her duties with WLEF, from April 1944 onwards as a member of EG W-6. On 7 May 1945 she left Halifax as a local escort to convoy SC.175, but was detached on 10 May to act, with HMCS *Rockcliffe*, as escort to the surrendered *U 889*. She was paid off on 3 July 1945 at Sydney and sold in 1945 to the Venezuelan Navy, serving as *Indepencia* until broken up in 1953.

Edmundston

Commissioned at Esquimalt on 21 October 1941, *Edmundston* was assigned after workups to Esquimalt Force. On 20 June 1942 she rescued thirty-one crew members of SS *Fort Camosun*, disabled by a torpedo from the Japanese submarine *I-25* off the coast of Washington. She left Esquimalt for the Atlantic on 13 September, arriving at Halifax on 13 October, and was assigned to WLEF. On 4 January 1943 she commenced a five-month refit at Halifax, including fo'c's'le extension, carried out workups at Pictou, then joined EG 5 at St. John's. For the next ten months she was employed in support of North Atlantic, Gibraltar, and Sierra Leone convoys. She underwent a refit at Liverpool, Nova Scotia from May to July 1944, worked up in Bermuda in August, and in October joined the newly formed EG C-8. She served the remainder of the war as an ocean escort, leaving Londonderry on 11 May 1945 for the last time. She was paid off at Sorel on 16 June and sold for mercantile use, entering service in 1948 as *Amapala*, last noted under Liberian flag in Lloyd's list for 1961-62.

DUNVEGAN

BUILDER:	Marine Industries Ltd., Sorel, QC
LAID DOWN:	30/8/40
LAUNCHED:	11/12/40
COMMISSIONED:	9/9/41
PAID OFF:	3/7/45
FO'C'S'LE EXTENSION COMPLETED	
Baltimore, MD:	27/12/43

Commanding Officers

LT J. A. Tullis, RCNR	9/9/41	5/2/43
LT J.W. E. Hastings, RCNR	6/2/43	30/6/43
LT J. A. Tullis, RCNR	1/7/43	5/7/44
LT J. A. Rankin, RCNR	6/7/44	11/3/45
LT R. L. B. Hunter, RCNVR	12/3/45	3/7/45

EDMUNDSTON

BUILDER:	Yarrows Ltd., Esquimalt, BC
LAID DOWN:	23/8/40
LAUNCHED:	22/2/41
COMMISSIONED:	21/10/41
PAID OFF:	16/6/45
FO'C'S'LE EXTENSION COMPLETED	
Halifax, NS:	3/6/43

Commanding Officers

A/LCDR R. D. Bennett, RCNR	21/10/41	21/5/44
LT J. Lecky, RCNVR	22/5/44	20/4/45
LT A. D. Ritchie, RCNVR	21/4/45	27/5/45
LT J. Lecky, RCNVR	28/5/45	16/6/45

Dunvegan, 7 August 1943.

Edmundston, Bermuda, August-September 1944.

Eyebright

Commissioned in the RN in Montreal on 26 November 1940, she arrived incomplete at Halifax on 11 December, and after working up, left on 21 January 1941 with convoy HX.104 for Sunderland. There she was completed on 16 April, and proceeded to Tobermory to work up. In May *Eyebright* was allocated to EG 4 (RN) based at Iceland, whence she sailed on 12 June to join convoy OB.332 for Halifax. She joined Newfoundland Command in June and for the next five months was employed as escort to convoys between St. John's and Iceland. In November she began a refit at Charleston, South Carolina which included fo'c's'le extension. Resuming escort duty late in January 1942, she arrived at Londonderry with her first transatlantic convoy, SC.66, on 6 February. In January 1943 she joined EG C-3, and that July commenced two months' refit at Baltimore, Maryland. Following repairs at Pictou and workups at Bermuda in the summer of 1944 she joined EG W-3, WLEF, and saw continuous service in the western Atlantic until the end of the war, with one further round trip to Londonderry as a temporary member of EG C-5. *Eyebright* was returned to the RN at Belfast on 17 June 1945 and sold in 1947 for conversion to a whale-catcher. She entered service in 1950 as the Dutch *Albert W. Vinke*, and was broken up at Cape Town in 1964-65.

Eyebright, 1942-43.

EYEBRIGHT

BUILDER:	Canadian Vickers Ltd., Montreal, QC	COMMISSIONED:	15/5/41
LAID DOWN:	20/2/40	PAID OFF:	17/6/45
LAUNCHED:	22/7/40	FO'C'S'LE EXTENSION COMPLETED	
		Charleston, SC:	1/1942

Commanding Officers

LT E. Randell, RCNR		26/11/40	24/6/41	LT H. L. Quinn, RCNVR	7/2/43	1/9/44
LCDR H. C. R. Davis, RCNR		25/6/41	6/2/43	LT R. J. Margesson, RCNVR	2/9/44	17/6/45

Fennel, 1942.

FENNEL

BUILDER:	Marine Industries Ltd., Sorel, QC	PAID OFF:	12/6/45
LAID DOWN:	29/3/40	FO'C'S'LE EXTENSION COMPLETED	
LAUNCHED:	20/8/40	New York, NY:	6/9/42
COMMISSIONED:	15/5/41		

Commanding Officers

LCDR J. N. Smith, RCNR	16/1/41	31/10/41	A/LCDR W. P. Moffatt, RCNVR	6/9/43	15/5/44
LT J. M. Gillison, RCNR	1/11/41	26/5/42	LCDR K. L. Johnson, RCNVR	16/5/44	12/6/45
LCDR R. B. Warwick, RCNVR	27/5/42	5/9/43			

Fennel

Built at Sorel, she was towed in December 1940 to Liverpool, Nova Scotia for completion and commissioned there on 15 January 1941. She left Halifax on 5 March with convoy HX.113 for the UK, and while there received finishing touches at Greenock. Following workups at Tobermory in June *Fennel* was assigned to NEF, first serving as an ocean escort between St. John's and Iceland, then between St. John's and Londonderry. In June 1942 she commenced a year's service with the newly formed WLEF. She underwent a refit, including fo'c's'le extension, at New York from mid-July to late September 1942. In June 1943 she was detached to EG C-2 for one round trip to Derry, and on returning she went to Baltimore, Maryland for a refit, completing on 6 September. After working up at Pictou she resumed her ocean escort duties with C-2, and on 6 March 1944 was one of seven escorts of HX.280 that hounded *U 744* to its death. In August she had two months' refit at Pictou, followed by three weeks' workups in Bermuda, and at year's end transferred to EG C-1 for the duration of the war. *Fennel* arrived at Greenock 29 May 1945 from one of the last convoys, and was returned to the RN at Londonderry on 12 June. She was sold in 1946 for conversion to a whale-catcher, entering service in 1948 as the Norwegian *Milliam Kihl*. She was broken up at Grimstad, Norway in 1966.

Galt

Commissioned on 15 May 1941 at Montreal, *Galt* arrived at Halifax 6 June. She was assigned in July to NEF and left St. John's on 25 August with SC.41, her first convoy, for Iceland. She was to serve on that route until January 1942. In February 1942 she commenced a refit at Liverpool, Nova Scotia which was completed on 11 May, and after working up in June was assigned to EG C-3. She arrived at Londonderry for the first time on 5 June from convoy HX.191, and served on the Newfie-Derry run for the balance of the year. She arrived 4 January 1943 at Liverpool, Nova Scotia for another refit which was completed at Halifax in mid-April, worked up in St. Margaret's Bay, and in June joined EG C-1. She left Halifax 13 March 1944 for New York for yet another refit, this one including fo'c's'le extension, completing early in May, and a month later left Halifax for Bermuda to work up. On her return she was allocated for the balance of the war to EG W-5, WEF. *Galt* was paid off 21 June 1945 at Sorel, and broken up at Hamilton in 1946.

Hepatica

Commissioned in the RN on 12 November 1940 at Quebec City, *Hepatica* arrived at Halifax on 17 November and left on 18 December with convoy HX.97, armed with a dummy 4-inch gun. The real thing was installed, and other deficiencies remedied at Greenock, completing on 6 March 1941. After working up in April, she joined EG 4, Greenock. In June, after brief service as a UK-Iceland escort, she was assigned to NEF for the rest of the year, escorting convoys between Iceland and St. John's. Late in January 1942 she escorted SC 64, the inaugural Newfie-Derry convoy, and for the next three months served on that run. In June she joined the Tanker Escort Force, operating from Halifax, for one round trip to Trinidad and then, late in July, joined Gulf Escort Force as a Quebec-Sydney convoy escort. In October she was reassigned to Halifax Force escorting Quebec-Labrador convoys, and in December to WLEF. She was to serve with WLEF for the remainder of the war, from June 1943 as a member of EG W-5 and from April 1944 with W-4. During this period *Hepatica* had two extensive refits, from 11 February to 1 April 1943 and 20 March to 8 June 1944, both at New York. The former refit included the lengthening of her fo'c's'le, and the latter was followed by three weeks' workups in Bermuda. She left St. John's 27 May 1945 as escort to HX.358, and on 27 June was handed over to the RN at Milford Haven. She was broken up at Llanelly, Wales in 1948.

GALT		
BUILDER:	Collingwood Shipyards Ltd., Collingwood, ON	
LAID DOWN:	27/5/40	
LAUNCHED:	28/12/40	
COMMISSIONED:	15/5/41	
PAID OFF:	21/6/45	
FO'C'S'LE EXTENSION COMPLETED		
New York City, NY:	8/5/44	

Commanding Officers

LT A. D. Landles, RCNR	15/5/41	10/3/43
LT A. M. Kirkpatrick, RCNVR	11/3/43	30/3/44
LT E. P. Taylor, RCNVR	31/3/44	24/4/45
LT J. G. Lorriman, RCNVR	25/4/45	19/6/45
LT E. P. Taylor, RCNVR	20/6/45	21/6/45

HEPATICA		
BUILDER:	Davie Shipbuilding and Repairing Co. Ltd., Lauzon, QC	
LAID DOWN:	24/2/40	
LAUNCHED:	6/7/40	
COMMISSIONED:	15/5/41	
PAID OFF:	27/6/45	
FO'C'S'LE EXTENSION COMPLETED		
New York City, NY:	1/4/43	

Commanding Officers

LT C.W. Copelin, RCNR	12/11/40	31/10/41
LCDR T. Gilmour, RCNR	1/11/41	11/4/43
LT H. E. Lade, RCNR	12/4/43	5/9/43
LT J. A. Ferguson, RCNR	6/9/43	4/11/44
LT E. M. Lutes, RCNVR	5/11/44	27/6/45

Galt, 1942.

Hepatica, 1941-42.

Kamloops

Commissioned at Victoria on 17 March 1941, *Kamloops* arrived at Halifax on 19 June and was assigned to Halifax Force, serving as a local escort until the end of the year. In January 1942 she commenced a year's duty as A/S training ship at Halifax and Pictou. In mid-February 1943 she completed a three-month refit at Liverpool, Nova Scotia, and after working up at Halifax joined WLEF in March. She transferred in June to EG C-2, Newfoundland Command, and served with this group as an ocean escort for the remainder of the war. In September 1943 she was with combined convoy ON.202/ONS.18, which lost six merchant ships and three of its escorts. In mid-December she began a refit at Charlottetown, completed on 25 April 1944, in the course of which her fo'c's'le was extended. Following workups in Bermuda in June she rejoined EG C-2. She was paid off at Sorel 27 June 1945 and sold in 1946 to an Amherstburg, Ontario tug operator.

Kamloops, 1943-44.

KAMLOOPS

BUILDER:	Victoria Machinery Depot Co. Ltd., Victoria, BC		COMMISSIONED:	17/3/41
			PAID OFF:	27/6/45
LAID DOWN:	29/4/40		FO'C'S'LE EXTENSION COMPLETED	
LAUNCHED:	7/8/40		Charlottetown, PEI:	25/4/44

Commanding Officers

LT J. M. Gillison, RCNR	17/3/41	31/10/41	LCDR J. H. S. MacDonald, RCNR	17/2/43	1/3/43
LT P. J. B. Watts, RCNR	1/11/41	4/2/42	LT D. M. Stewart, RCNR	2/3/43	5/11/43
LT I. W. McTavish, RCNR	5/2/42	27/3/42	LT S. D. Taylor, RCNR	6/11/43	20/12/43
A/LCDR J. H. Marshall, RCNVR	28/3/42	22/8/42	A/LCDR D. M. Stewart, RCNR	21/12/43	27/6/45
LT N. S. C. Dickinson, RCNVR	23/8/42	10/1/43			

Kamsack, May 1944.

KAMSACK

BUILDER:	Port Arthur Shipbuilding Co. Ltd., Port Arthur, ON		COMMISSIONED:	4/10/41
			PAID OFF:	22/7/45
LAID DOWN:	20/11/40		FO'C'S'LE EXTENSION COMPLETED	
LAUNCHED:	5/5/41		Baltimore, MD:	14/3/44

Commanding Officers

LT E. Randell, RCNR	4/10/41	17/5/43	LT J. F. Carmichael, RCNR	9/2/44	10/5/45
LCDR W. C. Halliday, RCNR	18/5/43	8/2/44	LCDR R. F. Wilson, RCNVR	11/5/45	22/7/45

Kamsack

Commissioned at Montreal on 4 October 1941, *Kamsack* arrived at Halifax on 13 October. She joined Sydney Force the following month but shortly transferred to Newfoundland Command and on 19 January 1942 left St. John's to pick up convoy SC.65 for Londonderry. In June, after three round trips she was reassigned to WLEF, then forming, and served in it for the rest of the war. From June 1943 she was a member of EG W-4, and from April 1944 a member of EG W-3. During this period she had two extensive refits: the first, begun at Liverpool, Nova Scotia on 12 November 1942, was completed at Halifax on 18 January 1943; the second, in the course of which her fo'c's'le was extended, was carried out at Baltimore, Maryland, between late December 1943 and mid-March 1944. *Kamsack* was paid off on 22 July 1945 at Sorel and sold to the Venezuelan Navy. Renamed *Federación*, she served until broken up in 1956.

Kenogami

Commissioned at Montreal on 29 June 1941, *Kenogami* arrived at Halifax on 4 July. She served briefly with Halifax Force before arriving at St. John's on 24 August to join Newfoundland Command. She sailed on 1 September to join convoy SC.42 for Iceland, but remained with the convoy all the way to the UK, as it lost eighteen ships in what proved to be one of the worst convoy battles of the war. In February 1942 after five months' ocean escort duty between St. John's and Iceland, she made her first trip to Londonderry, joining WLEF on her return. She received an extensive refit at Halifax through June and July, and in October resumed her ocean escort duties with EG C-1. The following month she took part in another fierce convoy battle, that of ONS.154, which lost fourteen ships. In March 1943 she made one round trip to Gibraltar, escorting follow-up convoys to the invasion of North Africa. On 11 May she left Derry for the last time attached to EG B-4 (RN) with convoy ON.183. After a two-month refit at Liverpool, Nova Scotia and workups at Pictou, she joined WLEF's EG W-8. In April 1944 she transferred to W-4, but in December rejoined W-8 for the balance of the war. During this period she underwent a major refit at Liverpool, Nova Scotia between June and October 1944, including fo'c's'le extension, followed by three weeks' workups in Bermuda. She was paid off 9 July 1945 at Sydney and broken up at Hamilton in 1950.

Lethbridge

Commissioned at Montreal on 25 June 1941, *Lethbridge* arrived at Halifax on 4 July. She served briefly with Sydney Force before joining NEF and leaving Sydney on 11 October with convoy SC.49 for Iceland. She was employed between St. John's and Iceland until February 1942 and thereafter on the Newfie-Derry run. On 20 June 1942 she left Londonderry for the last time, and on her return to Halifax joined Gulf Escort Force to escort Quebec-Sydney convoys. After refitting at Liverpool, Nova Scotia from 10 September to 22 October and working up at Pictou, she arrived at New York on 18 November to be placed under US control as escort to New York-Guantanamo convoys. In March 1943 she returned to Halifax to join WLEF for the remainder of the war, from June 1943 as a member of W-5. She acquired her extended fo'c's'le during a refit at Sydney from January to March 1944, which was followed by three weeks' working up at Bermuda in April. She was paid off on 23 July 1945 at Sorel and sold to Marine Industries Ltd., who resold her in 1952 for conversion to a whale-catcher. The conversion at last completed in 1955, she entered service under the Dutch flag as *Nicolaas Vinke*. She was broken up at Santander, Spain in 1966.

Kenogami, 1941.

Lethbridge, March 1944.

KENOGAMI

BUILDER:	Port Arthur Shipbuilding Co. Ltd., Port Arthur, ON	COMMISSIONED:	29/6/41
LAID DOWN:	20/4/40	PAID OFF:	9/7/45
LAUNCHED:	5/9/40	FO'C'S'LE EXTENSION COMPLETED Liverpool, NS:	1/10/44

Commanding Officers

LCDR R. Jackson, RCNVR	29/6/41	21/11/42
LT J. L. Percy, RCNVR	22/11/42	23/2/44
LT R. G. McKenzie, RCNVR	24/2/44	9/7/45

LETHBRIDGE

BUILDER:	Canadian Vickers Ltd., Montreal, QC	COMMISSIONED:	25/6/41
LAID DOWN:	5/8/40	PAID OFF:	23/7/45
LAUNCHED:	21/11/40	FO'C'S'LE EXTENSION COMPLETED Sydney, NS:	27/3/44

Commanding Officers

LT W. Mahan, RCNR	25/6/41	13/8/41	A/LCDR St. C. Balfour, RCNVR	16/6/43	26/12/43
LT R. Hocken, RCNR	14/8/41	7/9/41	LT F. H. Pinfold, RCNVR	15/3/44	19/8/44
A/LCDR H. Freeland, RCNR	8/9/41	20/10/42	LT J. Roberts, RCNVR	20/8/44	30/9/44
LCDR R. S. Kelley, RCNR	21/10/42	21/4/43	LT F. H. Pinfold, RCNVR	1/10/44	14/4/45
LCDR W. Woods, RCNR	22/4/43	15/6/43	LT J. Holland, RCNVR	8/5/45	23/7/45

Lévis

Commissioned on 16 May 1941, at Quebec City, *Lévis* arrived at Halifax on 29 May, worked up there and in June 1941 joined NEF. On 13 September 1941 after one round trip to Iceland, she left St. John's as ocean escort to convoy SC.44. On 19 September she was torpedoed by *U 74* 120 miles east of Cape Farewell, Greenland, resulting in the loss of eighteen lives. During the several hours she remained afloat, the remainder of her ship's company was taken off by her sisters, *Mayflower* and *Agassiz*.

Louisburg

Built at Quebec City and commissioned there on 2 October 1941, *Louisburg* arrived at Halifax on 15 October. She was assigned to Sydney Force until mid-January 1942 when she was transferred to Newfoundland Command. On 1 February she left St. John's for Londonderry as escort to convoy SC.67, another of

whose escorts, HMCS *Spikenard*, was lost. After a long refit at Halifax from 27 March to 27 June 1942 *Louisburg* made two more round trips to Derry before being assigned to duties in connection with Operation Torch, the invasion of North Africa. She arrived at Londonderry on 23 September, and then proceeded to the Humber for fitting of extra A/A armament. This work was completed on 18 October, the day before the accompanying photo was taken. On 9 December 1942 while anchored at Londonderry, she was accidentally rammed by HMS *Bideford*, necessitating five weeks' repairs at Belfast. *Louisburg* had scarcely commenced her Operation Torch duties when on 6 February 1943 she was sunk by Italian aircraft east of Oran, while escorting a convoy from Gibraltar to Bône, Algeria. Thirty-eight of her ship's company were lost.

Lévis about to sink, 20 September 1941.

Louisburg, 19 October 1942.

Lunenburg, 1942.

LÉVIS			
BUILDER:	George T. Davie & Sons Ltd., Lauzon, QC	LAUNCHED:	4/9/40
		COMMISSIONED:	16/5/41
		LOST:	19/9/41
LAID DOWN:	11/3/40	FO'C'S'LE EXTENSION:	
		Never done; ship was lost	
Commanding Officer			
LT C. W. Gilding, RCNR		16/5/41	19/9/41

LOUISBURG			
BUILDER:	Morton Engineering and Dry Dock Co., Quebec City, QC	LAUNCHED:	27/5/41
		COMMISSIONED:	2/10/41
		LOST:	6/2/43
LAID DOWN:	4/10/40	FO'C'S'LE EXTENSION:	
		Never done; ship was lost	
Commanding Officer			
LCDR W. F. Campbell, RCNVR		2/10/41	6/2/43

LUNENBURG						
BUILDER:	George T. Davie & Sons Ltd., Lauzon, QC		COMMISSIONED:	4/12/41		
LAID DOWN:	28/9/40		PAID OFF:	23/7/45		
LAUNCHED:	10/7/41		FO'C'S'LE EXTENSION COMPLETED			
			Liverpool, UK:	17/8/43		
Commanding Officers						
LT W. E. Harrison, RCNR	4/12/41	13/10/43	LT D. H. Smith, RCNVR		20/7/44	22/12/44
LT D. L. Miller, DSC, RCNVR	14/10/43	19/7/44	LT W. S. Thomson, RCNVR		23/12/44	23/7/45

Lunenburg

Commissioned on 4 December 1941 at Quebec City, *Lunenburg* arrived at Halifax on 13 December and after working up did escort duty between Halifax and St. John's. In July 1942 she was transferred to Halifax Force as escort to Quebec City-Hamilton Inlet (Labrador) convoys. She arrived at Sydney on 31 August to join Gulf Escort Force, but two weeks later was detached for Operation Torch duties. Arriving at Londonderry on 27 September, she proceeded to Liverpool for extra A/A armament and in November began a four-month stint escorting convoys between the UK and the Mediterranean. At the end of March 1943 she returned to Liverpool for a major refit, including fo'c's'le extension, completing on 17 August. After a brief sojourn in Canadian waters she was assigned to EG 6, Western Approaches Command, arriving at Plymouth late in November. For the next five months she operated in support of convoys between the UK and Gibraltar, and between Londonderry and other UK ports, as well as patrolling the Northwestern Approaches from her Londonderry base. When the group's corvettes were replaced by frigates in April 1944 *Lunenburg* went to Western Approaches Command, Greenock, to be based at Portsmouth for invasion duties. For the next five months she was employed primarily in the English Channel. She left Londonderry on 23 September for a refit begun at Saint John, New Brunswick, but completed at Halifax in mid-January 1945. Following workups in Bermuda she returned to the UK via the Azores, to serve with Plymouth Command until the end of the war. In May 1945 she visited St. Helier during the reoccupation of the Channel Islands. She left Greenock in mid-June for Halifax, was paid off at Sorel on 23 July, and broken up at Hamilton in 1946.

Matapedia

Commissioned at Quebec City on 9 May 1941, *Matapedia* arrived at Halifax on 24 May. She was assigned to Sydney Force as a local escort until late September, when she was transferred to Newfoundland Command for ocean escort work between St. John's and Iceland. On her first trip, she left Sydney on 29 September for Iceland with convoy SC.47. After three round trips she left St. John's on 6 February 1942 with SC.68 for Londonderry, returning in March with ON.70. It was to be her only trip to the UK, as she joined WLEF on her return and with the exception of a stint with Gaspé Force from November to December 1944, remained with WLEF until the end of the war. She underwent a major refit at Pictou from 8 May to 21 July 1942 and in June 1943 became a member of EG W-5. On 8 September 1943 she was rammed amidships in a thick fog off Sambro Lightship by SS *Scorton* and seriously damaged. After temporary repairs at Dartmouth from 10 September to 12 October, she was towed to Liverpool, Nova Scotia for full repairs and refit, including fo'c's'le extension. This was completed early in February 1944 and a month later she proceeded to Bermuda for two weeks' workups, on her return joining EG W-4 for the balance of the war. She underwent one further major refit from 15 February to 28 April 1945 at Halifax, again followed by workups in Bermuda, but by then the war was over and she was paid off at Sorel on 16 June. *Matapedia* was broken up at Hamilton, Ontario in 1945.

Matapedia, 1941.

MATAPEDIA

BUILDER:	Morton Engineering and Dry Dock Co., Quebec City, QC	COMMISSIONED:	9/5/41
		PAID OFF:	16/6/45
LAID DOWN:	2/2/40	FO'C'S'LE EXTENSION COMPLETED	
LAUNCHED:	14/9/40	Liverpool, NS:	3/2/44

Commanding Officers

LT R. J. Herman, RCNR	9/5/41	26/4/43
LT J. D. Frewer, RCNVR	27/4/43	12/5/44
LT C. F. Usher, RCNVR	13/5/44	16/6/45

Mayflower

Commissioned in the RN at Montreal on 9 November 1940, she arrived at Halifax on 11 December to work up and complete stores. On 9 February 1941 *Mayflower* left with convoy HX.108 for the UK, fitted like her sister *Hepatica*, with a dummy gun. This and other shortcomings were looked after on the Tyne River, where she was pronounced complete on 5 May, and she left Loch Ewe as a member of EG 4 with convoy OB.332 for Iceland on 10 June. Later that month she joined Newfoundland Command, and for the remainder of the year served between Iceland and St. John's as an ocean escort. During this period she took part in the battle of convoy SC.44 when four merchant ships and HMCS *Lévis* were lost, *Mayflower* taking off survivors of the latter. After a major refit and fo'c's'le extension at Charleston, South Carolina, from 9 December 1941 to 9 February 1942 *Mayflower* resumed her mid-ocean role on the Newfie-Derry run until April 1944. In April 1942 she became a member of EG A-3, transferring to C-3 in February 1943. She underwent two further long refits: from 29 October 1942 to 11 January 1943 at Pictou; and from 29 November 1943 to 14 February 1944 at Norfolk, Virginia. Following this she worked up in St. Margaret's Bay, then sailed on 21 April for the UK to join Western Approaches Command, Greenock, for invasion duties. She left Oban on 31 May, to escort block-ships for Normandy and arrived off the beaches on the day after D Day. For the remainder of the war she operated in UK waters, and on 15 May 1945 was paid off for return to the RN. Laid up at Grangemouth, Scotland, she was broken up at Inverkeithing in 1949.

Mayflower, 1941.

MAYFLOWER			
BUILDER:	Canadian Vickers Ltd., Montreal, QC	COMMISSIONED:	15/5/41
LAID DOWN:	20/2/40	PAID OFF:	15/5/45
LAUNCHED:	3/7/40	FO'C'S'LE EXTENSION COMPLETED	
		Charleston, SC:	9/2/42

Commanding Officers					
A/LCDR G. H. Stephen, RCNR	28/11/40	12/5/42	LT D. S. Martin, RCNR	3/3/44	15/5/45
A/LCDR V. Browne, RCNVR	13/5/42	2/3/44			

Moncton

Commissioned at Saint John, New Brunswick on 24 April 1942 she arrived at Halifax on 12 May. She was the last of the RCN's initial Flower class program to complete, owing to heavy demands on her builder, Saint John Dry Dock Co., for repair work to war-damaged ships. After working up she joined WLEF, Halifax, and when the force was divided into escort groups in June 1943 she became a member of EG W-5. She remained in this service until transferred to the west coast in January 1944, proceeding there via Guantanamo, Cristobal, Balboa, and San Pedro, California. Upon arrival she was assigned to Esquimalt Force, of which she remained a member until VJ Day. In the course of an extensive refit at Vancouver from 5 May to 7 July 1944 her fo'c's'le was extended. She was paid off at Esquimalt on 12 December 1945 and sold for conversion to a whale-catcher at Kiel. She entered service in 1955 as the Dutch-flag *Willem Vinke* and was broken up at Santander, Spain in 1966.

Moncton, November 1943. The protective rails spanning her quarterdeck show she has been equipped to act, if required, as a fleet tug.

MONCTON			
BUILDER:	Saint John Dry Dock and Shipbuilding Co. Ltd., Saint John, NB	COMMISSIONED:	24/4/42
		PAID OFF:	12/12/45
LAID DOWN:	17/12/40	FO'C'S'LE EXTENSION COMPLETED	
LAUNCHED:	11/8/41	Vancouver, BC:	7/7/44

Commanding Officers					
LCDR A. R. E. Coleman, RCNR	24/4/42	11/10/42	LCDR R. J. Roberts, RCNR	4/4/44	26/1/45
LT A. W. Ford, RCNR	12/10/42	3/2/44	LT W. McCombe, RCNR	27/1/45	26/6/45
LCDR A. T. Morrell, RCNR	4/3/44	3/4/44	LCDR C. G. Trotter, RCNVR	21/8/45	12/12/45

Moose Jaw

Built at Collingwood, *Moose Jaw* was commissioned at Montreal on 19 June 1941, and arrived at Halifax on 27 June for final fitting-out. After working up, she arrived at St. John's on 25 August to join Newfoundland Command, and on 5 September sailed with *Chambly* for exercises. The two were ordered to reinforce the badly beleaguered convoy SC.42 which lost eighteen ships, and just before joining on 10 September, they surprised and sank *U 501* astern of the convoy. *Moose Jaw*, which had rammed the U-boat, required ten days' repairs at Greenock, following which she arrived at Tobermory on 1 October to work up. For the next four months she operated between St. John's and Iceland, but in January 1942 she arrived at Londonderry from SC.64, the inaugural Newfie-Derry convoy. On 19 February 1942 she ran aground in the entrance to St. John's harbour en route to join convoy HX.176, and although refloated soon afterward proved to be holed and leaking in several places. Temporary repairs were carried out at St. John's from 20 February to 5 March, and permanent repairs at Saint John, New Brunswick, from 15 March to 25 June. Briefly assigned to WLEF, she was detached in September for duties in connection with Operation Torch, and made her passage to the UK with convoy SC.107, which lost fifteen ships to U-boats. During the next five months *Moose Jaw* was employed escorting UK-Mediterranean convoys, returning to Halifax on 20 April 1943.

Refitted there she joined Quebec Force at the end of May for escort duties in the Gulf of St. Lawrence, later transferring to Gaspé Force. She underwent a major refit, including fo'c's'le extension, at Liverpool, Nova Scotia, from 19 December 1943 to 23 March 1944. After working up in St. Margaret's Bay she left Halifax on 1 May for the UK to join Western Approaches Command, Greenock, for invasion duties. She served in the Channel until September 1944 when she joined EG 41, Plymouth, and escorted coastal convoys from her base at Milford Haven until the end of the war. She left for home in May 1945, was paid off at Sorel on 8 July, and broken up at Hamilton, Ontario in 1949.

Morden

Commissioned at Montreal on 6 September 1941, *Morden* arrived at Halifax on 16 September. She joined Newfoundland Command and left St. John's 23 November to escort SC.56, her first convoy, to Iceland. She continued on to the UK, however, to carry out two months' refit and repairs at Southampton. She left the Clyde on 5 March 1942 to pick up westbound convoy ON.73, and was thereafter continuously in service as an ocean escort until the fall of 1943, from August 1942 as a member of EG C-2. Postwar reassessment of U-boat kills credit *Morden* with the sinking of *U 756* in the North Atlantic, 1 September 1942.

After a brief refit at Lunenburg in June 1943 and workups at Pictou, she sailed for Plymouth to join EG 9. In October *Morden* rejoined EG C-2 and was given an extensive refit at Londonderry between late November 1943 and the end of January 1944. The work done included the lengthening of her fo'c's'le. She left Derry for the last time on 14 November 1944. In May 1945 on completion of a long refit at Sydney and Halifax, she joined EG W-9 of WLEF and left New York on 23 May as local escort to HX.358, the last HX convoy. Paid off on 29 June 1945 at Sorel, she was broken up at Hamilton in 1946.

Moose Jaw, 1943.

Morden, 1944.

MOOSE JAW			
BUILDER:	Collingwood Shipyards Ltd., Collingwood, ON	COMMISSIONED:	19/6/41
		PAID OFF:	8/7/45
LAID DOWN:	12/8/40	FO'C'S'LE EXTENSION COMPLETED	
LAUNCHED:	9/4/41	Liverpool, NS:	23/3/44

Commanding Officers		
LT F. E. Grubb, RCN	19/6/41	8/12/41
LT H. D. Campsie, RCNR	9/12/41	13/2/42
LT L. D. Quick, RCNR	14/2/42	29/8/43
LT J. E. Taylor, RCNVR	30/8/43	6/10/43
LT L. D. Quick, RCNR	7/10/43	3/2/44
LT H. Brynjolfson, RCNVR	14/3/44	12/10/44
LT A. Harvey, RCNR	13/10/44	8/7/45

MORDEN			
BUILDER:	Port Arthur Shipbuilding Co. Ltd., Port Arthur, ON	COMMISSIONED:	6/9/41
		PAID OFF:	29/6/45
LAID DOWN:	25/10/40	FO'C'S'LE EXTENSION COMPLETED	
LAUNCHED:	5/5/41	Londonderry, Ireland:	29/1/44

Commanding Officers		
LT J. J. Hodgkinson, RCNR	6/9/41	2/6/43
LT E. C. Smith, RCNVR	3/6/43	14/10/43
LT W. Turner, RCNR	15/10/43	2/1/44
LT E. C. Smith, RCNVR	3/1/44	21/5/44
LT K. B. Cully, RCNVR	22/5/44	18/2/45
LT F. R. Spindler, RCNVR	19/2/45	29/6/45

Nanaimo

Commissioned at Esquimalt on 26 April 1941, *Nanaimo* arrived at Halifax on 27 June and for the next three months carried out local duties. In October she was assigned to Newfoundland Command, leaving Halifax on 11 October to join convoy SC.49 for Iceland, her first trip as an ocean escort. After three round trips to Iceland, she escorted SC.68 to Londonderry in February 1942. Her return trip with ON.68 was to be her last Atlantic crossing, for in March she was reassigned to WLEF. With the formation of escort groups in June 1943 she became a member of EG W-9, transferring to W-7 in April 1944. In November 1944 she was allocated to Pacific Coast Command, arriving at Esquimalt on 7 December. There she underwent a refit that lasted until 21 February 1945 but left her one of the few corvettes to survive the war with a short fo'c's'le. She was paid off for disposal at Esquimalt on 28 September 1945 and subsequently sold for mercantile use. Converted to a whale-catcher at Kiel in 1953, she entered service as the Dutch-flag *Rene W. Vinke*, finally being broken up in South Africa in 1966.

Nanaimo, 1943-44.

NANAIMO

BUILDER:	Yarrows Ltd., Esquimalt, BC	COMMISSIONED:	26/4/41
LAID DOWN:	27/4/40	PAID OFF:	28/9/45
LAUNCHED:	28/10/40	FO'C'S'LE EXTENSION:	Never done

Commanding Officers

LCDR H. C. C. Daubney, RCNR	26/4/41	7/10/41	LT J. W.E. Hastings, RCNR	11/10/43	9/10/44
LT T. J. Bellas, RCNR	8/10/41	20/8/42	LT R. C. Eaton, RCNVR	10/10/44	2/3/45
LT E. U. Jones, RCNR	21/8/42	10/10/43	LT W. Redford, RCNR	23/3/45	28/9/45

Napanee, 1942.

NAPANEE

BUILDER:	Kingston Shipbuilding Co. Ltd., Kingston, ON	COMMISSIONED:	12/5/41
		PAID OFF:	12/7/45
LAID DOWN:	20/3/40	FO'C'S'LE EXTENSION COMPLETED	
LAUNCHED:	31/8/40	Montreal, QC:	19/10/43

Commanding Officers

LCDR A. H. Dobson, RCNR	12/5/41	8/12/41	A/LCDR G. A. Powell, RCNVR	3/6/44	12/7/45
LT S. Henderson, RCNR	9/12/41	2/6/44			

Napanee

Commissioned at Montreal on 12 May 1941, *Napanee* arrived at Halifax on 17 May. She was assigned initially to Sydney Force but transferred in September to Newfoundland Command, leaving Sydney for Iceland with convoy SC.47 on 29 September. She served on that route until January 1942 when she sailed with SC.65, the first of many Newfie-Derry convoys she would escort until August 1944. The worst of them was ONS.154, which lost fourteen ships in December 1942 but *Napanee* assisted in sinking one of its attackers, *U 356*, on 27 December. In March 1943 she made a side trip to Gibraltar with EG C-1, which she had joined in September 1942. She arrived at Montreal, 22 May 1943 for a five-month refit, including fo'c's'le extension, afterward working up at Pictou and joining EG C-3. She left Derry for the last time on 3 August 1944, refitted again at Pictou, then carried out three weeks' workups in Bermuda. On her return she joined EG W-2 on the "triangle run" until the end of the war. Paid off 12 July 1945 at Sorel, she was broken up at Hamilton in 1946.

Oakville

Commissioned at Montreal on 18 November 1941, she arrived at Halifax ten days later and joined Halifax Force on her arrival. On its formation in March 1942 she transferred to WLEF. In July she returned to Halifax Force to escort Halifax-Aruba convoys and, on her second arrival at Aruba late in August, was diverted to reinforce convoy TAW.15 (Aruba-Key West section). The convoy was attacked 28 August in the Windward Passage, losing four ships, but *Oakville* sank the seasoned *U 94*, in part by ramming. After temporary repairs at Guantanamo she arrived at Halifax on 16 September and there completed repairs on 1 December. She then joined the US Eastern Sea Frontier

Command to escort New York-Guantanamo convoys until 22 March 1943 when she arrived at Halifax to join WLEF. She served with three of its escort groups: W-7 from June 1943; W-8 from December 1943; and W-6 from April 1944. In mid-December she began a major refit at Galveston, Texas, which included fo'c's'le extension, and was completed on 29 March 1944. After minor repairs at Halifax, she proceeded to Bermuda for workups in May, thereafter returning to her duties with EG W-6. A refit begun at Lunenburg early in April 1945 was discontinued in June and the ship was paid off at Sorel on 20 July. She was sold to the Venezuelan Navy in 1945 and renamed *Patria*, serving until 1962.

Oakville, 1945.

OAKVILLE				
BUILDER:	Port Arthur Shipbuilding Co. Ltd., Port Arthur, ON	COMMISSIONED:	18/11/41	
LAID DOWN:	21/12/40	PAID OFF:	20/7/45	
LAUNCHED:	21/6/41	FO'C'S'LE EXTENSION COMPLETED Galveston, TX,:	29/3/44	

Commanding Officers

LT A. C. Jones, RCNR	18/11/41	11/5/42	LT H. F. Farncomb, RCNVR	22/4/43	22/10/44
LCDR C. A. King, DSC, RCNR	12/5/42	21/4/43	LT M. A. Griffiths, RCNVR	23/10/44	20/7/45

Orillia

Commissioned on 25 November 1940 at Collingwood, she arrived at Halifax on 11 December for completion and was assigned to Halifax Local Defence Force until 23 May 1941. *Orillia* sailed that day for St. John's to become one of the seven charter members of the NEF, and for the balance of the year escorted convoys between St. John's and Iceland. In September 1941 she was escort to convoy SC.42 which lost eighteen ships. She arrived at Halifax 24 December for a refit, upon completion of which on 22 March 1942 she joined EG C-1, leaving St.

John's 3 April with SC.77 for Londonderry. On her arrival she was sent to Tobermory for three weeks' workups, then returned to the Newfie-Derry run until January 1944. *Orillia* took part in major battles around convoys SC.94, which lost eleven ships in August 1942 and ON.137 that October, which lost only two ships despite being heavily attacked. She was a member of EG C-2 from November 1942 to May 1944 when she joined EG C-4 following two months' refit at Liverpool, Nova Scotia. She left Londonderry for the last time on 16 January 1944 to

Orillia, 1941.

ORILLIA				
BUILDER:	Collingwood Shipyards Ltd., Collingwood, ON	COMMISSIONED:	25/11/40	
LAID DOWN:	4/3/40	PAID OFF:	2/7/45	
LAUNCHED:	15/9/40	FO'C'S'LE EXTENSION COMPLETED Liverpool, NS:	3/5/44	

Commanding Officers

A/LCDR W. E. S. Briggs, RCNR	25/11/40	4/9/42	A/LCDR J. E. Mitchell, RCNVR	17/4/43	13/3/44
LT H. V. W. Groos, RCN	5/9/42	13/2/43	A/LCDR J. W. Sharpe, RCNR	8/5/44	2/7/45
LCDR R. Jackson, RCNR	14/2/43	16/4/43			

commence a long refit, again at Liverpool, which included the lengthening of her fo'c's'le. This refit was completed on 3 May, but further repairs were completed at Halifax late in June. She arrived at Bermuda on 29 June for three weeks' workups, on her return joining EG W-2, Western Escort Force, for the duration of the war. Paid off on 2 July 1945 at Sorel, she was broken up at Hamilton in 1951.

Pictou

Commissioned at Quebec City on 29 April 1941, *Pictou* arrived at Halifax on 12 May. She joined Newfoundland Command and left St. John's on 6 June with HX.131 for Iceland, one of the first two corvettes to escort an HX convoy. She remained on the St. John's-Iceland run for the rest of the year. After brief repairs at Halifax she returned to St. John's, where breakdowns forced her to turn back from three successive convoys. She finally crossed with HX.180 in March 1942 to Londonderry, carried out further repairs at Liverpool and, on completion early in June, joined EG C-4. On 5 August, while escorting convoy ON.116, she was rammed in a fog near St. John's by the Norwegian SS *Hindanger*, suffering severe damage to her stern. After completing repairs at

Halifax on 20 September she joined EG C-2. On her return from the UK with ON.149 in December 1942 she required further repairs at Halifax, followed immediately by refit at Liverpool, Nova Scotia. In May 1943 she joined EG C-3, and on 17 December left Londonderry for the last time. From early January to 31 March 1944 she was refitting at New York, receiving her extended fo'c's'le. She then proceeded to Bermuda for three weeks' workups, returning in mid-June to join EG W-5, Western Escort Force. Paid off on 12 July 1945 at Sorel, she was sold for conversion to a whale-catcher, entering service in 1950 as the Honduran-flag *Olympic Chaser*. Again sold in 1956, she served as *Otari Maru* No. 7 until converted to a barge in 1963.

Pictou, 1945.

PICTOU					
BUILDER:	Davie Shipbuilding and Repairing Co. Ltd., Lauzon, QC		COMMISSIONED:	29/4/41	
LAID DOWN:	12/7/40		PAID OFF:	12/7/45	
LAUNCHED:	5/10/40		FO'C'S'LE EXTENSION COMPLETED New York City, NY: 31/3/44		
Commanding Officers					
LCDR J. L. Diver, RCNR	29/4/41	17/8/41	LT A. G. S. Griffin, RCNVR	20/9/42	14/3/43
A/LCDR R. B. Campbell, RCNR	18/8/41	4/9/41	LT P. T. Byers, RCNR	15/3/43	19/11/43
LT A. G. S. Griffin, RCNVR	5/9/41	21/8/42	A/LCDR G. K. Fox, RCNVR	20/11/43	1/10/44
LT L. C. Audette, RCNVR	22/8/42	19/9/42	LT F. Cross, RCNR	2/10/44	12/7/45

Prescott

Commissioned at Montreal on 26 June 1941, *Prescott* arrived at Halifax on 4 July and was attached briefly to Halifax Force before arriving at St. John's on 31 August to join Newfoundland Command. She spent the rest of the year escorting convoys between St. John's and Iceland, but early in 1942 experienced mechanical difficulties requiring two months' repairs at Liverpool, Nova Scotia. Resuming her mid-ocean duties on 21 April, she made two round

trips to Londonderry before being transferred to WLEF in July. In September she was assigned to duties in connection with Operation Torch. Postwar reassessment of U-boat kills credits *Prescott* with the destruction of *U 163* in the Bay of Biscay, 13 March 1943. Returning to Canada on 4 April 1943, she began a six-month refit at Liverpool, Nova Scotia including extension of her fo'c's'le. After workups at Pictou she sailed from St. John's on 19 December for the UK to

Prescott on trials off Kingston, June 1941.

PRESCOTT					
BUILDER:	Kingston Shipbuilding Co. Ltd., Kingston, ON		COMMISSIONED:	26/6/41	
LAID DOWN:	31/8/40		PAID OFF:	20/7/45	
LAUNCHED:	7/1/41		FO'C'S'LE EXTENSION COMPLETED Liverpool, NS: 27/10/43		
Commanding Officers					
LT H. A. Russell, RCNR	26/6/41	30/5/42	LCDR W. McIsaac, RCNVR	12/9/42	28/12/44
LT G. H. Davidson, RCN	31/5/42	1/7/42	LT G. J. Mathewson, RCNVR	29/12/44	20/7/45
LT H. A. Russell, RCNR	2/7/42	11/9/42			

join EG 6, Londonderry. She served with the group, principally as escort to UK-Gibraltar/Freetown convoys, until April 1944 when its corvettes were replaced with frigates, then joined Western

Approaches Command, Greenock, for invasion duties. In September she returned to Liverpool, Nova Scotia for another refit and after working up, went back to the UK to serve with Nore

Command until the end of the war. Returning to Halifax late in May 1945 she was paid off at Sorel 20 July and ultimately broken up in Spain.

Quesnel

Named for a British Columbia village, she was commissioned on 23 May 1941 at Esquimalt, and for the next year patrolled off the west coast as a member of Esquimalt Force. In June 1942 she towed the torpedoed SS *Fort Camosun* into Victoria. Transferred to the east coast to replace an Operation Torch nominee, she arrived at Halifax on 13 October and was assigned to WLEF until June 1944. With the division of the force into escort groups in June 1943 she became a member of EG W-1. During this period she underwent a refit, including fo'c's'le extension, from early September to 23 December 1943 at Pictou. This refit was followed by workups in St. Margaret's Bay and Bermuda. In June 1944 *Quesnel* joined Quebec Force and spent five months escorting Labrador-Quebec convoys. In November she was transferred to Halifax Force, going to Sydney for refit and, on completion late in January 1945, to Bermuda for workups. She resumed escort duty late in March, temporarily attached to EG W-5 and W-8 of WLEF until the end of the war. She was paid off on 3 July 1945 at Sorel, and broken up in 1946 at Hamilton.

Quesnel, May 1945.

QUESNEL

BUILDER:	Victoria Machinery Depot Co. Ltd., Victoria, BC	COMMISSIONED:	23/5/41	
		PAID OFF:	3/7/45	
LAID DOWN:	9/5/40	FO'C'S'LE EXTENSION COMPLETED		
LAUNCHED:	12/11/40	Pictou, NS:	23/12/43	

Commanding Officers

LT J. A. Gow, RCNR	23/5/41	4/3/42	LT M. Smith, RCNR	17/11/42	11/4/43
LT A. E. Gough, RCNR	5/3/42	3/4/42	LT J. M. Laing, RCNR	12/4/43	3/7/45
LT J. A. Gow, RCNR	4/4/42	16/11/42			

Rimouski, July 1945.

RIMOUSKI

BUILDER:	Davie Shipbuilding and Repairing Co. Ltd., Lauzon, QC	COMMISSIONED:	26/4/41	
		PAID OFF:	24/7/45	
LAID DOWN:	12/7/40	FO'C'S'LE EXTENSION COMPLETED		
LAUNCHED:	3/10/40	Liverpool, NS:	24/8/43	

Commanding Officers

LT J. W. Bonner, RCNVR	27/4/41	11/11/41	LT C. D. Chivers, RCNVR	10/9/44	17/12/44
A/LCDR A. G. Boulton, RCNVR	12/11/41	1/12/42	LCDR D. M. MacDonald, RCNVR	18/12/44	12/6/45
LT R. J. Pickford, RCNVR	2/12/42	9/9/44	LT T. S. Cook, RCNVR	13/6/45	24/7/45

Rimouski

Commissioned on 26 April 1941 at Quebec City, *Rimouski* arrived at Halifax on 12 May and was assigned to Newfoundland Command. She shared with *Pictou* the honour of being one of the first two corvettes to escort an HX convoy (HX.131 in June 1941). On 20 January 1942 after three months' refit at Halifax, she left St. John's to join convoy SC.65 for Londonderry. After three round trips, she joined WLEF in June 1942. In the course of a five-month refit at Liverpool, Nova Scotia begun 24 March 1943, she received her extended fo'c's'le. Upon completion she was assigned to EG C-1, MOEF, transferring to C-3 in December. In April 1944 while at Londonderry, she was allocated to Western Approaches Command, Greenock, for invasion duties, and left Oban on 31 May to escort blockships for Normandy. She was employed until August as escort to Channel and coastal convoys, and then returned to Canada, where she served briefly as a Halifax-based training ship. A refit begun at Louisbourg early in November was completed at Liverpool and Halifax in February 1945. After working up, she returned to the UK to be based at Milford Haven as a member of EG 41, Plymouth, for the duration of the war. Returning to Canada in June 1945 she was paid off at Sorel on 24 July and broken up in 1950 at Hamilton.

Rosthern

Commissioned on 17 June 1941 at Montreal, *Rosthern* arrived at Halifax on 26 June. She joined Newfoundland Command and left St. John's for Iceland on 7 October as ocean escort to convoy SC.48. She proceeded on to the Clyde, where mechanical defects kept her for two months, and arrived at Halifax on 28 December for further repairs, not resuming service until mid-February 1942. She left Argentia, Newfoundland on 27 February with HX.177 for Londonderry, and was thereafter employed almost continuously on North Atlantic convoys until June 1944. In April 1942 she became a member of EG A-3, renumbered C-5 in May. *Rosthern* took part in three major convoy battles: SC.100 (September 1942); ON.166 (February 1943); and SC.121 (March 1943). She left Londonderry for the last time on 27 May 1944 and on her return to Canada became a training ship at Halifax for navigation and ship-handling, attached at first to WLEF and then, from December onward, to Halifax Force. She carried out workups at Bermuda in December, escorting HMCS *Provider* on the homeward trip. *Rosthern* had no long refits during the war, and never did have her fo'c's'le lengthened. Paid off on 19 July 1945 at Sorel, she was broken up at Hamilton in 1946.

Sackville

Commissioned on 31 December 1941 at Saint John, New Brunswick, *Sackville* arrived at Halifax on 12 January 1942. She joined NEF after working up, and on 26 May left St. John's to escort HX.191 as part of the newly formed EG C-3. In April 1943 she transferred to C-1, and that September briefly joined EG 9 in support of the beleaguered combined convoy ONS.18/ON.202, which lost six merchant vessels and three escorts. In October *Sackville* transferred to C-2 for the balance of her war career. She underwent two major refits: at Liverpool and Halifax, Nova Scotia from 14 January to 2 May 1943; and at Galveston, Texas, from late February to 7 May 1944 when her fo'c's'le was extended. Upon her return from working up in Bermuda in June 1944 she made a crossing to Londonderry. Soon after leaving for the westward journey she split a boiler and had to return to Derry for repairs. She left again on 11 August to limp home as escort to ONS.248, refitted at Halifax, and in September briefly became a training ship at HMCS *Kings*. In October at Halifax she began refit and reconstruction to a loop-laying vessel, and work was still in progress by VE Day. The ship was paid off on 8 April 1946, but recommissioned 4 August 1950 as depot ship, reserve fleet. She was refitted in 1950 but remained inactive until 1953, when as a Canadian Naval Auxiliary Vessel (CNAV), she began a survey of the Gulf of St. Lawrence that was to last several years. She also carried out a number of cruises to the Baffin Island-Greenland area. Extensive modification in 1968 reflected *Sackville*'s new status as a research vessel, in which capacity she served the Bedford Institute of Oceanography until the end of 1982. She was then acquired by the Maritime Museum of the Atlantic for reconversion to her original appearance, as the last surviving corvette.

Rosthern, 1943-44.

ROSTHERN

BUILDER:	Port Arthur Shipbuilding Co. Ltd., Port Arthur, ON	LAUNCHED:	30/11/40
		COMMISSIONED:	17/6/41
		PAID OFF:	19/7/45
LAID DOWN:	18/6/40	FO'C'S'LE EXTENSION Never done	

Commanding Officers

LT W. Russell, RCNR	17/6/41	20/11/41
CDR P. B. Cross, RCNVR	21/11/41	24/11/42
LCDR R. J. G. Johnson, RCNVR	25/11/42	17/4/44
LT S. P. R. Annett, RCNVR	18/4/44	3/11/44
A/LCDR R. F. Wilson, RCNVR	4/11/44	6/4/45
LT D. R. Smythies, RCNVR	7/4/45	19/7/45

Sackville, spring 1942.

SACKVILLE

BUILDER:	Saint John Dry Dock and Shipbuilding Co. Ltd., Saint John, NB	COMMISSIONED:	30/12/41
		PAID OFF:	8/4/46
LAID DOWN:	28/5/40	FO'C'S'LE EXTENSION COMPLETED	
LAUNCHED:	15/5/41	Galveston, TX:	7/5/44

Commanding Officers

LT W. R. Kirkland, RCNR	30/12/41	5/4/42	LT A. R. Hicks, RCNVR	18/5/44	17/9/44
LT A. H. Easton, DSC, RCNR	6/4/43	9/4/43	LT C. C. Love, RCNVR	18/9/44	5/11/44
A/LCDR A. H. Rankin, RCNVR	10/4/43	17/5/44	LT J. A. McKenna, RCNVR	6/11/44	8/4/46

Saskatoon

Commissioned at Montreal on 9 June 1941, *Saskatoon* arrived at Halifax on 22 June. She joined Halifax Force after working up and in August made a trip to the Bahamas, returning at the end of September. She remained on local escort duty until March 1942 and then joined WLEF on its formation. She served with this force on the "triangle run" until the end of the war, becoming a member of EG W-8 when it was established in June 1943 and transferring to W-6 in April 1944. During her career she had major refits, at Halifax from 11 August to 17 November 1942; and at Pictou from mid-December 1943 to 1 April 1944. Following the latter, which included the extension of her fo'c's'le, she worked up for three weeks at Pictou and another three in Bermuda. She was paid off on 25 June 1945 at Sorel and soon afterward sold for conversion to a merchant vessel. She began her new career as *Rio Norte*, then the Egyptian-registered *Mabruk*, and was later taken up by the Egyptian Navy as *Misr*. She was sunk by collision at Suez on 17 May 1953.

Saskatoon, March 1945.

Shawinigan, 23 June 1942.

Shawinigan

Commissioned on 19 September 1941 at Quebec City, *Shawinigan* arrived at Halifax on 27 October. She joined Sydney Force in November but on 13 January 1942 arrived at St. John's to join Newfoundland Command. She left 25 January to escort convoy SC.66 to Londonderry, the first of three round trips. In mid-May she left Derry for the last time, and in June was assigned to Halifax Force as escort to Quebec-Labrador convoys. She joined WLEF that November, almost immediately commencing a refit at Liverpool, Nova Scotia. This refit was completed in mid March 1943 and in June *Shawinigan* joined the recently established EG W-3. In April 1944 while undergoing another refit at Liverpool, she was transferred to W-2 and, on completion of the refit in mid-June, proceeded to Bermuda to work up. On 25 November, while on independent A/S patrol out of Sydney, she was torpedoed in the Cabot Strait by *U 1228* and lost with all hands.

SASKATOON								
BUILDER:	Canadian Vickers Ltd., Montreal, QC	LAID DOWN:	9/8/40	COMMISSIONED:	9/6/41	FO'C'S'LE EXTENSION COMPLETED		
		LAUNCHED:	6/11/40	PAID OFF:	25/6/45	Pictou, NS:	1/4/44	

Commanding Officers

LT J. S. Scott, RCNR	9/6/41	15/1/42	LT J. S. Scott, RCNR	15/4/42	20/4/42	LCDR T. MacDuff, RCNR	10/7/43	14/1/44
LT J. P. Fraser, RCNR	16/1/42	4/2/42	LT H. G. Dupont, RCNR	21/4/42	11/5/42	A/LCDR R. S. Williams, RCNVR	15/3/44	29/5/45
LCDR C. A. King, DSC, RCNR	5/2/42	14/2/42	LT J. S. Scott, RCNR	12/5/42	9/7/43	LT H. R. Knight, RCNR	30/5/45	25/6/45

SHAWINIGAN								
BUILDER:	George T. Davie & Sons Ltd., Lauzon, QC	LAID DOWN:	4/6/40	COMMISSIONED:	19/9/41	FO'C'S'LE EXTENSION COMPLETED		
		LAUNCHED:	16/5/41	LOST:	25/11/44	Liverpool, NS:	14/6/44	

Commanding Officers

A/LCDR C. P. Balfry, RCNR	19/9/41	4/1/44	LT W. E. Callan, RCNVR	15/3/44	4/6/44
LT R. S. Williams, RCNVR	5/1/44	14/3/44	LT W. J. Jones, RCNR	5/6/44	25/11/44

Shediac

Commissioned at Quebec City on 8 July 1941, *Shediac* arrived at Halifax on 18 July. She served briefly with Halifax Force and Sydney Force before joining Newfoundland Command in October, leaving Sydney on 5 October to escort convoy SC.48 to Iceland. After three round trips there, she accompanied SC.67 to Londonderry in January 1942, again the first of three return trips. Following a six-week refit at Liverpool, Nova Scotia she joined WLEF in July, returning in October to the Newfie-Derry run as a member of EG C-1. She took part in two major convoy battles: ONS.92 (May 1942); and ONS.154 (December 1942). On 4 March 1943 while escorting KMS.10, a UK-Gibraltar convoy, she assisted in the destruction of *U 87* west of the Azores. She left Londonderry for the last time on 28 March 1943, underwent refit at Liverpool, Nova Scotia from 27 April to July 1, and then joined WLEF's EG W-8. Transferred to the west coast, she left Halifax 3 April 1944 and arrived at Esquimalt 10 May. She refitted at Vancouver from mid-June to mid-August 1944, in the process receiving her extended fo'c's'le. She was paid off at Esquimalt on 28 August 1945 and sold in 1951 for conversion to a whale-catcher, entering service as the Dutch-flag *Jooske W. Vinke* in 1954. She was broken up at Santander, Spain, in 1965.

Sherbrooke

Commissioned at Sorel on 5 June 1941, *Sherbrooke* arrived at Halifax on 12 June. She joined Halifax Force later that month but transferred in September to Newfoundland Command and left Sydney on 29 September to escort convoy SC.47 as far as Iceland. After two round trips to Iceland, she left St. John's on 14 January 1942 to join SC.64, the first Newfie-Derry convoy, and was thereafter employed as an ocean escort on that run, principally with EG C-4. She took part in two particularly hard-fought convoy battles: ON.127 (August 1942); HX.229 (March 1943). Her west-bound journey after the latter convoy was her last; after a major refit at Lunenburg from April to June 1943 and workups at Pictou, she joined EG W-2 of WLEF, transferring in April 1944 to W-7 and in October 1944 to W-1. Late in May 1944 she began a refit at Liverpool, Nova Scotia that included fo'c's'le extension, followed by a month's repairs at Halifax and three weeks' workups in Bermuda in October. She was paid off at Sorel on 28 June 1945 and broken up at Hamilton in 1947.

Snowberry

Commissioned in the RN at Quebec City on 30 November 1940, she arrived at Halifax on 13 December for further work and sailed

Shediac, 1942.

SHEDIAC			
BUILDER:	Davie Shipbuilding and Repairing Co. Ltd., Lauzon, QC	COMMISSIONED:	8/7/41
		PAID OFF:	28/8/45
LAID DOWN:	5/10/40	FO'C'S'LE EXTENSION COMPLETED	
LAUNCHED:	29/4/41	Vancouver, BC:	18/8/44

Commanding Officers

LT J. E. Clayton, RCNR	8/7/41	22/3/43	A/LCDR T. P. Ryan, OBE, RCNR	31/3/44	31/7/44
A/LCDR A. Moorhouse, RCNR	23/3/43	9/2/44	A/LCDR P. D. Taylor, RCNVR	1/8/44	25/6/45
SKPR/LT J. B. Cooper, RCNR	10/2/44	30/3/44	LT W. McCombe, RCNR	26/6/45	28/8/45

Sherbrooke, July 1943.

SHERBROOKE			
BUILDER:	Marine Industries Ltd., Sorel, QC	COMMISSIONED:	5/6/41
LAID DOWN:	5/8/40	PAID OFF:	28/6/45
LAUNCHED:	25/10/40	FO'C'S'LE EXTENSION COMPLETED	
		Liverpool, NS:	22/8/44

Commanding Officers

LCDR E. G. M. Donald, RCN	5/6/41	2/7/42	LT R. A. Jarvis, RCNVR	30/8/43	30/7/44
LT J. A. M. Levesque, RCNR	3/7/42	29/8/43	LT D. A. Binmore, RCNVR	31/7/44	28/6/45

9 February 1941 with convoy HX.108 for the UK. There she completed fitting out at Greenock, completing 3 April, and worked up at Tobermory before joining Western Approaches Command, Greenock. She left Aultbea early in June to join convoy OB.332, arriving at Halifax on 23 June to join Newfoundland Command. From July to October she made three round trips to Iceland, and on 8 December arrived at Charleston, South Carolina, for six weeks' refit, including fo'c's'le extension. On 12 February 1942 she left for St. John's to escort SC.69 to

Londonderry. In March she joined the newly formed WLEF, shifting in June to Halifax Tanker Escort Force for one round trip to Trinidad and two round trips to Aruba with tanker convoys. In September she was placed under US control, escorting New York-Guantanamo convoys until March 1943 when she arrived at Charleston, South Carolina, for refit. On completion in mid-May, and after workups at Pictou, she joined the newly established EG 5 (later EG 6) and returned to UK waters in August. While serving with this support force on 20 November 1943 as escort to a UK-Gibraltar/Freetown convoy, she took part in the sinking of *U 536* north of the Azores. When the group replaced its corvettes with frigates in March 1944 *Snowberry* proceeded to Baltimore, Maryland, for five weeks' refit, afterward returning to Halifax. She went to Bermuda to work up in July, and on returning was briefly assigned to WLEF but left St. John's in mid-September for the UK. There she joined Portsmouth Command for the balance of the war. She was handed back to the RN at Rosyth on 8 June 1945 and used the following year as a target ship off Portsmouth. Her remains were broken up in 1947 at Thornaby-on-Tees.

Snowberry, February, 1944.

SNOWBERRY

BUILDER:	Davie Shipbuilding and Repairing Co Ltd., Lauzon, QC	COMMISSIONED:	15/5/41
		PAID OFF:	8/6/45
LAID DOWN:	24/2/40	FO'C'S'LL EXTENSION COMPLETED	
LAUNCHED:	8/8/40	Charleston, SC:	12/2/42

Commanding Officers

			A/LCDR J. A. Dunn, RCNVR	10/11/43	24/12/43
LT R. S. Kelley, RCNR	30/11/40	5/2/42	LT J. B. O'Brien, RCNVR	25/12/43	14/1/44
LCDR P. J. B. Watts, RCNVR	6/2/42	21/5/43	LCDR J. A. Dunn, RCNVR	15/1/44	30/4/45
LT J. B. O'Brien, RCNVR	22/5/43	9/11/43	LT B. T. R. Russell, RCNR	1/5/45	8/6/45

Sorel, 1943.

SOREL

BUILDER:	Marine Industries Ltd., Sorel, QC	PAID OFF:	22/6/45
LAID DOWN:	24/8/40	FO'C'S'LE EXTENSION COMPLETED	
LAUNCHED:	16/11/40	Halifax, NS:	2/43
COMMISSIONED:	19/8/41		

Commanding Officers

			LT G. A. V. Thomson, RCNVR	4/2/43	19/2/43
LT J. W. Dowling, RCNR	19/8/41	22/12/41	LCDR R. A. S. MacNeil, OBE, RCNR	20/2/43	23/11/43
LT A. E. Giffin, RCNVR	23/12/41	7/6/42	LT W. P. Wickett, RCNVR	24/11/43	13/3/44
LT M. H. Wallace, RCNR	8/6/42	14/1/43	LT J. A. M. Levesque, RCNR	14/3/44	24/1/45
LT P. D. Budge, RCN	15/1/43	3/2/43	LT C. W. King, RCNVR	25/1/45	22/6/45

Sorel

Commissioned at Sorel on 19 August 1941, *Sorel* arrived at Halifax on 30 August. She joined Sydney Force in October but transferred in November to Newfoundland Force, leaving St. John's on 18 November to escort convoy SC.55 to Iceland. On her next trip, mechanical defects forced her to go on to the UK, and she arrived at Leith, Scotland 17 January for ten weeks' repairs. She left Londonderry on 23 April to join convoy ON.88, and in May joined WLEF. Between 19 October 1942 and February 1943 she underwent refit, including fo'c's'le extension, successively at Liverpool, Pictou, and Halifax, Nova Scotia. In February she entered service as a training ship, first at Digby, then at St. Margaret's Bay, and at Pictou. In September 1943 she was temporarily allocated to EG C-3 for one round trip to Londonderry, and on her return underwent refit at Halifax and Dartmouth. This refit completed on 31 March 1944, she proceeded to Bermuda for workups and on her return was assigned to WEF's EG W-4 for the rest of the war. She was paid off on 22 June 1945 and broken up at Moncton, New Brunswick in 1946.

Spikenard

Commissioned in the RN on 6 December 1940 at Quebec City, she arrived at Halifax five days later to complete fitting out and working up. She left Halifax on 21 January 1941 escorting convoy HX.104 to the UK, where she received her finishing touches at South Shields, Tyne, from 4 February to 21 April. She arrived at Tobermory on 22 April to work up, and on 10 June left Aultbea to escort convoy OB.332. Arriving at Halifax on 25 June, she joined Newfoundland Command, and between July 1941 and January 1942 made three round trips to Iceland as ocean escort. On 1 February 1942 she left St. John's for convoy SC.67 on the recently inaugurated Newfie-Derry run, and on 10 February was torpedoed and sunk south of Iceland by *U 136*. There were only eight survivors.

Spikenard leaving Halifax.

SPIKENARD			
BUILDER:	Davie Shipbuilding and Repairing Co. Ltd., Lauzon, QC	COMMISSIONED:	15/5/41
		LOST:	10/2/42
LAID DOWN:	24/2/40	FO'C'S'LE EXTENSION:	
LAUNCHED:	10/8/40	Never done; ship was lost	

Commanding Officer

LCDR H. G. Shadforth, RCNR	8/12/40	10/2/42

Sudbury, November 1944.

SUDBURY			
BUILDER:	Kingston Shipbuilding Co. Ltd., Kingston, ON	COMMISSIONED:	15/10/41
		PAID OFF:	28/8/45
LAID DOWN:	25/1/41	FO'C'S'LE EXTENSION COMPLETED	
LAUNCHED:	31/5/41	Vancouver, BC:	10/5/44

Commanding Officers

LCDR A. M. McLarnon, RCNR	15/10/41	3/5/43	LT G. L. Mackay, RCNR	10/1/44	19/3/44
LT D. S. Martin, RCNR	4/5/43	9/1/44	A/LCDR J. W. Golby, DSC, RCNVR	20/3/44	19/6/45

Sudbury

Commissioned on 15 October 1941 at Montreal, *Sudbury* arrived at Halifax on 26 October. She joined Sydney Force as local escort to ocean convoys but in January 1942 joined Newfoundland Command, making one round trip to Londonderry. On her return she transferred to the newly formed WLEF, and in June to Halifax Tanker Escort Force. In the following three months she made two round trips to Trinidad and one to Aruba, escorting tankers both ways. That September *Sudbury* was placed under US control, escorting New York-Guantanamo convoys. She arrived at Liverpool, Nova Scotia 26 December for two months' refit, worked up at Halifax and then joined WLEF in June 1943 becoming a member of EG W-9. That September she was loaned to EG C-5 for her second transatlantic trip, afterward resuming service with W-9 until New Year's Day 1944 when she left for the west coast. She arrived at Esquimalt on 3 February 1944 and later that month commenced refit, including fo'c's'le extension, at Vancouver. On completion on 10 May, she joined Esquimalt Force for the duration of the war, being paid off on 28 August 1945 at Esquimalt. After the war *Sudbury* was sold and converted for use as a salvage tug, entering service in 1949 under her original name. She was broken up at Victoria in 1967.

Summerside

Commissioned at Quebec City on 11 September 1941, *Summerside* arrived at Halifax on 25 September. She was assigned to local escort duty out of Halifax and later Sydney, but left St. John's on 11 December as ocean escort to SC.59 for Iceland, returning with ON.50. It was to be her only trip there. She left St. John's on 25 January 1942 for convoy SC.66 to Londonderry, returning with ON.71 to join WLEF in March. In July she was transferred to Gulf Escort Force until, earmarked for duties in connection with Operation Torch, she left Halifax on 19 October for the UK. For the next four months she was employed on UK-Mediterranean convoys, returning to Canada in mid-March 1943 for a major refit at Saint John from 11 April

to 25 September. Her fo'c's'le was extended in the process. After working up at Halifax she joined EG C-5 and in April 1944 after seven transatlantic trips, was assigned at Londonderry to Western Approaches Command for invasion duties. She was employed in UK waters until returning to Canada for two months' refit at Liverpool, Nova Scotia, commencing in mid-October. After further repairs at Halifax were completed on 18 January 1945 she proceeded to Bermuda for three weeks' workups. In March she sailed for the UK to serve with EG 41 (RN) out of Plymouth until the war's end. She returned to Canada at the end of May, was paid off at Sorel on 6 July and broken up at Hamilton in 1946.

Summerside, July 1942.

SUMMERSIDE

BUILDER:	Morton Engineering and Dry Dock Co., Quebec City, QC	COMMISSIONED:	11/9/41
		PAID OFF:	6/7/45
LAID DOWN:	4/10/40	FO'C'S'LE EXTENSION COMPLETED	
LAUNCHED:	17/5/41	Saint John, NB:	25/9/43

Commanding Officers

LCDR F. O. Gerity, RCNR	11/9/41	3/6/43	LT H. S. Hardy, RCNVR	10/10/44	
LT G. E. Cross, RCNVR	4/6/43	31/8/43	LT F. O. Plant, RCNVR	18/12/44	6/7/45

The Pas

Commissioned at Montreal on 21 October 1941, *The Pas* arrived at Halifax on 4 November. She joined Halifax Force as a local escort, but in March 1942 was reassigned to WLEF, then forming. In June she was transferred to Halifax Tanker Escort Force, and during the next three months made three round trips between Halifax and Trinidad-Aruba. In September she came under US control as escort to New York-Guantanamo convoys,

but arrived at Liverpool, Nova Scotia on 27 November for two months' refit. Following workups locally, she rejoined WLEF and, on its division into escort groups in June 1943 became a member of EG W-4. The ship was badly damaged in collision with the American SS *Medina* in the western Atlantic on 21 July 1943 while escorting convoy ON.192, and was under repair at Halifax and Shelburne until early October. She then returned

The Pas, 1943-44.

THE PAS

BUILDER:	Collingwood Shipyards Ltd., Collingwood, ON	COMMISSIONED:	21/10/41
		PAID OFF:	24/7/45
LAID DOWN:	7/1/41	FO'C'S'LE EXTENSION Never done	
LAUNCHED:	16/8/41		

Commanding Officers

LCDR A. R. E. Coleman, RCNR	21/10/41	28/10/41	LT R. H. Sylvester, RCNVR	15/4/44	9/10/44
LCDR E. G. Old, RCNR	29/10/41	14/1/44	LT J. H. Ewart, RCNVR	10/10/44	24/7/45

to her duties with WLEF until September 1944 (from April as a member of EG W-3), when she underwent a refit at Sydney and, on com-

pletion of this late in November, joined HMCS *Cornwallis* as a training ship for the balance of the war. *The Pas* never did receive an

extended fo'c's'le. She was paid off on 24 July 1945 at Sorel and broken up at Hamilton the following year.

Trail

Commissioned at Vancouver on 30 April 1941, she left Esquimalt 31 May for the east coast, arriving at Halifax on 27 June. In August she joined Newfoundland Command, departing St. John's on 23 August to escort convoy HX.146 as far as Iceland. During the year she made four round trips there, and on 20 January 1942 left St. John's to join SC.65 for the first of two round trips to Londonderry. She returned to Halifax on 2 April and after a brief refit at Liverpool, Nova Scotia joined Halifax Force for Northern Waters in June. Between July and November she was employed escorting convoys between Labrador and Quebec City, also calling at Gaspé and Hamilton Inlet. She arrived at Halifax in November to join WLEF for the balance of the war, as a member successively of escort groups W-6 (from June 1943); W-5 (from April 1944); and W-4 (from December 1944). She underwent a refit at Lunenburg from mid-July to 3 September 1943 followed by workups at Pictou and a further refit at Liverpool, Nova Scotia between mid-July and 23 October 1944. Following the latter, which included extension of her fo'c's'le, she underwent additional repairs at Halifax, and then proceeded to Bermuda to work up in December. She left there on 7 January 1945 for Boston to resume service with WLEF until paid off on 17 July at Sorel. In 1950 the ship was broken up at Hamilton.

Trail, 12 May 1944.

TRAIL				
BUILDER:	Burrard Dry Dock Co. Ltd., Vancouver, BC	COMMISSIONED:	30/4/41	
LAID DOWN:	20/7/40	PAID OFF:	17/7/45	
LAUNCHED:	17/10/40	FO'C'S'LE EXTENSION COMPLETED Liverpool, NS 23/10/44		
Commanding Officers				
LT G. S. Hall, RCNR	30/4/41 8/10/43	LT D. G. B. Hueston, RCNVR	21/8/44	9/10/44
LT G. M. Hope, RCNVR	9/10/43 20/8/44	LT D. J. Lawson, RCNVR	10/10/44	17/7/45

Trillium

Commissioned at Montreal in the RN on 31 October 1940, *Trillium* arrived at Halifax on 14 November and in the Clyde on 20 December for final fitting out at Greenock, which was completed on 3 March 1941. In April, after three weeks' workups at Tobermory, she joined EG 4 (RN), Greenock, for outbound North American convoys. She left Aultbea on 10 June with OB.332 for St. John's to join Newfoundland Command. After two round trips to Iceland she arrived at Halifax on 28 August for three months' refit there and at Lunenburg. On completion of the refit in December she made one further round trip to Iceland, and on 20 January 1942 left St. John's for convoy SC.65 to Londonderry. After two return trips on the Newfie-Derry run she went to Galveston, Texas for refit that included the extension of her fo'c's'le, from 16 April to 23 June. Following workups at Pictou, she resumed mid-ocean service with EG A-3 from August 1942 until April 1943 when she arrived at Boston for a refit. This was completed on 10 June, after which she

Trillium, 23 February 1943, rescuing survivors of three ships sunk in convoy ON.166.

worked up at Pictou before joining EG C-4. Late in April 1944 she returned to Pictou for a two-month refit, followed by additional repairs at Halifax, and early in August went to Bermuda to work up. She arrived at St. John's 2 September 1944 to join EG C-3. On 14 January 1945 while escorting the Milford Haven section of ON.278, she sank a coaster in collision and required five weeks' repairs,

afterward resuming mid-ocean escort until the end of the war. This ship was unique in that she spent her entire career as a mid-ocean escort, participating in three major convoy battles: SC.100 (September 1942); ON.166 (February 1943); and SC.121 (March 1943). She left St. John's on 27 May 1945 for the UK, where she was returned to the RN at Milford Haven on 27 June. Sold in 1947

for conversion to a whale-catcher, she entered service in 1950 as the Honduran-registered *Olympic Runner*,

and in 1956 became the Japanese *Otori Maru No. 10*. Renamed *Kyo Maru No. 16* in 1959, she is last

noted in Lloyd's Register for 1972-73.

TRILLIUM					
BUILDER:	Canadian Vickers Ltd., Montreal, QC		COMMISSIONED:	15/5/41	
LAID DOWN:	20/2/40		PAID OFF:	27/6/45	
LAUNCHED:	26/6/40		FO'C'S'LE EXTENSION COMPLETED		
			Galveston, TX:	23/6/42	
Commanding Officers					
LCDR R. F. Harris, DSC, RCNVR	31/10/40	14/11/41	LT R. M. Wallace, RCNVR	25/3/43	17/4/43
LT H. D. Campsie, RCNR	15/11/41	8/12/41	A/LCDR P. C. Evans, RCNR	18/4/43	21/5/44
SKPR/LT G. E. Gaudreau, RCNR	9/12/41	25/2/42	LT K. E. Meredith, RCNVR	22/5/44	27/6/45
A/LCDR P. C. Evans, RCNR	26/2/42	24/3/43			

Wetaskiwin

Commissioned at Esquimalt on 17 December 1940, *Wetaskiwin* was the first west coast-built corvette to enter service. On patrol out of Esquimalt until she left on 17 March 1941 for the Atlantic, she arrived at Halifax on 13 April and left on 23 May for St. John's to become one of the founding members of NEF. In June she escorted her first convoy, HX.130, to Iceland and during the next eight months made six round trips there with eastbound convoys. She returned to Halifax on 24 January 1942 and in February commenced a major refit at Liverpool, Nova Scotia. After working up in May she joined EG C-3, arriving in Londonderry on 5 June for the first time from convoy HX.191. During this period *Wetaskiwin* participated in two major convoy actions: SC.42 (September 1941);

Wetaskiwin.

and SC.48 (October 1941). On 31 July 1942 while escorting ON.115, she shared with *Skeena* the sinking of *U 588*. In mid-January 1943 she arrived at Liverpool, Nova Scotia, for refit, which was completed on 9 March and followed by further repairs at Halifax. In May 1943 she joined EG C-5, and that December went to Galveston, Texas, for a long refit, including extension of her fo'c's'le. Following its completion on

6 March 1944 she returned briefly to Halifax before proceeding to Bermuda for workups late in April. Returning northward, she joined C-5, leaving Londonderry on 23 September for the last time to join EG W-7, WLEF, for the remainder of the war. She was paid off at Sorel on 19 June 1945 and sold to the Venezuelan Navy, which renamed her *Victoria*. She was discarded in 1962.

WETASKIWIN		
BUILDER:	Burrard Dry Dock Co.	COMMISSIONED: 17/12/40
	Ltd., Vancouver, BC	PAID OFF: 19/6/45
LAID DOWN:	11/4/40	FO'C'S'LE EXTENSION COMPLETED
LAUNCHED:	18/7/40	Galveston, TX: 6/3/44
Commanding Officers		
LCDR G. Windeyer, RCN	17/12/40	4/11/42
A/LCDR J. R. Kidston, RCNVR	5/11/42	21/3/44
LT A. Walton, RCNR	22/3/44	6/8/44
A/LCDR M. S. Duffus, RCNVR	7/8/44	15/9/44
LT A. Walton, RCNR	16/9/44	19/6/45

Weyburn

Commissioned at Montreal on 26 November 1941, she arrived at Halifax on 6 December and joined Halifax Force for local escort work, but was soon in need of repairs. These were carried out at Halifax during March and April, following which she joined WLEF. In July she transferred to Gulf Escort Force for Quebec City-Sydney convoys but in September was allocated to duties in connection with Operation Torch. She arrived at Londonderry on 27 September from convoy SC.100, and at Liverpool on 2 October for fitting of extra Oerlikon A/A guns. The work was completed on 21 October and in November *Weyburn* began four months' employment as escort to UK-Mediterranean convoys. On 22 February 1943 she struck a mine laid off Gibraltar three weeks earlier by *U 118*, and was lost with seven of her ship's company.

Weyburn, May 1942.

WEYBURN

BUILDER:	Port Arthur Shipbuilding Co. Ltd., Port Arthur, ON	COMMISSIONED:	26/11/41
		LOST:	22/2/43
LAID DOWN:	21/12/40	FO'C'S'LE EXTENSION:	
LAUNCHED:	26/7/41	Never done; ship was lost	

Commanding Officer

LCDR T. M. W. Golby, RCNR	26/11/41	22/2/43

Windflower in one of the earliest photographs of a corvette released, December 1940. She is not yet armed.

WINDFLOWER

BUILDER:	Davie Shipbuilding and Repairing Co. Ltd., Lauzon, QC	COMMISSIONED:	15/5/41
		LOST:	7/12/41
LAID DOWN:	24/2/40	FO'C'S'LE EXTENSION	
LAUNCHED:	4/7/40	Never done; ship was lost	

Commanding Officers

A/LCDR J. H. S. MacDonald, RCNR	20/10/40	13/10/41	LT J. Price, RCNR	14/10/41	7/12/41

Windflower

Commissioned on 20 October 1940 at Quebec City, she arrived at Halifax on 31 October and left on 6 December with convoy HX.94 for the UK. There, at Scotstoun, she completed fitting out on 2 March 1941 following which she went to Tobermory to work up. Later in March she was assigned to EG 4 (RN), Greenock, escorting convoys between the UK and Iceland. She left Aultbea on 10 June for St. John's with OB.332, and on arrival transferred to Newfoundland Command. After two round trips between St. John's and Iceland, she arrived at Liverpool, Nova Scotia on 29 August for a short refit, resuming her ocean escort duties in mid-October. She made one more round trip to Iceland, and on 7 December 1941 while making her second trip, was rammed and sunk in convoy SC.58 by the Dutch freighter *Zypenberg* in dense fog off the Grand Banks. Twenty-three of her complement were lost.

FLOWER CLASS 1940–1941 SHORT FO'C'S'LE PROGRAM

PARTICULARS OF CLASS:	
DISPLACEMENT:	950
DIMENSIONS:	205' 1" x 33' 1" x 11' 6"
SPEED:	16 kts
CREW:	6/79
ARMAMENT:	one 4-inch, one 2 pdr., two 20-mm, Hedgehog in many

Brantford, 11 October 1944.

Brantford

Commissioned on 15 May 1942 at Montreal, *Brantford* arrived at Halifax on 30 May. After working up at Pictou, she joined WLEF in July. When this force was divided into escort groups in June 1943 she became a member of EG W-3, transferring to W-2 in April 1944. Loaned in June 1944 to EG W-3 for one round trip to Londonderry, she left Halifax on 2 June with convoy HX.294 and returned at the end of the month with ONS.242. *Brantford* underwent two refits during her career: the first at Quebec City during the summer of 1943; the second at Sydney, completing 12 September 1944, following which she was assigned to HMCS *Cornwallis* for training duties until the end of the war. Her fo'c's'le was never lengthened. She was paid off on 27 August 1945 at Sorel, sold for conversion to a whale-catcher, and in 1950 entered service as the Honduran *Olympic Arrow*. Sold into Japanese hands, she was renamed *Otori Maru No. 11* in 1956, and *Kyo Maru No. 21* in 1961. She last appeared in Lloyd's register for 1972-73.

Dundas

Built at Victoria and commissioned on 1 April 1942 she joined Esquimalt Force after working up, and in August made a round trip as convoy escort to Kodiak, Alaska, in support of the Aleutian campaign. On 13 September she sailed for the east coast to replace an Operation Torch nominee, joining WLEF upon arrival at Halifax on 13 October. She served with EG W-7 from June 1943, with W-5 from September 1943, and with W-4 from April 1944. In the course of a major refit at Montreal from 13 June to 19 November 1943 *Dundas* acquired her extended fo'c's'le. She commenced another long refit early in January 1945 at Liverpool, Nova Scotia, resuming service in April. Paid off on 17 July at Sorel, she was sold later that year and broken up in 1946 at Port Colborne, Ontario.

BRANTFORD
BUILDER:	Midland Shipyards Ltd., Midland, ON	COMMISSIONED:	15/5/42
LAID DOWN:	24/2/41	PAID OFF:	17/8/45
LAUNCHED:	6/9/41	FO'C'S'LE EXTENSION: Never done	

Commanding Officers
LT W. D. F. Johnston, RCNR	15/5/42	26/4/43	IT J. P. Kieran, RCNR	29/9/44	27/4/45
IT J. A. R. Allan, RCNVR	27/4/43	1/5/44	LT R. M. Smillie, RCNVR	28/4/45	17/8/15
LT R. C. Eaton, RCNVR	2/5/44	28/9/44			

Dundas, 11 April 1942.

DUNDAS
BUILDER:	Victoria Machinery Depot Co. Ltd., Victoria, BC	COMMISSIONED:	1/4/42
		PAID OFF:	17/7/45
LAID DOWN:	19/3/41	FO'C'S'LE EXTENSION COMPLETED	
LAUNCHED:	25/7/41	Montreal, QC:	19/11/43

Commanding Officers
A/LCDR R. W. Draney, RCNR	1/4/42	17/5/43	LT R. B. Taylor, RCNVR	12/4/44	17/2/45
LT R. W. Hart, RCNVR	18/5/43	11/4/44	LT D. E. Howard, RCNVR	18/2/45	17/7/45

Midland

Commissioned at Montreal on 7 November 1941, she arrived at Halifax on 30 November and spent her entire career with WLEF, from June 1943 as a member of EG W-2. She underwent two extensive refits: the first at Liverpool, Nova Scotia from 30 November 1942 to 14 April 1943; the second at Galveston, Texas, from mid-March to 25 May 1944. The latter refit included the extension of her fo'c's'le. Upon its completion she returned briefly to Halifax before leaving on 1 July for three weeks' working up in Bermuda. She was paid off at Sydney on 15 July 1945 and broken up the following year at Fort William, Ontario.

Midland, early 1945.

MIDLAND

BUILDER:	Midland Shipyards Ltd., Midland, ON	COMMISSIONED:	7/11/41
LAID DOWN:	24/2/41	PAID OFF:	15/7/45
LAUNCHED:	25/6/41	FO'C'S'LE EXTENSION COMPLETED	
		Galveston, TX:	25/5/44

Commanding Officers

A/LCDR A. B. Taylor, RCNR	17/11/41	31/10/43	LT W. O. O. Barbour, RCNR	1/11/43	15/7/45

New Westminister, March 1945.

NEW WESTMINSTER

BUILDER:	Victoria Machinery Depot Co. Ltd., Victoria, BC	COMMISSIONED:	31/1/42
		PAID OFF:	21/6/45
LAID DOWN:	4/2/41	FO'C'S'LE EXTENSION COMPLETED	
LAUNCHED:	14/5/41	Sydney, NS:	10/12/43

Commanding Officer

A/LCDR R. O. McKenzie, RCNR	31/1/42	21/6/45

New Westminster

Built at Victoria, she was commissioned there 31 January 1942 and assigned to Esquimalt Force until the threat of Japanese invasion had abated. Ordered to Halifax to release an east coast corvette for Operation Torch service, she arrived there on 13 October, a month after leaving Esquimalt. Assigned to WLEF, she operated on the "triangle run" until May 1943, when she began a major refit at Sydney. This refit included fo'c's'le extension and was not completed until 10 December. The ship was then made a part of EG C-5, and in July 1944 sailed with HXS.300, the largest convoy of the war, comprised of 166 ships. She left Londonderry on 14 December 1944 for the last time, returning home to refit at Saint John until early March 1945. Allocated to Sydney Force until the end of hostilities, she was paid off at Sorel on 21 June 1945 and in 1947 sold for commercial purposes. She served under various names, the last being the Bahamian *Azua*, from 1954 to 1966, when she arrived at Tampa for breaking up.

Timmins, February 1942.

TIMMINS							
BUILDER:	Yarrows Ltd., Esquimalt, BC			PAID OFF:	15/7/45		
LAID DOWN:	14/12/40			FO'C'S'LE EXTENSION COMPLETED			
LAUNCHED:	26/6/41			Liverpool, NS.	16/10/44		
COMMISSIONED:	10/2/42						

Commanding Officers

LT J. A. Brown, RCNR	10/2/42	18/8/42	LCDR J. H. S. MacDonald, RCNR		20/3/43	18/4/43
LCDR A. T. Morrell, RCNR	19/8/42	30/8/42	A/LCDR H. S. Maxwell, RCNVR		19/4/43	29/6/44
LT J. M. Gillison, RCNR	31/8/42	11/1/43	LT R. G. James, RCNVR		2/9/44	15/12/44
LT N. S. C. Dickinson, RCNVR	12/1/43	19/3/43	LT J. Kincaid, RCNVR		16/12/44	15/7/45

Vancouver (2nd) September 1943 at Corner Brook, Nfld.

VANCOUVER (2nd)						
BUILDER:	Yarrows Ltd., Esquimalt, BC			COMMISSIONED:	20/3/42	
LAID DOWN:	16/6/41			PAID OFF:	26/6/45	
LAUNCHED:	26/8/41			FO'C'S'LE EXTENSION COMPLETED		
				Vancouver, BC:	16/9/43	

Commanding Officers

LT P.F.M. DeFreitas, RCNR	20/3/42	7/6/43	A/LCDR A.W. Ford, RCNR		5/2/44	9/10/44
LCDR A.T. Morrell, RCNR	8/6/43	4/2/44	LT G.C. Campbell, RCNVR		10/10/44	26/6/45

Timmins

Commissioned at Esquimalt on 10 February 1942, *Timmins* served with Esquimalt Force until transferred to the east coast. Upon arrival at Halifax on 13 October, she was assigned to WLEF. With its division into escort groups in June 1943 she became a member of EG W-6, transferring to W-2 in April 1944. She commenced a two-month refit at Liverpool, Nova Scotia late in June 1943, followed by workups at Picton. A second refit at Liverpool was carried out between late June and mid October 1944. It included the extension of her fo'c's'le, and three weeks' working up in Bermuda followed. *Timmins* was paid off on 15 July 1945 at Sorel, and sold later that year for commercial use. She entered service in 1948 as the Honduran-flag *Guayaquil* and, ironically, foundered at Guayaquil, Ecuador on 3 August 1960.

Vancouver (2nd)

Commissioned at Esquimalt on 20 March 1942, she joined Esquimalt Force and, on 20 June, escorted the torpedo-damaged SS *Fort Camosun* to Victoria. In August she left for Kodiak, Alaska, to perform escort service for several weeks in support of the Aleutian campaign. On 24 February 1943 she again arrived at Kodiak to serve under US control until the end of May. In mid-September she emerged from three months' refit at Vancouver with an extended fo'c's'le. Reassigned in February 1944 to WLEF, she arrived at Halifax on 25 March. After serving briefly with escort groups W-3 and W-1, she was transferred in June to Quebec Force as escort to Quebec City-Goose Bay convoys for three months. Late in November, after a month's refit at Charlottetown, she proceeded to Bermuda to work up, and on her return rejoined W-1 for the balance of the hostilities. She was paid off 26 June 1945 at Sorel, and broken up at Hamilton, Ontario, in 1946.

REVISED FLOWER CLASS 1940–1941 PROGRAM

PARTICULARS OF CLASS:
DISPLACEMENT: 1,015
DIMENSIONS: 208' 4" x 33'1" x 11'
SPEED: 16 kts
CREW: 6/79
ARMAMENT: one 4-inch, one 2 pdr., two 20-mm, Hedgehog in most
First corvettes built with long fo'c's'le

Calgary

Commissioned at Sorel on 16 December 1941, *Calgary* arrived at Halifax on 28 December. She served with WLEF until November 1942 when she was assigned to duties in connection with Operation Torch. She arrived at Londonderry on 3 November but proved to have mechanical defects that precluded her intended use on UK-Mediterranean convoys. Instead, she had to undergo three months' repairs at Cardiff, completing at the end of March 1943, and in April returned to Canada and joined WLEF. In June 1943 she was transferred to EG 5, Western Support Force, and sailed for the UK with convoy SC.133. For the next few months she was employed in support of Atlantic convoys and on 20 November shared in sinking *U 536* north of the Azores. *Calgary* returned to Canada early in 1944 for refit at Liverpool, Nova Scotia, completing on 17 March. After working up at Halifax, she left on 1 May for the UK to join Western Approaches Command, Greenock, for invasion duties. Initially based at Sheerness, she was moved to Nore Command in September for the duration of the war. Returning home late in May 1945 she was paid off at Sorel on 19 June and eventually broken up in Spain.

Calgary, May 1944.

Charlottetown, 1942.

CALGARY

BUILDER:	Marine Industries Ltd., Sorel, QC	LAUNCHED:	23/8/41
		COMMISSIONED:	16/12/41
LAID DOWN:	22/3/41	PAID OFF:	19/6/45

Commanding Officers

LT G. Lancaster, RCNR	16/12/41	19/6/42
A/LCDR H. K. Hill, RCNVR	20/6/42	17/3/44
LT A. A. R. Dykes, RCNR	18/3/44	15/9/44
LT L. D. M. Saunders, RCNVR	16/9/44	25/5/45
LT G. M. Orr, RCNVR	26/5/45	19/6/45

Charlottetown

Commissioned at Quebec City on 13 December 1941, *Charlottetown* arrived at Halifax on 18 December. She was a member of WLEF until mid-July 1942 when she was transferred to Gulf Escort Force owing to increased U-boat activity in the Gulf of St. Lawrence. She was employed as escort to Quebec-Sydney convoys until 11 September 1942 when she was torpedoed and sunk by *U 517* in the St. Lawrence River, near Cap Chat, Quebec. Nine of her ship's company were lost. She had earlier delivered convoy SQ.35 to Rimouski and was en route back to Gaspé, her base, at the time.

CHARLOTTETOWN

BUILDER:	Kingston Shipbuilding Co. Ltd., Kingston, ON	LAUNCHED:	10/9/41
		COMMISSIONED:	13/12/41
		LOST:	11/9/42
LAID DOWN:	7/6/41		

Commanding Officer

LT J. W. Bonner, RCNR	13/12/41	11/9/42

Fredericton

Commissioned on 8 December 1941 at Sorel, *Fredericton* arrived at Halifax on 18 December. She was assigned to WLEF until July 1942, when she joined Halifax Force (Aruba Tanker Convoys). In September, after one round trip to Aruba, she was placed under US operational control to escort New York-Guantanamo convoys. She arrived in New York for the last time on 21 February 1943, rejoining WLEF in March. After a major refit at Liverpool, Nova Scotia from 9 June to 10 October 1943 and workups at Pictou, she joined EG C-1 and for the next ten months was employed as an ocean escort. She left Londonderry on 30 September 1944 for convoy ON.256, and upon arriving in Canada went to Saint John, New Brunswick for two months' refit. This was completed in mid-December and in January 1945 the ship proceeded to Bermuda for three weeks' workups. In February she joined EG C-9, with which she was to spend the balance of the war as ocean escort. *Fredericton* was paid off on 14 July 1945 at Sorel. Although said to have been broken up in 1946, it appears that she was sold to become a whale-catcher in 1948, successively the Panamanian-flag *Tra los Montes*, *Olympic Fighter* (1950), *Otori Maru No. 6* (1956), and *Kyo Maru No. 20* (1961). Last noted in Lloyd's Register for 1978-79. Owing to an error by Lloyd's, the above details were attributed to HMCS *Saskatoon* in our 1993 printing.

Fredericton, November 1943.

FREDERICTON

BUILDER:	Marine Industries Ltd., Sorel, QC	COMMISSIONED:	8/12/41
LAID DOWN:	22/3/41	PAID OFF:	14/7/45
LAUNCHED:	2/9/41		

Commanding Officers

A/LCDR J. H. S. MacDonald, RCNR	8/12/41	1/7/42	LT J. C. Smyth, RCN	21/7/44	14/7/45
LCDR J. F. Harrington, RCNVR	2/7/42	20/7/44			

Halifax, 1944.

HALIFAX

BUILDER:	Collingwood Shipyards Ltd., Collingwood, ON	LAUNCHED:	4/10/41
		COMMISSIONED:	26/11/41
LAID DOWN:	26/4/41	PAID OFF:	12/7/45

Commanding Officers

LCDR C.W. Copelin, OBE, RCNR	26/11/41	6/2/43	A/LCDR R. M. Hanbury, RCNVR	22/6/44	3/9/44
LT M. F. Oliver, RCNR	7/2/43	21/6/44	LT L. E. Horne, RCNVR	4/9/44	12/7/45

Halifax

Commissioned on 26 November 1941 at Montreal, *Halifax* was the first RCN corvette to be completed with a long fo'c's'le. Assigned to WLEF on her arrival at Halifax on 18 December, she was transferred in July 1942 to Halifax Force (Aruba Tanker Convoys). On 14 August she arrived at Aruba with HA.3, her third tanker convoy, and was assigned to escort TAW.15, a Trinidad-Aruba-Key West convoy that developed into the only major convoy battle of the war in those waters. Arriving in New York on 14 September, she was placed under US control for New York-Guantanamo convoys until March 1943 when she joined WLEF. Between 2 May and 15 October she underwent an extensive refit at Liverpool, Nova Scotia, followed by workups at Pictou. On New Year's Day 1944 she arrived at St. John's to join EG C-1, leaving Londonderry on 11 August for two weeks' refit at Lunenburg. This refit was followed by three weeks' further repairs at Halifax and, late in December, workups in Bermuda. In January 1945 she briefly joined Halifax Force, transferring in February to EG C-9 for the rest of the war. Paid off on 12 July at Sorel, she was sold for conversion as a salvage vessel.

Kitchener.

KITCHENER

BUILDER:	Marine Industries Ltd., Sorel, QC	COMMISSIONED:	28/6/42
LAID DOWN:	28/2/41	PAID OFF:	11/7/45
LAUNCHED:	18/11/41		

Commanding Officers

LCDR W. Evans, RCNVR	28/6/42	16/1/44	LT J. E. Moles, RCNVR	17/1/44	11/7/45

La Malbaie, ca 1943.

LA MALBAIE

BUILDER:	Marine Industries Ltd., Sorel, QC	COMMISSIONED:	28/4/42
LAID DOWN:	22/3/41	PAID OFF:	28/6/45
LAUNCHED:	25/10/41		

Commanding Officers

LT I. W. McTavish, RCNR	28/4/42	11/2/43	LT E. F. Piper, RCNVR	8/6/44	21/2/45
A/LCDR J. S. Davis, RCNVR	12/2/43	7/6/44	LT T. H. Dunn, RCNVR	22/2/45	28/6/45

Kitchener

Commissioned at Quebec City on 28 June 1942, *Kitchener* arrived at Halifax on 16 July and carried out six weeks' workups at Pictou before briefly joining WLEF in September. It may have been during this unusually long workup that she starred in the film *Corvette K-225* with Randolph Scott. In October she was assigned to duties in connection with Operation Torch, and arrived at Londonderry on 3 November. For the next four and a half months she escorted UK-Mediterranean convoys, returning to Canada in mid-April 1943 with convoy ONS.2. In May she joined Western Support Force but in June transferred to EG C-5, MOEF, and during the following four months made three round trips to Londonderry. A major refit, commenced in October at Liverpool, Nova Scotia was completed on 28 January 1944 followed by two weeks' working up in Bermuda. In mid-April she arrived at Londonderry, where she was assigned to invasion duties with Western Approaches Command, based at Milford Haven. She arrived off the beaches on D Day, escorting a group of landing craft. From August until the end of the war she served with EG 41, Plymouth, returning home late in May 1945 to be paid off at Sorel 11 July. She was broken up at Hamilton in 1949.

La Malbaie

Commissioned at Sorel on 28 April 1942, *La Malbaie* arrived at Halifax on 13 May and, after working up there and at Pictou, joined WLEF late in June. After undergoing mechanical repairs at Halifax from 11 August to 20 December, she was assigned to EG C-3, arriving at Londonderry for the first time on 12 January 1943 from HX.221. She served with C-3 until her final departure from Derry on 26 October 1944. During this period she underwent a major refit at Liverpool, Nova Scotia, mid-September to mid-December 1943. Late in December 1944 she joined Halifax Force for the duration of hostilities, was paid off 28 June 1945 at Sorel, and ultimately broken up in Scotland. A pre-launching photo of *La Malbaie* served as the model for the 20-cent Canadian stamp of 1942.

Port Arthur

Commissioned on 26 May 1942 at Montreal, she arrived at Halifax on 10 June and was allocated to WLEF at the end of July. In September she was appointed to Operation Torch duties, arriving at Londonderry on 1 November from convoy SC.105, and during the next four months escorted UK-Mediterranean convoys. On 19 January 1943 while so employed, *Port Arthur* sank the Italian submarine *Tritone* off Bougie, Algeria. She arrived at Halifax on 23 March 1943 and, after brief repairs there, joined Western Support Force at St. John's. Early in August she began a major refit at Liverpool, Nova Scotia, completing on 31 December. After working up at Halifax, she joined EG W-9, WEF. In April 1944 she was assigned to Western Approaches Command for invasion duties and left St. John's on 24 April for Londonderry. During the following four months she was occupied as a convoy escort in support of the invasion, and in September joined Portsmouth Command. In February 1945 she returned to Canada, where VE Day found her still under refit at Liverpool, Nova Scotia. She was paid off 11 July at Sorel and broken up at Port Colborne in 1947.

Port Arthur, 1942-43.

PORT ARTHUR

BUILDER:	Port Arthur Shipbuilding Co. Ltd., Port Arthur, ON	LAUNCHED:	18/9/41
		COMMISSIONED:	26/5/42
LAID DOWN:	28/4/41	PAID OFF:	11/7/45

Commanding Officers

| LT E. T. Simmons, DSC, RCNVR | 26/5/42 | 8/7/43 | A/LCDR K. T. Chisholm, RCNVR | 9/7/43 | 11/7/45 |

Regina, 1942.

REGINA

BUILDER:	Marine Industries Ltd., Sorel, QC	COMMISSIONED:	22/1/42
LAID DOWN:	22/3/41	LOST:	8/8/44
LAUNCHED:	14/10/41		

Commanding Officers

| LCDR R. F. Harris, RCNR | 22/1/42 | 23/2/42 | LCDR H. Freeland, DSO, RCNR | 21/10/42 | 3/9/43 |
| LT R. S. Kelley, RCNR | 24/2/42 | 20/10/42 | LT J. W. Radford, RCNR | 4/9/43 | 8/8/44 |

Regina

Regina arrived at Halifax on 6 January, and was commissioned on 22 January 1942. She served with WLEF from mid-March until September, when she was reassigned to Operation Torch. Crossing as escort to convoy SC.108, she arrived at Belfast on 22 November for refit, following which she was employed as escort to UK-Mediterranean convoys. While thus engaged on 8 February 1943 she sank the Italian submarine *Avorio* in the western Mediterranean north of Phillipville, Algeria. Returning to Canada late in March, she briefly rejoined WLEF before commencing a refit at Sydney on 9 June. The work was completed at Pictou in mid-December and workups carried out there, followed by further repairs at Halifax and Shelburne. *Regina* joined EG C-1 in February 1944, and at the beginning of March left Argentia to escort SC.154 to the UK, but fouled her screw while fuelling and was towed into Horta by the rescue ship *Dundee*, escorted by *Valleyfield*. Arriving at Londonderry toward the end of March, *Regina* was assigned to Western Approaches Command for invasion duties. She was employed as an escort to Channel and coastal convoys until 8 August 1944 when she was torpedoed and sunk off Trevose Head, Cornwall, by *U 667*. Thirty of her ship's company were lost.

Ville de Québec, 1942-43.

VILLE DE QUÉBEC

BUILDER:	Morton Engineering and Dry Dock Co., Quebec City, QC		LAUNCHED:	12/11/41
LAID DOWN:	7/6/41		COMMISSIONED:	24/5/42
			PAID OFF:	6/7/45

Commanding Officers

LCDR D. G. Jeffrey, RCNR	24/5/42	29/9/42	LT J. L. Carter, RCNVR	13/6/43	12/3/44
LT I. H. Bell, RCNVR	30/9/42	11/10/42	LT C. S. Glassco, RCNVR	13/3/44	1/5/44
LCDR A. R. E. Coleman, RCNR	12/10/42	12/6/43	LCDR H. C. Hatch, RCNVR	2/5/44	6/7/45

Woodstock, 2 October 1943.

WOODSTOCK

BUILDER:	Collingwood Shipyards Ltd., Collingwood, ON		LAUNCHED:	10/12/41
LAID DOWN:	23/5/41		COMMISSIONED:	1/5/42
			PAID OFF:	27/1/45

Commanding Officers

LT L. P. Denny, RCNR	1/5/42	18/10/42	LT C. E. Wright, RCNVR	17/8/43	5/10/44
CDR G. H. Griffiths, RCN	19/10/42	19/1/43	LT W. McCombe, RCNR	6/10/44	27/1/45
SKPR/LT J. M. Watson, RCNR	20/1/43	16/8/43	LCDR J. S. Cunningham, RCNVR	17/5/45	18/3/46

Ville de Québec

Commissioned on 24 May 1942 at Quebec City, she arrived at Halifax on 12 June, having escorted Quebec-Sydney convoy QS.7 en route. Late in July, after working up at Pictou, she was assigned to WLEF and used almost exclusively as an escort to convoys between Boston and Halifax. In September *Ville de Québec* was allocated to Operation Torch, arriving at Londonderry on 10 November, and for the succeeding four months was employed on UK-Mediterranean convoys. On 13 January 1943 she sank *U 224* west of Algiers. She returned to Canada in April, carried out brief repairs at Halifax, and then arrived at Gaspé on 12 May to join Quebec Force, escorting Quebec-Sydney and Quebec-Labrador convoys. In September she returned to Halifax and later that month joined EG W-2, WLEF. In mid-January 1944 she began an extensive refit at Liverpool, Nova Scotia, completing early in May, and on 22 May left for a month's workups in Bermuda. On her return she joined EG C-4 for one round trip to Londonderry, transferring in September to EG 41, Plymouth. Based at Milford Haven, she served with that group for the balance of the war, returning to Canada late in May 1945 to be paid off on 6 July at Sorel. Sold for mercantile use in 1946, she was variously named *Despina* (1946), *Dorothea Paxos* (1947), *Tanya* (1948), and *Medex* (in Lloyd's Register until 1952).

Woodstock

Commissioned on 1 May 1942 at Montreal, she arrived at Halifax on 23 May and, after working up at Pictou, joined WLEF. Assigned to Operation Torch, she arrived on 23 September at Londonderry from convoy HX.207 and proceeded to the Humber for six weeks' refit, including extra A/A armament. While serving as escort to UK-Mediterranean convoys, on 1 January 1943 she sank *MTB 105* 250 miles northwest of the Azores, after the merchant ship carrying it had been sunk. *Woodstock* returned to Canada in March, and in April, after repairs at Halifax, joined EG C-1 for one round trip to the UK. In June she was transferred to EG 5, Western Support Force at St. John's, but later that month was reassigned to EG C-4 at Londonderry. She escorted only one convoy as a member of that group before commencing refit late in June at Liverpool, Nova Scotia. Completed at Halifax in mid-September, the refit was followed by three weeks' workups at Pictou, the ship then rejoining C-4. In April

1944 while at Londonderry, she was allocated to Western Approaches Command for invasion duties, and was so employed for the next three months. She left Derry for the last time on 3 August 1944 for two months' refit at Liverpool, Nova Scotia. She left Halifax on 18 October for the west coast, arriving at Esquimalt a month later to join Esquimalt Force. On 27 January 1945 she was paid off there for conversion to a loop-layer but upon recommissioning on 17 May was employed as a weather ship until finally paid off on 18 March 1946. Sold in 1948 for conversion to a whale-catcher, she entered service in 1952 as the Honduran-flag *Olympic Winner*. She passed into Japanese ownership in 1956, was renamed *Otori Maru No. 20*, and in 1957, *Akitsu Maru*. She was broken up at Etajima in 1975.

REVISED FLOWER CLASS, INCREASED ENDURANCE 1942–1943 PROGRAM

Note: Pressurized boiler rooms eliminated the need for the distinctive ventilators grouped around the funnels of earlier corvettes.

PARTICULARS OF CLASS:	
DISPLACEMENT:	970
DIMENSIONS:	208' 4" x 33' 1" x 11'
SPEED:	16 kts
CREW:	6/79
ARMAMENT:	one 4-inch, one 2 pdr., two 20-mm, Hedgehog

Atholl

Commissioned on 14 October 1943 at Quebec City, *Atholl* arrived at Halifax in November and returned there in mid-December for two months' repairs after working up at Pictou. In February 1944 she was assigned to EG 9, Londonderry, and made her passage there in March as escort to convoy HX.281. She had scarcely arrived when it was decided that the group should consist only of frigates, and she returned to Canada in April with ONM.231, joining EG C-4 at St. John's. She served the rest of the war as mid-ocean escort except for time out under refit at Sydney and Halifax from December 1944 to April 1945. Early in June 1945 she left Londonderry for the last time, and was paid off on 17 July at Sydney and laid up at Sorel. She was broken up at Hamilton, Ontario, in 1952.

Cobourg

Commissioned at Midland on 11 May 1944, she arrived at Halifax 17 June, having paid a visit to her namesake port en route. She arrived in Bermuda in mid-July for three weeks' workups and on her return was allocated to EG C-6, St. John's. *Cobourg* served with the group as a mid-ocean escort for the duration of the war, leaving Londonderry on 27 March 1945 to join convoy ON.293 for her last trip westward. She arrived at Halifax 2 May for refit and was paid off 15 June at Sorel to await disposal. Sold into mercantile service in 1945, she began her new career in 1947 under the name of *Camco*. In 1956 she assumed the name *Puerto del Sol* under Panamanian flag, and on 1 July 1971, burned and sank at New Orleans. She was later raised and scrapped.

Atholl, 1944.

ATHOLL			
BUILDER:	Morton Engineering and Dry Dock Co., Quebec City, QC	LAUNCHED:	4/4/43
		COMMISSIONED:	14/10/43
LAID DOWN:	15/8/42	PAID OFF:	17/7/45

Commanding Officers

LT W. D. H. Gardiner, RCNVR	14/10/43	16/9/44	LT W. G. Garden, RCNVR	17/9/44	17/7/45

Cobourg, May 1944.

COBOURG			
BUILDER:	Midland Shipyards Ltd., Midland, ON	COMMISSIONED:	11/5/44
LAID DOWN:	25/11/42	PAID OFF:	15/6/45
LAUNCHED:	14/7/43		

Commanding Officer

LT G. H. Johnson, RCNVR	11/5/44	15/6/45

Fergus

Commissioned at Collingwood on 18 November 1944, *Fergus* was the last corvette launched for the RCN. She arrived at Halifax in mid-December, and early in January 1945 proceeded to Bermuda to work up. Arriving at St. John's on 2 February, she joined EG C-9, with which she was to serve on North Atlantic convoy duty until VE Day. She left Greenock early in June for return to Canada, was paid off on 14 July at Sydney and placed in reserve at Sorel. Sold for mercantile use in November, she was renamed *Camco II* and in 1948, *Harcourt Kent*. She was wrecked on Cape Pine, Newfoundland, 22 November 1949.

Fergus, Bermuda, January 1945.

FERGUS

BUILDER:	Collingwood Shipyards Ltd., Collingwood, ON	LAUNCHED:	30/8/44
		COMMISSIONED:	18/11/44
LAID DOWN:	10/12/43	PAID OFF:	14/7/45

Commanding Officer

A/LCDR H. F. Farncomb, RCNVR	18/11/44	14/7/45

Frontenac, December 1944.

FRONTENAC

BUILDER:	Kingston Shipbuilding Co. Ltd., Kingston, ON	LAUNCHED:	2/6/43
		COMMISSIONED:	26/10/43
LAID DOWN:	19/2/43	PAID OFF:	22/7/45

Commanding Officers

A/LCDR E. T. P. Wennberg, RCNVR	26/10/43	15/3/45	LT D. R. Baker, RCNVR	16/3/45	22/7/45

Frontenac

Frontenac was commissioned at Kingston on 26 October 1943, arrived at Halifax in mid-December and carried out working up exercises in St. Margaret's Bay in January 1944. She was then assigned to EG 9, Londonderry, and made the crossing in March as escort to convoy SC.154. It was decided, however, that EG 9 should be made up only of frigates, and *Frontenac* returned to St. John's, where in May she joined EG C-1. She left Belfast 19 December to escort ON.273, her last westbound convoy, and early in January 1945 commenced three weeks' refit at Liverpool, Nova Scotia. On completion she was assigned to Halifax Force and sent to Bermuda to work up, but saw little further service before being paid off at Halifax on 22 July. She was then taken to Sorel, but was sold in October to the United Ship Corp. of New York. She was still afloat in 1957, flying the Honduran flag.

Guelph

Commissioned at Toronto on 9 May 1944, *Guelph* arrived at Halifax early in June and left on 2 July, escorting the ancient RN submarines *P.553* and *P.554* to Philadelphia. She then proceeded to Bermuda for workups, leaving there on 2 August for New York, where she joined EG C-8. She served with this group as a local escort until late September, when she was transferred to EG W-8, which, although forming in Londonderry, was to be based at St. John's. She made her passage eastward as escort to convoy HXF.310. On her final transatlantic trip she left Belfast on 9 April 1945 to be based at Halifax until paid off on 27 June at Sorel. On 2 October she was sold to a New York buyer, retaining her name under Panamanian flag. She was last noted in Lloyd's Register for 1964-65 as *Burfin*, a name she had borne since 1956.

Hawkesbury

Commissioned at Quebec City on 14 June 1944, *Hawkesbury* arrived at Halifax in mid-July and proceeded to Bermuda on 6 August for three weeks' working up. On 18 September she left St. John's to join convoy HXF.308 for passage to Londonderry, where she was to join EG C-7, then forming. She served the remainder of her career on North Atlantic convoy duty, leaving Londonderry early in June 1945 for Canada, and was paid off on 10 July at Sydney. Taken to Sorel, she was later sold for mercantile purposes, entering service after conversion in 1949 to the Cambodian-owned *Campuchea*. She was broken up at Hong Kong in 1956.

Guelph while a member of EG C-8.

Hawkesbury, 1944.

GUELPH			
BUILDER:	Collingwood Shipyards Ltd., Collingwood, ON	LAID DOWN:	29/5/43
		LAUNCHED:	20/12/43
		COMMISSIONED:	9/5/44
		PAID OFF:	27/6/45
Commanding Officers			
LT G. H. Hayes, DSC, RCN		9/5/44	14/5/45
LT F. D. Wickett, RCNVR		15/5/45	20/5/45
LT D. H. Smith, RCNVR		15/6/45	27/6/45

HAWKESBURY			
BUILDER:	Morton Engineering and Dry Dock Co., Quebec City, QC	LAUNCHED:	16/11/43
		COMMISSIONED:	14/6/44
LAID DOWN:	20/7/43	PAID OFF:	10/7/45
Commanding Officer			
A/LCDR W. G. Curry, RCNVR	14/6/44	10/7/45	

Lindsay, 1944.

LINDSAY			
BUILDER:	Midland Shipyards Ltd., Midland, ON	COMMISSIONED:	15/11/43
LAID DOWN:	30/9/42	PAID OFF:	18/7/45
LAUNCHED:	4/6/43		

Commanding Officer
A/LCDR G. A. V. Thomson, RCNVR   15/11/43   18/7/45

Louisburg (2nd) celebrating VE-Day.

LOUISBURG (2nd)			
BUILDER:	Morton Engineering and Dry Dock Co., Quebec City, QC	LAUNCHED:	13/7/43
		COMMISSIONED:	13/12/43
LAID DOWN:	11/1/43	PAID OFF:	25/6/45

Commanding Officers
LT J. B. Elmsley, RCNVR   13/12/43   10/2/45   LT M. W. Knowles, RCNVR   11/2/45   25/6/45

Lindsay

Commissioned at Midland on 15 November 1943, *Lindsay* arrived at Halifax in December and late in January 1944 sailed to Bermuda for three weeks' workups. Upon her return she was briefly attached to EG W-5, but left Halifax on 23 April to join Western Approaches Command at Londonderry. For the next four months she served in UK waters as an unallocated unit, in September joining the RN's EG 41, Plymouth Command, for service in the Channel. On 22 January 1945 she was damaged in collision with HMS *Brilliant* southwest of the Isle of Wight. Following temporary repairs at Devonport from 22 January to 19 February, she sailed for Canada via Londonderry, arriving at Halifax early in March. She left there on 15 March for Saint John where she was under refit until 22 June, then proceeded to Sydney and was paid off on 18 July. She was sold for mercantile use in 1946 and renamed *North Shore*, later passing into Greek registry for Mediterranean passenger service under the name of *Lemnos*.

Louisburg (2nd)

Commissioned at Quebec City on 13 December 1943, she was sailed to Halifax in advance of completion in order to escape the freeze-up, arriving late in December, and was not ready for service until February 1944. Late in March she went to Bermuda for workups and upon returning to Halifax was assigned as an unallocated unit to Western Approaches Command, Londonderry. She sailed for the UK on 23 April and spent the next four months on escort duties associated with the invasion. That September she was allocated to EG 41, Plymouth, and late in March 1945 returned home for refit at Saint John. Upon completion of this refit she was paid off at Sorel on 25 June and placed in reserve there. She was sold in 1947 to the Dominican Navy and renamed *Juan Alejandro Acosta*. Deleted from the active list in 1978, she was driven ashore in a hurricane on 31 August 1979.

Norsyd

This name is a contraction of North Sydney. *Norsyd* was commissioned at Quebec City on December 22 1943 and en route to Halifax was diverted to Indiantown, New Brunswick for fitting-out, which was not completed until mid-March. She arrived in Bermuda later that month to work up, and on her return was assigned to EG W-7, WEF. She served with W-7, escorting local convoys, until November 1944 when she was transferred to EG C-2, St. John's, taking her first convoy, HX.323, eastward early in December. On 27 May 1945 she began a refit at Halifax and soon after its completion, on 25 June, was paid off and laid up at Sorel. She was sold into mercantile service in 1948 as *Balboa*, but acquired by the Israeli Navy in 1950 and reconverted to a warship. Renamed *Haganah*, she served until broken up in 1956.

North Bay

Commissioned on 25 October 1943 at Collingwood, *North Bay* arrived at Halifax on 29 November, and in December carried out workups in St. Margaret's Bay. On completion of these she was assigned to EG 9, Londonderry, making her passage there as escort to convoy SC.154 early in March 1944. When EG 9 became a frigates-only group, *North Bay* returned to St. John's in April and became a member of EG C-4. From 11 December to mid February 1945 she underwent a refit at Sydney and proceeded to Bermuda to work up. On completing this exercise she sailed directly to St. John's to join EG C-2, but later in April she was transferred to C-3, and on 30 April left St. John's to join convoy SC.194 for a final trip to Londonderry. She returned in May with ON.304 and was paid off 1 July and laid up at Sorel. In 1946 she was sold for mercantile use and in 1947 was renamed *Galloway Kent*.

Norsyd.

NORSYD

BUILDER:	Morton Engineering and Dry Dock Co., Quebec City, QC		LAUNCHED:	31/7/43
			COMMISSIONED:	22/12/43
LAID DOWN:	14/1/43		PAID OFF:	25/6/45

Commanding Officers

LT J. R. Biggs, RCNR	22/12/43	20/10/44	LT W. P Wickett, RCNVR	21/10/44	25/6/45

North Bay **at Montreal, November 1943.**

NORTH BAY

BUILDER:	Collingwood Shipyards Ltd., Collingwood, ON		LAUNCHED:	27/4/43
			COMMISSIONED:	25/10/43
LAID DOWN:	24/9/42		PAID OFF:	1/7/45

Commanding Officers

LT B. Hynes, RCNR	25/10/43	29/6/44	LT J. W. Radford, RCNR	24/1/45	18/2/45
LT J. N. Finlayson, RCNVR	30/6/44	11/8/44	LCDR A. C. Campbell, RCNVR	19/2/45	1/7/45
A/LCDR B. Hynes, RCNVR	12/8/44	23/1/45			

Owen Sound, 1945.

Owen Sound

Commissioned at Collingwood on 17 November 1943, *Owen Sound* arrived at Halifax on 13 December, worked up in St. Margaret's Bay in January 1944 and in February was assigned to EG 9, Londonderry. On 10 March, while acting as escort to convoy SC.157, she assisted HMCS *St. Laurent* and HMS *Forester* in the destruction of *U 845*. In May she transferred to EG C-2 at Londonderry and, in October, to the newly formed C-7. She left Derry 6 February 1945 for her last westward trip, as escort to ON.283 and, on arrival at Halifax, commenced refit. On completion of the refit in mid-May she sailed for Bermuda for three weeks' working up and on her return was paid off on 19 July and placed in reserve at Sorel. Later that year she was sold to the United Ship Co. of New York, to become in 1949 the Greek-flag merchant ship, *Cadio*, last appearing in Lloyd's list for 1967-68.

Rivière du Loup

Commissioned at Quebec City on 21 November 1943, she arrived at Halifax on 18 December requiring a month's repairs. She carried out working up exercises in Bermuda, returning on 18 February, to complete the exercises in St. Margaret's Bay. Continuing mechanical problems necessitated further repairs, which continued at Halifax until early in August. Having lost much of her original crew during this period, she had to return to Bermuda to work up again. Early in September 1944 *Rivière du Loup* returned to Halifax and joined EG W-3, WEF. In October she was assigned to EG C-3 and left St. John's on 13 November to pick up her first transatlantic convoy, HX.319. On arrival in the UK, still dogged by troubles, she underwent a month's repairs at Belfast. Her career as a mid-ocean escort ended with her arrival at Halifax late in May 1945 from convoy ON.304, and she was paid off 2 July and placed in reserve at Sorel. In 1947 she was sold to the Dominican Navy and renamed *Juan Bautista Maggiolo*. She was broken up in 1972.

OWEN SOUND						
BUILDER:	Collingwood Shipyards Ltd., Collingwood, ON	LAUNCHED:	15/6/43			
LAID DOWN:	11/11/42	COMMISSIONED:	17/11/43			
		PAID OFF:	19/7/45			
Commanding Officers						
A/LCDR J. M. Watson, RCNR		17/11/43	13/4/45	LT F. H. Pinfold, RCNVR	14/4/45	19/7/45

Rivière du Loup, 1944.

RIVIÈRE DU LOUP			
BUILDER:	Morton Engineering and Dry Dock Co., Quebec City, QC	LAUNCHED:	2/7/43
		COMMISSIONED:	21/11/43
		PAID OFF:	2/7/45
LAID DOWN:	5/1/43		
Commanding Officers			
LT R. N. Smillie, RCNVR		21/11/43	20/6/44
LT R. N. Smillie, RCNVR		19/7/44	8/1/45
LCDR F. R. K. Naftel, RCNVR		9/1/45	25/1/45
LT R. D. Weldon, RCNVR		26/1/45	2/7/45

St. Lambert

Commissioned at Quebec City on 27 May 1944 she arrived at Halifax on 19 June, and in July sailed for Bermuda to work up. On her return in mid-August *St. Lambert* was assigned to EG C-6, Londonderry, and left St. John's 18 September to join convoy HX.308 for her passage there. She served on North Atlantic convoys for the rest of her career, leaving St. John's on 27 May 1945 as escort to HX.308, the last HX convoy of the war. In mid-June she sailed from Londonderry on her final trip homeward and was paid off on 20 July and laid up at Sorel for disposal. Sold in 1946 for conversion to a merchant ship, she became the Panamanian *Chrysi Hondroulis,* in 1955 the Greek-flag *Loula*, and finally as *Stefanos III* was lost on 14 March 1964 west of Rhodes.

Trentonian

Commissioned at Kingston on 1 December 1943, *Trentonian* arrived at Halifax late in December and, after further fitting-out at Liverpool and Halifax, left the latter port for Bermuda on 18 February 1944 to work up. Returning at the beginning of March, she was assigned to Western Approaches Command and left for Londonderry on 23 April. For three months she carried out escort duty in connection with the invasion and on 13 June, while escorting the cable vessel *St. Margaret* off Normandy, she was shelled in error by a US destroyer. The shell, fortunately a dud, passed through her engine room and did little damage. Late in August she transferred to EG 41 (RN) and, based at different times at Plymouth and Milford Haven, escorted Channel convoys. While so engaged on 22 February 1945 she was torpedoed and sunk by *U 1004*, with the loss of six lives.

St. Lambert.

ST. LAMBERT

BUILDER:	Morton Engineering and Dry Dock Co., Quebec City, QC	LAUNCHED:	6/11/43
		COMMISSIONED:	27/5/44
LAID DOWN:	8/7/43	PAID OFF:	20/7/45

Commanding Officers

LT R. C. Hayden, RCNVR	27/5/44	27/10/44	A/LCDR A. P. Duke, RCNVR	24/6/45	20/7/45
LT W. D. H. Gardiner, RCNVR	28/10/44	23/6/45			

Trentonian, Bermuda, February 1944.

TRENTONIAN

BUILDER:	Kingston Shipbuilding Co. Ltd., Kingston, ON	LAUNCHED:	1/9/43
		COMMISSIONED:	1/12/43
LAID DOWN:	19/2/43	LOST:	22/2/45

Commanding Officers

A/LCDR W. E. Harrison, RCNR	1/12/43	30/1/45	LT C. S. Glassco, RCNVR	31/1/45	22/2/45

Whitby

Commissioned at Midland on 6 June 1944, she did not arrive at Halifax until 16 August, owing to a layover en route at Shelburne for repairs. Following workups in Bermuda in September she sailed direct to St. John's, arriving on 30 September, and was assigned to EG C-4. She left St. John's on 5

October for Londonderry to join the group, with which she was to serve for the balance of the war. *Whitby* left Londonderry for Canada in mid-June 1945 and was paid off on 16 July and placed in reserve at Sorel. She was sold in 1946 for merchant service and reportedly renamed *Bengo.*

Whitby in Georgian Bay, 1944.

WHITBY

BUILDER:	Midland Shipyards Ltd., Midland, ON	COMMISSIONED:	6/6/44
LAID DOWN:	1/4/43	PAID OFF:	16/7/45
LAUNCHED:	18/9/43		

Commanding Officer

A/LCDR R. K. Lester, RCNVR	6/6/44	16/7/45

REVISED FLOWER CLASS INCREASED ENDURANCE 1943–1944 PROGRAM

PARTICULARS OF CLASS:

DISPLACEMENT:	970
DIMENSIONS:	208' 4" x 33' 1" x 11'
SPEED:	16 kts
CREW:	6/79
ARMAMENT:	one 4-inch, one 2 pdr., two 20-mm, Hedgehog

Asbestos

Commissioned at Quebec City on 16 June 1944, she arrived at Halifax on 9 July and later that month proceeded to Bermuda to work up. *Asbestos* left Bermuda on 21 August for St. John's, where she joined EG C-2, and left on 10 September for HXF.307, her maiden convoy to Britain. For the rest of the war she was steadily employed as a North Atlantic escort and left Londonderry for the last time at the beginning of June 1945. Paid off on 8 July, she was laid up at Sorel for disposal. In 1947 she was sold to Panamanian owners but was wrecked on the Cuban coast en route there on 13 February 1949. She was later salvaged and taken to New Orleans for scrapping in 1949.

Beauharnois

Commissioned at Quebec City on 25 September 1944, *Beauharnois* arrived at Halifax on 20 October and left for Bermuda on 6 November to work up. On 30 November she sailed from Bermuda for St. John's, where she joined EG C-4, leaving on 9 December to pick up her first convoy, HX.324. She was employed on North Atlantic convoys for the next few months, the last one being ONS.45 for which she left Londonderry on 23 March 1945. Among her last duties was acting as escort to the cable vessel *Lord Kelvin* off Cape Race in May. She was paid off on 12 July and laid up at Sorel. Sold for mercantile purposes in 1946, she was renamed *Colon*, but became a warship again in 1950, when she was acquired by the Israeli Navy and renamed *Wedgwood*. She was broken up in Israel in 1956.

Asbestos, 1944.

ASBESTOS

BUILDER:	Morton Engineering and Dry Dock Co., Quebec City, QC	LAUNCHED:	22/11/43
		COMMISSIONED:	16/6/44
LAID DOWN:	20/7/43	PAID OFF:	8/7/45

Commanding Officer

A/LCDR J. Cuthbert, RCNR	16/6/44	8/7/45

Beauharnois in the St. Lawrence, 25 September 1944.

BEAUHARNOIS

BUILDER:	Morton Engineering and Dry Dock Co., Quebec City, QC	LAUNCHED:	11/5/44
		COMMISSIONED:	25/9/44
LAID DOWN:	8/11/43	PAID OFF:	12/7/45

Commanding Officers

A/LCDR E. C. Smith, RCNVR	25/9/44	20/5/45	LT J. M. Pretty, RCNVR	21/5/45	12/7/45

Belleville

Commissioned at Kingston on 19 October 1944, she visited the Ontario port for which she was named before leaving for Halifax, where she arrived early in November. *Belleville* continued fitting out at Halifax until mid-January, then sailed to Bermuda for a month's working up. Further repairs followed on her return, after which she was allocated to EG C-5, leaving St. John's on 28 March to join her first convoy, HX.346. She made three transatlantic crossings before the war's end, leaving Londonderry for the last time at the beginning of June 1945. She was paid off on 5 July 1945 and placed in reserve at Sorel until 1947, when she was sold to the Dominican Republic and renamed *Juan Bautista Cambiaso*. She was broken up in 1972.

Belleville, 23 October 1944, on the occasion of a visit to her namesake city.

Lachute

Commissioned at Quebec City on 26 October 1944, *Lachute* arrived at Halifax in mid-November and left for Bermuda on 2 December for three weeks' workups. Assigned on her return to EG C-5 at St. John's, she left there on 5 January 1945 to escort her first convoy, SC.164. She served the remainder of her career as a mid-ocean convoy escort, leaving Londonderry on 26 May to join ON.305, the last westbound convoy of the war. On 10 July she was paid off and placed in reserve at Sorel. In 1947 she was sold to the Dominican Republic and joined its navy as *Colon*. Deleted from the active list in 1978, she was driven ashore in a hurricane on 31 August 1979.

BELLEVILLE

BUILDER:	Kingston Shipbuilding Co. Ltd., Kingston, ON	LAUNCHED:	17/6/44
		COMMISSIONED:	19/10/44
LAID DOWN:	21/1/44	PAID OFF:	5/7/45

Commanding Officers

| LT J. E. Korning, RCN | 19/10/44 | 6/5/45 | LCDR R. M. Powell, RCNVR | 7/5/45 | 5/7/45 |

Lachute, March 1945.

LACHUTE

BUILDER:	Morton Engineering and Dry Dock Co., Quebec City, QC	LAUNCHED:	9/6/44
		COMMISSIONED:	26/10/44
LAID DOWN:	24/11/43	PAID OFF:	10/7/45

Commanding Officer

| LT R. G. Hatrick, RCNVR | 26/10/44 | 10/7/45 |

Merrittonia, 1945.

MERRITTONIA

BUILDER:	Morton Engineering and Dry Dock Co., Quebec City, QC	LAUNCHED:	24/6/44
		COMMISSIONED:	10/11/44
LAID DOWN:	23/11/43	PAID OFF:	11/7/45

Commanding Officers

| LT F. K. Ellis, RCNVR | 10/11/44 | 5/4/45 | LCDR R. M. Powell, RCNVR | 26/4/45 | 6/5/45 |
| LCDR J. F. Stairs, RCNVR | 6/4/45 | 25/4/45 | LT R. J. Keelan, RCNVR | 7/5/45 | 11/7/45 |

Parry Sound, Georgian Bay, 1944.

PARRY SOUND

BUILDER:	Midland Shipyards Ltd., Midland, ON	COMMISSIONED:	30/8/44
LAID DOWN:	11/6/43	PAID OFF:	10/7/45
LAUNCHED:	13/11/43		

Commanding Officer

| A/LCDR W. J. Gilmore, RCNVR | 30/8/44 | 10/7/45 |

Merrittonia

She was named for Merritton, Ontario, the modification having been suggested by the town council. Commissioned at Quebec City on 10 November 1944, she arrived at Halifax in mid-December and sailed to Bermuda for a month's workups. On her return *Merrittonia* was assigned to EG C-7 and left St. John's on 7 February to meet the group, which was westbound with convoy ON.283 from Britain. Thereafter continuously employed on North Atlantic convoy duty, she left Londonderry for the final time at the beginning of June 1945. She was paid off on 11 July and laid up at Sorel for disposal. Purchased by K.C. Irving Ltd., Moncton, on 16 November 1945, she was wrecked on the Nova Scotia coast on 30 November.

Parry Sound

Commissioned at Midland on 30 August 1944, *Parry Sound* arrived at Halifax late in September and left in October for three weeks' working up in Bermuda. From Bermuda she sailed direct to St. John's, arriving 11 November, and was assigned to EG C-7. As the group was in Londonderry at the time, she sailed on 17 November, in company with several US-built Russian sub-chasers, to join. Her first convoy was ONS.39, which she picked up at the end of the year. She left St. John's on 17 January 1945 for convoy HX.332 but developed defects and had to turn back. It was mid-March before repairs were completed, and *Parry Sound* returned to convoy duty on 7 April. She departed Londonderry for the last time in June and was paid off at Sydney on 10 July. Sold for conversion to a whale-killer, she entered service in 1950 as the Honduran-flag *Olympic Champion*. In 1956 she was sold to Japanese owners and renamed *Otori Maru No. 15*. Again renamed *Kyo Maru No. 22* in 1961, she is last noted in Lloyd's Register for 1978-79.

Peterborough.

PETERBOROUGH

BUILDER:	Kingston Shipbuilding Co. Ltd., Kingston, ON	LAUNCHED:	15/1/44
LAID DOWN:	14/9/43	COMMISSIONED:	1/6/44
		PAID OFF:	19/7/45

Commanding Officer

| LT J. B. Raine, RCNR | 1/6/44 | 19/7/45 |

Smiths Falls, February 1945.

SMITHS FALLS

BUILDER:	Kingston Shipbuilding Co. Ltd., Kingston, ON	LAUNCHED:	19/8/44
LAID DOWN:	21/1/44	COMMISSIONED:	28/11/44
		PAID OFF:	8/7/45

Commanding Officer

| A/LCDR P. T. Byers, RCNR | 28/11/44 | 8/7/45 |

Peterborough

Commissioned at Kingston on 1 June 1944, she arrived at Halifax on 26 June and in Bermuda on 17 July to work up. _Peterborough_ left Bermuda on 7 August for St. John's, where in September she joined EG C-6 and sailed for her first convoy, HXF.308, on 18 September. Continuously employed as a mid-ocean escort for the rest of her career, she left St. John's on 27 May 1945 to join convoy HX.358, the last HX convoy of the war. In mid-June she left Londonderry for home, where she was paid off on 19 July and laid up at Sorel. She was sold to the Dominican Republic in 1947 and renamed _Gerardo Jansen_, serving until disposed of for scrap in 1972.

Smiths Falls

Commissioned at Kingston on 28 November 1944, she was the last RCN corvette to enter service. She arrived at Halifax late in December and remained there fitting out until 10 February 1945, then proceeded to Bermuda for workups. On her return _Smiths Falls_ was assigned to EG C-2, Londonderry, and made her passage there as escort to convoy SC.171, early in April, the first of three crossings before the end of hostilities. She left Londonderry early in June for the last time, and was paid off 8 July and placed in reserve at Sorel for disposal. Sold for conversion to a whale-killer, she entered service in 1950 as the Honduran-flag _Olympic Lightning_, but was sold to Japanese owners in 1956 and renamed _Otori Maru No. 16_. Again renamed _Kyo Maru No. 23_ in 1961, she last appears in Lloyd's Register for 1977-78.

Stellarton

Commissioned at Quebec City on 29 September 1944, *Stellarton* arrived at Halifax late in October and sailed for Bermuda early in November to work up. She left Bermuda on 4 December for St. John's, where she joined EG C-3 and on 4 January 1945 sailed to pick up her first convoy, HX.329. She was employed for the rest of the war as a mid-ocean escort, and left Londonderry for the last time on 21 May to join ON.304. On 1 July she was paid off and placed in reserve at Sorel until 1946, when she joined the Chilean Navy as *Casma*. She was broken up in 1969.

Strathroy

Commissioned at Midland on 19 November 1944, *Strathroy* arrived at Halifax in December and immediately escorted her first convoy, HF.147, to Saint John, New Brunswick. She arrived there on 18 December for completion of fitting out that could not be done at the builder's prior to freeze-up. She then carried out workups in Bermuda, and on completing these joined Halifax Force in April 1945 for local escort duties. On 12 July she was paid off and laid up at Sorel for disposal. Purchased in 1946 by the Chilean Navy and renamed *Chipana*, she was broken up in 1969.

Stellarton, 1945.

STELLARTON

BUILDER:	Morton Engineering and Dry Dock Co., Quebec City, QC	LAUNCHED:	27/4/44
		COMMISSIONED:	29/9/44
LAID DOWN:	16/11/43	PAID OFF:	1/7/45

Commanding Officers

LT R. A. Jarvis, RCNVR	29/9/44	19/12/44	A/LCDR M. G. McCarthy, RCNVR	20/12/44 1/7/45

Strathroy, Bermuda, March 1945.

STRATHROY

BUILDER:	Midland Shipyards Ltd., Midland, ON	LAUNCHED:	15/6/44
		COMMISSIONED:	19/11/44
LAID DOWN:	19/11/43	PAID OFF:	12/7/45

Commanding Officers

LCDR W. F. Wood, RCNR	19/11/44	27/12/44	LT J. D. Moore, RCNVR	1/2/45	12/7/45
LT H. D. Pepper, RCNVR	28/12/44	31/1/45			

Thorlock, Bermuda, January 1945.

Thorlock

Thorlock was commissioned at Midland on 13 November 1944 and arrived at Halifax on 16 December. On 7 January 1945 she left for Bermuda to work up, setting out on 1 February for the return journey northward. Later that month she was allocated to EG C-9 and on 26 February left Halifax to pick up her first convoy, SC.168. She served for the remainder of the war as an ocean escort, making five transatlantic trips. On 12 May 1945 when on the final leg of an Atlantic crossing with convoy ON.300 from the UK, she was diverted, along with HMCS *Victoriaville*, to accept the surrender of *U 190* and escort the U-boat to Bay Bulls, Newfoundland. She was paid off on 15 July 1945 and placed in reserve at Sorel. Sold in 1946, she served in the Chilean Navy as *Papudo* until disposed of for scrap in 1967.

THORLOCK

BUILDER:	Midland Shipyards Ltd., Midland, ON
LAID DOWN:	25/9/43
LAUNCHED:	15/5/44
COMMISSIONED:	13/11/44
PAID OFF:	15/7/45

Commanding Officer

A/LCDR J. E. Francois, RCNR	13/11/44 15/7/45

West York

Commissioned at Collingwood, Ontario on 6 October 1944, *West York* arrived at Halifax in mid-November and left a month later for Bermuda to work up. In February 1945 she joined EG C-5 at St. John's, leaving 16 February to rendezvous with her maiden convoy, HX.338. She made three round trips across the Atlantic before the end of her career, the last one as escort to ON.305, which she joined from Londonderry at the end of May 1945. Paid off on 9 July and laid up at Sorel, she was sold later that year for commercial use. As

SS *West York*, she was towing the decommissioned HMCS *Assiniboine* when the towline parted and the destroyer was wrecked on Prince Edward Island, 7 November 1945. The former *West York* sailed under a variety of names and flags, returning to Canadian registry in 1960 as *Federal Express*. She sank at Montreal on 5 May 1960, after being in collision, and her after section was raised and broken up later that year.

West York, May 1945.

WEST YORK

BUILDER:	Midland Shipyards Ltd., Midland, ON	COMMISSIONED:	6/10/44
LAID DOWN:	23/7/43	PAID OFF:	9/7/45
LAUNCHED:	25/1/44		

Commanding Officers

LT M. Smith, RCNR		6/10/44	29/12/44	LCDR W. F. Wood, RCNR	30/12/44	9/7/45

REVISED FLOWER CLASS INCREASED ENDURANCE, EX-ROYAL NAVY

Note: These four ships were acquired in 1943 in exchange for four Canadian-built Algerine class minesweepers.

PARTICULARS OF CLASS:

DISPLACEMENT:	970
DIMENSIONS:	208' 4" x 33' 1" x 11'
SPEED:	16 kts
CREW:	6/79
ARMAMENT:	one 4-inch, one 2 pdr., two 20-mm, Hedgehog

Forest Hill

Named for a village absorbed by Toronto, *Forest Hill* was laid down as HMS *Ceanothus* but was transferred to the RCN and commissioned on 1 December 1943 on the Clyde, Scotland. Following workups at Tobermory she joined EG C-3 at Londonderry, leaving on 29 January 1944 to join her first convoy, ONS.28. She served as an ocean escort until late in December, when she arrived at Liverpool, Nova Scotia for an extended refit, on the completion of which, two months later, she sailed for Bermuda to work up. Returning in April 1945 she joined Halifax Force for local duties. Paid off on 9 July and laid up at Sorel, she was broken up at Hamilton in 1948.

Forest Hill, 1943.

FOREST HILL

BUILDER:	Ferguson Bros. Ltd., Port Glasgow, Scotland	LAUNCHED:	30/8/43
		COMMISSIONED:	1/12/43
LAID DOWN:	5/2/43	PAID OFF:	9/7/45
		Ex-HMS *Ceanothus*	

Commanding Officers

A/LCDR E. U. Jones, RCNVR		1/12/43	17/9/44	LT F. R. Brebner, RCNVR	18/9/44	9/7/45

Giffard.

GIFFARD

BUILDER:	Alexander Hall & Co. Ltd., Aberdeen, Scotland	COMMISSIONED:	10/11/43
		PAID OFF:	5/7/45
LAID DOWN:	30/11/42	Ex-HMS *Buddleia*	
LAUNCHED:	19/6/43		

Commanding Officers

A/LCDR C. Peterson, RCNR	10/11/43	9/5/44	LT G. H. Matheson, RCNR	10/5/44	5/7/45

Long Branch, December 1944.

LONG BRANCH

BUILDER:	A. & J. Inglis Ltd., Glasgow, Scotland	COMMISSIONED:	5/1/44
LAID DOWN:	27/2/43	PAID OFF:	17/6/45
LAUNCHED:	28/9/43	Ex-HMS *Candytuft*	

Commanding Officers

A/LCDR W. J. Kingsmill, RCNVR	5/1/44	21/1/44	LCDR R. J. G. Johnson, RCNVR	17/4/44	7/10/44
CDR E. G. Skinner, DSC, RCNR	22/1/44	2/2/44	A/LCDR J. B. O'Brien, RCNVR	8/10/44	21/2/45
A/LCDR A. B. Taylor, RCNR	3/2/44	14/3/44	LT K. B. Culley, RCNVR	22/2/45	14/6/45
A/LCDR W. J. Kingsmill, RCNVR	15/3/44	16/4/44			

Giffard

Named for a Quebec village, she was originally laid down as HMS *Buddleia* but was transferred to the RCN and commissioned on 10 November 1943 at Aberdeen. After working up at Tobermory *Giffard* joined EG C-1 at Londonderry and on 15 February 1944 sailed to join her first convoy, ON.224. On 7 May she rescued forty-three survivors of the torpedoed *Valleyfield*, five of whom later died and the following week resumed her duties as an ocean escort until 27 November, when she left Halifax for Liverpool, Nova Scotia to undergo a major refit. Completed in March 1945, this was followed by workups in Bermuda. She arrived in St. John's on 15 April, to be employed locally until her departure on 13 May with convoy HX.355 for the UK. *Giffard* left Greenock early in June on her final westward voyage, was paid off 5 July and laid up at Sorel to await disposal. She was broken up in 1952 in Hamilton.

Long Branch

Named for a village absorbed by Toronto, she was originally laid down as HMS *Candytuft* but was transferred to the RCN and commissioned on the Clyde on 5 January 1944. In April, following a month's workups at Tobermory, *Long Branch* joined EG C-5 at Londonderry, and sailed to pick up her maiden convoy, ONS.233. She developed mechanical defects on the crossing and was under repair at St. John's for six weeks. She left St. John's 14 June to resume her duties, but returned from her next westbound convoy with the assistance of HM tug *Tenacity*. Repaired, she left St. John's a week later to join HXS.300, the largest convoy of the war, and continued as an ocean escort until her final departure from Derry on 27 January 1945. Arriving at Halifax on 11 February, she commenced a refit on completion of which, in April, she was assigned to Halifax Force for local duties. On 17 June she was paid off at Sorel for disposal. Sold for commercial use in 1947, she was renamed *Rexton Kent II* (later dropping the 'II') and finally scuttled off the east coast in 1966.

Mimico

Named after a town now part of Toronto, *Mimico* was laid down as HMS *Bulrush* but was transferred to the RCN and commissioned on 8 February 1944 at Sunderland, UK. On 18 April, after working up at Stornoway, she arrived at Oban, Scotland where she was assigned to Western Approaches Command for escort duty in connection with the invasion. She arrived off the Normandy beaches with a convoy on the day after D Day. She remained on escort duty in the Channel, assigned briefly in September to Portsmouth Command, based at Sheerness. In February and March 1945 she refitted at Chatham, then returned to Sheerness and resumed her previous role until late in May, when she left the UK for the last time. She was paid off on 18 July 1945 and laid up at Sorel. Sold for use as a whale-killer, she entered service in 1950 as *Olympic Victor* but passed into Japanese hands in 1956 and was renamed *Otori Maru No. 12*. Again renamed *Kyo Maru No. 25* in 1962, she last appears in Lloyd's Register for 1977-78.

Mimico, 1944.

MIMICO				
BUILDER:	John Crown & Sons Ltd., Sunderland, UK	COMMISSIONED:	8/2/44	
LAID DOWN:	22/2/43	PAID OFF:	18/7/45	
LAUNCHED:	11/10/43	Ex-HMS *Bulrush*		

Commanding Officers

LT F. J. Jones, RCNVR	8/2/44	2/10/44	LCDR W. R. Stacey, RCNR	26/1/45	1/2/45
LT G. F. Crosby, RCNVR	3/10/44	20/11/44	LT M. W. Knowles, RCNVR	2/2/45	14/2/45
LT F. J. Jones, RCNVR	21/11/44	25/1/45	A/LCDR J. B. Elmsley, RCNVR	15/2/45	18/7/45

CASTLE CLASS

Note: These were acquired in 1944 in exchange for twelve Canadian-built Algerine class minesweepers.

PARTICULARS OF CLASS:	
DISPLACEMENT:	1,060
DIMENSIONS:	251' 9" x 36' 8" x 10'
SPEED:	16 kts
CREW:	7/105
ARMAMENT:	one 4-inch, six 20-mm (2 x II, 2 x I) Squid

Arnprior

Laid down as HMS *Rising Castle*, she was transferred to the RCN and commissioned at Belfast on 8 June 1944. After working up at Tobermory she joined EG C-1 at Londonderry in August, leaving on 19 August to join her first convoy, ONM.249. *Arnprior* was continuously employed as an ocean escort for the balance of the war. At the beginning of June 1945 she left Greenock for St. John's, where she underwent a two-month refit, and from September was based at Halifax. She was paid off there on 14 March 1946, and sold later that year to the Uruguayan Navy, which renamed her *Montevideo* and operated her as a training ship until 1975.

Arnprior, 1944.

ARNPRIOR			
BUILDER:	Harland & Wolff Ltd., Belfast, Ireland	COMMISSIONED:	8/6/44
LAID DOWN:	21/6/43	PAID OFF:	14/3/46
LAUNCHED:	8/2/44	Ex-HMS *Rising Castle*	

Commanding Officers

A/LCDR S. D. Thom, RCNVR	8/6/44	27/8/45	A/LCDR T. B. Edwards, RCNR	28/8/45	14/3/46

Bowmanville

Laid down as HMS *Nunney Castle*, she was transferred to the RCN and commissioned at Sunderland, UK, on 28 September 1944. Following workups at Tobermory *Bowmanville* joined EG C-4 at Londonderry, sailing on 24 November to join her first convoy, ON.268. She served continuously as an ocean escort for the rest of the war. Early in June 1945 she left Londonderry for the last time, and was based at Halifax until paid off on 15 February 1946. She was sold into mercantile service in 1947 under the Chinese flag and first renamed *Ta Shun*, then *Yuan Pei*. In 1949 she was taken over by the Chinese Communist government, rearmed and renamed *Kuang Chou*.

Copper Cliff

Laid down as HMS *Hever Castle*, she was transferred to the RCN and commissioned at Blyth, UK, on 25 February 1944. After working up at Tobermory in August she was assigned to EG C-6 but in fact joined EG C-7, then forming at Londonderry, in October. She left Londonderry to pick up her first convoy, ONS.266, on 16 November, and was thereafter continuously employed as an ocean escort. *Copper Cliff* left Londonderry for her final westward crossing early in June 1945 and later that month sailed from Halifax for Esquimalt. There, on 21 November she was paid off into reserve. In 1946 she became the Chinese-flag merchant ship *Ta Lung*, soon afterward renamed *Wan Lee*, and was taken over by the Chinese government in 1949.

Bowmanville, October 1944, fitted with Type 277 radar.

BOWMANVILLE

BUILDER:	Wm. Pickersgill & Sons Ltd., Sunderland, UK	COMMISSIONED:	28/9/44
LAID DOWN:	12/8/43	PAID OFF:	15/2/46
LAUNCHED:	26/1/44	Ex-HMS *Nunney Castle*	

Commanding Officers

| | | LT A. D. Ritchie, RCNVR | 4/4/45 | 20/4/45 | LT W. J. Ransom, RCNVR | 25/10/45 | 15/2/46 |
| LCDR M. S. Duffus, RCNVR | 28/9/44 | 3/4/45 | LCDR M. S. Duffus, RCNVR | 21/4/45 | 24/8/45 | | |

Copper Cliff, 1944.

COPPER CLIFF

| BUILDER: | Blyth Shipbuilding & Dry Dock Co. Ltd., Blyth, UK | LAID DOWN: | 29/6/43 | COMMISSIONED: | 25/2/44 | Ex-HMS *Hever Castle* |
| | | LAUNCHED: | 24/2/44 | PAID OFF: | 21/11/45 | |

Commanding Officers

| LCDR F. G. Hutchings, RCNR | 25/2/44 | 3/12/44 | A/LCDR F. W. Bogardus, RCNVR | 4/12/44 | 11/1/45 | LCDR F. G. Hutchings, RCNR | 12/1/45 | 25/7/45 | LT W. M. Combe, RCNR | 20/8/45 | 20/9/45 |

Hespeler

Laid down as HMS *Guildford Castle*, she was transferred to the RCN and commissioned on 28 February 1944 at Leith. Following workups at Tobermory she arrived at Londonderry in April to become a member of EG C-5. *Hespeler* sailed on 21 April to meet her first convoy, ONS.233, and for the next eleven months was employed as an ocean escort. On 23 July 1944 she left St. John's with EG C-5 to escort the largest convoy of the war, HXS.300, and on 9 September, while temporarily on patrol duty south of the Hebrides, she sank *U 484* in co-operation with *Dunver*. She left Derry for the last time on 8 March 1945 to escort ON.289 westward, and upon arriving at Halifax began a refit, completing at Liverpool, Nova Scotia in July. She then sailed for the west coast and on 15 November was paid off into reserve at Esquimalt. Sold for mercantile use in 1946, she was renamed *Chilcotin*, then in 1958 she became the Liberian-flag *Capri*, and the Panamanian *Stella Maris* in 1960. Again under the Liberian flag she was renamed *Westar* in 1965. She was gutted by fire at Sarroch, Sardinia on 28 January 1966 and broken up at La Spezia, Italy.

Hespeler, 1944.

HESPELER

BUILDER.	Henry Robb Ltd., Leith, Scotland		COMMISSIONED:	28/2/44
LAID DOWN:	25/5/43		PAID OFF:	15/11/45
LAUNCHED:	13/11/43		Ex HMS *Guildford Castle*	

Commanding Officers

LCDR N. S. C. Dickinson, RCNVR	28/2/44	13/11/44	LT G. P. Manning, RCNVR	14/11/44	24/8/45

Humberstone.

HUMBERSTONE

BUILDER:	A. & J. Inglis Ltd., Glasgow, Scotland		COMMISSIONED:	6/9/44
LAID DOWN:	30/8/43		PAID OFF:	17/11/45
LAUNCHED:	12/4/44		Ex-HMS *Norham Castle*	

Commanding Officers

LCDR H. A. Boucher, RCNVR	6/9/44	15/10/44	LCDR H. A. Boucher, RCNVR	27/11/44	15/6/45
LT C. L. Campbell, RCNVR	16/10/44	26/11/44	A/LCDR J. W. Golby, RCNVR	19/8/45	14/10/45

Humberstone

Laid down as HMS *Norham Castle*, she was transferred to the RCN and commissioned at Glasgow on 6 September 1944. After working up at Tobermory she arrived in October at Londonderry to join EG C-8, then forming. She left Derry 22 October to join convoy ON.261 for her first Atlantic crossing and continued in service as an ocean escort for the remainder of the war. *Humberstone* left Londonderry 12 May 1945 for her last convoy, ONS.50, and in June sailed to Esquimalt, where she was paid off on 17 November. She was sold to Chinese owners in 1946 and converted for merchant service as *Taiwei*, subsequently undergoing five more name changes before becoming the Korean *South Ocean* in 1954. She was broken up at Hong Kong in 1959.

Huntsville.

HUNTSVILLE			
BUILDER:	Aisla Shipbuilding Co. Ltd., Troon, Scotland	COMMISSIONED:	6/6/44
		PAID OFF:	15/2/46
LAID DOWN:	1/6/43	Ex-HMS *Woolvesey Castle*	
LAUNCHED:	24/2/44		

Commanding Officers

A/LCDR C. B. Hermann, RCNVR	6/6/44	20/7/45	LT C. F. Usher, RCNVR	21/7/45	9/9/45

Kincardine, **1944.**

KINCARDINE			
BUILDER:	Smith's Dock Co., South Bank-on-Tees, UK	COMMISSIONED:	19/6/44
		PAID OFF:	27/2/46
LAID DOWN:	25/8/43	Ex-HMS *Tamworth Castle*	
LAUNCHED:	26/1/44		

Commanding Officers

A/LCDR R. P. Brown, RCNR	19/6/44	27/8/45	SKPR/LT A. H. Campbell, RCNR	4/10/45	-
A/LCDR A. E. Gough, RCNR	28/8/45	13/9/45			

Huntsville

Laid down as HMS *Woolvesey Castle*, she was transferred to the RCN and commissioned on 6 June 1944 on the Clyde. She worked up at Stornoway early in July and joined EG C-5 at Londonderry later that month, leaving on 11 August for ONS.248, her first convoy. In November *Huntsville* missed a convoy while under repair at Halifax and acted as local escort to one convoy from St. John's to New York—seemingly the only ship of her class to visit there. Rejoining the Atlantic convoy cycle in December, she left Londonderry for the last time on 16 April 1945 to meet ON.297. In May she commenced refit at Halifax, completed in August, and in September was placed in reserve. She was paid off for disposal on 15 February 1946 and sold that year, entering service in 1947 as SS *Wellington Kent*. Renamed *Belle Isle II* in 1951, she was sunk in collision off Trois-Rivières on 19 August 1960.

Kincardine

Laid down as HMS *Tamworth Castle*, she was transferred to the RCN and commissioned at Middlesbrough on 19 June 1944. After working up at Tobermory and Stornoway she arrived at Londonderry late in August to join EG C-2 but had to return to her builders for repairs. Returning to Londonderry in mid-September, she remained on local duties until 2 October, when she left to join ON.257, her first convoy. *Kincardine* served as an ocean escort for the remainder of the war, leaving Derry for the last time at the beginning of June 1945. Briefly allocated to HMCS *Cornwallis* for training in July, she then underwent a minor refit at Liverpool, Nova Scotia. Placed in maintenance reserve at Halifax in October, she was paid off there on 27 February 1946. Later that year she was sold to the French government and resold in 1947 to Moroccan interests, to be renamed *Saada*. She was later acquired by the Burmese Navy in 1958 and renamed *Van Myo Aung*.

Leaside

Laid down as HMS *Walmer Castle*, she was transferred to the RCN and commissioned on 21 August 1944 at Middlesbrough. Following workups at Tobermory in September *Leaside* arrived at Londonderry early in October to join EG C-8, then forming. She sailed on 22 October to meet ON.261, her first convoy, and served the rest of the war as an ocean escort. On 11 May 1945 she made her last departure from Derry to join ONS.50. She left St. John's in June for Esquimalt, where she was paid off for disposal on 16 November. In 1946 she became the BC coastal passenger vessel *Coquitlam*, passed into Liberian registry and was renamed *Glacier Queen* in 1950. In 1973 she was acquired by US interests and for a time was a floating hotel at Valdez, Alaska. On 8 November 1978 she sank at anchor in Seldovia Bay, was subsequently refloated and scuttled in the Gulf of Alaska.

Orangeville

Laid down as HMS *Hedingham Castle*, she was transferred to the RCN and commissioned at Leith on 24 April 1944. After working up at Tobermory in May she joined EG C-1 at Londonderry, leaving on June 4 to meet ONS.239, her first convoy. She spent the remainder of the war on North Atlantic convoy duty, leaving Derry for the last time on 21 April 1945 to escort ONS.48. After refitting at Liverpool, Nova Scotia from May to August, *Orangeville* was placed in maintenance reserve at Halifax and finally paid off on 12 April 1946. She was sold later that year for conversion to mercantile use under the Chinese flag and renamed *Ta Tung*. In 1951 she was taken over by the Nationalist Chinese government, rearmed and renamed *Te-An*.

Leaside, June 1945.

Orangeville, 1944.

LEASIDE			
BUILDER:	Smith's Dock Co., South Bank-on-Tees, UK	LAUNCHED:	10/3/44
		COMMISSIONED:	21/8/44
		PAID OFF:	16/11/45
LAID DOWN:	23/9/43	Ex-HMS *Walmer Castle*	

Commanding Officers		
LT G. G. K. Holder, RCNVR	21/8/44	15/6/45
LT H. Brynjolfson, RCNVR	16/6/45	30/8/45
LCDR C. P. Balfry, RCNR	1/9/45	16/11/45

ORANGEVILLE					
BUILDER:	Henry Robb Ltd., Leith, Scotland		COMMISSIONED:	24/4/44	
LAID DOWN:	23/7/43		PAID OFF:	12/4/46	
LAUNCHED:	26/1/44		Ex-HMS *Hedingham Castle*		

Commanding Officers					
A/LCDR F. R. Pike, RCNVR	24/4/44	16/7/45	A/LCDR G. A. Powell, RCNVR	17/7/45	16/10/45

Petrolia, July 1944.

PETROLIA

BUILDER:	Harland & Wolff Ltd., Belfast, Ireland	COMMISSIONED:	29/6/44
LAID DOWN:	21/6/43	PAID OFF:	8/3/46
LAUNCHED:	24/2/44	Ex-HMS Sherborne Castle	

Commanding Officers

LT P. W. Spragge, RCNVR	29/6/44	25/6/45	LT R. H. Ellis, RCNVR	8/8/45	11/9/45
LT N. M. Simpson, RCNVR	26/6/45	7/8/45	LT J. J. Hodgkinson, RCNR	12/9/45	8/3/46

St. Thomas.

ST. THOMAS

BUILDER:	Smith's Dock Co., South Bank-on-Tees, UK	COMMISSIONED:	4/5/44
LAID DOWN:	23/6/43	PAID OFF:	22/11/45
LAUNCHED:	28/12/43	Ex-HMS Sandgate Castle	

Commanding Officers

LCDR L. P. Denny, RCNR	4/5/44	26/1/45	LT J. R. K. Stewart, RCNVR	21/6/45	22/11/45
A/LCDR B. Hynes, RCNVR	27/1/45	20/6/45			

Petrolia

Laid down as HMS *Sherborne Castle*, she was transferred to the RCN and commissioned on 29 June 1944 at Belfast. Following workups at Tobermory, she joined EG C-4 at Londonderry in August, leaving on 2 September for her first convoy, ONS.251. An ocean escort for the rest of the war, she left Londonderry for the last time early in June 1945. In August *Petrolia* underwent a refit at Charlottetown and was placed in maintenance reserve at Halifax in October. Paid off at Liverpool, Nova Scotia on 8 March 1946, she was sold not long afterward to a New York buyer and renamed *Maid of Athens*. In 1947 she was transferred to Indian registry and renamed *Bharat Laxmi*, serving as such until broken up at Bombay in 1965.

St. Thomas

Laid down as HMS *Sandgate Castle*, she was transferred to the RCN and commissioned at Middlesbrough on 4 May 1944. In June *St. Thomas* carried out workups at Tobermory, leaving later that month for Londonderry where, in July, she became part of EG C-3. She sailed on 3 August to join ONF.247, her first convoy, and was employed as an ocean escort for the rest of the war. On 27 December 1944 while escorting HX.327, she sank *U 877* in the North Atlantic. She left Londonderry for the last time on 11 April 1945, commencing refit on arrival at Halifax 30 April. Following completion of the refit in July she sailed for the west coast and was paid off at Esquimalt on 22 November. In 1946 she was sold to the Union Steamship Co., Vancouver, converted to a coastal passenger vessel, and renamed *Camosun*. She was renamed *Chilcotin* in 1958 and, later that year, *Yukon Star*. After several years of idleness, she was broken up at Tacoma in 1974.

Tillsonburg

Laid down as HMS *Pembroke Castle*, she was transferred to the RCN and commissioned on the Clyde on 29 June 1944. Following working up at Stornoway *Tillsonburg* arrived at Londonderry on 19 August, sailing a week later for St. John's to join EG C-6, then forming. Unlike her sisters, therefore, she first escorted an eastbound convoy, HXF.308, leaving St. John's on 18 September to join it. An ocean escort for the balance of the war, she left Londonderry for her last crossing in mid June 1945. Briefly based at St. John's, Sydney, and Halifax, she was paid off at Halifax on 15 February 1946, and later that year was sold to Chinese owners for mercantile service. Initially named *Ta Ching*, she was renamed *Chiu Chin* in 1947. In 1951 she was taken over by the Nationalist Chinese government, rearmed and renamed *Kao-An*.

Tillsonburg, 1944.

TILLSONBURG

BUILDER:	Ferguson Bros. Ltd., Port Glasgow, Scotland	COMMISSIONED:	29/6/44
		PAID OFF:	15/2/46
LAID DOWN:	3/6/43	Ex-HMS *Pembroke Castle*	
LAUNCHED:	12/2/44		

Commanding Officers

LCDR W. Evans, RCNVR	29/6/44	16/1/45	LT G. E. Gilbride, RCNVR	10/7/45	4/9/45
LT A. D. Ritchie, RCNVR	17/1/45	2/3/45	LT F. Angus, RCNVR	5/9/45	28/11/45
LCDR W. Evans, RCNVR	3/3/45	9/7/45			

Minesweepers

The RCN had four minesweepers in 1939, Canadian-built copies of the RN's Basset class, and consideration was being given to building more of these when the Naval Staff learned of the RN's newer Bangor class. The Bangor was larger and faster, had much greater endurance, and burned oil unlike the coal-burning Bassets. Accordingly, twenty-eight Bangor class minesweepers were ordered in 1940 and twenty more under subsequent programs. Another six, built at Vancouver for the RN, were loaned to the RCN for the duration of the war. Ten Bangors of the first program were of a smaller, diesel-engined variety and one of these, *Granby*, survived until 1966. Most of the Bangors were named after Canadian towns and cities, the rest after bays.

Like the corvettes, the Bangors were small enough to be produced at shipyards on the Great Lakes, and sixteen were built at Toronto and Port Arthur. The Toronto yard turned out six others of the class for the RN.

As enemy mines were laid only once (1943) in Canadian waters, the Bangors were used principally as escorts to coastal shipping or as local escorts to ocean convoys. Sixteen of them, however, assisted in sweeping the approaches to Normandy before D Day, and stayed to help clear German and Allied minefields in the Channel for some months afterward.

The Bangors were bluff-bowed ships, very wet in a head sea, and arguably less comfortable even than corvettes in rough weather. These faults were eliminated in the Algerine class, all twelve RCN units of which were built at Port Arthur. They were intended by the RCN as convoy escorts, hence not fitted with minesweeping gear. Although they were larger than corvettes, the latter outperformed them as ocean escorts, the Algerines finding particular favour as Senior Officers' ships in Western Local groups. Most found employment for many years after the war on hydrographic survey duties or as training ships for reservists. Forty-one of this class were built at Toronto and eleven at Port Arthur for the RN.

Two classes of wooden-hulled ships were built in Canada for magnetic minesweeping, the Llewellyn and Lake classes. None of the latter class had been commissioned by VJ Day, and the ten most nearly complete were turned over to the USSR.

BANGOR CLASS 1939–1940 PROGRAM

PARTICULARS OF CLASS:

DISPLACEMENT:	672
DIMENSIONS:	180' x 28' 6" x 8' 3"
SPEED:	16 kts
CREW:	6/77
ARMAMENT:	one 4-inch, one 3-inch or one 12 pdr., two 20-mm

Bellechasse

Named for a county in Quebec, *Bellechasse* was built at Vancouver and commissioned there 13 December 1941. She spent her entire career on the west coast, alternating between Prince Rupert Force and Esquimalt Force. Paid off on 23 October 1945 at Esquimalt, she was sold the following year to the Union Steamship Co., Vancouver, but her intended conversion for mercantile service was not carried out.

Burlington

Burlington was commissioned at Toronto on 6 September 1941 and arrived at Halifax on 30 September. After working up, she made Halifax her base, and in March 1942 was assigned to WLEF, transferring in May to Gulf Escort Force. Late in December she commenced refitting progressively at Halifax, Lunenburg, and Dartmouth. Following completion of the work in May 1943 she worked up at Pictou and was assigned in June to EG W-9 of WLEF. In February 1944 she was transferred to Halifax Local Defence Force, and in September sent to Bermuda for a month's workup. On her return she joined Newfoundland Force, based at St. John's, and served there until 8 June 1945 when the Command was disbanded. She then engaged in miscellaneous duties until paid off on 30 October 1945 and she was sold to a New Jersey buyer in 1946.

Bellechasse, 30 November 1944.

BELLECHASSE

BUILDER:	Burrard Dry Dock Co. Ltd., Vancouver, BC	LAID DOWN:	16/4/41	COMMISSIONED:	13/12/41
		LAUNCHED:	20/10/41	PAID OFF:	23/10/45

Commanding Officers

LT H. H. Rankin, RCNR	13/12/41	2/5/43	LCDR W. Redford, RCNR	6/1/44	22/3/45
LT R. J. Roberts, RCNR	3/5/43	16/12/43	LCDR J. S. Cunningham, RCNVR	23/3/45	17/4/45
LT H. H. Rankin, RCNR	17/12/43	5/1/44	LT J. M. MacRae, RCNVR	18/4/45	24/8/45

Burlington, July 1942.

BURLINGTON

BUILDER:	Dufferin Shipbuilding Co. Toronto, ON	LAID DOWN:	4/7/40	COMMISSIONED:	6/9/41
		LAUNCHED:	23/11/40	PAID OFF:	30/10/45

Commanding Officers

LCDR W. J. Fricker, RCN	6/9/41	1/5/42	LT K. G. Clark, RCNVR	3/1/45	6/5/45
LT M. Russell, RCNR	2/5/42	31/12/43	LT P. P. Jeffries, RCNVR	7/5/45	12/8/45
SKPR/LT J. B. Cooper, RCNR	1/1/44	22/1/44	LT S. W. McEvenue, RCNVR	13/8/45	4/9/45
LT J. W. Golby, RCNVR	23/1/44	6/2/44	SKPR/LT J. E. N. Vezina, RCNR	5/9/45	30/10/45
LT J. M. Richardson, RCNVR	7/2/44	3/1/45			

Chedabucto

Built at Vancouver and commissioned there on 27 September 1941, *Chedabucto* left Esquimalt for the Atlantic on 11 November, arriving at Halifax on 17 December. On 10 April 1942 she sank the British SS *Trongate*, afire at Halifax with a cargo of explosives. Assigned briefly to WLEF, she transferred in June 1942 to Gulf Escort Force, escorting convoys between Quebec City and Sydney. In September 1942 she was assigned to Sydney Force and then, in January 1943 reassigned to WLEF. Soon afterward she underwent a lengthy refit at Lunenburg and Halifax, on completion of which in June 1943 she worked up at Pictou and was allocated to Gaspé Force. On 21 October 1943 *Chedabucto* was involved in a night collision with the cable vessel *Lord Kelvin*, and sank thirty miles from Rimouski with the loss of one officer.

Chedabucto, 1941.

CHEDABUCTO

BUILDER:	Burrard Dry Dock Co. Ltd., Vancouver, BC	LAUNCHED:	14/4/41
LAID DOWN:	24/1/41	COMMISSIONED:	27/9/41
		LOST:	21/10/43

Commanding Officer

| LT J. H. B. Davies, RCNR | 27/9/41 | 31/10/43 |

Chignecto

Commissioned at Vancouver on 31 October 1941, *Chignecto* spent her whole career on the west coast, alternating between Esquimalt Force and Prince Rupert Force. She was paid off on 3 November 1945 at Esquimalt, and sold in 1946 to the Union Steamship Co., Vancouver, for conversion to a coastal merchant ship. The conversion was not proceeded with, and she has proved impossible to trace beyond 1951, when an offer to purchase her was received from a San Francisco firm.

Chignecto, 19 July 1944.

CHIGNECTO

| BUILDER: | North Van Ship Repairs Ltd., Vancouver, BC | LAID DOWN: | 11/9/40 | COMMISSIONED: | 31/10/41 |
| | | LAUNCHED: | 12/12/40 | PAID OFF: | 3/11/45 |

Commanding Officers

LT L. F. McQuarrie, RCNR	31/10/41	8/8/43	SKPR/LT G. F. Cassidy, RCNR	29/6/44	1/3/45
LT H. H. Rankin, RCNR	9/8/43	29/8/43	LT R. C. Eaton, RCNVR	2/3/45	23/9/45
LT L. F. McQuarrie, RCNR	30/8/43	28/6/44	(Not Known)	24/9/45	3/11/45

Clayoquot, July 1943.

Cowichan, 11 July 1941.

Clayoquot

Named after Clayoquot Sound, Vancouver Island, she was commissioned at Prince Rupert on 22 August 1941. After working up, she left Esquimalt on 10 October for Halifax, arriving 14 November. Initially assigned to Halifax Local Defence Force, she was transferred in March 1942 to WLEF and in May to Gulf Escort Force. While serving with Gulf Escort Force she rescued fifty-five survivors of HMCS *Charlottetown*, torpedoed and sunk near Cap Chat on 11 September 1942. In October, *Clayoquot* joined Sydney Force. She arrived at Halifax on 29 December for a major refit, which was progressively carried out there and at Liverpool and Pictou, Nova Scotia. Completing her refit in May 1943 she rejoined Sydney Force in July after working up. In January 1944 she was transferred to HMCS *Cornwallis* for offi-cer's training in A/S warfare, and in October was reassigned to Halifax Force. On 24 December, while taking station on convoy XB.139, she was torpedoed and sunk three miles from Sambro Light Vessel by *U 806*, losing eight of her crew.

Cowichan

Commissioned at Vancouver on 4 July 1941, she sailed from Esquimalt for Halifax on 6 August, arriving on 10 September. After working up in Bermuda she was initially assigned to Halifax Local Defence Force, but was transferred in January 1942 to Newfoundland Force and in September to WLEF. With WLEF's division into escort groups in June 1943 *Cowichan* became a member of EG W-6. She remained with the group until February 1944 when she was ordered to the UK for invasion duties. She left Halifax on 19 February with *Caraquet*, *Malpeque* and *Vegreville* via the Azores for Plymouth, arriving on 13 March. Assigned to the 31st Minesweeping Flotilla, she was present on D Day. *Cowichan* returned to Canada for refit late in February 1945 but resumed her duties overseas in June. Proceeding home in September, she was paid off on 9 October 1945 and placed in reserve at Shelburne. Sold in 1946 to a New York buyer and converted for mercantile purposes under Greek flag, she still existed in 1956 under her original name.

CLAYOQUOT			
BUILDER:	Prince Rupert Dry Dock and Shipyards Co., Prince Rupert, BC	LAID DOWN:	20/6/40
		LAUNCHED:	3/10/40
		COMMISSIONED:	22/8/41
		LOST:	24/12/44

Commanding Officers

A/LCDR G. A. Thomson, RCNR	22/8/41	18/11/41
A/LCDR R. B. Campbell, RCNR	19/11/41	13/4/42
LT H. T. Lade, RCNR	14/4/42	7/4/43
LT C. L. Campbell, RCNVR	8/4/43	5/3/44
LT D. R. Baker, RCNVR	6/3/44	11/4/44
LT C. L. Campbell, RCNVR	12/4/44	15/6/44
LT M. Smith, RCNR	16/6/44	28/7/44
A/LCDR A. C. Campbell, RCNVR	29/7/44	24/12/44

COWICHAN			
BUILDER:	North Van Ship Repairs Ltd., Vancouver, BC	LAUNCHED:	9/8/40
		COMMISSIONED:	4/7/41
		PAID OFF:	9/10/45
LAID DOWN:	24/4/40		

Commanding Officers

LT Ronald Jackson, RCNR	4/7/41	1/12/41
LT Richard Jackson, RCNR	2/12/41	14/2/42
A/LT J. R. Kidston, RCNVR	15/2/42	25/10/42
A/LCDR K. W. N. Hall, RCNR	26/10/42	22/4/45
SKPR/LT H. W. Stone, RCNR	23/4/45	9/10/45

Georgian

Commissioned at Toronto on 23 September 1941, *Georgian* arrived at Halifax on 13 October. On completing workups she was assigned to Sydney Force, but in January 1942 she joined Newfoundland Force and remained with it until February 1944. Through a tragic error on 21 June 1942 she rammed and sank the British submarine *P.514* off Newfoundland. Nominated for duties in connection with the invasion of Europe, she left Halifax on 18 February 1944 with *Bayfield*, *Mulgrave* and *Thunder* for Plymouth via the Azores, arriving on 7 March. Assigned to a series of minesweeping flotillas, particularly the 14th, she was present on D Day. She returned to Canada in January 1945 for refit at Lunenburg, Nova Scotia, and then returned to the UK for service with the 31st Flotilla in April. That fall she sailed again for Canada, where she was paid off at Sydney on 23 October and laid up at Shelburne until sold for scrap.

Georgian, March 1944.

GEORGIAN

BUILDER:	Dufferin Shipbuilding Co. Toronto, ON	COMMISSIONED:	23/9/41
LAID DOWN:	10/10/40	PAID OFF:	23/10/45
LAUNCHED:	28/1/41		

Commanding Officers

A/LCDR A. G. Stanley, RCNR	23/9/41	21/9/42	A/LCDR H. A. Boucher, RCNVR	26/1/43	26/6/44
LCDR W. Redford, RCNR	22/9/42	7/12/42	A/LCDR D. W. Main, RCNR	27/6/44	23/3/45
LT P. M. Crawford, RCNVR	8/12/42	21/1/43	LT T. C. McLaughlin, RCNR	24/3/45	23/10/45
LT G. H. Johnson, RCNVR	22/1/43	25/1/43			

Mahone, 1945.

MAHONE

BUILDER:	North Van Ship Repairs Ltd., Vancouver, BC	LAUNCHED:	14/11/40
		COMMISSIONED:	29/9/41
LAID DOWN:	13/8/40	PAID OFF:	6/11/45

Commanding Officers

LT D. M. Stewart, RCNR	29/9/41	3/12/42	LT L. R. Hoar, RCNVR	5/6/44	25/3/45
LT W. J. Gilmore, RCNVR	4/12/42	9/1/44	LT N. R. Chappell, RCNVR	26/3/45	20/8/45
LT W. Turner, RCNR	10/1/44	28/3/44			

Mahone

Commissioned at Vancouver on 29 September 1941, she left Esquimalt on 11 November for Halifax where, upon her arrival on 17 December, she was assigned to WLEF. Between May 1942 and January 1943 she served with Halifax Force, and then underwent a major refit at Liverpool, Nova Scotia, from 19 January to 3 April. She was then transferred to Gaspé Force because of U-boat activity in the St. Lawrence, but returned to Halifax Force in November 1943 and soon afterward went to Sydney Force. On 29 January 1944 she was rammed by SS *Fort Townshend* off Louisbourg, Nova Scotia and after temporary repairs was sent to Halifax for further repair work which lasted four months. Early in June she proceeded to Bermuda to work up, returning to Halifax a month later. *Mahone* was paid off at Halifax on 6 November 1945 and laid up at Shelburne. In 1946 she was placed in strategic reserve at Sorel until 1951, when she was reacquired by the RCN, which kept her in reserve at Sydney until 29 March 1958. That day marked her transfer to the Turkish Navy as *Beylerbeyi*, to remain in service until discarded in 1972.

Malpeque

Commissioned at Vancouver on 4 August 1941, *Malpeque* left for Halifax on 13 September, arriving on 19 October. She was briefly assigned to Sydney Force, then to Newfoundland Force, with which she served until 19 February 1944 when, with *Caraquet*, *Cowichan* and *Vegreville*, she sailed for the UK via the Azores for invasion duties. Arriving at Plymouth on 13 March, she was assigned to the 31st Minesweeping Flotilla, and was present on D Day. She proceeded to Canada in April 1945 for refit at Liverpool, Nova Scotia, but returned to the UK in June and remained there until September. She then returned home and was paid off on 9 October 1945 to reserve at Shelburne. Taken to Sorel in 1946 and placed in strategic reserve, she was reacquired by the RCN in 1952 and laid up at Sydney. Never again commissioned, she was sold for scrap in February 1959.

Malpeque, 25 February 1944.

MALPEQUE

BUILDER:	North Van Ship Repairs Ltd., Vancouver, BC	LAUNCHED:	5/9/40
LAID DOWN:	24/4/40	COMMISSIONED:	4/8/41
		PAID OFF:	9/10/45

Commanding Officers

A/LCDR W. R. Stacey, RCNR	4/8/41	5/8/42	A/LCDR W. R. Stacey, RCNR	14/9/43	24/10/43
LT J. G. McQuarrie, RCNR	6/8/42	13/9/42	LT D. Davis, RCNVR	25/10/43	25/4/45
A/LCDR W. R. Stacey, RCNR	14/9/42	12/8/43	LT O. R. Archibald, RCNVR	26/4/45	9/10/45
LT J. A. Dunn, RCNVR	13/8/43	13/9/43			

Minas, March 1944.

MINAS

BUILDER:	Burrard Dry Dock Co. Ltd., Vancouver, BC	LAUNCHED:	22/1/41
LAID DOWN:	18/10/40	COMMISSIONED:	2/8/41
		PAID OFF:	7/11/55

Commanding Officers

LT J. C. Barbour, RCNR	2/8/41	24/11/41	LT J. B. Lamb, RCNVR	18/6/43	25/10/44
LT J. C. Barbour, RCNR	2/12/41	13/9/42	LT J. G. Kingsmill, RCNVR	26/10/44	1/9/45
LT W. F. Wood, RCNR	14/9/42	17/6/43	LCDR K. A. Stone, RCN	15/3/55	7/11/55

Minas

Named for Minas Basin in the Bay of Fundy, she was built at Vancouver and commissioned there 2 August 1941. She sailed for Halifax on 13 September, arriving on 19 October. After brief service with Sydney Force, she was assigned in January 1942 to Newfoundland Force. That November she transferred to WLEF, and when WLEF was divided into escort groups in June, she became a member of EG W-7. That December she was reassigned to W-4. On 1 February 1943 she collided with HMS *Liscomb* outside Halifax, necessitating a month's repairs. *Minas* left Halifax for the UK on 20 February 1944 with *Blairmore*, *Fort William* and *Milltown*, via the Azores. On arrival in the UK on 8 March, she was assigned to the 31st Minesweeping Flotilla for invasion duties, and was on hand on D Day. In September she proceeded to Canada to refit at Dartmouth, Nova Scotia, returning to Plymouth in January 1945. There she joined the 31st Flotilla until she sailed again for Canada on 4 September. She was paid off into reserve at Shelburne on 6 October 1945 and later moved to Sorel, but was reacquired by the RCN in 1952 and recommissioned on 15 March 1955 for training on the west coast. Paid off on 7 November 1955, she was sold in August 1958, and broken up at Seattle the following year.

Miramichi, September 1944.

MIRAMICHI

				LAUNCHED:	2/9/41
BUILDER:	Burrard Dry Dock Co. Ltd., Vancouver, BC			COMMISSIONED:	26/11/41
LAID DOWN:	11/3/41			PAID OFF:	24/11/45

Commanding Officers

LT W. G. Johnstone, RCNR	26/11/41	26/10/42	LT R. J. Williams, RCNVR	24/1/44	21/6/45
LT G. H. Matheson, RCNR	27/10/42	23/1/44	SKPR/LT W. R. Chaster, RCNR	22/6/45	24/11/45

Miramichi

Commissioned at Vancouver on 26 November 1941, *Miramichi* spent her entire service career on the west coast, alternating between Esquimalt Force and Prince Rupert Force. In the summer and fall of 1943 while serving with Esquimalt Force, she was used occasionally for training purposes. She was paid off at Esquimalt on 24 November 1945 and in 1946 was acquired by the Union Steamship Co. for conversion that was never accomplished. She was broken up at Vancouver in 1949-50.

Nipigon.

NIPIGON

				LAUNCHED:	1/10/40
BUILDER:	Dufferin Shipbuilding Co. Toronto, ON			COMMISSIONED:	11/8/41
LAID DOWN:	4/7/40			PAID OFF:	13/10/45

Commanding Officers

LCDR A. T. Morrell, RCNR	11/8/41	14/2/42	LT W. Turner, RCNR	29/3/44	11/4/44
A/LCDR C. A. King, DSC, RCNR	15/2/42	11/5/42	LT D. R. Baker, RCNVR	12/4/44	4/2/45
LT J. Brock, RCNVR	12/5/42	4/10/42	LT J. R. Brown, RCNVR	5/2/45	13/10/45
LT W. J. Piercy, RCNVR	5/10/42	28/3/44			

Nipigon

Commissioned at Toronto on 11 August 1941, *Nipigon* arrived at Halifax on 5 September. She was the first of the Bangor class to join Sydney Force, on 3 October, and remained with it until her return to Halifax on 17 January 1942. She was then assigned for varying periods to WLEF, Halifax Force and Newfoundland Force. She was again attached to WLEF when it was divided into escort groups, and became a member of EG W-1. Early in 1944 she underwent a major refit at Lunenburg and Liverpool, Nova Scotia, on completion of which she sailed in May to work up in Bermuda. Returning in mid-June she was assigned to Halifax Force until it was disbanded a year later, afterward performing various duties on the Atlantic coast. *Nipigon* was paid off at Sydney on 13 October 1945 and laid up at Shelburne. She was placed in strategic reserve at Sorel in 1946 but was reacquired and refitted in 1952, though not again commissioned. Transferred to the Turkish Navy on 29 November 1957, she served as *Bafra* until 1972.

Outarde, 3 September 1942.

Outarde

Named for Outarde Bay, Quebec, she was commissioned at Vancouver on 4 December 1941. *Outarde* spent her whole career on the west coast, alternately serving with the Prince Rupert and Esquimalt Forces. She was paid off 24 November 1945 at Esquimalt, sold in 1946 for conversion to a merchant ship, and renamed *Ping Hsin* by her Shanghai owners. She vanished from Lloyd's Register after 1950.

OUTARDE

BUILDER:	North Van Ship Repairs Ltd., Vancouver, BC	LAID DOWN:	15/10/40	COMMISSIONED:	4/12/41
		LAUNCHED:	27/1/41	PAID OFF:	24/11/45

Commanding Officers

LT H. M. Kennedy, RCNR	4/12/41	25/2/42	LT H. B. Tindale, RCNVR	24/2/44	9/3/44
LT A. A. R. Dykes, RCNR	26/2/42	9/3/42	LT A. C. Jones, RCNR	10/3/44	23/8/44
LT H. M. Kennedy, RCNR	10/3/42	18/5/42	LT H. B. Tindale, RCNVR	24/8/44	24/8/45
LT R. Jackson, RCNVR	19/5/42	5/2/43	LT J. P. Kieran, RCNR	25/8/45	4/10/45
A/LCDR J. A. Macdonnell, RCNR	6/2/43	23/2/44			

Quatsino, 28 April 1944. The "jigsaw" camouflage was peculiar to west coast Bangors.

Quatsino

Named for Quatsino Sound, Vancouver Island, she was built at Prince Rupert and commissioned on 3 November 1941. *Quatsino* spent her entire service life on the west coast, alternately a member of the Prince Rupert and Esquimalt Forces. She was paid off at Esquimalt on 26 November 1945 and converted for commercial purposes in 1947, to be renamed *Chen Hsin* and domiciled at Shanghai. She vanished from Lloyd's Register after 1950.

QUATSINO

BUILDER:	Prince Rupert Dry Dock and Shipyards Co., Prince Rupert, BC	LAID DOWN:	20/6/40	COMMISSIONED:	3/11/41
		LAUNCHED:	9/1/41	PAID OFF:	26/11/45

Commanding Officers

LT S. Douglas, RCNR	3/11/41	14/12/41	LT A. H. Gosse, RCNR	3/4/43	29/9/43	A/LCDR B. C. Cook, RCNVR	3/1/45	26/11/45
A/LCDR T. MacDuff, RCN	15/12/41	27/5/42	LT H. H. Rankin, RCNR	30/9/43	22/10/43			
LT A. E. Gough, RCNR	28/5/42	2/4/43	LT A. H. Gosse, RCNR	23/10/43	2/1/45			

Quinte as training ship at Cornwallis, 6 September 1944.

Quinte

Commissioned at Vancouver on 30 August 1941, *Quinte* left Esquimalt 10 October for Halifax, arriving on 14 November. She was assigned at first to WLEF and then, in June 1942 to Halifax Force. On 30 November 1942, after completing a six-week refit at Lunenburg, she ran aground and sank at the entrance to St. Peter's Canal, Cape Breton. She was later refloated and on 25 April 1943 *Quinte* arrived at Pictou in tow for repairs, which were not completed until June 1944. She was then sent to HMCS *Cornwallis* as a training ship, arriving at Digby on 21 August, and remained there until the end of 1945. In 1946 she was employed with the Naval Research Establishment at Halifax until paid off on 25 October. *Quinte* was broken up at Sydney in 1947.

Thunder, 25 February 1944.

Thunder

Commissioned at Toronto on 14 October 1941, *Thunder* arrived at Halifax 30 October. After working up, she joined Sydney Force, but in January 1942 was transferred to WLEF and subsequently to Halifax Local Defence Force, Shelburne Force, Halifax Force, and back to Sydney Force. She sailed with *Bayfield, Georgian* and *Mulgrave* from Halifax on 18 February 1944 for Plymouth via the Azores. Arriving on 13 March, she was allocated to the 32nd Minesweeping Flotilla as Senior Officer's ship but was later transferred to the 4th Flotilla, and was present on D Day. *Thunder* returned to Canada in August 1944 to refit at Sydney but was back at Plymouth in late November, assigned to the 31st Flotilla. In May 1945 in the Bay of Biscay, she accepted the surrender of the German auxiliary minesweeper *FGi 07*. She sailed for Canada in September 1945 to be paid off on 4 October at Halifax, and was broken up at Sorel in 1947.

QUINTE				
BUILDER:	Burrard Dry Dock Co. Ltd., Vancouver, BC		LAUNCHED:	8/3/41
			COMMISSIONED:	30/8/41
LAID DOWN:	14/12/40		PAID OFF:	25/10/46

Commanding Officers

LT C. A. Nicol, RCNR	30/8/41	17/1/43	LT D. C. McPherson, RCNVR		19/7/45
LT I. B. B. Morrow, RCN	10/11/44	26/11/44	LT R. B. Taylor, RCNVR	20/7/45	3/8/45
SKPR/LT C. C. Clattenburg, RCNR	27/11/44	14/3/45	LT L. McQuarrie, RCNR	7/3/46	25/10/46

THUNDER				
BUILDER:	Dufferin Shipbuilding Co. Toronto, ON		LAUNCHED:	19/3/41
			COMMISSIONED:	14/10/41
LAID DOWN:	4/12/40		PAID OFF:	4/10/45

Commanding Officers

CDR H. D. Mackay, RCNR	14/10/41	25/6/45	LT A.W. Moore, RCNR	26/6/45	4/10/45

Ungava, 20 September 1941.

Ungava

Commissioned at Vancouver on 5 September 1941, *Ungava* left on 10 October for Halifax, arriving on 14 November. Initially assigned to Halifax Force, she was transferred in May 1943 to Gaspé Force, then back to Halifax Force that December. In May 1944 she joined Sydney Force, returning again to Halifax Force in February 1945. Following a refit from April to May 1945 at Liverpool, Nova Scotia, she went to Bermuda to work up, and on her return after VE Day she was assigned miscellaneous duties until paid off on 3 April 1946. She was sold later that year to a New Jersey buyer, presumably for scrap.

UNGAVA

BUILDER:	North Van Ship Repairs Ltd., Vancouver, BC		LAUNCHED:	9/10/40	
LAID DOWN:	24/4/40		COMMISSIONED:	5/9/41	
			PAID OFF:	3/4/46	

Commanding Officers

LT C. Winterbottom, RCNR	5/9/41	19/1/42	LT J. M. Home, RCNVR	17/1/45	30/1/45
LT F. E. Scoates, RCNR	20/1/42	8/2/43	LT S. Henderson, RCNR	31/1/45	9/4/45
LT D. M. Coolican, RCNVR	9/2/43	12/3/44	LT F. K. Ellis, RCNR	10/4/45	16/7/45
LT J. M. Home, RCNVR	13/3/44	17/12/44	LT F. Cross, RCNR	17/7/45	30/10/45
LT J. W. Radford, RCNR	18/12/44	16/1/45			

Wasaga, March 1944.

WASAGA

BUILDER:	Burrard Dry Dock Co. Ltd., Vancouver, BC		LAUNCHED:	23/1/41	
LAID DOWN:	3/9/40		COMMISSIONED:	1/7/41	
			PAID OFF:	6/10/45	

Commanding Officers

LCDR W. Redford, RCNR	1/7/41	9/3/42	LT J. B. Raine, RCNR	18/6/43	22/12/43
LT J. B. Raine, RCNR	10/3/42	13/5/43	LT J.J.H. Green, RCNR	23/12/43	6/10/45
LT J. A. Dunn, RCNVR	14/5/43	17/6/43			

Wasaga

The first of the RCN Bangors, *Wasaga* was commissioned at Vancouver on 1 July 1941. She left Esquimalt on 6 August for Halifax, arriving on 10 September. Sent to Bermuda for working up, she was assigned to Halifax Force on her return. In March 1942 she was transferred to Newfoundland Force, and in January 1944 to Sydney Force. Ordered to the UK for invasion duties, she sailed from Halifax on 21 February 1944 for Plymouth via the Azores, in company with *Canso, Guysborough* and *Kenora.* Arriving at Plymouth early in March, she was assigned at first to the 32nd and then to the 31st Minesweeping Flotilla, and was on hand on D Day. She sailed for Canada on 30 September 1944 to refit at Charlottetown, returning to Plymouth on 4 February 1945. That September she returned to Canada and was paid off at Halifax on 6 October, to be laid up at Shelburne until sold for scrap in 1947.

BANGOR CLASS, EX-ROYAL NAVY

PARTICULARS OF CLASS:	
DISPLACEMENT:	672
DIMENSIONS:	180' x 28' 6" x 8' 3"
SPEED:	16 kts
CREW:	6/77
ARMAMENT:	one 12 pdr., two 20-mm

Bayfield

Named for the village of Bayfield, Nova Scotia, she was built at Vancouver for the RN but transferred to the RCN for manning, and commissioned on 26 February 1942. After working up, *Bayfield* joined Esquimalt Force in May but was transferred to Prince Rupert Force in November, returning to Esquimalt in March 1943 for reassignment to the east coast. She left Esquimalt on 18 March, arriving at Halifax on 30 April and, after a major refit at Baltimore, Maryland, joined Halifax Force until ordered to the UK for invasion duties. On 18 February 1944 with *Georgian*, *Mulgrave* and *Thunder*, she left Halifax for Plymouth via the Azores, arriving on 7 March. Allocated to the 31st Minesweeping Flotilla, she was present on D Day, and she remained with Plymouth Command until paid off on 24 September 1945. Returned to the RN, she was placed in reserve at Sheerness until 1948, when she was broken up at Gateshead.

Bayfield, March 1944.

BAYFIELD

BUILDER:	North Van Ship Repairs Ltd., Vancouver, DC	LAUNCHED:	26/5/41
		COMMISSIONED:	26/2/42
LAID DOWN:	30/12/40	PAID OFF:	24/9/45

Commanding Officers

LT D. W. Main, RCNR	26/2/42	3/11/42	LT J. C. K. McNaught, RCNVR	16/10/44	22/12/44
LT A. H. Gosse, RCNR	4/11/42	31/12/42	LT F. A. Cunningham, RCNVR	23/12/44	1/9/45
LT D. W. Main, RCNR	1/1/43	19/1/44	LT J. G. Kingsmill, RCNVR	2/9/45	24/9/45
LT S. Pierce, RCNR	20/1/44	15/10/44			

Canso, March 1944.

CANSO

BUILDER:	North Van Ship Repairs Ltd., Vancouver, BC	LAUNCHED:	9/6/41
		COMMISSIONED:	5/3/42
LAID DOWN:	30/12/40	PAID OFF:	24/9/45

Commanding Officers

LT H. S. MacFarlane, RCNR	5/3/42	3/2/43	LT J. Kincaid, RCNR	6/6/43	4/10/44
LT J. Kincaid, RCNR	4/2/43	23/5/43	A/LCDR J. M. Gracey, RCNVR	5/10/44	24/9/45
LT H. H. Rankin, RCNR	24/5/43	5/6/43			

Canso

Built for the RN but transferred to the RCN for manning, *Canso* was commissioned at Vancouver on 5 March 1942. After working up, she was assigned to Esquimalt Force from May 1942 to July 1943 when she was nominated for service in the Atlantic. She left Esquimalt on 8 July 1943 arriving at Halifax on 19 August, and was allocated to Halifax Force. On 21 February 1944 with *Guysborough*, *Kenora* and *Wasaga*, she sailed from Halifax via the Azores for Plymouth, arriving on 7 March. She was allocated in turn to the 32nd 16th, and 31st Minesweeping Flotillas, and was on hand at D Day. In August she returned briefly to Canada for a refit at Saint John, New Brunswick, and in November resumed her task of clearing German minefields. She was paid off on 24 September 1945 and returned to the RN at Sheerness, to be broken up at Sunderland in 1948.

Caraquet

Named for a New Brunswick bay, she was built for the RN but transferred to the RCN for manning and commissioned 2 April 1942 at Vancouver. In May she joined Esquimalt Force and in September was transferred to Prince Rupert Force, but returned to Esquimalt in March 1943 with orders to proceed to the east coast. She left Esquimalt for Halifax on 17 March, arriving on 2 May, and was allocated to WLEF, transferring in June to Halifax Force and in December to Newfoundland Force. During this period she underwent a six-week refit at Baltimore, Maryland from mid-July 1943. On 19 February 1944 with *Cowichan*, *Malpeque* and *Vegreville*, she left for Plymouth via the Azores, arriving on 13 March. She was assigned to the 31st Minesweeping Flotilla for invasion duties and was present on D Day. *Caraquet* proceeded to Canada at the end of September to refit at Lunenburg, returning to Plymouth in March 1945 for further mine-clearance work. Paid off on 26 September and returned to the RN at Sheerness, she was sold to the Portuguese Navy in 1946 and renamed *Almirante Lacerda*. She remained in service as a survey vessel until 1975.

Caraquet leaving Baltimore after refit, September 1943.

CARAQUET

BUILDER:	North Van Ship Repairs Ltd., Vancouver, BC		LAUNCHED:	2/6/41	
			COMMISSIONED:	2/4/42	
LAID DOWN:	31/1/41		PAID OFF:	26/9/45	

Commanding Officers

LT A. A. R. Dykes, RCNR	2/4/42	3/11/43	LT G. W. Leckie, RCNVR	13/11/44	26/9/45
CDR A. H. G. Storrs, RCNR	4/11/43	18/9/44			

Guysborough, March 1944.

GUYSBOROUGH

BUILDER:	North Van Ship Repairs Ltd., Vancouver, BC		LAUNCHED:	21/7/41
			COMMISSIONED:	22/4/42
LAID DOWN:	28/5/41		LOST:	17/3/45

Commanding Officer

LT B. T. R. Russell, RCNR	22/4/42	17/3/45

Guysborough

Built at Vancouver for the RN but transferred to the RCN for manning, she was commissioned on 22 April 1942 and assigned to Esquimalt Force. On 17 March 1943 she left for Halifax, arriving on 30 April. After brief service with WLEF, she joined Halifax Force. In mid-September *Guysborough* underwent six weeks' refit at Baltimore, Maryland. On 21 February 1944 with *Canso*, *Kenora* and *Wasaga*, she left Halifax for the Azores en route to Plymouth, where she arrived on 8 March. She was assigned to the 14th Minesweeping Flotilla and was present on D Day. That December she returned to Canada for refit at Lunenburg, after which, bound again for Plymouth, she was torpedoed and sunk on 17 March 1945 by *U 878* off Ushant in the Channel. Fifty-one of her complement lost their lives.

Ingonish

Built at Vancouver for the RN but transferred to the RCN for manning, *Ingonish* was commissioned on 8 May 1942. She saw her first service with the Esquimalt and Prince Rupert Forces. She left Esquimalt 17 March 1943 for Halifax where, after her arrival on 30 April, she was allocated briefly to Western Local Defence Force and then in June, to Halifax Force. In mid-November she had a nine-week refit at Baltimore, Maryland. In May 1944 she was transferred to Sydney Force and in February 1945 back again to Halifax Force.

Following an extensive refit at Saint John she went in May to work up in Bermuda and in June sailed for the UK. She was returned to the RN at Sheerness on 2 July 1945 and placed in reserve until taken to Dunston-on-Tyne for scrapping in 1948.

Ingonish, March 1944.

Lockeport, April 1944.

Lockeport

Built for the RN at Vancouver but transferred to the RCN for manning, she was commissioned on 27 May 1942 and served with Esquimalt Force until 17 March 1943 when she left for Halifax. On her arrival there on 30 April she was assigned briefly to WLEF and in June to Halifax Force. In November and December 1943 she was loaned to Newfoundland Force but was withdrawn owing to engine trouble. On 9 January 1944 while en route to Baltimore for refit, her engines broke down during a storm, and she made 190 miles under improvised sail before being towed the rest of the way to her destination. Upon her return to Halifax in April, *Lockeport* was ordered to Bermuda to work up, and on the homeward journey she escorted the boats of the 78th Motor Launch Flotilla. Returning to Sydney Force in May 1944 she was frequently an escort to the Port-aux-Basques/Sydney ferry. She left Canada on 27 May 1945 for the UK, and was returned to the RN at Sheerness on 2 July, to be broken up three years later.

INGONISH			
BUILDER:	North Van Ship Repairs Ltd., Vancouver, BC	LAUNCHED:	30/7/41
		COMMISSIONED:	8/5/42
		PAID OFF:	2/7/45
LAID DOWN:	6/6/41		

Commanding Officers		
A/LCDR T. P. Ryan, OBE, RCN	8/5/42	2/5/43
LT F. E. Burrows, RCNVR	3/5/43	12/3/44
SKPR/LT G. B. McCandless, RCNR	13/3/44	4/4/44
LT R. C. G. Merriam, RCNR	5/4/44	15/9/44
LT H. V. Shaw, RCNVR	16/9/44	19/12/44
LT P. W. Lee, RCNVR	20/12/44	25/2/45
LT H. V. Shaw, RCNVR	26/2/45	26/3/45
LT C. D. Chivers, RCNVR	27/3/45	2/7/45

LOCKEPORT			
BUILDER:	North Van Ship Repairs Ltd., Vancouver, BC	LAUNCHED:	22/8/41
		COMMISSIONED:	27/5/42
		PAID OFF:	2/7/45
LAID DOWN:	17/6/41		

Commanding Officers		
LT D. Trail, RCNR	27/5/42	11/8/42
LCDR A. T. Morrell, RCNR	12/8/42	18/8/42
LT D. Trail, RCNR	19/8/42	21/8/43
LT R. M. Wallace, RCNVR	22/8/43	23/6/44
LT C. A. Nicol, RCNR	24/6/44	2/7/45

BANGOR CLASS 1940–1941 PROGRAM

PARTICULARS OF CLASS:

DISPLACEMENT:	672
DIMENSIONS:	180' x 28' 6" x 8' 3"
SPEED:	16 kts
CREW:	6/77
ARMAMENT:	one 4-inch, one 3-inch or one 12 pdr., two 20-mm

Courtenay

Commissioned at Prince Rupert on 21 March 1942 *Courtenay* spent her whole career on the west coast, serving alternately with the Esquimalt and Prince Rupert Forces. She was paid off on 5 November 1945 at Esquimalt and sold in 1946 to the Union Steamship Co., Vancouver, for use as a merchant ship. However, she was not converted to this use, and has proved impossible to trace beyond 1951, when a purchase offer was made by a San Francisco firm.

Courtenay, 8 June 1944.

COURTENAY

BUILDER:	Prince Rupert Dry Dock and Shipyards Co., Prince Rupert, BC	LAUNCHED:	2/8/41
		COMMISSIONED:	21/3/42
LAID DOWN:	28/1/41	PAID OFF:	5/11/45

Commanding Officers

A/LCDR A. R. Ascah, RCNR	21/3/42	7/2/43	A/LCDR A. R. Ascah, RCNR	2/3/43	4/3/45
LT A. H. Gosse, RCNR	8/2/43	1/3/43	LT W. N. Black, RCNVR	5/3/45	2/9/45

Drummondville at Sydney, Nova Scotia, 1943.

DRUMMONDVILLE

BUILDER:	Canadian Vickers Ltd., Montreal, QC	COMMISSIONED:	30/10/41
LAID DOWN:	10/1/41	PAID OFF:	29/10/45
LAUNCHED:	21/5/41		

Commanding Officers

LT J. P. Fraser, RCNR	30/10/41	16/1/42	LT H. C. Hatch, RCNVR	10/5/43	7/4/44
LT J. P. Fraser, RCNR	5/2/42	12/1/43	SKPR/LT F. W. M. Drew, RCNR	8/4/44	9/4/45
LT D. M. Stewart, RCNR	13/1/43	1/3/43	LT G. E. Cross, RCNR	10/4/45	23/6/45
LT J. P. Fraser, RCNR	2/3/43	9/5/43			

Drummondville

Commissioned at Montreal on 30 October 1941, she arrived at Halifax on 11 November and served at various times with WLEF, Gulf Escort Force, Halifax Local Defence Force, and Sydney Force before joining Newfoundland Force in February 1944. Following a major refit at Louisbourg, she proceeded to Bermuda in mid-August to work up, returning to St. John's early in October. The Newfoundland Force was disbanded in June 1945 and from then until October *Drummondville* was employed at miscellaneous duties on the east coast. She was paid off at Halifax on 29 October 1945 and in 1946 placed in strategic reserve at Sorel. Reacquired by the RCN in 1952, she was placed in reserve at Sydney but never recommissioned, and in 1948 she was sold for conversion to a merchant ship. As SS *Fort Albany* she was sunk by collision near Sorel on 8 December 1963, and raised and broken up there the following year.

Gananoque

Commissioned at Toronto on 8 November 1941, *Gananoque* arrived at Halifax on 23 November. She was assigned to Halifax Force, St. John's Local Defence Force, Gulf Escort Force, and Sydney Force. In January 1943 she was assigned to WLEF, returning to Halifax Force in July of the same year, and to Sydney Force once again in May 1944. During this period she had the distinction of twice refitting at other than Atlantic coast ports. In May 1943 she underwent a six-week refit at Quebec City, and in July 1944 an eight-week refit at Charlottetown. In February 1945 she was allocated to Newfoundland Force, based at St. John's, until the force was disbanded in June, whereupon she went to Atlantic Coast Command. *Gananoque* was paid off at Sydney on 13 October 1945 and laid up at Shelburne. Placed in strategic reserve at Sorel in 1946, she was reacquired by the RCN in 1952 but not recommissioned, and in February 1959 was sold for scrap.

Gananoque.

GANANOQUE

BUILDER:	Dufferin Shipbuilding Co. Toronto, ON		LAUNCHED:	23/4/41	
LAID DOWN:	15/1/41		COMMISSIONED:	8/11/41	
			PAID OFF:	13/10/45	

Commanding Officers

LT E. M. More, RCNR	8/11/41	15/3/43	SKPR/LT E. S. N. Pleasance, RCNR	28/11/43	24/5/44
LCDR W. Woods, RCNR	16/3/43	28/3/43	LCDR A. P. Duke, RCNVR	25/5/44	23/6/45
SKPR/LT E. S. N. Pleasance, RCNR	29/3/43	2/11/43	LT G. E. Cross, RCNVR	24/6/45	10/8/45
SKPR/LT J. B. Cooper, RCNR	3/11/43	27/11/43			

Goderich.

GODERICH

BUILDER:	Dufferin Shipbuilding Co. Toronto, ON		LAUNCHED:	14/5/41	
LAID DOWN:	15/1/41		COMMISSIONED:	23/11/41	
			PAID OFF:	6/11/45	

Commanding Officers

LT R. R. Kenny, RCNR	23/11/41	20/8/42	LT W. P. Wickett, RCNVR	7/3/44	21/3/44
LT J. G. Hughes, RCNR	21/8/42	7/9/42	LT J. E. Taylor, RCNVR	22/3/44	15/8/45
LT R. R. Kenny, RCNR	8/9/42	6/4/43	LT R. C. Hayden, RCNVR	16/8/45	22/8/45
LT J. C. Pratt, RCNVR	7/4/43	6/3/44			

Goderich

Commissioned at Toronto on 23 November 1941, *Goderich* arrived at Halifax on 6 December. She spent her whole career based at Halifax as a member, alternately, of Halifax Local Defence Force and Halifax Force. She was damaged on 18 November 1942 in a collision with the tanker *Iocoma* in Halifax harbour, which necessitated three weeks' repairs there. *Goderich* saw almost continuous service, undergoing only one major refit at Liverpool, Nova Scotia from 5 March to 15 May 1943. On 29 January 1943 she rescued survivors from the after section of the US tanker *Brilliant*, which had broken in half during a storm. She was paid off at Halifax on 6 November 1945 and in 1946 placed in strategic reserve at Sorel. In 1951 she was reacquired by the RCN and underwent modernization at Lauzon. Never recommissioned, however, she lay in reserve at Sydney until sold in February 1959 for scrap.

Grandmère

Grandmère was commissioned at Montreal on 11 December 1941. En route to Halifax she broke down in the Gulf of St. Lawrence on 21 December, and was towed to Sydney by HMCS *Kamsack*. Later that month, while alongside at Sydney undergoing repairs, she suffered serious damage to her No. 2 boiler, and was taken to Pictou for repairs, which were not completed until May 1942. She finally arrived at Halifax, her original destination, on 5 May. She served for varying periods with WLEF, Sydney Force, Halifax Force, and Halifax Local Defence Force. On 11 October 1942 while with Sydney Force, she rescued 101 survivors of the passenger ferry *Caribou*, torpedoed in the Cabot Strait. In July 1943 she had a seven-week refit at Louisbourg and underwent a second major refit at Sydney and Halifax in September 1944, following which she worked up in Bermuda in February 1945. The ship was paid off at Sydney on 23 October 1945 and placed in reserve at Shelburne. Sold in 1947, she was modified for use as a yacht, first renamed *Elda* and later, *Jack's Bay*.

Grandmère, May 1942.

GRANDMÈRE

BUILDER:	Canadian Vickers Ltd., Montreal, QC		LAUNCHED:	21/8/41	
			COMMISSIONED:	11/12/41	
LAID DOWN:	2/6/41		PAID OFF:	23/10/45	

Commanding Officers

LT J. Cuthbert, RCNR	11/12/41	20/4/44	LT R. C. Hayden, RCNVR	23/8/45	23/10/45
LT N. W. Winters, RCNVR	21/4/44	20/7/45			

Kelowna, 4 October 1944.

KELOWNA

BUILDER:	Prince Rupert Dry Dock and Shipyards Co., Prince Rupert, BC		LAUNCHED:	28/5/41	
			COMMISSIONED:	5/2/42	
LAID DOWN:	27/12/40		PAID OFF:	22/10/45	

Commanding Officers

LT W. Davenport, RCNR	5/2/42	4/8/43	LCDR R. B. Campbell, RCNR	22/11/43	11/1/44
SKPR/LT E. W. Suffield, RCNR	5/8/43	21/11/43	SKPR/LT E. W. Suffield, RCNR	12/1/44	22/10/45

Kelowna

Commissioned on 5 February 1942 at Prince Rupert, *Kelowna* spent her entire career on the west coast, alternately a member of Prince Rupert Force and Esquimalt Force. She was paid off at Esquimalt on 22 October 1945 and sold the following year for commercial purposes, first renamed *Condor* and in 1950, *Hung Hsin*. Owned in Shanghai, she disappeared from Lloyd's Register after 1950.

Medicine Hat

Commissioned at Montreal on 4 December 1941, she arrived at Halifax on 13 December and was allocated to WLEF and then in June 1942 to Sydney Force. In January 1943 she returned to WLEF but was transferred to Halifax Force in June, and remained there until May 1944, apart from a brief absence from November to December 1943 when she was loaned to Newfoundland Force. In May 1944 she returned to Sydney Force until January 1945 when she was transferred to Newfoundland Force until VE Day. She was thereafter employed at miscellaneous duties on the Atlantic coast until 6 November 1945 when she was paid off at Halifax and laid up at Shelburne. In 1946 *Medicine Hat* was placed in strategic reserve at Sorel until reacquired in 1951 and taken to Sydney. She remained in Sydney until she was transferred to the Turkish Navy on 29 November 1957. Renamed *Biga*, she remained in service until 1963.

Medicine Hat, October 1943.

MEDICINE HAT

BUILDER:	Canadian Vickers Ltd., Montreal, QC	LAUNCHED:	25/6/41
		COMMISSIONED:	4/12/41
LAID DOWN:	10/1/41	PAID OFF:	6/11/45

Commanding Officers

LT J. Bevan, RCNR	4/12/41	1/5/43	LT R. J. Keelan, RCNVR	29/8/44	7/5/45
LT J. E. Heward, RCNVR	2/5/43	20/12/43	LT K. G. Clark, RCNVR	8/5/45	11/6/45
LT A. A. R. Dykes, RCNR	21/12/43	10/1/44	CDR A. M. McLarnon, RCNR	12/6/45	10/7/45
LT J. E. Heward, RCNVR	11/1/44	28/8/44	LT W. R. Aylwin, RCNVR	19/7/45	-

Red Deer, 17 August 1943.

RED DEER

BUILDER:	Canadian Vickers Ltd., Montreal, QC	LAUNCHED:	5/10/41
		COMMISSIONED:	24/11/41
LAID DOWN:	10/1/41	PAID OFF:	30/10/45

Commanding Officers

LT A. Moorhouse, RCNR	24/11/41	2/2/43	LT D. B. D. Ross, RCNVR	6/6/44	2/7/45
LT J. A. Mitchell, RCNR	3/2/43	-	SKPR/LT R. A. Doucette, RCNR	1/10/45	30/10/45

Red Deer

Commissioned at Montreal on November 24 1941, *Red Deer* arrived at Halifax on 3 December. She was assigned to WLEF, later serving at various times with Halifax Local Defence Force, Gulf Escort Force, and Sydney Force. On 12 January 1942 she rescued survivors from the British SS *Cyclops*, which was torpedoed 125 miles southeast of Cape Sable, the first victim of the epic U-boat campaign off the US east coast. In May 1944 she began a refit at Liverpool, Nova Scotia and was sent to Bermuda to work up late in July. In February 1944 she had been allocated to Newfoundland Force, and she continued a member of this force until VE Day. She was paid off at Halifax on 30 October 1945 and laid up at Shelburne, later being placed in strategic reserve at Sorel. Reacquired by the RCN in 1952, she was never recommissioned, and was sold in February 1959 for breaking up at Sorel.

Swift Current

Commissioned at Montreal on 11 November 1941, she arrived at Halifax on 24 November and was based there for A/S training. In May 1942 *Swift Current* was moved to Pictou in the same capacity, and continued in this role until February 1943 when she was transferred to Halifax Force. She went to Gaspé Force in June 1943 but returned to Halifax in November. In February 1944 following a major refit at Lunenburg she was transferred to Newfoundland Force, remaining there until June 1945. Miscellaneous duties occupied her until she was paid off at Sydney on 23 October 1945 and laid up at Shelburne. *Swift Current* was placed in strategic reserve at Sorel the following year, but reacquired by the RCN in 1951 owing to the Korean emergency. However, she was not recommissioned and was handed over to the Turkish Navy on 29 March 1958. Renamed *Bozcaada*, she remained in Turkish service until 1971.

Swift Current, May 1944.

SWIFT CURRENT

BUILDER:	Canadian Vickers Ltd., Montreal, QC	COMMISSIONED:	11/11/41
LAID DOWN:	10/1/41	PAID OFF:	23/10/45
LAUNCHED:	29/5/41		

Commanding Officers

LCDR A. G. King, RCNR	20/9/41	18/4/42	LT K. D. Heath, RCNVR		8/4/44	13/5/45
LT I. H. Bell, RCNVR	19/4/42	27/9/42	LT J. N. Fraser, RCNVR		14/5/45	26/7/45
LT J. Evelyn, RCNR	28/9/42	7/4/44	LT P. J. Lawrence, RCNR		27/7/45	23/10/45

Vegreville.

VEGREVILLE

BUILDER:	Canadian Vickers Ltd., Montreal, QC	COMMISSIONED:	10/12/41
LAID DOWN:	2/6/41	PAID OFF:	6/6/45
LAUNCHED:	7/10/41		

Commanding Officers

CDR F. A. Price, RCNVR	10/12/41	19/1/42	LT T. B. Edwards, RCNR		12/1/43	6/11/44
LCDR T. H. Beament, RCNVR	20/1/42	11/1/43	LT J. W. Ross, RCNVR		7/11/44	6/6/45

Vegreville

Commissioned at Montreal on 10 December 1941, *Vegreville* arrived at Halifax on 18 December and was assigned to WLEF. She was reassigned to Gulf Escort Force in June 1942 and transferred that September to Newfoundland Force. In January 1944 she was assigned to invasion duties, and sailed on 19 February from Halifax for Plymouth via the Azores, in company with *Caraquet*, *Cowichan*, and *Malpeque*. Arriving at Plymouth on 13 March, *Vegreville* was assigned successively to the 32nd 14th, and 31st Minesweeping Flotillas, and was present on D Day. In September 1944 she proceeded to Canada to refit at Sydney, returning to Plymouth on 4 February 1945. On 23 April, while operating off the French coast, she sustained severe damage to her port engine. Dockyard survey at Devonport indicated that she was not worth repairing at that stage of the war, and she was laid up at Falmouth in June. Paid off on 6 June 1945 she was broken up at Hayle, UK, in 1947.

BANGOR CLASS 1940–1941 PROGRAM (DIESEL)

PARTICULARS OF CLASS:

DISPLACEMENT:	592
DIMENSIONS:	162' x 28' x 8' 3"
SPEED:	16 kts
CREW:	6/77
ARMAMENT:	one 12 pdr., two 20-mm

Brockville

Commissioned on 19 September 1942 at Sorel, she arrived at Halifax on 20 October in need of two weeks' repairs, having grounded at Rimouski en route. After working up, she was assigned briefly to WLEF and then to Halifax Force. In March she was transferred back to WLEF and when that force was divided into escort groups in June, she became a member of EG W-3. In May 1944 *Brockville* returned to Sydney Force remaining with it until June 1945. She had two wartime refits: one at Dalhousie, New Brunswick lasting seven weeks in August and September 1943; the other a three-month refit at Lunenburg at the end of 1944 followed by workups in Bermuda in March 1945. On 28 August 1945 she was paid off at Halifax, transferred to the marine section of the RCMP and renamed *Macleod*. *Brockville* was reacquired by the RCN in 1950 and recommissioned on 5 April 1951. After modernization at Lauzon in 1952 she was assigned to Point Edward naval base at Sydney and later transferred to the west coast. She was paid off into reserve at Esquimalt on 31 October 1958, and broken up three years later.

Digby

Commissioned at Quebec City on 26 July 1942, she arrived at Halifax on August 15, and after completing workups at Pictou was assigned to WLEF. When WLEF was divided into escort groups in June 1943 *Digby* became a member of EG W-5. In April 1944 she arrived at Lunenburg to commence a refit that continued at Shelburne and at Halifax and was completed on 7 August. She then proceeded to Bermuda for workups. On returning she was allocated to Sydney Force and in February 1945 to Newfoundland Force. She was paid off on 31 July 1945 and placed in reserve at Sydney. *Digby* was proposed for transfer to the marine section of the RCMP in 1945 to be renamed *Perry*, but was not taken over. She lay in strategic reserve at Sorel until reacquired by the RCN in 1951 and refitted for training duties. She was recommissioned on 29 April 1953, finally being paid off on 14 November 1956 and scrapped.

Brockville, 15 July 1955.

BROCKVILLE

BUILDER:	Marine Industries Ltd., Sorel, QC	COMMISSIONED:	19/9/42
LAID DOWN:	9/12/40	PAID OFF:	28/8/45
LAUNCHED:	20/6/41		

Commanding Officers

LT C. Peterson, RCNR	19/9/42	13/3/43	LT J. O. L. Lake, RCNR	8/2/45	14/5/45
LT R. C. Chenoweth, RCNVR	14/3/43	17/7/43	LT E. E. MacInnis, RCNR	30/7/45	28/8/45
LT C. Peterson, RCNR	18/7/43	23/7/43	LCDR J. H. Maxner, RCN	1/11/50	21/4/54
LT B. P. Young, RCNR	24/7/43	17/9/43	LCDR R. D. Hayes, RCNR	22/4/54	11/1/55
LT F. K. Ellis, RCNVR	18/9/43	2/8/44	LCDR E. S. Cassels, RCN	12/1/55	12/12/56
LT M. G. McCarthy, RCNVR	3/8/44	17/12/44	LCDR L. I. Jones, RCN	29/8/58	31/10/58
LT J. R. Bell, RCNVR	18/12/44	7/2/45			

Digby.

DIGBY

BUILDER:	Davie Shipbuilding and Repairing Co. Ltd., Lauzon, QC	LAUNCHED:	5/6/42
		COMMISSIONED:	26/7/42
LAID DOWN:	20/3/41	PAID OFF:	14/11/56

Commanding Officers

A/LCDR S. W. Howell, RCNR	26/7/42	9/7/43	LCDR E. G. T. Fisher, RCN	29/4/53	7/12/54
SKPR/LT J. W. Sharpe, RCNR	10/7/43	6/4/44	LCDR E. T. Coggins, RCN	8/12/54	28/9/55
LT E. O. Ormsby, RCNVR	7/4/44	1/7/45	LCDR A. F. Rowland, RCN	29/9/55	14/11/56

Esquimalt

Commissioned at Sorel on 26 October 1942, *Esquimalt* arrived at Halifax on 21 November. Chronically plagued by mechanical problems, she underwent repairs there until 27 March 1943 and again throughout most of May. She was then assigned to Newfoundland Force until September 1944 when she was transferred to Halifax Local Defence Force. Late in September she underwent a three-month refit at Halifax. While on A/S patrol on 16 April 1945 she was torpedoed and sunk by *U 190* five miles off Chebucto Head, near Halifax, with the loss of thirty-nine of her ship's company.

Granby

Commissioned at Quebec City on 2 May 1942 *Granby* arrived at Halifax on 13 May. She completed working up and was assigned first to Sydney Force and then to Western Local Defence Force. In June 1943 when the latter was divided into escort groups, she became a member of EG W-3 until May 1944, when she returned to Sydney Force. During this period she had an extensive refit at Lunenburg from June to October 1944, afterward proceeding to Bermuda to work up. She returned in November and was assigned to Shelburne Force in February 1945. In April she was transferred to Halifax Force and remained under repair at Halifax until paid off on 31 July 1945. Although allocated to the marine section of the RCMP as *Col. White*, she was not actually taken over. She was recommissioned on 23 May 1953 for conversion to a deep-diving tender, and served as such until finally paid off on 15 December 1966 and sold.

Esquimalt, May 1944.

Granby working up off Pictou, July 1943.

GRANBY

BUILDER:	Davie Shipbuilding and Repairing Co. Ltd., Lauzon, QC		LAUNCHED:	9/6/41
			COMMISSIONED:	2/5/42
LAID DOWN:	17/12/40		PAID OFF:	31/7/45

Commanding Officers

Mate J. R. Biggs, RCNR	2/5/42	7/2/43	LT E. S. Turnill, RCNVR	19/6/45	7/8/45
LCDR H. C. R. Davis, RCNR	8/2/43	16/3/43	LCDR G. G. K. Holder, RCN	23/5/53	2/3/54
A/LT J. R. Biggs, RCNR	17/3/43	10/10/43	LCDR G. A. Hoyte, RCN	3/3/54	13/5/54
LT G. G. K. Holder, RCNVR	11/10/43	9/5/44	LCDR D. Brownlow, RCN	14/5/54	30/9/54
LT D. A. P. Davidson, RCNVR	10/5/44	30/7/44	LCDR W. E. Williams, RCN	1/10/54	11/10/56
LT A. M. Brodie, RCNVR	31/7/44	24/4/45	LCDR C. S. Smedley, RCN	12/10/56	16/8/59
LT E. S. Turnill, RCNVR	25/4/45	27/5/45	LCDR W. W. Palmer, RCN	17/8/59	-
LT A. M. Brodie, RCNVR	28/5/45	18/6/45			

ESQUIMALT

BUILDER:	Marine Industries Ltd., Sorel, QC	LAUNCHED:	8/8/41
		COMMISSIONED:	26/10/42
LAID DOWN:	20/12/40	LOST:	16/4/45

Commanding Officers

LT F. J. L. Davies, RCNR	16/10/42	5/2/43
LT P. D. Taylor, RCNVR	6/2/43	12/3/44
LT J. M. S. Clark, RCNVR	13/3/44	14/12/44
LCDR W. McIsaac, RCNVR	29/12/44	1/2/45
LT R. C. MacMillan, DSC, RCNVR	2/2/45	16/4/45

Lachine

Commissioned at Quebec City on 20 June 1942, *Lachine* arrived at Halifax on 4 July and after repairs and workups, was assigned to Sydney Force in September. In October she was transferred to WLEF and in June 1943 became a member of EG W-6, one of the force's newly created escort groups. She served with Halifax Force from June 1944 until VE Day, and on 31 July 1945 was paid off at Shelburne. During the war she underwent two refits: the first at Dalhousie, New Brunswick, from October to November 1943; the second, at Lunenburg, from December 1944 to March 1945 followed by workups in Bermuda. An intended transfer to the marine section of the RCMP as *Starnes* did not materialize, and *Lachine* was sold in 1945 for conversion to a salvage tug.

Lachine, October 1943.

LACHINE

BUILDER:	Davie Shipbuilding and Repairing Co. Ltd., Lauzon, QC	LAUNCHED:	14/6/41	
LAID DOWN.	27/12/40	COMMISSIONED:	20/6/42	
		PAID OFF:	31/7/45	

Commanding Officers

LT B. P. Young, RCNR	20/6/42	8/5/43	LT F. M. Travers, RCNVR	22/3/45	23/4/45
LT L. F. Moore, RCNR	9/5/43	3/4/44	LT G. F. Pipe, RCNVR	24/4/45	31/7/45
LT F. R. Spindler, RCNVR	4/4/44	18/2/45			

Melville.

MELVILLE

BUILDER:	Davie Shipbuilding and Repairing Co. Ltd., Lauzon, QC	LAUNCHED:	7/6/41	
LAID DOWN:	17/12/40	COMMISSIONED:	4/12/41	
		PAID OFF:	18/8/45	

Commanding Officers

LT R. T. Ingram, RCNR	4/12/41	19/6/42	LT J. S. Foster, RCNR	18/1/44	25/1/44
A/LCDR E. R. Shaw, RCNR	20/6/42	13/10/43	LT N. W. Winters, RCNVR	26/1/44	20/4/44
SKPR/LT J. B. Cooper, RCNR	8/11/43	/12/43	LT J. S. Foster, RCNR	20/5/44	/5/45
LT J. E. Taylor, RCNVR	-	17/1/44	LT D. B. Harding, RCNR	/5/45	-

Melville

The first of the diesel-engined Bangors, *Melville* was commissioned at Quebec City on 4 December 1941. She arrived at Halifax on 13 December, worked up, and was assigned to WLEF. In May 1942 she was transferred to Shelburne Force, returning to WLEF that September. On 3 February 1943 she arrived at Lunenburg for refit, which was completed in Halifax. She did not resume service until 8 July, when she joined WLEF's recently created EG W-5. In March 1944 she underwent further repairs at Lunenburg, following which, on 6 June, she sailed to Bermuda to work up. Returning to Halifax 2 July, she was assigned to Sydney Force until June 1945. *Melville* was paid off at Sydney on 18 August 1945 and handed over to the marine section of the RCMP. Renamed *Cygnus*, she was broken up in 1961.

Noranda

Commissioned at Quebec City on 15 May 1942, *Noranda* arrived at Halifax on 30 May, and after working up at Pictou was assigned to Halifax Force. In February 1943 she was transferred to WLEF and on its division into escort groups that June became a member of EG W-9. *Noranda* went to Sydney Force in May 1944 and after a major refit at Lunenburg from September to December, proceeded to Bermuda to work up. Returning to Halifax on 2 February 1945 she served briefly with Halifax Force before joining Sydney Force. She was paid off at Halifax on 28 August 1945 and transferred to the marine section of the RCMP as *Irvine*. Sold in 1962 for use as a yacht and renamed *Miriana*, she sank at Montego Bay, Jamaica, in May 1971. *Miriana* may have been salvaged, as a ship answering this description and named *Viking L&R* appears on Cayman Islands registry in Lloyd's, 1977.

Noranda, 1942.

NORANDA

BUILDER:	Davie Shipbuilding and Repairing Co. Ltd., Lauzon, QC	LAUNCHED:	13/6/41
		COMMISSIONED:	15/5/42
LAID DOWN:	27/12/40	PAID OFF:	28/8/45

Commanding Officers

LT W. R. Nunn, RCNR	15/5/42	10/1/43	LT R. A. Wright, RCNVR	18/10/44	7/11/44
LT J. E. Francois, RCNR	11/1/43	1/9/44	LT G. E. Gilbride, RCNVR	8/11/44	10/7/45
LT J. C. K. McNaught, RCNVR	2/9/44	17/10/44			

Transcona.

TRANSCONA

BUILDER:	Marine Industries Ltd., Sorel, QC	COMMISSIONED:	25/11/42
LAID DOWN:	18/12/40	PAID OFF:	31/7/45
LAUNCHED:	26/4/41		

Commanding Officers

LT H. B. Tindale, RCNVR	25/11/42	17/1/44	LT J. N. Fraser, RCNVR	3/5/45	18/5/45
LCDR A. E. Gough, RCNR	18/1/44	6/4/45	SKPR/LT H. V. Mossman, RCNR	19/5/45	12/6/45

Transcona

Built at Sorel and commissioned there on August 12 1942 *Transcona* was the last Bangor class minesweeper to join the RCN. She arrived at Halifax on 19 December, having escorted HMCS *Provider* en route, and remained in shipyard hands there from 22 December 1942 to 6 March 1943 owing to engine defects. Following workups at Halifax, she was assigned in April 1943 to WLEF and, in June, to newly created EG W-2. In May 1944 she joined Halifax Force, remaining until June 1945 after which she performed various local tasks until she was paid off at Sydney on 31 July 1945. During this period she was under refit and repair at Lunenburg from February to May 1945. On 1 September *Transcona* was transferred to the marine section of the RCMP and renamed *French*. She was sold for scrapping at La Have, Nova Scotia in 1961.

Trois-Rivières

Built at Sorel and commissioned there on 12 August 1942 she arrived at Halifax on 29 August and, after working up in Pictou, was assigned to WLEF. In November 1942 she was transferred to Newfoundland Force, serving until the Command was disbanded in June 1945. She was under repair at Dalhousie, New Brunswick, Halifax and Saint John between October 1943 and January 1944 and had a major refit at Lunenburg from February to May 1945, followed by workups in Bermuda. *Trois-Rivières* was paid off on 31 July 1945 and handed over later that year to serve the RCMP as *MacBrien*. She was sold for scrapping in 1960.

Trois-Rivières.

TROIS-RIVIÈRES

BUILDER:	Marine Industries Ltd., Sorel, QC	COMMISSIONED:	12/8/42
LAID DOWN:	9/12/40	PAID OFF:	31/7/45
LAUNCHED:	30/6/41		

Commanding Officers

A/LCDR G. M. Kaizer, RCNR	12/8/42	11/2/43	LT R. C. G. Merriam, RCNVR	13/9/44	11/12/44
LT J. E. Taylor, RCNVR	12/2/43	10/3/43	LT J. M. S. Clark, RCNVR	12/12/44	23/4/45
A/LCDR G. M. Kaizer, RCNR	11/3/43	15/11/43	LT M. Gagnon, RCNVR	24/4/45	31/7/45
LT W. G. Garden, RCNVR	16/11/43	12/9/44			

Truro.

TRURO

BUILDER:	Davie Shipbuilding and Repairing Co. Ltd., Lauzon, QC	LAUNCHED:	5/6/42
		COMMISSIONED:	27/8/42
LAID DOWN:	20/3/41	PAID OFF:	31/7/45

Commanding Officers

SKPR/LT G. A. Myra, RCNR	27/8/42	1/8/43	LT E. E. MacInnis, RCNR	28/3/44	31/7/45
LT G. D. Campbell, RCNVR	2/8/43	27/3/44			

Truro

Commissioned at Quebec City on 27 August 1942 she arrived at Halifax on 15 September and was allocated to WLEF. In June 1943 she became a member of newly created EG W-4. In May 1944 she was transferred to Sydney Force, and from December 1944 to February 1945 underwent a major refit at Lunenburg. *Truro* was then assigned briefly to Halifax Force before returning to Sydney Force until June 1945. Paid off on 31 July at Sydney, she was handed over to the RCMP later that year and renamed *Herchmer*. She was sold for mercantile use in 1947 and, as *Gulf Mariner*, was abandoned ashore in the Fraser River after plans to convert her to a suction dredge had fallen through. She was broken up in 1964.

BANGOR CLASS 1941–1942 PROGRAM

PARTICULARS OF CLASS:

DISPLACEMENT: 672

DIMENSIONS: 180' x 28' 6" x 8' 3"

SPEED: 16 kts

CREW: 6/77

ARMAMENT: one 4-inch, one 3-inch or one 12 pdr., two 20mm

Blairmore

Commissioned at Port Arthur on 17 November 1942, *Blairmore* arrived at Halifax on 24 December, and after working up was assigned to WLEF. Upon the division of the force into escort groups in June 1943 she became a member of EG W-4 and remained with the group until February 1944.

Transferred to the UK for invasion duties, she left Halifax on 20 February in company with *Fort William*, *Milltown*, and *Minas* for Plymouth via the Azores, arriving on 8 March. Assigned to the 31st Minesweeping Flotilla, she was present on D Day, and continued with Plymouth Command until 21 September 1945 when she sailed for Canada. During this period she returned to Canada for a refit at Halifax in April 1945, returning to Plymouth in July. *Blairmore* was paid off at Sydney, Nova Scotia on 16 October 1945, sold to Marine Industries Ltd., and placed in strategic reserve at Sorel in 1946. She was reacquired by the RCN in July 1951, owing to the Korean crisis, and converted to a coastal escort. Again placed in reserve at Sydney, she was transferred to the Turkish Navy as *Beycoz* on 29 March 1958, remaining in service until 1971.

Blairmore in the Channel, 17 March 1944.

Fort William, March 1944.

BLAIRMORE			
BUILDER:	Port Arthur Shipbuilding Co. Ltd., Port Arthur, ON	LAUNCHED:	14/5/42
		COMMISSIONED:	17/11/42
		PAID OFF:	16/10/45
LAID DOWN:	2/1/42		
Commanding Officers			
A/LCDR W. J. Kingsmill, RCNVR		17/11/42	24/10/43
LT J. C. Marston, RCNR		25/10/43	14/6/45
SKPR/LT H. V. Mossman, RCNR		15/6/45	16/10/45

FORT WILLIAM			
BUILDER:	Port Arthur Shipbuilding Co. Ltd., Port Arthur, ON	LAUNCHED:	30/12/41
		COMMISSIONED:	25/8/42
		PAID OFF:	23/10/45
LAID DOWN:	18/8/41		
Commanding Officers			
LT H. Campbell, RCNR		25/8/42	29/6/43
LT S. D. Taylor, RCNR		30/6/43	4/10/43
A/LCDR H. Campbell, DSC, RCNR		5/10/43	18/5/45
LT G. E. Kelly, DSC, RCNR		19/5/45	23/10/45

Fort William

Commissioned at Port Arthur on 25 August 1942, *Fort William* arrived at Halifax on 24 September with a good many defects, and did not commence working up until mid-October. A month later she was assigned to Halifax Force for local convoys. On 11 January 1943 she suffered considerable damage in collision with the government vessel *Lisgar* at Halifax, and was under repair there for a month. In June 1943 she was transferred to Newfoundland Force. She returned to Halifax in February 1944 for a short refit, and on 20 February left with *Blairmore*, *Milltown*, and *Minas* for Plymouth via the Azores, arriving on 8 March. Assigned to the 31st Minesweeping Flotilla, she was present on D Day. *Fort William* refitted at St. John's in March 1945, rejoining the 31st Flotilla in July and remaining until 21 September, when she left Plymouth for Canada. She was paid off on 23 October 1945 at Sydney, and was placed in strategic reserve at Sorel in 1946. Reacquired in June 1951 and extensively modernized, she lay in reserve at Sydney until 29 November 1957, when she was transferred to the Turkish Navy and renamed *Bodrum*. She was removed from service in 1971 and broken up.

Kenora

Commissioned on 6 August 1942 at Port Arthur, she arrived at Halifax on September 7 and proceeded to Pictou for workups. She was then assigned to WLEF and in June 1943 became a member of EG W-8. She left Halifax on 21 February 1944 with *Canso*, *Guysborough* and *Wasaga*, via the Azores for Plymouth, arriving on 8 March. *Kenora* was assigned to the 14th Minesweeping Flotilla, with which she was present on D Day, and in October returned to Canada for a refit at Liverpool, Nova Scotia. She proceeded to the UK again in February 1945 and was assigned to the 31st Flotilla until September 4, when she left Plymouth for Canada. *Kenora* was paid off at Halifax on 6 October 1945 and placed in reserve at Shelburne. In 1946 she went into strategic reserve at Sorel until reacquired by the RCN in 1952 and moved to Sydney. On 29 November 1957, she was transferred to the Turkish Navy as *Bandirma*. She was removed from service in 1972.

Kenora, March 1944.

KENORA

BUILDER:	Port Arthur Shipbuilding Co. Ltd., Port Arthur, ON	LAUNCHED:	20/12/41
LAID DOWN:	18/8/41	COMMISSIONED:	6/8/42
		PAID OFF:	6/10/45

Commanding Officers

| A/LCDR F. R. K. Naftel, RCNVR | 6/8/42 | 14/9/43 | A/LCDR R. M. Meredith, RCNR | 8/2/45 | 6/10/45 |
| LT D. W. Lowe, RCNVR | 15/9/43 | 7/2/45 | | | |

Kentville, 1945.

KENTVILLE

BUILDER:	Port Arthur Shipbuilding Co. Ltd., Port Arthur, ON	LAUNCHED:	17/4/42
LAID DOWN:	15/12/41	COMMISSIONED:	10/10/42
		PAID OFF:	28/10/45

Commanding Officers

LT J. G. Hughes, RCNR	10/10/42	21/3/44	LT J. R. Brown, RCNVR	15/12/44	3/2/45
LT W. J. Gilmore, RCNVR	22/3/44	28/4/44	LT F. G. Rainsford, RCNVR	4/2/45	8/7/45
LT J. G. Hughes, RCNR	29/4/44	21/7/44	LT P. W. Lee, RCNVR	9/7/45	10/8/45
LT F. G. Rainsford, RCNVR	22/7/44	14/12/44	LT W. G. Hunt, RCN	10/5/54	30/9/54

Kentville

Commissioned at Port Arthur on 10 October 1942, *Kentville* arrived at Halifax on 15 November, having escorted a Quebec-Sydney convoy en route. After working up, she was assigned to Halifax Force in January 1943. With the exception of the period between May and November 1943 when she served with Sydney Force, she spent her entire career based at Halifax. In May 1944 she underwent a refit at Charlottetown, on completion of which in July she proceeded to Bermuda for working up, returning to Halifax in mid-August. *Kentville* was paid off at Sydney on 28 October 1945 and went into reserve, first at Shelburne and then in 1946 at Sorel. She was reacquired by the RCN in 1952, refitted and placed in reserve at Sydney, and was again in commission during the summer of 1954. Transferred on 29 November 1957 to the Turkish Navy and renamed *Bartin*, she remained in service until 1972.

Milltown

Commissioned on 18 September 1942 at Port Arthur, *Milltown* arrived at Halifax on 27 October and after working up joined Halifax Force in December. In March 1943 she transferred to WLEF and in June, to Gaspé Force. In November 1943 she returned to Halifax Force until 20 February 1944, when with *Blairmore*, *Fort William* and *Minas* she sailed via the Azores for Plymouth, arriving on 8 March. She was present on D Day with the 31st Minesweeping Flotilla. She returned to Canada to refit at Saint John, New Brunswick, from March to June 1945, leaving Halifax 23 June for Plymouth, via the Azores. She left Plymouth for home on 21 September and was paid off 16 October at Sydney and laid up at Shelburne. *Milltown* was placed in strategic reserve at Sorel in 1946, but reacquired by the RCN in 1952 and kept in reserve at Sydney until February 1959, when she was sold for scrap.

Milltown, March 1944.

MILLTOWN

BUILDER:	Port Arthur Shipbuilding Co. Ltd., Port Arthur, ON	LAUNCHED:	27/1/42
		COMMISSIONED:	18/9/42
LAID DOWN:	18/8/41	PAID OFF:	16/10/45

Commanding Officers

A/LCDR J. H. Marshall, RCNVR	18/9/42	14/4/43	A/CDR A. H. G. Storrs, RCNR	19/9/44	16/10/45
LT E. H. Maguire, RCNVR	15/4/43	18/9/44			

Mulgrave, March 1944.

MULGRAVE

BUILDER:	Port Arthur Shipbuilding Co. Ltd., Port Arthur, ON	LAUNCHED:	2/5/42
		COMMISSIONED:	4/11/42
LAID DOWN:	15/12/41	PAID OFF:	7/6/45

Commanding Officers

LT D. T. English, RCNR	4/11/42	10/10/43	LT R. M. Meredith, RCNR	11/10/43	25/12/44

Mulgrave

Commissioned at Port Arthur on 4 November 1942, *Mulgrave* arrived at Halifax on 30 November and was assigned to Halifax Force for the first quarter of 1943. She then transferred to WLEF, becoming a member of newly created EG W-2 in June 1943. On 18 February 1944 with *Bayfield*, *Georgian* and *Thunder*, she left Halifax for Plymouth via the Azores. On 29 February, when entering Horta, *Mulgrave* suffered grounding damage and had to be towed to Greenock, Scotland. After repairs at Ardrossan she finally made Plymouth on 24 April to commence training and exercises. She was temporarily assigned to the 32nd Minesweeping Flotilla, then in June to the 31st, with which she was present on D Day. On 8 October 1944 the unlucky *Mulgrave* was damaged by a ground mine near Le Havre and had to be beached. On 3 November she left Le Havre in tow for Portsmouth, where she was declared a constructive total loss. Placed in reserve at Falmouth in January 1945 with a reduced complement, she was formally paid off on 7 June and scrapped at Llanelly, Wales, two years later.

Port Hope

Commissioned at Toronto on 30 July 1942, *Port Hope* arrived in Halifax on 29 August and on completion of workups, joined Halifax Force. In May 1943 owing to U-boat activity in the Gulf of St. Lawrence she was transferred to Gaspé Force, but returned to Halifax Force in November. In January 1944 she was transferred to Newfoundland Force. That October she underwent an extensive refit at Saint John and Halifax, on completion of which she went to Bermuda to work up. Returning, *Port Hope* served a short further stint with Halifax Force from April to June 1945, then performed miscellaneous duties on the east coast until paid off at Sydney on 13 October 1945. She lay in strategic reserve at Sorel until 1952, when the RCN reacquired her, but was not recommissioned, and was sold in February 1959, for breaking up at Sorel.

Port Hope.

PORT HOPE

BUILDER:	Davie Shipbuilding and Repairing Co. Ltd., Lauzon, QC	LAUNCHED:	14/12/41
		COMMISSIONED:	30/7/42
LAID DOWN:	9/9/41	PAID OFF:	13/10/45

Commanding Officers

LT W. Turner, RCNR	30/7/42	1/12/42	LT R. K. Lester, RCNVR	9/4/43	17/3/44
LT A. H. Rankin, RCNVR	2/12/42	8/4/43	LT R. M. Montague, RCNVR	18/3/44	17/7/45

Sarnia, October 1943.

SARNIA

BUILDER:	Davie Shipbuilding and Repairing Co. Ltd., Lauzon, QC	LAUNCHED:	21/1/42
		COMMISSIONED:	13/8/42
LAID DOWN:	18/9/41	PAID OFF:	28/10/45

Commanding Officers

LT C. A. Mott, RCNR	13/8/42	10/2/43	LT R. D. Hurst, RCNVR	25/6/44	9/10/44
LT D. I. McGill, RCNVR	11/2/43	17/7/43	LT R. P. J. Douty, RCNVR	10/10/44	21/9/45
LT R. C. Chenoweth, RCNVR	18/7/43	12/3/44	LT D. M. Mossop, RCNVR	22/9/45	28/10/45
LT H. A. Plow, RCNVR	13/3/44	24/6/44			

Sarnia

Commissioned at Toronto on 13 August 1942, *Sarnia* arrived at Halifax on 22 September, having escorted a Quebec-Sydney convoy en route, and was assigned to Newfoundland Force. In September 1944 she underwent a major refit at Lunenburg, and on completion went to Bermuda in November to work up. On her return to Canada she was assigned to Halifax Force and, later, to Halifax Local Defence Force until June 1945. On 15 April 1945 she rescued survivors of HMCS *Esquimalt*, torpedoed outside Halifax. She then performed miscellaneous duties until paid off on 28 October 1945 at Sydney and laid up at Shelburne. In 1946 she was placed in strategic reserve at Sorel, and in 1951 reacquired by the RCN and extensively refitted. She did not recommission, however, and on 29 March 1958 was transferred to the Turkish Navy to serve until 1972 as *Buyukdere*.

Stratford

Commissioned at Toronto on 29 August 1942, *Stratford* arrived at Halifax on 22 September and was assigned to Newfoundland Force. She remained with this force as a convoy escort throughout her wartime career, and saw continuous service. She did not require a major refit until December 1944, when this was done at Dartmouth, Nova Scotia. On its completion she carried out workups in Bermuda from 15 February to 8 March 1945. Returning from Bermuda, she was involved in a collision with HMCS *Ottawa* in the Halifax approaches on 11 March, receiving extensive damage to her fo'c's'le. Though inactive thereafter, she was not paid off until 4 January 1946, and was then sold for scrap.

Stratford.

STRATFORD

BUILDER:	Davie Shipbuilding and Repairing Co. Ltd., Lauzon, QC	LAUNCHED:	14/2/42
		COMMISSIONED:	29/8/42
LAID DOWN:	29/10/41	PAID OFF:	4/1/46

Commanding Officers

LT R. M. Meredith, RCNR	29/8/42	30/10/42	LT R. G. Magnusson, RCNVR	22/6/44	1/4/45
LT R. J. C. Pringle, RCNVR	31/10/42	3/5/43	LT J. P. Charbonneau, RCNVR	2/4/45	25/4/45
LT W. G. Garden, RCNVR	4/5/43	4/8/43	LT J. M. S. Clark, RCNVR	26/4/45	13/6/45
LT D. W. G. Storey, RCNVR	5/8/43	20/12/43	LT G. G. Currie, RCNVR	4/10/45	-
LT H. A. Ovenden, RCNR	21/12/43	21/6/44			

Westmount.

WESTMOUNT

BUILDER:	Davie Shipbuilding and Repairing Co. Ltd., Lauzon, QC	LAUNCHED:	14/3/42
		COMMISSIONED:	15/9/42
LAID DOWN:	28/10/41	PAID OFF:	13/10/45

Commanding Officers

A/LCDR F. G. Hutchings, RCNVR	15/9/'42	7/12/43	LT R. L. B. Hunter, RCNVR	17/3/44	25/3/45
LT F. H. Pinfold, RCNVR	8/12/43	16/3/44	LT R. P. Jackson, RCNVR	26/3/45	7/7/45

Westmount

Commissioned at Toronto on 15 September 1942, *Westmount* arrived at Halifax on 10 October and proceeded to Pictou to work up. Following this, she underwent engine repairs at Halifax from 20 November to 2 February 1943. She was then assigned to Halifax Local Defence Force and, later, to Halifax Force. In May 1943 she was transferred to Sydney Force, but returned to Halifax Force in January 1944. In February 1945 she commenced a major refit at Lunenburg and, after this was completed late in April, proceeded to Bermuda to work up. Upon her return to Halifax on 30 May she was assigned to miscellaneous duties until paid off at Sydney on 13 October 1945 and laid up at Shelburne. In 1946 she was placed in strategic reserve at Sorel until reacquired by the RCN in 1951. On 29 March 1958, she was transferred to the Turkish Navy, serving as *Bornova* until 1972.

ALGERINE CLASS

PARTICULARS OF CLASS:

DISPLACEMENT:	990
DIMENSIONS:	225' x 35' 6" x 8' 6"
SPEED:	16 kts
CREW:	8/99
ARMAMENT:	one 4-inch, four 20-mm, Hedgehog

Border Cities

Commissioned at Port Arthur on 18 May 1944, *Border Cities* arrived at Halifax in mid-June, and on 8 July proceeded to Bermuda to work up. Returning to Halifax on 3 August, she was assigned as Senior Officer's ship to EG W-2 of WLEF. In June 1945 she was assigned to Atlantic Coast Command and, in August, placed temporarily in maintenance reserve at Sydney. On 10 November she left, with four sisters, for the west coast, and on January 15 1946 was paid off into reserve at Esquimalt. She was sold for scrap in 1948 and broken up at Victoria soon afterward.

Border Cities, July 1944.

BORDER CITIES

BUILDER:	Port Arthur Shipbuilding Co. Ltd., Port Arthur, ON	LAUNCHED:	3/5/43
		COMMISSIONED:	18/5/44
LAID DOWN:	26/8/42	PAID OFF:	15/1/46

Commanding Officers

LCDR B. P. Young, MBE, RCNR	18/5/44	23/7/45	LT J. Butterfield, RCNR	24/10/45	15/1/46

Fort Frances, 28 March 1945.

FORT FRANCES

BUILDER:	Port Arthur Shipbuilding Co. Ltd., Port Arthur, ON	LAUNCHED:	30/10/43
		COMMISSIONED:	28/10/44
LAID DOWN:	11/5/43	PAID OFF:	5/4/46

Commanding Officers

LT D. E. Ryerson, RCNVR	28/10/44	25/7/45	LCDR W. O. O. Barbour, RCNR	6/3/46	5/4/46
LT L. F. Horne, RCNVR	19/10/45	-			

Fort Frances

Commissioned at Port Arthur on 28 October 1944, she arrived at Halifax on 26 November, and sailed for Bermuda in January 1945 to work up. Returning to Halifax, *Fort Frances* served briefly with escort groups W-8 and W-9 of Western Escort Force before being paid off into maintenance reserve on 3 August 1945. She was again in commission from 23 October 1945 to 5 April 1946, and in 1948 was handed over to the Department of Mines and Technical Surveys as a hydrographic survey ship. In 1958 she reverted to naval service as a civilian-manned oceanographic research vessel. She was sold for breaking up in 1974.

Kapuskasing

Commissioned at Port Arthur on 17 August 1944, *Kapuskasing* arrived at Halifax early in September and on 1 October proceeded to Bermuda to work up. She returned to Halifax in mid-November and was assigned as Senior Officer's ship to EG W-1 of Western Escort Force. When the force was disbanded in June 1945 she was placed temporarily in maintenance reserve at Sydney, then taken to Halifax for refit in November. On completion of the refit she was paid off into reserve on 27 March 1946. In 1949 she was loaned to the Department of Mines and Technical Surveys and converted for hydrographic survey work. Returned to the Navy in 1972, she was expended as a target on 3 October 1978.

Kapuskasing, April 1945.

KAPUSKASING				
BUILDER:	Port Arthur Shipbuilding Co. Ltd., Port Arthur, ON	LAUNCHED:	22/7/43	
		COMMISSIONED:	17/8/44	
LAID DOWN:	19/12/42	PAID OFF:	27/3/46	
Commanding Officers				
LCDR A. H. Rankin, OBE, RCN	17/8/44	2/9/45	LT G. M. Kennelly, RCNVR	22/10/45 –

Middlesex, March 1945.

MIDDLESEX				
BUILDER:	Port Arthur Shipbuilding Co. Ltd., Port Arthur, ON	LAUNCHED:	27/5/43	
		COMMISSIONED:	8/6/44	
LAID DOWN:	29/9/42	LOST:	12/12/46	
Commanding Officers				
LT W. J. Piercy, RCNR	8/6/44	5/1/46	LCDR B. P. Young, MBE, RCN	16/1/46
LT J. Butterfield, RCNR	6/1/46	15/1/46		

Middlesex

Middlesex was commissioned at Port Arthur on 8 June 1944, arrived at Halifax in mid-July and sailed for Bermuda in August to work up. Assigned to EG W-3 of Western Escort Force, she joined the group in New York on 30 August, direct from Bermuda. *Middlesex* was principally engaged as southern local escort to UK bound convoys out of New York. She was Senior Officer's ship of W-3 from mid-November 1944 until the force was disbanded in June 1945, whereupon she refitted at Halifax and was placed in maintenance reserve there. In March 1946, she returned to service as emergency ship at Halifax. On 2 December 1946, en route to assist the fishing vessel *Ohio*, she ran ashore on Half Island Point, near Halifax, and was declared a constructive total loss on 12 December.

New Liskeard

Commissioned at Port Arthur on 21 November 1944, *New Liskeard* arrived at Halifax on 15 December and proceeded to Bermuda for workups in March 1945. Upon her return in April she was assigned to EG W-8 of Western Escort Force. When EG W-8 was disbanded in June she was allocated to HMCS *Cornwallis* as a training ship from July to September. She then was placed in maintenance reserve, first at Sydney and then at Halifax, until the end of the year. Refitted at Halifax, she was recommissioned on 9 April 1946 as a training ship for cadets. On 22 April 1958 she was paid off and converted to an oceanographic research vessel, serving as such until 1 May 1969. Later that year she was taken to Dartmouth Cove, Nova Scotia for breaking up.

Oshawa

Commissioned at Port Arthur on 6 July 1944, she arrived at Halifax on 18 August. She worked up in Bermuda in September, and on her return was allocated to EG W-6 of Western Escort Force as Senior Officer's ship. The group was disbanded in June 1945 and *Oshawa* was paid off into maintenance reserve at Sydney on 28 July. She was recommissioned on 24 October, and in November sailed for Esquimalt. She arrived there 21 December and on 26 February 1946 was paid off into reserve. During one more commission from 11 April 1956 to 7 November 1958, she was extensively converted for oceanographic research, in which role she continued, civilian-manned, until sold and broken up at Victoria in 1966.

New Liskeard at Port Arthur, 20 November 1944.

NEW LISKEARD

BUILDER:	Port Arthur Shipbuilding Co. Ltd., Port Arthur, ON		LAUNCHED:	14/1/44
			COMMISSIONED:	21/11/44
LAID DOWN:	8/7/43		PAID OFF:	22/4/58

Commanding Officers

LT W. M. Grand, RCNVR	21/11/44	15/6/45	LCDR C. E. Coles, RCN	15/4/51	14/12/51
LT W. J. Piercy, RCNR	7/1/46	21/2/46	LCDR T. W. Wall, RCN	15/12/51	2/3/53
LT A. H. McDonald, RCN	22/2/46	30/4/46	LCDR R. L. Ellis, RCN	3/3/53	6/8/54
LCDR J. C. L. Annesley, RCN	1/5/46	15/9/46	LCDR M. A. Turner, RCN	7/8/54	3/6/56
LCDR B. P. Young, MBE, RCN	16/9/46	11/11/47	LCDR G. R. Wood, RCN	4/6/56	27/8/57
LT I. B. B. Morrow, RCN	12/11/47	23/6/49	LCDR C. H. LaRose, RCN	28/8/57	-
LT W. W. MacColl, RCN	24/6/49	14/4/51			

Oshawa, 1944.

OSHAWA

BUILDER:	Port Arthur Shipbuilding Co. Ltd., Port Arthur, ON	LAUNCHED:	10/6/43
		COMMISSIONED:	6/7/44
		PAID OFF:	7/11/58
LAID DOWN:	6/10/42		

Commanding Officers

A/LCDR J. C. Pratt, RCNVR	6/7/44	27/5/45
A/LCDR R. S. Williams, RCNVR	28/5/45	28/7/45
LT J. Kincaid, RCNR	24/10/45	26/2/46
LCDR G. H. Barrick, RCN	11/4/46	7/11/58

Portage, 1944.

Portage

Named for Portage la Prairie, Manitoba, she was commissioned at Port Arthur on 22 October 1943 and arrived at Halifax on 28 November. After working up in St. Margaret's Bay *Portage* was assigned to EG W-2 of Western Escort Force as Senior Officer's ship, late in January 1944. In mid-April she was transferred, still as S.O., to W-3, and continued as such until late October, when she underwent an extensive refit at Liverpool, Nova Scotia. She then proceeded to Bermuda for workups, rejoining W-3 in March 1945. The group was disbanded in June and *Portage* was placed in maintenance reserve at Sydney and then at Halifax, where she was paid off on 31 July 1946. She was reactivated for training purposes during the summers of 1947 and 1948, and spent most of the period between 1949 and 1959 in the same role, much of the time on the Great Lakes. She was finally paid off on 26 September 1958, and scrapped at Sorel three years later.

Rockcliffe

Commissioned at Port Arthur on 30 September 1944, *Rockcliffe* arrived at Halifax on 30 October and proceeded to Bermuda to work up. Upon returning to Halifax in mid-December she was assigned to EG W-6 until June 1945. She escorted the surrendered *U 889* part of the way to Shelburne, Nova Scotia on 10 May 1945. Paid off to reserve at Sydney on 28 July 1945, she was recommissioned for passage to Esquimalt, where she arrived on 21 December 1945. On 14 January 1946 she was again paid off into reserve, but was recommissioned on 3 March 1947 to serve as a training ship. She was finally paid off on 15 August 1950 and scrapped ten years later.

PORTAGE

BUILDER:	Port Arthur Shipbuilding Co. Ltd., Port Arthur, ON	LAUNCHED:	21/11/42
		COMMISSIONED:	22/10/43
LAID DOWN:	23/5/42	PAID OFF:	26/9/58

Commanding Officers

LT B. P. Young, RCNR	22/10/43	19/12/43	LCDR A. H. Rankin, OBE, RCN	24/3/48	18/8/48
A/LCDR G. M. Kaizer, RCNR	20/12/43	4/6/45	LCDR D. M. MacDonald, RCN	12/4/49	27/10/49
LT J. G. Macdonnell, RCNVR	5/6/45	13/7/45	LT W. W. MacColl, RCN	28/10/49	16/2/50
LCDR G. M. Kaizer, RCNR	14/7/45	2/8/45	LT E. P. Earnshaw, RCN	17/2/50	23/6/51
LT W. E. Williams, RCNR	23/10/45	2/11/45	LT J. H. MacLean, RCN	24/6/51	15/3/53
LT W. R. Aylwin, RCNVR	3/11/45	5/2/46	LCDR A. B. Torrie, RCN	16/3/53	25/11/54
A/LT W. E. Hughson, RCNR	6/2/46	8/4/46	LCDR H. E. T. Lawrence, DSC, RCN	23/4/55	25/10/56
LT C. J. Benoit, DSC, RCN	9/4/46	2/6/46	LCDR K. R. Crombie, RCN	26/10/56	5/5/57
LT M. H. Cooke, RCN	3/6/46	31/7/46	LCDR J. A. Farquhar, RCN	6/5/57	24/9/57
LT J. B. Bugden, RCN	12/4/47	30/9/47	LCDR C. W. Fleming, RCN	1/4/58	26/9/58

Rockcliffe, March 1945.

ROCKCLIFFE

BUILDER:	Port Arthur Shipbuilding Co. Ltd., Port Arthur, ON	LAUNCHED:	19/8/43
		COMMISSIONED:	30/9/44
		PAID OFF:	28/7/45
LAID DOWN:	23/12/42		

Commanding Officers

LT J. E. Heward, RCNVR	30/9/44	28/7/45
A/LCDR A. E. Gough, RCNR	24/10/45	14/1/46
LCDR J. W. Golby, DSC, RCNR	3/3/47	30/3/47
CDR H. Kingsley, RCN	31/3/47	15/10/48
LCDR J. B. Bugden, RCN	16/10/48	3/12/48
CDR H. Kingsley, RCN	4/12/48	25/4/49
LCDR J. B. Bugden, RCN	26/4/49	10/7/49
LCDR H. R. Beck, RCN	11/7/49	6/9/49
A/CAPT H. Kingsley, RCN	7/9/49	21/4/50
CDR J. S. Davis, RCN	22/4/50	15/8/50

St. Boniface

Commissioned at Port Arthur on 10 September 1943, *St. Boniface* arrived at Halifax late in October, and worked up at Pictou from November to December. She was then assigned as Senior Officer's ship to EG W-5 of Western Escort Force until mid-April 1944. She then transferred to W-4, again as S.O., until early December when, following minor repairs at Halifax, she proceeded to Bermuda to work up. Upon returning to Canada, she rejoined W-4 until the group was disbanded in June 1945. On 18 April 1945 St. Boniface was in collision with SS *Empire Chamois* in the Halifax approaches as the freighter's convoy, SC.173, was forming up for passage to the UK. *St. Boniface* suffered extensive damage to her bows, but made Halifax under her own power and was under repair there for three months. In August 1945 she became a training ship at HMCS *Cornwallis* until January 1946, when she was placed in reserve at Halifax. She was finally paid off on 25 September 1946, and sold for mercantile use. She was last noted under Panamanian flag as *Bess Barry M.* in 1954.

St. Boniface.

ST. BONIFACE

BUILDER:	Port Arthur Shipbuilding Co. Ltd., Port Arthur, ON	LAUNCHED:	5/11/42
		COMMISSIONED:	10/9/43
LAID DOWN:	21/5/42	PAID OFF:	25/9/46

Commanding Officers

LCDR J. J. Hodgkinson, RCNR	10/9/43	12/5/44	LCDR R. N. Smillie, RCNVR	20/8/45	29/1/46
A/LCDR J. D. Frewer, RCNVR	13/5/44	14/4/45	LT H. R. Tilley, RCN	21/3/46	26/4/46
LCDR J. M. Watson, RCNR	15/4/45	25/6/45	SKPR/LT P. Perrault, RCNR	27/4/46	25/9/46
LT C. W. King, RCNVR	26/6/45	19/8/45			

Sault Ste. Marie, **August 1943.**

SAULT STE. MARIE

BUILDER:	Port Arthur Shipbuilding Co. Ltd., Port Arthur, ON	LAUNCHED:	5/8/42
		COMMISSIONED:	24/6/43
LAID DOWN:	27/1/42	PAID OFF:	1/10/58

Commanding Officers

LCDR R. Jackson, RCNVR	24/6/43	11/2/44	LT D. E. Rigg, RCN	12/6/53	9/8/53
A/LCDR A. Moorhouse, RCNR	12/2/44	5/7/45	LT H. J. Andrews, RCN	10/8/53	11/10/54
LT D. Davis, RCNVR	6/7/45	28/7/45	LCDR E. T. Coggins, RCN	12/10/54	6/12/54
LT A. D. Ritchie, RCNVR	7/9/45	12/1/46	LT T. Elworthy, RCN	7/12/54	10/1/55
LT A. O. Grav, RCN	7/5/49	4/12/49	LCDR K. A. Stone, RCN	8/11/55	25/10/56
LT A. R. Heater, RCN(R)	5/12/49	21/10/51	LCDR R. M. Greene, RCN	26/10/56	24/9/57
LCDR B. T. R. Russell, RCN	22/10/51	11/6/53	LCDR W. V. A. Lesslie, RCN	1/4/58	1/10/58

Sault Ste. Marie

Commissioned at Port Arthur on 24 June 1943, she was the first Algerine class ship to join the RCN. Originally intended to be named *The Soo*, she was renamed owing to objections from her namesake city. *Sault Ste Marie* arrived at Halifax on 8 August 1943 and proceeded to Bermuda for workups in September. On her return she joined EG W-9 of Western Escort Force, serving as Senior Officer's ship until mid-April 1945. She then transferred as S.O. to W-7 until the group was disbanded in June. After a short period in reserve at Sydney she was ordered to the west coast, arriving at Esquimalt on 12 December. She was paid off into reserve on 12 January 1946, but recommissioned for reserve training on 7 May 1949. The ship returned to the east coast in mid-December 1955, and spent the summers of 1956 to 1958 on the Great Lakes. She was paid off on 1 October 1958, and broken up in 1960 at Sorel.

Wallaceburg

Commissioned at Port Arthur on 18 November 1943, she arrived at Halifax on 13 December, and after working up was assigned to EG W-8, Western Escort Force in February 1944. In April, *Wallaceburg* was transferred to EG W-6 as Senior Officer's ship, but returned in December to W-8. During July and August 1945 she was attached to HMCS *Cornwallis* for training, and then placed in reserve, first at Sydney and then at Halifax. She was paid off on 7 October 1946, but recommissioned on 1 November 1950 for cadet training. *Wallaceburg* spent the summers of 1956 and 1957 on the Great Lakes and was paid off on 24 September 1957. On 31 July 1959, she was transferred to the Belgian Navy, to serve as *Georges Lecointe* until she was discarded in 1969.

Wallaceburg.

WALLACEBURG						
BUILDER:	Port Arthur Shipbuilding Co. Ltd., Port Arthur, ON		LAUNCHED:	17/12/42		
			COMMISSIONED:	18/11/43		
LAID DOWN:	6/7/42		PAID OFF:	24/9/57		

Commanding Officers

A/LCDR F. R. K. Naftel, RCNVR	18/11/43	2/5/44	LCDR J. C. Marston, DSC, RCN(R)	1/11/50	20/12/50
LCDR R. A. S. MacNeil, RCNR	3/5/44	9/1/45	CDR R. A. Webber, DSC, RCN	21/12/50	3/4/51
A/LCDR F. E. Burrows, RCNVR	10/1/45	21/5/45	LCDR J. H. Maxner, RCN	4/4/51	27/9/51
LCDR J. H. G. Bovey, RCNVR	22/5/45	16/7/45	LCDR I. A. McPhee, RCN	28/9/51	21/2/54
LT R. N. Smillie, RCNVR	17/7/45	19/8/45	LCDR W. A. Manfield, RCN	22/2/54	25/11/54
LT A. D. Ritchie, RCNVR	20/8/45	7/9/45	CDR F. J. Jones, RCN	14/4/55	16/10/55
LT G. Kelly, RCNVR	23/10/45	1/2/46	LCDR D. S. Bethune, RCN	17/10/55	24/9/57
LCDR R. M. Steele, RCNR	3/6/46	7/10/46			

Winnipeg

Commissioned at Port Arthur on 29 July 1943, she arrived at Halifax in mid-September and after working up at Pictou, was assigned to EG W-7 of Western Escort Force. That December she was transferred to W-6, acting as Senior Officer's ship from February to April 1944. *Winnipeg* then joined W-5, again as S.O., and served with that group until it was disbanded in June 1945. In August she was placed in reserve at Sydney, but was reactivated for passage to Esquimalt, where she arrived on 21 December. She was paid off into reserve there on 11 January 1946, but in 1956 she was brought around to the east coast, and on 7 August 1959 entered service with the Belgian Navy as *A.F. Dufour*. She was broken up in 1966.

Winnipeg, 8 November 1944.

WINNIPEG						
BUILDER:	Port Arthur Shipbuilding Co. Ltd., Port Arthur, ON		LAUNCHED:	19/9/42		
			COMMISSIONED:	29/7/43		
LAID DOWN:	31/1/42		PAID OFF:	11/1/46		

Commanding Officers

LCDR W. D. F. Johnston, RCNR	29/7/43	4/4/44	LCDR G. K. Fox, RCNVR	4/10/44	23/7/45
LCDR R. A. Judges, RCNVR	5/4/44	3/9/44	LT C. F. Usher, RCNVR	10/9/45	11/1/46

LLEWELLYN CLASS

Llewellyn represents her class of ten 105-foot wooden minesweepers, as photographs could not be found for all of them. The first two were completed at Quebec City in 1942; the other eight on the west coast in 1944. The two east coast ships, *Llewellyn* and *Lloyd George*, were commissioned at Quebec City on 24 August 1942 and arrived at Halifax on 5 September, having escorted a Quebec-Sydney convoy en route. Their names reflect the fact they were equipped with "double-L" magnetic minesweeping gear, but ingenuity seems to have failed when it came to naming the rest of the class. They were assigned to Halifax Local Defence Force, and spent their wartime careers on precautionary sweeps of the Halifax approaches. *Llewellyn* served after the war as guard ship for the reserve fleet at Halifax until she was paid off on 14 June 1946. She was recommissioned in 1949 for use as a tender at Saint John, and finally was paid off on 31 October 1951. *Lloyd George* also served as guard vessel, but was paid off on 16 July 1948, to spend many years in reserve at Halifax employed by the Naval Research Establishment.

The other eight ships of the class were employed on the west coast, alternating between Esquimalt Force and Prince Rupert Force until the end of 1945 when all were paid off. *Revelstoke* alone was recommissioned for passage to Halifax where, like her east-coast sisters, she acted as guard ship for a time. She was recommissioned in the summer and fall of 1952 for use as a tender at St. John's, and was finally paid off on 23 October 1953, for transfer to the Department of Indian Affairs.

PARTICULARS OF CLASS:

DISPLACEMENT:	228
DIMENSIONS:	119' 4" x 22' x 8' 8"
SPEED:	12 kts
CREW:	3/20
ARMAMENT:	four 0.5-inch m.g. (2 x II)

Coquitlam

BUILDER:	Newcastle Shipbuilding Co. Ltd., Nanaimo, BC		
COMMISSIONED:	25/7/44 at Nanaimo		
PAID OFF:	30/11/45		
SOLD:	1946		

Commanding Officer

LT G. J. McNamara, RCNVR	25/7/44	3/7/45

Cranbrook

BUILDER:	Star Shipyards Ltd, New Westminster, BC
COMMISSIONED:	12/5/44 at New Westminster
PAID OFF:	3/11/45
SOLD:	1947

Commanding Officers

LT C. G. Trotter, RCNVR	12/5/44	2/10/44
LT R. Stark, RCNVR	3/10/44	17/10/44
LT C. G. Trotter, RCNVR	18/10/44	3/5/45
SKPR/LT J. R. Smith, RCNR	4/5/45	14/6/45
SKPR/LT K. Bennett, RCNR	15/6/45	3/11/45

Daerwood

BUILDER:	Vancouver Shipyards Ltd. Vancouver, BC
COMMISSIONED:	22/4/44 at Vancouver
PAID OFF:	28/11/45
SOLD:	1947

Commanding Officers

LCDR E. S. McGowan, RCNVR	22/4/44	29/10/44
SKPR/LT J. Craig, RCNR	30/10/44	13/11/44
LCDR E. S. McGowan, RCNVR	14/11/44	14/2/45
SKPR/LT W. E. Eccles, RCNR	2/4/45	9/8/45
LT T. A. Mulhern, RCNVR	10/8/45	28/11/45

Kalamalka

BUILDER:	A.C. Benson Shipyard Ltd. Vancouver, BC
COMMISSIONED:	2/10/44 at Vancouver
PAID OFF:	16/11/45
SOLD:	1947

Commanding Officers

LT C. J. Henrickson, RCNVR	2/10/44	20/7/45
LT E. L. MacDonald, RCNVR	21/7/45	20/9/45

Lavallee

BUILDER:	A.C. Benson Shipyard Ltd. Vancouver, BC
COMMISSIONED:	21/6/44 at Vancouver
PAID OFF:	27/12/45
SOLD:	1947

Commanding Officers

SKPR/LT A. Miller, RCNR	21/6/44	20/3/45
SKPR/LT J. R. Smith, RCNR	21/3/45	3/5/45
A/LCDR C. G. Trotter, RCNVR	4/5/45	18/6/45
SKPR/LT J. Craig, RCNR	19/6/45	15/7/45
A/LCDR C. G. Trotter, RCNVR	16/7/45	20/8/45
SKPR/LT J. E. Moore, RCNR	14/11/45	18/12/45

Llewellyn

BUILDER:	Chantier Maritime de St. Laurent, Ile d'Orléans, QC
COMMISSIONED:	24/8/42 at Quebec City
PAID OFF:	31/10/51
SOLD:	1959

Commanding Officers

CH/SKPR A. Currie, RCNR	24/8/42	14/9/42
LT J. A. MacKinnon, RCNR	15/9/42	24/9/43
SKPR/LT W. H. Crocker, RCNR	25/9/43	11/10/43
LT J. A. MacKinnon, RCNR	12/10/43	26/2/45
LT F. W. Anderson, RCNVR	27/2/45	29/3/45
LT J. A. MacKinnon, RCNR	30/3/45	11/4/45
LT F. W. Anderson, RCNVR	12/4/45	19/8/45
LT F. W. Anderson, RCNVR	8/9/45	-
CDR E. W. Briggs, RCNR	25/7/49	21/8/49
LT J. C. Marston, RCNR	22/8/49	31/10/51

Lloyd George

BUILDER:	Chantier Maritime de St. Laurent, Ile d'Orléans, QC
COMMISSIONED:	24/8/42 at Quebec City
PAID OFF:	16/7/48
SOLD:	1959

Commanding Officers

CH/SKPR W. H. Crocker, RCNR	24/8/42	23/8/43
LT G. F. Crosby, RCNVR	24/8/43	11/10/43
CH/SKPR W. H. Crocker, RCNR	12/10/43	7/11/43
CH/SKPR W. H. Crocker, RCNR	26/11/43	23/2/45
LT J. F. Stevens, RCNVR	24/2/45	8/5/45
SKPR/LT C. K. Darrach, MBE, RCNR	9/5/45	6/1/46
Bos'n J. R. Addison, BEM, RCN	7/1/46	7/5/47
LT L. J. MacGregor, RCN(R)	8/5/47	21/6/48
LT K. A. Stone, RCN	22/6/48	16/7/48

Revelstoke

BUILDER:	Star Shipyards Ltd., New Westminster, BC
COMMISSIONED:	4/7/44 at New Westminster
PAID OFF:	23/10/53
SOLD:	1956

Commanding Officers

SKPR/LT G. Billard, RCNR	4/7/44	14/9/44
SKPR/LT J. E. Moore, RCNR	15/9/44	19/2/45
SKPR/LT J. Craig, RCNR	20/2/45	24/4/45
LT A. B. Plummer, RCNVR	25/4/45	15/7/45
SKPR/LT J. Craig, RCNR	16/7/45	6/8/45
LT A. B. Plummer, RCNVR	7/8/45	2/9/45
LCDR C. A. Binmore, RCN	17/6/52	-
LCDR C. A. Binmore, RCN	11/6/53	-

Rossland

BUILDER:	Vancouver Shipyards Ltd., Vancouver, BC
COMMISSIONED:	15/7/44 at Vancouver
PAID OFF:	1/11/45
SOLD:	1946

Commanding Officers

SKPR/LT E. E. Kinney, RCNR	15/7/44	26/1/45
SKPR/LT E. E. Kinney, RCNR	1/3/45	1/11/45

St. Joseph

BUILDER:	Newcastle Shipbuilding Co. Ltd., Nanaimo, BC
COMMISSIONED:	24/5/44 at Nanaimo
PAID OFF:	8/11/45
SOLD:	1947

Commanding Officers

LT A. B. Plummer, RCNVR	24/5/44	23/4/45
SKPR/LT J. Craig, RCNR	24/4/45	18/6/45

LAKE CLASS

These were copies of the Admiralty type 126-foot wooden-hulled minesweepers, of which twenty-four were completed in east coast yards for the Royal Navy. Of the sixteen for which orders were placed by the RCN, only ten were completed as warships, VJ Day having intervened, and these were transferred to the USSR. The three on which work was stopped were completed for civilian use. The remaining three were apparently never built.

PARTICULARS OF CLASS:
DISPLACEMENT:	360
DIMENSIONS:	140' x 27' 11' x 12' 6'
ARMAMENT:	two 20-mm

Pine Lake in Georgian Bay, 1945.

Alder Lake

BUILDER:	Midland Boat Works,
COMPLETED:	22/9/45
REMARKS:	To USSR, 20/9/45 as *T-196*

Ash Lake

BUILDER:	Midland Boat Works, Midland, ON
COMPLETED:	/45
REMARKS:	To Dept. of Mines as *Cartier*

Beech Lake

BUILDER:	Vancouver Shipyards Ltd., Vancouver, BC
COMPLETED:	8/2/46
REMARKS:	To USSR, 5/2/46, as *T-200*

Birch Lake

BUILDER:	Port Carling Boat Works Ltd., Port Carling, ON
COMPLETED:	—
REMARKS:	Completed as M/V *Aspy III*

Cedar Lake

BUILDER:	J.J. Taylor & Sons Ltd., Toronto, ON
COMPLETED:	4/11/45
REMARKS:	To USSR 1/11/45 as *T-197*

Cherry Lake

BUILDER:	J.J. Taylor & Sons Ltd., Toronto, ON
COMPLETED:	—
REMARKS:	Cancelled 22/10/45

Elm Lake

BUILDER:	Mac-Craft Corp., Sarnia, Ontario
COMPLETED:	18/11/45
REMARKS:	To USSR 17/11/45 as *T-193*

Fir Lake

BUILDER:	Mac-Craft Corp., Sarnia, Ontario
COMPLETED:	/47
REMARKS:	Completed as mission ship *Regina Polaris*

Hickory Lake

BUILDER:	Grew Boat Works Ltd., Penetanguishene, ON
COMPLETED:	14/8/45
REMARKS:	To USSR 15/8/45 as *T-194*

Larch Lake

BUILDER:	Grew Boat Works Ltd., Penetanguishene, ON
COMPLETED:	2/11/45
REMARKS:	To USSR, 2/11/45 as *T-198*

Maple Lake

BUILDER:	Clare Shipbuilding Co., Meteghan, NS
COMPLETED:	—
REMARKS:	Cancelled 18/9/44

Oak Lake

BUILDER:	Clare Shipbuilding Co., Meteghan, NS
COMPLETED:	—
REMARKS:	Cancelled 18/9/44

Pine Lake

BUILDER:	Port Carling Boat Works Ltd., Port Carling, ON
COMPLETED:	22/9/45
REMARKS:	To USSR, 20/9/45 as *T-195*

Poplar Lake

BUILDER:	Star Shipyards, New Westminster, BC
COMPLETED:	9/1/46
REMARKS:	To USSR, 9/1/46, as *T-199*

Spruce Lake

BUILDER:	Star Shipyards, New Westminster, BC
COMPLETED:	19/3/46
REMARKS:	To USSR 19/3/46, as *T-202*

Willow Lake

BUILDER:	Newcastle Shipbuilding Co.Ltd., Nanaimo, BC
COMPLETED:	11/3/46
REMARKS:	To USSR 11/3/46, as *T-201*

Armed Yachts

Although empowered to requisition British-registered craft of any description from private owners, the RCN failed to turn up vessels with any real potential for A/S use in 1939. A discreet survey of the US yacht market showed promise, but purchase seemed impossible without contravening neutrality regulations. It was accordingly arranged for a sufficient number of Canadian yachts, however inadequate, to be requisitioned from their owners, who then replaced them with yachts purchased in the US. These replacements had, of course, already been selected with care by the RCN—which, "discovering" that the replacements were better than the yachts originally requisitioned, took over the replacements instead. By the spring of 1940 fourteen large yachts had been acquired in this somewhat questionable fashion, armed, and given animal names. They ranged in age from seven to thirty-nine years, and five of them (*Beaver, Cougar, Grizzly, Renard* and *Wolf*) had served in the USN as auxiliary patrol craft from 1917 to 1919.

Two other large yachts were acquired in 1940. One of them, *Sans Peur*, had belonged to the Duke of Sutherland; the other, *Ambler*, was the only Canadian-registered yacht considered to be worth taking up. Both retained their own names while in naval service.

Makeshift though the yachts were, they shouldered the responsibility for local A/S defence until the summer of 1941, when corvettes began to be available to replace them, and they afterward proved their worth as training vessels and guard ships.

Ambler, 16 May 1944.

Ambler

The only yacht acquired from a Canadian owner, *Ambler* was commissioned on 6 May 1940 at Midland. She was converted and armed at Quebec City, leaving on 20 July for Rivière du Loup, where she was to be based for patrol duties on the St. Lawrence River. In October 1941 she was transferred to Halifax as tender to HMCS *Stadacona* and, in 1942 to HMCS *Cornwallis* as a training ship. She was paid off to reserve at Sydney on 20 July 1945 and sold into Greek registry in 1947.

AMBLER

FORMER NAME:	Same	DISPLACEMENT:	273	ARMAMENT:	three .303 m.g.
BUILDER:	Tebo Yacht Basin Co., Brooklyn, NY	DIMENSIONS:	130' x 23' x 10'	COMMISSIONED:	6/5/40
		SPEED:	9 kts	PAID OFF:	20/7/45
LAUNCH DATE:	1922	CREW:	4/17		

Commanding Officers

A/LT R. S. Kelley, RNVR	6/5/40	29/5/40	LT W. J. Kingsmill, RCNVR	27/7/42	26/10/42
A/CDR H. W. S. Soulsby, RCN	30/5/40	23/7/40	LCDR J. E. Mitchell, RCNVR	27/10/42	29/11/42
LCDR E. G. M. Donald, RCN	24/7/40	11/10/40	LT A. M. Kirkpatrick, RCNVR	30/11/42	8/3/43
LCDR T. H. Beament, RCNVR	12/10/40	17/11/40	LT W. T. Cook, RCNVR	9/3/43	5/5/43
LCDR L. L. Atwood, RCNVR	10/3/41	28/9/41	LT R. Montpetit, RCNVR	6/5/43	25/2/45
CH/SKPR A. C. A. Chouinard, RCNR	29/9/41	18/5/42	LT E. K. Forbes, DSC, RCNVR	26/2/45	2/4/45
LT A. H. Rankin, RCNVR	19/5/42	26/7/42	LT S. H. Jagger, RCNVR	3/4/45	20/7/45

Beaver

The oldest of her type, *Beaver* had reached the age of thirty-nine when she was commissioned on 1 April 1941 at Halifax and assigned to Halifax Local Defence Force. She was employed much of the time as a radar training ship but served briefly, first with Saint John, New Brunswick Force and then with Sydney Force toward the end of 1942, returning to Halifax on 27 December to refit. On 29 July 1943 she arrived at Digby to become a training ship for DEMS (Defensively Equipped Merchant Ship) gunners, and was later used for seamanship training. *Beaver* was paid off on 17 October 1944, sold in 1946, and resold ten years later for scrap.

Beaver, April 1941.

BEAVER

FORMER NAME:	*Aztec*	SPEED:	12 kts	
BUILDER:	Crescent Shipyard, Elizabeth, NJ	CREW:	5/45	
LAUNCH DATE:	1902	ARMAMENT:	one 4-inch gun	
DISPLACEMENT:	808	COMMISSIONED:	1/4/41	
DIMENSIONS:	260' x 28' x 13'	PAID OFF:	17/10/44	

Commanding Officers

(Not Known)	30/9/40	16/3/41	LT D. Davis, RCNR	4/1/43	16/1/43
LCDR G. H. Griffiths, RCN	17/3/41	31/7/41	LT J. F. Watson, RCNR	17/1/43	19/9/43
A/CDR R. I. Swansburg, RCNR	1/8/41	15/10/42	A/LCDR H. C. Walmseley, RCNR	20/9/43	5/3/44
LT J. F. Watson, RCNR	16/10/42	4/12/42	LCDR C. G. Williams, RCNR	6/3/44	7/8/44
LCDR J. S. Wilson, RCNR	5/12/42	28/12/42	LCDR C. G. Williams, RCNR	29/9/44	13/3/45
LT J. F. Watson, RCNR	29/12/42	3/1/43	SKPR/LT J. E. Abbott, RCNR	14/3/45	/6/45

Caribou, 13 May 1944.

CARIBOU

FORMER NAME:	*Elfreda*	SPEED:	11 kts	
BUILDER:	Defoe Shipbuilding Co., Bay City, MI	CREW:	5/35	
LAUNCH DATE:	1928	ARMAMENT:	one 12 pdr.	
DISPLACEMENT:	306	COMMISSIONED:	27/5/40	
DIMENSIONS:	142' x 23' x 9'	PAID OFF:	20/7/45	

Commanding Officers

LT A. K. Young, RCNR	27/5/40	-	LT D. Davis, RCNVR	11/2/43	11/8/43
LT J. H. Marshall, RCNVR	19/9/41	25/3/42	LT R. K. Bythell, RCNVR	12/8/43	/44
LT J. Evelyn, RCNR	26/3/42	18/9/42	LT J. C. Fritz, RCNVR	8/44	20/7/45
Mate J. M. Moncrieff, RCNR	19/9/42	10/2/43			

Caribou

Commissioned on 27 May 1940 at Halifax, *Caribou* left the following day for Quebec City for conversion and arming. On completion of this in mid-November 1940, she returned to Halifax and was employed until August 1941 as guard ship at the entrance to Bedford Basin. Early in October 1941, following refit, she had her first taste of patrol duty, but a serious galley fire on 19 November put her out of action until February 1942 while repairs were made at Lunenburg. In March she was transferred to Saint John, New Brunswick Force. On 31 July she arrived at Halifax for survey and was declared unfit for active patrol duty. Relegated to training service at HMCS *Cornwallis*, she had been transferred to Saint John in the same capacity by September 1943 and in April 1944 to Digby again. She remained there until the war's end, was paid off on 20 July 1945 and sold for commercial use the following year.

Cougar

Commissioned on the west coast on 11 September 1940, *Cougar* was employed initially on A/S patrol from Esquimalt, and then transferred in May 1942 to Prince Rupert Force. In June 1944 she returned to Esquimalt as an examination vessel and was paid off on 23 November 1945. Sold to a California buyer in 1946, she resumed her original name, *Breezin' Thru*, for a time before sinking in a hurricane at Kingston Jamaica in 1950.

Cougar, 17 July 1942.

COUGAR

FORMER NAME:	*Breezin' Thru*		SPEED:	10 kts
BUILDER:	Geo. Lawley & Sons, Neponset, MA		CREW:	5/35
LAUNCH DATE:	1916		ARMAMENT:	one 6 pdr.
DISPLACEMENT:	204		COMMISSIONED:	11/9/40
DIMENSIONS:	140' x 20' x 10'		PAID OFF:	23/11/45

Commanding Officers

LT T. M. W. Golby, RCNR	20/8/40	1/1/41		SKPR D. J. Smith, RCNR	24/11/43	12/1/44
LT H. G. Denyer, RCNR	2/1/41	11/5/41		SKPR/LT G. F. Cassidy, RCNR	13/1/44	22/6/44
CH/SKPR G. F. Cassidy, RCNR	12/5/41	5/11/42		SKPR/LT K. Bennett, RCNR	23/6/44	15/9/44
CH/SKPR R. W. Sparks, RCNR	6/11/42	7/2/43		SKPR/LT K. Bennett, RCNR	3/10/44	15/5/45
SKPR/LT E. W. Suffield, RCNR	8/2/43	22/2/43		SKPR/LT W. R. Chaster, RCNR	16/5/45	22/6/45
CH/SKPR R. W. Sparks, RCNR	23/2/43	23/11/43				

Elk, spring, 1944.

ELK

FORMER NAME:	*Arcadia*		SPEED:	11 kts
BUILDER:	Newport News S.B. Co., Newport News, VA		CREW:	5/35
LAUNCH DATE:	1926		ARMAMENT:	one 4-inch
DISPLACEMENT:	578		COMMISSIONED:	10/9/40
DIMENSIONS:	188' x 27' x 11'		PAID OFF:	4/8/45

Commanding Officers

LCDR N. V. Clarke, RCNR	10/9/40	24/6/41		LT T. B. Edwards, RCNR	1/11/41	11/12/42
LT R. Hocken, RCNR	14/7/41	17/8/41		LT J. A. Dunn, RCNVR	12/12/42	14/4/43
LT T. Gilmour, RCNR	18/8/41	31/10/41		SKPR/LT W. K. S. Hines, RCNR	15/4/43	18/6/45

Elk

Elk left Halifax for Pictou on 21 June 1940 for conversion and arming, after which she was commissioned at Halifax on 10 September and transferred to the America and West Indies Station. She arrived in Bermuda on 23 September, returning to Halifax on 13 May 1941. Following a major refit there, she sailed for Trinidad on 2 December. On 11 May 1942 she returned to Halifax and was assigned to Sydney Force, serving extensively as escort to Sydney-Corner Brook convoys. In February 1943 she was sent to Halifax for repairs, and in May transferred to Digby as a training ship. A month later, however, she was moved to Shelburne, remaining there until November and then returning to Digby, where she was to be based until the end of the war. She served almost continuously as escort to the ancient British training submarine *L.23*. *Elk* was paid off on 4 August 1945 and sold. After long service as a short-haul passenger ferry, *Grand Manan III*, she was sold in 1968 for breaking up.

Grizzly

Grizzly was commissioned on 7 July 1941 on the west coast, but the condition of her engines made it impractical for her to function effectively. She was therefore towed to Prince Rupert in July for use as a stationary guard ship and examination vessel. In the spring of 1944 she was taken to Victoria, where her hull was found to be in poor condition. Paid off on 17 June, she was broken up at Victoria the following year.

GRIZZLY	
FORMER NAME:	*Machigonne*
BUILDER:	Consolidated S.B. Corp., New York, NY
LAUNCH DATE:	1909
DISPLACEMENT:	195
DIMENSIONS:	140' x 19' x 10'
SPEED:	12 kts
CREW:	5/35
ARMAMENT:	one 6 pdr.
COMMISSIONED:	17/7/41
PAID OFF:	17/6/44

Husky

Husky left Halifax on 30 May 1940 for conversion and arming at Quebec City. Commissioned at Halifax on 23 July, she was assigned to Sydney Force for A/S patrol duty. She was transferred that December to Trinidad, but returned to join Saint John, New Brunswick Force on 24 September 1941. A year later she returned to Halifax Local Defence Force for a few months before being reassigned in March 1943 to training duties at HMCS *Cornwallis* (then located at Halifax). She moved with that establishment to Digby, and for the remainder of the war exercised with RN submarines in the Bay of Fundy. Paid off to reserve at Sydney on 3 August 1945, she was sold into mercantile service in 1946. After a term as the inspection vessel *Good Neighbor* for the port of New Orleans, she was sold in 1968 for use as a sport-diving tender in Honduran waters but later returned to New Orleans to become a floating restaurant.

Grizzly, 4 September 1942.

Husky, 17 February 1944.

HUSKY						
FORMER NAME:	*Wild Duck*			SPEED:	10 kts	
BUILDER:	Defoe Boat & Engine Works, Bay City, MI			CREW:	5/35	
				ARMAMENT:	one 4-inch	
LAUNCH DATE:	1930			COMMISSIONED:	23/7/40	
DISPLACEMENT:	360			PAID OFF:	3/8/45	
DIMENSIONS:	153' x 25' x 10'					

Commanding Officers

LT H. Freeland, RCNR	23/7/40	5/9/41	LT W. E. Joliffe, RCNVR	30/9/44	12/11/44
LT W. E. Harrison, RCNR	6/9/41	18/10/41	LT E. B. Pearce, RCNVR	13/11/44	30/4/45
LT A. H. Rankin, RCNR	19/10/41	30/4/42	LT R. C. Hayden, RCNVR	1/5/45	12/6/45
LT J. P. Kieran, RCNR	1/5/42	29/9/44	SKPR/LT C. C. Clattenburg, RCNR	13/6/45	3/8/45

Lynx

Lynx left Halifax with *Husky* on 30 May 1940 for conversion and arming at Quebec City. On her return she was commissioned at Halifax on 26 August and allocated to Sydney Force. She returned at year's end to Halifax for the winter, and in July 1941 was assigned to Gaspé Force. The ship was plagued by mechanical troubles, however, and spare parts proved unobtainable. She was accordingly transferred to Halifax on 25 November. On 18 January 1942 *Lynx* rescued the passengers and crew of SS *Empire Kingfisher*, which sank off Cape Sable. Soon afterward condemned for further sea duty, she was paid off on 23 April 1943 and offered for sale, but no buyer was forthcoming until July 1943. For some years a banana trader in the Caribbean, she was finally lost near Sydney, Australia, under the name *Rican Star*.

Lynx,

LYNX

FORMER NAME:	*Ramona*		SPEED:	10 kts
BUILDER:	Newport News S.B. Co., Newport News, VA		CREW:	5/35
LAUNCH DATE:	1922		ARMAMENT:	one 4-inch
DISPLACEMENT:	495		COMMISSIONED:	26/8/40
DIMENSIONS:	181' x 24' x 9'		PAID OFF:	23/4/42

Commanding Officers

CDR J. R. Prudence, RCNR	25/5/40	-	LCDR A. D. MacLean, RCNVR	25/5/42	/9/42
LT J. L. A. Levesque, RCNR	26/8/40	24/5/42			

Moose

Moose left Halifax on June 3 1940 for conversion and arming at Quebec City, where she was commissioned on 8 September. She was then assigned to Halifax Local Defence Force until May 1942, transferring then to Sydney, where by September 1943 she was employed as training ship and examination vessel under control of HMCS *Cornwallis*. *Moose* was paid off on 20 July 1945 and sold the following year to Marine Industries Ltd., who renamed her *Fraternité*. Sold to a US buyer in 1956, she became *Ottelia*.

Moose, 1940.

MOOSE

FORMER NAME:	*Cleopatra*		SPEED:	12 kts
BUILDER:	Geo. Lawley & Sons, Neponset, MA		CREW:	5/35
LAUNCH DATE:	1930		ARMAMENT:	one 12 pdr.
DISPLACEMENT:	263		COMMISSIONED:	8/9/40
DIMENSIONS:	130' x 22' x 9'		PAID OFF:	20/7/45

Commanding Officers

LT J. Evelyn, RCNR	31/5/40	17/10/40	LT J. H. Langille, RCNR	18/10/40	20/7/45

Otter

Otter accompanied *Moose* to Quebec City for conversion and arming, returning to Halifax on 2 October 1940, to be commissioned two days later for service with Halifax Local Defence Force. She was destroyed by accidental explosion and fire off Halifax Lightship on 26 March 1941 with the loss of two officers and seventeen men.

Otter arriving at Halifax under the Red Ensign as *Conseco*. No photo of her as a naval vessel has been found.

OTTER

FORMER NAME:	*Conseco*	SPEED:	10 kts
BUILDER:	Robert Jacob, City Island, NY	CREW:	5/35
LAUNCH DATE:	1921	ARMAMENT:	one 4-inch
DISPLACEMENT:	419	COMMISSIONED:	4/10/40
DIMENSIONS:	160' x 25' x 10'	LOST:	26/3/41

Commanding Officer

LT D. S. Mossman, RCNR	4/10/40	26/3/41

Raccoon.

RACCOON

FORMER NAME:	*Halonia*	SPEED:	11 kts
BUILDER:	Bath Iron Works, Bath, Me.	CREW:	5/35
LAUNCH DATE:	1931	ARMAMENT:	one 12 pdr.
DISPLACEMENT:	377	COMMISSIONED:	17/5/40
DIMENSIONS:	148' x 25' x 10'	LOST:	7/9/42

Commanding Officers

LCDR J. L. Diver, RCNR	17/5/40	17/10/40	LT D. W. Main, RCNR	23/7/41	16/11/41
LT F. Roberts, RCNR	18/10/40	16/4/41	LT A. H. Cassivi, RCNR	17/11/41	4/12/41
LT N. G. W. Bennett, RCNR	17/4/41	22/7/41	LT J. N. Smith, RCNR	5/12/41	7/9/42

Raccoon

Raccoon, commissioned 17 May 1940, left Halifax on 18 October 1940 for Pictou, where she was converted and armed. She returned to Halifax at the end of the year for service with Halifax Local Defence Force. In July 1941 she became a member of Gaspé Force, but returned to HLDF on 1 February 1942. On 25 May 1942 she returned to Gaspé to join the Gulf Escort Force, with which she saw extensive service as escort to Quebec-Sydney convoys. On 7 September 1942 while escorting convoy QS.33, she was torpedoed and sunk by *U 165* in the St. Lawrence River. There were no survivors.

Reindeer.

REINDEER

FORMER NAME:	*Mascotte*	SPEED:	11 kts	
BUILDER:	Newport News S.B. Co., Newport News, Va.	CREW:	5/35	
		ARMAMENT:	one 4-inch	
LAUNCH DATE:	1926	COMMISSIONED:	25/7/40	
DISPLACEMENT:	337	PAID OFF:	20/7/45	
DIMENSIONS:	140' x 24' x 9'			

Commanding Officers

LCDR E. G. Skinner, RCNR	25/7/40	17/1/41	LT D. M. Coolican, RCNVR	24/11/42	8/2/43
LCDR F. A. Price, RCNVR	18/1/41	16/5/41	LT R. G. James, RCNVR	9/2/43	19/5/44
LT L. G. Cumming, RCNVR	17/5/41	8/7/41	LT J. H. Ewart, RCNVR	20/5/44	7/10/44
LCDR F. A. Price, RCNVR	9/7/41	31/7/41	LT W. C. Hawkins, RCNVR	8/10/44	1/3/45
LT L. G. Cumming, RCNVR	1/8/41	20/4/42	LT R. C. Hayden, RCNVR	2/3/45	29/4/45
LT W. Evans, RCNVR	21/4/42	30/4/42	LT W. C. Hawkins, RCNVR	30/4/45	20/7/45
LT F. J. G. Johnson, RCNVR	1/5/42	23/11/42			

RENARD

FORMER NAME:	*Winchester*	SPEED:	15 kts	
BUILDER:	Bath Iron Works, Bath, Me.	CREW:	5/35	
LAUNCH DATE:	1916	ARMAMENT:	one 12 pdr., two 21-inch TT	
DISPLACEMENT:	411	COMMISSIONED:	27/5/40	
DIMENSIONS:	225' x 21' x 8'	PAID OFF:	1/8/44	

Commanding Officers

LCDR N. V. Clark, RCNR	27/5/40	-	Mate J. H. Maxner, RCNR	28/4/42	-
LCDR D. G. Jeffrey, RCNR	2/10/40	-	Mate H. A. Sowerbutts, RCNR	9/9/42	-

SANS PEUR

FORMER NAME:	*Trenora*	SPEED:	13 kts	
BUILDER:	Thornycroft & Co., Southampton, UK	CREW:	5/43	
LAUNCH DATE:	1933	ARMAMENT:	one 4-inch, one 12 pdr.	
DISPLACEMENT:	856	COMMISSIONED:	5/5/40	
DIMENSIONS:	210' x 30' x 13'	PAID OFF:	31/1/47	

Commanding Officers

A/LCDR W. C. Halliday, RCNR	23/10/39	3/6/42	LCDR H. S. MacFarlane, RCNR	10/1/44	4/11/45
LCDR T. MacDuff, RCN	4/6/42	14/5/43	SKPR/LT P. Perrault, RCNR	26/2/46	-
LCDR W. Redford, RCNVR	15/5/43	9/1/44	LT D. L. MacKnight, RCNVR	22/7/46	-

Reindeer

Reindeer accompanied *Husky* and *Lynx* to Quebec City for conversion and arming in the summer of 1940. She was commissioned at Halifax on 25 July for service with Sydney Force, returning to Halifax on 26 December for the winter. She joined Gaspé Force in July 1941, but by year's end was back again with Halifax Local Defence Force. In May 1942 she moved to Sydney Force, and that November to Saint John, New Brunswick Force. On 24 December 1942 *Reindeer* was assigned as training ship to HMCS *Cornwallis*, then located at Halifax, transferring with the establishment to Digby in 1943. She was employed there on A/S training with RN submarines until the end of the war, except for a brief stint at Saint John, New Brunswick during the first half of 1944. She was paid off to reserve at Sydney on 20 July 1945 and sold later that year.

Renard

In her prime, *Renard* had shown a turn of speed to match her destroyer-like appearance, but she was twenty-four years old when commissioned on 27 May 1940 at Halifax. She left the following day for Quebec City for conversion and arming, returning on 3 December to Halifax, where she was assigned to Halifax Local Defence Force. In April 1942 she began a long refit at Liverpool and Pictou, Nova Scotia, on completion of which in July she became a torpedo and gunnery ship attached to HMCS *Cornwallis*, with torpedo tubes fitted for the purpose. She moved with the establishment to Digby in July 1943 but returned that November to Halifax to serve as a torpedo-firing ship. Surveyed in 1944 and found not worth repairing, she was paid off on 1 August. She was sold in 1945, purportedly to become a floating power plant for a Cape Breton mine, but was derelict at Sydney in 1955.

Sans Peur

This large yacht, the property of the Duke of Sutherland, was requisitioned in 1939 at Esquimalt and commissioned for patrol service on 5 May 1940. From May 1942 *Sans Peur* served the dual function of patrol vessel and training vessel, but after November was used for training alone. Originally chartered, the ship was purchased in 1943. Following an extensive refit at Esquimalt, she left on 24 January 1944 for Halifax, arriving late in February. In March she was sent to HMCS *Cornwallis*, where she carried out A/S training in conjunction with RN submarines, and after February 1946 she was a training ship at Halifax. Paid off on 31 January 1947, she was sold to Maple Leaf Steamships of Montreal, but on resale the following year she reverted, under Panamanian flag, to her original name, *Trenora*. Later refitted by her builders at Southampton, she resumed her career as a yacht for Italian owners, but by 1975 was in use as VIP accommodation at Okinawa, Japan.

Renard, March 1941.

Sans Peur.

Vison

Vison left Halifax on 23 June 1940 for Pictou, where she was to be converted and armed. She returned to Halifax on 2 October and was commissioned three days later. She was then assigned to the base at Gaspé, but returned to Halifax that November when the base was closed for the winter. In December 1940 she was sent southward, operating out of Trinidad and Bermuda until her return to Halifax on 13 May 1941. In July she became a member of Gaspé Force, proceeding to Halifax for passage to Trinidad in December 1941. She rejoined Halifax Local Defence Force in April 1942 but was transferred to Sydney Force in July. In February 1943 *Vison* returned to Halifax as a training ship attached to HMCS *Cornwallis* and moved with the establishment to Digby in April. She remained there until the end of the war as a seamen's training ship, exercising with RN submarines in the Bay of Fundy, and was paid off for disposal on 4 August 1945.

Wolf

Aged twenty-five years at the time of her commissioning on 2 October 1940, *Wolf* spent the entire war as a member of Esquimalt Force, at first on training and patrol duty and after September 1943 as an examination vessel. Paid off on 16 May 1945, she was sold in 1946 to become the merchant vessel *Gulfstream*. She was wrecked off Powell River, British Columbia, on 11 October 1947.

Vison, 27 April 1943.

VISON

FORMER NAME:	*Avalon*	SPEED:	10 kts
BUILDER:	Pusey & Jones Corp., Wilmington, Del.	CREW:	5/35
LAUNCH DATE:	1931	ARMAMENT:	one 12 pdr.
DISPLACEMENT:	422	COMMISSIONED:	5/10/40
DIMENSIONS:	181' x 24' x 13'	PAID OFF:	4/8/45

Commanding Officers

LCDR R. I. Swansburg, RCNR	5/10/40	31/7/41	CDR W. G. Sheldon, RCNVR	22/11/41	14/4/42
LCDR F. A. Price, RCNVR	1/8/41	21/11/41	LT W. E. Nicholson, RCNR	15/4/42	4/8/45

Wolf, 1 June 1943.

WOLF

FORMER NAME:	*Blue Water*	LAUNCH DATE:	1915	SPEED:	10 kts	COMMISSIONED:	2/10/40
BUILDER:	Geo. Lawley & Sons, Neponset, Mass.	DISPLACEMENT:	320	CREW:	5/38	PAID OFF:	16/5/45
		DIMENSIONS:	172' x 23' x 10'	ARMAMENT:	one 12 pdr., one 2 pdr.		

Commanding Officers

LT J. A. Gow, RCNR	2/10/40	21/4/41	CH/SKPR A. W. Ogden, RCNR	19/9/41	5/10/41	SKPR/LT G. F. Cassidy, RCNR	22/4/43	22/5/43
CH/SKPR J. M. Richardson, RCNR	22/4/41	18/9/41	SKPR/LT W. R. Chaster, RCNR	6/10/41	21/4/43	SKPR/LT W. R. Chaster, RCNR	23/5/43	16/5/45

Motor Torpedo Boats

CMTB-1

A prototype MTB, she was shipped to Canada in 1940 by the British Power Boat Co., which had contracts for twelve of the type to be built at Montreal. CMTB-*1* arrived on 16 July 1940, was rebuilt to RCN specifications and sent to Halifax as a training vessel that fall. She arrived there on 17 December after a trip fraught with difficulties owing to ice and weather, and had been aground for a time near Richibucto, New Brunswick on 27 November. She was at some point designated *V-250*. The boat returned to Montreal for refit in August 1941, following which she was turned over to the RN as MTB *332*. She seems to have been the only one of the twelve to serve, however briefly, in the RCN. The others became MTBs *333-343* (RN) in 1941.

CMTB-1	
DISPLACEMENT:	32
DIMENSIONS:	70' x 20' 4" x 4' 9"
SPEED:	40 kts
CREW:	2/8
ARMAMENT:	four .5-inch m.g. (2 x II), four 18-inch TT

MTB-1

S-09, December 1942.

S-09

This was one of six US PT boats acquired by the RN under Lend Lease in 1941. Numbered PT-*3, 4, 5, 6, 7* and *9*, they were subsequently loaned by the RN to the RCN. PT-*9* was redesignated S-*09*, while her five sisters served the RCAF as crash boats from 1941–1945. Alone of the group, S-*09* was built in Britain in 1939, by the British Power Boat Co. at Hythe for the Elco Boat Co. of New Jersey. She was handed over to the RCN without engines, arriving in tow at Montreal on 23 August 1941. There the Canadian Power Boat Co. fitted her with two 500 HP engines that enabled her to make only 22 knots. Commissioned on 25 September 1942 she served out of Halifax, Gaspé, and Quebec before proceeding to Toronto in May 1944 to serve as firing range patrol vessel off Frenchman's Bay. She was turned over to the British Naval Liaison Officer at New York in June 1945.

S-09	
DISPLACEMENT:	45
DIMENSIONS:	70' x 20' x 4' 6"
SPEED:	22 kts
ARMAMENT:	four .5-inch m.g. (2 x II), four 18-inch TT

D and G Class Motor Torpedo Boats

The proposal made in 1942 that the RCN should form a British-based flotilla of motor craft was not acted upon because Canada had no such boats. A year later, however, the Admiralty offered to supply and maintain boats if the RCN would man them. Two flotillas were accordingly formed early in 1944: the 29th, equipped with 72-foot G type motor torpedo boats (MTBs *459-466*, *485*, *486*, and *491*); and the 65th, with 115-foot Fairmile D boats (MTBs *726*, *727*, *735*, *736*, *743-748*, and *797*). These flotillas took part in a variety of pre-invasion operations off the coast of France, and in protecting the flank of the invasion forces. After D Day they helped prevent E-boats (their German counterparts) and larger craft from attacking cross-Channel traffic replenishing the beachhead. 29th Flotilla MTBs *460* and *463* fell prey to mines on 1 and 7 July 1944 and five others—MTBs *459*, *461*, *462*, *465*, and *466*—were destroyed by fire at Ostend, Belgium, on 14 February 1945.

MTB 459, 1944.

D Type MTBs

DISPLACEMENT:	102		
DIMENSIONS:	115' x 21' 3" x 5' 3"	CREW:	4/28
SPEED:	29 kts	ARMAMENT:	two 6 pdrs., two 20-mm (1 x II), four 18-inch TT

MTB, 1944.

G Type MTBs

DISPLACEMENT:	44		
DIMENSIONS:	71' 9" x 20' 7" x 5' 8"	CREW:	3/14
SPEED:	39 kts	ARMAMENT:	one 6 pdr., two 20-mm (1 x II), four 18-inch TT

Commanding Officers

MTB 459	LT C. A. Law, DSC, RCNVR	26/1/44	11/9/44
	LT J. J. Shand, RCNVR	12/9/44	14/2/45
MTB 460	LT D. Killam, DSC, RCNVR	25/2/44	1/7/44
MTB 461	LT C. A. Burk, DSC + 2 Bars, RCNVR	28/2/44	17/9/44
	LT T. K. Scobie, RCNVR	18/9/44	3/2/45
	LT J. R. Cunningham, RCNVR	4/2/45	9/2/45
	LT C. V. Barlow, RCNVR	10/2/45	14/2/45
MTB 462	LT R. J. Moyse, RCNVR	1/3/44	28/8/44
	LT J. H. Shand, RCNVR	29/8/44	9/10/44
	LT R.P.B. Graham, RCNVR	10/10/44	23/1/45
	LT R. Paddon, RCNVR	24/1/45	14/2/45
MTB 463	LT D. G. Creba, RCNVR	16/3/44	7/7/44
MTB 464	LT L. C. Bishop, DSC, RCNVR	26/3/44	24/2/45
	LT C. V. Barlow, RCNVR	25/2/45	6/3/45
	LT L. C. Bishop, DSC, RCNVR	7/3/45	9/4/45
MTB 465	LT C. D. Chaffey, RCNVR	27/3/44	14/2/45
MTB 466	LT S. B. Marshall, RCNVR	29/3/44	27/7/44
	LT T. K. Scobie, RCNVR	28/7/44	17/9/44
	LT S. B. Marshall. RCNVR	18/9/44	7/1/45
	LT J. M. Adams, RCNVR	8/1/45	14/2/45
MTB 485	LT D. G. Creba, RCNVR	31/7/44	10/3/45
MTB 486	LCDR C. A. Law, DSC, RCNVR	5/8/44	24/2/45
	LT C. D. Chaffey, RCNVR	25/2/45	3/3/45
	LT T. K. Scobie, RCNVR	4/3/45	8/3/45
MTB 491	LT C. A. Burk, DSC, + 2 Bars, RCNVR	4/10/44	26/1/45
	LT R. J. Moyse, RCNVR	27/1/45	10/3/45
MTB 726	LT A. P. Morrow, RCNVR	1/2/44	22/5/45
MTB 727	LT L. R. McLarnon, DSC, RCNVR	7/1/44	4/4/45
	LT G. D. Pattison, RCNVR	5/4/45	21/5/45
MTB 735	LT J. W. Collins, DSC, RCNVR	14/2/44	2/10/44
	LT J. R. Culley, RCNVR	3/10/44	24/6/45
MTB 736	LT S. O. Greening, RCNVR	31/3/44	17/5/44
	LT A.M. Byers, RCNVR	23/10/44	6/45
MTB 743	LT M. C. Knox, DSC, RCNVR	15/5/44	31/5/45
MTB 744	LT G. M. Moors, RCNVR	14/2/44	/5/44
MTB 745	LT O. B. Mabee, RCNVR	15/1/44	19/5/45
MTB 746	LT S. O. Greening, RCNVR	19/5/44	20/12/44
	LT G. D. Pattison, RCNVR	21/12/44	15/1/45
	LT J. W. Collins, DSC, RCNVR	16/1/45	18/5/45
MTB 748	LCDR J. R. H. Fitzpatrick, DSC, RCNVR	19/2/44	23/5/45
MTB 797	LT R. C. Smith, RCNVR	30/12/44	12/4/45
	LT R. C. Smith, RCNVR	20/5/45	21/5/45

Motor Launches

The versatile 112-foot B class motor launch was designed in England by the Fairmile Company and the boats were accordingly known as Fairmiles. Eighty were built in Canada, fifty-nine of them in Great Lakes boatyards. Fourteen of the remainder were built on the west coast and seven at Weymouth, Nova Scotia. They were numbered Q 050 to 129.

The Fairmiles played a useful role as escorts in the St. Lawrence River and the Gulf of St. Lawrence, and as escorts to convoys between Newfoundland and the mainland. They also carried out A/S patrol, port defence, and rescue duties, releasing larger escort craft urgently needed elsewhere.

In 1942 it was decided to send two flotillas for the winter to the Caribbean, where the U-boats were enjoying great success owing to a shortage of US escorts. The 72nd and 73rd Flotillas of six boats each left Halifax in mid-December for Trinidad via Boston and other east coast ports. Stress of weather en route forced the 72nd Flotilla to return home after reaching Savannah, Georgia, but the boats of the 73rd Flotilla operated until the following spring out of Miami and Key West under the (US) Commander, Gulf Sea Frontier.

Their mother ship, HMCS *Provider*, was stationed at Key West. She also acted as base ship for the 70th and 78th Flotillas in Bermuda during the winter of 1943–1944. Early in June 1943 ML *053* distinguished herself by recovering, intact, two mines of a barrage laid by *U 119* in the Halifax approaches on 1 June. MLs *052, 062*, and *063* were transferred to the Free French Forces in February 1943 and stationed at St. Pierre and Miquelon under operational control of the Flag Officer, Newfoundland. Most of the Fairmiles were sold at war's end, but half a dozen remained in service as training ships on the Great Lakes in the 1960s: *Beaver* (ML *106*), *Cougar* (ML *104*), *Moose* (ML *111*), *Raccoon* (ML *079*), *Reindeer* (ML *116*), and *Wolf* (ML *062*). A seventh, *Elk* (ML *124*), served on the west coast. The animal names, recalling those of the armed yachts whose duties the Fairmiles had taken over, were bestowed in 1954.

ML 067.

B Type MLs *050-111*

DISPLACEMENT:	79
DIMENSIONS:	112' x 17' 10" x 4' 10"
SPEED:	20 kts
CREW:	3/14
ARMAMENT:	three 20-mm

B Type MLs *112-129*

DISPLACEMENT:	79
DIMENSIONS:	112' x 17' x 4' 10"
SPEED:	22 kts
CREW:	3/14
ARMAMENT:	three 20-mm

Commanding Officers

ML 050	LT J. W. Braidwood, RCNVR	17/11/41	18/4/42
	SUB/LT D. R. Grierson, RCNVR	19/4/42	7/6/42
	SUB/LT T. H. Crone, RCNVR	8/6/42	25/8/42
	LT J. T. Sharp, RCNVR	26/8/42	19/12/43
	LT A. G. Beardmore, RCNVR	10/1/44	6/3/44
	SUB/LT R. M. Greene, RCNVR	7/3/44	4/4/44
	LT A. G. Beardmore, RCNVR	5/4/44	5/12/44
	LI J. J. McLaughlin, RCNVR	21/4/45	10/6/45
ML 051	LT T. C Sewell, RCNVR	1/4/42	8/10/42
	LT W. H. B. Thomson, RCNVR	14/12/42	16/12/43
	LT R. Dickinson, RCNVR	17/12/43	8/2/44
	LT R. A. Wylie, RCNVR	9/2/44	2/3/44
	LT W. H. B. Thomson, RCNVR	3/3/44	26/3/45
	LT D. S. Marlow, RCNVR	27/3/45	10/8/45
ML 052	LCDR A. D. MacLean, RCNVR	31/10/41	/12/41
	SUB/LT A. B. Strange, RCNVR	28/2/42	16/1/43
ML 053	LT C. L. Campbell, RCNVR	17/9/41	10/3/42
	SUB/LT S. E. C. Garlick, RCNVR	11/3/42	11/5/42
	LT R. P. Baldwin, RCNVR	12/5/42	26/2/43
	LT G. M. Schuthe, RCNVR	27/4/43	9/1/44
	LT W. P. Munsie, RCNVR	26/1/44	8/1/45
	LT H. D. McFarland, RCNVR	3/5/45	13/7/45
ML 054	SUB/LT D. D. Morin, RCNVR	17/9/41	/12/41
	LT S. O. Greening, RCNVR	24/3/42	30/3/42
	LT D. G. King, RCNVR	19/4/42	29/6/42
	LT W. C. Rigney, RCNVR	29/6/42	10/10/42
	LT A. D. Stairs, RCNVR	11/10/42	1/11/42
	LT W. C. Rigney, RCNVR	2/11/42	27/3/43
	LT H. F. Bartram, RCNVR	22/7/43	13/4/44
	LT C. N. Blagrave, RCNVR	14/4/44	6/12/44
ML 055	SUB/LT C. T. W. Hyslop, RCNVR	29/10/41	/12/41
	LT F. N. Greener, RCNVR	19/4/42	11/12/42
	LT F. N. Greener, RCNVR	7/1/43	28/3/43
	LT R. W. Rankin, RCNVR	29/3/43	14/1/44
	A/LT J. E. White, RCNVR	15/1/44	14/9/44
	LT A. Budge, RCNVR	15/9/44	-
	LT R. G. Spence, RCNVR	25/4/45	12/6/45
ML 056	LT S. B. Fraser, RCNVR	20/11/41	17 /12/41
	LT G. P. Manning, RCNVR	11/3/42	16/10/42
	SUB/LT G. D. Patterson, RCNVR	17/10/42	19/10/43
	LT R. A. Raney, RCNVR	20/10/43	24/12/43
	LT J. R. Jenner, RCNVR	3/5/45	14/6/45
ML 057	LT R. A. Jarvis, RCNVR	29/10/41	/12/41
	SUB/LT J. F. Gallagher, RCNVR	17/3/42	8/6/43
	LT R. C. Denney, RCNVR	9/6/43	22/9/43
	SUB/LT J. A. Davis, RCNVR	23/9/43	9/12/43
	LT K. F. Hurst, RCNVR	10/12/43	4/5/44
	LT M. O. Beverley, RCNVR	4/5/44	26/9/44
	LT C. D. Gillis, RCNVR	27/9/44	23/11/44
	LT J. S. Gardiner, RCNVR	2/5/45	5/6/45
ML 058	J. H. G. Bovey, RCNVR	20/10/41	/12/41
	LT H. K. Hill, RCNVR	1/4/42	19/6/42
	LT S. E. C. Garlick, RCNVR	20/6/42	14/2/43
	LT G. E. Rising, RCNVR	15/2/43	25/1/44
	LT R. Synette, RCNVR	26/1/44	26/5/44
	LT J. G. Chance, RCNVR	27/5/44	10/7/45
ML 059	LT H. A. Batey, RCNVR	21/4/42	18/10/43
	LT R. Dickinson, RCNVR	19/10/43	17/11/43
	LT D. B. Drummond, RCNVR	18/11/43	18/8/44
	LT W. B. McTavish, RCNVR	19/8/44	7/3/45
	LT K. M. Ross, RCNVR	8/3/45	25/6/45
ML 060	LT H. F. Farncomb, RCNVR	6/9/41	17/12/41
	SUB/LT F. K. Ellis, RCNVR	18/12/41	17/4/42
	LT J. S. Davis, RCNVR	18/4/42	11/2/43
	SUB/LT A. M. Byers, RCNVR	12/2/43	10/10/43
	LT R. J. M. Allen, RCNVR	11/10/43	15/2/44
	SUB/LT R. M. Greene, RCNVR	16/2/44	6/3/44
	LT R. J. M. Allen, RCNVR	7/3/44	29/1/45
	LT J. W. MacKenzie, RCNVR	30/1/45	13/3/45
	LT R. J. M. Allen, RCNVR	14/3/45	17/4/45
	LT G. A. Sweeney, RCNVR	18/4/45	20/6/45
ML 061	LT T. G. Denney, RCNVR	20/10/41	17/12/41
	LT S. B. Fraser, RCNVR	18/12/41	21/12/41
	LT J. W. Braidwood, RCNVR	22/12/41	15/1/42
	LT W. L. Moore, RCNVR	16/1/42	17/4/42
	LT G. W. Leckie, RCNVR	18/4/42	30/12/42
	LT S. B. Marshall, RCNVR	30/1/43	10/10/43
	LT E. U. Anderson, RCNVR	11/10/43	25/8/44
	LT C. A. Balfry, RCNVR	26/8/44	17/1/45
	LT J. A. Barrett, RCNVR	18/1/45	19/6/45
ML 062	LT W. L. Moore, RCNVR	1/4/42	7/7/42
	LT H. D. Pepper, RCNVR	8/7/42	16/1/43
ML 063	SUB/LT N. M. Simpson, RCNVR	1/4/42	16/1/43
ML 064	LT T. G. Sewell, RCNVR	20/2/42	31/3/42
	SUB/LT N. L. Williams, RCNVR	1/5/42	2/10/43
	SUB/LT P. G. D. Armour, RCNVR	3/10/43	7/10/43
	SUB/LT N. L. Williams, RCNVR	8/10/43	20/2/44
	LT E. G. Jarvis, RCNVR	6/3/44	21/4/44
	LT J. G. Chance, RCNVR	22/4/44	23/5/44
	LT E. G. Jarvis, RCNVR	24/5/44	16/1/45
	LT R. A. F. Raney, RCNVR	17/1/45	22/6/45
ML 065	LT J. J. McLaughlin, RCNVR	1/5/43	12/5/43
	LT F. H. B. Dewdney, RCNVR	13/5/43	23/11/43
	LT J. F. Stevens, RCNVR	10/1/44	25/1/44
	LT J. H. Beeman, RCNVR	26/1/44	1/8/44
	LT G. E. McCabe, RCNVR	2/8/44	10/2/45
	LT G. E. McCabe, RCNVR	26/2/45	4/3/45
	LT W. B. McTavish, RCNVR	5/3/45	18/7/45
ML 066	LT C. F. Draney, RCNVR	6/3/42	23/11/42
	LT W. E. W. Snaith, RCNVR	24/11/42	10/2/43
	CH.SKPR B. B. McCandless, RCNR	11/2/43	3/3/43
	LT W. E. W. Snaith, RCNVR	4/3/43	3/7/43
	LT R. R. Maitland, RCNVR	4/7/43	12/1/44
	LT J. W. Shaw, RCNVR	13/1/44	15/5/44
	LT J. M. Lewis, RCNVR	16/5/44	13/6/44
	LT E. S. Blanchet, RCNVR	14/6/44	19/6/44
	LT J. M. Lewis, RCNVR	20/6/44	20/7/44
	LT W. A. Smith, RCNVR	21/7/44	10/9/44
ML 067	SUB/LT C. C. T. McNair, RCNR	27/3/42	15/6/43
	LT J. F. Beveridge, RCNVR	16/6/43	1/11/43
	SKPR/LT G. F. Cassidy, RCNR	2/11/43	16/11/43
	LT J. F. Beveridge, RCNVR	17/11/43	6/4/44
	LT E. S. Blanchet, RCNVR	7/4/44	13/6/44
	LT H. W. Patterson, RCNVR	4/11/44	12/7/45
	LT J. M. Ferris, RCNVR	13/7/45	12/9/45
ML 068	SKPR/LT H. E. Young, RCNR	7/3/42	28/2/43
	LT E. P. Ashe, RCNVR	29/2/43	8/9/43
	LT R. D. Linton, RCNVR	9/9/43	30/8/44
	LT J. M. Lewis, RCNVR	31/8/44	21/9/44
	LT R. D. Linton, RCNVR	22/9/44	27/8/45
ML 069	CH/SKPR F. W. M. Drew, RCNR	28/3/42	15/6/43
	LT R. M. Francis, RCNVR	16/6/43	25/10/43
	LT H. W. Patterson, RCNVR	26/10/43	19/9/44
	LT E. U. Anderson, RCNVR	20/9/44	24/6/45
ML 070	CH/SKPR G. B. McCandless, RCNR	19/11/42	28/11/42
	LT D. F. G. Fladgate, RCNVR	18/1/43	22/10/43
	LT F. G. Mitchell, RCNVR	23/10/43	21/11/44
	LT R. Muir, RCNVR	22/11/44	9/8/45
	LT J. E. E. Richardson, RCNVR	10/8/45	18/8/45
ML 071	SKPR/LT L. S. W. Pusey, RCNR	10/4/42	6/2/43
	LT J. E. E. Richardson, RCNVR	7/2/43	23/7/43
	SKPR/LT G. F. Cassidy, RCNR	24/7/43	15/8/43
	LT J. E. E. Richardson, RCNVR	16/8/43	3/3/44
	LT G. E. Devlin, RCNVR	4/10/44	5/11/44
	LT D.J. Morrison, RCNVR	20/11/44	11/7/45
ML 072	LT H. F. Newell, RCNVR	22/11/41	/12/41
	LT C. L. Campbell, RCNVR	1/4/42	18/6/42
	LT D. S. Howard, RCNVR	19/6/42	30/4/43
	LT E. G. Jarvis, RCNVR	18/5/43	18/11/43
	LT J. A. Davis, RCNVR	14/12/43	23/4/44
	LT F. Amyot, RCNVR	24/4/44	16/3/45
	LT A. M. C. Kenning, RCNVR	17/3/45	5/9/45
ML 073	LT V. Browne, RCNVR	22/11/45	/12/41
	LT S. O. Greening, RCNVR	1/4/42	17/6/43
	LT J. H. Stevenson, RCNVR	18/6/43	19/2/44
	LT R. D. Hayes, RCNVR	20/2/44	15/5/45
	LT J. C. Austin, RCNVR	16/5/45	28/5/45
	LT R. D. Hayes, RCNVR	29/5/45	22/8/45
ML 074	LT T. G. Denny, RCNVR	21/4/42	20/1/43
	LT V. J. Wilgress, RCNVR	21/1/43	28/10/43
	LT E. Leyland, RCNVR	29/10/43	1/7/45
ML 075	LT J. G. Humphrey, RCNVR	28/4/42	2/5/43
	LT L. J. Wallace, RCNVR	3/5/433	27/5/43
	LT R. C. Denny, RCNVR	28/5/43	31/5/43
	A/LCDR J. M. Todd, RCNVR	1/6/43	4/1/44
	A/LCDR J. M. Todd, RCNVR	25/1/44	11/10/44
	LT J. D. Lineham, RCNVR	12/10/44	8/2/45
	LT C. R. Godbehere, RCNVR	9/2/45	16/3/45
	LT J. D. Lineham, RCNVR	17/3/45	19/8/45
ML 076	LT J. Leitch, RCNVR	13/7/42	4/4/43
	LT G. R. Brassard, RCNVR	5/4/43	8/6/43
	LT T. F. H. Galway, RCNVR	9/6/43	21/6/43
	LT W. E. W. Snaith, RCNVR	24/2/44	20/7/44
	LT F. B. Pugh, RCNVR	21/7/44	19/7/45
ML 077	A/LCDR J. W. Braidwood, RCNVR	21/4/42	7/10/43
	SUB/LT R. Paddon, RCNVR	8/10/43	29/10/43
	SUB/LT P. Thomas, RCNVR	30/10/43	29/12/43
	LT P. B. C. Samson, RCNVR	30/12/43	5/3/44
	LT F. Amyot, RCNVR	6/3/44	23/4/44
	LT P. B. C. Samson, RCNVR	24/4/44	29/4/45
	LT D. R. Lester, RCNVR	30/4/45	19/7/45

ML 078	SUB/LT J. N. Finlayson, RCNVR	21/4/12	11/4/43
	LT G. P. Manning, RCNVR	12/4/43	23/4/43
	SUB/LT J. A. Davis, RCNVR	24/4/43	5/5/43
	LT D. G. Creba, RCNVR	6/5/43	7/10/43
	LT L. O. Stonehouse, RCNVR	8/10/43	5/5/44
	LT C. H. Adair, RCNVR	6/5/44	25/10/44
	LT S. C. Kilbank, RCNVR	26/10/44	5/2/45
	LT J. L. Gourlay, RCNVR	24/4/45	20/7/45
ML 079	LT S. B. Fraser, RCNVR	21/4/42	3/7/42
	LT H. R. Cruise, RCNVR	4/7/42	13/8/43
	LT C. J. Holloway, RCNVR	14/8/43	7/11/43
	LT C. A. Balfry, RCNVR	8/11/43	15/8/44
	LT J. B. LeMaistre, RCNVR	16/8/44	15/12/44
	LT F. J. Johnson, RCNVR	23/4/45	11/6/45
ML 080	SUB/LT J. W. Collins, RCNVR	21/4/42	8/9/42
	SUB/LT G. E. Burrell, RCNVR	9/9/42	6/10/43
	LT J. E. M. Jones, RCNVR	7/10/43	15/12/44
	LT G. E. McCabe, RCNVR	23/4/45	31/5/45
	LT J. J. Caya, RCNVR	1/6/45	12/7/45
ML 081	LT F. K. Ellis, RCNVR	21/4/42	23/11/42
	LT J. M. Todd, RCNVR	24/11/42	31/5/43
	LT R. C. Denny, RCNVR	1/6/43	8/6/43
	LT J. J. McLoughlin, RCNVR	19/8/43	5/10/43
	LT G. C. Brain, RCNVR	6/10/43	20/4/44
	LT A. D. Stairs, RCNVR	21/4/44	26/11/44
	LT W. J. King, RCNVR	27/11/44	14/1/45
	LT A. D. Stairs, RCNVR	23/4/45	21/6/45
ML 082	LT A. B. Strange, RCNVR	21/4/42	4/2/43
	LT J. F. Stevens, RCNVR	25/8/43	9/1/44
	LT J. F. Stevens, RCNVR	26/1/44	25/9/44
ML 083	LT W. M. Grand, RCNVR	9/5/42	10/5/43
	LT M. C. Knox, RCNVR	11/5/43	7/10/43
	LT J. R. Akin, RCNVR	8/10/43	11/9/44
	LT G. A. Sweeney, RCNVR	12/9/44	15/12/44
	LT R. J. M. Allen, RCNVR	23/4/45	15/7/45
ML 084	LT G. E. Cross, RCNVR	4/6/42	26/3/43
	LT R. N. McDiarmid, RCNVR	27/3/43	16/4/44
	LT V.W. Marples, RCNVR	4/4/44	15/12/44
	LT J. C. Mackey, RCNVR	23/4/45	22/6/45
ML 085	LT W. E. D. Atkinson, RCNVR	21/4/42	21/10/42
	SUB/LT G. C. Clark, RCNVR	22/10/42	7/3/44
	LT J. J. McLaughlin, RCNVR	8/3/44	4/4/44
	LT R. M. Greene, RCNVR	5/4/44	29/11/44
	LT H. J. Dow, RCNVR	1/5/45	4/7/45
ML 086	LT T. G. Sewell, RCNVR	25/10/42	8/2/43
	LT S. C. Robinson, RCNVR	9/2/43	2/3/43
	LT T. G. Sewell, RCNVR	3/3/43	13/3/43
	LT J. R. Sare, RCNVR	14/3/43	21/3/43
	LT G. L. James, RCNVR	22/3/43	16/11/43
	LT P. Husoy, RCNVR	17/11/43	3/12/44
	LT V. B. Chew, RCNVR	4/12/44	31/1/45
	LT P. Husoy, RCNVR	1/2/45	7/7/45
ML 087	LT A. D. Stairs, RCNVR	11/11/42	9/1/44
	LT W. G. Finlay, RCNVR	10/1/44	6/2/45
	LT V. B. Chew, RCNVR	7/2/45	6/3/45
	LT J. C. Austin, RCNVR	7/3/45	25/4/45
	LT V. B. Chew, RCNVR	26/4/45	8/7/45

ML 088	LCDR W. L. Moore, RCNVR	10/5/43	6/9/43
	SUB/LT J. G. McClelland, RCNVR	7/9/43	8/10/43
	SUB/LT R. S. Graves, RCNVR	9/10/43	28/10/43
	LCDR W. L. Moore, RCNVR	29/10/43	24/11/43
	LT W. G. Cunningham, RCNVR	25/11/43	16/8/44
	LT T. M. Kirkwood, RCNVR	17/8/44	14/3/45
	LT J. G. W. MacKenzie, RCNVR	15/3/45	4/4/45
	LT T. M. Kirkwood, RCNVR	5/4/45	25/6/45
ML 089	LT A. G. Beardmore, RCNVR	26/9/42	9/1/44
	LT J. H. Curtis, RCNVR	10/1/44	16/3/45
	LT J. A. D. Alguire, RCNVR	17/3/45	29/4/45
	LT J. H. Curtis, RCNVR	30/4/45	1/7/45
ML 090	LCDR A. C. Campbell, RCNVR	11/11/42	10/5/44
	LT C. A. L. Maase, RCNVR	11/5/44	24/1/45
	LT D. A. Dobson, RCNVR	25/1/45	6/3/45
	LT C. A. L. Maase, RCNVR	7/3/45	13/7/45
ML 091	LT S. C. Robinson, RCNVR	17/5/43	8/10/43
	SUB/LT J. G. McClelland, RCNVR	9/10/43	11/11/43
	LT F. H. B. Dewdney, RCNVR	12/11/43	7/3/44
	LT R. A. Wylie, RCNVR	8/3/44	22/5/44
	LT E. B. Kendall, RCNVR	23/5/44	16/7/45
ML 092	LT H. J. Browne, RCNVR	28/9/42	8/10/43
	LT E. Loyland, RCNVR	9/10/43	28/10/43
	LT G. L. Parker, RCNVR	29/10/43	1/2/44
	LT R. Dickinson, RCNVR	2/2/44	2/7/45
ML 093	LT D. M. Fraser, RCNVR	2/11/42	27/12/42
	LT R. Carfrae, RCNVR	28/12/42	1/11/43
	LT A. W. Murray, RCNVR	2/11/43	18/4/44
	LT E. G. Arthurs, RCNVR	19/4/44	21/1/45
	LT J. C. Austin, RCNVR	22/1/45	6/3/45
	LT E. G. Arthurs, RCNVR	7/3/45	2/7/45
ML 094	LT G. Marcil, RCNVR	29/11/42	4/3/43
	LT A. P. Morrow, RCNVR	5/3/43	7/10/43
	LT C. J. VanTighem, RCNVR	8/10/43	11/12/44
	LT C. Carras, RCNVR	12/12/44	5/1/45
	LT W. J. Langston, RCNVR	6/1/45	6/2/45
ML 095	LT J. J. McLaughlin, RCNVR	7/7/43	18/7/43
	LT H. D. Pepper, RCNVR	19/7/43	3/9/43
	LT H. R. Cruise, RCNVR	4/9/43	19/9/43
	LT H. D. Pepper, RCNVR	20/9/43	21/10/43
	LT N. L. Williams, RCNVR	25/2/44	5/1/45
	LT W. J. Langston, RCNVR	6/1/45	6/2/45
	LT N. L. Williams, RCNVR	7/2/45	1/7/45
ML 096	LT H. R. Cruise, RCNVR	9/11/42	11/8/43
	LT A. M. Harper, RCNVR	12/8/43	27/8/43
	SUB/LT R. W. Kettlewell, RCNVR	28/8/43	7/11/43
	LT J. M. Lewis, RCNVR	8/11/43	16/11/43
	LT T. H. Browne, RCNVR	17/11/43	10/1/45
	LT J. H. Morrison, RCNVR	11/1/45	9/4/45
	LT W. J. Langston, RCNVR	10/4/45	19/4/45
	LT J. H. Morrison, RCNVR	14/5/45	1/7/45
ML 097	LT E. P. Jones, RCNVR	5/1/44	15/9/44
	LT J. H. Bailey, RCNVR	16/9/44	2/3/45
	LT W. J. Langston, RCNVR	3/3/45	9/4/45
	LT J. H. Bailey, RCNVR	10/4/45	2/7/45

ML 098	SUB/LT T. A. Welch, RCNVR	7/11/42	18/11/43
	LT E. G. Jarvis, RCNVR	19/11/43	4/1/44
	A/LCDR J. M. Todd, RCNVR	5/1/44	24/1/44
	LT E. G. Jarvis, RCNVR	25/1/44	5/3/44
	LT E. Desrosiers, RCNVR	6/3/44	16/3/45
	LT M. L. M. DeMartigny, RCNVR	17/3/45	17/4/45
	LT E. Desrosiers, RCNVR	18/4/45	25/4/45
	LT J. C. Austin, RCNVR	26/4/45	28/4/45
	LT E. Desrosiers, RCNVR	29/4/45	16/7/45
ML 099	SUB/LT P. G. D. Armour, RCNVR	7/3/42	6/11/42
	LT G. M. Moors, RCNVR	7/11/42	18/10/43
	SUB/LT P. G. D. Armour, RCNVR	19/10/43	9/1/45
	LT J. B. LeMaistre, RCNVR	8/1/45	2/7/45
ML 100	LT E. G. Scott, RCNVR	8/11/42	16/11/43
	LT D. A. Dobson, RCNVR	17/11/43	17/12/44
	LT W. G. Lumsden, RCNVR	18/12/44	9/1/45
	LT J. R. Jenner, RCNVR	10/1/45	7/4/45
	LT D. A. Dobson, RCNVR	8/4/45	12/7/45
ML 101	LT A. A. McLeod, RCNVR	20/10/42	15/8/43
	SUB/LT C. R. Godbehere, RCNVR	11/10/43	
	LT G. L. James, RCNVR	17/11/43	19/6/44
	LT P. B. Paine, RCNVR	20/6/44	20/12/44
	LT F. H. B. Dewdney, RCNVR	25/1/45	31/7/45
ML 102	LT H. M. Gordon, RCNVR	14/11/42	23/4/43
	SUB/LT J. G. W. MacKenzie, RCNVR	24/4/43	2/6/43
	LT H. M. Gordon, RCNVR	3/6/43	18/10/43
	LT B. C. Heintzman, RCNVR	19/10/43	5/7/44
	LT J. K. MacDonald, RCNVR	6/7/44	24/6/45
ML 103	LT H. A. Agar, RCNVR	18/11/42	21/6/43
	LT F. H. Galway, RCNVR	22/6/43	6/1/45
	LT W. G. Lumsden, RCNVR	7/1/45	26/4/45
	LT J. B. Barbeau, RCNVR	27/4/45	8/7/45
ML 104	LCDR J. W. Braidwood, RCNVR	8/10/43	1/2/44
	LT C. F. W. Cooper, RCNVR	2/2/44	3/4/44
	LT J. J. McLaughlin, RCNVR	4/4/44	18/2/45
	LT F. H. Galway, RCNVR	19/2/45	14/9/45
ML 105	LT J. D. Addison, RCNVR	5/9/43	29/8/44
	LT W. P. T. McGhee, RCNVR	30/8/44	16/9/45
ML 106	LT F. B. Pugh, RCNVR	28/8/43	3/6/44
	LT C. F. W. Cooper, RCNVR	4/6/44	17/2/45
	LT C. N. Blagrave, RCNVR	18/2/45	30/8/45
ML 107	LT H. P. R. Brown, RCNVR	11/9/43	30/8/45
ML 108	LT I. L. Campbell, RCNVR	14/8/43	19/12/44
ML 109	LT J. G. W. MacKenzie, RCNVR	23/8/43	22/1/45
	LT J. S. Stephen, RCNVR	23/1/45	17/7/45
ML 110	LT R. Dickinson, RCNVR	18/10/43	
	LT H. A. Batey, RCNVR	19/10/43	23/6/44
	LT W. B. Bailey, RCNVR	24/6/44	23/2/45
	LT J. U. McFall, RCNVR	24/2/45	6/3/45
	LT D. A. Dobson, RCNVR	7/3/45	7/4/45
	SUB/LT R. R. Pierson, RCNVR	8/4/45	29/4/45
	LT W. B. Bailey, RCNVR	30/4/45	13/7/45
ML 111	LT A. M. Harper, RCNVR	9/9/43	5/4/44
	LT C. F. W. Cooper, RCNVR	6/4/44	28/5/44
	LT A. M. Harper, RCNVR	29/5/44	5/10/44
	LT S. L. Burke, RCNVR	6/10/44	6/2/45
	LT P. B. Paine, RCNVR	7/2/45	13/7/45

Ship	Commanding Officer		
ML 112	LT R. C. Denny, RCNVR	25/10/43	18/4/43
	LT G. R. Brassard, RCNVR	19/4/44	28/12/44
	LT R. M. Greene, RCNVR	29/12/44	5/1/45
	LT W. R. Duggan, RCNVR	6/1/45	22/2/45
	LT J. E. M. Jones, RCNVR	23/2/45	20/3/45
	LT W. R. Duggan, RCNVR	21/3/45	16/7/45
ML 113	LT C. J. Holloway, RCNVR	8/11/43	15/9/44
	LT E.R. Whitehouse, RCNVR	16/9/44	20/3/45
	LT J. E. M. Jones, RCNVR	21/3/45	23/7/45
ML 114	LT R. Carfrae, RCNVR	23/11/43	8/7/44
	LCDR W. L. Moore, RCNVR	23/10/44	26/12/44
	LT W. J. King, RCNVR	27/12/44	14/1/45
	LT J. H. Osler, RCNVR	15/1/45	28/1/45
	LT G. E. Rising, RCNVR	29/1/45	13/2/45
	LT J. H. Osler, RCNVR	14/2/45	5/5/45
	LT F. Amyot, RCNVR	6/5/45	6/6/45
	LT J. H. Osler, RCNVR	7/6/45	20/8/45
ML 115	LT R. W. Kettlewell, RCNVR	8/11/43	7/2/44
	LT C. R. Godbehere, RCNVR	8/2/44	4/1/454
	LT C. R. Godbehere, RCNVR	26/3/45	8/6/45
	LT F. Amyot, RCNVR	9/6/45	25/7/45
	LT C. R. Godbehere, RCNVR	26/7/45	13/8/45
ML 116	LT E. P. Jones, RCNVR	10/4/44	8/9/44
	LT J. D. Addison, RCNVR	9/9/44	22/1/45
	LT J. D. Addison, RCNVR	26/3/45	31/5/45
	LT G. E. McCabe, RCNR	1/6/45	2/9/45
ML 117	SUB/LT E. H. Gudewlll, RCNVR	17/12/43	25/1/44
	LT G. E. Rising, RCNVR	26/1/44	26/12/44
	LT J. G. Menzies, RCNVR	27/12/44	13/3/45
	LT W. J. King, RCNVR	14/3/45	2/4/45
	LT J. G. Menzies, RCNVR	3/4/45	19/7/45
ML 118	LT V. J. Wilgress, RCNVR	6/11/43	7/2/44
	LT W. J. King, RCNVR	3/4/44	19/4/44
	LT J. H. Osler, RCNVR	20/4/44	8/1/45
	LT W. J. King, RCNVR	11/2/45	25/7/45
ML 119	LT J. J. McLaughlin, RCNVR	16/11/43	7/3/44
	LT F. H. B. Dewdney, RCNVR	8/3/44	7/1/45
ML 120	LT G. M. Schuthe, RCNVR	10/1/44	19/2/44
	LT J. H. Stevenson, RCNVR	20/2/44	21/9/44
	LT W. J. King, RCNVR	22/9/44	29/10/44
	LT J. H. Stevenson, RCNVR	30/10/44	21/1/45
	LT J. M. Todd, RCNVR	22/1/45	26/7/45
ML 121	LT R. N. McDiarmid, RCNVR	17/4/44	9/1/45
	LT J. G. W. MacKenzie, RCNVR	17/4/45	26/7/45
	LT J. M. Todd, RCNVR	27/7/45	26/8/45
ML 122	LT C. K. D. Smith, RCNVR	17/5/44	9/10/44
	LT R. T. McKean, RCNVR	10/10/44	5/9/45
ML 123	LT J. W. Shaw, RCNVR	5/6/44	3/7/45
ML 124	LT E. S. Blanchet, RCNVR	20/6/44	1/8/45
ML 125	LT J. E. Kendrick, RCNVR	2/6/44	8/6/45
	LT F. J. Fiander, RCNVR	9/6/45	13/9/45
ML 126	LT R. C. Denny, RCNVR	7/8/44	8/11/44
	LT W. H. Davidson, RCNVR	9/11/44	12/9/45
ML 127	LT J. M. Lewis, RCNVR	25/9/44	5/11/44
	LT G. E. Devlin, RCNVR	6/11/44	22/11/44
	LT C. K. D. Smith, RCNVR	23/11/44	11/9/45
ML 128	LT R. K. Baker, RCNVR	4/7/44	11/11/44
	LT G. E. Devlin, RCNVR	12/1/45	11/9/45
ML 129	LT G. L. James, RCNVR	25/9/44	30/5/45
	LT E. L. MacDonald, RCNVR	31/5/45	3/7/45

Infantry Landing Craft

Twenty-four of these were loaned to Canada by the USN expressly for the Normandy invasion, and RCN crews manned a further six previously on loan to the RN. Built in three New Jersey shipyards in 1943, all were commissioned between December 1943 and March 1944. These 158-foot craft could carry 155 troops below deck, landing them in shallow water via gangways on either bow.

Formed into three flotillas, the Canadian LCI (L)s shared to the full the hazards of the D Day landings. Sandy beaches were seldom encountered, and many of the craft suffered damage from rocks, man-made obstacles, and limpet mines. The majority, however, continued to ferry Allied personnel to and from the beaches until well into August 1944. By the end of September all of the craft had been paid off for return to the USN.

1st Canadian (260th RN) Flotilla: LCI (L) 117, 121, 166, 177, 249, 266, 277, 285, 298, 301.

2nd Canadian (262nd RN) Flotilla: LCI (L) 115, 118, 135, 250, 252, 262, 263, 276, 299, 306.

3rd Canadian (264th RN) Flotilla: LCI (L) 125, 255, 270, 271, 288, 295, 302, 305, 310, 311.

LCI (L) 115, 1944.

PARTICULARS OF CLASS:

DISPLACEMENT:	380
DIMENSIONS:	158' 6" x 23' 8" x 6' 6"
SPEED:	14 kts
CREW:	2/20
ARMAMENT:	four 40-mm

Commanding Officers:

115 LT V. D. Ramsay, RCNVR	252 LT R. E. St. J. Wakefield. RCNVR	288 LT W. E. Charron, RCNVR
117 LT R. L. Gordon, RCNVR	255 LT H. E. Trenholme, RCNVR	295 LT P. G. R. Campbell, RCNVR
118 LT C. R. Bond, RCNVR	262 LT P. R. Hinton, RCNVR	298 LT J. S. Monteath, RCNVR
121 LT D. H. Botly, RCNVR	263 LT J. B. B. Shaw, RCNVR	299 LT W. B. McGregor, RCNVR
125 LT C. R. Parker, DSC, RCNVR	266 LT J. G. Wenman, RCNVR	301 LT D. G. M. Smith, RCNVR
135 LT J. D. Kell, RCNVR	270 LT A. C. Clark, RCNVR	302 LT J. M. Ruttan, DSC, RCNVR
166 LT G. M. Oliver, RCNVR	271 LT W. R. Sinclair, RCNVR	305 LT C. B. MacKay, RCNVR
177 LT W. C. Gardner, RCNVR	276 LT A. A. Wedd, DSC, RCNVR	306 LT A. K. Stephens, RCNVR
249 LT J. E. O'Rourke, RCNVR	277 LT W. H. M. Ballantyne, RCNVR	310 LT L. Williams, RCNVR
250 LT H. M. Harrison, RCNVR	285 LT H. S. Square, RCNVR	311 LT D. J. Lewis, RCNVR

Auxiliaries

Adversus

Built as an RCMP patrol craft in 1931, *Adversus* served the RCN in a similar capacity on the east coast until 20 December 1941, when she was lost aground in a blizzard on McNutt's Island, near Shelburne, Nova Scotia.

ADVERSUS	
DISPLACEMENT:	155
DIMENSIONS:	112' 3" x 19" x 11'
SPEED:	12 kts
CREW:	4/15
ARMAMENT:	one .303 m.g.
BUILT:	1931, Orillia, ON
COMMISSIONED:	7/9/39
LOST:	20/12/41

Alachasse

Sister to *Adversus*, *Alachasse* was taken over from the RCMP early in the war for patrol duty on the east coast. She was paid off on 28 November 1945 and sold to Marine Industries Ltd., in whose service she remained until 1957.

ALACHASSE	
DISPLACEMENT:	157
DIMENSIONS:	116' 4" x 19' x 11' 3"
SPEED:	12 kts
CREW:	4/14
ARMAMENT:	one .303 m.g.
BUILT:	1931, Sorel, QC
COMMISSIONED:	3/9/39
PAID OFF:	28/11/45

Adversus, 1940.

Alachasse, 3 April 1944.

Andrée Dupré, November 1940.

Andrée Dupré

Originally a Sorel-built naval trawler of the TR class, she was sold for commercial use after the First World War and renamed *Napoléon L.* Again renamed and in the hands of Marine Industries Ltd. as a tug, she was taken up by the RCN in 1939 for use as an examination vessel at Halifax. Sold after the war, she resumed her former occupation as a tug, renamed *Remorqueur 16*, at Bordeaux, France.

ANDRÉE DUPRÉ	
DISPLACEMENT:	285
DIMENSIONS:	125' x 23' 7" x 12' 0"
SPEED:	9 kts
CREW:	4/29
BUILT:	1918, Sorel, QC
ARMAMENT:	none
COMMISSIONED:	10/10/39
PAID OFF:	7/45

Bras d'Or, 1940.

Dundalk, 12 April 1950.

Dundurn, 14 September 1959.

Dundalk

Commissioned on 13 November 1943 at Walkerville, Ontario this small tanker was used to deliver fuel oil from Halifax refineries to bases on the east coast and in Newfoundland. Occasionally *Dundalk* served as a lighter. She was paid off on 9 April 1946 and subsequently served as a CNAV until 13 November 1959.

Dundurn

Commissioned on 25 November 1943 at Walkerville, Ontario, Dundurn performed the same duties as her sister, *Dundalk*. She was transferred to Esquimalt in 1946 and, on 2 January 1947 was paid off to serve as a CNAV. Sold in 1985, she was reportedly broken up at Vancouver in 1995.

BRAS D'OR

DISPLACEMENT:	265	CREW:	4/20
DIMENSIONS:	124' 6" x 23' 6" x 12' 5"	BUILT:	1919, Sorel, QC
		COMMISSIONED:	9/10/39
SPEED:	7 kts	LOST:	19/10/40

Commanding Officers

LT A. K. Young, RCNR	9/10/39	25/4/40
LT C. A. Hornsby, RCNR	26/4/40	19/10/40

DUNDALK

DISPLACEMENT:	950	ARMAMENT:	one 12 pdr., two 20-mm
DIMENSIONS:	178' 9" x 33' 2" x 13'	BUILT:	1943 Walkerville, ON
SPEED:	11 kts	COMMISSIONED:	13/11/43
CREW:	3/27	PAID OFF:	9/4/46

Commanding Officers

SKPR/LT J. S. G. Ascah, RCNR	6/10/43	9/7/45
SKPR/LT B. W. Allen, RCNR	10/7/45	-

DUNDURN

DISPLACEMENT:	950	ARMAMENT:	one 12 pdr., two 20-mm
DIMENSIONS:	178' 9" x 33' 2" x 13'	BUILT:	1943 Walkerville, ON
SPEED:	11 kts	COMMISSIONED:	25/11/43
CREW:	3/27	PAID OFF:	2/1/47

Commanding Officers

SKPR/LT A. J. Porter, RCNR	25/11/43	2/4/44
LCDR R. M. Musher, RCNR	3/4/44	10/6/45
SKPR/LT J. Blackmore, RCNVR	11/6/45	-

Bras d'Or

The New York ship owner for whom this trawler was ordered at Sorel went bankrupt soon after her launching in 1919, and she and five sisters were sold incomplete. She was completed in 1926 for service with the Department of Marine and Fisheries as *Lightship No. 25*.

Requisitioned on 15 September 1939 as an auxiliary minesweeper and renamed *Bras d'Or*, she patrolled the Halifax approaches from 1939 to 1940. She joined the St. Lawrence Patrol in June 1940, based at Rimouski, and on 10 June intercepted

and seized the Italian freighter *Capo Noli*. On the night of 18-19 October 1940, while keeping the Rumanian freighter *Ingener N. Vlassopol* under surveillance in the Gulf of St. Lawrence, *Bras d'Or* disappeared.

Eastore and Laymore

Originally built at Brunswick, Georgia for the US Army, *Eastore* was commissioned on 7 December 1944 as a supply vessel, and served on the east coast until paid off on 8 April 1946 to become a CNAV. She was sold on 30 July 1964.

Laymore, a sister ship, was built at Kewaunee, Wisconsin, and commissioned in the RCN on 12 June 1945. While stationed on the east coast she performed a variety of functions, including those of transport, boom defence, and laying moorings. She was paid off on 17 April 1946 to become a CNAV, and that summer was transferred to the west coast, becoming an oceanographic research vessel in 1966. She was offered for sale in 1977. A third sister, intended to be named *Westore*, was not acquired.

Fleur de Lis

This triple-screw RCMP vessel was commissioned on 16 November 1939, as a patrol craft at Halifax. *Fleur de Lis* operated from Shelburne in 1942 and in 1943 joined Sydney Force for examination service in the Gut of Canso, based at Mulgrave, Nova Scotia. On 29 November 1945 she was paid off and acquired by Marine Industries Ltd., who still had her in 1953 when her register was closed.

Eastore, 6 April 1964.

EASTORE, LAYMORE

DISPLACEMENT:	803	SPEED:	10 kts		BUILT:	1944 Brunswick, Ga.
DIMENSIONS:	176' x 32' x 9'	ARMAMENT:	one 4-inch, two 20-mm			

Commanding Officers:

EASTORE			LAYMORE		
CDR J. E. McQueen, RCNVR	7/12/44	1/1/45	SKPR/LT F. H. Anderson, RCNR	12/6/45	-
SKPR/LT J. A. MacLeod, RCNR	2/1/45	14/10/45	SKPR/LT G. Collier, RCNR	26/11/45	-
SKPR/LT A. R. Hallett, RCNR	15/10/45	8/4/46			

Fleur de Lis, 1940.

FLEUR DE LIS

DISPLACEMENT:	316	SPEED:	12 kts	ARMAMENT:	one .303 m.g.
DIMENSIONS:	164' 8" x 21' 1" x 11' 7"	CREW:	6/30	BUILT:	1929, Montreal, QC

Commanding Officers

Mate A. Currie, RCNR	16/11/39	20/4/40	LT J. W. Dowling, RCNR	11/3/42	5/7/42
LT R. J. Herman, RCNR	21/4/40	-	LCDR M. G. G. Stanton, RCNVR	6/7/42	13/4/43
Mate A. Currie, RCNR	10/9/40	10/3/42	SKPR/LT A. Currie, RCNR	14/4/43	29/11/45

French

A former RCMP vessel, she was commissioned at Halifax on 18 September 1939 for local patrol work. By the spring of 1942 *French* was based at Mulgrave, Nova Scotia as an examination vessel, and that December was transferred to Saint John, New Brunswick Force. In May 1943 she joined Sydney Force and returned to examination service work in the Gut of Canso, based once more at Mulgrave. In January 1944 she rejoined Halifax Local Defence Force, but after completing a major refit at Lunenburg that July she returned again to Mulgrave. Sold to commercial interests after the war, *French* was operating out of Halifax as *Le Français* as recently as 1953. On 15 August of that year she was badly damaged in a hurricane off Cape May, New Jersey, and abandoned to the underwriters.

French, 1940.

FRENCH			
DISPLACEMENT:	226	CREW:	5/25
DIMENSIONS:	138' 1" x 22' 1" x 10' 8"	ARMAMENT:	one 6 pdr. one .303 m.g.
SPEED:	11 kts	BUILT:	1938, Lauzon, QC

Commanding Officers

LT J. W. Bonner, RCNR	18/9/39	26/2/41
LT D. W. Main, RCNR	27/2/41	22/7/41
SKPR/LT K. W. N. Hall, RCNR	23/7/41	22/10/42
SKPR/LT W. G. Kent, RCNR	23/10/42	20/9/46

Jalobert, 24 October 1944.

Jalobert

Built as *Polana* in 1911 for the Department of Agriculture, she later became a quarantine patrol vessel for the Department of Health. In 1923 she was acquired by the Department of Marine and Fisheries as a pilot vessel and renamed *Jalobert*, commemorating one of Jacques Cartier's master mariners. She served as an examination vessel in the St. Lawrence, 12 December 1941 to 15 December 1942, and then returned to the Department of Transport. Sold out of government service in 1954, she served until 1980 as *Macassa* and later as *Queen City*. In 1982 she became a floating restaurant at Windsor, Ontario.

JALOBERT	
DISPLACEMENT:	378
DIMENSIONS:	107' 5" x 23' x 11' 9"
SPEED:	8 kts
CREW:	4/16
BUILT:	1911, Kingston, ON

LAURIER			
DISPLACEMENT:	201	CREW:	4/25
DIMENSIONS:	113' x 21' x 10' 4"	ARMAMENT:	one 12 pdr. one .303 m.g
SPEED:	10 kts	BUILT:	1936, Quebec City, QC

Commanding Officers

LT R. A. S. MacNeil, RCNR	12/4/40	10/4/41	SKPR/LT A. Smith, RCNR	3/12/45	31/1/46
SKPR/LT D. E. Freeman, RCNR	11/4/41	30/6/45	SKPR/LT N. H. Pentz, RCNR	1/2/46	25/3/46
SKPR/LT J. W. G. Ascah, RCNR	1/7/45	4/11/45			

Laurier, August 1940.

Laurier

Formerly an RCMP patrol vessel, she was commissioned on 9 July 1939 at Halifax for local A/S duties, and occasionally served as escort to the Sydney sections of Halifax convoys (SHX). By 1943 she was a member of Sydney Force, based at Mulgrave, Nova Scotia for examination and patrol duty in the Gut of Canso. In February *Laurier* returned to Halifax Local Defence Force, but rejoined Sydney Force that September. Paid off on 25 March 1946, she was returned to the RCMP, and was disposed of in 1984.

Macdonald, 6 June 1941.

Macdonald

Like her sister *Laurier*, *Macdonald* was a former RCMP vessel. She was commissioned on 11 October 1939 for patrol duty out of Halifax. Paid off on 28 January 1945 she was turned over to the Fisheries Department in 1946 and renamed *Howay*. She was sold in 1982.

MACDONALD

| DISPLACMENT | 201 | SPEED: | 10 kts | ARMAMENT: | one 12 pdr. one .303 m.g |
| DIMENSIONS: | 113' x 21' x 10' 4" | CREW: | 4/25 | BUILT: | 1936, Quebec City, QC |

Commanding Officers

LT A. R. Ascah, RCNR	11/10/39	1/3/42	SKPR/LT K. Bennett, RCNR	18/12/43	26/5/44
CH/SKPR G. Billard, RCNR	2/3/42	4/11/42	CH/SKPR R. W. Sparkes, RCNR	27/5/44	28/1/45
CH/SKPR E. W. Suffield, RCNR	5/11/42	17/12/43			

Macsin

A sister to *Andrée Dupré* and like her, a TR class naval trawler built at Sorel in 1918, *Macsin* was sold into commercial hands postwar and renamed *Gedéon L.* She was later renamed and acquired by Marine Industries Ltd., from whom the RCN took her over on 10 April 1940. She served throughout the Second World War as an examination vessel, and later was sold to the French government to serve as a tug at St. Nazaire.

Marvita

This wooden-hulled craft saw service as a rum-runner during the early 1930s but was in the employ of the Newfoundland government when the RCN chartered her in 1941. *Marvita* served as an examination vessel until 1945, returning to her previous owners in 1946. She was transferred to the federal Department of Revenue in 1949, and was lost on Cape Ballard, Newfoundland, on 15 July 1954.

Macsin, 28 August 1941.

Marvita, May 1941.

Mastadon, 25 February 1943.

MACSIN	
DISPLACEMENT:	293
DIMENSIONS:	125' 2" x 23' 7" x 12' 8"
SPEED:	8 kts
CREW:	3/22
BUILT:	1918, Sorel, QC

MARVITA	
DISPLACEMENT:	121
DIMENSIONS:	105' x 20' x 8'
SPEED:	10 kts
CREW:	2/9
BUILT:	1930, Mahone Bay, NS

Mastadon

Formerly Department of Public Works *Dredge No. 306*, she was taken over by the RCN and converted to an auxiliary tanker for use on the west coast. Commissioned on 9 December 1942, *Mastadon* delivered oil to naval storage tanks and occasionally assisted in the distribution of commercial oil products as well. She was paid off on 12 March 1946 and entered mercantile service, being noted under Peruvian flag in the 1950s. She was off Lloyd's Register in 1964.

MASTADON				
DISPLACEMENT:	1,233		CREW:	5/37
DIMENSIONS:	210' x 36' 6" x 13' 9"		ARMAMENT:	one 12 pdr., two 20-mm
SPEED:	6 kts		BUILT:	1910, Renfrew, Scotland

Commanding Officers

CH/SKPR H. R. H. Stratford, RCNR	9/12/42	5/1/44	LT H. H, Rankin, RCNR	6/1/44	12/3/46

Mont Joli

Mont Joli was chartered on 5 July 1940 for use as an examination vessel and purchased on 29 June 1943. An east coast auxiliary, she was paid off on 29 March 1946, and shortly afterward sold for commercial use. She still existed under the same name as late as 1966, when she was destroyed by fire.

MONT JOLI	
DISPLACEMENT:	275
DIMENSIONS:	120' 4" x 24' 6" x 11' 1"
SPEED:	9 kts
CREW.	4/29
BUILT:	1938, Meteghan, NS

Moonbeam

Formerly the Department of Transport *Hopper Barge No. 1*, she was acquired by the RCN on 4 December 1940 and converted to a fuel oil carrier for use on the east coast and at St. John's, Newfoundland. *Moonbeam* was paid off on 13 November 1945 and sold the following year to become *Oakbranch* and, about 1960, *B.L.L. 24*. Her register was closed in 1971, the ship having been broken up.

Murray Stewart

Built in 1918, she was purchased in 1922 by the Department of Transport, which loaned her to the RCN in 1942. *Murray Stewart* served most of the war as an examination vessel at Saint John, New Brunswick, and was paid off on 22 August 1945. Sold in 1946, she was in service in 1951 as *David Richard* at her native Port Arthur, and in 1979 was renamed *Georgian Queen*.

MURRAY STEWART	
DISPLACEMENT:	234
DIMENSIONS:	119' x 26' x 15' 7"
SPEED:	6 kts
CREW:	2/21
BUILT:	1918, Port Arthur, ON

Mont Joli, April 1942.

Moonbeam, April 1941.

MOONBEAM			
DISPLACEMENT:	589	CREW:	2/18
DIMENSIONS:	178/ x 33' 6" x 12'	BUILT:	1913, Lévis, QC
SPEED:	6 kts		

Commanding Officers

LT T. D. Kelly, RCNR	4/12/40	-	LT W. W. Hackney, RCNR	7/7/42	-
CH/SKPR S. F. Ellis, RCNR	4/1/41	-	CH/SKPR E. W. Hannaford, RCNR	15/10/43	-

Murray Stewart.

Nitinat.

Nitinat

A newly built fisheries patrol vessel, *Nitinat* was chartered on 18 September 1939 for patrol and examination duties on the west coast. She was returned to her owners in June 1945, and her career was ended by fire in the Fraser River on 1 February 1977.

NITINAT	
DISPLACEMENT:	135
DIMENSIONS:	99' 5" x 17' 7" x 10' 6"
SPEED:	10 kts
CREW:	3/15
ARMAMENT:	one .303 m.g.
BUILT:	1939, New Westminster, BC

Norsal

A vessel hired from the Powell River Co. for miscellaneous duties, *Norsal* returned to commercial service after the war, to be renamed *Maui Lu* in 1973. Reverting to her former name, she sank in Hecate Strait on 7 December 1990.

NORSAL	
DISPLACEMENT:	168
DIMENSIONS:	122' 4" x 19' 2" x 10' 6"
SPEED:	10 kts
CREW:	3/17
ARMAMENT:	one .303 m.g.
BUILT:	1921, Vancouver, BC

Norsal, January 1941.

Preserver

Commissioned on 11 July 1942 at Sorel, she arrived at Halifax on 4 August, having escorted a Quebec-Sydney convoy en route. She was assigned to Newfoundland Force as a Fairmile base supply ship, arriving at St. John's on 18 September but transferring almost immediately to Botwood, Newfoundland. She returned to St. John's in mid-December, staying until the end of July 1943 when she moved to Red Bay. Back at St. John's in November, she returned to Red Bay in mid-June 1944 and at the beginning of September, moved to Sydney. After a refit at Halifax at the beginning of 1945 *Preserver* returned once more to St. John's but was transferred to Shelburne, Nova Scotia in June. Paid off on 6 November 1945 at Shelburne, she was sold to the Peruvian Navy in 1946 and renamed *Mariscal Castilla*, then *Cabo Blanco*. She was broken up in 1961.

Preserver at trials off Sorel, July 1942.

PRESERVER

DISPLACEMENT:	4,670	CREW:	20/87
DIMENSIONS:	268' 5" x 43' 11" x 17' 8"	ARMAMENT:	one 4-inch, two 20-mm
SPEED:	10 kts	BUILT:	1941-42 Sorel, QC

Commanding Officers

CAPT B. L. Johnson, DSO, RCNR	11/7/42	16/12/43	LCDR H. C. Walmesley, RCNR	18/4/45	18/10/45
CDR G. Borrie, RCNR	17/12/43	17/4/45			

Provider, 17 January 1943.

PROVIDER

DISPLACEMENT:	4,670	CREW:	20/87
DIMENSIONS:	268' 5" x 43' 11" x 17' 8"	ARMAMENT:	one 4-inch, two 20-mm
SPEED:	10 kts	BUILT:	1941-42 Sorel, QC

Commanding Officers

CDR J. A. Heenan, OBE, RCNR	1/12/42	4/5/43	A/CDR T. Gilmour, RCNR	18/11/43	14/2/45
LCDR W. H. Koughan, RCNR	5/5/43	3/7/43	CAPT L. J. M. Gauvreau, RCN	15/2/45	19/11/45
CDR E. G. Skinner, DSC, RCNR	4/7/743	17/11/43	LCDR D. G. King, RCN	20/11/45	22/3/46

Provider

Sister to *Preserver*, she was commissioned at Sorel on 1 December 1942 and arrived at Halifax on 14 December. Two flotillas of Fairmiles were to proceed to the Caribbean to alleviate a shortage of escorts there, and *Provider* was ordered south to be their base supply ship. She accordingly sailed on 19 January 1943 but had to return owing to storm damage and sailed again ten days later, arriving at Trinidad on 20 February. One Fairmile flotilla, the 73rd, joined her at Guantanamo, Cuba, proceeding with her in March to a new base at Key West. Returning to Halifax on 23 April, she was then assigned to Gaspé Force, arriving on 22 May, and subsequently transferred to Sept Iles, where she remained from 29 June to November. At the end of 1943 she proceeded to Halifax and thence to Bermuda to serve as base ship for the 70th and 78th Flotillas. *Provider* returned to Halifax on 31 July 1944 but sailed again that September for Bermuda, where she was attached to the recently established base, HMCS *Somers Isle,* until May 1945. She then went to Halifax as base supply ship until she was paid off on 22 March 1946, to be sold later that year to Peruvian owners and renamed *Maruba*. Subsequently acquired by the Peruvian Navy, she served as *Orgenos* until disposed of for scrap in 1961.

Rayon d'Or, 1940.

Reo II, 24 April 1941.

Ross Norman.

Rayon d'Or

Requisitioned on 11 September 1939, this former fishing trawler became an auxiliary minesweeper based at Halifax. Her duties also included loop laying and maintenance. Early in 1943 following a winter refit, *Rayon d'Or* was assigned to Sydney Force and remained in that service until February 1944 when she rejoined the Halifax Local Defence Force. Paid off in April 1945 she resumed her commercial career until 1954.

Reo II

A former rum-runner, *Reo II* was chartered by the RCN on 30 July 1940, and commissioned on 23 January 1941 as an auxiliary minesweeper. She also served as an examination vessel and coil skid-towing vessel. Declared surplus on 19 October 1945, she was paid off and in 1946 sold for mercantile purposes. *Reo II* was subsequently broken up. All that remains is her wheelhouse, which is now on the dock outside the Lunenburg Marine Museum.

Ross Norman

A wooden-hulled coaster chartered on 19 June 1940, *Ross Norman* served successively as auxiliary minesweeper, coil skid-towing craft and mobile deperming craft with Halifax Local Defence Force. She was purchased on 26 August 1943. Paid off on 8 April 1946, she was sold in 1947 and, as *Chicoutimi Trader*, was lost by stranding on Grindstone Island, Quebec, on 18 November 1952.

RAYON D'OR	
DISPLACEMENT:	342
DIMENSIONS:	140' x 24' 1" x 13'
SPEED:	9 kts
CREW:	4/31
ARMAMENT:	one 12 pdr.
BUILT:	1912, Beverley, UK

REO II	
DISPLACEMENT:	129
DIMENSIONS:	96' 1" x 17' 5" x 7' 5"
SPEED:	9 kts
CREW:	4/32
BUILT:	1931, Meteghan, NS

ROSS NORMAN	
DISPLACEMENT:	297
DIMENSIONS:	131' 8" x 28' x 12' 6"
SPEED:	10 kts
CREW:	4/21
BUILT:	1937, Lunenburg, NS

Sankaty

Formerly a Stamford-Oyster Bay, Massachusetts ferry, *Sankaty* was commissioned on 24 September 1940 at Halifax as a minelaying, loop-laying and maintenance vessel. She was paid off on 18 August 1945 and became a Prince Edward Island ferry under the name of *Charles A. Dunning*. Sold for scrap in 1964, she sank on 27 October en route to Sydney.

Shulamite

Another former rum-runner and sister of *Marvita*, she was acquired by the RCN from the Newfoundland government to be used as an examination vessel. Returned to her previous owners in August 1945, she was later sold and renamed *Norsya* in 1950. She foundered off Matane, Quebec, on 19 September 1953.

Standard Coaster

Hired on 31 July 1940 and commissioned on 11 February 1942, this wooden-hulled coaster was based at Halifax, functioning primarily as a coil skid-towing vessel. She was paid off on 25 March 1946 and returned to merchant service. She was broken up at Saint John, New Brunswick, and her register closed in 1957.

SANKATY

DISPLACEMENT:	459
DIMENSIONS:	195' x 38' 2" x 9' 9"
SPEED:	8 kts
CREW:	3/39
ARMAMENT:	one .303 m.g.
BUILT:	1911, Quincy, Mass.

SHULAMITE

DISPLACEMENT:	121
DIMENSIONS:	105' x 20' x 8'
SPEED:	10 kts
CREW:	2/9
BUILT:	1930, Mahone Bay, NS
COMMISSIONED:	7/8/41
PAID OFF:	3/8/45

STANDARD COASTER

DISPLACEMENT:	150
DIMENSIONS:	130' x 22' x 9' 9"
SPEED:	9 kts
BUILT:	1927, Liverpool, NS

Sankaty, March 1941. Note the mines on the quarterdeck.

Shulamite, 26 April 1944.

Standard Coaster, 21 April 1944.

Star XVI.

Star XVI

Left homeless by the fall of Norway, the whale-catcher *Star XVI* was chartered in August 1941 from the Norwegian government-in-exile, and by early 1942 was a member of St. John's Local Defence Force. She transferred in June 1942 to Sydney Force, with which she remained until the war's end, and was returned to her owners after being paid off on 31 August 1945.

Suderöy IV

Like *Star XVI*, *Suderöy IV* and her two sisters were stranded overseas when the Germans overran Norway, and were chartered by the RCN in June 1940. Commissioned in June 1941, she served with Halifax Local Defence Force until paid off on 31 August 1945 and returned to her owners.

Note: Evidence received from Dr. Robert Stark, at one time CO of *Suderöy VI*, raises the probability of some or all of these ships having been misidentified in the first printing. It would appear that, contrary to logic, *Suderöys IV, V,* and *VI* bore pendant numbers J03, J04, and J05. Accordingly, the second printing presented new photographs of *Suderöys IV* and *V*, while the photo earlier thought to represent *Suderöy V* now illustrates *Suderöy VI*.

Suderoy IV.

SUDERÖY IV

DISPLACEMENT:	252		CREW:	4/25
DIMENSIONS:	122' 6" x 23' 9" x 10'		BUILT:	1930 Oslo, Norway
SPEED:	9 kts			

Commanding Officers

Mate C. A. Mott, RCNR	7/5/41	2/4/42	LT W. Russell, RCNR	1/3/43	7/9/43
LT R. J. C. Pringle, RCNVR	3/4/42	24/4/42	LT D. G. Van Bommel, RCNVR	8/9/43	5/11/43
LT C. A. Mott, RCNR	25/4/42	9/6/42	LT D. G. Van Bommel, RCNVR	12/6/44	25/7/44
LT C. F. R. Dalton, RCNVR	10/6/42	10/8/42	LT D. G. Van Bommel, RCNVR	13/8/44	28/3/45
LT W. McIsaac, RCNVR	11/8/42	11/9/42	SKPR/LT W. H. Crocker, RCNR	29/3/45	11/4/45
LT J. Evelyn, RCNR	12/9/42	25/9/42	LT W. McIsaac, RCNVR	12/4/45	31/8/45
LT L. D. Clarke, RCNVR	26/9/42	28/2/43			

STAR XVI

DISPLACEMENT:	249		CREW:	4/25
DIMENSIONS:	116' x 23' 9" x 13' 2"		BUILT:	1930, Oslo, Norway
SPEED:	10 kts			

Commanding Officers

LCDR T. H. Beament, RCNVR	31/3/41	19/1/42
LT J. M. Gracey, RCNVR	20/1/42	1/10/44
LT C. J. Metcalf, RCNVR	2/10/44	31/7/45

Suderöy V

Chartered in 1940 and commissioned on 2 June 1941, *Suderöy V* joined St. John's Local Defence Force. From June 1942 until she was paid off on 7 August 1945 she was a member of Sydney Force. After the war she resumed her occupation as a whale-catcher.

Suderöy VI

Chartered in 1940 and commissioned on March 19 1941, this whale-catcher had been the British *Southern Gem* before her sale to Norwegian owners. She served with Halifax Local Defence Force throughout the war as an auxiliary minesweeper. Paid off on 31 August 1945, she was returned to her owners.

Suderöy V.

Suderöy VI.

SUDERÖY V

DISPLACEMENT:	252	SPEED:	9 kts
DIMENSIONS:	115' 1" x 23' 9" x 13' 2"	CREW:	4/25
		BUILT:	1930 Oslo, Norway

Commanding Officers

LT R. M. Meredith, RCNR	2/6/41	11/6/42
LT M. W. Knowles, RCNVR	12/6/42	2/11/43
LT D. E. Francis, RCNVR	3/11/43	7/8/45

SUDERÖY VI

DISPLACEMENT:	254	CREW:	4/25
DIMENSIONS:	121' 9" x 24' 3" x 11' 6"	BUILT:	1929, Middlesbrough, UK
SPEED:	9 kts		

Commanding Officers

LT R. J. C. Pringle, RCNVR	19/3/41	20/8/41
LT A. M. McLarnon, RCNR	21/8/41	6/9/41
LT R. J. C. Pringle, RCNVR	7/9/41	15/3/42
LT W. Russell, RCNR	16/3/42	2/4/42
LT R. J. C. Pringle, RCNVR	3/4/42	24/4/42
LT W. Russell, RCNR	25/4/42	24/12/42
LT P. M. MacCallum, RCNVR	25/12/42	29/1/43
LT R. Stark, RCNVR	30/1/43	7/11/43
SKPR/LT W. H. Crocker, RCNR	8/11/43	24/11/43
LT J. C. Smith, RCNR	25/11/43	23/2/44
LT D. I. McGill, RCNVR	24/2/44	26/5/44
LT D. J. Van Bommel, RCNVR	27/5/44	11/6/44
LT D. I. McGill, RCNVR	12/6/44	20/12/44
LT J. S. Barrick, RCNVR	21/12/44	8/4/45
SKPR/LT W. H. Crocker, RCNR	9/4/45	26/4/45
LT J. A. MacKinnon, RCNR	27/4/45	10/5/45
LT J. S. Barrick, RCNVR	11/5/45	14/7/45
LT D. J. Van Bommel, RCNVR	15/7/45	4/8/45

Sunbeam.

Sunbeam

Formerly the Department of Transport *Hopper Barge No. 4*, she was acquired by the RCN in 1940 and converted to a fuel oil carrier. *Sunbeam* was commissioned on 11 November 1940 and served as a lighter at Halifax and St. John's, and occasionally as a transport. Paid off on 13 December 1945 and sold into commercial service, she was renamed *Birchbranch* in 1949. Her register was closed in 1968 as she had been broken up.

Venostar

She was commissioned on 17 November 1939 as a gate vessel and auxiliary minesweeper at Halifax, and later employed at Sydney. She had served in the RN as a minesweeper during the First World War. *Venosta* is said to have been paid off on 22 January 1942 and designated *C.Y.509*. Sold postwar, she was still in service under her original name in 1953, but was later known progressively as *Reyneld V, Fort Prevel* and *Michel P*. She was broken up and her register closed in 1972.

SUNBEAM

DISPLACEMENT:	589	CREW:	2/27
DIMENSIONS:	178' x 33' 6" x 12'	BUILT:	1911, Port Glasgow, NS
SPEED:	6 kts		

Commanding Officers

SKPR E. W. Hannaford, RCNR	8/5/41	27/6/43	LT J. A. Aldhouse, RCNR	/45	-
CH/SKPR E. L. Thompson, RCNR	28/6/43	/45	SKPR/LT F. J. J. Henderson, RCNR	22/5/45	-

Vencedor, 27 July 1945.

Vencedor

This rather bizarre-looking vessel was built in Britain in 1913 as the three-masted topsail schooner *Exmouth II*, tender to the Thames River training ship *Exmouth*. She was renamed after her sale in 1927 to the Lieutenant-Governor of British Columbia. Used by the RCN as a miscellaneous auxiliary on the west coast, she was sold after the war and was still in service in 1981.

VENCEDOR

DISPLACEMENT:	380
DIMENSIONS:	146' 10" x 27' x 14' 6"
SPEED:	6 kts
CREW:	3/25
BUILT:	1913, Wivenhoe, UK

VENOSTA

DISPLACMENT:	316
DIMENSIONS:	135' 3" x 23' 5" x 12' 3"
SPEED:	9 kts
CREW:	4/28
ARMAMENT:	one 12 pdr.
BUILT:	1917, Selby, UK

Venosta, 1940.

Venture II

Formerly the US yacht *Seaborn*, she had been acquired in 1939 by Northumberland Ferries Ltd. and renamed *Charles A. Dunning* just in time to be taken over for naval service and revert to her former name. On 7 December 1939 she was commissioned as HMS *Seaborn*, flagship of the Rear Admiral, 3rd Battleship Squadron, Halifax. At the end of September 1941 she became HMCS *Sambro*, depot ship at Halifax for destroyers and auxiliaries, and on 6 March 1943 was again renamed *Venture II* as depot ship for Fairmiles. When the sailing yacht *Venture* was redesignated in May 1943 as HC 190, the depot ship dropped her Roman suffix and remained plain *Venture* until paid off on 14 January 1946. Sold for commercial purposes, she still existed in 1953 under the Panamanian flag.

Viernoe

A near sister to *Venosta*, she also served with the RN from 1915 to 1919. *Viernoe* was commissioned in the RCN on 11 October 1939, and in 1941 was serving as a boom defence vessel at Sydney. She is said to have been paid off on 22 January 1942 and designated *C.Y. 512* (significance unknown). Subsequently sold for mercantile use, she was broken up and her register closed in 1954.

Whitethroat

A controlled minelayer converted from an Isles class trawler, *Whitethroat* was commissioned at Beverley, Yorkshire, on 7 December 1944. She made her passage to Canada with convoy ONS.42 in February 1945 to replace HMCS *Sankaty*. She assisted in the dismantling of harbour defences until 6 May 1946, when she was paid off to become a CNAV, and was employed in 1947 making repairs to submarine telegraph cables. In 1950 she carried out oceanographic work for the Naval Research Establishment, but on 17 April 1951 was recommissioned to provide mine and loop-laying training in the Korean emergency. She remained with Seaward Defence until 30 September 1954, when she again became a CNAV. Transferred to the west coast in March 1955, she was attached to the Pacific Naval Laboratory until sold in 1967.

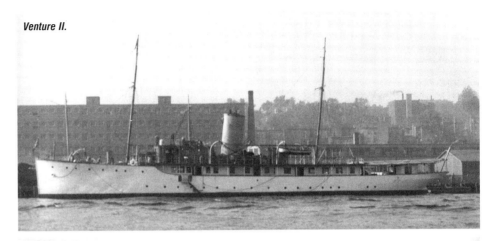

Venture II.

Viernoe, 1940.

Whitethroat, 10 April 1963.

VENTURE II	
DISPLACEMENT:	510
DIMENSIONS:	182' 3" x 27' 2" x 10' 3"
SPEED:	12 kts
BUILT:	1925, Leith, Scotland

VIERNOE	
DISPLACEMENT:	273
DIMENSIONS:	130' 4" x 22' x 12' 6"
SPEED:	9 kts
CREW:	4/28
ARMAMENT:	one 12 pdr.
BUILT:	1914, Selby, UK

WHITETHROAT			
DISPLACEMENT:	580	ARMAMENT:	one 20-mm
DIMENSIONS:	164' x 27' 6" x 12' 6"	BUILT:	1944 Beverley, UK
SPEED:	12 kts		

Commanding Officers

LCDR B. G. Jemmett, RCNVR	7/12/44	26/6/45	LCDR R. S. Hurst, RCN	17/4/51	26/8/51
SKPR/LT I. E. Abbott, RCNR	27/6/45	6/5/46	LCDR W. E. Williams, RCN	27/8/51	-

The Fishermen's Reserve

Santa Maria.

The Fishermen's Reserve was formed in 1938 because of the growing likelihood of war. By October 1941 it comprised seventeen ships and, until the advent of the first corvettes, was the only naval force available on the west coast. The ships were mostly fishing craft of various kinds, many of them seiners like *Santa Maria*. In

December 1941 five more ships joined, and shortly thereafter twenty more, seized from their Japanese-Canadian owners following Pearl Harbor.

The force performed a valuable inshore patrol service, as their skippers were thoroughly familiar with the intricacies of the British Columbia coastline.

It remained, however, very much an ad hoc organization until August 1942 when officialdom took a hand, and formal training of its personnel was begun at Esquimalt in an establishment called Givenchy II. Personnel had increased rapidly since Pearl Harbor, and it was envisaged that they might be better used as

crews for landing craft in Combined Operations exercises with the army.

The danger of Japanese attack on the west coast failed to materialize, however, and through 1943 and 1944 Fishermen's Reserve personnel were discharged or siphoned off into the RCNVR. By the end of 1944 the force had ceased to

exist, the only five of its ships still in service manned by the RCNVR at Prince Rupert.

There no longer seems to be an official list of the ships that composed the Fishermen's Reserve, but the following are probably most of the likely candidates.

Allaverdy	*Combat*	*Johanna*	*Moresby II*	*Surf*
BC Lady	*Comber*	*Kuitan*	*Nenamook*	*Takla*
Barkley Sound	*Crest*	*Leelo*	*Ripple II*	*Talapus*
Billow	*Dalehurst*	*Loyal I*	*San Tomas*	*Tordo*
Bluenose	*Departure Bay*	*Loyal II*	*Santa Maria*	*Valdes*
Camenita	*Early Field*	*Maraudor*	*Seiner*	*Vanisle*
Canfisco	*Ehkoli*	*Margaret I*	*Signal*	*West Coast*
Cape Beale	*Fifer*	*Meander*	*Smith Sound*	*Western Maid*
Cancolim	*Flores*	*Merry Chase*	*Spray*	
Capella	*Foam*	*Mitchell Bay*	*Springtime V*	
Charmiss Bay	*Howe Sound I*	*Moolock*	*Stanpoint*	

PART III 1945–1990

INTRODUCTION

REVERTING WITH ASTONISHING SPEED from a wartime to a peacetime footing, the RCN had fewer ships in commission at the end of 1946 than at the outbreak of the war: an aircraft carrier, two cruisers, three destroyers, a frigate, a minesweeper and a former U-boat. These were, of course wholly inadequate as a training force, and in succeeding years many ships—especially frigates—were brought out of retirement and given major refits. Among them were three diesel Bangors, three Algerines and two motor minesweepers.

The outbreak of the Korean War in 1950 accelerated this process, although only two of eighteen Bangors recovered in this emergency were recommissioned. Eight of our eleven destroyers, once again in commission, served with distinction in the Korean theatre. The aircraft carrier *Warrior* was replaced in 1948 by *Magnificent* and she by *Bonaventure* in 1957.

Twenty-one frigates were extensively rebuilt as ocean escorts between 1953 and 1958, and in 1955 *St. Laurent*, the first of twenty destroyer escorts of novel design, was commissioned. The building programs of 1950 and 1951 produced the only other new ships, the twenty Bay class coastal minesweepers. Six of these were transferred to the French Navy in 1954 but replaced by six of new construction. The latter, all that remained of the class by 1964, were to serve on the west coast as training ships until paid off, 1996-98.

Two former US submarines were acquired, one in 1961 and the other in 1968. These were disposed of and replaced by three submarines built in Britain and commissioned between 1965 and 1967. These then-modern craft provided our A/S ships with "tame" adversaries against whom to test their skills.

All but two of the frigates had been discarded by 1967, and in 1970 the last of the older destroyers was sold for scrap, along with *Bonaventure*. The Navy's duties, apart from training officer cadets and new-entry ratings, now consisted of upholding Canada's maritime commitment to NATO, enforcing fishery regulations, and generally "showing the flag", which after 1965 was no longer the White Ensign.

The seven St. Laurent class DDEs were rebuilt between 1962 and 1966 to carry helicopters, but *St. Laurent* herself was retired in 1974, along with three of the Restigouche class. The more modern four ships of the Iroquois class entered service in 1972-73, and a contract for six new frigates, later increased to twelve, was awarded in 1983.

Bonaventure, 1968.

Aircraft Carriers

Active consideration of an expanded role for Canada in the Pacific war began as early as May 1944, and it was agreed that larger ships would be required than any serving in the RCN at that time. The Canadian Naval Staff favoured returning the escort aircraft carriers *Nabob* and *Puncher*, then on loan from the Royal Navy, and taking over light fleet carriers in their place.

Two of these, *Warrior* and *Magnificent*, were offered on loan (with option to purchase) in January 1945, and arrangements were concluded in May, but neither ship had been completed by VJ Day. *Warrior* was finally commissioned at Belfast on 24 January 1946, arriving at Halifax on 31 March with the Seafires and Fireflies of 803 and 825 Squadrons. Unsuited for an eastern

Canadian winter, she was transferred to Esquimalt in November.

Reductions in defence spending soon made it evident that the RCN would be able to afford only one carrier, and it was decided to exchange *Warrior* for the slightly larger *Magnificent*. *Warrior* accordingly returned in February 1947 to the east coast, where she was engaged most of the year in sea training and later in preparations for her return to the RN. In February 1948 she arrived at Belfast, where she transferred stores to *Magnificent*, and was paid off on 23 March. She served in the RN until 1958, when she was sold to Argentina and renamed *Independencia*.

Magnificent, a near sister to *Warrior*, had been launched at Belfast six months after her, in

November 1944. She was commissioned on 21 March 1948, and spent the ensuing nine years in an unceasing round of training cruises and exercises, visiting such far-flung ports as Oslo, Havana, Lisbon, and San Francisco, and taking part in large-scale NATO manoeuvres such as "Mainbrace" and "Mariner" in 1952 and 1953. On 29 December 1956 she left Halifax for Port Said, carrying a deck load of 233 vehicles as well as 406 army personnel and stores—Canada's contribution to the UN Emergency Force in the Middle East. "Maggie" sailed from Halifax for the last time on 10 April 1957, to be paid off at Plymouth on 14 June. After being laid up for eight years there she arrived at Faslane, Scotland in July 1965 for breaking up. When the Suez crisis erupt-

ed, *Magnificent* had just finished landing stores for her successor, a more modern carrier whose construction had been suspended in 1946. The successor's name was to have been HMS *Powerful*, but the RCN decided to name her *Bonaventure* after the bird sanctuary in the Gulf of St. Lawrence. Work on this ship had stopped three months after her launching in February 1945, with the result that when construction recommenced in 1952, improvements could be built into her. The most notable of these was the angled flight deck, which provided a longer landing run without sacrificing forward parking space, and permitted the removal of the unpopular crash barrier. Also noteworthy were a steam catapult and a mirror landing sight,

the latter going far toward eliminating human error in landing.

"Bonnie" was commissioned at Belfast on 17 January 1957, and arrived at Halifax on 26 June, carrying on deck an experimental hydrofoil craft that was to serve in the development of HMCS *Bras d'Or*. Unlike her predecessors, *Bonaventure* had Banshee jet fighters and Tracker A/S aircraft as her complement. Like them, she enjoyed a busy career of flying training and participation in A/S and tactical exercises with ships of other NATO nations. What was expected to be her mid-life refit, carried out from 1966 to 1967, took sixteen months and cost over $11 million. She was paid off on 3 July 1970 and sold for scrap.

Bonaventure

BUILDER:	Harland & Wolff Ltd., Belfast, Ireland		DISPLACEMENT:	16,000
LAID DOWN:	27/11/43		DIMENSIONS:	704' x 80' x 25'
LAUNCHED:	27/2/45		SPEED:	24 kts
COMMISSIONED:	17/1/57		ARMAMENT:	eight 3-inch guns (4 x II) About 30 aircraft carried
PAID OFF:	3/7/70		REMARKS:	Ex-HMS *Powerful*.

Commanding Officers

CAPT H. V. W. Groos, RCN	17/1/57	14/1/58	CAPT H. A. Porter, RCN	2/4/65	31/7/66
CAPT W. M. Landymore, OBE, RCN	15/1/58	11/9/59	CDR A. T. Bice, RCN	1/8/66	20/11/66
CAPT J. C. O'Brien, RCN	12/9/59	29/8/61	CAPT R. H. Falls, RCN	21/11/66	8/4/69
CAPT F. C. Frewer, RCN	30/8/61	6/8/63	CAPT J. M. Cutts	9/4/69	8/1/70
CAPT R. W. Timbrell, DSC, RCN	7/8/63	1/4/65	CDR H. W. Vondette	9/1/70	3/7/70

Magnificent.

Magnificent

BUILDER:	Harland & Wolff Ltd., Belfast, Ireland
LAID DOWN:	29/7/43
LAUNCHED:	16/11/44
COMMISSIONED:	21/3/48
PAID OFF:	14/6/5/
DISPLACEMENT:	15,700
DIMENSIONS:	698' x 80' x 25'
SPEED:	24 kts
ARMAMENT:	six 40-mm (3 x II), eighteen 40-mm
	About 30 aircraft carried
REMARKS:	Ex-HMS *Magnificent*.

Commanding Officers

COM H. G. DeWolf, CBE, DS, DSC, RCN	7/4/48	29/8/48
COM G. R. Miles, OBE, RCN	30/8/48	28/6/49
CDR A. G. Boulton, DSC, RCN	29/6/49	6/9/49
COM K. F. Adams, RCN	7/9/49	28/10/51
CAPT K. L. Dyer, DSC, RCN	29/10/51	10/3/53
COM H. S. Rayner, DSC & Bar, RCN	11/3/53	29/1/55
CAPT A. H. G. Storrs, DSC & Bar, RCN	30/1/55	2/8/56
CAPT A. B. F. Fraser-Harris, DSC & Bar, RCN	3/8/56	14/6/57

Warrior

BUILDER:	Harland & Wolff Ltd., Belfast, Ireland
LAID DOWN:	12/12/42
LAUNCHED:	20/5/44
COMMISSIONED:	24/1/46
PAID OFF:	23/3/48
DISPLACEMENT:	13,350
DIMENSIONS:	693'3" x 80'4" x 23'
SPEED:	24 kts
ARMAMENT:	twenty-four 2pdr. (6xIV), nineteen 40-mm
	About 30 aircraft carried
REMARKS:	Ex-HMS *Warrior*.

Commanding Officers

CAPT F. L. Houghton, CBE, RCN	24/1/46	17/1/47
COM H. G. DeWolf, CBE, DSO, DSC, RCN	18/1/47	23/3/48

Warrior, 1945.

Destroyers

TRIBAL CLASS

PARTICULARS OF CLASS:

DISPLACEMENT:	2,200
DIMENSIONS:	355' 6" x 37' 6" x 11' 2"
SPEED:	32 kts
CREW:	14/245
ARMAMENT:	six 4.7-inch (3 x II), two 4-inch (1 x II), four 2 pdrs. (1 x IV), six 20-mm, four 21-inch TT (1 x IV)
REVISED:	four 4-inch (2 x II), two 3-inch (1 x II), four 40-mm, four 21-inch TT (1 x IV), two Squid

Athabaskan (2nd)

The last of her class to be completed, "Athabee" was commissioned at Halifax on 20 January 1948, and sailed in mid May for the west coast, where she trained new entries and officer cadets until the outbreak of the Korean War. She sailed from Esquimalt on 5 July 1950 for the first of three tours of duty in Korean waters, returning 11 December 1953 from the last of them. In October 1954 she emerged from an extensive conversion classed as a destroyer escort, and resumed her training role until January 1959, when she left for the east coast to become part of a homogenous Tribal class squadron. After five more years of

Athabaskan (2nd), 7 April 1961.

training cruises and NATO exercises she was placed in reserve at Halifax and on 21 April 1966 paid off for disposal. She was broken up at La Spezia, Italy in 1970.

ATHABASKAN (2nd)

BUILDER:	Halifax Shipyards Ltd., Halifax, NS	COMMISSIONED:	20/1/48
LAID DOWN:	15/5/43	PAID OFF:	21/4/66
LAUNCHED:	4/5/46		

Commanding Officers

CDR J. S. Davis, RCN	20/1/48	28/10/48	LCDR C. E. Richardson, RCN	25/10/54	15/1/56
LCDR G. H. Davidson, RCN	29/10/48	25/11/48	CDR P. S. Booth, RCN	16/1/56	5/9/57
CDR M. A Medland, RCN	26/11/48	14/9/49	CDR D. S. Boyle, RCN	6/9/57	1/3/59
LCDR G. A. Powell, RCN	15/9/49	14/1/50	CDR J. H. G. Bovey, DSC, RCN	2/3/59	10/8/59
LCDR T. S. R. Peacocke, RCN	15/1/50	12/3/50	CDR D. R. Saxon, DSC, RCN	11/8/59	24/5/61
CDR R. P. Welland, DSC, RCN	13/3/50	2/7/51	CAPT G. C. Edwards, RCN	25/5/61	15/3/62
CDR D. G. King, RCN	3/7/51	23/7/52	CDR A. E. Fox, RCN	16/3/62	3/1/63
LCDR H. Shorten, RCN	24/7/52	24/9/52	LCDR S. Dee, RCN	4/1/63	19/7/64
CDR J. C. Reed, DSC, RCN	25/9/52	20/12/53	CDR J. Y. Clarke, RCN	12/8/64	21/4/66
LCDR H. Shorten, RCN	21/12/53	15/2/54			

Cayuga

Commissioned at Halifax on 20 October 1947, she sailed on 4 February 1948 for Esquimalt, her assigned base. She left there 5 July 1950 as Senior Officer's ship of the first three Canadian destroyers to serve in Canadian waters. She carried out three tours of duty there, the last in 1954 after the armistice. In 1952, between the second and third tours, she was rebuilt as a destroyer escort. For four years after her return from Korea in mid December 1954, *Cayuga* carried out training on the west coast, transferring to the east coast in January 1959 for five more years in the same capacity. Paid off at Halifax on 27 February 1964, she was broken up at Faslane, Scotland the following year.

Cayuga.

CAYUGA

BUILDER:	Halifax Shipyards Ltd., Halifax, NS	COMMISSIONED:	20/10/47
LAID DOWN:	7/10/43	PAID OFF:	27/2/64
LAUNCHED:	28/7/45		

Commanding Officers

CDR O. C. S. Robertson, GM, RCN	20/10/47	1/1/49	LCDR G. A. Hoyte, RCN		17/4/58	23/6/58
CDR M. A. Medland, RCN	15/9/49	4/7/50	CDR M. H. E. Page, RCN		24/6/58	1/3/59
CAPT J. V. Brock, DSO, DSC, RCN	5/7/50	24/5/51	CDR E. Petley-Jones, RCN		2/3/59	13/12/59
CDR J. Plomer, OBE, DSC, RCN	25/5/51	18/6/52	LCDR F. J. Dunbar, RCN		14/12/59	28/8/60
LT F. Little, RCN	18/6/52	14/7/52	CDR A. H. McDonald, RCN		29/8/60	22/8/61
LCDR W. P. Hayes, RCN	23/21/53	31/12/54	CDR D. C. Rutherford, RCN		23/8/61	1/2/62
CDR G. H. Davidson, RCN	1/1/55	16/10/56	CDR W. M. Beckett, RCN		2/2/62	27/2/64
CDR P. C. Benson, RCN	17/10/56	16/4/58				

Micmac.

MICMAC

BUILDER:	Halifax Shipyards Ltd., Halifax, NS	COMMISSIONED:	12/9/45
LAID DOWN:	20/5/42	PAID OFF:	31/3/64
LAUNCHED:	18/9/43		

Commanding Officers

LCDR R. L. Hennessy, DSC, RCN	12/9/45	27/3/47	CDR L. B. Jenson, RCN	9/7/56	4/8/57
LCDR J. C. Littler, RCN	28/3/47	5/9/47	CDR N. Cogdon, RCN	5/8/57	13/6/58
LCDR F. C. Frewer, RCN	16/11/49	30/11/51	CDR A. B. German, RCN	10/3/59	15/12/59
CDR G. M. Wadds, RCN	14/8/53	26/8/54	CDR G. R. Smith, RCN	16/12/59	9/2/61
CDR J. C. Smyth, RCN	27/8/54	1/9/55	CDR W. J. Stuart, RCN	10/2/61	14/8/62
CDR E. T. G. Madgwick, DSC, RCN	2/9/55	8/7/56	LCDR J. M. Cutts, RCN	15/8/62	31/3/64

Micmac

Micmac was commissioned at Halifax on 12 September 1945. Alone of her class, she never fired a shot in anger but spent her entire career as a training ship. On 16 July 1947 she collided in fog with SS *Yarmouth County* off Halifax, suffering very extensive damage to her bows. While under repair she was partially converted to a destroyer escort, returning to her duties early in 1950. Her conversion was completed during 1952 and she was recommissioned on 14 August 1953. At the end of 1963, after ten further strenuous years of training, NATO exercises, and "showing the flag," she was declared surplus, and on 31 March 1964 paid off at Halifax. She was broken up at Faslane, Scotland in 1965.

Nootka (2nd)

Commissioned on 7 August 1946 at Halifax, *Nootka* served as a training ship on the east coast and in the Caribbean until her conversion to a destroyer escort in 1949 and 1950. Earmarked for Korean duty, she transited the Panama Canal in December 1950 for the first of two tours of duty in that theatre of war. Returning to Halifax via the Mediterranean at the end of 1952, she became the second RCN ship to circumnavigate the globe. During 1953 and 1954 she underwent further conversion and modernization, afterward resuming her original training duties. In 1963, with *Haida*, she toured the Great Lakes in the course of a summer's cruising. She was paid off at Halifax on 6 February 1964 and broken up at Faslane, Scotland the following year.

Nootka (2nd), 21 May 1960.

NOOTKA (2nd)

BUILDER:	Halifax Shipyards Ltd., Halifax, NS	LAID DOWN:	20/05/42	COMMISSIONED:	7/8/46
		LAUNCHED:	26/4/44	PAID OFF:	6/2/64

Commanding Officers

CDR H. S. Rayner, DSC, RCN	7/8/46	17/6/47	LCDR E. M. Chadwick, RCN	15/12/54	4/11/56
LCDR M. G. Stirling, RCN	18/6/47	5/9/47	CDR T. S. R. Peacock, RCN	5/11/56	31/7/57
CAPT H. F. Pullen, OBE, RCN	6/9/47	16/8/48	LCDR C. E. Coles, RCN	1/8/57	16/8/57
CDR A. H. G. Storrs, DSC & Bar, RCN	17/8/48	15/8/49	CDR I. A. McPhee, RCN	17/8/57	6/1/59
CDR A. B. F. Fraser-Harris, DSC & Bar, RCN	29/8/50	16/9/51	CDR R. A. Creery, RCN	7/1/59	9/9/61
LCDR C. E. Richardson, RCN	17/9/51	14/10/51	CDR S. M. King, RCN	10/9/61	8/11/62
LT F. P. R. Saunders, RCN	15/10/51	28/10/51	CDR V. J. Murphy, RCN	9/11/62	9/4/63
CDR R. M. Steele, DSC, RCN	29/10/51	16/1/53	CDR D. S. Bethune, RCN	10/4/63	6/2/64

C CLASS

PARTICULARS OF CLASS:	
DISPLACEMENT:	1,730
DIMENSIONS:	362' 9" x 35' 8" x 11' 6"
SPEED:	31 kts
CREW:	14/230
ARMAMENT:	four 4.5-inch, four 40-mm, four 20-mm, four 21-inch TT (1 x IV)
As revised:	
Crescent	two 4-inch (1 x II), two 3-inch (1 x II), two 40-mm, 2 Limbos
Crusader	three 4.5-inch, six 40-mm, four 21-inch TT (1 x IV)

Crescent and Crusader

In January 1945, after a year's discussion, the British Admiralty agreed to lend the RCN a flotilla of C class destroyers for use against the Japanese. The Pacific war ended, however, before any of the eight ships had been completed, and only two were transferred. The previous ships to bear their names, *Crescent* and *Crusader*, had been lost during the war as HMCS *Fraser* and *Ottawa*; this time they retained their names although the transfer was made permanent in 1951.

Crescent and *Crusader* were virtually identical to *Algonquin* and *Sioux*, differing principally in having only one set of torpedo tubes and in being armed with 4.5-inch guns instead of 4.7-inch. Both ships were commissioned on the Clyde in 1945, *Crescent* on 10 September and *Crusader* on 15 November.

Crescent arrived at Esquimalt in November 1945 and *Crusader* in January 1946, both having made the journey via the Azores and the West Indies. *Crusader* was almost immediately paid off into reserve, a state in which she was to spend several years, while *Crescent* carried out training duties until taken in hand for a major conversion. She emerged in 1956 as a "fast A/S frigate," following an RN pattern which entailed stripping her to deck level, extending the fo'c's'le right aft, erecting new superstructure, and fitting completely new armament. She was now a near sister to *Algonquin*, which had undergone similar transformation earlier.

While her sister was being rebuilt, *Crusader* carried out two tours of duty in the Korean theatre, the first between June 1952 and June 1953, the second after the armistice, from November 1953 to August 1954. Reverting then to her former training role, she was paid off on 15 January 1960 at Halifax. She had earlier served as a test vehicle for a prototype VDS (variable depth sonar) outfit, a more permanent installation of which was made in *Crescent* in 1960.

Crusader was sold for scrapping in 1963, but *Crescent* remained longer in service, being paid off at Esquimalt on 1 April 1970. She left Victoria with *Algonquin* on 21 April 1971 for Taiwan to be broken up.

***Crusader*, December 1945.**

Crescent, 16 January 1958, showing the transfiguration completed in 1956.

CRESCENT					
BUILDER:	John Brown & Co. Ltd., Glasgow, Scotland		COMMISSIONED:	10/9/45	
LAID DOWN:	16/9/43		PAID OFF:	1/4/70	
LAUNCHED:	20/7/44		Ex-HMS *Crescent*		

Commanding Officers

LCDR C. P. Nixon, DSC, RCN	10/9/45	17/12/46	CAPT M. G. Stirling, RCN	11/3/57	17/5/57
LCDR J. C. O'Brien, RCN	18/12/46	4/1/48	LCDR L. I. Jones, RCN	18/5/57	15/8/57
LCDR J. A. Charles, RCN	5/1/48	15/11/48	CAPT M. G. Stirling, RCN	16/8/57	20/6/58
LCDR D. W. Groos, DSC, RCN	16/11/48	1/12/49	CAPT J. C. Pratt, RCN	21/6/58	18/2/59
LCDR G. H. Hayes, DSC, RCN	26/9/50	24/9/51	CDR J. R. Coulter, RCN	19/2/59	14/9/59
LT J. K. H. Mason, MBE, RCN	25/9/51	12/10/51	CAPT R. W. Murdock, RCN	15/9/59	11/6/61
CDR J. C. Littler, RCN	13/10/51	14/9/52	CDR P. H. Cayley, RCN	12/6/61	11/7/62
LCDR J. R. Coulter, RCN	15/9/52	15/2/53	CAPT A. D. McPhee, RCN	12/7/62	11/4/63
LCDR D. L. Davies, RCN	16/2/53	25/2/53	CDR V. J. Murphy, RCN	12/4/63	22/10/64
CAPT P. D. Taylor, DSC, RCN	31/10/55	10/3/57	CDR H. C. LaRose, RCN	23/10/64	12/8/66

CRUSADER				
BUILDER:	John Brown & Co. Ltd., Glasgow, Scotland	LAUNCHED:	5/10/44	
		COMMISSIONED:	15/11/45	
		PAID OFF:	15/1/60	
LAID DOWN:	15/11/43	Ex-HMS *Crusader*		

Commanding Officers

A/LCDR M. G. Stirling, RCN	15/11/45	1/2/46
CDR H. V. W. Groos, RCN	2/4/51	2/4/52
LCDR J. H. G. Bovey, RCN	3/4/52	7/7/53
LCDR J. Husher, RCN	8/7/53	20/7/53
LCDR H. H. Smith, RCN	21/7/53	28/8/53
LCDR W. H. Willson, DSC, RCN	29/8/53	12/9/54
LCDR R. H. Leir, RCN	13/9/54	17/3/55
LCDR J. Butterfield, RCN	18/3/55	31/5/55
CDR L. B. Jenson, RCN	1/6/55	5/7/56
CDR N. S. C. Dickenson, RCN	6/7/56	14/7/57
CDR F. W. H. Bradley, RCN	15/7/57	14/12/58
LCDR A. J. Tanner, RCN	15/12/58	11/8/59
LCDR C. G. Pratt, RCN	12/8/59	15/1/60

Destroyer Escorts

ST. LAURENT CLASS

PARTICULARS OF CLASS:

DISPLACEMENT:	2,263
DIMENSIONS:	366' x 42' x 13' 2"
SPEED:	28 kts
CREW:	12/237
ARMAMENT:	four 3-inch50 (2 x II), 2 Limbo, homing torpedoes

Assiniboine, Ottawa, Skeena & *St. Laurent* two 40-mm

As DDHs:	two 3-inch50 (1 x II), 1 Limbo, homing torpedoes, 1 Sea King helicopter

HMCS *St. Laurent*, launched in 1951, was the first A/S vessel designed and built in Canada. She and her six sisters, classed as destroyer escorts (DDEs) were originally armed with two twin 3-inch50 guns and two Limbo A/S mortar mounts, the latter located in a well beneath the quarterdeck. From 1962 to 1966 all seven were extensively rebuilt as destroyer helicopter escorts (DDHs), emerging with a hangar and flight deck. Space for the hangar was made by twinning the original single stack, while the flight deck necessitated the removal of one gun and one Limbo mount. The stern was rebuilt to accommodate equipment for handling variable depth sonar, a Canadian development that overcomes the problem of water layers at varying depths, which confuse fixed sonar systems.

DELEX

With a view to prolonging the lives of the remaining sixteen steam-powered destroyers, the Destroyer Life Extension Project (DELEX) was introduced in December 1979. The procedure, which was carried out mainly by civilian shipyards, took about ten months per ship. In this way it was hoped that, by 1987, twelve years would have been added to the life expectancy of the Nipigon class and eight years to that of the others.

The procedure entailed carrying out structural and mechanical repairs necessary to ensure safe operation at sea, especially in the case of the six oldest ships, and providing equipment necessary to maintain ASW capability in the ten newest. Major tasks under this heading included:

Replacement of three radar systems

Modernization of fire control systems

Replacement of electronic warfare systems

Replacement of command, control and navigational systems

Replacement of sonar systems

Replacement of message handling systems.

A superb view of a DDE in its original guise: *St. Laurent* in 1955, while still in her builder's hands.

ST. LAURENT (2nd)

BUILDER:	Canadian Vickers Ltd., Montreal, QC	COMMISSIONED AFTER CONVERSIONS	
LAID DOWN:	24/11/50	TO DDH:	4/10/63
LAUNCHED:	30/11/51	PAID OFF:	14/6/74
COMMISSIONED:	29/10/55		

Commanding Officers

CDR R. W. Timbrell, DSC, RCN	29/10/55	23/1/57
CAPT A. G. Boulton, DSC, RCN	23/1/57	15/3/58
CAPT H. L. Quinn, DSC, RCN	15/3/58	9/1/59
LCDR E. Petley-Jones, RCN	9/1/59	2/3/59
CDR M. H. E. Page, RCN	2/3/59	29/6/60
CDR J. B. Fotheringham, RCN	29/6/60	/10/62
CDR D. D. Lee, RCN	4/10/63	15/9/65
CDR W. J. Walton, RCN	15/9/65	2/2/67
LCDR B. Hayes, RCN	2/2/67	25/8/67
CDR M. Barrow, RCN	25/8/67	11/8/69
CDR S. W. Riddell	11/8/69	/7/71
CDR G. G. Freill	/7/71	/11/72
LCDR R. L. Burnip	/11/72	14/6/74

St. Laurent (2nd)

Name ship of her trend-setting class of "Cadillacs," *St. Laurent* was built by Canadian Vickers Ltd., Montreal, and commissioned on 29 October 1955. In February 1956 she proceeded to the U.S. Trials Centre at Key West, Florida, for three months' evaluation, after which she visited Washington and then the U.K., in the course of the latter excursion escorting HMY *Britannia* on a state visit to Sweden. On 2 February, 1960, *St Laurent*, by then stationed on the west coast, departed Esquimalt with two of her sisters on a 2 1/2-month Pacific cruise, visiting Long Beach, Pearl Harbour, Yokosuka, Okinawa and Hong Kong. She was test-fitted with VDS prior to being converted to a DDH at Burrard Dry Dock, Vancouver. Recommissioned on 4 October 1963, she returned to the east coast. Paid off on 14 June 1974, the now ageing ship remained in Halifax as a source of spare parts for her sisters. On 1 January 1980, she left under tow for Brownsville, Texas, to be broken up, but on the 12th foundered in a gale off Cape Hatteras.

Assiniboine (2nd), 13 December 1967.

ASSINIBOINE (2nd)						
BUILDER:	Marine Industries Ltd., Sorel, QC	COMMISSIONED	16/8/56		FOR DELEX:	1979
LAID DOWN:	19/5/52	COMMISSIONED AFTER			PAID OFF:	14/12/00
LAUNCHED:	12/2/54	CONVERSION TO DDH:	28/6/63			

Commanding Officers

CDR E. P Earnshaw, RCN	16/8/56	23/5/58	CDR G. G. Freill	20/11/72	22/12/72
CDR J. R. Coulter, RCN	24/5/58	19/2/59	LCDR R. Thomas	22/12/72	14/4/73
CAPT J. C. Pratt, RCN	19/2/59	17/8/60	CDR R. Cornell	14/4/73	20/5/74
CAPT J. A. Charles, RCN	17/8/60	18/8/61	LCDR R. Thomas	20/5/74	10/6/74
CDR V. Browne, RCN	18/8/61	30/4/62	CDR M. Taylor	10/6/74	16/7/75
CDR E. A. Wiggs, RCN	30/4/62	22/6/62	CDR E. K. Kelly	16/7/75	27/6/77
CDR W. S. Blandy, RCN	28/6/62	15/1/66	CDR M. Duncan	27/6/77	31/7/79
CDR T. L. Hebbert, RCN	15/1/66	15/7/67	CDR G. Braithwaite	31/7/79	10/8/81
CDR G. L. Edwards, RCN	15/7/67	6/7/70	CDR R. Moore	10/8/81	4/7/83
LCDR E. Cullwick	6/7/70	18/8/70	CDR W. G. Lund	4/7/83	1/6/84
CDR L. J. Cavan	18/8/70	10/1/72	CDR R. M. Bernard	16/6/84	1/8/85
LCDR H. Kieran	10/1/72	17/7/72	CDR B. D. Neal	1/8/85	11/6/87
CDR T. S. Hayward	17/7/72	20/11/72	CDR D. G. McNeil	11/6/87	2/1/89

Assiniboine (2nd)

Assiniboine was the first ship delivered post-war to the RCN by Marine Industries Ltd., Sorel, and was commissioned there on 16 August 1956. In January 1959, after two years' service on the east coast, she was transferred west, and that July had the honour of carrying Queen Elizabeth and Prince Philip from Vancouver to Nanaimo. In June 1962 she began her conversion to a helicopter-carrying destroyer (DDH), the first of her class to undergo the procedure, which was largely carried out by the Victoria Machinery Depot. Recommissioned on 28 June 1963, she returned to Halifax. In January 1975, *Assiniboine* took off the crew of the freighter *Barma*, which was shipping water 185 miles off Boston. Between April and November 1979, she completed her Destroyer Life Extension (DELEX) program at Canadian Vickers Ltd., Montreal. While acting as escort for the Tall Ships race from Bermuda to Halifax in the summer of 1984, *Assiniboine* took a leading role in the search for survivors of the lost British sailing vessel *Marques*, but sadly only one was found. After thirty-two years' service, and with more than 700,000 nautical miles under her keel, she was paid off on 14 December, 1988, afterward serving as a floating classroom for fleet technicians at Halifax until January 1995, when she was turned over to Crown Assets for disposal.

Fraser (2nd), 10 September 1969.

Fraser (2nd)

Laid down by Burrard Dry Dock Co. Ltd., Vancouver and completed by Yarrows Ltd., Esquimalt, *Fraser* was commissioned on 28 June 1957, and served on the west coast until proceeding to Canadian Vickers Ltd., Montreal, where on 2 July 1965 she began her conversion to DDH configuration. She was recommissioned on 22 October 1966, and was thereafter based at Halifax. She demonstrated the Canadian-designed Beartrap helicopter haul-down system at Washington, D.C., in October 1967. *Fraser* underwent her DELEX refit at Canadian Vickers Ltd., between 19 October 1981 and 28 May 1982, and was thereafter something of a test vehicle. She was also the first RCN ship to be fitted (1986) with an experimental towed array sonar system (ETASS), and was made the test bed for the NIXIE torpedo decoy system and later a tactical aircraft beacon (TACAN). In 1988 she was equipped to operate the HELTAS helicopter, equipped for a passive acoustic role. *Fraser* was among the ships enforcing UN sanctions against Haiti between October 1993 and March 1994. Paid off on 5 October 1994, and by then the sole survivor of her class, she replaced *Assiniboine* in her classroom role until 18 December 1997, when she arrived at Bridgewater, N.S., to become a floating museum.

FRASER (2nd)

BUILDER:	Burrard Dry Dock Co. Ltd., Vancouver, BC		COMMISSIONED AFTER CONVERSION		
LAID DOWN:	11/12/51		TO DDH	22/10/66	
LAUNCHED:	19/2/53		FOR DELEX:	1981	
COMMISSIONED:	28/6/57		PAID OFF:	5/10/94	

Commanding Officers

CDR R. Phillips, RCN	28/6/57	3/1/59	CDR H. R. Waddell	12/8/77	18/12/78
CDR D. L. MacKnight, RCN	3/1/59	4/1/61	CDR J. B. Elson	18/12/78	26/1/81
CDR D. J. Sheppard, RCN	4/1/61	6/9/62	CDR J. Nethercott	26/1/81	1/5/82
CAPT G. H. Hayes, RCN	6/9/62	3/10/62	CDR W. B. Hodgkin	1/5/82	12/12/83
CDR R. C. Thurber, RCN	3/10/62	5/8/64	CDR V. U. Auns	12/12/83	16/8/85
CDR R. Carle, RCN	5/8/64	2/7/65	CDR B. M. Power	16/8/85	4/7/88
CDR J. F. Watson, RCN	22/10/66	4/7/68	CDR I. G. Parker	4/7/88	19/7/90
CDR F. W. Crickard, RCN	4/7/68	17/11/69	CDR J. A. Y. Plante	19/7/90	19/12/90
CDR R. G. Guy	17/11/69	30/6/71	CDR H. W. McEwen	19/12/90	10/5/91
CDR C. M. Thomas	30/6/71	12/4/73	CDR E. P. Webster	10/5/91	23/7/93
CDR L. I. MacDonald	11/3/74	15/8/76	CDR H. R. Smith	23/7/93	24/10/94
CDR P. W. Cairns	15/8/76	12/8/77			

Margaree (2nd)

A product of Halifax Shipyards Ltd., *Margaree* was commissioned on 5 October, 1957 for service on the west coast, and began her conversion to a DDH at Victoria Machinery Depot on 25 September, 1964. Recommissioned on 15 October 1965, she returned to Halifax. On 1 April 1979, some 200 nautical miles south of Halifax, using gunfire she sank the bow section of the tanker *Kurdistan*, which had been towed there for that purpose after breaking in half on 15 March south of Cabot Strait. *Margaree* commenced her DELEX refit at Canadian Vickers Ltd., Montreal, on 5 May, 1980, being towed to HMC Dockyard, Halifax when it appeared she might become ice-bound before its completion the following year. In later years she was several times Canada's representative in Standing Naval Force Atlantic (SNFL). In August 1991 *Margaree* took part in a re-enactment of the signing of the Atlantic Charter at Argentia, Nfld. Paid off on 2 May 1992, she left Halifax in tow for India on 13 March 1994, to be broken up.

Margaree (2nd), 10 September 1969, in a photo graphically portraying the changed appearance of the class after conversion to DDHs. They were originally near-sisters to the Restigouche class.

MARGAREE (2nd)

BUILDER:	Halifax Shipyards Ltd., Halifax, NS			
LAID DOWN:	12/9/51			
LAUNCHED:	29/3/56			
COMMISSIONED:	5/10/57			

COMMISSIONED AFTER CONVERSION TO DDH: 15/10/65
FOR DELEX: 1980
PAID OFF: 2/5/92

Commanding Officers

CDR J. E. Korning, RCN	5/10/57	10/11/59	CDR R. J. Lancashire	18/12/75	10/8/77
CDR E. V. P. Sunderland, RCN	10/11/59	17/8/60	CDR P. W. Cairns	10/8/77	13/7/78
CDR J. H. MacLean, RCN	17/8/60	22/5/62	CDR R. A. Rutherford	13/7/78	12/8/80
CDR J. L. Panabaker, RCN	22/5/62	26/9/64	CDR P. J. Stow	12/8/80	29/5/82
CDR R. C. MacLean, RCN	15/10/65	3/7/67	CDR R. W. Allen	29/5/82	1/4/84
CDR P. M. Birch-Jones, RCN	4/7/67	23/8/68	CDR J. M Ewan	1/4/84	1/1/86
CDR R. I. Hitesman, RCN	23/8/68	25/7/70	CDR A. E. Delamere	1/1/86	4/1/88
CDR J. K. Kennedy	25/7/70	24/1/72	CDR T. N. Brockway	4/1/88	6/7/89
LCDR D. Nugent	24/1/72	5/4/72	CDR G. G. Borgal	6/7/89	17/12/91
CDR R. G. Campbell	5/4/72	4/1/74	CDR D. O. Thamer	17/12/91	2/5/92
CDR R. E. George	4/1/74	18/12/75			

Ottawa (3rd)

Ottawa (3rd), 12 June 1965.

Built by Canadian Vickers Ltd., Montreal, *Ottawa* was commissioned there on 10 November 1956. In 1957 she was fitted with an experimental deck over her stern to test the feasibility of operating a helicopter from a ship of her type. Transferred to the west coast, she began her DDH conversion at Victoria on 24 May 1963. Recommissioned on 28 October 1964 and destined to be based at Halifax, she left Esquimalt on 2 February 1965. In 1968 *Ottawa* became Canada's first designated francophone naval unit. She returned to her builder for DELEX refit, 19 April to 26 November 1982. From 20 June to 29 July 1988, *Ottawa* carried out a St. Lawrence River and Great Lakes cruise. She was paid off on 31 July 1992, and on 4 April 1994, left Halifax in tow for India, to be broken up.

OTTAWA (3rd)

BUILDER:	Canadian Vickers Ltd., Montreal, QC	COMMISSIONED:	10/11/56	FOR DELEX: 1982
LAID DOWN:	8/6/51	COMMISSIONED AFTER		PAID OFF: 31/7/92
LAUNCHED:	29/4/53	CONVERSION TO DDH: 28/10/64		

Commanding Officers

CDR C. R. Parker, DSC, RCN	10/11/56	7/7/58	CDR P. Simard, RCN	15/7/68	15/5/70	CDR J. E. D. Bell	23/1/78	4/7/80
CDR W. H. Willson, DSC, RCN	7/7/58	28/4/59	CDR M. H. Tremblay	15/5/70	7/2/72	CDR E. J. M. Young	4/7/80	10/9/82
CDR I. B. Morrow, RCN	28/4/59	19/8/61	LCDR N. Boivin	7/2/72	5/6/73	CDR R. A. M. Burton	10/9/82	9/7/84
CDR I. A. MacPherson, RCN	19/8/61	25/3/63	LCDR R. L. Burnip	5/6/73	14/6/74	CDR K. C. E. Beardmore	9/7/84	11/7/86
LCDR T. C. Shuckburg, RCN	25/3/63	-	LCDR T. C. Milne	14/6/74	30/8/74	CDR A. B. Dunlop	11/7/86	5/8/88
CDR J. P. Côte, RCN	28/10/64	31/7/67	CDR W. J. Draper	30/8/74	6/1/77	CDR M. A. Pulchny	5/8/88	11/7/90
CDR C. Cotaras, RCN	21/7/67	15/7/68	CDR L. C. A. Westropp	6/1/77	23/1/78	CDR A. G. D. Perusse	11/7/90	31/7/92

Saguenay (2nd).

SAGUENAY (2nd)					
BUILDER:	Halifax Shipyards Ltd., Halifax, NS		COMMISSIONED AFTER		
LAID DOWN:	4/4/51		CONVERSION TO DDH:	14/5/65	
LAUNCHED:	30/7/53		FOR DELEX:	1979	
COMMISSIONED:	15/12/56		PAID OFF:	31/8/90	

Commanding Officers

CDR G. H. Hayes, DSC, RCN	15/12/56	13/3/58	CDR D. MacNeil	18/7/72	17/6/74
CDR J. H. D. Bovey, DSC, RCN	31/3/58	2/3/59	CDR J. Harwood	17/6/74	10/1/75
CDR D. S. Boyle, RCN	2/3/59	14/10/59	CDR R. J. Luke	10/1/75	18/1/77
CDR E. M. Chadwick, RCN	14/10/59	23/8/61	CDR C. Milne	18/1/77	4/8/78
CDR H. R. Tilley, RCN	23/8/61	22/8/63	CDR J. Goode	4/8/78	18/4/80
CDR H. H. Plant, RCN	14/5/65	13/7/66	CDR A. G. Schwartz	18/4/80	24/7/82
CDR D. A. Avery, RCN	13/7/66	23/8/67	CDR E. E. Davie	24/7/82	18/7/83
LCDR L. A. Dzioba, RCN	23/8/67	15/12/67	CDR J. M. Barlow	18/7/83	17/7/85
CAPT D. H. P. Ryan, RCN	15/12/67	23/1/69	CDR R. M. L. Bernard	17/7/85	22/5/87
CDR R. Yanow	23/1/69	13/8/70	CDR R. I. Clayton	22/5/87	6/1/89
LCDR R. Hardy	13/8/70	1/11/70	CDR E. J. Lerhe	6/1/89	26/6/90
CDR K. M. Young	1/11/70	—			

Saguenay (2nd)

Built by Halifax Shipyards Ltd., *Saguenay* was commissioned on 15 December 1956. She transferred to the west coast in 1959. Burrard Dry Dock Ltd started her conversion to a DDH on 22 August 1963. Recommissioned on 14 May 1965, she returned that July to Halifax. She began her DELEX refit at Versatile Vickers, Montreal, on 29 October 1979, returning to service on 23 May 1980. On 16 August 1986, while on SNFL exercises in the Baltic, she collided with the German submarine *U 17*. Returning home for repairs, she was again in service in March 1987. *Saguenay* was paid off on 31 August 1990 and, on 25 June 1994, scuttled as recreational divers' wreck outside Lunenburg, N.S.

Skeena (2nd).

SKEENA (2nd)

BUILDER:	Burrard Dry Dock Co. Ltd., Vancouver, BC		COMMISSIONED:	30/3/57	FOR DELEX:	1981
LAID DOWN:	1/6/51		COMMISSIONED AFTER		PAID OFF:	1/11/93
LAUNCHED:	19/8/52		CONVERSIONS TO DDH: 1	4/8/65		

Commanding Officers

CDR J. P. T. Dawson, RCN	30/3/57	20/8/58	LT B. Elson, RCN	27/1/68	16/4/68	CDR J. G. R. Boucher	7/7/80	26/9/83
CDR W. M. Kidd, RCN	20/8/58	1/10/59	LCDR W. G. Brown, RCN	16/4/68	23/6/69	CDR I. Foldesi	26/9/83	1/8/85
LCDR G. M. DeRosenroll, RCN	1/10/59	5/1/60	LCDR R. Dougan	23/6/69	11/8/69	CDR P. J. Yans	1/8/85	15/7/87
CDR T. H. Crone, RCN	5/1/60	22/2/60	CDR R. L. Hughes	11/8/69	23/7/70	CDR D. C. Morse	15/7/87	9/1/89
CDR A. L. Collier, RCN	22/2/60	11/1/62	CDR F. J. Mifflin	23/7/70	5/7/72	CDR D. MacKay	9/1/89	15/7/91
CDR R. M. Leir, RCN	22/1/62	10/5/63	CDR N. R. Boivin	15/6/73	5/9/75	CDR J. A. C. Gauthier	15/7/91	15/12/91
CDR M. A. Martin, RCN	10/5/63	26/7/64	CDR J. Chouinard	5/9/75	13/5/76	CDR J. J. Gauvin	15/12/91	26/7/93
CDR C. J. Mair, RCN	14/8/65	29/8/66	CDR D. E. Pollard	13/5/76	29/5/78			
LCDR K. D. Lewis, RCN	29/8/66	27/1/68	CDR B. E. Derible	29/5/78	7/7/80			

Skeena (2nd)

Built at Burrard Dry Dock, Vancouver, *Skeena* was commissioned on 30 March 1957. On 14 August 1965, after a year's work at Davie Shipbuilding, Lauzon, she was recommissioned in DDH format and allocated for service out of Halifax. In 1972 she was designated a French Language Unit. Along with *Fraser* and *Protecteur*, she provided security, rescue crews and emergency support at the Montreal Olympics of 1976. *Skeena* underwent her DELEX refit at Montreal between 12 April and 20 November 1981. In the summer of 1991 she took part in the NATO exercise Ocean Safari '91, soon afterward visiting St. Lawrence and Great Lakes ports to encourage recruiting and public awareness. After steaming more than 980,000 nautical miles, the venerable ship was paid off on 1 November 1993, and on 3 July 1996 left Halifax in tow for India to be broken up.

RESTIGOUCHE CLASS

PARTICULARS OF CLASS:	
DISPLACEMENT:	2,366
DIMENSIONS:	366' x 42' x 13' 6"
SPEED:	28 kts
CREW:	13/201
ARMAMENT:	two 3-inch70 (A mounting), two 3-inch50 (Y mounting) (2 x II), 2 Limbo, homing torpedoes
Gatineau, Kootenay, Restigouche and *Terra Nova* as modified to IRE configuration:	
DISPLACEMENT:	2,390
DIMENSIONS:	372' x 42' x 14'1"
SPEED:	28 kts
CREW:	13/201
ARMAMENT:	two 3-inch70 (1 x II), 1 Limbo, 1 ASROC, homing torpedoes

A second class of seven DDEs, the Restigouche class, entered service between 1958 and 1959. They approximated very closely the original *St. Laurent* design, except for the replacement of the forward A mounting with the twin 3-inch70 gun. Four of them were rebuilt from 1962 to 1972 as Improved Restigouche Escorts (IRE), with an A/S rocket (ASROC) and launcher aft in place of the after turret, a disproportionately tall mast, and a stern redesigned to accommodate variable depth sonar (VDS). None of the four rebuilt carried a helicopter. The three not rebuilt, *ChaudiÉre, Columbia* and *St. Croix*, were reduced to Category C reserve in 1974.

Chaudière (2nd)

Built at Halifax Shipyards and the last of her class, *Chaudière* was commissioned on 14 November 1959. On 2 October 1967, she left Halifax to serve on the west coast. Her intended conversion to an IRE was abandoned for reasons of economy, and in 1970 her complement was reduced to training level. On 23 May 1974, she was paid off and thereafter used as a source of spare parts for others of her class. Her bow was removed in 1989 to replace that of *Kootenay*, which had been damaged in a collision. *Chaudière* was sunk as a sport divers' wreck in Sechelt Inlet, B.C., on 5 December 1992.

Chaudière (2nd), 26 May 1967.

CHAUDIÈRE (2nd)				
BUILDER:	Halifax Shipyards Ltd., Halifax, NS		COMMISSIONED:	14/11/59
LAID DOWN:	30/7/53		PAID OFF:	23/5/74
LAUNCHED:	13/11/57			

Commanding Officers

CDR V. J. Wilgress, RCN	14/11/59	25/4/61	LCDR J. L. Woodbury, RCN	24/11/67	8/12/67
CDR P. J. Pratley, RCN	24/4/61	11/4/63	LCDR P. G. Bissell, RCN	8/12/67	20/1/70
CDR R. H. Falls, RCN	11/4/63	25/8/64	CDR H. Rusk	20/1/70	30/6/71
CDR G. R. MacFarlane, RCN	25/8/64	17/1/66	CDR D. R. Donaldson	30/6/71	24/5/73
CDR J. I. Manore, RCN	17/1/66	26/8/67	CDR J. G. Comeau	24/5/73	23/5/74
LCDR W. G. Brown, RCN	26/8/67	24/11/67			

Columbia (2nd)

Built by Burrard Dry Dock Ltd. Vancouver, *Columbia* was commissioned on 7 November 1959, and soon afterward was transferred to the east coast. In 1960 she represented Canada at Nigerian Independence observances, returning home on 25 October. In March 1967 she was transferred to Esquimalt. Paid off on 18 February 1974, *Columbia* was fitted with "no-thrust wheels" so that her engines might be run at dockside. Late in June 1996, she was sunk by the Artificial Reef Society of B.C. near Campbell River.

Columbia (2nd).

Gatineau (2nd).

Gatineau (2nd)

The first post-war product of Davie Shipbuilding Ltd., Lauzon, Que., *Gatineau* was towed to Halifax for completion to avoid freeze-up and commissioned on 17 February 1959. In March 1968 she was the first Canadian warship to become a member of NATO's Standing Naval Force Atlantic (STANAV-FORLANT). *Gatineau* was transferred west in 1969, and on 9 September began her IRE conversion at Ship Repair Unit (Pacific), recommissioning on 14 April 1971. Her DELEX refit was also carried out at SRU(P) between September 1981 and 12 November 1982. In April 1987 she resumed her duties in Halifax. In July 1993, she played host to three visiting Soviet warships and afterward escorted them to sea while carrying out exercises along the way. In the fall of 1993 *Gatineau*, along with *Fraser* and *Preserver*, assisted in the enforcement of UN sanctions off Haiti. Early in 1995 she took part in the NATO exercise Strong Resolve off the coast of Norway, acting as flagship for the four other Canadian ships involved. April found her operating in support of Fisheries and Coast Guard ships off Newfoundland during the "Turbot Dispute" with Spain. She was finally paid off on 1 July 1998, and as of May 2002, lay idle at Halifax.

COLUMBIA (2nd)

BUILDER:	Burrard Dry Dock Co. Ltd., Vancouver, BC	LAID DOWN:	11/6/53	COMMISSIONED:	7/11/59
		LAUNCHED:	1/11/56	PAID OFF:	18/2/74

Commanding Officers

CDR W. P. Hayes, RCN	7/11/59	25/4/61	CDR R. D. Okros, RCN	20/2/67	31/8/68
CDR D. W. Knox, RCN	25/4/61	8/1/63	CDR T. C. Shuckburg, RCN	31/8/68	23/7/70
CDR A. E. Fox, RCN	8/1/63	2/9/64	CDR E. A. Makin	23/7/70	6/8/72
CDR P. R. Hinton, RCN	4/9/64	15/9/65	CDR R. F. Choat	7/8/72	18/2/74
CDR A. C. McMillin, RCN	15/9/65	20/2/67			

GATINEAU (2nd)

BUILDER:	Davie Shipbuilding and Repairing Co. Ltd., Lauzon, QC	LAUNCHED:	3/6/57	FOR DELEX:	1983
		COMMISSIONED:	17/2/59	PAID OFF:	1/7/98
LAID DOWN:	30/4/53	As IRE:	14/4/71		

Commanding Officers

CAPT H. L. Quinn, DSC, RCN	17/2/59	14/9/59	CDR J. B. McKenzie	11/11/77	26/7/99
CAPT F. B. Caldwell, RCN	15/9/59	27/1/61	CDR C. D. E. Cronk	26/7/79	11/6/81
LCDR R. A. Shimmin, RCN	28/1/61	24/5/61	CDR D. M. Robson	11/6/81	4/7/83
LCDR H. C. Mecredy, RCN	25/5/61	24/8/61	CDR T. C. Heath	4/7/83	1/8/85
CDR A. H. McDonald, RCN	25/8/61	21/8/62	CDR J. A. Keenliside	1/8/85	21/4/87
CDR J. W. Roberts, RCN	22/8/62	28/4/64	CDR G. Jeffrey	21/4/87	4/7/88
CDR W. G. Kinsman, DSO, RCN	29/4/64	11/8/65	CDR A. E. Tanguay	4/7/88	7/7/90
CDR J. A. Fulton, RCN	12/8/65	8/9/66	CDR R. H. Edwards	7/7/90	10/7/92
CDR W. A. Hughes, RCN	8/9/66	29/9/69	CDR R. G. Allen	10/7/92	7/1/94
CDR T. S. Murphy	14/4/71	3/7/71	CDR J. A. Westlake	7/1/94	5/7/95
LCDR J. C. Slade	3/7/71	11/7/75	CDR D. O. Thamer	5/7/95	30/6/96
CDR L. G. Temple	11/7/75	11/11/77			

Kootenay (2nd)

First of her class to be launched, *Kootenay* was built at Burrard Dry Dock, Vancouver, and commissioned there on 7 March 1959. After working up, she was transferred to the east coast. On 23 October 1969, while in European waters, she suffered a gearbox explosion that killed 7 crewmen and injured 53 others. She was towed to Plymouth—part of the way by *Saguenay* and then to Halifax by a salvage tug. It was the RCN's worst-ever peacetime accident. While she was under repairs, it was decided to convert her to an IRE, in which guise she was recommissioned on 7 January 1972. Transferred to the west coast, she arrived in Esquimalt on 12 February 1973. On 1 June 1989, *Kootenay* collided in fog off Cape Flattery with the M.V. *Nord Pol*, sustaining a sizeable gash in her bow, which was replaced with a matching section from *Chaudière*. From 3 to 7 June 1990, *Kootenay* visited Vladivostok as part of a Canadian Task Group, the first to do so since World War II. In the summer of 1994 she took part in enforcing UN sanctions against Haiti. Her final trip found her off Uruguay for a two month naval exercise called UNITAS. On 18 December 1996, she was paid off and, on 6 November 2000, towed out of Esquimalt to be sunk as an artificial reef off Puerto Vallarta, Mexico.

Kootenay (2nd), 4 November 1964.

KOOTENAY (2nd)

BUILDER:	Burrard Dry Dock Co. Ltd., Vancouver, BC	LAUNCHED:	15/6/54	FOR DELEX:	1984
		COMMISSIONED:	7/3/59	PAID OFF:	18/12/96
LAID DOWN:	21/8/52	As IRE:	7/1/72		

Commanding Officers

CDR R. J. Pickford, RCN	7/3/59	11/7/60	CDR B. P. Moore	16/7/76	27/6/78
CDR H. Shorten, RCN	11/7/60	19/9/62	CDR B. Johnston	27/6/78	11/8/80
CDR D. H. Ryan, RCN	19/9/62	15/1/65	CDR B. H. Beckett	11/8/80	28/6/82
CDR C. G. Pratt, RCN	15/1/65	1/6/66	CDR S. K. Jessen	28/6/82	9/1/83
CDR W. P. Rikely, RCN	1/6/66	1/7/67	CDR P. C. Young	24/1/84	5/7/85
CDR G. C. McMorris, RCN	1/7/67	15/11/68	CDR B. R. Melville	5/7/85	30/7/87
CDR M. Tremblay, RCN	15/11/68	21/3/69	CDR J. Dickson	30/7/87	21/7/89
CDR N. St. C. Norton	21/3/69	14/1/70	CDR J. D. Fraser	21/7/91	29/5/92
CDR J. L. Creech	12/1/72	17/2/73	LCDR M. R. Bellows	29/5/92	31/7/92
CDR R. H. Kirby	17/2/73	14/6/74	CDR D. J. Kyle	31/7/92	21/6/94
CDR J. Spalding	14/6/74	16/7/76	CDR R. H. Dawe	21/6/94	18/12/96

Restigouche (2nd)

Restigouche suffered portside damage in a collision with the freighter *Manchester Port* in November 1957 while still in the hands of her builder, Canadian Vickers Ltd., and was finally commissioned at Montreal on 7 June 1958. She was present at the formal opening of the St. Lawrence Seaway in 1959, and at a mini-UN naval review at Toronto the following month, immediately afterward carrying the Lieutenant Governor of Newfoundland on a tour of that province's northeast outports. She underwent her IRE modernization in 1970-72 at Halifax Shipyards, and in 1973 was transferred to the west coast, arriving at Esquimalt on 2 August. Between 3 December 1984 and 29 November 1985 she completed her DELEX refit at SRU(P). Upgraded (as per *Terra Nova*) for possible service in the Persian Gulf, in March 1991 she instead joined SNFL, the first west coast based unit to do so. On 24 February 1992, *Restigouche* was dispatched to the Red Sea to assist a multinational force convened to ensure that Iraq did not resume hostilities. She returned to Esquimalt on 18 August. She was paid off on 31 August 1994. On 6 November 2000, she and her sister, *Kootenay*, departed Esquimalt in tow for Mexico, where *Restigouche* was sunk off Acapulco on 11 June 2001, as an artificial reef.

St. Croix (2nd)

Built by Marine Industries Ltd., Sorel, *St. Croix* was commissioned on 4 October 1958. In 1959, as a member of the 5th Canadian Destroyer Squadron, she served as escort to HMY *Britannia* on a Royal visit to Canada and in August 1960, with *Terra Nova*, helped mark the 500th Anniversary of the death of Prince Henry the Navigator off Lisbon. *St. Croix* was transferred to the west coast in August 1964. She returned to Halifax in 1973, she was paid off on 15 November 1974, into Category "C" Reserve. Her guns and propellers were removed and her machinery spaces made into classrooms for Fleet School trainees. She served in this capacity from 1984 to September 1990. In 1991 *St. Croix* was sold to Jacobson Metal of Chesapeake, Va., and early in April left Halifax in tow to be broken up.

Restigouche (2nd), 21 September 1968.

RESTIGOUCHE (2nd)

BUILDER:	Canadian Vickers Ltd., Montreal, QC	As IRE:	12/5/72
LAID DOWN:	15/7/53	FOR DELEX:	1986
LAUNCHED:	22/11/54	PAID OFF:	31/8/94
COMMISSIONED:	7/6/58		

Commanding Officers

CDR J. W. McDowall, RCN	7/6/58	4/8/60	CDR C. J. Crowe	27/3/77	29/4/77
CDR W. W. MacColl, RCN	4/8/60	8/8/62	CDR H. T. Porter	29/4/77	29/7/78
CDR B. C. Thillaye, RCN	8/8/62	19/5/65	CDR J. R. Anderson	29/7/78	29/9/80
CDR H. W. Vondette, RCN	19/5/65	10/8/66	CDR D. A. Henderson	29/9/80	10/1/83
CDR R. A. Evans, RCN	10/8/66	3/1/68	CDR S. K. Jessen	10/1/83	6/7/84
CDR P. L. McCulloch, RCN	3/1/68	3/8/70	CDR H. C. Silvestor	6/7/84	7/7/87
CDR R. H. Kirby	12/5/72	7/9/72	CDR R. D. Buck	7/7/87	9/3/89
CDR R. C. Burnip	7/9/72	2/4/73	CDR B. E. Mathews	9/3/89	19/6/89
CDR R. J. Deluca	2/4/73	15/7/75	CDR G. C. Oakley	19/6/89	23/8/91
CDR C. J. Crowe	15/7/75	27/1/77	CDR D. Baltes	23/8/91	4/1/93
CDR R. G. Balfour	27/1/77	27/3/77	CDR R. K. Taylor	4/1/93	31/8/94

ST. CROIX (2nd)

BUILDER:	Marine Industries Ltd., Sorel, QC	COMMISSIONED:	4/10/58
LAID DOWN:	15/10/54	PAID OFF:	15/11/74
LAUNCHED:	17/11/56		

Commanding Officers

CDR K. H. Boggild, RCN	4/10/58	28/5/59	CDR J. I. Donald, RCN	21/9/66	15/7/68
CDR W. S. T. McCully, RCN	28/5/59	14/3/61	CDR J. M. Cumming, RCN	15/7/68	31/8/71
CDR T. E. Connors, RCN	14/3/61	22/7/62	LCDR R. L. Donaldson	31/8/71	2/7/73
CDR D. C. Rutherford, RCN	22/7/62	31/5/63	CDR T. S. Murphy	2/7/73	9/9/74
CDR D. M. Maclennan, RCN	31/5/53	4/5/64	CDR P. E. Simard	9/9/74	15/11/74
CDR J. S. Hertzberg, RCN	4/5/64	21/9/66			

St. Croix (2nd), 1962.

Terra Nova departing Halifax Harbour 24 August 1990 for the Persian Gulf.

Terra Nova

Seventh and last of her class, *Terra Nova* was built by the Victoria Machinery Depot and commissioned on 6 June, 1959, and shortly thereafter sailed east, to be on hand for the opening of the St. Lawrence Seaway and a review of NATO warships at Toronto in August. In July 1961 she carried the Lieutenant Governor of Newfoundland on a series of visits to its southwest outports. In May 1965 she entered Halifax Shipyards to begin her conversion to an IRE class destroyer escort. She was fitted with the new AN/SQS-505 sonar, which she tested for seven months before completing the IRE conversion, which she was the first of her class to undergo. She returned for duties in Esquimalt on 4 May 1971. Between 21 November 1983 and 9 November 1984, *Terra Nova* received her DELEX refit at Esquimalt. Transferred to the east coast, she returned to Halifax on 12 December 1989. Designated for service in the Persian Gulf, she was temporarily armed with two quadruple Harpoon missile-launchers, mounted just abaft the after deckhouse; a Phalanx gun atop the Limbo well; two single Bofors on the boat deck amidships, and shoulder-fired Blowpipe and Javelin missiles. Along with *Athabaskan* and *Preserver*, she left Halifax on 24 August 1990, not to return until 7 April 1991. On 22 February 1994, *Terra Nova* stopped and boarded M.V. *Pacifico* while on a drug interdiction patrol and seized 5.9 tonnes of cocaine. Later that year, while taking part in blockade duty off Haiti, she rescued boatloads of refugees on two separate occasions. On 11 July 1997 she was placed in a "state of extended readiness" until finally paid off on 1 July 1998. As of May 2002 she remained alongside in Halifax awaiting her fate.

TERRA NOVA

BUILDER:	Victoria Machinery Depot Co. Ltd., Victoria, BC		LAUNCHED:	21/6/55		FOR DELEX:	1985
			COMMISSIONED:	6/6/59		PAID OFF:	1/7/98
LAID DOWN:	14/11/52		As IRE:	9/67			

Commanding Officers

CDR W. H. Willson, DSC, RCN	6/6/59	22/6/60	CDR J. B. O'Reilly	19/6/74	8/1/76	CDR J. T. Jones	30/7/84	5/5/86
CDR C. G. Smith, RCN	22/6/60	18/9/62	CDR R. G. Balfour	8/1/76	8/2/77	CDR E. B. Waa	15/5/86	21/4/88
CDR J. B. Young, RCN	18/9/62	3/4/64	CDR C. J. Crow	8/2/77	25/3/77	CDR A. L. Vey	21/4/88	28/9/89
CDR C. E. Leighton, RCN	3/4/64	6/12/66	CDR R. G. Balfour	25/3/77	29/7/77	CDR R. J. Neveu	28/9/89	12/7/90
CDR N. Brodeur, RCN	6/12/66	1/8/68	CDR J. D. Large	29/7/77	20/6/79	CDR S. D. Andrews	12/7/90	2/7/91
CDR J. M. Reid, RCN	1/8/68	5/6/71	CDR J. K. Steele	20/6/79	18/6/81	CDR H. R. Smith	2/7/91	19/7/93
LCDR J. Bishop	5/6/71	3/8/71	CDR G. J. Eldridge	18/6/81	19/8/82	CDR R. M. Williams	19/7/93	16/7/95
CDR L. A. Dzioba	3/8/71	19/6/74	CDR D. R. E. Cooper	19/8/82	30/7/84	CDR H. W. McEwen	16/7/95	11/7/97

MACKENZIE CLASS

PARTICULARS OF CLASS:

DISPLACEMENT:	2,380
DIMENSIONS:	366' x 42' x 13' 6"
SPEED:	28 kts
CREW:	12/233
ARMAMENT:	four 3-inch50 (2 x II), 2 Limbo, homing torpedoes

The four Mackenzie class DDEs, which entered service between 1962 and 1963, essentially repeat the original Restigouche design, while the two Nipigon class DDHs of 1964 incorporated from their launching the design elements of the rebuilt St. Laurents, and carried a helicopter.

MACKENZIE

BUILDER:	Canadian Vickers Ltd., Montreal, QC	COMMISSIONED:	6/10/62
LAID DOWN:	15/12/58	FOR DELEX:	1985
LAUNCHED:	25/5/61	PAID OFF:	3/8/93

Commanding Officers

CDR A. B. German, RCN	6/10/62	29/5/64	CDR R. L. Donaldson	17/9/74	21/5/76
CDR H. J. Wade, RCN	29/5/64	17/1/66	CDR J. Chouinard	21/5/76	14/1/77
LCDR R. D. Okros, RCN	17/1/66	7/3/66	CDR J. W. McIntosh	14/1/77	31/12/78
CDR G. M. De Rosenroll, RCN	7/3/66	11/8/67	CDR H. R. Waddell	31/12/78	27/8/81
LCDR W. J. Draper, RCN	11/8/67	22/11/67	CDR T. C. Milne	27/8/81	19/12/83
CDR O. J. Cavenagh, RCN	22/11/67	24/7/69	CDR J. Nethercott	19/12/83	1/8/85
CDR R. L. McLean	24/7/69	20/1/71	CDR K. A. Nason	1/8/85	25/4/86
CDR G. G. Armstrong	20/1/71	6/8/72	CDR A. J. Hollington-Sawyer	15/9/86	9/7/88
LCDR R. J. Deluca	6/8/72	11/9/72	CDR R. W. Bowers	9/7/88	20/7/90
CDR R. H. Kirby	11/9/72	23/1/73	CDR R. P. Harrison	20/7/90	4/1/93
CDR R. D. C. Sweeny	23/1/73	17/9/74	CDR J. H. A. P. Lebel	4/1/93	3/8/93

Mackenzie

Built by Canadian Vickers, Montreal, *Mackenzie* was commissioned on 6 October 1962. Initially based at Halifax, she sailed for the west coast on 2 March 1963, and spent the remainder of her service life in Pacific waters. Between 25 May, 1986, and 16 January 1987, she received her DELEX refit at SRU(P). After 30 years of service, in the course of which she visited 96 foreign ports and steamed 845,640 nautical miles either as a unit of the 4th Canadian Destroyer Squadron or of Training Group Pacific, *Mackenzie* was paid off on 3 August 1993. On 16 September 1995, like several of her sisters, she was sunk off Rum Island, near Sidney, B.C., as a sport-divers' venue.

Qu'Appelle (2nd)

A product of the Davie Shipbuilding Co., Lauzon, *Qu'Appelle* was commissioned on 14 September 1963, becoming a unit of Pacific Command the following spring. She was in a subtle way unique of her class, being fitted with a 3inch50 calibre gun forward since the intended 3inch70 calibre weapon was unavailable. On 28 August 1972, in company with *Gatineau* and *Provider*, she left Esquimalt on a four-month south Pacific cruise during which exercises were carried out with units of the Australian, New Zealand and U.S. navies. *Qu'Appelle*'s DELEX refit was carried out between 25 May 1983 and 13 January 1984 by Burrard Yarrow at CFB Esquimalt. In the summer of 1986, with *Yukon* and *Saskatchewan*, she returned to Australia to attend ceremonies marking the 75th birthday of that country's navy. She was paid off on 31 July 1992 and sold in 1994 to a Chinese firm for breaking up.

QU'APPELLE (2nd)							
BUILDER:	Davie Shipbuilding and Repairing Co. Ltd., Lauzon, QC	LAID DOWN:	14/1/60	COMMISSIONED:	14/9/63	PAID OFF:	31/7/92
		LAUNCHED:	2/5/62	FOR DELEX:	1982		

Commanding Officers							
CDR A. G. Kilpatrick, RCN	14/9/63	28/8/65	CDR R. F. Choat	14/2/74	19/9/75	CDR D. J. McLean	1/6/85	24/4/86
CDR H. D. Joy, RCN	28/8/65	16/1/67	CDR K. M. Young	19/9/75	4/8/76	LCDR W. J. Poole	24/4/86	1/8/86
CDR R. Ratcliffe, RCN	16/1/67	16/12/68	CDR R. H. Kirby	4/8/76	25/1/77	CDR D. C. Beresford-Green	1/8/86	20/6/88
CDR J. Allan	16/12/68	28/7/70	CDR J. M. Chouinard	25/1/77	4/10/78	CDR W. Johnston	20/6/88	13/7/90
CDR J. Rodocanachi	28/7/70	8/5/72	CDR J. J. Drent	4/10/78	28/7/80	CDR J. G. V. Tremblay	13/7/90	15/7/91
CDR R. D. C. Sweeny	8/5/72	22/1/73	CDR R. J. Luke	28/7/80	12/7/82	CDR B. F. Lofthouse	15/7/91	31/7/92
CDR J. L. Creech	22/1/73	2/7/73	CDR H. L. Davies	12/7/82	11/7/83		
CDR J. D. Sine	2/7/73	14/2/74	CDR J. M. Bishop	11/7/83	1/6/85		

Saskatchewan (2nd), 19 October 1965.

Saskatchewan (2nd)

Built by Victoria Machinery Depot and completed by Yarrows at Esquimalt, *Saskatchewan* was commissioned on 16 February 1963, following which, from June to October, she was based at Halifax. She then returned west until February 1970, when she sailed to Halifax with the erstwhile crew of *Kootenay*, relieving *Nipigon* as flagship of SNFL that summer, but returned to the Pacific in 1973. She was given her DELEX refit

SASKATCHEWAN (2nd)								
BUILDER:	Victoria Machinery Depot Co. Ltd., Victoria, BC		LAUNCHED:	1/2/61		PAID OFF:	1/4/94	
			COMMISSIONED:	16/2/63				
LAID DOWN:	29/10/59		FOR DELEX:	1984				

Commanding Officers

CDR M. W. Mayo, RCN	16/2/63	18/12/64	CDR R. F. Gladman	2/4/71	6/7/72	CDR J. D. Sine	3/7/80	5/8/82
CDR M. A. Turner, RCN	18/12/64	7/3/66	CDR T. S. Hayward	6/7/72	9/4/73	CDR G. J. Eldridge	19/8/82	25/6/84
CDR P. J. Traves, RCN	7/3/66	15/7/67	LCDR H. L. Davies	9/4/73	31/7/73	CDR D. R. A. McLean	25/6/84	15/6/85
CDR N. S. Jackson, RCN	15/7/67	23/9/68	CDR J. Harwood	31/7/73	24/5/74	CDR S. F. Verran	15/6/85	25/7/88
CDR H. Rusk, RCN	23/9/68	15/1/70	CDR J. G. Comeau	24/5/74	1/9/76	CDR D. V. Adamthwaite	25/7/88	15/8/90
CDR N. St. C. Norton	15/1/70	9/3/71	CDR F. Hope	1/9/76	3/8/78	CDR S. E. King	15/8/90	21/7/92
LCDR A. Bajkov	9/3/71	2/4/71	CDR H. T. Porter	3/8/78	3/7/80	CDR N. R. Sorsdahl	21/7/92	1/4/94

at Burrard Yarrow Inc., Esquimalt, between 27 May 1985 and 17 June 1986. That fall *Saskatchewan* was part of a Canadian squadron that visited Australia for the RAN's 75th Anniversary celebrations. In her final years, *Saskatchewan* was a member of Training Group Pacific, instructing officer cadets in ship handling, navigation and marine engineering. She was paid off on 1 April 1994, purchased by the Artificial Reef Society of B.C. and sunk on 14 June 1997, near Nanaimo.

Yukon

Built by Burrard Dry Dock Ltd., Vancouver, *Yukon* was commissioned on 25 May 1963 and, manned by east-coast personnel, sailed for Halifax on 27 July. On 5 January 1965, she departed for Esquimalt. In mid-1970, with *Mackenzie* and *Provider*, she carried out exercises with units of the Australian, New Zealand, Japanese and U.S. navies, incidentally making visits to Kobe, Osaka and Sasebo. On completion of her mid-life refit in 1975, *Yukon* became a member of Training Group Pacific. Her DELEX refit was carried out by Burrard Yarrow at Esquimalt, between 28 May 1984 and 16 January 1985. During her career, *Yukon* steamed more than 792,000 nautical miles and visited some 30 foreign ports. She was paid off on 3 December 1993 and eventually sold to the San Diego Oceans Foundation. On 25 April 1999 she left Vancouver in tow for San Diego, where she was to be ceremoniously sunk on July 15 as a sport-divers' wreck, but she flooded in rough weather at the intended site and sank the day before.

Yukon, 27 February 1974.

YUKON

BUILDER:	Burrard Dry Dock Co. Ltd., Vancouver, BC	COMMISSIONED:	25/5/63
LAID DOWN:	25/10/59	FOR DELEX:	1983
LAUNCHED:	27/7/61	PAID OFF:	3/12/93

Commanding Officers

CDR R. W. J. Cocks, RCN	25/5/63	5/7/65	CDR C. J. Crowe	22/5/81	25/7/83
CDR R. Carle, RCN	5/7/65	1/9/66	CDR J. K. Steele	25/7/83	5/11/84
CDR S. I. Ker, RCN	1/9/66	15/1/68	CDR M. F. Morres	5/11/84	23/4/86
CDR P. G. May, RCN	15/1/68	12/9/69	CDR K. A. Nason	23/4/86	13/7/87
CDR C. H. P. Shaw	12/9/69	28/6/71	CDR K. V. Watson	13/7/87	31/7/89
LCDR D. Large	28/6/71	9/8/71	CDR D. W. Fitzgerald	31/7/89	31/7/91
CDR C. Cotaras	9/8/71	9/8/73	CDR J. G. V. Tremblay	31/7/91	31/7/92
CDR M. F. MacIntosh	9/8/73	1/10/76	CDR B. F. Lofthouse	31/7/92	19/8/93
CDR H. Kieran	1/10/76	15/5/78	CDR J. H. A. P. Lebel	19/8/93	3/12/93
CDR N. R. Boivin	15/5/78	22/5/81			

ANNAPOLIS CLASS

PARTICULARS OF CLASS:

DISPLACEMENT:	2,400
DIMENSIONS:	371' x 42' x 13' 8"
SPEED:	28 kts
CREW:	12/234
ARMAMENT:	two 3-inch50 (1 x II), 1 Limbo, homing torpedoes, 1 Sea King helicopter

A two-ship class incorporating from their launching the design elements of the St. Laurents as then being rebuilt, most notably the twinned funnels, hangar and VDS. In the course of DELEX refit, *Annapolis's* VDS and Limbo installations were removed to make room for CANTASS and NIXIE systems. As well, she received new radar, entailing a disproportionately tall mast like that of the four IREs, a new Mk.60 gunnery director, and four Super RBOC chaff launchers.

Annapolis (2nd), 23 May 1962.

ANNAPOLIS (2nd)

BUILDER:	Halifax Shipyards Ltd., Halifax, NS	COMMISSIONED:	19/12/64
LAID DOWN:	2/9/61	FOR DELEX:	1984
LAUNCHED:	27/4/63	PAID OFF:	1/7/98

Commanding Officers

CDR R. C. K. Peers, RCN	19/12/64	6/9/66	CDR W. P. Dumbrille	16/4/79	1/10/80	CDR A. L. Vey	28/9/89	27/9/90
CDR D. N. Mainguy, RCN	6/9/66	18/12/67	CDR J. C. Braconnier	1/10/80	28/6/82	CDR J. D. Fraser	27/9/90	25/1/91
CDR D. Ross, RCN	4/1/68	21/8/69	CDR J. C. Bain	28/6/82	23/4/84	CDR R. R. Town	25/1/91	26/7/93
CDR A. G. Lowe	21/8/69	20/2/71	CDR G. O. Hurford	23/4/84	1/8/85	CDR S. C. Bertrand	26/7/93	4/1/95
CDR A. P. Campbell	1/4/71	8/9/72	LCDR R. J. Kerr	1/8/85	16/12/85	CDR D. W. Robertson	4/1/95	22/7/96
CDR J. Drent	8/9/72	18/7/75	LCDR D. G. McNeil	16/12/85	26/7/86	CDR J. W. Hayes	22/7/96	19/12/96
CDR R. A. Willson	8/8/75	14/5/77	CDR B. F. Beaudry	26/7/86	4/7/88			
CDR A. R. H. Wood	14/5/77	16/4/79	CDR R. J. Neveu	4/7/88	28/9/89			

Annapolis (2nd)

Built at Halifax Shipyards Ltd., *Annapolis* was commissioned on 19 December 1964. She was the twentieth and last of the "Cadillacs". In the summer of 1970, along with *Skeena* and *Protecteur*, she celebrated Manitoba's Centennial with visits to Fort Churchill, Rankin Inlet, Chesterfield Inlet and Wakeham Bay. In June 1974, while serving as flag-ship of SNFL, *Annapolis* went to the aid of a Sea King helicopter which had lost an engine and ditched while attempting to land aboard USS *Julius A. Furer*. After rescuing its crew, divers from *Annapolis* recovered the helicopter, which had been kept afloat by flotation bags, loaded it onto a borrowed barge and towed it to Den Helder, Holland. There it was taken aboard the destroyer for transport to Shearwater, N.S. The ship's DELEX/265 refit was carried out by Saint John Shipbuilding Ltd., 19 August, 1985 to 8 January 1987. *Annapolis* took part in the major NATO exercise Ocean Safari '87, and that fall acted as escort to HMY *Britannia* on a tour of the Great Lakes. On 14 August 1989, she left Halifax for Esquimalt. The spring of 1994 saw her participating in Operation Forward Action off Haiti. In December 1996 she was put into an 'extended state of readiness'. She was removed from service on 1 July 1998, and as of May 2002 lay alongside in Esquimalt.

Nipigon (2nd)

Nipigon (2nd).

Built by Marine Industries Ltd., Sorel, *Nipigon* was commissioned on 30 May 1964. Apart from her sister, *Annapolis*, she was the only one of the twenty "Cadillacs" originally designed and built to carry and operate a helicopter. She underwent her DELEX/265 refit at Davie Shipbuilding Co., Lauzon, between 27 June 1983 and 22 August 1984. This refit entailed very extensive modifications; most obviously the fitting of a towering, IRE-type lattice mast and a Mk.60 gunnery control system forward of it. Stresses resulting from the new mast in particular caused flaws in hull and superstructure that were not finally resolved until mid-1986. Another refit was begun at Port Weller, Ont., Drydock on 30 August 1988, and completed at Halifax on 16 February 1990. In the course of this refit, she was fitted to accommodate a mixed-gender ship's company. *Nipigon* joined SNFL on 18 August 1991, and in May 1993 was Canada's representative at ceremonies commemorating the Battle of the Atlantic, which took place off the Welsh coast and at Liverpool. In 1995 she was off Newfoundland, supporting Canada's position in the "Turbot Dispute" with Spain. During the closing years of her career, *Nipigon* was a test ship for sonar systems and long-range detection of submarines. She was paid off on 1 July 1998, and on 16 October 2001, left Halifax in tow for Rimouski, where it was intended to sink her as an artificial reef.

NIPIGON (2nd)

BUILDER:	Marine Industries Ltd., Sorel, QC	COMMISSIONED:	30/5/64
LAID DOWN:	5/8/60	FOR DELEX:	1982
LAUNCHED:	10/12/61	PAID OFF:	1/7/98

Commanding Officers

CDR D. R. Saxon, DSC, RCN	30/5/64	19/5/66	CDR W. G. Lund	19/7/82	2/4/84
CDR J. B. Carling, RCN	19/5/66	11/9/67	CDR H. W. Hendel	2/4/84	15/7/86
CDR R. F. Choat, RCN	11/9/67	19/12/68	CDR D. E. Miller	15/7/86	5/10/87
LCDR O. S. Chorneyko	19/12/68	4/2/69	CDR E. J. Lerhe	5/10/87	6/1/89
CDR R. C. Brown	4/2/69	31/8/70	CDR M. A. Wylie	6/1/89	12/7/89
LCDR L. I. MacDonald	31/8/70	29/9/70	CDR S. C. Doucette	12/7/89	21/6/91
CDR A. H. Brookbank	29/9/70	19/6/72	CDR K. S. White	21/6/91	16/7/93
CDR D. A. Avery	19/6/72	10/4/74	LCDR C. L. Mofford	16/7/93	18/8/93
CDR J. D. Sine	10/4/74	23/5/75	LCDR E. P. Deslauriers	18/8/93	2/5/94
CDR F. H. Hope	23/5/75	1/9/76	CDR M. P. Palmer	2/5/94	18/1/96
CDR H. L. Davies	1/9/76	15/5/78	CDR G. A. Prudat	18/1/96	21/8/97
CDR R. C. Waller	15/5/78	12/6/80	CDR J. D. Penman	21/8/97	1/7/98
CDR D. E. Gibb	12/6/80	19/7/82			

TRIBAL (280) CLASS

PARTICULARS OF CLASS:

DISPLACEMENT:	4,500
DIMENSIONS:	426' x 50' x 15'
SPEED:	30 kts
CREW:	14/230
ARMAMENT:	one 5-inch, 1 Limbo, homing torpedoes, 2 Sea Sparrow, 2 Sea King helicopters
TRUMPED:	one 3-inch, 1 Phalanx CIWS, 29 Standard missile cells, six 21-inch TT (2 x III), 2 Sea King helicopters

Sometimes known as the "280" or Iroquois class, these ships are much larger than earlier DDEs and DDHs. They were initially armed with a 5-inch gun, a Mk.X A/S mortar and two Sea Sparrow SAM missile launchers. The Tribal Class Update and Modernization Project (TRUMP) converted these four ships to the primary role of area air defence. New and improved combat systems include SM2 Block 2 missiles, a single Melara 76-mm Rapid Fire gun, a Phalanx CIWS, new Chaff launchers and a new outfit of radar and sonar. The helicopters and homing torpedoes have been retained. Visually noteworthy is the single large, square funnel which replaces the original twin outward-angled funnels.

Algonquin (2nd)

The last of her class, she was built by the Davie Shipbuilding Co., Lauzon, and commissioned on 3 November 1973. In November 1974, *Algonquin* rescued the crew of the fishing vessel *Paul & Maria*, which was sinking 80 miles east of Halifax. In the fall of 1977, she took part in the Caribbean exercise Caribops '77, in the process being the first of her class to cross the equator. On 26 September 1978, she relieved *Huron* as flagship of SNFL, staying with the Force until the end of the year. By the end of her tenth year in service, *Algonquin* had steamed more than 200,000 nautical miles and spent an actual three years at sea. During that period, she had taken part in more than twenty multinational exercises and completed four tours of duty with SNFL, three of them as flagship. On 1 March 1986 she responded to a call for help from the Dept. of Fisheries and Oceans, two of whose officers had boarded the Panamanian trawler *Peonia 7*. Ignoring orders to put in to St. John's, the vessel's captain had headed to sea with the DFO officers still on board. *Algonquin* overtook her and enforced the original orders. On 26 October 1987 she commenced her TRUMP refit at MIL Davie, Lauzon, completed on 11 October 1991. On 29 March 1993, *Algonquin* sailed to join SNFL, again as flagship, in the Adriatic enforcing the blockade of the former Yugoslavia. She transferred to the west coast in August 1994. Early in 1995 she took part in an U.S. battle group training exercise off southern California. That fall, *Algonquin* test-fired her SM2 missile on the Pacific Missile Range in the Hawaiian Islands. On 18 March 1996 she left Esquimalt to participate in Exercise Westploy '96, acting as flagship of a group including *Preserver, Regina* and *Winnipeg*. During three months the ships visited Japan, the Soviet Union and South Korea and afterward took part in Rimpac '96 off Hawaii. In mid-January 1997, she began a refit costing almost $25 million, re-entering service in May 1998. More exercises with Pacific rim countries followed during 2000 and 2001. *Algonquin* departed Esquimalt on 23 March 2002 to participate in Operation Apollo in the Arabian Sea.

Algonquin showing the effects of TRUMP refit completed in October 1991.

ALGONQUIN (2nd)								
BUILDER: Davie Shipbuilding and Repairing Co. Ltd., Lauzon, QC			LAID DOWN: 1/9/69 LAUNCHED: 23/4/71			COMMISSIONED: 3/11/73 As TRUMP: 1991		
Commanding Officers								
CDR R. L. McClean, RCN	3/11/73	7/5/76	CDR K. J. Summers	17/12/83	1/7/85	CDR J. B. McCarthy	31/3/94	4/8/95
CDR H. M. D. MacNeil, RCN	8/5/76	10/8/77	CDR J. C. A. Nadeau, RCN	1/7/85	10/8/87	CDR A. W. Round	4/8/95	1/8/97
CDR J. Harwood, RCN	11/8/77	19/3/78	LCDR J. G. V. Tremblay	10/8/87	6/4/88	LCDR P. A. Hendry	1/8/97	13/8/98
CDR L. C. A. Westrop, RCN	20/3/78	24/7/80	LCDR J. A. P. Lebel	30/6/88	15/7/89	CAPT J. J. P. Thiffault	13/8/98	18/7/00
CDR D. E. Pollard, RCN	25/7/80	10/4/82	CDR J. Y. Forcier	17/7/89	15/7/93	CAPT G. A. Paulson	18/7/00	-
CDR A. J. Goode, RCN	10/4/82	17/12/83	CDR P. C. Leblanc	15/7/93	31/3/94			

Athabaskan (3rd).

Athabaskan (3rd)

Built by the Davie Shipbuilding Co., Lauzon, *Athabaskan* was commissioned on 30 September 1972. On 26 November 1981, she was dispatched, along with *Algonquin* and *Preserver,* to the aid of the M.V. *Euro Princess,* which was badly holed and drifting down on the drill-rig Rowan Juneau, off Sable Island. Rescue helicopters took off the ship's crew, while *Athabaskan's* Sea King evacuated 44 from the drill-rig despite 60-knot winds. This procedure had to be done "free- deck" at both ends, owing to a malfunction of her Beartrap. The abandoned merchant ship was recovered by CGS *Alert.* On 24 August 1990, *Athabaskan* departed Halifax as the flagship for Operation Friction, along with *Terra Nova* and *Protecteur,* representing Canada in the Persian Gulf conflict, returning on 7 April 1991. Although she had been emergency refitted with many of the TRUMP weapons and systems, in October she was turned over to MIL, Lauzon, for her TRUMP refit, and on 3 August 1994, was provisionally accepted by the Navy. In the fall of 1995 she took part, with *Kootenay,* in Exercise Unitas, along with ships from Argentina, Brazil, Chile, Spain, the U.S. and Uruguay.

In 1999 *Athabaskan* spent six months with SNFL, rejoining the Force at the beginning of 2000. On 3 August that year she boarded (via helicopter) the *GTS Katie* 160 kilometres off Newfoundland, to compel delivery of a cargo of Canadian military equipment destined from Kosovo to Bécancour, Que., which her charterer had refused to land because of a dispute over payment. October 2001 saw her in Halifax Shipyards to start a $9.4 million refit. She was scheduled to return to duties in Summer 2002.

ATHABASKAN (3rd)					
BUILDER: Davie Shipbuilding and Repairing Co. Ltd., Lauzon, QC			LAUNCHED: 27/11/70 COMMISSIONED: 30/9/72		
LAID DOWN: 1/6/69			As TRUMP: 1994		
Commanding Officers					
CDR R. D. Yanow	30/9/72	6/9/74	LCDR A. G. Munroe	6/9/91	9/7/92
CDR G. L. Edwards	6/9/74	29/3/76	LCDR J. G. King	9/792	30/6/93
CDR J. C. Slade	29/3/76	7/7/78	LCDR H. C. Edmundson	30/6/93	16/11/93
CDR J. B. O'Reilly	7/7/78	7/7/80	CDR P. C. Leblanc	16/11/93	15/12/95
CDR J. W. McIntosh	7/7/80	2/8/81	CDR D. Rouleau	15/12/95	1/12/97
CDR K. R. Scotten	2/8/81	31/3/84	CAPT J. J. Gauvin	1/12/97	18/8/99
CDR D. Cogdon	31/3/84	16/5/86	CAPT D. W. Robertson	18/8/99	6/1/00
CDR G. R. Maddison	16/5/86	14/4/88	CDR P. V. Dempsey	6/1/00	30/8/01
CDR J. D. Peacocke	14/4/88	11/7/90	LCDR S. Bishop	30/8/01	
CDR K. J. Pickford	11/7/90	6/9/91			

Huron (2nd)

Second of her class, and built at Marine Industries Ltd., Sorel, *Huron* was commissioned on 16 December 1972. She represented Canada at the Silver Jubilee naval review at Spithead, U.K., on 28 June 1977. On 12 March 1980, while on patrol off Nova Scotia, she took off the crew of the freighter *Maurice Desgagnes*, whose cargo had shifted and holed her hull. The freighter subsequently sank. *Huron* took part in exercises in the Mediterranean in April 1980, and carried out trials of the vertically launched Sea Sparrow system, with which the TRUMP refit was to equip her class, in Roosevelt Roads, P.R., 19-24 February, 1981. Between 18 May and 3 June that year, she carried Governor-General Edward Schreyer on a tour of five Scandinavian ports. On 17 July 1987, she joined Pacific Command. In the summer of 1990, *Huron, Kootenay* and *Annapolis* paid the first visit to Vladivostok by Canadian warships since World War 2. In the spring of 1991 she relieved *Athabaskan* in the Persian Gulf. Between July 1993 and 25 November 1994, she underwent her TRUMP refit at MIL Davie, Lauzon, and in 1995 returned to Esquimalt, arriving on 21 July. For the next five years *Huron* participated in most of the major exercises taking place in Pacific waters. On September 7, 1999, *Huron* put to sea with RCMP and

Canada Immigration officers onboard. After two days of tracking a coastal ship carrying 146 Chinese migrants, the ship was hailed and then escorted into Nootka Sound where RCMP officers boarded it. The ship was found unfit for further travel and the migrants were taken aboard *Huron* and transported back to Esquimalt. On 4 December 2000, *Huron* was placed under care and maintenance owing to personnel shortage as well as with a view to economy.

Huron (2nd), 22 November 1972.

HURON (2nd)

BUILDER:	Marine Industries Ltd., Sorel, Que.	COMMISSIONED:	16/12/72
LAID DOWN:	6/69	As TRUMP:	1995
LAUNCHED:	9/4/71		

Commanding Officers

CDR R. J. Hitesman	14/12/72	25/7/75	CDR G. A. Paulson	25/6/91	27/9/91
CDR L. J. Cavan	25/7/75	15/7/77	CDR F. Scherber	27/9/91	24/4/92
CDR M. H. D. Taylor	15/7/77	22/7/78	CDR G. A. Paulson	24/9/92	29/6/92
CDR J. D. Spaulding	22/7/78	24/7/81	LCDR R. V. Marsh	29/6/92	11/6/93
CDR R. J. Deluca	24/7/81	14/1/83	CDR J. B. McCarthy	11/6/93	31/3/94
CDR G. L. Garnett	14/1/83	2/7/84	CDR R. A. Maze	28/4/95	26/7/96
CDR J. A. King	2/7/84	6/1/87	CDR J. S. Dewar	26/7/96	8/1/98
CDR G. Jeffrey	6/1/87	21/4/87	CAPT D. G. McNeil	8/1/98	12/8/99
CDR J. A. Keenliside	21/4/87	22/7/88	CAPT R. D. Murphy	12/8/99	1/2/01
CDR D. E. Collinson	22/7/88	3/8/90	CDR P. Fotheringham	1/2/01	19/6/01
CDR R. H. Melnick	8/8/90	25/6/91	LCDR W. S. Bates	19/6/01	-

Iroquois (2nd)

First of her class, she was built by Marine Industries Ltd. at Sorel and commissioned on 29 July 1972. In 1978, a fairly typical year for the period, she took part in exercises off Portugal, with French units in the Bay of Biscay, and with German units off the coast of Denmark, returning home on 7 July after logging some 14,300 nautical miles. On 4 December 1983, while on fisheries patrol off the Grand Banks, *Iroquois* answered an SOS from the Panamanian-registered *Ho Ming 5*, in danger of capsizing. In gale-force winds, the destroyer's Sea King took off eleven of the twenty-man crew, the remaining nine being rescued by her Zodiacs. Eighteen of her ship's company were decorated for their bravery during the episode. She underwent her TRUMP refit between 1 November 1989 and 3 July 1992. Between 25 September 1993 and 25 April 1994 *Iroquois* served with the blockading force off the former Yugoslavia, succeeding *Algonquin* as flagship of the SNFL force. She was appointed flagship of Maritime Operations Group 1 (MOG 1) on 17 June 1995. MOG 1 left Halifax on 22 February 1996 and headed south for exercises, stopping in Grenada where she played host to Prime Minister Jean Chrétien and a number of Caribbean heads of state. She returned to Halifax on 15 December.

Iroquois (2nd).

On 21 March 2000, *Iroquois*, as a member of a Canadian Task Group, left Halifax for spring exercises. While enroute south, the task group was re-directed to offer assistance to the bulk carrier *Leader L* which had gone down northeast of Bermuda. Thirteen survivors were picked up along with six bodies; twelve sailors were missing. *Iroquois* delivered the survivors and bodies to Bermuda before rejoining the task group. On 17 October 2001 *Iroquois* departed Halifax for the Arabian Sea as flagship of the Canadian Task Group (with *Charlottetown* and *Preserver*) designated for Operation Apollo, to support a U.S.-led coalition against international terrorism in Afghanistan (Operation Enduring Freedom). She returned to Halifax on 27 April 2002.

IROQUOIS (2nd)

BUILDER:	Marine Industries Ltd., Sorel, Que.	COMMISSIONED:	29/7/72
LAID DOWN:	15/1/69	As TRUMP:	1995
LAUNCHED:	28/11/70		

Commanding Officers

CDR D. N. MacGillivray	29/7/72	24/3/75	CDR P. Ballard	25/6/86	10/10/88
CDR G. G. Freill	24/3/75	4/5/77	LCDR G. Romanow	15/7/90	5/8/91
CDR R. E. George	4/5/77	30/6/79	CDR L. J. Edmunds	8/9/91	29/7/94
CDR E. K. Kelly	1/7/79	16/4/81	CDR R. Girouard	29/7/94	7/7/96
CDR L. G. Mason	16/3/81	30/6/82	CDR A. G. Munroe	7/7/96	13/2/98
CDR G. L. Garnett	30/6/82	13/1/83	CAPT S. E. King	13/2/98	7/7/99
CDR L. E. Murray	18/4/83	4/1/85	CAPT L. D. Sweeney	7/7/99	26/1/01
CDR B. R. Brown	4/1/85	25/6/86	CAPT C. L. Mofford	26/1/01	-

Submarines

U 190 and U 889

On May 12 and 13 1945, *U 190* and *U 889* formally surrendered at sea to units of the RCN, hostilities having ended a few days earlier. Both were of the large IX C type, built at Bremen in 1942 and 1944. They were almost immediately commissioned in the RCN for testing and evaluation, following which, on January 12 1946, *U 889* was turned over to the USN. She was expended on torpedo tests off New England the following year. *U 190* was paid off on July 24 1947, and on October 21 she was sunk by Canadian naval aircraft near the position where she had sunk HMCS *Esquimalt* in April 1945.

PARTICULARS OF CLASS:
DISPLACEMENT: 1,120/1,232
DIMENSIONS: 252' x 22' x 15'
SPEED: 18/7 kts
ARMAMENT: six 21-inch TT
Original armament included two 37-mm (1 x II), four 20-mm (2 x II)

U 190, 20 October 1947.

U 190

BUILDER:	Deschimag A.G. Weser, Bremen Germany	COMMISSIONED IN RCN:	19/5/45		
LAUNCHED:	8/6/42	PAID OFF:	24/7/47		
Commanding Officers					
LT M. Wood, RNVR	14/5/45	24/6/45	LT E. A. D. Holmes, RNVR	6/10/45	17/1/46
LT M. Pope, RNR	25/6/45	27/9/45	LT J. R. Johnston, RCN(R)	18/1/46	24/7/47
LT C. Larose, RCNVR	28/9/45	5/10/45			

U 889, May 1945.

U 889

BUILDER:	Deschimag A.G. Weser, Bremen Germany	COMMISSIONED IN RCN:	14/5/45		
LAUNCHED:	1944	PAID OFF:	12/1/46		
Commanding Officers					
LT E. A. D. Holmes, RNVR	14/5/45	5/10/45	LT J. R. Johnston, RCNVR	28/10/45	31/12/45
LT J. A. Cross, RCNVR	6/10/45	27/10/45	LT J. R. Johnston, RCN(R)	1/1/46	12/1/46

Grilse (2nd)

During and after the war it had been the custom of the RN to provide "tame" submarines for A/S training in Nova Scotia waters. By 1961, with a growing fleet of new A/S ships based at Esquimalt, it had become desirable to have a submarine stationed there as well.

USS *Burrfish* was accordingly borrowed and commissioned as HMCS *Grilse* on 11 May 1961, at New London, Connecticut. *Burrfish*, launched in 1943, had carried out six war patrols in the Pacific between 1944 and 1945. Converted to a radar picket submarine, she resumed service with the USN, including three tours with the Mediterranean Fleet from 1950 to 1956. She was paid off by the RCN on 2 October 1969, and returned to her owners. On 19 November 1969, she was expended in a training exercise, destroyed by a Mk 46 torpedo dropped by helicopter off San Clemente Island.

Grilse (2nd), 17 October 1961.

GRILSE (2nd)

BUILDER:	Portsmouth Navy Yard, NH	DISPLACEMENT:	1800/2425
LAID DOWN:	24/2/43	DIMENSIONS:	311' 6" x 27' 3" x 16' 10"
LAUNCHED:	18/6/43	SPEED:	20/10 kts
COMMISSIONED		CREW:	7/72
IN RCN:	11/5/61	ARMAMENT:	ten 21-inch TT (Originally one 5-inch as well)
PAID OFF:	2/10/69	Ex-USS *Burrfish*	

Commanding Officers

LCDR E. G. Gigg, RCN	11/5/61	2/12/62	LCDR M. Tate, RCN	9/9/66	20/8/68
LCDR G. C. McMorris, RCN	3/16/62	27/9/64	LCDR E. Falstrem, RCN	20/8/68	2/12/68
LCDR J. Rodocanachi, RCN	28/9/64	9/9/66			

Rainbow (2nd), 18 March 1969.

Rainbow (2nd)

Purchased from the USN, HMCS *Rainbow* was commissioned on 2 December 1968. As USS *Argonaut*, she had been launched in 1944, in time to carry out one war patrol from Pearl Harbor in June 1945. After the war she operated out of New London, Connecticut, from 1946 to 1955, undergoing modification in 1952 to what the USN calls Guppy II configuration. She served in the RCN until 31 December 1974.

RAINBOW (2nd)

BUILDER:	Portsmouth Navy Yard, NH	PAID OFF:	31/12/74	CREW:	8/74
LAID DOWN:	28/6/44	DISPLACEMENT:	1,526/2,391	ARMAMENT:	ten 21-inch TT
LAUNCHED:	1/10/44	DIMENSIONS:	311' 8" x 27' 4" x 17'		(Originally one 5-inch as well)
COMMISSIONED IN RCN:	2/12/68	SPEED:	20/10 kts	Ex-USS *Argonaut*	

Commanding Officers

LCDR C. E. Falstrem	2/12/68	1/4/70	LCDR C. J. Crow	1/7/72	1/8/73
LCDR R. C. Hunt	1/4/70	1/7/72	LCDR L. W. Barnes	1/8/73	31/12/75

O CLASS

PARTICULARS OF CLASS:

DISPLACEMENT:	1,610/2,410
DIMENSIONS:	295' 3" x 26' 6" x 18'
SPEED:	12/17 kts
CREW:	6/62
ARMAMENT:	eight 21-inch TT (homing torpedoes)

These three, which included two of the first submarines to be built to the order of the RCN, were near duplicates of the Oberon Class, at the time the Royal Navy's latest conventionally powered submarines. All were built at H.M. Dockyard, Chatham, U.K. In 1979 approval was given for the three to undergo a Submarine Operational Update Program (SOUP). In the course of this, they were fitted with new fire control, sonar, communications and optical equipment, as well as new batteries, which improved their endurance. Carried out at HM Dockyard, Halifax, the procedure upgraded their status from that of passive "tame" ASW targets to an aggressive capability. A fourth sister, HMS *Olympus*, was acquired in 1989, to serve as a stationary training vessel at dockside in Halifax. She was turned over to Crown Assets on 27 April 2000, for disposal. Though respectable enough craft in their prime, the "O" boats had long since reached the end of their useful lives and by July 1999 all three had been decommissioned. As of May 2002, they lay alongside in Halifax awaiting their fates.

Ojibwa, 25 August 1965.

Okanagan, 28 September 1968.

Onondaga.

Ojibwa

Laid down as HMS *Onyx*, she was sold to the RCN while completing, and commissioned at Chatham on 23 September 1965. Like her sisters, *Ojibwa* served all her time operating from Halifax except for two deployments (1977 and 1997) on the west coast. She underwent her SOUP refit 20 December 1981 and 31 May 1982. In 1994, *Ojibwa* was cut in half, her engines removed and replaced with newer ones from HMS *Osiris*, which had been purchased for spare parts. She was paid off on 21 May 1998.

Okanagan

She was commissioned at Chatham on 22 June 1968. Her SOUP refit was carried out between 12 June 1985 and 7 April 1986. In October and November 1990 she undertook a cruise on the Great Lakes, the first Canadian submarine to do so. She was paid off on 12 September 1998.

Onondaga

She was commissioned at Chatham on 22 June 1967, and served for six months in 1994 on the west coast. She was paid off on 28 July 2000, and there were rumoured to be plans afoot to take her to Ottawa for preservation as a museum ship.

OJIBWA

BUILDER: H. M. Dockyard, Chatham, U.K.
LAID DOWN: 27/9/62
LAUNCHED: 29/2/64
COMMISSIONED: 23/9/65
PAID OFF: 21/5/98

Commanding Officers

Officer	From	To	Officer	From	To	Officer	From	To
LCDR S. G. Tomlinson, RCN	23/9/65	14/11/66	LCDR W. J. Sloan	8/3/76	1/8/77	LCDR C. D. Soule	3/8/87	30/4/88
LCDR J. Rodocanachi, RCN	15/11/66	25/8/67	LCDR J. T. O. Jones	1/8/77	9/7/79	LCDR A. L. MacDonald	30/4/88	2/2/89
LCDR J. C. Wood, RCN	26/8/67	17/8/69	LCDR K. F. MacMillan	9/7/79	1/12/79	LCDR R. E. Bush	2/2/89	5/8/89
LCDR J. E. D. Bell	18/8/69	17/7/71	LCDR J. M. Ewan	1/12/79	24/6/80	LCDR R. A. Davidson	5/8/89	5/12/90
LCDR C. E. Falstrem	17/7/71	1/6/72	LCDR N. P. Nicolson	30/6/80	6/1/84	LCDR D. C. Marsaw	5/12/90	29/10/93
LCDR R. C. Perks	1/6/72	3/7/74	LCDR E. P. Webster	6/1/84	9/4/85	LCDR P. T. Kavanagh	29/10/93	20/7/94
LCDR J. E. D. Bell	23/9/74	15/1/75	LCDR W. C. Irvine	9/4/85	22/9/86	LCDR J. G. M. Dussault	20/7/94	27/5/97
LCDR L. W. Barnes	15/1/75	8/3/76	LCDR J. A. Y. Plante	22/9/86	3/8/87	LCDR J. R. L. Pelletier	27/5/97	21/5/98

OKANAGAN

BUILDER: H. M. Dockyard, Chatham, U.K.
LAID DOWN: 25/3/65
LAUNCHED: 17/9/66
COMMISSIONED: 22/6/68
PAID OFF: 14/9/98

Commanding Officers

Officer	From	To	Officer	From	To	Officer	From	To
LCDR N. H. H. Frawley, RCN	22/6/68	18/8/69	LT(N) J. S. Ferguson	7/7/78	13/7/78	LCDR A. L. MacDonald	1/4/86	8/2/88
LCDR G. R. Meek	19/8/69	6/11/69	LCDR J. S. Ferguson	14/7/78	14/7/80	LCDR N. P. Nicholson	8/2/88	24/7/89
LCDR L. G. Temple	7/11/69	21/12/69	LCDR F. Scherber	14/7/80	20/12/81	LCDR W. C. Irvine	24/7/89	22/7/90
LCDR C. J. Crowe	22/12/69	20/12/70	LCDR A. B. Dunlop	20/12/81	3/5/82	LCDR L. B. Mosher	22/7/90	3/6/91
LCDR H. R. Waddell	21/12/70	15/10/71	LCDR M. B. Maclean	3/5/82	10/8/83	LCDR R. E. Bush	3/6/91	15/6/92
LCDR C. E. Falstrem	16/10/71	6/5/73	LCDR E. P. Webster	10/8/83	6/1/84	LCDR L. M. Hickey	15/6/92	3/1/95
LCDR J. E. D. Bell	7/5/73	1/8/74	LCDR J. A. Y. Plante	6/1/84	12/3/84	LCDR L. B. Mosher	3/1/95	12/1/96
LCDR R. C. Hunt	2/8/74	28/10/75	LCDR D. F. Webb, RAN	12/3/84	14/4/85	LCDR S. A. Virgin	12/1/96	12/5/97
LCDR K. G. Nesbit	29/10/75	21/7/77	LCDR E. P. Webster	14/4/85	30/7/85	LCDR D. P. Mulholland	12/5/97	14/9/98
LCDR J. M. Ewan	22/7/77	6/7/78	LT A. L. MacDonald	30/7/85	1/4/86			

ONONDAGA

BUILDER: H. M. Dockyard, Chatham, U.K.
LAID DOWN: 18/6/64
LAUNCHED: 25/9/65
COMMISSIONED: 22/6/67
PAID OFF: 28/7/00

Commanding Officers

Officer	From	To	Officer	From	To	Officer	From	To
LCDR G. R. Meek, RCN	22/6/67	23/8/68	LCDR R. C. Hunt	1/11/75	4/12/75	LCDR J. A. Y. Plante	12/12/83	31/7/86
LCDR L. G. Temple	23/8/68	4/11/69	LCDR W. J. Sloan	4/12/75	15/3/76	LCDR L. M. Hickey	3176/86	13/5/87
LCDR G. R. Meek	4/11/69	23/12/69	LCDR R. C. Hunt	15/3/76	23/7/76	LCDR R. D. Carter, RAN	13/5/87	29/12/87
LCDR L. G. Temple	23/12/69	29/1/70	LCDR L. W. Barnes	23/7/76	26/7/76	LCDR J. A. Deirks, RAN	29/12/87	17/7/88
LCDR G. R. Meek	29/1/70	21/7/70	LCDR W. G. D. Lund	26/7/76	19/7/78	LCDR R. E. Bush	17/7/88	2/2/89
LCDR C. E. Falstrem	21/7/70	21/12/70	LCDR J. M. Ewan	19/7/78	3/12/79	LCDR A. L. MacDonald	2/2/89	1/1/90
LCDR C. J. Crowe	21/12/70	1/9/71	LCDR K. F. MacMillan	3/12/79	17/3/81	LCDR R. M. Truscott	1/1/90	20/7/92
LCDR M. Tate	1/9/71	15/10/71	LCDR A. B. Dunlop	17/3/81	20/12/81	LCDR W. A. Woodburn	20/7/92	5/8/94
LCDR H. R. Waddell	15/10/71	16/6/72	LCDR P. Webster	14/1/82	1/7/82	LCDR P. T. Kavanagh	5/8/94	15/12/97
LCDR P. W. Cairns	16/6/72	2/7/74	LCDR R. A. Perks	1/7/82	6/6/83	LCDR A. R. Wamback	15/12/97	29/7/00
LCDR R. C. Perks	2/7/74	14/7/75	LCDR P. Webster	6/6/83	15/8/83			
LCDR K. G. Nesbit	14/7/75	1/11/75	LT(N) L. M. Hickey	15/8/83	12/12/83			

SUBMARINE OPERATIONAL UPDATE PROGRAM (SOUP) SCHEDULE

OJIBWA
To HMC Dockyard 18/6/79
Start 20/2/81
Finish 31/5/82

ONONDAGA
To HMC Dockyard 18/1/82
Start 25/6/83
Finish 27/4/84

OKANAGAN
To HMC Dockyard 2/4/84
Start 12/6/85
Finish 7/4/86

Fast Hydrofoil Escort

Bras d'Or (2nd)

In 1919 a hydrofoil craft developed by Alexander Graham Bell and F. W. Baldwin attained the unheard of speed of 60 knots in trials on Cape Breton's Bras d'Or Lake. It was powered by two aircraft engines and air propellers. The potential of such a craft as an A/S vessel was finally considered in the early 1950s, when a small test vessel was built in Britain to Naval Research Establishment specifications. It arrived at Halifax aboard HMCS *Bonaventure* in 1957, and its performance led to the awarding of a contract to De Havilland Aircraft of Canada in 1963.

HMCS *Bras d'Or*, named for the scene of the first tests and designated a fast hydrofoil escort (FHE), was commissioned in 1968. When "hull-borne" at low speeds, the craft is driven by a 2,400-BHP diesel engine, but at about 23 knots the foils lift the hull clear of the water, and propulsion is taken over by a 30,000-SHP gas turbine engine powering twin screws. Trial speeds as great as 63 knots were attained.

Despite the evident success of the prototype FHE, she was laid up in 1971 and, in 1982, presented to a marine museum at L'Islet-sur-Mer, on the St. Lawrence River below Quebec.

Bras d'Or (2nd) at about forty-five knots, 14 January 1971.

BRAS D'OR (2nd)

BUILDER:	Marine Ind. Ltd., Sorel	DIMENSIONS:	151' x 21' x 23'
COMMISSIONED:	19/7/68	SPEED:	60 kts
PAID OFF:	1/5/72	CREW:	4/25
DISPLACEMENT:	180	ARMAMENT:	none fitted

Commanding Officers

CDR C. Cotaras, RCN	19/7/68	6/7/70	CDR G. L. Edwards	6/7/70	1/5/72

Cordova, 14 July 1953.

CORDOVA

BUILDER:	H.C. Grebe & Co., Chicago, IL	DISPLACEMENT:	325
LAUNCHED:	8/4/44	DIMENSIONS:	136' x 24' 6" x 8'
COMMISSIONED:	9/8/52	SPEED:	15 kts
PAID OFF:	12/4/57	CREW:	30

Commanding Officers

LCDR A. F. Rowland, RCN	13/1/55	31/5/55	LT R. Freeman, RCN	1/6/55	12/4/57

Minesweepers

Cordova

One of hundreds of motor minesweepers built for the USN during the Second World War, *Cordova* was launched as YMS.420 in 1944 at Chicago. She was purchased by the RCN on 3 December 1951, and commissioned from 9 August 1952 to 12 April 1957, serving primarily as tender to the Vancouver Naval Reserve Division. Afer being sold, she became the barge *Harbour Queen* and later *Nakaya*. In 1985 she was sunk as a sport-divers' wreck in Howe Sound, B.C.

BAY CLASS

PARTICULARS OF CLASS:

DISPLACEMENT:	390
DIMENSIONS:	152' x 28' x 8'
SPEED:	16 kts
CREW:	3/35
ARMAMENT:	1-40 mm

In 1951 and 1952, fourteen replacements were laid down for the aging minesweepers of wartime construction. Six were transferred to the French Navy in 1954, but were replaced by six of the same name in 1956-57. These ships were very similar to the Royal Navy's Ton Class of the same vintage. They were reclassed as patrol escorts in 1972. Six survivors soldiered on until the late 1990s, providing ship-handling experience for junior officers, on a rotating basis, as members of Training Group Pacific.

Chaleur, 1954.

CHALEUR

BUILDER:	Port Arthur Shipbuilding Co. Ltd., Port Arthur, Ont.	LAUNCHED:	21/6/52
		COMMISSIONED:	18/6/54
LAID DOWN:	8/6/51	PAID OFF:	30/9/54

Commanding Officer

LT M. A. Martin, RCN	18/6/54	30/9/54

Chaleur (2nd), 7 November 1959.

CHALEUR (2nd)

BUILDER:	Marine Industries Ltd., Sorel, Que.	LAUNCHED:	11/5/57
LAID DOWN:	20/2/56	COMMISSIONED:	12/9/57
		PAID OFF:	18/12/98

Commanding Officers

LCDR R. Carle, RCN	12/9/57	27/6/59	CDR R. B. Hayward, RCN	30/3/61	23/7/63
LCDR K. D. Lewis, RCN	28/6/59	29/3/61	CDR W. H. Wilson, RCN	24/7/63	20/3/64

Chaleur

Built by the Port Arthur Shipbuilding Co., she was commissioned on 18 June 1954, and paid off on 30 September. She was transferred on 9 October, 1954 to the French Navy, serving as *La Dieppoise* until 1985.

Chaleur (2nd)

Built by Marine Industries Ltd., Sorel, she was commissioned on 12 September 1957 and with five surviving sisters, was a member of Training Group Pacific until paid off for disposal on 18 December 1998. She was broken up at Port Hope, B.C. in 1999.

Chignecto (2nd), 16 December 1953.

Chignecto (3rd).

Comox (2nd), 11 May 1956.

Chignecto (2nd)

Built by Marine Industries Ltd., Sorel, she was commissioned on 1 December 1953, and paid off on March 31 1954, the day of her transfer to the French Navy. Renamed *La Bayonnaise*, she served until 1976.

Chignecto (3rd)

Built by G.T. Davie & Sons, Lauzon, she was commissioned on 1 August 1957, and was a member of Training Group Pacific until paid off on 19 December 1998. Sold to Budget Steel of Victoria, she was scrapped shortly thereafter.

Comox (2nd)

Built by Victoria Machinery Depot, she was commissioned on 2 April 1954, and paid off on 11 September 1957. On 31 March 1958, she was transferred to the Turkish Navy, which renamed her *Tirebolu*.

CHIGNECTO (2nd)

BUILDER:	Marine Industries Ltd., Sorel, Que.	LAUNCHED:	13/6/52
		COMMISSIONED:	1/12/53
LAID DOWN:	4/6/51	PAID OFF:	31/3/54

Commanding Officers

LCDR C. J. Benoit, DSC, RCN	1/12/53	2/2/54
LCDR E. J. Semmens, RCN	3/2/54	31/3/54

CHIGNECTO (3rd)

BUILDER:	George T. Davie & Sons Ltd., Lauzon, Que.	LAUNCHED:	17/11/56
		COMMISSIONED:	1/8/57
LAID DOWN:	25/10/55	PAID OFF:	19/12/98

Commanding Officers

LCDR R. C. K. Peers, RCN	1/8/57	10/3/58
LCDR C. D. Gillis, RCN	11/3/58	3/11/59
LCDR J. I. Manore, RCN	4/11/59	10/9/61
LCDR D. G. Wales, RCN	11/9/61	25/7/63
LCDR E. A. Makin, RCN	26/7/63	-

COMOX (2nd)

BUILDER:	Victoria Machinery Depot Co. Ltd., Victoria, B.C.	LAUNCHED:	24/4/52
		COMMISSIONED:	2/4/54
LAID DOWN:	8/6/51	PAID OFF:	11/9/57

Commanding Officers

CDR J. V. Steele, GM, RCN	2/4/54	9/8/55
LCDR C. G. Smith, RCN	10/8/55	5/5/57
LCDR P. S. Cox, RCN	6/5/57	11/9/57

Cowichan (2nd)

Built by the Davie Shipbuilding Co., Lauzon, she was commissioned on 10 December 1953, and on 31 March 1954, paid off and transferred to the French Navy. Renamed *La Malouine*, she served until 1977.

Cowichan (2nd).

COWICHAN (2nd)			
BUILDER:	Davie Shipbuilding and Repairing Co. Ltd., Lauzon, Que.	LAUNCHED:	12/11/51
		COMMISSIONED:	10/12/53
		PAID OFF:	31/3/54
LAID DOWN:	20/6/51		
Commanding Officers			
LCDR P. H. Cayley, RCN		10/12/53	/12/53
LCDR A. H. Slater, RCN		/12/53	15/3/54
LT J. M. Cutts, RCN		16/3/54	31/3/54

COWICHAN (3rd)			
BUILDER:	Yarrows Ltd., Esquimalt, B.C.	LAUNCHED:	26/2/57
		COMMISSIONED:	12/12/57
LAID DOWN:	10/7/56	PAID OFF:	22/8/97
Commanding Officers			
LCDR G. W. S. Brooks, RCN		12/12/57	27/8/59
LCDR W. C. Wilson, RCN		28/8/59	30/8/61
LCDR R. D. Okros, RCN		31/8/61	/8/63
LT A. P. Howard, RCN		/8/63	/2/64

Cowichan (3rd)

Built by Yarrows Ltd., Esquimalt, she was commissioned on 12 December 1957, and was a member of Training Group Pacific until paid off on 22 August 1997.

Cowichan (3rd).

Fortune

Built by Victoria Machinery Depot, she was commissioned on 3 November 1954, and paid off on 28 February 1964. Sold for commercial purposes in 1966, she figured, as *Greenpeace Two*, in an unsuccessful attempt to hinder a nuclear test in the Aleutians in November 1971. She is currently registered as *Edgewater Fortune*.

Fortune, 14 February 1968.

FORTUNE						
BUILDER:	Victoria Machinery Depot Co. Ltd., Victoria, B.C.			LAUNCHED:	14/4/53	
				COMMISSIONED:	3/11/54	
LAID DOWN:	24/4/52			PAID OFF:	28/2/64	
Commanding Officers						
LCDR J. B. Young, RCN	3/11/54	23/8/55	LCDR S. G. Moore, RCN	14/8/57	15/2/59	
LCDR P. R. Hinton, RCN	24/8/55	21/3/57	LCDR D. M. Waters, RCN	16/2/59	9/1/62	
LCDR C. G. Smith, RCN	22/3/57	13/8/57	LCDR A. B. Torrie, RCN	10/1/62	28/2/64	

Fundy (2nd), 9 March 1954.

Fundy (3rd), 26 February 1962.

Gaspé (2nd), 14 January 1954.

Fundy (2nd)

Built by the Saint John Dry Dock Co., she was commissioned on 19 March 1954, and paid off 31 March, the date of her transfer to the French Navy, serving as *La Dunkerquoise* until 1984.

Fundy (3rd)

Built by G.T. Davies & Sons, Lauzon, she was commissioned on 27 November 1956, and was a member of Training Group Pacific until paid off on 19 December 1996.

Gaspé (2nd)

Built by the Davie Shipbuilding Co., Lauzon, she was commissioned on 26 November 1953, and paid off on 22 August 1957. She was transferred to the Turkish Navy, which renamed her *Trabzon*, on 31 March 1958.

FUNDY (2nd)

BUILDER:	Saint John Dry Dock and Shipbuilding Co. Ltd., Saint John, N.B.	LAUNCHED:	9/12/53
		COMMISSIONED:	19/3/54
		PAID OFF:	31/3/54
LAID DOWN:	19/6/51		

Commanding Officer

| LCDR A. Slater, RCN | | 19/3/54 | 31/3/54 |

FUNDY (3rd)

BUILDER:	Davie Shipbuilding and Repairing Co. Ltd., Lauzon, Que.	LAUNCHED:	14/6/56
		COMMISSIONED:	27/11/56
		PAID OFF:	19/12/96
LAID DOWN:	7/3/55		

Commanding Officers

LCDR R. C. Thurber, RCN	18/12/56	10/2/58
LCDR N. St. C. Norton, RCN	18/2/58	18/8/59
LCDR J. Butterfield, RCN	19/8/59	2/1/62
LT R. J. Luke, RCN	3/1/62	7/2/64

GASPÉ (2nd)

BUILDER:	Davie Shipbuilding and Repairing Co. Ltd., Lauzon, Que.	LAUNCHED:	12/11/51
		COMMISSIONED:	26/11/53
		PAID OFF:	22/8/57
LAID DOWN:	21/3/51		

Commanding Officers

LCDR H. B. Carnall, RCN	26/11/53	17/10/55
CDR W. S. T. McCully, RCN	18/10/55	4/6/57
LCDR H. C. LaRose, RCN	5/6/57	22/8/57

James Bay

Built by Yarrows Ltd., Esquimalt, she was commissioned on 3 May 1954, and paid off on 28 February 1964. She was subsequently sold for use in offshore oil exploration.

Miramichi (2nd)

Built by the Saint John Dry Dock Co., she was commissioned on 30 July 1954, and paid off on 1 October. On 9 October 1954, she was transferred to the French Navy, serving as *La Lorientaise* until 1984.

Miramichi (3rd)

Built by Victoria Machinery Depot, she was commissioned on 29 October 1957, and served with Training Group Pacific until paid off on 16 December 1998.

James Bay.

Miramichi (2nd), 2 August 1954.

JAMES BAY			
BUILDER:	Yarrows Ltd., Esquimalt, B.C.	LAUNCHED:	12/3/53
		COMMISSIONED:	3/5/54
LAID DOWN:	16/8/51	PAID OFF:	28/2/64
Commanding Officers			
LCDR G. R. Smith, RCN		3/5/54	4/10/55
LCDR J. J. Coates, RCN		5/10/55	22/7/58
LT I. C. S. Inglis, DSC, RCN		23/7/58	6/9/60
LT R. A. Orton, RCN		7/9/60	3/7/62
LCDR J. E. Hobbs, RCN		4/7/62	28/2/64

MIRAMICHI (2nd)			
BUILDER:	Saint John Dry Dock and Shipbuilding Co. Ltd., Saint John, N.B.	LAUNCHED:	4/5/54
		COMMISSIONED:	30/7/54
		PAID OFF:	1/10/54
LAID DOWN:	13/6/52		
Commanding Officers			
LCDR J. L. Panabaker, RCN		30/7/54	11/8/54
LT D. A. Scott, RCN		12/8/54	1/10/54

MIRAMICHI (3rd)			
BUILDER:	Victoria Machinery Depot Co. Ltd., Victoria, B.C.	LAUNCHED:	22/2/57
		COMMISSIONED:	29/10/57
		PAID OFF:	16/12/98
LAID DOWN:	2/2/56		
Commanding Officers			
LCDR M. A. Considine, RCN		29/10/57	8/10/59
LCDR R. K. Niven, RCN		9/10/59	29/6/61
LT C. Cotaras, RCN		30/6/61	16/7/63
LT D. B. Rogers, RCN		17/7/63	28/2/64

Miramichi (3rd), 14 November 1957.

Quinte (2nd).

Resolute, 26 February 1962.

Thunder (2nd) celebrating Christmas, 1953, at Halifax.

Quinte (2nd)

Built by the Port Arthur Shipbuilding Co., she was commissioned on 15 October 1954, paid off on 26 February 1964, and declared surplus the following year.

Resolute

Built by Kingston Shipyards Ltd., she was commissioned on 16 September 1954, paid off on 14 February 1964 and declared surplus the following year.

Thunder (2nd)

Built by Canadian Vickers Ltd., Montreal, she was commissioned on 15 December 1953, and paid off on 31 March 1954, the date of her transfer to the French Navy. Renamed *La Paimpolaise*, she served until 1986.

QUINTE (2nd)

BUILDER:	Port Arthur Shipbuilding Co. Ltd., Port Arthur, Ont.	LAUNCHED:	8/8/53
		COMMISSIONED:	15/10/54
		PAID OFF:	26/2/64
LAID DOWN:	14/6/52		

Commanding Officers

LCDR D. P. Brownlow, RCN	15/10/54	23/6/57
LCDR R. P. Mylrea, RCN	24/6/57	2/9/59
LCDR R. J. Paul, RCN	3/9/59	2/8/61
LCDR G. G. Armstrong, RCN	3/8/61	30/7/63
LCDR R. L. Donaldson, RCN	31/7/63	26/2/64

RESOLUTE

BUILDER:	Kingston Shipbuilding Co. Ltd., Kingston, Ont.	LAUNCHED:	20/6/53
		COMMISSIONED:	16/9/54
		PAID OFF:	14/2/64
LAID DOWN:	29/8/51		

Commanding Officers

LCDR J. L. Panabaker, RCN	16/9/54	14/9/55
LCDR N. D. Langham, RCN	15/9/55	5/8/57
CDR K. H. Boggild, RCN	6/8/57	13/5/58
CDR A. C. Campbell, RCN	14/5/58	-
CDR H. J. Hunter, RCN		22/3/61
LT G. W. Garrad, RCN	23/3/61	2/1/63
LCDR M. F. McIntosh, RCN	3/1/63	14/2/64

THUNDER (2nd)

BUILDER:	Canadian Vickers Ltd., Montreal, Que.	LAUNCHED:	17/7/52
		COMMISSIONED:	15/12/53
		PAID OFF:	31/3/54
LAID DOWN:	17/5/51		

Commanding Officers

LCDR S. Howell, RCN	15/12/53	22/12/53
LT W. N. Holmes, RCN	23/12/53	23/2/54
LCDR J. L. Panabaker, RCN	24/2/54	31/3/54

Thunder (3rd)

Built by Port Arthur Shipbuulding Co., she was commissioned on 3 October 1957, and served with Training Group Pacific until paid off on 22 August 1997.

Trinity

Built by G. T. Davie & Son, Lauzon, she was commissioned on 16 June 1954, and paid off on 21 August 1957, for transfer to the Turkish Navy. The transfer took place on 31 March 1958, and the ship was named *Terme*.

Ungava (2nd)

Built by the Davie Shipbuilding Co., Lauzon, she was commissioned on 4 June 1954, and paid off on 23 August 1957. She was transferred on 31 March 1958, to the Turkish Navy, which renamed her *Tekirdag*.

Thunder (3rd), 16 June 1958.

Trinity.

Ungava (2nd), 4 May 1955.

THUNDER (3rd)			
BUILDER:	Port Arthur Shipbuilding Co. Ltd., Port Arthur, Ont.	LAUNCHED: COMMISSIONED: PAID OFF:	27/10/56 3/10/57 22/8/97
LAID DOWN:	1/9/55		
Commanding Officers			
LCDR T. F. Owen, RCN		3/10/57	27/10/59
LCDR N. S. Jackson, RCN		28/10/59	3/2/62
LCDR M. Barrow, RCN		4/2/62	6/3/64
LT J. B. Elson, RCN		14/4/67	/9/67

TRINITY			
BUILDER:	George T. Davie & Sons Ltd., Lauzon, Que.	LAUNCHED: COMMISSIONED: PAID OFF:	31/7/53 16/6/54 21/8/57
LAID DOWN:	31/1/52		
Commanding Officers			
LCDR A. H. M. Slater, RCN		16/6/54	10/5/56
LCDR R. C. Thurber, RCN		11/5/56	12/12/56
LT R. C. K. Peers, RCN		13/12/56	11/7/57
LT P. Herdman, RCN		12/7/57	21/8/57

UNGAVA (2nd)			
BUILDER:	Davie Shipbuilding and Repairing Co. Ltd., Lauzon, Que.	LAUNCHED: COMMISSIONED: PAID OFF:	20/5/53 4/6/54 23/8/57
LAID DOWN:	17/12/51		
Commanding Officers			
LCDR E. J. Semmens, RCN		4/6/54	4/5/55
LCDR R. M. Young, RCN		5/5/55	11/4/57
LCDR T. F. Owen, RCN		12/4/57	23/8/57

Patrol Craft

Blue Heron
Cormorant
Loon
Mallard

PARTICULARS OF CLASS:	
DISPLACEMENT:	66 full load
DIMENSIONS:	92' x 17' x 5' 4"
SPEED:	14 kts
CREW:	2/19
ARMAMENT:	1-20 mm, Hedgehog

The Bird Class "seaward defence patrol craft" were launched 1954-56 at four Ontario boatyards. They were intended to replace the remaining Fairmile motor launches, and their principal peacetime functions were Reserve and cadet training and air/sea rescue. *Blue Heron* served on loan to the RCMP 1957-68. All were paid off in the 1960s and sold 1970-71.

Blue Heron, 25 September 1956.

Cormorant, 23 May 1962.

Loon, 29 February 1962.

Mallard, 4 June 1960.

BLUE HERON	
BUILDER:	Hunter Boat Works, Orillia
LAUNCHED:	7/5/56
COMMISSIONED:	30/7/56
PAID OFF:	19/11/56

CORMORANT	
BUILDER:	Midland Boat Works, Midland
LAUNCHED:	15/5/56
COMMISSIONED:	16/7/56
PAID OFF:	23/5/63

LOON	
BUILDER:	Taylor Boat Works, Toronto
LAUNCHED:	4/10/54
COMMISSIONED:	30/11/55
PAID OFF:	30/8/65

MALLARD	
BUILDER:	Grew Boat Works, Penetanguishine
LAUNCHED:	30/4/56
COMMISSIONED:	16/7/56
PAID OFF:	2/9/65

Escort Maintenance Ships

Cape Breton
Cape Scott

These modified Fort type cargo ships were launched at Vancouver in 1944 as HMS *Beachy Head* and *Flamborough Head*. The latter continued in service with the RN after the war, but *Beachy Head* was turned over to the Royal Netherlands Navy in 1947 as repair ship *Vulkan*. In 1950 she was returned to the RN and resumed her original name until 1952, when she was transferred to the RCN and, in 1953, renamed *Cape Scott*. She lay alongside her sister, *Cape Breton*, at Halifax for some years, providing supplementary workshop and classroom facilities until *Cape Breton* was transferred to the west coast in 1958. After refit at Saint John, *Cape Scott* was at last commissioned on 28 January 1959, to serve at Halifax until paid off into reserve on July 1 1970. In 1972 she was redesignated Fleet Maintenance Group (Atlantic), but was sold when the group moved ashore in 1975 and left under tow in 1978 to be broken up in Texas.

Flamborough Head was also acquired from the RN in 1952, and renamed *Cape Breton* upon commissioning on 31 January 1953. She served at Halifax until 25 August 1958, as repair ship and training establishment for technical apprentices. Converted to escort maintenance ship at Esquimalt, she was commissioned there on 16 November 1959, for service on the west coast. On 10 February 1964, *Cape Breton* was paid off into reserve and subsequently functioned as a towed mobile support facility and accommodation vessel at Esquimalt, designated Fleet Maintenance Group (Pacific). In 1993, she was replaced by a shore building. Sold to the Artificial Reef Society of B.C., she was sunk as a sport-divers' wreck on 20 October 2001, off Snake Island, near Nanaimo.

Cape Breton, 22 January 1960.

CAPE BRETON (2nd)

BUILDER:	Burrard Dry Dock Co. Ltd., Vancouver, B.C.	PAID OFF:	10/2/64
		DISPLACEMENT:	8,580
LAID DOWN:	5/7/44	DIMENSIONS:	441' 6" x 57' x 20'
LAUNCHED:	7/10/44	SPEED:	11 kts
COMMISSIONED:	31/1/53	CREW:	270

Commanding Officers

CDR E. N. Clarke, RCN	31/1/53	21/3/54	CDR J. C. Chauvin, RCN	27/8/57	11/6/58
CDR D. H. Fairney, RCN	22/3/54	8/3/56	CDR H. R. Beck, RCN	12/6/58	1/8/58
CAPT J. S. Ross, RCN	9/3/56	2/7/56	LCDR R. P. LeMay, RCN	2/8/58	25/8/58
CDR F. Harley, RCN	3/7/56	31/7/57	CDR M. F. Oliver, RCN	16/11/59	24/7/62
LCDR K. W. Salmon, RCN	1/8/57	26/8/57	CDR I. A. McPhee, RCN	25/7/62	10/2/64

Cape Scott, 15 December 1959.

CAPE SCOTT

BUILDER:	Burrard Dry Dock Co. Ltd., Vancouver, B.C.	DISPLACEMENT:	8,580
LAID DOWN:	8/6/44	DIMENSIONS:	441' 6" x 57' x 20'
LAUNCHED:	27/9/44	SPEED:	11 kts
COMMISSIONED:	28/1/59	CREW:	270
PAID OFF:	1/7/70		

Commanding Officers

CDR F. J. Jones, RCN	28/1/59	23/8/60	CDR C. A. Law, RCN	11/5/64	10/4/66
CDR A. H. Rankin, RCN	24/8/60	10/5/64	CDR H. H. Smith, RCN	11/4/66	-

Operational Support Ships

The first of this type, *Provider*, was commissioned on 28 September 1963, at Lauzon, Quebec. Originally designated a Fleet Replenishment Ship, she was the largest vessel thus far built in Canada for the RCN, and enabled its ships to remain at sea for extended periods, as well as greatly increasing their range and mobility. She had stowage space for some 12,000 tonnes of fuel oil, diesel oil and aviation gasoline, in addition to spare parts, ammunition, missiles, general stores and food.

Experience with *Provider* led to significant changes in the next two of her type, *Protecteur* and *Preserver*, commissioned at Saint John, N.B., on 30 August, 1969 and 30 July 1970, respectively. Though similar in size to the tanker-like *Provider*, they have higher freeboard, massive bridges, and paired funnels, which make possible a single, much wider hangar door. Unlike *Provider*, they were armed with a twin 3-inch "bow chaser" gun, which was dispensed with in 1984, having proved vulnerable to damage from head seas. They can refuel three other fleet units simultaneously (two abeam and one astern) at 20 knots, with automatic tensioning gear to compensate for the ships' motion as fuel is transferred at 25 tonnes per minute. Each can carry three A/S helicopters as spares for the fleet or for transferring pallet-loads of solid stores.

Preserver (2nd)

Commissioned at Saint John on 30 August 1969, she was selected to carry Governor-General Roland Michener on a visit to the Netherlands and Belgium in 1971. On this trip she twice hosted royalty, on 16 April Queen Juliana and Prince Bernhard of the Netherlands, and on the 22nd, King Baudouin and Queen Fabiola of Belgium. That June she carried out the first-ever replenishment of a hydrofoil at sea, the recipient being HMCS *Bras d'Or*. In 1974-75 *Preserver* served as supply ship for Canadian troops stationed in Cyprus as part of a UN peacekeeping force. Throughout the Cold War, she and *Protecteur* engaged in all major NATO and east coast fleet exercises, and have remained indispensable. On 7 April 1993, she returned to Halifax from duty off Somalia. Between 18 October and 23 November she served in Operation Forward Action (UN sanctions against Haiti). *Preserver* next departed on 27 January 1994, to join the multinational force carrying out sanctions against the former Yugoslavia. She operated there again from May to June 1995. She was one of the fleet units that assisted in the Swiss Air disaster off Nova Scotia in September 1998. She departed Halifax on 17 October 2001, with *Charlottetown* and *Iroquois*, to support Operation Enduring Freedom, the U.S.-led response to the terrorist destruction of the Twin Trade Towers, New York City, on September 11. She returned to Halifax on 27 April 2002.

Preserver (2nd).

PRESERVER (2nd)

BUILDER:	Saint John Dry Dock and Shipbuilding Co. Ltd., Saint John, N.B.	DISPLACEMENT:	24,000 full load
		DIMENSIONS:	555' x 76' 30'
LAID DOWN:	17/10/67	SPEED:	20 kts
LAUNCHED:	29/56/69	CREW:	15/212
COMMISSIONED:	30/7/70	ARMAMENT:	two 3 inch50, until 1984

Commanding Officers

CAPT M. W. Mayo	30/7/70	5/9/72	CAPT C. D. E. Cronk	4/8/89	9/1/91
CAPT P. J. Traves	5/9/72	4/7/74	CAPT D. J. McClean	9/1/91	7/4/91
CAPT M. Tremblay	4/7/74	2/8/75	CAPT C. D. E. Cronk	7/4/91	19/7/91
CAPT H. W. Vondette	2/8/75	6/7/77	CAPT R. W. Allen	19/7/91	19/7/93
CAPT T. S. Murphy	6/7/77	21/7/78	CAPT P. C. B. Young	19/7/93	15/7/94
CAPT J. M. Cumming	21/7/78	13/12/79	CAPT J. A. Keenliside	15/7/94	18/7/96
CDR T. Heath	14/12/79	31/7/80	CDR J. P. Allaire	18/7/96	4/7/97
CAPT L. J. Cavan	31/7/80	3/8/81	CAPT S. E. King	4/7/97	6/1/98
CAPT R. C. Hunt	3/8/81	18/7/83	CDR N. S. Greenwood	6/1/98	27/3/98
CAPT J. B. O'Reilly	18/7/83	11/1/85	CDR R. R. Town	27/3/98	5/7/99
CAPT B. P. Moore	11/1/85	14/7/87	CDR D. J. Galina	5/7/99	5/7/01
CAPT B. E. Derible	14/7/87	4/8/89	CDR J. B. McCarthy	5/7/01	-

Protecteur

Protecteur was commissioned in Saint John on 30 August 1969. During 1973 she joined SNFL for a five month tour along with HMCS *Margaree*. This was the first time two Canadian units worked with this group and the first time an AOR was assigned to this fleet. Through the 1970s and 80s *Protecteur* worked with her sister *Preserver* to ensure fleet support for virtually every major east coast Canadian fleet deployment. Along with *Athabaskan* and *Terra Nova* she departed Halifax on 24 August 1990 for Operation Friction, Canada's contribution to operations against Iraq following that country's invasion of Kuwait. In preparation, her bow 3-inch50 was re-installed, as were two CIWS (Close-In Weapon Systems) mounts and other upgrades. Upon her return in the fall of 1991 *Protecteur* made visits to

Protecteur refuelling *Athabaskan* in the Persian Gulf, November 1990.

ports in Newfoundland, and a year later journeyed south to offer aid to victims in Florida of Hurricane Andrew. She sailed from Halifax on 15 October 1992 to begin a two-year refit at SRU(P), Esquimalt, returning to service in August 1995. (She had been transferred to the west coast fleet on 9 July 1993.) On 16 September 1999 she departed Esquimalt to join the multinational forces responding to the crisis in East Timor. After serving as the force logistics co-ordinator for five months, she returned home on 2 March 2000. A major refit was undertaken in 2001 and on 22 May 2002 *Protecteur* departed Esquimalt to replace *Preserver* in Operation Apollo in the Arabian Sea.

PROTECTEUR				
BUILDER:	Saint John Dry Dock and Shipbuilding Co. Ltd., Saint John, N.B.	DISPLACEMENT:	24,000 full load	
		DIMENSIONS:	555' x 76' x 30'	
LAID DOWN:	17/10/67	SPEED:	20 kts	
LAUNCHED:	7/11/68	CREW:	15/212	
COMMISSIONED:	30/8/69	ARMAMENT:	two 3 inch50, until 1984	

Commanding Officers

CAPT D. R. Hinton	30/8/69	13/7/71	CAPT C. D. E. Cronk	9/1/91	7/4/91
CAPT J. P Côté	13/7/71	24/7/72	CAPT D. J. McClean	7/4/91	20/11/92
CAPT D. N. Mainguy	24/7/72	31/5/74	CAPT R. S. Edwards	20/11/92	26/2/93
CAPT A. M. Brookbank	31/5/74	12/2/76	LCDR N. Leak	5/2/93	19/7/93
CAPT J. C. Wood	12/2/76	28/7/77	CDR W. G. Buckeridge	19/7/93	31/8/94
CAPT L. A. Dzioba	29/7/77	4/8/80	CDR G. H. Gadd	31/8/94	10/7/95
CAPT R. G. Guy	4/8/80	2/11/81	CAPT K. C. E. Beardmore	10/7/95	3/7/97
CAPT R. C. Waller	2/11/81	1/7/84	CAPT D. G. McNeil	3/7/97	7/1/98
CAPT B. Johnson	1/7/84	27/6/86	CDR R. P. Harrison	7/1/98	27/8/99
CAPT H. L. Davies	27/6/86	26/4/88	CDR R. A. Maze	27/8/99	15/8/01
CAPT J. K. Steele	26/4/88	10/7/90	CDR M. R. Bellows	15/8/01	-
CAPT D. J. McClean	10/7/90	9/1/91			

Provider (2nd)

<table>
<tr><td colspan="4">PROVIDER (2nd)</td></tr>
<tr><td>BUILDER:</td><td colspan="3">Davie Shipbuilding and Repairing Co. Ltd., Lauzon, Que.</td></tr>
<tr><td>LAID DOWN:</td><td colspan="3">21/6/61</td></tr>
<tr><td>LAUNCHED:</td><td colspan="3">5/7/62</td></tr>
<tr><td>COMMISSIONED:</td><td colspan="3">28/9/63</td></tr>
<tr><td>PAID OFF:</td><td colspan="3">24/06/98</td></tr>
</table>

DISPLACEMENT:	22,700 full load
DIMENSIONS:	551' x 76' x 30'
SPEED:	20 kts
CREW:	11/131
ARMAMENT:	None fitted

Commanding Officers

CAPT T. C. Pullen, RCN	28/9/63	8/12/64	CAPT J. Drent	12/4/82	9/7/84
CAPT K. H. Boggild, RCN	8/12/64	24/8/66	CAPT D. E. Gibb	9/7/84	15/7/86
CAPT D. W. Knox, RCN	24/8/66	16/8/67	CAPT R. D. Moore	15/7/86	5/12/88
CAPT W. J. H. Stuart, RCN	16/8/67	5/9/69	CAPT K. R. Scotten	5/12/88	13/7/90
CAPT J. A. Fulton	5/9/69	2/8/72	CAPT I. S. Foldesi	13/7/90	27/7/92
CAPT F. W. Crickard	2/8/72	30/9/74	CAPT M. B. McLean	27/7/92	5/8/94
CAPT C. H. P Shaw	30/9/74	5/8/76	CDR I. G. Parker	5/8/94	15/12/95
CAPT K. M. Young	5/8/76	21/7/78	CAPT S. D. Andrews	15/12/95	25/6/97
CAPT R. H. Kirby	21/7/78	20/6/80	CDR D. O. Thamer	25/6/97	24/6/98
CAPT R. L. Donaldson	20/6/80	12/4/82			

Commissioned on 28 September 1963, at Saint John, NB. Late in 1969, with the arrival of the two follow-on AORs, she was transferred to the west coast. In the spring of 1990 she took part in the Pacific Rim countries' exercise RIMPAC 90, along with units of the 2nd and 4th Destroyer Squadrons, which afterward visited Vladivostok, the first western warships to do so since 1939. Afterward, en route to visit Manila, she rescued a large number of Vietnamese boat people that had spent nine days without food or water after their boat had broken down. In late 1993 and early 1994 she took part in the UN embargo of Haiti. She returned to Halifax in June 1996. Paid off on 24 June 1998. She was sold to Greek interests and on 26 July 2002 left Halifax under tow for Greece, to become a water storage vessel.

Arctic Patrol Vessel

Labrador

HMCS *Labrador* was built in recognition of the growing strategic importance of Canada's Arctic region, and to the assert her sovereignty there. The design was adapted from that of the US Coast Guard's Wind class of icebreakers. Like them, she was built for power rather than speed, her six diesel-electric engines driving her at 16 knots maximum Heeling tanks connected by reversible-propeller type pumps enable water ballast to be hurled from side to side at 40,000 gallons a minute, so that she can rock herself free when trapped by ice. She carries two helicopters.

Commissioned on 8 July 1954, *Labrador* sailed that summer on the first of four voyages she would make to the Arctic as a naval vessel. On that initial voyage she became the first warship to negotiate the Northwest Passage across the top of the continent and, returning to Halifax via the Panama Canal, the first to circumnavigate North America. On her second voyage, in 1955, she transported personnel and equipment for the construction of the eastern portion of the Distant Early Warning (DEW) Line. That summer and next, she also carried out extensive hydrographic surveys in the eastern Arctic, spending five and one-half months there in

Labrador, March 1957.

1956 alone. A departure from custom in 1957 found her paying visits to Portsmouth, Oslo, and Copenhagen, and on 22 November she was paid off for refit.

She was fated not to fly the White Ensign again, for it was decided to transfer her to the Department of Transport. As CCGS *Labrador*, she was used for icebreaking in the lower St. Lawrence and on occasion embarked scientists for summer studies in the Arctic until being decommissioned on 28 May 1987. *Labrador* was later towed to Taiwan and broken up.

LABRADOR

BUILDER:	Marine Industries Ltd., Sorel, Que.	DISPLACEMENT:	6,490 full load
LAID DOWN:	18/11/49	DIMENSIONS:	269' x 63' x 26'8"
LAUNCHED:	14/12/51	SPEED:	16 kts
COMMISSIONED:	8/7/54	CREW:	228
PAID OFF as CNAV:	22/11/57		

Commanding Officers

CAPT O. C. S. Robertson, GM, RCN	8/7/54	29/10/55	CAPT T. C. Pullen, RCN	13/2/56	3/11/57
CDR J. M. Leeming, RCN	29/10/55	30/11/55	CDR C. A. Law, DSC, RCN	4/11/57	22/11/57
CAPT O. C. S. Robertson, GM, RCN	1/12/55	12/2/56			

Auxiliaries

GATE VESSELS

PARTICULARS OF CLASS:

DISPLACEMENT:	429 full load
DIMENSIONS:	125' 6" x 26' 4" x 13'
SPEED:	11 kts
CREW:	3/20
ARMAMENT:	1-40 mm

Porte Dauphine
Porte de la Reine
Porte Québec
Porte Saint Jean
Porte Saint Louis

Their names, appropriately, are those of gates in the French fortifications at Quebec City and Louisbourg. Though designed specifically to operate the gates in anti-submarine booms, these craft served primarily as training vessels in peacetime. *Porte Saint Jean* and *Porte Saint Louis* were based at Halifax, with summer forays into the Great Lakes, the others at Esquimalt. *Porte Dauphine* wore a coat of bright red paint 1958-74, while on loan to the Department of Transport as an environmental research ship on the Great Lakes. All five Gate class vessels were paid off by 19 December 1996.

Porte Dauphine, 11 May 1953.

Porte de la Reine.

Porte Québec, 14 July 1953.

PORTE DAUPHINE

BUILDER:	Pictou Foundry Co., Pictou, NS
LAID DOWN:	16/5/51
LAUNCHED:	24/4/52
COMMISSIONED:	10/12/52
PAID OFF:	12/95

PORTE DE LA REINE

BUILDER:	Victoria Machinery Depot Co. Ltd., Victoria, B.C.
LAID DOWN:	4/3/51
LAUNCHED:	28/12/51
COMMISSIONED:	7/10/52
PAID OFF:	19/12/96

PORTE QUÉBEC

BUILDER:	Burrard Dry Dock Co. Ltd., Vancouver, B.C.
LAID DOWN:	15/2/51
LAUNCHED:	28/8/51
COMMISSIONED:	19/9/52
PAID OFF:	19/12/96

PORTE SAINT JEAN

BUILDER:	George T. Davie & Sons Ltd., Lauzon, Que.
LAID DOWN:	16/5/50
LAUNCHED:	22/11/50
COMMISSIONED:	5/12/51
PAID OFF:	31/03/96

PORTE SAINT LOUIS

BUILDER:	George T. Davie & Sons Ltd., Lauzon, Que.
LAID DOWN:	21/3/51
LAUNCHED:	23/7/52
COMMISSIONED:	29/8/52
PAID OFF:	31/03/96

Porte Saint Jean, 8 June 1961.

Porte Saint Louis at Kingston, 1953.

Cedarwood, 14 June 1949.

SURVEY VESSEL

Cedarwood

Launched in 1941 at Lunenburg, Nova Scotia, as MV *J. E. Kinney*, this ship was taken up for war service with the Royal Canadian Army Service Corps and renamed *General Schmidlin*. Her function seems to have been that of supplying army detachments at scattered harbours in the Maritimes and Newfoundland. She was commissioned in the RCN on 22 September 1948, for oceanographic survey duties on the west coast, and renamed *Cedarwood*. Paid off on 19 October 1956, she was fitted in 1958 with paddle wheels and other dummy fittings in order to play the role of the steamer *Commodore* during British Columbia's centennial celebration.

CEDARWOOD			
BUILDER:	Lunenburg, NS	DISPLACEMENT:	566
LAUNCHED:	1941	DIMENSIONS:	166' x 30' 6" x 10'
COMMISSIONED:	22/9/48	SPEED:	11 kts
PAID OFF:	19/10/56	CREW:	24

Cormorant (2nd), 1978.

DIVING SUPPORT VESSEL

Cormorant (2nd)

Formerly the Italian-flag stern trawler *Aspa Quarto,* built in 1965, she was purchased for Maritime Command in July 1975 and converted, principally at Davie Shipbuilding, Lauzon, Que., for her new purpose. She was commissioned there on 10 November 1978. She served as mother ship to SDL-1 (Submersible Diver Lockout), a mini-sub capable of reaching a depth of 2,000 feet, and which has been extensively used to chart the bottom of Halifax harbour. Between 23 August and 5 October, 1989, *Cormorant,* along with CFAV *Quest,* was deployed to Canada's eastern High Arctic waters, conducting defence research in Baffin Bay, Lancaster Sound and Davis Strait. In the course of the operation, dubbed NORPLOY 89, she visited Canada's northernmost Inuit community, Grise Fjord, on Ellesmere Island. Her SDL-1 also found and filmed the *Breadalbane,* crushed and sunk by ice off Beechey Island in 1853 while searching for John Franklin's lost Northwest Passage expedition. During her career she was used for a variety of purposes ranging from retrieval of illegal drug caches; covering vents in the sunken barge *Irving Whale* to recovering the bell from the wreck of the *Edmund Fitzgerald.*

Cormorant had among her complement the first women to be assigned to a Canadian naval vessel. She was paid off on 2 July 1997.

CORMORANT (2nd)					
BUILDER:	Cantiere Navale Apuania, Marina-Carrara, Italy		DIMENSIONS:	245' x 39' x 16' 6"	
			SPEED:	14 kts	
LAUNCHED:	1965		CREW:	65	
COMMISSIONED:	10/11/78		Ex-*Aspa Quarto*		
PAID OFF:	2/7/97				
DISPLACEMENT:	2,350				

Commanding Officers

LCDR J. G. Morrison	24/7/78	17/8/81	LCDR A. G. D. Perusse	/6/86	10/6/88
LCDR J. W. Alexander	17/8/81	27/6/83	LCDR M. P. Palmer	10/6/88	10/8/90
LCDR B. J. Fisher	27/6/83	30/7/84	LCDR P. O. Gaynor	10/8/90	8/10/92
LCDR R. W. Bowers	30/7/84	-	LCDR A. T. Pinnell	8/10/92	-

SAIL
TRAINING
VESSEL

Oriole

Construction of this vessel for George Gooderham, Commodore of the Royal Canadian Yacht Club, was begun by the Dominion Shipbuilding Co. of Toronto, but work was stopped owing to a strike and she was completed at Neponset, Mass., and launched in June 1921 as *Oriole IV*. She served as the Club's flagship 1924-28. In 1941 she was sold to the Navy League of Canada for Sea Cadet training, and in 1943 was chartered to the RCN as a training vessel. Returned postwar to the Navy League, she was reacquired in 1950, refitted, and purchased outright in 1956, to be attached to HMCS *Venture* at Esquimalt. Commissioned in 1952, she had been renamed simply HMCS *Oriole*.

The beautiful ketch provides training for regular and reserve personnel on the west coast. In 1964 she sailed from Esquimalt to Quebec City to take part in celebrations marking the 450th Anniversary of Jacques Cartier's arrival. An annual highlight is her participation in the Swiftsure Classic, a race up the Juan de Fuca Strait to the Swiftsure light.

Oriole has the distinction of being the longest serving vessel in the Canadian Navy.

Oriole.

ORIOLE

Displacement:	68 tons	Sail area:	7000 sq. ft.
Dimensions:	77' x 19' x 10.3'	Mast height:	94 ft.

Commanding Officers

LT E. L. Davies	22/4/40	-
LCDR E. T. Coggins	23/7/54	1/11/54
LCDR B. L. Judd	1/11/54	5/12/55
LCDR R. C. MacLean	5/12/55	6/1/57
LCDR C. A. Prosser	6/1/57	18/2/63
LCDR W. D. Walker	18/2/63	3/5/65
LCDR J. Butterfield	3/5/65	18/8/67
LCDR G. S. Hilliard	18/8/67	26/7/69
LCDR P. S. Cox	26/6/69	25/9/72
LCDR A. R. Horner	25/9/72	16/7/73
CDR R. D. C. Sweeney	16/7/73	10/8/73
CDR W. D. Walker	10/8/73	7/6/81
LCDR P. B. Hunter	7/6/81	4/5/83
LCDR J. R. Gracie	4/5/83	15/10/84
LCDR P. J. Watt	15/10/84	29/8/88
LCDR K. J. Brown	29/8/88	2/8/91
LCDR M. Cooper	2/8/91	18/5/94
LCDR M. Brooks	18/5/94	20/5/98
LCDR L. Trim	20/5/98	16/8/99
LCDR S. Crawshaw	16/8/99	-

PART IV 1990–2002

INTRODUCTION

WHEN THE BERLIN WALL CAME DOWN in 1989 and the Cold War ended with unexpected suddenness, the Canadian fleet remained essentially unchanged from that of 1975. Increasingly derided by journalists as "rusted-out" and irrelevant, the Navy literally and figuratively was running out of steam. It was with a certain degree of astonishment, then, that Canada's initial response to Iraq's invasion of Kuwait in 1990 was to hastily refit the destroyers *Athabaskan* and *Terra Nova*, along with the supply ship *Protecteur*, for service in the Persian Gulf. That they were able to acquit themselves well in a theatre of action very different from the North Atlantic for which they had trained was due as much to the resilience of the ships' basic design as to the high quality of the men and women who sailed in them.

There was also the fact that a new generation of weapons and equipment was available to be fitted into the ships before their departure. Approval had been granted in the late 1980s for the rebuilding of the *Iroquois* (DDH-280) class under the Tribal Update and Modernization Program (TRUMP), and for the construction of a whole new class under the Canadian Patrol Frigate (CPF) program. Although none of these ships were ready for operational deployment, many of the new modular systems (such as the Phalanx Close-in Weapons System and Harpoon anti-ship missiles) could be fitted to the older ships. Indeed, even as they sailed to the Gulf, the lead ship of the CPFs, HMCS *Halifax*, was undergoing acceptance trials. The remaining steam destroyers gradually were paid off so that their crews could undertake conversion to the new types (the last to go was *Nipigon* in 1998).

Over the course of the last decade of the 20th century, Canada's Navy accepted the four rebuilt ships of the *Iroquois* class, as well as twenty-four new ships: besides the twelve CPFs, there were twelve Maritime Coastal Defence Vessels (MCDVs), for use primarily with the Naval Reserve for training and the renewal of a mine countermeasures (MCM) capability. As these latter ships became available, the *Bay* class minesweepers and *Anticosti* and *Moresby* were withdrawn from service. By the end of the decade, the *Oberons* also were gone, being replaced by the *Victoria* (ex-*Upholder*) class of four diesel submarines acquired from the Royal Navy. Only *Protecteur* and *Preserver* remained of the Cold War fleet, and a project for their replacement was being defined under the Afloat Logistics and Sealift Concept (ALSC).

If the "Persian Excursion" was the last war cry of the Cold War fleet, Canada's "New World Order" Navy very quickly found itself engaged at a higher operational tempo, as real-world brush-fire crises replaced the routine of peacetime exercises. The Turbot Crisis on the East Coast, illegal Chinese immigration on the West, and continued instability in Haiti all ensured gainful employment in home waters. Canada consistently commits a destroyer or frigate (and occasionally an oiler) to the Standing Naval Force Atlantic. Twice in the past decade, STANAVFOR-LANT deployed out-of-area to the Adriatic Sea for operations against the former Yugoslav Republic, each time coincidentally under the command of a Canadian commodore employing one of the *Iroquois* class as his flagship. The *Halifax* class frigates were engaged prominently elsewhere, through their individual integration in rotation into US Navy carrier battle groups in the Persian Gulf, enforcing United Nations sanctions against Iraq. Besides their traditional fleet replenishment role, *Preserver* and *Protecteur* were dispatched for humanitarian assistance operations, respectively to Somalia and East Timor. The *Oberons* discovered a new utility in covert fisheries patrols. MCDVs ranged across the Atlantic for NATO MCM exercises, and were among the ships to respond to the Swissair Flight 111 disaster in Peggy's Cove.

On the date of writing this introduction in November 2001 a Canadian task group comprising HMC ships *Iroquois, Charlottetown* and *Preserver* passed through the Suez Canal to the Arabian Sea for operations against the Taliban forces of Osama bin-Laden in Afghanistan, and three other frigates (*Halifax, Vancouver* and *Ottawa*) also are engaged with USN carrier battle groups. A fourth frigate, *Toronto*, has joined the SNFL operating in the Eastern Mediterranean in support of the war. Through the 1990s, the Canadian Navy effectively was rebuilt into the "multi-purpose, combat-capable" force envisioned in the 1994 Defence White Paper, and the Canadian government was finding it to be of increasing utility in meeting the challenges of the twenty-first century.

LCDR (ret'd) Richard Gimblett

Patrol Frigates

CITY CLASS

A class of six frigates, to be named for major Canadian cities, was ordered in July 1983, and a further six on 29 December 1987. Saint John Shipbuilding Ltd., the principal contractor, built three of the first group and all of the second. The remaining three (FFHs 332, 334 and 335) were built by Marine Industries Ltd., Sorel. The ships were assembled in dock from large modules, and "floated up" rather than launched, once completed. All were afloat by mid-1996.

Their dimensions, 440 x 54 x 16 feet on a displacement of 4,750 tons, make these ships somewhat larger than the "280" class DDHs. They are fitted with Mk.46 homing torpedoes, ship and helicopter-launched; two octuple Sea Sparrow surface-to-air missile launchers and two quadruple Harpoon surface-to-surface missile launchers. Close-in weapons include a Bofors 57 mm Mk.2, Phalanx Mk.15 anti-missile system, and four 6-barrelled Chaff/IR launchers.

The frigates use Pielstick diesel engines for cruising, while two gas turbines provide a maximum speed in excess of 30 knots. Endurance on diesels is 7,000 NM at 15 knots. Ship's company totals some 225, including aircrew.

Calgary (2nd).

Calgary (2nd)

The final ship from Marine Industries Ltd., she was floated up on 28 August 1992, and arrived on 28 June, 1994 at Halifax, where she was provisionally accepted on 30 August. She was to be based at Esquimalt, where she was commissioned on 12 May 1995. On 10 July she sailed for the Arabian (Persian) Gulf as the first in her class to assist in enforcing sanctions against Iraq. Homebound that December, she went to the aid of the sinking Greek bulk-carrier *Mount Olympus,* 1,500 km south of Halifax. *Calgary's* helicopter rescued all 30 of the crew, landing them aboard the Bulgarian freighter *Rodopi. Calgary* returned to Esquimalt on 22 December, the first CPF to circumnavigate the globe. In the summer of 1999 *Calgary* participated in the Pacific exercise Tandem Thrust despite the break-down of one of her diesel generators. From there she journeyed to Singapore, to take part in IMDEX 99 (the International Maritime Defence Exhibition). On 20 June 2000, *Calgary* again departed Esquimalt for a five-month deployment to the Arabian Gulf, operating with American units in enforcing UN sanctions against Iraq, returning home on 30 November.

CALGARY (2nd)

Builder:	Marine Industries Ltd., Sorel, Que.	Floated up:	28/8/92
Laid Down:	15/6/91	Commissioned:	12/5/95

Commanding Officers

CDR G. A. Paulson	30/8/94	9/7/96	CDR T. M. Howard	16/7/99	29/1/01
CDR R. E. Bush	9/7/96	18/10/97	CDR G. R. Peskett	29/1/01	-
CDR P. A. Maddison	18/10/97	16/7/99			

Charlottetown (3rd)

She was floated up on 1 October 1994, and commissioned in Charlottetown on 9 September 1995. In the fall of 1996 she took part, as a member of Standing Naval Force Atlantic, in exercises with ships of a number of eastern European navies. On 12 August 1997 *Charlottetown* made a courtesy visit to the port for which she is named, and was the first Canadian warship to pass under the Confederation Bridge. Soon afterward she took part in the US Exercise United Spirit. She returned home on 17 December, and late in February 1998 began a six-month stint with SNFL in place of *Toronto*, which had been ordered to the Persian Gulf. On 12 January, 2001, *Charlottetown* herself sailed for the Arabian Gulf, there joining the USS *Harry S. Truman* Battle Group in sanctions against Iraq. She again left Halifax on 17 October, with *Iroquois* and *Preserver*, for the Middle East, this time on Operation Apollo to support a US-led coalition against international terrorism. The trio was joined in the Arabian Sea in December by *Halifax*, and conducted arms embargo operations and screening of other naval units in the area. *Charlottetown* returned to Halifax on 4 March 2002.

Charlottetown (3rd).

CHARLOTTETOWN (3rd)

Builder:	Saint John Dry Dock and Shipbuilding Co. Ltd., Saint John, N.B.		Floated up:	1/10/94	
Laid Down:	18/12/93		Commissioned:	9/9/95	

Commanding Officers

CDR M. A. Wylie	1/1/95	18/12/96	CDR D. C. Gardam	17/12/98	5/7/00
CDR G. J. Romanow	18/12/96	17/12/98	CDR M. F. R. Lloyd	5/7/00	-

Fredericton (2nd).

FREDERICTON (2nd)

Builder:	Saint John Dry Dock and Shipbuilding Co. Ltd., Saint John, N.B.		Floated up:	26/6/93	
Laid Down:	25/4/92		Commissioned:	10/9/94	

Commanding Officers

CDR D. J. Galina	20/9/93	20/8/95	CDR P. C. Avis	3/5/99	15/7/01
CDR K. D. W. Laing	20/8/95	30/5/97	CDR B. Ryan	15/7/01	11/1/02
CDR G. D. Switzer	30/5/97	3/5/99	CDR H. Harsch	11/1/02	-

Fredericton (2nd)

Floated up at Saint John on 26 June 1993, *Fredericton* was commissioned there on 10 September 1994, and was to be based at Halifax. On 5 April 1995, while in the Gulf of Aden on a tour of mideast ports to demonstrate Canadian warship technology, *Fredericton* answered a distress call from the yacht *Longo Barda,* which was under attack by pirates. On 28 November 1995, "Freddie" departed Halifax for a six-month tour in the Adriatic with SNFL, acting as flagship from 29 February to 11 March, and then from 17 to 19 March as flagship to Standing Naval Force Mediterranean (SNFM). She returned home on 4 April 1996. In the fall of 1996 she took part in a NATO exercise in the Norwegian Sea, suffering storm damage on the homeward journey. She was again employed as a NATO unit during part of 1997 (6 January to 15 April) and 2000 (21 March to 14 August). *Fredericton* participated with SNFL again between 5 March and 27 July 2001.

Halifax (2nd)

First of her class to enter service, and the first warship built in Canada since 1971, *Halifax* was floated up on 30 April 1988 and commissioned on 29 June 1992. On 2 April 1994, she sailed to relieve *Iroquois* in the multinational arms embargo of the former Yugoslavia. While enroute, one of the diesel cruise engines blew and the ship had to proceed on its gas turbine engines. She returned home on 9 September. In the spring of 1995 she made visits to several European ports, including Goteborg, Oslo and Gydnia, in connection with the 50th Anniversary of VE Day. Afterward taking part in the NATO exercise Linked Seas 95 off Portugal, she returned to base at the end of June. On 18 March 1996, she departed for another tour of duty in the Adriatic, part of the time as flagship. In March 1998 *Halifax* and *Iroquois* took part in Exercise Strong Resolve off Norway, returning to Halifax on 16 April. That fall she had the melancholy duty of assisting at the scene of the crash of a Swissair jet in the sea near Peggy's Cove. Another tour with NATO's SNFL occupied her time between 26 July and 15 December 2000. On 15 August 2001, she left Halifax to join SNFL, but was detached to join in Operation Enduring Freedom against international terrorism. She joined *Charlottetown*, *Iroquois*, and *Preserver* in the Arabian Sea in December. She returned home from this endeavour on 11 February 2002.

Montreal (2nd)

She was floated up on 26 February 1992 and provisionally accepted on 27 July 1993. After a series of trials, she was commissioned at Montreal on 21 July 1994, and designated a French Language Unit. On 4 January 1995, *Montreal* sailed from Halifax to join NATO's SNFL in the Adriatic Sea, blockading the former Yugoslavia. During this tour she twice acted as flagship and returned home on 19 July. During 1997, 12,500 anechoic tiles were applied to *Montreal's* hull in order to reduce noise. This experiment was not entirely successful, and no other CPFs were so fitted. On 10 August 1998, *Montreal* departed Halifax to join the NATO fleet off Florida, and with its Immediate Reaction Force paid an epoch-making visit to St. Petersburg, to celebrate the 300th Anniversary of the Russian Navy. She was back in Halifax on 15 December. During the summer of 2000 *Montreal* represented Canada in the Millennium International Fleet Review in New York City, then escorted the Tall Ships to Halifax, where she acted as flagship for the Commander-in-Chief, Governor-General Adrienne Clarkson, to review the Tall Ships sail past. The following week she was deployed to support *Athabaskan* in Operation Megaphone, the boarding and escorting of GTS *Katie* to Bécancour, Quebec.

Halifax (2nd).

HALIFAX (2nd)

Builder:	Saint John Dry Dock and Shipbuilding Co. Ltd., Saint John, N.B.		Floated up:	30/4/88	
Laid Down:	19/3/87		Commissioned:	29/6/92	

Commanding Officers

CDR R. I. Clayton	1/5/89	21/12/92	CDR G. M. Aikins	30/6/98	15/6/99
CDR G. B. Burke	22/11/92	28/10/94	CDR J. Y. Bastien	15/6/99	11/5/01
CDR L. D. Sweeney	18/10/94	3/7/96	CDR P. Ellis	11/5/01	-
CDR J. E. H. A. Langlois	3/7/96	30/6/98			

Montreal (2nd).

MONTREAL (2nd)

Builder:	Saint John Dry Dock and Shipbuilding Co. Ltd., Saint John, N.B.		Floated up:	26/2/92	
Laid Down:	9/2/91		Commissioned:	21/7/94	

Commanding Officers

CDR S. D. Andrews	31/3/93	28/6/93	CDR P. D. McFadden	9/7/97	9/7/99
CDR C. D. Gunn	28/6/93	13/7/93	CDR N. H. Jolin	9/7/99	22/6/01
CDR D. W. Shubaly	13/7/93	9/7/97	CDR G. H. A. Hatton	22/6/01	-

Ottawa (4th)

Ottawa was floated up on 31 May 1996, and commissioned at Cornwall on 28 September 1996. On 16 November, in company with the new MCDV *Nanaimo*, she left Halifax for Esquimalt, where the two are based. On 16 June 1998 *Ottawa* sailed to join the USS *Abraham Lincoln* Carrier Battle Group in the Arabian Gulf, enforcing the UN trade embargo against Iraq. Although not the first assigned to such duties, *Ottawa* was the first Canadian warship to be completely integrated operationally into such a group. She returned to Esquimalt shortly before Christmas. *Ottawa* departed Esquimalt on 17 February 2002 to join Operation Apollo, Canada's contribution to the war on terrorism, returning on 17 August.

Ottawa (4th).

OTTAWA (4th)

Builder:	Saint John Dry Dock and Shipbuilding Co. Ltd., Saint John, N.B.	Floated up:	31/5/96			
Laid Down:	29/4/95	Commissioned:	28/9/96			

Commanding Officers

CDR J. C. G. Goulet	31/7/96	21/12/97	CDR N. S. Greenwood	1/7/99	21/6/01
CDR J. J. R. R. Bergeron	21/12/97	1/7/99	CDR P. A. Hendry	21/6/01	-

Regina (2nd).

REGINA (2nd)

Builder:	Marine Industries Ltd., Sorel, Que.	Floated up:	25/10/91			
Laid Down:	6/10/89	Commissioned:	30/9/94			

Commanding Officers

CDR M. H. Jellinek	24/6/93	8/8/95	CDR K. R. Stewart	25/2/00	14/8/01
CDR T. H. W. Pile	8/8/95	25/8/97	CDR B. F. Truelove	14/8/01	-
CDR J. W. Hayes	25/8/97	25/2/00			

Regina (2nd)

Regina was floated up on 25 October 1991 and provisionally accepted by the Navy on 2 March 1994. Following trials off Halifax, she left on 13 June for Esquimalt, where she was commissioned on 30 September. On 10 May 1995, along with *Vancouver,* she departed for exercises with Southeast Asian naval units. On 18 March 1996, in company with *Algonquin, Winnipeg* and *Protecteur, Regina* again headed for the western Pacific, this time to exercise with ships of the Japanese, Russian, Korean and Philippine navies. In the course of this deployment, she made a call at Ho Chi Minh City, the first North American warship to do so since the end of the Vietnam War. On 21 February 1997, she sailed to join a US carrier battle group in the enforcement of trade sanctions against Iraq. In the summer of 1999 she was back in the Arabian Gulf on the same mission, this time with the USS *Constellation* Battle Group. She returned home on 17 December 1999.

St. John's

St. John's was floated up on 26 August 1995. The first to be named for Newfoundland's capital city, she was commissioned there on 24 June 1996. She joined SNFL on 7 August 1997 at Norfolk, Va., returning home on 18 December. She took part in NATO Exercise Strong Resolve in Norwegian waters in the early spring of 1998, and that fall joined Standing Naval Force Mediterranean (SNFM), returning to Halifax on 15 December. On 23 March 1999, *St. John's* and three consorts sailed south for a month's training. The following spring found her in the Caribbean area yet again, making courtesy visits and taking part in the international Exercise Unitas. She sailed on 1 May 2002 to join in Operation Apollo.

St. John's.

ST. JOHN'S

Builder:	Saint John Dry Dock and Shipbuilding Co. Ltd., Saint John, N.B.	Floated up:	26/8/95
Laid Down:	24/8/94	Commissioned:	24/6/96

Commanding Officers

CDR R. S. Edwards	12/12/95	7/7/97	CDR M. G. Langford	24/6/00	7/12/01
CDR R. A. Davidson	7/7/97	15/1/99	CDR D. Ryan	7/12/01	-
CDR C. L. Mofford	15/1/99	24/6/00			

Toronto (2nd).

Toronto (2nd)

Third of her class to join the Navy, she was floated up on 18 December 1990, and commissioned at Toronto on 29 July 1993. A year later she was on duty in the Adriatic for five and a half months, helping enforce UN sanctions against the former Yugoslavia. In 1995, with *Halifax* and *Terra Nova*, she made a round of visits to European ports in commemoration of VE Day, en route taking part in the NATO exercise Linked Seas off Portugal. *Toronto* made a tour of eight Great Lakes ports in the fall of 1996. In January 1998 she sailed to join SNFL, and was detached on 10 February to the Persian Gulf to assist in carrying out sanctions against Iraq. She arrived back home on 16 June. *Toronto* again sailed for the Middle East on 5 December 2001, to join the US-led coalition against terrorism in Afghanistan, returning to Halifax on 27 May 2002.

TORONTO (2nd)

Builder:	Saint John Dry Dock and Shipbuilding Co. Ltd., Saint John, N.B.
Laid Down:	22/4/89
Floated up:	18/12/90
Commissioned:	29/7/93

Commanding Officers

CDR R. D. Murphy	29/5/92	18/6/95
CDR L. J. Fleck	18/6/95	26/6/97
CDR B. J. Johnson	26/6/97	7/1/99
CDR L. M. Hickey	7/1/99	17/7/00
CDR I. A. Paterson	17/7/00	-

Vancouver (3rd)

Vancouver was floated up on 8 July 1989 and commissioned at Vancouver on 23 August 1993. In May-July 1994 she took part in Exercise Rimpac 94 off Hawaii before making courtesy visits to ports in Japan and South Korea. Westploy 95 saw her leave Esquimalt with *Regina* on 10 May for visits to several ports in Southeast Asia, *Vancouver* then making calls in Australia and New Zealand before returning home on 4 August. Early in 1995 she exercised with a US carrier battle group, successfully launching a Sea Sparrow missile on the Pacific Firing Range off California. In the course of Westploy 97 she again visited several Southeast Asian ports, and while involved in Rimpac 98 made calls in Japan, China, Russia and South Korea. On 29 October 2001, *Vancouver* sailed from Esquimalt to become a part of the USS *John C. Stennis* Carrier Battle Group, as part of the US-led coalition against terrorist forces in Afghanistan. The Battle Group arrived in Hong Kong on 29 November, and in the Arabian Gulf on 19 December 2001. *Vancouver* returned home to Esquimalt on 28 May 2002.

Vancouver (3rd).

VANCOUVER (3rd)

Builder:	Saint John Dry Dock and Shipbuilding Co. Ltd., Saint John, N.B.	Floated up:	8/7/89
Laid Down:	19/5/88	Commissioned:	23/8/93

Commanding Officers

CDR S. D. Andrews	2/7/91	31/3/93	CDR A. B. Donaldson	29/6/97	15/7/99
CDR B. E. Matthews	31/3/93	8/7/95	CDR J. T. Heath	15/7/99	-
CDR M. R. Bellows	8/7/95	29/6/97			

Ville de Québec (2nd).

VILLE DE QUÉBEC (2nd)

Builder:	Marine Industries Ltd., Sorel, Que.	Floated up:	16/5/91
Laid Down:	16/12/88	Commissioned:	14/7/94

Commanding Officers

CAPF J. J. P. Thiffault	4/4/92	22/6/95	CAPF G. J. Romanow	20/12/98	21/6/99
CAPF J. P. A. Guindon	22/6/95	20/6/97	CAPF G. M. Aikins	21/6/99	15/6/00
CAPF J. R. P. S. Allaire	30/6/97	20/12/98	CAPF D. G. Cameron	15/6/00	-

Ville de Québec (2nd)

First of the three built by Marine Industries Ltd. Davies, Lauzon, and appropriately designated a French Language Unit, *Ville de Québec* was floated up on 16 May 1991. She relieved *Annapolis* on the UN embargo of Haiti in April 1993, and was commissioned at Quebec City on 14 July 1994. On 9 February, 1995, she left Halifax to take part in the NATO Exercise Strong Resolve off Norway, and on 5 July left again for a six-month tour of duty with SNFL in the Adriatic, enforcing the arms embargo against the former Yugoslavia. In the fall of 1998 she assisted at the scene of the Swissair jet disaster. January 1999 saw *"VDQ"* join SNFL once again, this time for a three-month tour. On 30 August 2001, she bore the ashes of the late Adm. H.G. DeWolf up the harbour of Halifax for committal in Bedford Basin. The date marked the same day in August 1943 when De Wolf commissioned his much-celebrated HMCS *Haida*.

Winnipeg (2nd).

Winnipeg (2nd)

Though she was assembled at Saint John, *Winnipeg's* engine room modules were constructed at Georgetown, PEI, and transported by barge for incorporation into her hull. She was floated up on 5 December 1993 and delivered to the Navy on 11 October 1994. *Winnipeg* left Halifax on 16 January 1995 for Esquimalt, where she was commissioned on 23 June 1995 and assigned to Maritime Operations Group 2 that October. In 1996 she took part in Rimpac 96 off Hawaii. On 1 April 1997, she replaced *Fredericton* in SNFL, with which she served four months. A highlight of 1998 was her participation in Exercise Unitas off South America, and in 2000 she was part of a task force involved in Pacex 2000. Early in March 2001, *Winnipeg* departed Esquimalt to join the USS *Constellation* Carrier Battle Group for a six-month tour enforcing UN sanctions against Iraq. She returned to Esquimalt on 14 September.

WINNIPEG (2nd)						
Builder:	Saint John Dry Dock and Shipbuilding Co. Ltd., Saint John, N.B.		Floated up:	5/12/93		
Laid Down:	20/3/93		Commissioned:	23/6/95		
Commanding Officers						
CDR M. R. R. Brossard	10/6/94	17/12/96	CDR L. J. Falloon		18/12/98	8/1/01
CDR D. C. Hudock	17/12/96	18/12/98	CDR K. E. Williams		8/1/01	-

Submarines

VICTORIA CLASS

PARTICULARS OF CLASS:

Displacement:	2221 tonnes (Surface), 2475 tonnes (Submerged)
Dimensions:	230'6" x 25' x 17'7"
Speed:	12/20 kts
Crew:	49
Armament:	6 Torpedo tubes (forward)

Victoria arriving in Halifax from the UK, October 2000.

On 6 April 1998, the Canadian Government announced its decision to acquire four Upholder class submarines from the United Kingdom which had been placed in reserve by the Royal Navy when it switched to an all-nuclear submarine fleet in the early 1990s. A purchase agreement was worked out over an eight-year period and Canada agreed to pay $610 million for the submarines, training services, simulators, spare parts and a technical package. Another $140 million was then set toward further modifications and training facilities in Canada.

Three of the new submarines will be stationed on the East Coast and one on the West. Operationally, their role will be to serve alongside Canadian Task Groups, provide support to multi-national forces, and lend surveillance assistance to government departments.

Victoria

Formerly HMS *Unseen*, laid up by the Royal Navy in June 1994, she was accepted by Canada on 6 October 2000 at Barrow-in-Furness. The submarine departed England 9 October 2000 and travelled to Halifax submerged for the most part, where she arrived on 23 October. Commissioned on 2 December in Halifax, *Victoria* is expected to be based in Esquimalt. Early in April 2002 while she was in drydock a dent was discovered in her hull below the waterline. This is expected to delay her arrival on the West Coast while repairs are made.

Windsor

The former HMS *Unicorn*, she was laid up by the Royal Navy in October 1994. She arrived in Halifax, where she will be based, on 19 October 2001. On her first training mission in early March 2002 *Windsor* had to return to port after only five hours, due to a faulty seal in a communications mast.

Corner Brook

The former HMS *Ursula*, she was laid up by the Royal Navy in June 1994. She will be based in Halifax.

Chicoutimi (2nd)

The former HMS *Upholder*, she was laid up by the Royal Navy in June 1994. She will be based in Halifax.

VICTORIA

Builder:	Cammell Laird, Birkenhead	Launched:	14/11/89
		Commissioned:	2/12/00
Laid Down:	1/86	Ex-*Unseen*	

Commanding Officers

CDR W. A. Woodburn	6/10/00	21/9/01
LCDR S. McVicar	21/9/01	-

WINDSOR

Builder:	Cammell Laird, Birkenhead	Launched:	16/04/92
		Ex-*Unicorn*	
Laid Down:	2/89		

Commanding Officer

LCDR A.R. Wamback	16/7/01 -

CORNER BROOK

Builder:	Cammell Laird, Birkenhead	Launched:	28/02/91
		Ex-*Ursula*	
Laid Down:	28/08/87		

Commanding Officer

LCDR L. Pelletier	02/05/02 -

CHICOUTIMI (2nd)

Builder:	Vickers, Barrow-in-Furness VSEL	Launched:	2/12/86
		Ex-*Upholder*	
Laid Down:	02/11/83		

Maritime Coastal Defence Vessels

The MCDVs came about as a result of four influences within the Navy: by the late 1970s the Navy had almost no mine warfare capability, the Bay Class minesweepers having been relegated to training purposes with their minesweeping gear removed; the ships being used by the Naval Reserves were becoming very old (the early 1950s "Porte" Class gate vessels and the small, single-purpose ex-RCMP motor launches) for which the new MCMV (Mine Countermeasures Vessels) would make excellent replacements; the City Class frigate construction program was well underway, with no further such expensive ships likely in the foreseeable future, and yet the Naval staff wished to encourage a continuing naval draw on whatever capital construction dollars might be made available from a reluctant treasury; and there was a perceived national requirement for new inshore, restricted waters operational naval ships which the City Class could not easily meet.

There were at least five main criteria for these new ships: they must be built in Canada, shipbuilding being labour-intensive, they must be as inexpensive to build as practicable, with maximum use of commercial, rather than naval, components and building facilities; they must be operable by Naval Reserves with less technical background training than the Regular Force; they must be inexpensive to build and operate; and their design must be flexible to meet demands for several roles, especially in addition to that of traditional mine warfare using bottom searching and sweeping.

A visit by a squadron of the Royal Navy's Reserve-manned, very similar River Class minesweepers at our 75th Anniversary observations in Halifax in the summer of 1985 was of much interest, and at least showed a proven example of how these criteria could be met. In fact, the Canadian ships of two years later are very similar, with largely commercial construction and engines, a large, open space aft to allow for multiple uses, including lift-aboard containers that could house various options for mine-hunting, sweeping, extra accommodation, supplies, or whatever else occasion might require.

In each ship there are usually two Regular Force technical petty officers for the electronics fit and the engine room. Apart from that, the Reserves man all of them, divided evenly between the East and West coasts, with summer training and familiarization visits by some East coast units to the Great Lakes.

Special or unique equipment is found in these ships: two separated, square rather than round funnels, being less expensive to manufacture, and leaving space between them for the minesweeping control position looking aft above the open quarterdeck; their propellers are shrouded in a circular "hood" and on what is referred to as a "Z" drive, mounted on a rotatable vertical shsft similar to that of an outboard motor. They have no rudders as such, their steering being managed similarly as with an outboard, by rotating the vertical unit. The ships can turn in less than their own length and can be stopped in a matter of a few feet, a valuable asset when mine-hunting in restricted waters. They are fitted with the latest in minor war vessels' navigation and communications equipment, and are reportedly comfortable to live in.

—CDR F.W. McKee

PARTICULARS OF CLASS	
Displacement:	970 tonnes
Dimensions:	55.3m x 11.3m x 3.4m
Speed:	15 kts
Crew:	37
Armament :	1 40mm gun 2 sites for machine guns

All vessels were built by Halifax Shipyards Limited, Halifax, NS

A contract for $650 million was let to Halifax Shipyards Ltd in May 1992 to build twelve of these ships. They were designed to commercial standards and intended to conduct coastal patrols, minesweeping, law enforcement, pollution surveillance/response and search and rescue duties. The ships are fitted with modular payloads to carry out the assigned duties. The navy has seven modules available: four route survey modules; two mechanical minesweeping and one bottom inspection module. Steel cutting started in December 1993 and by July 1999 all were in commission.

NAME	LAID DOWN	LAUNCHED	COMMISSIONED
BRANDON	6/12/97	10/7/97	5/6/99
EDMONTON	8/12/95	16/8/96	21/6/97
GLACE BAY	28/4/95	22/1/96	26/10/96
GOOSE BAY	22/2/97	4/9/97	26/7/98
KINGSTON	20/12/94	12/8/95	21/9/96
MONCTON	31/5/97	5/12/97	12/7/98
NANAIMO	11/8/95	17/5/96	10/5/97
SASKATOON	5/9/97	30/3/98	5/12/98
SHAWINIGAN	26/4/96	15/11/96	14/6/97
SUMMERSIDE	28/03/98	26/8/98	18/7/99
WHITEHORSE	26/7/96	24/2/97	17/4/98
YELLOWKNIFE	2/11/96	5/6/97	18/4/98

Brandon (2nd)

Brandon left Halifax on 17 March 1999 and headed to Esquimalt, where she arrived on 3 May. She commissioned 5 June 1999, and is the sixth and final MCDV to be stationed on the West Coast.

Brandon (2nd).

BRANDON (2nd)

Laid Down:	6/12/97			Commissioned:	5/6/99		
Launched:	10/7/97			Based out of Esquimalt			

Commanding Officers

LCDR R. Ramage		11/1/99	9/12/00	LCDR D. Young		14/2/01	14/4/01
LCDR D. Turetski		9/12/00	14/2/01	LCDR S. King		14/4/01	18/6/01

Edmonton

The first ship to bear this name, she was accepted by the Navy on 24 November 1996 and conducted trials and work-ups off Halifax before heading west. On 3 March 1997, in company with HMCS *Moresby*, she departed Halifax bound for Esquimalt via the Panama Canal. Commissioned on 21 June 1997 at Esquimalt, she was assigned to Maritime Operations Group 4. She participated, with *Nanaimo* and *Saskatoon*, in RIMPAC 2002 off Hawaii from June to 31 July 2002.

Edmonton.

EDMONTON

Laid Down:	8/12/95			Commissioned:	21/6/97		
Launched:	16/8/96			Based out of Esquimalt			

Commanding Officers

CDR G. Wong		31/10/96	13/6/98	LCDR B. Cook		14/4/99	1/10/00
LCDR W. Bowes		13/6/98	19/8/98	LCDR S. King		16/10/00	14/4/01
LCDR D. Leblanc		19/8/98	14/4/99	LCDR S. King		18/6/01	-

Glace Bay (2nd)

Contractor trials were conducted 6 to 9 May 1996 and the ship was commissioned in Sydney, NS, on 26 October 1996. Leaving Halifax on 10 September 1997, she made her first Great Lakes trip and returned to Halifax in early October. In September 1998, she was one of the ships that participated in Operation Persistence after the crash of Swissair Flight 111 off Peggy's Cove, NS. On 8 March 1999, in company with *Kingston* and *Anticosti*, she departed Halifax and proceeded to the Baltic Sea to participate in NATO minesweeping exercises. They returned in May.

Glace Bay (2nd).

GLACE BAY (2nd)

Laid Down:	28/4/95			Commissioned:	26/10/96	
Launched:	22/1/96			Based out of Halifax		
Commanding Officers						
CDR C. R. McNary		16/5/96	25/7/97	LCDR J. A. Offer	26/6/00	1/01
LCDR J. R. Thorpe		25/7/97	25/2/98	Extended Readiness	1/01	-
LCDR J. C. MacInnis		25/2/98	26/6/00			

Goose Bay.

GOOSE BAY

Laid Down:	22/2/97			Commissioned:	26/7/98	
Launched:	4/9/97			Based out of Halifax		
Commanding Officers						
LCDR T. P. Gijzen		21/11/97	30/6/99	LCDR C. J. Ross	30/6/99	-

Goose Bay

Launched on 4 September 1997, Goose Bay was accepted by the Navy on 21 November 1997 and commissioned in Happy Valley/Goose Bay on 26 July 1998. In early June 1999, she took part in a pollution exercise off Eastport, Maine with Canadian and American Coast Guard units. In the fall of 2000 she was one of the Canadian units which participated in the exercise Unified Spirit off the eastern seaboard. *Goose Bay*, in company with *Moncton*, departed Halifax on 1 April 2001 to participate in NATO's mine warfare Exercise Blue Game off the coasts of Norway and Denmark between 23 April and 9 May. *Goose Bay* and *Summerside* sailed into the southern edge of Arctic waters in early August 2002 to participate in Exercise Narwhal Ranger, a combined air force/army/navy exercise. This was the first time in thirteen years that navy units had sailed into northern waters.

Kingston

Lead ship of the class, *Kingston* was the first ship to be built in Halifax in thirty-two years. Trials started on 13 November 1995 and on 10 September 1996 she left Halifax in company with *Glace Bay* and *Anticosti* and was commissioned in Kingston, Ontario on 21 September. On 8 March 1999 she proceeded with *Glace Bay* and *Anticosti* to the Baltic Sea to participate in Exercise Blue Game, a major minesweeping exercise with other NATO units. These were the smallest Canadian warships to cross the Atlantic since the Second World War.

Kingston.

Moncton (2nd)

The ninth of her class, *Moncton* was launched on 5 December 1997 and the Navy took delivery on 27 February 1998. She commissioned on 12 July 1998 at Pointe du Chêne, N.B, accompanied by *Goose Bay* and *Shawinigan*. *Moncton* was among those present at the scene of the Swissair disaster in September of 1998. She was a participant in Exercise Unified Spirit off the eastern seaboard in the fall of 2000. *Moncton*, in company with *Goose Bay*, departed Halifax on 1 April 2001 to participate in NATO's mine warfare Exercise Blue Game off the coasts of Norway and Denmark between 23 April and 9 May.

KINGSTON

| Laid Down: | 20/12/94 | | | Commissioned: | 21/9/96 | |
| Launched: | 12/8/95 | | | Based out of Halifax | | |

Commanding Officers

CDR F. A. McDonnell	21/9/96	14/1/97	Extended Readiness	6/00	1/01
CDR M. Cameron	14/1/97	10/11/98	LCDR J. A. Offer	8/1/01	-
LCDR S. Healey	10/11/98	30/4/00			

Moncton (2nd).

MONCTON (2nd)

| Laid Down: | 31/5/97 | | | Commissioned: | 12/7/98 | |
| Launched: | 5/12/97 | | | Based out of Halifax | | |

Commanding Officers

| CDR J. S. Greenlaw | 3/11/97 | 29/6/01 | LCDR R. W. Green | 29/6/01 | - |

Nanaimo (2nd)

Allocated to the west coast, *Nanaimo* left Halifax on 12 November 1996, arriving on 19 December. The first MCDV to be based at Esquimalt, she was commissioned at Nanaimo on 10 May 1997. *Nanaimo* and *Saskatoon*, along with *Edmonton*, participated in RIMPAC 2002 off Hawaii from June to 31 July 2002.

Saskatoon (2nd)

Launched on 30 March 1998, *Saskatoon* departed Halifax on 31 August 1998 and headed for Esquimalt via the Panama Canal. She reached the West Coast on 19 October and was commissioned on 5 December.

Shawinigan (2nd)

Shawinigan was commissioned at Trois Rivières, Quebec on 14 June 1997. On 28 June 1998, she celebrated the 75th anniversary of the naval reserves by participating in a sail past in Halifax Harbour and was featured on a commemorative stamp issued for the occasion. In July *Shawinigan* was a member of the escort ships for the commissioning of *Moncton*.

Nanaimo (2nd).

Saskatoon (2nd).

Shawinigan (2nd).

NANAIMO (2nd)			
Laid Down:	11/8/95	Commissioned:	10/5/97
Launched:	17/5/96	Based out of Esquimalt	
Commanding Officers			
CDR P. MacNeill		10/5/97	13/5/98
CDR B. Cook		13/5/98	30/9/98
CDR D. Gagliardi		30/9/98	1/4/00
CDR B. Cook		1/10/99	-

SASKATOON (2nd)			
Laid Down:	5/9/97	Commissioned:	5/12/98
Launched:	30/3/98	Based out of Esquimalt	
Commanding Officers			
LCDR E. M. Richardson		28/5/98	-

SHAWINIGAN (2nd)			
Laid Down:	26/4/96	Commissioned:	14/6/97
Launched:	15/11/96	Based out of Halifax	
Commanding Officers			
LCDR J. F. Boisjoli		20/2/97	1/99
LCDR C. Ross		1/99	6/99
Extended Readiness		6/99	5/00
LCDR S. A. S. Healey		5/00	6/01
LCDR J. F. Boisjoli		6/01	-

Summerside (2nd).

Whitehorse.

Yellowknife.

Summerside (2nd)

The last of her class, her keel was laid on 28 March 1998 and the completed vessel launched on 26 September of that year. On 18 July 1999 *Summerside* was commissioned in her namesake city. She is based at Halifax. *Summerside* and *Goose Bay* sailed into the southern edge of Arctic waters in early August 2002 during Exercise Narwhal Ranger, a combined air force/army/navy exercise. This was the first time in thirteen years that navy units had sailed into northern waters.

Whitehorse

Work-ups off the East Coast included a visit to St.John's, Nfld. in July 1997. *Whitehorse* departed Halifax on 25 August 1997 and arrived at her new homeport of Esquimalt on 24 October. After commissioning on 17 April 1998, she traveled up the West Coast of British Columbia visiting Skagway, Alaska in company with *Yellowknife*.

Yellowknife

The first ship to be named after the capital of the Northwest Territories, she was accepted by the Navy on 16 October 1997. She left Halifax on 30 January 1998 for Esquimalt, where she was commissioned on 18 April, later accompanying *Whitehorse* on a courtesy call at Skagway, Alaska.

SUMMERSIDE (2nd)			
Laid Down:	28/3/98	Commissioned:	18/7/99
Launched:	26/8/98	Based out of Halifax	
Commanding Officers			
LCDR T. A. Kerr		18/7/99	1/12/01
LCDR M. Hopper		1/12/01	

WHITEHORSE			
Laid Down:	26/7/96	Commissioned:	17/4/98
Launched:	24/2/97	Based out of Esquimalt	
Commanding Officers			
LCDR D. Carroll			

YELLOWKNIFE			
Laid Down:	2/11/96	Commissioned:	18/4/98
Launched:	5/6/97	Based out of Esquimalt	
Commanding Officers			
LCDR D. Bancroft			
LCDR G. Bannister			

Minesweeping Auxiliaries

These were built as offshore drill-rig supply vessels by Allied Shipbuilding, Vancouver, purchased in 1988 and commissioned after conversion. With the entry into service of the MCDVs, they became surplus to requirements and were paid off.

PARTICULARS OF CLASS:	
Displacement:	1,076 tons, full load
Dimensions:	191' x 41' x 17'
Speed:	13.5 kts
Endurance:	12,000 NM
Complement:	5/18

Anticosti (2nd)

Formerly named *Jean Tide*, she was converted at Marystown, Nfld. in 1991. On 3 September 1991, she departed Halifax for a tour of the St. Lawrence and Great Lakes. On 18 March 1990, she sailed for Norfolk, Va., to take part in the MCM Exercise First Shield 1. She was fitted with astern refueling gear in 1995. She was among the ships taking part in rescue efforts after the Swissair Flight 111 crash in St. Margaret's Bay in September 1998. *Anticosti* made her first and only visit to Anticosti Island on 15 September 1999. She was paid off on 21 March 2000. During January 2002 she was sold to commercial interests.

Anicosti (2nd).

ANICOSTI (2nd)
Commanding Officers

CDR D. A. Edmonds	7/5/89*	9/10/90	LCDR M. N. Cameron	14/2/94	29/5/97
LCDR D. Gagliardi	9/10/90	15/12/90	LCDR J. F. Newton	29/5/97	21/5/98
LT(N) R. Jean	15/12/90	6/91	LCDR F. G. Rasmussen	21/5/98	31/3/00
LCDR P. Stow	6/91	5/5/91	* Start date is that of commissioning, although Cdr Edmonds was appointed Captain earlier and sailed the *Jean Tide* from Europe to Canada.		
LCDR M. D. Page	5/5/91	14/2/94			

Moresby.

MORESBY
Commanding Officers

CDR L. Maguire	1/1/90	3/9/90	LCDR J. R. Thorpe	22/9/95	18/4/97
LCDR T. M. Taylor	3/9/90	?/?/90	LCDR K. B. Larkin	18/4/97	1/10/98
LCDR F. A. McDonnell	?/?/90	11/10/94	LCDR B. A. Walker	1/10/98	18/6/99
LT McNichol	11/10/94	28/11/94	LCDR E. C. King	18/6/99	28/3/00
LCDR D. P. Gagliardi	28/11/94	22/9/95			

Moresby

Formerly named *Joyce Tide*, she too was converted at Marystown, Nfld., to provide Reserve personnel with training in minesweeping and coastal defence. Early in 1990, she joined the joint British/Netherlands NATO Exercise Safe Pass 90. In 1992, trials of her side-scan sonar led to the discovery of a WW2 casualty, the tanker *British Freedom*, outside Halifax. Transferred to Esquimalt, she left Halifax in company with HMCS *Edmonton* on 3 March 1997. She was paid off on 10 March 2000 and turned over to Crown Assets for disposal. Like her sister, she was sold commercially in January 2002.

Torpedo Sound Range Vessels

Sechelt
Sikanni
Sooke
Stikine

These 108-foot craft were built by Manly Shipyard, Vancouver. All named for small towns in British Columbia, they were commissioned in 1991 and replaced World War II vintage craft. They were used to recover expended torpedoes on the Nanoose Bay Torpedo Range. *Sechelt* and *Sooke* were converted into diving tenders in 1997. *Stikine* and *Sikanni* are still serving at Nanoose Bay, albeit with civilian crews.

Name	Displacement	Dimensions	Commissioned
SECHELT	291 tons*	108' x 33' 6"	8/2/1991
SIKANNI	275 tons	108' x 33' 6"	26/4/1991
SOOKE	291 tons*	108' x 33' 6"	21/6/1991
STIKINE	275 tons	108' x 33' 6"	25/7/1991

* After conversion to diving tenders.
(Above information courtesy Kevin McNamara, FDU–Atlantic.)

Sooke.

Sechelt.

A rare example of an entire class, this photograph shows all the TSRVs in line abreast: left to right, *Stikine*, *Sooke*, *Sikani*, *Sechelt*.

TORPEDO SOUND RANGE VESSELS

APPENDIX 1

Royal Navy Ships under Royal Canadian Navy Control

During the Second World War a number of RN ships served alongside ships of the RCN, some of them under RCN control, as members of Canadian escort groups. Nine of these ships—three frigates and six corvettes—spent most of their war careers in this fashion, and paid a disproportionately heavy price. Two frigates and two corvettes were lost, and the third frigate was irreparably damaged.

Frigates

HMS *Itchen* was completed on 28 December 1942 at Paisley, Scotland. After workups at Tobermory and a brief refit on the Clyde, she joined EG C-1 in March 1943 as Senior Officer's ship. She escorted eight North Atlantic convoys with C-1, but was transferred in August 1943 at Londonderry to an RCN support group, EG 9. On 19 September this group was ordered to the assistance of combined convoy ON.202/ONS.18, and on 22 September *Itchen* was torpedoed and sunk by U 666, south of Greenland. Ironically, she had on board 80 survivors of HMCS *St. Croix*, sunk two days earlier, and all but one of these lost their lives.

HMS *Lagan* was completed at South Bank-on-Tees, 2 December 1942, and joined EG C-2 early in January 1943. She escorted eleven North Atlantic convoys, and in March 1943 made a round trip from Britain to Gibraltar in support of Operation Torch convoys. On 20 September 1943, while escorting convoy ON.202, she was torpedoed by *U 270* in the North Atlantic but managed to reach Liverpool. Subsequently declared a constructive total loss, she was broken up at Troon in May 1946.

HMS *Tweed* was completed on 28 April 1943 at Glasgow and, after working up at Tobermory, joined an RCN support group, EG 5, in June. From then until December she served with the group in support of North Atlantic convoys, operating from Londonderry and St. John's. On 7 January 1944, while on blockade-runner patrol northwest of Spain, she was torpedoed and sunk by *U 305*.

Corvettes

HMS *Celandine* was completed at Grangemouth, Scotland, on 30 April 1941. After working up she joined Newfoundland Command as an ocean escort. On 27 June 1941 she shared with *Gladiolus* and *Nasturtium* the sinking of *U 556*. In February 1942 she became a member of TU 24.1.11, predecessor of EG C-1, making one round trip to Londonderry before proceeding to Norfolk, Virginia, for two months' refit. On completion of the refit in July 1942, she joined EG C-4 and served with it until March 1943, when she underwent another refit, this time at Liverpool, U.K. Following this, she returned to C-1 in August 1943. *Celandine* left St. John's for the last time on 1 February 1944 to escort convoy HX.277, and spent the balance of the war in U.K. waters under RN command. She was broken up at Portaferry in October 1948.

Itchen.

Nasturtium.

Ayrshire.

HMS *Dianthus* was completed at Leith, Scotland, on 17 March 1941 and after working up briefly joined EG 7 (RN) at Liverpool. In June 1941 she was allocated to Newfoundland Command, arriving at Halifax on 26 June. In February 1942 she became a member of TU24.1.11, predecessor of EG C-1, serving as an ocean escort until that August, when she commenced two months' refit at Bristol, U.K. Refit completed, she joined EG A-3 and served with it and its successor, C-5, until January 1944. She left St. John's for the last time with convoy HX.274, and spent the balance of the war in U.K. waters under RN command. In 1949 she was sold for conversion to a whale-catcher.

HMS *Gladiolus*, completed on 6 April 1940 at South Bank-on-Tees, was the first corvette launched. After working up at Portland, she joined Western Approaches Command, Liverpool and, later, EG 1 and EG 2 at Londonderry. In June 1941 she was allocated to the recently formed Newfoundland Command, and in July joined its EG 25. In October she was transferred to Task Unit 4.1.15, and on 16 October, while escorting convoy SC.48, was torpedoed and sunk by *U 558* in the North Atlantic. During her short career, *Gladiolus* sank *U 26* and *U 65*, and shared a third kill, *U 556*, with *Celandine* and *Nasturtium*.

HMS *Nasturtium* was completed on 26 September 1940 at South Bank-on-Tees and after working up joined EG 7, Western Approaches Command, Liverpool, as a North Atlantic escort. On 27 June 1941, with *Gladiolus* and *Celandine*, she took part in the sinking of *U 556*. In July 1941 she joined Newfoundland Command and in June 1942, EG C-1, following refits at Mobile, Alabama, and Liverpool. In August 1942, after four Atlantic crossings with EG C-1, she transferred to A-3 for two further crossings. She returned to the U.K. in September 1942, having been assigned duties in connection with Operation Torch. In June 1943, on completion of a two-month refit at Belfast, *Nasturtium* was allocated to EG C-4. She left St. John's for the last time on 18 March 1944 as escort to convoy HX.283 and spent the remainder of the war in U.K. waters under RN command. She was sold in 1948 for conversion to a merchant ship.

HMS *Polyanthus* was completed at Leith, Scotland, on 23 April 1941, and after work ups joined Newfoundland Command, which assigned her to EG 17. In May 1942 following a refit at Galveston, Texas, she joined EG C-2, and was still a member of the group when, on 20 September 1943 she was torpedoed and sunk in convoy ON.202 by *U 963*.

HMS *Primrose* was completed on 15 July 1940 at Renfrew, Scotland, and after working up joined EG 6, Liverpool and then, in February 1941, EG 7. In June 1941, she joined newly formed Newfoundland Command and, in October 1942, EG C-2, serving with this group as an ocean escort until August 1943. Following a refit at Corpach, Scotland, *Primrose* remained in U.K. waters until January 1945, when she returned to mid-ocean duties with EG B-2 until the end of the war. She was sold for conversion to a whale-catcher in 1949.

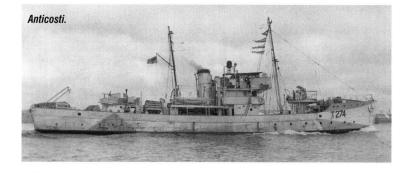
Anticosti.

Royal Navy Anti-Submarine Trawlers

It was expected that the spring of 1943 would bring renewed U-boat activity in the Gulf of St. Lawrence, and there was concern over the shortage of suitable RCN escorts for the area. The RN accordingly lent the RCN six of its ocean-going anti-submarine trawlers, complete with crews. Formerly large fishing trawlers, they were named *Ayrshire, Cape Argona, Cape Mariato, Lord Middleton, Paynter*, and *St. Kenan*. With the exception of *Cape Argona*, which arrived at Halifax on 7 May, all arrived in Canadian waters in mid-April. For the remainder of the month they were assigned to Halifax Force while undergoing repairs, and early in May they joined Sydney Force. *Cape Argona*, meanwhile, did escort work between St. Pierre and Halifax, joining the rest at Sydney on 31 May. The six trawlers performed an important role in the escort of Quebec-Sydney convoys and patrols in Cabot Strait during the remainder of 1943, and then returned to the U.K.

Name	Pt. No.	Builder	Date	Displ.	Dimensions
Ayrshire	FY.225	Smith's Dock, Middlesborough, U.K	1938	540	176' x 28' x 15'
Cape Argona	FY 190	Cochrane & Sons, Selby, U.K.	1936	494	166' x 27' x 14'
Cape Mariato	4.172	Cochrane & Sons, Selby, U.K.	1936	497	170' x 27' x 14'
Lord Middleton	FY 219	Cochrane & Sons, Selby, U.K.	1936	464	161' x 26' x 14'
Paynter	FY 242	Cochrane & Sons, Selby, U.K.	1937	477	167' x 28' x 14'
St. Kenan	FY 264	Cook, Welton & Gemmel, Beverly, U.K	1936	565	127' x 29' x 14'

Western Isles Class A/S Trawlers

Sixteen anti-submarine trawlers of the Isles class were built in Canada for the RN, which loaned eight of them to the RCN for the duration of the war, as escorts for coastal convoys were in short supply at the time of their completion in 1942. They were not, however, commissioned in the RCN, and were manned by RN crews. These ships were given the names of Canadian islands and therefore known as the Western Isles class. All were launched in 1942, commissioned in 1943 and returned to the RN in 1945.

DISPLACEMENT: 530 tons
DIMENSIONS: 164' x 27' 8" x 8' 7"
ARMAMENT: one 12 pdr., three 20-mm

Name	Pt. No.	Builder
Anticosti	T.274	Collingwood Shipyards Ltd.
Baffin	T.275	Collingwood Shipyards Ltd.
Cailiff	T.276	Collingwood Shipyards Ltd.
Ironbound	T.284	Kingston Shipbuilding Co. Ltd
Liscomb	T.285	Kingston Shipbuilding Co. Ltd
Magdalen	T.279	Midland Shipyards Ltd.
Manitoulin	T.280	Midland Shipyards Ltd.
Miscou	T.277	Collingwood Shipyards Ltd.

APPENDIX 2
Special Assignments

Caribbean Sea, 1942

By May 1942, shortage of oil, both at Halifax and in the U.K., made necessary the initiation of fast tanker convoys between Halifax and Trinidad, and shortly afterward between Halifax and Aruba. Most of the escorts were provided by the RCN's Halifax Force, and seven corvettes were involved.

Convoys Escorted

Ship	May 1942	June 1942	July 1942	August 1942
Fredericton			HA.2	AH.2
Halifax			HA.1	HA.3
Halifax			AH.1	TAW.7
Halifax				TAW.15
Hepatica		HT.2		
Hepatica		TH.3		
Oakville			HA.1	HA.3
Oakville			AH.1	TAW.7
Oakville				TAW.15
Snowberry		HT.2	HA.1	HA.3
Snowberry		TH.3	AH.1	TAW.15
Sudbury	HT.1	TH.2	TH.4	AH.2
Sudbury		HT.3	HA.2	
The Pas	HT.1	TH.2	TH.4	AH.2
The Pas		HT.3	HA.2	

Convoy designations: AH: Aruba-Halifax, TH: Trinidad-Halifax, HA: Halifax-Aruba, HT: Halifax-Trinidad, TAW: Trinidad-Aruba-Key West (Florida)

Guantanamo Convoys, 1942-1943

In August 1942, the USN asked for the loan of corvettes to escort convoys between New York City and Guantanamo, Cuba (designated as NG or GN convoys according to destination). The RCN provided seven corvettes, which were placed under the control of the Commander, Eastern Sea Frontier, USN.

Ship	Arrived N.Y. to join	Period of Service
Fredericton	29/8/42	9/42 - 2/43
Halifax	14/9/42	9/42 - 3/43
Lethbridge	18/11/42	11/42 - 3/43
Oakville	7/12/42	12/42 - 2/43
Snowberry	7/9/42	9/42 - 3/43
Sudbury	29/8/42	9/42 - 12/42
The Pas	29/8/42	9/42 - 12/42

Operation Neptune, The Invasion of Northern France, June 1944. RCN Ships Engaged

Ship	Command or Group	Ship	Command or Group
2 LSI (M)		**19 Corvettes**	(all with Western Approaches Command, Greenock)
Prince David	Combined Operations (RN)		
Prince Henry	Combined Operations (RN)	*Alberni*	
		Algoma	
13 Destroyers		*Baddeck*	
Algonquin	26th DF (RN)	*Calgary*	
Chaudière	EG 11	*Camrose*	
Gatineau	EG 11	*Kitchener*	
Haida	10th DF (RN)	*Louisburg*	
Huron	10th DF (RN)	*Lunenburg*	
Kootenay	EG 11	*Moose Jaw*	
Ottawa (2nd)	EG 11	*Port Arthur*	
Qu'Appelle	EG 12	*Prescott*	
Restigouche	EG 12	*Regina*	
St. Laurent	EG 11	*Rimouski*	
Saskatchewan	EG 12	*Summerside*	
Sioux	26th DF (RN)	*Trentonian*	
Skeena	EG 12	*Woodstock*	
11 Frigates		**16 Minesweepers**	
Cape Breton	EG 6	*Bayfield*	31st MF
Grou	EG 6	*Blairmore*	31st MF
Matane	EG 9	*Canso*	16th MF (RN)
Meon	EG 9	*Caraquet*	31st MF
Outremont	EG 6	*Cowichan*	31st MF
Port Colborne	EG 9	*Fort William*	31st MF
Saint John	EG 9	*Georgian*	14th MF (RN)
Stormont	EG 9	*Guysborough*	14th MF (RN)
Swansea	EG 9	*Kenora*	14th MF (RN)
Teme	EG 6	*Malpeque*	31st MF
Waskesiu	EG 6	*Milltown*	31st MF
		Minas	31st MF
		Mulgrave	31st MF
		Thunder	4th MF (RN)
		Vegreville	14th MF (RN)
		Wasaga	31st MF

Note: The above table does not include minor vessels such as MTBs and LCI (L)s

Operation Torch, North African Landings, November 1942

In August 1942, the Admiralty requested the loan of a number of corvettes to support this operation. The RCN lent 16 of its own corvettes and 1 RN corvette from RCN EG C-1. All served in the Mediterranean or escorted U.K.-Gibraltar convoys in support of Operation Torch.

Ship	Left St. John's for the U.K.	Transit Convoy	Returned to Halifax or St. John's	Transit Convoy	Remarks
Alberni	23/10/42	HX.212	23/3/43	ON.172	
Algoma	30/10/42	SC.107	30/4/43	ON.179	Returned to St. John's
Baddeck	18/10/42	SC.105	4/4/43	ON.174	
Calgary	23/10/42	SC.106	4/4/43	ON.179	Returned to St. John's
Camrose	22/10/42	SC.106	18/4/43	ONS.2	
Kitchener	23/10/42	SC.106	19/4/43	ONS.2	
Louisburg	15/9/42	HX.207			Lost 6/2/43
Lunenburg	16/9/42	SC.100	20/9/43	ON.201	
Moose Jaw	30/10/42	SC.107	19/4/43	ONS.2	
Port Arthur	18/10/42	SC.105	23/3/43	ON.172	
Prescott	15/9/42	HX.207	4/4/43	ON.174	
Regina	30/10/42	SC.108	4/4/43	ON.174	
Summerside	23/10/42	HX.212	23/3/43	ON.172	
Ville de QuÈbec	23/10/42	HX.212	22/4/43	ONS.2	
Weyburn	16/9/42	SC.100			Lost 22/2/43
Woodstock	15/9/42	HX.207	24/3/43	ON.172	
Nasturtium (HMS)	16/9/42	SC.100	16/7/43	ONS.12	Return delayed by refit in U.K.

Murmansk Convoys, 1943-1945

The following RCN ships escorted convoys to North Russia between November 1943 and May 1945.

Ship	No. of round trips	Convoys escorted
Destroyers		
Algonquin	1	M N
Athabaskan	1	C D
Haida	3	A B E F Q R
Huron	4	A B E F G H Q R
Iroquois	3	A B E F Q R
Sioux	2	M N O P
Frigates-EG 6		
Cape Breton	1	*J
Grou	1	*J
Outremont	1	*J
Waskesiu	1	*J
Frigates-EG 9		
Loch Alvie	2	K L S T
Monnow	2	K L S T
Nene	2	K L S T
Port Colborne	1	K L
Saint John	1	K L
Stormont	1	K L
Matane	1	S T
St. Pierre	1	S T

* Group sailed independently to Kola Inlet

Key to Convoys Northbound to Russia

Code	Convoy	Sailed Loch Ewe	Arrived Kola Inlet
A	JW.54A	15/11/43	24/11/43
C	JW.55A	12/12/43	20/12/43
E	JW.55B	20/12/43	29/12/43
G	JW.56B	22/1/44	1/2/44
K	JW.62	29/11/44	7/12/44
M	JW.63	30/12/44	8/1/45
		Sailed Clyde	
O	JW.65	11/3/45	21/3/45
Q	JW.66	16/4/45	25/4/45
S	JW.67	12/5/45	20/5/45

Key to Convoys Southbound to U.K.

Code	Convoy	Sailed Archangel	Arrived Loch Ewe
B	RA.54B	26/11/43	9/12/43
		Sailed Kola Inlet	
D	RA.55A	23/12/43	1/1/44
F	RA.55B	31/12/43	8/1/44
H	RA.56	3/2/44	11/2/44
J	RA.59	28/4/44	6/5/44
			Arrived Clyde
L	RA.62	10/12/44	20/12/44
N	RA.63	11/1/45	23/1/45
P	RA.65	23/3/45	1/4/45
R	RA.66	29/4/45	8/5/45
T	RA.67	23/5/45	31/5/45

Operation Forward Action, UN Sanctions Against Haiti, 1993

Ship	Leave Hfx/Esq.	Arrive Haiti	Leave Haiti	Arrive Hfx/Esq
Preserver	28/9/93	18/10/93	***	23/11/93
Gatineau	28/9/93	18/10/93	***	23/11/93
Fraser	28/8/93	18/10/93	17/12/93	23/12/93
Provider	1/12/93 (E)	17/12/93	13/1/94	3/94 (E)
Fraser	8/1/94	13/1/94	25/3/94	31/3/94
Annapolis	10/3/94 (E)	25/3/94	23/4/94	***
Ville de Quebec	***	23/4/94	28/4/94	13/5/94
Terra Nova	5/4/94	28/4/94	13/7/94	18/7/94
Kootenay	21/6/94 (E)	13/7/94	15/9/94	***
Terra Nova	7/9/94	15/9/94	29/9/94	19/10/94

*** *information unavailable.*

Remarks:

Provider conducted exercises in the Atlantic with other Canadian units after leaving Haiti.

On *Fraser*'s two tours, she conducted 73 boardings and 450 hailings, while spending a total of 134 days on station.

Ville de Quebec conducted 14 boardings during her 5 days on patrol.

Terra Nova spent 87 days at sea and upon her departure, completed her 90th boarding. On July 5 she rescued 67 occupants of one boat and on July 8, 57 occupants of another.

Canada's contribution to the naval blockade of Haiti ended on 1 October 1994, when *Terra Nova* departed. The country had by then been peacefully occupied by an American force. Overall, Canadian personnel conducted 9,424 hailings and 1,388 armed boardings, and diverted 119 ships. This was 19 percent of all UN hailings, 18 percent of boardings and 13 percent of diversions.

Operation Sharp Guard, UN Sanctions Against Yugoslavia, 1993

Ship	Leave Halifax	Join SNFA	Leave SNFA	Arrives Halifax
Algonquin	29/3/93	24/6/93	***	15/10/93
Iroquois	25/9/93	10/93	15/4/94	25/4/94
Preserver	27/1/94	10/2/94	***	14/6/94
Halifax	2/4/94	15/4/94	30/8/94	9/9/94
Toronto	15/8/94	30/8/94	16/1/95	26/1/95
Montreal	4/1/95	16/1/95	8/7/95	19/7/95
Preserver	5/7/95	***	***	30/6/95
Ville de Quebec	26/6/95	7/7/95	17/12/95	19/12/95
Fredericton	28/11/95	14/12/95	***	4/4/96
Halifax	18/3/96	***	***	25/7/96

*** *information unavailable*

Remarks:

Algonquin left Halifax to join the NATO fleet: the fleet was then deployed to the Adriatic and arrived there 24 June1993 to enforce UN sanctions against the former Yugoslavia. During the deployment, *Algonquin* conducted 88 boardings.

During deployment, *Iroquois* conducted 98 boardings.

During deployment, *Toronto* conducted 370 hailings, 56 boardings and 25 diversions.

During deployment, *Montreal* conducted 187 hailings, 57 boardings and 4 diversions.

Operation Apollo, International Coalition Against Terrorism, 2001

Ship	Depart	Return	Remarks
Halifax	Halifax 15/8/01	Halifax 11/2/02	Sailed to join SNFA. Detached to join US-led coalition against terrorism
Preserver	Halifax 17/10/01	Halifax 27/4/02	
Iroquois	Halifax 17/10/01	Halifax 27/4/02	
Charlottetown	Halifax 17/10/01	Halifax 4/3/02	
Vancouver	Esquimalt 29/10/01	Esquimalt 28/5/02	Joined USS *John Stennis* Battle Group
Toronto	Halifax 5/12/01	Halifax 27/5/02	
Ottawa	Esquimalt 17/2/02	Esquimalt 17/8/02	Replaced *Charlottetown*
Algonquin	Esquimalt 23/3/02		Replaced *Iroquois*
Protecteur	Esquimalt 22/5/02		Replaced *Preserver*
St. John's	Halifax 1/5/02		Replaced *Vancouver*

APPENDIX 3

Pendant Numbers

Pendant numbers make possible the visual identification of ships, especially members of a large class. The number is worn on either side of the fo'c's'le and usually on the stern, often displayed as well in the form of flags. During the Second World War the painted-on version was generally seen only in destroyers and smaller ships, except in the USN.

In the list that follows, the Canadian pendants for 1939 to 1945 have been excerpted from much larger lists that included all British and Commonwealth ships; hence the gaps in the series. The only RCN ships affected by a change (1940) in the letter preceding the numerals were *Assiniboine, Saguenay,* and *Skeena,* whose letter D changed to I.

RCN pendant numbers having S, Z, and the Fisheries flag "superior," bore no relation to the RN lists. To make matters even more confusing, many east and west coast ships simultaneously bore the same numbers. These may be distinguished in the list by A (Atlantic) and P (Pacific) appended to the ships' names. A further complication arises from the fact that the armed yachts, in particular, were assigned changed numbers at various times.

The letter prefix was no longer displayed after the pendant numbers were revised at the end of 1949. USN-style ship type designations are "understood" in reading these. Thus, HMCS Preserver (2nd) is recognized by her number to be AOR 510.

Pendant Numbers, Wartime

F

56	Prince Robert
70	Prince Henry
89	Prince David
94	Preserver
100	Provider

G

07	Athabaskan
24	Huron
63	Haida
89	Iroquois

H

00	Restigouche
31	Ottawa (2nd)
48	Fraser
49	Margaree
60	Ottawa (1st)
61	Gatineau
69	Qu'Appelle
70	Saskatchewan
75	Kootenay
83	St. Laurent
95	Buxton
99	Chaudière

I

04	Annapolis
18	Assiniboine
24	Hamilton
50	Columbia
57	Niagara
58	Skeena
64	St. Clair
79	Saguenay
80	St. Croix
93	St. Francis

J

01	Ross Norman
03	Suderoy IV
04	Suderoy V
05	Suderoy VI
08	Bayfield
10	Standard Coaster
11	Venosta
12	Viernoe
13	Rayon d'Or
16	Fleur de Lis
21	Canso
29	Armentières
35	Nanoose
38	Caraquet
46	Festubert
51	Guysborough
65	Comox
69	Ingonish
70	Ypres
88	Fundy
94	Gaspé
100	Lockeport
144	Georgian
146	Cowichan
148	Malpeque
149	Ungava
152	Quatsino
153	Nipigon
156	Thunder
159	Mahone
160	Chignecto
161	Outarde
162	Wasaga
165	Minas
166	Quinte
168	Chedabucto
169	Miramichi
170	Bellechasse
174	Clayoquot
250	Burlington
253	Drummondville
254	Swift Current
255	Red Deer
256	Medicine Hat
257	Vegreville
258	Grandmère
259	Gananoque
260	Goderich
261	Kelowna
262	Courtenay
263	Melville
264	Granby
265	Noranda
266	Lachine
267	Digby
268	Truro
269	Trois-Rivières
270	Brockville
271	Transcona
272	Esquimalt
278	Llewellyn
279	Lloyd George
280	Port Hope
281	Kenora
309	Sarnia
310	Stratford
311	Fort William
312	Kentville
313	Mulgrave
314	Blairmore
317	Milltown
318	Westmount
326	Kapuskasing
327	Middlesex
330	Oshawa
331	Portage
332	St. Boniface
334	Sault Ste. Marie
336	Wallaceburg
337	Winnipeg
344	Border Cities
355	Rockcliffe
357	Daerwood
358	Rossland
359	St. Joseph
364	Coquitlam
371	Lavallée
372	Cranbrook
373	Revelstoke
395	Kalamalka
396	Fort Frances
397	New Liskeard
480	Alder Lake
481	Beech Lake
483	Birch Lake
484	Cedar Lake
485	Elm Lake
487	Fir Lake
488	Hickory Lake
489	Larch Lake
491	Oak Lake
492	Pine Lake
493	Poplar Lake
494	Spruce Lake
495	Willow Lake

K

03	Dunver
14	Atholl
101	Nanaimo
102	Alberni
103	Dawson
106	Edmundston
110	Shediac
111	Matapedia
112	Arvida
115	Lévis (1st)
116	Chambly
118	Napanee
119	Orillia
120	Rimouski
124	Cobalt

125	Kenogami
126	Algoma
129	Agassiz
130	Chilliwack
133	Quesnel
136	Shawinigan
137	Barrie
138	Moncton
141	Summerside
143	Louisburg (1st)
145	Arrowhead
146	Pictou
147	Baddeck
148	Amherst
149	Brandon
150	Eyebright
151	Lunenburg
152	Sherbrooke
153	Sorel
154	Camrose
155	Windflower
156	Chicoutimi
157	Dauphin
158	Saskatoon
159	Hepatica
160	Lethbridge
161	Prescott
162	Sudbury
163	Galt
164	Moose Jaw
165	Battleford
166	Snowberry
167	Drumheller
168	The Pas
169	Rosthern
170	Morden
171	Kamsack
172	Trillium
173	Weyburn
174	Trail
175	Wetaskiwin
176	Kamloops
177	Dunvegan
178	Oakville
179	Buctouche
180	Collingwood
181	Sackville
182	Bittersweet
191	Mayflower
194	Fennel
198	Spikenard
218	Brantford
219	Midland
223	Timmins
225	Kitchener
228	New Westminster
229	Dundas
231	Calgary
233	Port Arthur
234	Regina
237	Halifax
238	Woodstock
240	Vancouver
242	Ville de Québec
244	Charlottetown (1st and 2nd)
245	Fredericton
254	Ettrick
269	Meon
270	Nene
273	La Malbaie
317	Chebogue
318	Jonquière
319	Montreal
320	New Glasgow
321	New Waterford
322	Outremont
323	Springhill
324	Prince Rupert
325	St. Catharines
326	Port Colborne
327	Stormont
328	Swansea
329	Valleyfield
330	Waskesiu
331	Wentworth
332	Belleville
333	Cobourg
334	Frontenac
337	Kirkland Lake
338	Lindsay
339	North Bay
340	Owen Sound
341	Parry Sound
342	Peterborough
343	St. Lambert
344	Sea Cliff
345	Smiths Falls
346	Whitby
350	Cape Breton
357	Rivière du Loup
358	Asbestos
365	Ste. Thérèse
368	Trentonian
369	West York
394	Thorlock
400	Lévis (2nd)
401	Louisburg (2nd)
402	Giffard
404	Annan
407	Beacon Hill
409	Capilano
410	Coaticook
414	Glace Bay
415	Hawkesbury
418	Joliette
419	Kokanee
424	Loch Achanalt
428	Loch Alvie
440	Lachute
441	Monnow
444	Matane
448	Orkney
454	St. Stephen
455	Strathroy
456	Saint John
457	Stellarton
458	Teme
459	Thetford Mines
485	Mimico
486	Forest Hill
487	Long Branch
488	St. Thomas
489	Hespeler
490	Kincardine
491	Orangeville
492	Leaside
493	Bowmanville
494	Arnprior
495	Copper Cliff
496	Tillsonburg
497	Humberstone
498	Petrolia
499	Huntsville
517	Loch Morlich
518	Grou
519	Lasalle
520	Norsyd
525	Ribble
531	Stone Town
538	Toronto
539	Beauharnois
661	Antigonish
662	Prestonian
663	Cap de la Madeleine
664	Carlplace
665	Eastview
666	Hallowell
667	Inch Arran
668	La Hulloise
669	Lanark
670	Fort Erie
671	Lauzon
672	Longueuil
673	Magog
675	Poundmaker
676	Penetang
677	Royalmount
678	Runnymede
680	St. Pierre
681	Stettler
682	Strathadam
683	Sussexville
684	Victoriaville
685	Buckingham
686	Fergus
687	Guelph
688	Merrittonia
R	
04	Cayuga
10	Micmac
15	Crescent
16	Algonquin
19	Crusader
64	Sioux
79	Athabaskan (1st)
89	Iroquois
96	Nootka
S	
00	Acadia
02	Charny
05	Elk
08	Reindeer
09	Laurier
10	Beaver
11	Vison
12	Caribou
13	Renard
T	
274	Anticosti
275	Baffin
276	Cailiff
277	Miscou
279	Magdalen
280	Manitoulin
284	Ironbound
285	Liscomb
Z	
00	Acadia (A); Malaspina (P)
01	Givenchy (P)
02	Mont Joli (A); Sans Peur (P)
03	Suderöy IV (A); Nitinat (P)
04	Suderöy V (A); Meander (P)
05	Suderöy VI (A); Stanpoint (P)
06	Haro (P)
07	Lynx (A); Macdonald (P)
08	Reindeer (A); Ripple (P)
09	Ross Norman (A); Spray (P)
10	Beaver (A); Cancolim (P)
11	Rayon d'Or (A); Leola Vivian (P)
12	Anna Mildred (A); Norsal (P)
13	Husky, Renard (A); Crusader (P)
14	Moose (A); Grizzly (P)
15	Interceptor (A); Cougar (P)
16	Star XVI (A); Wolf (P)
17	Standard Coaster (A)
18	Alachasse (A); Imperator (P)
19	Murray Stewart (A)
20	Chaleur (A); Skidegate (P)
21	Madawaska (A); Vencedor (P)
22	Scatarie (A); Andamara (P)
23	French (A)
24	Mont Joli (A)
25	Caribou (A); Flores (P)
26	Charny (A)
27	Elk (A)
28	Husky (A)
29	Sankaty (A)
30	Vison (A); Fifer (P)
31	Fleur de Lis (A)
32	Ambler (A)
33	Reo II (A)
34	Laurier (A)
39	Shulamite (A)
40	Dundalk (A)
41	Dundurn (A)
42	Sunbeam (A)
43	Moonbeam (A)
44	Marvita (A)
52	Sans Peur (A)
55	Arras (A)
56	Eastore (A)
57	Laymore (A)
62	Sackville (A)

Fisheries Pendant Superior (West Coast)

FY

00	Fifer
01	Vanisle
02	San Tomas
03	Maraudor
04	West Coast
05	Mitchell Bay
06	Allaverdy
07	B.C. Lady
08	Santa Maria
09	Springtime V
10	Barmar
11	Talapus
12	Ehkoli
13	Nenamook
14	Kuitan
15	Leclo
16	Moolock
17	Canfisco
18	Smith Sound
19	Howe Sound I
20	Tordo
21	Valdes
22	Foam; Loyal II
23	Barkley Sound
24	Surf
25	Billow
26	Cape Beale
27	Takla
28	Johanna
29	Margaret I
30	Signal
31	Capella
32	Seiner
33	Hatta VII (Spray)
34	Joan W. II
35	Dalehurst
36	Western Maid
37	Comber
38	Crest
39	Chamiss Bay
40	Early Field
41	Camenita
42	Moresby III
43	Loyal I
44	Bluenose
45	Sea Flash
46	Merry Chase
47	Sea Wave
48	Departure Bay

Pendant Numbers, 1949 onward

20	Cormorant (2nd)
21	Magnificent
22	Bonaventure
31	Warrior; Uganda
32	Ontario
50	Labrador
71	Grilse
72	Ojibwa
73	Onondaga
74	Okanagan
75	Rainbow
100	Cape Breton (2nd)
101	Cape Scott
110	Anticosti
112	Moresby
113	Sackville
114	Bluethroat
141	Llewellyn
142	Lloyd George
143	Gaspé (2nd)
144	Chaleur (1st)
145	Fundy (2nd)
146	Comox (2nd)
147	Cowichan (2nd)
148	Ungava (2nd)
149	Quinte (2nd)
150	Miramichi (2nd)
151	Fortune
152	James Bay
153	Thunder (2nd)
154	Resolute
156	Chignecto (2nd)
157	Trinity
158	Cordova
159	Fundy (3rd)
160	Chignecto (3rd)
161	Thunder (3rd)
162	Cowichan (3rd)
163	Miramichi (3rd)
164	Chaleur (2nd)
168	New Liskeard
169	Portage
170	Fort Frances
171	Kapuskasing
172	Wallaceburg
173	Rockcliffe
174	Oshawa
176	Sault Ste. Marie
177	Winnipeg
178	Brockville
179	Digby

180	Granby; Porte St. Jean
181	Drummondville
182	Kentville
183	Port Hope; Porte St. Louis
184	Gananoque; Porte de la Reine
185	Swift Current; Porte Québec
186	Malpeque; Porte Dauphine
187	Westmount
188	Nipigon
189	Minas
190	Sarnia
191	Kenora
192	Mahone
193	Blairmore
194	Milltown
195	Fort William
196	Red Deer
197	Medicine Hat
198	Goderich
205	St. Laurent (2nd)
206	Saguenay (2nd)
207	Skeena (2nd)
213	Nootka
214	Micmac
215	Haida
216	Huron (1st)
217	Iroquois (1st)
218	Cayuga
219	Athabaskan (2nd)
224	Algonquin (1st)
225	Sioux
226	Crescent
229	Ottawa (3rd)
230	Margaree
233	Fraser (2nd)
234	Assiniboine (2nd)
235	Chaudière (2nd)
236	Gatineau (2nd)
256	St. Croix (2nd)
257	Restigouche (2nd)
258	Kootenay (2nd)
259	Terra Nova
260	Columbia (2nd)
261	Mackenzie
262	Saskatchewan (2nd)
263	Yukon
264	Qu'Appelle (2nd)
265	Annapolis (2nd)
266	Nipigon (2nd)
280	Iroquois (2nd)
281	Huron (2nd)
282	Athabaskan (3rd)
283	Algonquin (2nd)
301	Antigonish

302	Stone Town
303	Beacon Hill
304	New Waterford
305	La Hulloise
306	Swansea
307	Prestonian
308	Inch Arran
309	Ste. Thérèse
310	Outremont
311	Stettler
312	Fort Erie
313	Sussexvale
314	Buckingham
315	New Glasgow
316	Penetang
317	Cap de la Madeleine
318	Jonquière
319	Toronto
320	Victoriaville
321	Lanark
322	Lauzon
323	St. Stephen
324	St. Catharines
330	Halifax (2nd)
331	Vancouver (3rd)
332	Ville de Québec (2nd)
333	Toronto (2nd)
334	Regina (2nd)
335	Calgary (2nd)
336	Montreal (2nd)
337	Fredericton
338	Winnipeg (2nd)
339	Charlottetown (3rd)
340	St. John's
341	Ottawa (4th)
400	Bras d'Or (2nd)
420	Cordova
501	Dundalk
502	Dundurn
508	Provider (2nd)
509	Protecteur
510	Preserver (2nd)
516	Laymore
531	Whitethroat
610	Sechelt
611	Sikani
612	Sooke
613	Stikine
700	Kingston
701	Glace Bay (2nd)
702	Nanaimo (2nd)
703	Edmonton
704	Shawinigan (2nd)
705	Whitehorse

706	Yellowknife
707	Goose Bay
708	Moncton (2nd)
709	Saskatoon (2nd)
710	Brandon (2nd)
711	Summerside (2nd)
780	Loon
781	Cormorant (1st)
782	Blue Heron
783	Mallard
876	Victoria
877	Corner Brook
878	Windsor
879	Chicoutimi (2nd)

BIBLIOGRAPHY

Published Sources

Abbazia, Patrick *Mr. Roosevelt's Navy: The Private War of the U.S. Atlantic Fleet, 1939-1942.* Annapolis: U.S. Naval Institute Press, 1975.

Alden, John D. *Flush Decks and Four Pipes.* Annapolis: U.S. Naval Institute Press, 1965.

Beesly, Patrick. *Very Special Intelligence: The Story of the Admiralty's Operational Intelligence Centre 1939-1945.* London: Hamish Hamilton, 1977.

Blakely, Tom. *Corvette Cobourg.* Cobourg. Royal Canadian Legion, 1985.

Brice, Martin H. *The Tribals, Biography of a Destroyer Class.* London: Ian Allen, 1971.

Brown, J. D. *Carrier Operations in World War II, Volume 1: The Royal Navy.* London: Ian Allen, 1968.

Chalmers, William S. *Max Horton and the Western Approaches.* London: Hodder & Stoughton, 1954.

Colledge, J. J. *Ships of the Royal Navy, an Historical Index.* (2 vols.) Newton Abbot: David & Charles, 1969-1970.

Dittmar, F. J. and J. J. Colledge. *British Warships 1914-1919.* London: Ian Allen, 1972.

Easton, Alan. *50 North: an Atlantic Battleground.* London: Macdonald and Jane's, 1977.

Elliott, Peter. *Allied Escort Ships of World War II.* London: Macdonald and Jane's, 1977.

_____*Allied Minesweeping in World War 2.* Cambridge: Patrick Stephens, 1979.

Essex, James W. *Victory in the St. Lawrence: Canada's Unknown War.* Erin: Boston Mills Press, 1984.

Freeman, David J. *Canadian Warship Names.* St. Catharines: Vanwell Publishing Ltd, 2000.

German, Cdr. Tony. *The Sea Is At Our Gates.* Toronto: McClelland & Stewart, 1990.

Gretton, Sir Peter. *Convoy Escort Commander.* London: Cassell, 1964.

_____*Crisis Convoy: the Story of the Atlantic Convoy HX.231.* London: Davies, 1974.

Gröner, Erich. *Die Schiffe der Deutschen Kriegsmarine und Luftwaffe 1939-1945.* Munich: Lehmann, 1972.

Hadley, Michael L. *U-Boats Against Canada.* Kingston/Montreal: McGill-Queen's University Press, 1985.

Hague, Arnold. *Destroyers for Great Britain.* London: Greenhill Books, 1990.

_____ *The Allied Convoy System 1939 - 1945: Its Organization, Defence and Operation.* St. Catharines: Vanwell Publishing Ltd, 2000.

Harbron, John D. *The Longest Battle: The RCN in the Atlantic 1939-1945.* St. Catharines.: Vanwell Publishing Ltd, 1993.

Herzog, Bodo. *U-Boote im Einsatz 1939-1945.* Dorheim: Podzun, 1970.

Hodges, Peter. *Tribal Class Destroyers.* London: Almark, 1971.

Jane's Fighting Ships. London: Sampson Low, Marston & Co. Ltd. various editions 1914 to 1980-1981.

Klepsch, Peter. *Die Fremden Flotten im 2 Weltkrieg und ihr Shicksal.* Munich: Lehmann, 1968.

Lamb, James B. *The Corvette Navy: True Stories from Canada's Atlantic War.* Toronto: Macmillan, 1977.

_____*On the Triangle Run.* Toronto: Macmillan of Canada, 1986.

Lawrence, Hal *A Bloody War: One Man's Memories of the Canadian Navy 1939-1945.* Toronto: Macmillan, 1979.

Lenton, H. T. *British Fleet and Escort Destroyers.* Vols. 1-2, London: Macdonald, 1970.

_____"British Escort Ships." W.W.2 Fact Files. London: Macdonald & Jane's, 1974.

Lenton, H. T. and J. J. Colledge. *Warships of World War II.* London: Ian Allen, 1964.

Lloyd's Register of Shipping. various editions, 1910-1980.

Lund, Paul and Harry Ludlum. *Night of the U-Boats: the Story of Convoy SC-7.* Slough: Foulsham, 1973.

Lynch, Thomas G. *Canada's Flowers: History of the Corvettes of Canada.* Bennington: International Graphics, 1981.

Macintyre, Donald *U-Boat Killer.* London: Weidenfeld & Nicolson, 1956.

_____*The Battle of the Atlantic.* London: Batsford, 1961.

Macpherson, Ken. *Canada's Fighting Ships.* Toronto: Samuel Stevens, 1975.

Macpherson, Ken. *Frigates of the Royal Canadian Navy, 1943-1974.* St. Catharines: Vanwell Publishing Ltd, 1989.

_____*Minesweepers of the Royal Canadian Navy, 1938-1945.* St. Catharines: Vanwell Publishing Ltd, 1990.

_____ *The River Class Destroyers of the Royal Canadian Navy.* Toronto: C. J. Musson & Assoc., 1985.

Macpherson, Ken and Marc Milner. *Corvettes of the Royal Canadian Navy, 1939-1945.* St. Catharines: Vanwell Publishing Ltd, 1993.

Maginley, C. D. and Bernard Collin. *The Ships of Canada's Marine Services.* St. Catharines: Vanwell Publishing Ltd, 2001.

Mallmann Showell, J. P. *U-Boats under the Swastika.* London: Ian Allen,

1973.

McKay, John and John Harland. *Anatomy of the Ship: The Flower Class Corvette Agassiz*. London: Conway Maritime Press, 1993.

McKee, Fraser. *The Armed Yachts of Canada*. Erin: Boston Mills Press, 1983.

_____*HMCS* Swansea. St. Catharines: Vanwell Publishing Ltd, 1995.

McKee Fraser and Bob Darlington. *The Canadian Naval Chronicle, 1939-1945*. St. Catharines: Vanwell Publishing Ltd, 1996.

Middlebrook, Martin *Convoy: The Battle for Convoys SC.122 and HX.229*. London: Allen Lane, 1976.

Milner, Marc. *North Atlantic Run*. Toronto: University of Toronto Press, 1985.

Mitchell, W. H. and L. A. Sawyer. *The Oceans, the Forts & the Parks. Wartime Standard Ships*, Vol. II. Liverpool: Sea Breezes, 1966.

Morison, Samuel Eliot. *History of United States Naval Operations in World War II, I, The Battle of the Atlantic, Sept. 1939-May 1943*. Boston: Little, Brown, 1947.

_____*History of United States Naval Operations in World War II, X, The Atlantic Battle Won, May 1943-May 1945*. Boston: Little, Brown, 1956.

Padfield, Peter. *War Beneath the Sea: The Submarine Conflict During World War II*. Toronto: John Wiley, 1995.

Perkins, J. David. *The Canadian Submarine Service in Review*. St. Catharines: Vanwell Publishing Ltd, 2000.

Poolman, Kenneth *Escort Carrier 1941-1945*. London: Ian Allen, 1972.

Preston, Anthony and Alan Raven. "Flower Class Corvettes." *Ensign 3*. London: Bivouac Books, 1973.

Rayner, D. A. *Escort: the Battle of the Atlantic*. London: William Kimber, 1955.

Rehder, Jacob. *Die Verluste der Kriegsflotten 1914-1918*. Munich: Lehmann, 1969.

Revely, Henry. *The Convoy that Nearly Died: the Story of ONS-154*. London: William Kimber, 1979.

Rohwer, Jürgen *The Critical Convoy Battles of March 1943*. Annapolis: U.S. Naval Institute Press, 1977.

_____*Die U-Boot-Erfolge der Achenmachte 1939-1945*. Munich: Lehmann, 1968.

Rohwer, Jürgen & Gerd. Hümmechen. *Chronology of the War at Sea 1939-1945*. (2 vols.) London: Ian Allen, 1972-74.

Roskill, Stephen W. *The War at Sea 1939-1945*. (4 vols.) *History of the Second World War*. United Kingdom Military Series. London: H.M. Stationery Office, 1954-1961.

_____*The Secret Capture: the Capture of U-110*. London: Collins, 1959.

Schofield, Brian B. *The Arctic Convoys*. London: Macdonald & Jane's, 1977.

Schofield, B. B. and L. F. Martyn. *The Rescue Ships*. Edinburgh: Blackwood, 1968.

Seth, Ronald. *The Fiercest Battle: The Story of North Atlantic Convoy ONS.5 22 April-7 May1943*. London: Hutchinson, 1961.

Schull, Joseph. *The Far Distant Ships: An Official Account of Canadian Naval Operations in the Second World War*. Ottawa: Department of National Defence, 1952.

Tucker, Gilbert N. *The Naval Service of Canada, Its Official History*. (2 vols.) Ottawa: Minister of National Defence, 1952.

Watts, Anthony. *The U-boat Hunters*. London: Macdonald & Jane's, 1976.

Young, John A. *A Dictionary of Ships of the Royal Navy of the Second World War*. Cambridge: Patrick Stephens, 1975.

Special Note

Readers interested in a complete bibliography of published material on the Canadian Armed Forces are referred to: *The Canadian Military Experience 1867-1967: A Bibliography* written by Owen A. Cooke of the Directorate of History, National Defence Headquarters, Ottawa: Queen's Printer, 1979.

Journals

Marine News. Journal of the World Ship Society. Kendal: Michael Crowdy, ed, years 1946-1981.

Warship International. Journal of the International Naval Research Organization. Toledo: Christopher C. Wright, ed, years 1964-1981.

Warships Supplement: Marine News. Journal of the World Ship Society. Kendal: James J. Colledge, ed, years 1966-1981.

Unpublished Sources
Directorate of History, Department of National Defence

Naval Service Headquarters, Ottawa, Operations Division.

Daily State 1. HMC Ships and HM and Allied Ships Operated by RCN Authorities. Feb. 27, 1942 - June 22, 1943.

Daily State 2. HM and Allied Ships Operating in Canadian Coastal Zones or Refitting in US Ports. Feb. 28, 1942 - June 22, 1943.

RCN Weekly State Reports. June 28, 1943 - Feb. 6, 1945 and Jan. 1946 - Dec. 3, 1946.

RCN "Ship Movements" Cards. Sept. 3, 1939 - Sept. 3, 1945.

"HX" Convoys Binder, Summaries. Sept. 16, 1939 - May 23, 1945.

"SC" Convoys Binder, Summaries. Aug. 15, 1940 - May 26, 1945.

Weekly Naval Report to Minister. Sept. 16, 1939 - Sept. 6, 1945.

RCN Navy Lists. Years 1940 - 1965.

Naval Historical Section

Individual Ship's Files.

RCN Commands, War Diaries

(Reports of Proceedings/Operational War Diary) Halifax, Sept. 1939 - Sept. 1945; Esquimalt, Sept. 1939 - Sept. 1945; St. John's, July, 1941- June 1945 .

Western Approaches Command - Royal Navy

Western Approaches Monthly News Bulletins, Jan. 1944 - April 1945 Daily State Reports. July 9, 1944 - July 2, 1945.

Admiralty Naval Staff, Operations Division

RN Ship Movements Binders. Sept. 1939 - Sept. 1945.

Admiralty, Historical Section

The "Town" Class Destroyers: the Story of the "Four Stackers." March 1949.

Naval Historical Branch, Ministry of Defence, London

Admiralty, Naval Staff, Operations Division

Pink Lists. Aug. 29, 1939 - July 5, 1948.

Admiralty, Naval Staff, Trade Division

Convoy Commodore Binders, Summaries of Atlantic Convoys HG - HX - HXF - JW - KMS - MKS - OA - OB - OG - ON - ONS - OS - PQ - OP - RA - SC - SL. Sept. 1939 - June 1945.

Daily State Reports, Status of North Atlantic Convoys, May 1941 - Dec. 1941.

Public Record Office, Kew Gardens, London

"OB" and "ON" Convoys - Reports of Proceedings, ADM File Nos. 199/59, 199/284, 199/582, 199/1141, 199/1145, 199/1147. Years 1940 - 1942.

PHOTO CREDITS

The photographs in this book were, for the most part, collected by Ken Macpherson over a period of many years. His vast collection of ship photographs is now housed at the Naval Museum of Alberta in Calgary.

A majority of these illustrations are originally from Canadian Forces photographs. Negatives of those taken prior to 1957 are, in general, held by Public Archives of Canada, and more recent ones by the Canadian Forces Photographic Unit, Rockcliffe.

The following photographs were taken by, or acquired from, other sources.

Acadia, McBride Collection, Maritime Museum of the Atlantic; *Algonquin* (2nd), Ron Barrie; Anticosti (2nd), Sandy Mclearn; *Antigonish*, Dave Shirlaw; *Arnprior*, Ministry of Defence, U.K.; *Asbestos*, W. K. Milroy; *Bowmanville*, Ministry of Defence, U.K.; *Brandon*, Imperial War Museum; *Buckingham*, Dave Shirlaw; *Burlington*, P. M. McEntyre; *Carlplace*, R. J. Horne; *Celandine*, D. Trimingham; *Charlottetown*, W.B. Edwards; *Copper Cliff*, Imperial War Museum; *Constance* and *Curlew*, Art Mears; *Cormorant*, Ian MacCorquodale; *Diana*, Ministry of Defence, U.K.; *Drumheller*, J. L. Dooley; *Drummondville*, B. A. Earthy; *Edmundston*, M. J. Robertson; *Eyebright*, Jack Tice; *Fergus*, D. Trimingham; *Florence*, Eaton's of Canada; *Forest Hill*, Ministry of Defence, U.K.; *Foxhound*, Imperial War Museum; *Fraser* (1st), James Plomer; *Gananoque*, Bob Petry; *Gatineau*, Ian MacCorquodale; *Giffard*, P. L. Robinson; *Glace Bay*, E. W. Finch- Noyes; *Grou*, D. Copp; *Guelph*, R. A. Simon; *Halifax*, D. Trimingham; *Halifax* (2nd), Saint John Shipbuilding Ltd.; *Hallowell*, R. G. Pentland; *Hamilton*, John Small; *Humberstone*, R. A. Simon; *Huron*, Ken Levert; *Iroquois*, CFPU; *Itchen*, J. O. Bayford; *Joliette*, McBride Collection; *Kingston*, Cpl. C. Stephenson; *La Hulloise*, Imperial War Museum; *Lindsay*, F. M. Thompson; *Loch Achanalt*, C. S. J. Lancaster; *Longueuil*, J. Reid; *Louisburg* (1st), Imperial War Museum; *ML067*, H. W. Patterson; *Magog*, H. M. Brown; *Manitoulin*, Watson's Studio, Midland; *Matapedia*, Bob Petry; *Melville*, R. W. King; *Middlesex*, John Freeman; *Mimico*, Ministry of Defence, U.K.; *Moncton* (2nd), CFPU; *Monnow*, Imperial War Museum; *Montreal*, C. Zickerman; *Moresby*, Ian MacCorquodale; *Murray Stewart*, James Plomer; *Nanaimo*, W. S. Knapp; *Nanaimo* (2nd), Ken Levert; *New Liskeard*, Port Arthur Shipbuilding Co.; *New Waterford*, Imperial War Museum; *New Westminster*, B. Trumpour; *Niagara*, Imperial War Museum; *Norsyd*, Larratt Higgins; *North Bay*, W. McMullan; *Orangeville*, Ministry of Defence, U.K.; *Oriole*, CFPU; *Oshawa*, Port Arthur Shipbuilding Co.; *Owen Sound*, P. Hardy; *Parry Sound*, J. W. Bald; *Patrician*, Provincial Archives of B.C.; *Petrolia*, N. Combe; *Pine Lake*, Watson's Studio, Midland; Port Hope, Keith Mendes; *Poundmaker*, R. A. Simon; *Protecteur*, Richard Gimblett; *Puncher*, Imperial War Museum; *Quesnel*, M. H. Jones; *Restless*, R. W. Sandilands; *Ribble*, Imperial War Museum; *Royalmount*, Bob Petry; *St. Laurent* (1st), C. V. Laughton; *Sans Peur*, McBride Collection; *Saskatoon* (2nd), Naval Museum of Alberta; *Sechelt*, Ian MacCorquodale; *Sea Cliff*, Donald Warren; *Shawinigan* (2nd), CFPU *Shediac*, Paul Taylor; *Skeena* (2nd), Ted Stone; *Sooke*, Graham Wragg; *Star XVI*, Bob Petry; *Stellarton*, Joseph Picton; *Stettler*, Dave Shirlaw; *Stratford*, W. G. Garden; *Suderöy IV*, R. Stark; *Summerside*, P. M. McEntyre; *Sussexvale*, Dave Shirlaw; *Teme*, Imperial War Museum; *Terra Nova*, Richard Gimblett; *Thetford Mines*, L. Gray; *Thorlock*, D. Trimingham; *Tillsonburg*, Imperial War Museum; Toronto, McBride Collection *Trentonian*, D. Trimingham; *Trillium*, U.S. Coast Guard; *Truro*, W. McMullan; *Tuna*, J. R. Curry; *Vancouver* (1st), U.S. Navy; *Vancouver* (2nd), R. A. Parker; *Venture*, C. J. Dillon; *Victoria*, J. David Perkins; *Victoriaville*, Dave Shirlaw; *Ville de Québec*, J. Allan; *Waskesiu*, E. G. Giles; *Wentworth*, R. J. C. Pringle; *Wetaskiwin*, W. Hemstreet; *Whitehorse*, Ken Levert; *Yellowknife*, Ken Levert.

INDEX OF SHIPS